WHO'S WHO IN THE COSMIC ZOO?

Book Two:
A Guide to ETs, Aliens, Gods and Angels

WHO IS GOD?

by Ella LeBain

Copyright © 2015 by Ella LeBain

All Rights Reserved. No part(s) of this book may be reproduced, distributed or transmitted in any form, or by any means, or stored in a database or retrieval systems without prior expressed written permission of the author of this book.

Cover Art by Lori Garcia - www.TLCUnlimited.com

Published by Skypath Books, LLC
3051 W. 105th Ave. #351961
Westminster, CO 80035
720.977.9110
www.skypathbooks.com

Where The Sky Is The Limit!

"The Heavens Declare the Glory of God." (Psalm 19:1)

CONTENTS

Book Two: Who Is God?

INTRODUCTION 1
WHO IS GOD? 1
    DEFINITION OF GOD: 6
CHAPTER ONE 9
GODS OR ETS? 9
    THE COSMIC DRAMA 9
    THE SEA OF FORGETFULNESS 10
    HOW ARE WE JUDGED? 11
    FAITH? WHOSE FAITH? 12
    THE LORD OF THE COSMOS 14
CHAPTER TWO 21
ANCIENT TECHNOLOGY & BIBLICAL ASTRONAUTS 21
    MOVING STARS 26
    DIVINE PREGNANCIES 26
    DIVINE SPACESHIPS 27
    DIVINE ENCOUNTERS 28
    WHO WAS EZEKIEL? 30
    LIVING CREATURES? 32
    EZEKIEL'S VISION OF THE DRY BONES 33
    WHO WAS ENOCH? 34
    TECHNOLOGY OF THE ARK 38
    THE LORD'S FLEET OF SPACESHIPS 41
    BIBLICAL ALIEN GODS 43
CHAPTER THREE 47
ANCIENT ASTRONAUT THEORY 47

THE WINGS OF ANGELS OR AIRPLANES?	48
ON THE WINGS OF EAGLES	49
EZEKIEL'S WHEELS WITHIN WHEELS	49
LET DOWN THEIR WINGS	52
WHO OR WHAT ARE THE CHERUBIM?	56
THE LORD'S AERONAUTICS	58
ELIJAH'S JOURNEY INTO HEAVEN	60
CHARIOTS OF FIRE	60
FIRE FROM HEAVEN	63
THE TRUTH IS STRANGER THAN SCIENCE FICTION	66

CHAPTER FOUR 71
MOTHER SHIPS OF THE LORD 71

THE LAW OF READINESS	73
THE CLOUD SHIPS	75
THE CLOUDS OF HEAVEN	77
JESUS TAKEN UP INTO HEAVEN	83
THE COSMIC POLICE	85

CHAPTER FIVE 89
COSMIC WARFARE ON EARTH 89

CHAPTER SIX 97
THE BEASTS OF THE SEA AND EARTH 97

THE BEAST OUT OF THE EARTH	98
CAST DOWN TO EARTH	100
WHO IS THE KING OF THE ABYSS?	102

CHAPTER SEVEN 105
DISCERNMENT OF GODS, ANGELS & DEMONS 105

WHO OR WHAT IS GOD?	105
THE NEW AGE DILEMMA	107
THE DIVINE FEMININE AND THE FALSE GODDESS	108
DISCERNING THE SPIRITS	112
IMPOSTER ARCHANGELS	116

THE CHRISTIAN DILEMMA	119
SYMPTOMS OF TRAFFICKING	121
THE COUNTERFEIT SPIRIT	122
THE LANGUAGE OF ANGELS OR FALLEN ANGELS?	123

CHAPTER EIGHT 129
WHO ARE THE GODS? 129

WHO ARE THE CREATOR GODS?	132
IDOLATRY	133

CHAPTER NINE 137
THE RETURN OF THE GODS 137

THE HINDU GODS	139
BUDDHA PROPHESIED JESUS	140
THE EGYPTIAN GODS	143
THE GREEK AND PAGAN GODS	151
THE MAYAN AND INCAN GODS	152
WHY WILL THE GODS BE PUNISHED?	154
DEEP ROOTED SPIRITUAL WOUNDS	156
DISASTER BECAUSE OF IDOLATRY	161

CHAPTER TEN 165
GODS OR ETS? – WHAT'S NEXT? 165

ARE FALSE GODS JUST EXTRATERRESTRIALS?	165

CHAPTER ELEVEN 171
WHO ARE THE BIBLICAL GOD(S)? 171

ELOHIM	171
THE YHWH CODE	172
THE ELOHIM ARE NOT YHVH (YAHUAH)	174
THE DIVINE COUNCIL OF ELOHIM	175
THE NAMES OF THE GOD OF ISRAEL	179

CHAPTER TWELVE 185
THE TETRAGRAMMATON 185

WHY YAHUAH? WHY NOT YAHWEH OR JEHOVAH?	186

THE PERSONALITY OF YAHUAH	194
THE NAME YAH	196
YAHUAH'S NAME WITHIN THE PROPHETS	198

CHAPTER THIRTEEN 201
THE NAME ABOVE ALL NAMES 201

DISTORTIONS AND TRUNCATION OF THE NAME	205
IN THE NAME OF	209
WHAT'S IN A NAME?	213
COUNTERFEIT NAMES LEADS TO COUNTERFEIT MESSIAHS	214
DISCERNING THE SPIRIT BEHIND HRM	218
JEALOUSY OF JEWS & GENTILES	222
THE NEW AGE CHRISTIAN	228

CHAPTER FOURTEEN 233
WHO IS THE GOD OF GODS? 233

GOD IS A FOUR LETTER WORD	233
THE MASORETIC CONTROVERSY	235

CHAPTER FIFTEEN 239
WHO IS YAHWEH? 239

YAHWEH, THE COUNTERFEIT GOD	243
YAHWEH, THE DRAGON	244
YAHWEH THE GOLDEN CALF	248
YAHWEH CULTS	249
GNOSTIC YAHWEH	252
WHO IS YAHWEH YALDABAOTH?	254

CHAPTER SIXTEEN 259
WHO WERE THE ARCHONS? 259

THE VIRTUAL HEAVENS	260
IS YAHWEH ANNUNAKI?	262
LIFEFORCE IS IN THE BLOOD	262
ANNUNAKI IN THE BIBLE	263
ARE ALL "GODS" EXTRATERRESTRIALS?	264

- Who Are The Annunaki?..264

CHAPTER SEVENTEEN 269
WHO IS JEHOVAH?...269
- Jehovah - The Counterfeit God 269
- Appendix Of Supporting Evidence:...272
- Jehovah Witnesses-False Doctrines 274

CHAPTER EIGHTEEN 277
LIKE FATHER, LIKE SON 277
- Whom Did Jesus Pray To?...277
- Who Are The Children Of Abraham?...279
- Who Are The Children Of The Devil?..280
- The Holy Trinity: One God Or Three? 281
- I AM A Jealous God..282
- Shepherds And Their Sheep 284
- Where's The Power?...290

CHAPTER NINETEEN 297
WHO IS THE HOLY SPIRIT?..297
- The Holy Spirit Is The Spirit Of Christ 300
- The Holy Spirit Is A Living Person 301
- Where The Spirit Is, There Is Freedom...301
- The One And Only Unforgiveable Sin 303
- Fruits Of The Holy Spirit...304
- The Spiritual Gifts Of The Holy Spirit 304
- Discerning Tongues: The Gift of Languages 305
- The Sheep And The Goats 307

CHAPTER TWENTY 311
THE GOD OF THIS WORLD..311
- Lucifer, Fallen Angel Of Enlightenment..311
- Good God, Bad God...313
- The Devil's In The Details 319
- Lucifer/Satan's History 320

    Lucifer, Rahab And The Stones Of Fire 322
    Who Or What Is Rahab? 327

CHAPTER TWENTY-ONE 331
THE OFFICE OF SATAN 331
    The Original Counterfeiter 331
    Lucifer, Fallen Angels & Inter-Dimensionals 333
    Why Do Evil Angels Exist? 334
    The Principality Of Jealousy 335
    The Spirit Of Antichrist 337
    Fear Based Or Fear Of The Truth? 338
    Living In The Light 341
    The Age Of Narcissism & Godlessness In End Times 344
    Spiritual Narcissism 345
    Derivatives Of Lucifer/Satan 350

CHAPTER TWENTY-TWO 359
WHO IS ALLAH? 359

CHAPTER TWENTY-THREE 367
BABYLONIAN HISTORY: WHERE IT ALL BEGAN 367
    Babylon: The Great Mother Of Prostitutes And The
    Abominations Of The Earth 367
    Babylon: The First "United Nations" 368
    Who Was Nimrod? 369
    Who Is Semiramis? 371
    Striking Similarities 372
    Baal Worship 374
    There's Nothing New Under The Sun 376
    The Return Of Nimrod 376
    Mother And Child Worship 378
    The Son Of God And The "Sons Of God" 379
    The Sign of The Cross 380
    Why Jesus Came Forth From The Tomb Before Daybreak 380
    Constantine's Creed 381

    FALSE BELIEFS – FALSE RELIGIONS 384

CHAPTER TWENTY-FOUR 387
WHAT IS ISLAM? 387
    ISLAM TEACHES WIFE BEATING 388
    RADICAL ISLAMIC SEXUALITY IS PURE EVIL 388
    ANAL SEX CAUSES INFERTILITY 389
    GENITAL MUTILATION 389
    MAN-BOY-PEDOPHILIA 390
    TOTAL GENDER SEGREGATION 390
    SEX WITH FEMALE CHILDREN 390
    PROSTITUTION AKA "TEMPORARY MARRIAGES" 390
    LUCIFER AND THE MORNING STARS 391
    ISLAM: A RELIGION OF PEACE? 392
    THE CALL TO JIHAD IN THREE STAGES 395
    WHEN MUSLIMS REACH STAGE THREE 396
    WHAT IS SHARIAH LAW? 397

CHAPTER TWENTY-FIVE 399
WHO IS THE BEAST? 399
    THE GREAT COUNTERFEITER 400
    THE WORLD STAGE PREPARES FOR ANTICHRIST 401
    THE ANTICHRIST PROPHESY 403
    THE GODS WHO COME THROUGH PORTALS 411
    CERN AND THE ANTICHRIST 412
    THE ANCIENT PORTAL OF MEGIDDO 415
    WHY SATAN IS OBSESSED WITH ISRAEL'S ANCIENT SPACE PORTALS 417
    THE RIDER ON A WHITE HORSE 421

CHAPTER TWENTY-SIX 425
THE OFFICE OF CHRIST 425
    THE ARCHETYPE OF THE COSMIC CHRIST 427
    MITHRAS 429
    HORUS THE EGYPTIAN SUN GOD 432
    WILL THE REAL SAVIOR PLEASE STEP UP? 432

- Proof: Crucifixion, Resurrection of Jesus Christ 436
- Starships With Horsepower 438

CHAPTER TWENTY-SEVEN 441
THE CHRISTMAS GODS 441
- The Piscean Age Is The Age Of Jesus Christ 441
- The Return Of The Sun - December 25 443
- The Real Birthday of Jesus Christ 446

CHAPTER TWENTY-EIGHT 455
WHAT HAPPENS WHEN YOU DIE? 455
- Reincarnation: God's Original Plan 455
- Purgatory, Reincarnation in the Holy Bible 456
- Second Chances and Rebirth 457
- The Valley of Dry Bones 458
- Reincarnation: Been There, Done That 462
- Anathema To Rome 463
- Jesus Taught Reincarnation 466
- The End of Reincarnation 468
- On Karma 474
- Ye Must Be Born Again 476
- Prophets of God Reincarnated 478
- Can a Deceased Spirit Return to Earth? 479

CHAPTER TWENTY-NINE 485
WHO CREATED SEXISM? 485
- God's Anointing on Women to Teach and Lead 487

CONCLUDING WORDS 501
- Extraterrestrial Sheep? 503
- My Experiences With Religious Spirits 504
- Children Of God vs Children Of The Devil 517
- Who Is The Synagogue of Satan? 518
- Eight Woes To The Religious Spirits 521
- Who Are the Children of God? 528
- Who is Christian? 529

    THE LAST DAYS OF THE END TIMES 539
    UFO WARS 540
    CELESTIAL ARMIES OF FLYING WHITE HORSES 541
    END TIME CONCLUSION 542
    IT'S ALL ABOUT LOVE 545
NOTES AND BIBLIOGRAPHY 549
ABOUT THE AUTHOR 559

DEDICATION

This book is dedicated to the Lord of the Cosmos, the Lord of Heaven and Earth, without whose loving support, guidance and protection, this manuscript would not have been possible, for which I am forever grateful.

In addition to, I am dedicating this book to all those wounded by religion, all atheists, agnostics, and especially to those who consider themselves religious. May you all find something useful within the pages of this book to heal your soul.

ACKNOWLEDGEMENTS

My deepest gratitude goes to my loving and devoted husband and daughter, without whose love and support, this manuscript would not have been possible. They have stuck with me through all the spiritual battles and never stopped believing in my vision and goal. They are my true loves and soul mates whom I am blessed to be journeying with through this earth experience.

"All truth passes through three stages. First it is ridiculed. Second, it is violently opposed. Third, it is accepted as being self-evident."

~Arthur Shopenhauer (1788-1860)

INTRODUCTION

WHO IS GOD?

> "The sin of both men and of angels was rendered possible by the fact that God gave us free will."
>
> C.S. Lewis

How can we know "who" God is? How can we discern the difference between the gods of the Bible? Who is this cast of characters in the Old Testament and New Testament of the Bible? Are they all the same? What happened during the transliterations? Did some of the original meaning get lost? Who is the God of gods? Who is Satan? Are Allah and the God of the Old Testament one and the same? Who is Jesus? Who is the Holy Spirit? Are they God, too? Who created sexism? Why isn't the trinity mentioned in the Bible?

Who stretches out the heavens like a tent curtain? Who lays the beams of His upper chambers in the waters? Who makes the clouds His chariot? Who walks upon the wings of the wind? Who makes the winds His messengers? Who makes the flaming fire His ministers? Who rides across the heavens and on the clouds in His majesty to help you? Who is the God of Jeshurun?[1]

Who are the cherubim? What are the wheels of Ezekiel? Who rides in these flying chariots? What happens when you die? In Book Two of *Who's Who In The Cosmic Zoo?*, you will find definitive answers to all these questions and more.

For those who have read Book One of *Who's Who In The Cosmic Zoo?*, this book will pick up where you left off. However, for those readers who have not read my first book in this series of *Who's Who In The Cosmic Zoo?*, let me begin by recapping a few important definitions for the purpose of clarity and language.

The words *alien* and *extraterrestrial* are not one and the same meanings. Even though many people use these words interchangeably, they specifically describe two completely different types of beings. For definition and language purposes, an *alien* is a being or creature that does not share the same DNA as humans. By definition an alien is foreign to humans. However, Earth humans use this word to describe people that come from different countries and cultures, but truthfully, this word implies genetics and bloodlines. And while someone from England may be "alien" to America, their DNA is not necessarily "alien," as we all share humanity. We may not think alike, but that is not entirely due to different genetics, but to education, conditioning, and spiritual differences.

As I concluded in Book One, the biggest social problem on planet Earth is racism, which originates from extraterrestrials and aliens who have inserted their DNA bloodlines into humanity's cultures, subsequently creating differences between humans, not only culturally, but genetically. These extraterrestrial races, who have been at odds with one another over the real estate and control of planet Earth, have used their descendants against one another in a spiritual war against each other. This is why it's important to discern and understand the true meaning of the word *alien*.

An alien can qualify as "non-human intelligence," like Grays and their many clones, as well as robots. Reptilians are aliens to humans; however, not all reptilians and Gray aliens are extraterrestrials. As I've proved in Book One of *Who's Who In The Cosmic Zoo?*, they, in fact, live "inside" the Earth. I call them *intraterrestrials*. This means they are alien to us, but are not extraterrestrials.

True, there are aliens that appear to be human, they inhabit human form, but are clearly not human. Demonic possession is a good example of this. A demon possesses the mind and body of a human, and controls that human, making him or her perform inhumane acts upon other humans, making him or her do things that most humans would never even think of doing.

We, also, use the term *resident alien* to describe someone whose nationality is different from ours. This distinguishes their differences from American culture. Many believe that this term *alien* is misused when describing other human beings who were born outside the United States, and are pushing to have this definition redefined, to call them, instead *undocumented workers*, because they are still human.

An extraterrestrial, by definition, is a being that is not of this world, and not of this Earth; they may or may not be "alien." There are many humans that are extraterrestrials that are not necessarily alien to us, but live off planet. For example, and I know this example tends to rock some people's theology, but the very words of Jesus Christ describe this exactly:

"I AM not of this world." (John 8:23; John 17:16)

"My Kingdom is not of this world." (John 18:36)

This is the very definition of an extraterrestrial human. Jesus Christ was called both the Son of Man (human) and Son of God (Divine). While many Christians cringe at the thought of their God as an extraterrestrial, the truth of the matter is, His very words describe Him as such, in no uncertain terms.

In *The Merriam-Webster Dictionary*, the full definition of an extraterrestrial is "coming from or existing outside the planet Earth."

While Jesus Christ was extraterrestrial, He was, however, not "alien" to us, because He was fully human. Not only that, but according to the Bible, humans are made in the image and likeness of God (Elohim), which means, that our DNA comes from the Elohim, who are beyond this Earth, and therefore, by definition, are extraterrestrial.

INTRODUCTION: Who Is God?

In Book Two, I am proving, that, not only is this scriptural (based on the original Hebrew Scriptures), but also an important discernment for these End Times.

As Earth humans (aka terrestrials), we are not extraterrestrial per se; we do, however, have extraterrestrial DNA, which is stated in Genesis 1:27:

> "So God created man in his own image, in the image of God He created him, male and female, He created them."

Based on this scripture alone, almost everyone can agree that some God created the human race. However, what I will prove to you in this book is which god or gods that was, based on the original language that this scripture was originally written in, and why that is relevant now.

In Book One, I began by laying out in my dissertation — how to discern between ETs and Aliens. In Book Two, I'm going to take you on a journey of how to discern between the different so-called ancient gods of our human history, a handful of which are mentioned right inside the Bible scriptures.

Today's English Bibles, unfortunately, do not allow much of these details to be seen or discerned by those who only rely solely on the English translations, (and that includes all the other languages that get translated from English to Spanish, German, French, etc.) because so many "key" words, particularly the names of God and the other gods mentioned in the Old Testament, are all translated into the same English word, God, misleading the English reader to believe that they are all one and the same. I will prove to you, within these pages, through the discernment of language and the linguistics of the original Scripture language that this knowledge was completely lost in mis-translations and mis-transliterations - that the same "God" mentioned throughout the English Bible is clearly not the same god.

My purpose is to reveal truths that have been hidden from Bible readers since 1611, when the first English Bible was published known as the King James Bible.

> "The time is coming when everything that is covered up will be revealed, and all that is secret will be made known to all."
>
> (Luke 12:2 NLT)

My hope and intention is that this knowledge will clear up confusion in the minds of many people, particularly those who have rejected the Bible based on these erroneous mistranslations, as well as those religious folks who mistakenly believe they are all one and the same.

While all gods have spirits attached to them, (including the inanimate gods, like idols), there are, however, creator gods, and there is *the* Creator God, who is the God of gods, whose very Spirit permeates the universe and multiverse we all exist in. He is also called the Lord of Spirits. This Spirit transcends this terrestrial plane known as Earth, as well as this flesh and blood life. The discernment of spirits is important when discerning "who" God is, for everything is spiritual, both of the light and of the darkness.

Another word for spirit is *attitude*. There is the spirit of unbelief, which creates the attitude of atheism. But in reality, there is no such thing as true atheists. Atheists claim that there is no god, but what they are actually saying, is "I don't know God." How do I know this? Simply because when Atheists 'see' the Lord, they immediately become believers. The list of atheists who have had experiences with God showing up for them, or speaking to them, or revealing Himself to them in dreams, is too long to print here. Atheism is simply a state of mind, controlled by a 'spirit' of unbelief.

In a world where there is so much dissension between religions, religious people seem to always be in conflict with one another; it's no wonder there are atheists because religious folks often fail at lovingly representing who God really is. Of course, that all depends on one's religion, as their notion of who God is differs from one religion to another. From this, one can conclude that not all gods are the same. Unfortunately, due to the founders and creators of the world's religions, many religions obscure who God really is. Again, this is done through the agency of spirits and their spiritual strongholds. I am taking on one of these and exposing it within this book, which I call the "religious spirit," aka the spirit of religion, which I began to define in Book One of *Who's Who In The Cosmic Zoo?* (See, pp. 361-381)[2].

The root word 'religion' comes from the Latin word, *religare'*, which is broken down to *re 'ligare''* which means, to bind, to tie down or to shackle. Is it any wonder that religious 'spirits' hold people in all sorts of oppressive bondages? There is a difference between 'faith' in God, and following a particular religious doctrine. There is a huge difference, between a 'relationship' with the Creator God, and following a religion. Does one actually need to belong to a religion to have a relationship with God? Let's discern.

Religion has corrupted the Truth about who God is. There are forces within the religious structures of planet Earth that are actually mind control setups, programs created to manipulate humans. However, there is another side within the world's religious paths that are woven within that point humans to their Creator and invite humans into a relationship through the Spirit of the Creator.

So many people I know, including myself, consider themselves to be "spiritual," but not religious. But a spiritual person can be attached to a variety of spirits (not all are of the light and the truth), which again requires both the gift and the spiritual muscle to actually *discern* spirits.

Here is what scripture has to say about atheism and the spirit of unbelief in God and its consequences:

> "For the wrath of God is revealed from heaven against all ungodliness and unrighteousness of men who suppress the truth in unrighteousness, because that which is known about God is evident **within** them; for God made it evident to them.

INTRODUCTION: Who Is God?

(By putting a piece of His Spirit within humans, known as the soul, in order for that 'God spark' to recognize and have relationship with their Creator)

For since the creation of the world His *invisible* attributes, His eternal power and Divine nature, have been clearly seen, being understood through what has been made (through His creation), so that they are without excuse. For even though they knew God, they did not honor Him as God or give thanks, but they became futile in their speculations, and their foolish heart was darkened (the word *heart* in the Bible is interchangeable with the word *spirit*). Professing to be wise, they became fools, and exchanged the glory of the incorruptible God for an image in the form of corruptible man and of birds and four-footed animals and crawling creatures.

Therefore God gave them over in the lusts of their hearts to impurity, so that their bodies would be dishonored among them. ***For they exchanged the truth of God for a lie***, and worshiped and served the creature rather than the Creator, who is blessed forever."

(Romans 1:18-25)

While praying one day, a woman asked, "Who are you God?
He answered, "I Am."
"But who is I Am?" she asked.
He replied, "I Am Love, I Am Peace, I Am Grace, I Am Joy, I Am Strength, I Am Safety, I Am Shelter, I Am Power, I Am the Creator, I Am the Comforter, I Am the Beginning and the End. I Am the Way, the Truth, and the Light."
With tears in her eyes, she looked toward heaven and said, "Now I understand. But who am I?"
God tenderly wiped the tears from her eyes and whispered, "You Are Mine."

In today's world, most people identify God with religion. But there are dozens of different religions, all venerating many different gods. In Book Two of *Who's Who In The Cosmic Zoo?: A Guide to ETs, Aliens, Gods & Angels,* I'm going to take you on a journey to explore "who" these gods actually are. Are they all the same? Or are they all different gods? Are the gods of Judaism, Islam, and Christianity all the same? What about those three million Hindu gods? Don't worry. I'm not going to go through all of them.

If the different religions worship different gods, is it possible that some may actually end up worshipping the same god without realizing it because of a simple name translation? Or not? But what happens when mis-translations come into the picture, and the names of God are changed into names with completely different meanings or even counterfeit names that may invoke a completely different god or spirit? Can this affect your relationship with God? What about blood? What's up with all the blood sacrifices? Why does God demand blood? Whose blood has authority over all the bloodlines? Do you think there is such a thing as the ultimate blood sacrifice? Does all this bloodlust through religion's histories indicate the presence of a carnivorous alien on Earth? Does the God of Love actually require blood?

Do we as humans even need religion to have a relationship with our Creator? Does God even care what religion you belong to? Does your religion, church, or temple affiliation have anything to do with whether or not you get to go to heaven? What does God really care about when you stand before His heavenly throne in the afterlife? If you make mistakes, does God give you a second chance? Does God have enemies? If so, who are God's enemies? If you are sabotaged or deceived into worshipping God's enemies, will God forgive you? If so, at what cost? And for the million-dollar question answered in this book, "who" is God? But before we can discern the "who," let's first define the "what."

DEFINITION OF GOD:

The word *god* is a title; it is not a name. Not all gods are named "God," yet people call Him God or Goddess anyway; suffice it to say, both *god* and *goddess* are simply titles. However, there was someone named *Gawd* in the Old Testament, who was a pagan god, and somehow the title of every other god stuck, and every idol was then called God.

Isaiah 65:11-12 warns the Israelites of leaving the God of Abraham for another god called Gawd, whose name has been translated as "Fortune" in various bibles:

> "But as for you who abandon the LORD (Yahuwah) and forget about worshiping at my holy mountain, who prepare a feast for the god called ' Fortune,' (Gawd in Hebrew) and fill up wine jugs for the god called 'Destiny' (Lamni in Hebrew)[11], I will destine you for the sword, and all of you will bow down to the slaughter. Because I called you, but you did not answer; I spoke, but you did not hear. And you did evil in My sight and chose that in which I did not delight.[12]"
>
> (Verse 11: Net Bible; Verse 12: NAS)

We know that Israel has a recorded history of having left the God of Abraham, YHUH, in favor of a deity whose personal name was GOD/Gawd in 721 B.C. The word *GAAD* (Gawd in Hebrew) refers to a "God of Forces," literally a "troop." We see GAAD in the King James Bible translated as "troop." This brings a whole new meaning to the modern-day phrase "Support the Troops!" The name GAAD (Gawd) is also often translated into English Bibles as "Fortune." As in "when your troops enlisted the help of GAWD to invade and conquer your enemies, you could make a 'Fortune.'"

For those of you who have read Book One of *Who's Who In The Cosmic Zoo?*, you will remember that the business of war, known as today's Military Industrialized Complex (MIC), was more specifically called the Extraterrestrial Militarized Industrialized Complex (EMIC), because ETs and aliens have been in contracts and agreements with Earth's governments for a long time. These contracts include knowledge

INTRODUCTION: Who Is God?

of advanced space technology in exchange for allowing them to harvest humanity for resources, just as humanity harvests cattle for milk. The cattle are kept alive and used for their energy over and over again until there is no more. The human energy field and the human soul are of great importance to some of these beings, as are human bodily fluids, which contain human DNA for cloning and genetic engineering for their hybridization program.

Language makes a difference, as you can see from just one word in the Old Testament, which today has become the title for every other "god."

In order to take in new information, a psychological attitude often comes on, called "cognitive dissonance." The concept of cognitive dissonance was first introduced by psychologist Leon Festig (1919-1989). In the late 1950s, he along with other researchers proved that when people are confronted with challenging, new information, most people seek to preserve their current understanding of the world by rejecting, explaining away, or avoiding the new information or by convincing themselves that no conflict really exists. This occurs when there is a mental conflict that occurs when beliefs or assumptions are contradicted by new information. Cognitive dissonance is, nonetheless, considered an explanation for attitude changes.

In this book, you can expect to see new information on the actual meanings and words in the scriptures that were both misconstrued, deliberately obscured, and lost in translations. These new meanings may create cognitive dissonance. "It's not what you don't know that gets you in trouble, it's what you do know, that just ain't so." (Mark Twain)

Before the truth can set you free,
You need to recognize which false belief is holding you hostage.

We will, throughout this book, explore the names of God and discern, based solely on His names and their meanings, if it's all one God or, perhaps, a cast of characters known as God. I will take you on a journey and explore how language and mis-translations, along with numerous spiritual battles, have changed people's perceptions of who God is and what His real name is in comparison to all the other names of all the other gods.

In this book, you will discover just "who" is the God of gods, the Most High, the Almighty, and the Creator of Heaven and Earth and why that matters now more than ever before. We will explore the history of the world's major religions, along with a few popular offshoot cults, and determine if they are all worshipping the same one God, and why that, too, matters now, more than ever before.

Religion has corrupted the truth about "who" God is. I will identify which forces within all the religious structures of Earth have been deliberately constructed as mind-control setups and programs to manipulate humankind. However, there has always been a path woven within the world's religions that points the way back to their Creator God and invites them into a relationship with Spirit, well maybe not all the religions, but most certainly the big ones have that.

In the past, anyone who had personal contact with extraterrestrial beings, who were more advanced than humans, were considered to be "gods" to them. Here is a more recent example portrayed in the 1978 film *Superman*:

> "Can you read my mind? Do you know what it is that you do to me? I don't know who you are. Just a friend from another star. Here I am, like a kid out of school. Holding hands with a god. I'm a fool. Will you look at me? Quivering. Like a little girl, shivering. You can see right through me. Can you read my mind? Can you picture the things I'm thinking of? Wondering why you are ... all the wonderful things you are. You can fly. You belong in the sky. You and I ... could belong to each other. If you need a friend ... I'm the one to fly to. If you need to be loved ... here I am. Read my mind."
>
> ~ Lois Lane, *Superman*

These famous words turned into a famous love song, edifying romance with extraterrestrials. Is it any wonder how Earth women of the past gave into having sex with fallen angels? But what we must learn to do is discern between what and who is a god or God Himself, and what and who mere extraterrestrial beings are.

> "Now listen to me. I tell you, boys and girls — whichever one of you gets it out ... is going to wind up with the single most important interview since ... God talked to Moses!"
>
> ~ Perry White, *Superman*

Yes, since God talked to Moses, Joshua, Elijah, Ezekiel, Isaiah, Daniel, Zechariah, Micah, Malachi, David, John, and Jesus.

NOTES:

1. Deuteronomy 33:26; Psalms 104:2-4, KJV
2. Ella LeBain, *Who's Who In The Cosmic Zoo?, Book One, Third Edition,* Tate Publishing, 2013.

CHAPTER ONE

GODS OR ETS?

"And there was war in heaven:
Michael and his angels fought against the dragon;
And the dragon fought and his angels, prevailed not;
Neither was their place found any more in heaven.
And the great dragon was cast out, that old serpent,
called the Devil, and Satan,
Who deceives the whole world:
He was cast out into the earth, and
The angels were cast out with him."
(Revelation 12:7-9, KJ2000)

THE COSMIC DRAMA

"The early history of our universe was a bloody mosaic of interplanetary war."
~Jor-El (to Kal-El), *Superman*

The Cosmic Drama is between the Almighty Creator God and his rebellious fallen extraterrestrial sons and angels. This is why the Cosmic Christ was sent as God in the flesh to redeem His creation from the bondage of the fallen angels (the satans) and their lead prince/cherub/son, Lucifer, aka Satan the Chief Adversary. Because they were created as immortal beings, they were allowed dominion over certain star systems and planets but were allowed only limited access in the heavens. This was the beginning of Cosmic Evil.

It says, in the book of Revelation, that the Lord will create a new heavens and a new earth at the end of this Cosmic Drama. He will obliterate Cosmic Evil and its stronghold and dominion over the lower stars and planets by recreating the heavens, rearranging the stars, and destroying the strongholds that the satans and fallen angel extraterrestrials have created, which the Zohar called Cosmic Evil or dark stars, also known as a cursed state. The Book of Revelation, together with the Books of Enoch, prophesied of a final cosmic battle between the faithful and the fallen extraterrestrial angels.

This is why the Cosmic Christ is relevant, as the Lord Jesus Christ, aka Yahshua HaMashiach, the Messiah, and Savior of the world is not limited to planet Earth.

His very words were "I am not of this world" (John 17:14, KJV), and "I have other sheep <u>that are not of this sheep pen</u>. I must bring them also. They too will listen to my voice, and there shall be one flock and one shepherd" (John 10:16, NIV).

These words of Christ prove that, not only are we not alone in the Cosmos, but that there is One Cosmic Christ who brings us all together to live in peace and harmony in the Kingdom of Heaven. Heaven is a vast place. His divine plan of salvation extends out to the entire Cosmos as it is written into the constellations and stars as a reminder for all creation to have, know, and understand that God's plan of redemption, victory over cosmic evil, and His establishment of His Kingdom of Light, Love, and Grace is secure for all those in the Cosmos who believe in and acknowledge Him.

Jesus Christ is not limited to saving earth humans. There are extraterrestrial (ET) civilizations that have been hijacked and held in bondage by the cosmic adversaries, the satans, and the fallen angels (Nephilim, Anunnaki), who hold humans hostage as slaves. The Cosmic Christ is going to liberate them, as well, after the final battle is won and the Lord establishes the Kingdom of Heaven on Earth and rearranges the heavens. He will rule from His heavenly city, the New Jerusalem, which represents the hub and epicenter of the cosmos, when both Heaven and the New Jerusalem comes to Earth.

"For, behold, I create new heavens and a new earth:
And the former shall not be remembered, nor come into mind."

(Isaiah 65:17, KJV)

THE SEA OF FORGETFULNESS

"And I saw a new heaven and a new earth: for the first heaven and the first earth were passed away; and there was no more sea."

(Revelation 21:1, KJV)

Why no more sea? Because our sins are washed away in the sea of forgetfulness.

"You (the Lord Yahuah) will again have compassion on us; you will tread our sins underfoot and hurl all our iniquities into the depths of the sea."

(Micah 7:19, NIV)

This scripture illustrates the concept of where we have coined the phrase "sea of forgetfulness." This theme is repeated in the promises of God in Isaiah 1:18 (ESV):

"Come now, let us reason together, says the LORD: though your sins are like scarlet, they shall be as white as snow; though they are red like crimson, they shall become like wool."

Psalm 103:11-12 (NAS) reiterates God's Promise:

"For as high as the heavens are above the earth, so great is His lovingkindness toward those who fear Him. As far as the east is from the west, so far has He removed our transgressions from us."

How Are We Judged?

Believe it or not, there are two judgments mentioned in the Bible, the Terrible Day of the Lord, also known as "Judgment Day," and the Great White Throne Judgment:

> "And I saw a great white throne, and him that sat on it, from whose face the earth and the heaven fled away; and there was found no place for them.
>
> And I saw the dead, small and great, stand before God; and the books were opened: and another book was opened, which is *the book* of life: and the dead were judged out of those things which were written in the books, according to their works.
>
> And the sea gave up the dead which were in it; and death and hell delivered up the dead which were in them: and they were judged every man according to their works.
>
> And death and hell were cast into the lake of fire. This is the second death.
>
> And whosoever was not found written in the book of life was cast into the lake of fire."
>
> (Revelation 20:11-15, KJV)

Scripture tells us that, according to the Torah, if you break just one of these laws, you are guilty of breaking all (Deuteronomy 27:26; James 2:10). Then the New Covenant came through Yahshua HaMashiach, who did not come to abolish the law, but to fulfill the law.

> "Do not think that I have come to abolish the Law or the Prophets; I have not come to abolish them but to fulfill them."
>
> (Matthew 5:17, NIV)

This is also known as the Law of Grace. Grace through the Messiah is how people will be judged. All will be judged based on our acceptance or rejection of what He did for us as our advocate between our mistakes (sins, errors, iniquities, and transgressions) and the law giver, who is the Most High God.

Just because today's humans have grown to ignore, even dismiss, God's laws entirely, that doesn't make those laws go away or God's judgment of humans go away either.

Many Jews follow the Torah to the "T." Some do this to be worthy and earn their favor with God; others do this to avoid having an encounter with Yahshua, their Messiah, and asking for forgiveness by repenting of unbelief. Either way, God's laws prevail, God's son Yahshua is the Law of Grace available to all who believe in Him and repent of their sins.

> "For by grace are ye saved through faith; and that not of yourselves: *it is* the gift of God: Not of works, lest any man should boast."
>
> (Ephesians 2:8-9, KJV)

FAITH? WHOSE FAITH?

Hebrews 12:2 says that Jesus Christ is the author (founder) and finisher (perfecter) of our faith. This scripture tells us that it is His faith that is deposited into us to have fellowship with Him. His faith provides the righteousness and grace that we need.

> "Knowing that a man is not justified by the works of the law, but by the faith of Jesus Christ, even we have believed in Jesus Christ, <u>that we might be justified by the faith of Christ</u>, and not by the works of the law: for by the works of the law shall no flesh be justified."
>
> (Galatians 2:16, KJV)

Because Christ gave up His "god" powers to fulfill the mission of the Cross, we are justified by God through His faith, His faith that He displayed on the Cross for us, as well His faith that He deposits into each of one of us. For it is written, "The Just shall live by Faith."

> (Hebrews 10:38, KJV)

> "Who, being in the very nature of God, did not consider equality with God something to be used to his own advantage; rather, he made himself nothing by taking the very nature of a servant, being made in human likeness. And being found in appearance as a man, he humbled himself by becoming obedient to death — even death on a cross! Therefore God exalted him to the highest place and gave him the name that is above every name, that at the name of Jesus every knee should bow, in heaven and on earth and under the earth, and every tongue acknowledge that Jesus Christ is Lord, to the glory of God the Father."
>
> (Philippians 2:6-1, 1 NIV)

So Jesus explained, "I tell you the truth, the Son can do nothing by himself. He does only what he sees the Father doing.

> Whatever the Father does, the Son also does."
>
> (John 5:19, NLT)

> "Don't you think that I could call on my Father to send more than twelve legions of angels to help me now?"
>
> (Matthew 26:53, God's Word)

CHAPTER ONE: Gods or ETs?

Just to give my readers an idea of how many twelve legions of angels are, one legion equals 12,000 angels. Twelve legions of angels would be 144,000 angels. This is what it means when the Bible calls the Father Yahuah the Lord of Hosts. Hosts are celestial armies of angels (extraterrestrial warriors).

> "No one takes it from me, but I lay it down of my own accord. I have authority to lay it down and authority to take it up again. This command I received from my Father." (John 10:18, NIV)

This means that the specific mission Yeshua had was to be obedient to the Father unto death, to give up His life so that others could be set free spiritually. Part of the reason the Jewish Pharisees did not recognize this is because they were expecting the Messiah to free them from Roman oppression. Everything in this world first begins in the spiritual realm, and then manifests into the material, physical realm.

The spiritual oppression first had to be broken, by defeating the forces of darkness with the innocence of one of the members of the godhead, the Son of God, who was Yeshua. (See, my chapter on *Spiritual Legal Ground* in Book One of *Who's Who In the Cosmic Zoo?*, pp.45-54) Yahshua had to reclaim spiritually what the first Adam lost for humankind. He did that, as many know of His power over the spiritual and supernatural realms today. Demons tremble at his name; even aliens are disoriented when rebuked in the name of the Lord. Healings and miracles continue to happen, to this day, in the name of Yeshua/Jesus.

Now even the demons knew who Yahshua was. In later chapters, I identify just who and what demons are, but suffice it to say, for now, they are spiritual intelligences, which is exactly where the word *demon* comes from. The Greek word *daemon* means intelligences. The fact that the supernatural realm identified Yahshua as the Son of God, which, by the way, goes on till this day, is extremely revealing, particularly to those who were blinded by a spirit of unbelief, which keeps people from seeing with their spiritual eyes who Yahshua is and thwarts them from hearing from His Holy Spirit directly, so instead their ears are itching to hear what they want to hear and, therefore, follow after the doctrines of demons.

> "And whenever those possessed by evil spirits caught sight of him, the spirits would throw them to the ground in front of him shrieking, "You are the Son of God!""
> (Mark 3:11, NLT)

Jesus said, "**My kingdom is not of this world**. If it were, my servants would fight to prevent my arrest by the Jewish leaders. **But now my kingdom is from another place.**"
(John 18:36, NIV)

That Kingdom is the Kingdom of Heaven, which will be coming to earth at the end of this processional age. The City of God, also known as the New Jerusalem is prophesied to come out of the heavens and land on earth, where the throne of Yeshua/Jesus will be, and He will rule over the earth and all the nations in what the prophesy calls the Millennial Reign. This is the thousand years of peace, love, and brotherhood and sisterhood that is sung about in the song, "Aquarius/Let the Sunshine In." It will be the Age of Understanding, the Golden Age where God lives with mankind. This is the next processional age to come.

THE LORD OF THE COSMOS

When Christ returns, He will come to judge and make war. He will wear the crowns of total universal sovereignty (Revelation 19:12). He is not only the Judge and the Captain, but also the sovereign King. Remember, He won these crowns by his obedience to his Father's will as our substitute (John 17:2). When King David conquered the Ammonites, he took the crown of the defeated king and placed it upon his own head, in addition to the crown he already had as king of Israel (2 Samuel 12:30).

In the same sense, Christ has, by virtue of his conquests, taken all the crowns of the universe and placed them upon his own head, in addition to the crown he possesses as God and Creator of all things. And He is coming to make war with and execute judgment upon all those who dispute his right to total sovereignty, which includes the rebel ETs and pseudo-gods (Isaiah 45:9).

The scriptures tell us that Lucifer, God's Chief Archangel (Cherub), convinced one-third of Heaven's angels to rebel against the Almighty Creator God. Yet two-thirds of Heaven's angels (aka extraterrestrial messengers) remained faithful and did not rebel and are, to this day, still very much aligned with the Creator's Divine Will for Creation, for Space, and to overcome Cosmic Evil and Spiritual Darkness and Wickedness in heavenly places. That means the dark forces are outnumbered 2:1.

The Fallen Angel/Nephilim and Satan's dominion over Earth is a mock-up for the cosmic battles, which is not limited to their rebellion against the Almighty Creator God; instead, it is inclusive and shows how they are battling among themselves for power and control over who has dominion over which galaxy, star system and, more importantly, over Earth and Earth humans. They became "gods" with a small "g" in the experiment of creating life on other worlds, and many have had lots of control issues over their human subjects, as our earth history is rich with stories of such brutal human suffering under the direct and indirect influences of these gods (fallen angels).

They demanded worship and created slavery and bondage of all kinds to ensure that this plan for humanity would work for them; they used their knowledge of genetic engineering to manipulate human DNA, so humans would have a really hard time finding their power and their way back to the Creator. This is why earth humans only have two strands of DNA. Even today's top geneticists have discovered there are ten strands of missing DNA in humans. This explains why humans only use 10 percent of their brains, and that number is even debatable for some earth humans.

Suffice it to say, these "gods" (fallen extraterrestrial angels) have created karma with earth humans. The path of evolution is the Creator's constant of the Universe, all creation eventually evolves or transforms into something else, whether it lives or is destroyed. Everything is energy; energy can never be destroyed only transformed. However, even the force of a black hole can recreate that which it vaporized; its molecular structure may be rearranged, but spirit will find a way to bump it into matter eventually, and so it is with the fallen angel gods, as they are not immune to the Creator's force of evolution.

Some will evolve out of the karma they created for earth humans and continue to create, and others will be castigated even deeper into darker, denser worlds to work out their karma or receive their punishment which is promised in Revelation chapters 20-22 and the *Books of Enoch*, which is the promise that all evil will finally be destroyed. Somehow all this serves as the Great Experiment that the Almighty Creator God has allowed to take place for divine purposes.

> "I form the light, and create darkness:
> I make peace, and create evil: I the LORD do all these *things*."
> (Isaiah 45:7 KJV)

Reincarnation is about grace. The fact that human souls are allowed many lifetimes which loop into a rather larger cycle of lifetimes within this Great Experiment we call life on planet earth shows a Creator full of mercy and fairness. Why should mortals (earth humans) be terminated after dying in a war or a battle or all the myriads of ways earth humans can expire?

Think of how many lives are cut short suddenly, how many people die with unrequited love, having to endure incredible hardships, suffering, and slavery under the dominion of these fallen angels and pseudo-gods who have set up power structures on Earth under Satan's hierarchy. Grace and mercy allows for second, third, and as many chances as the soul requires for evolution and to find its way back to the Creator God.

Believe it or not, reincarnation is in the Bible, but most of the scriptures (but not all) were deleted by the Church of Nicaea in 325 AD when it was voted out (3-2) at the Ecumenical Council of Constantinople because the Church had an agenda at that time to control religion, and the beliefs of reincarnation no longer served their present-day agenda, which was to put the fear of God into people by telling them that they had only one chance to live, and if they failed to accept their version of Christianity, they would go to hell.

At that time, the Church was sabotaged by a *Religious Spirit*, which came through Constantine, which is a demonic, fallen angel influence with an agenda to control, manipulate, and hold souls in bondage. Yet, in spite of their mandates, reincarnation continued, as many, who were tortured by their countless inquisitions and persecutions, were reincarnated. In addition to all the other horrible ways humans found death — through the plagues, the wars, and the genocides — many people today have uncovered unconscious memories of their past lives and past deaths. (See my chapter *What Happens When You Die*)

Ask yourself this question, do you need to "believe" in God for God to exist? Most intelligent people will answer no. God exists whether we understand or believe in Him or not. Likewise, ask yourself this question: Do you need to "believe" in reincarnation for reincarnation to be real?

The fallen angels (gods) were created immortal; they don't reincarnate like humans do; instead they transform and evolve through events and battles, which make them part of the Creator's Grand Experiment as well. Many of them will be destroyed in the lake of fire created for Satan and his fallen angels, (Revelation Chapters 19 – 20), yet some will be redeemed through Christ for those who have repented of their rebellion toward the Creator. We are told that, after Jesus Christ bled to death on the Cross of Calvary, He went inside the earth, to the depths of Hades (Hell) and Purgatory (the Holy Fire), and redeemed both human souls and repentant angels (ETs).

This is why I am calling him the Cosmic Christ. Isaiah 61:1(ESV) says he came "To proclaim liberty to the captives and the opening of the prison to those who are bound." Jesus then preached to those being held in prison. "By which also he went and preached unto the spirits in prison" (1 Peter 3:19 KJV). "For this cause was the gospel preached also to them that are dead, that they might be judged according to men in the flesh, but live according to God in the spirit" (1 Peter 4:6 KJV).

"Verily, verily, I say unto you, the hour is coming, and now is, when the dead shall hear the voice of the Son of God; and they that hear shall live" (John 5:25 KJV). First Peter 4:6 and John 5:25 make it clear that these prisoners Jesus is preaching to are the dead. Again, the Divine Plan of Salvation is not limited to earth humans. In fact, the entire story of salvation is literally written into the very stars themselves. (See my chapter in Book Five- *The Heavens*: "The Word of God Written in the Stars.")

Therefore, it is imperative that earth humans become aware of the differences between these "gods" (fallen extraterrestrial angels) and the Creator and His Angels (Extra Terrestrial Messengers), who have not fallen from heaven. Remember the equation, as history tells us that one-third of heaven's angels followed Lucifer's rebellion, the other two-thirds of Heaven's Angels stayed loyal to the Creator and continue to be a part of the Lord's Celestial Army and Hierarchy which stretches across the vast constellations of stars today.

These are the extraterrestrial gods and guardians of two-thirds of the Heavens, which are the worlds of light. They preside over the most advanced and evolved civilization in the Creator's Universe. These are the Human Vine (see my *Cosmic Drama Chart*, pp. 90-91 in Book One of *Who's Who In the Cosmic Zoo?*), the Super Humans, the Sons of God (i.e., the Elohim, the Ultra-Terrestrials from the vast array of star systems in the dominion of Light). They are giants in their own right, both in stature and in spirit.

The Cosmology of the Zohar talks about the existence of and awareness of Cosmic Evil and Cosmic Light. This reflects the ancient Cosmic Drama between the forces of Light and Darkness. The Almighty Creator God has a lot of ETs on His side against the battles with the Fallen Angels and Satan's hierarchy. As I've said before, the Fallen Angels and Satan's hierarchy are clearly outnumbered in the Cosmos by, at least a ratio of 2:1, if not more.

This is the reason the Almighty Creator God created the Cosmic Christ or Cosmic Messiah. It's the heart of the Creator, who has pure love and grace for His creation. The plan of salvation is part of the Divine Program and Divine Plan for all of His creation. The Cosmic Christ is a Cosmic Archetype; similar histories have been repeated on other planets and star systems. Perhaps the details are different, but remember Christ was sent on a specific mission. He was to become the living sacrifice to be the "gateway" between humans and the Creator.

When He died on the cross, the Bible tells us there was a great earthquake, the dead were raised that were buried, and Christ went into the underworld and rescued one-third of the spirits along with some angels that chose redemption from Hades. This is about creating the bridge back to the Supreme Creator through grace in Christ. This Divine Program is not limited to planet Earth, as there are numerous other planets bound by the forces of darkness or Cosmic Evil that need redemption by the light.

According to Dr. James Hurtak in *The Keys of Enoch*, Ursa Major and Ursa Minor are midway stations which control negativity on lower planets, which are controlled by the Nephilim (Fallen Angels).

> Key 106:20: "The Big Dipper (Ursa Major) and the Little Dipper (Ursa Minor) are the thresholds gates of the lower evolutions in opposition to the Pleiades, the 7 lamp stands to the throne of the Father. At the end of time, we will see the war of the heavens and the coming of the Host of Michael. This will free the planetary intelligence from the influences of Ursa Major and Ursa Minor, the negative influences controlling the root races of this planet."
>
> Key 106:24: "Intelligences in these distant universes are called upon not only to judge the Earth, but also to judge the gods who reign in these fallen stations of the sky. We, too, who are on the threshold between the spiritual powers and humanity, will be called upon to judge the angels who have been cast into our dimension of space during this cleansing of the sky, fulfilling the words of I Corinthians 6:3 where it says: "Do you know that you shall judge angels?"[3]

Everyone goes to their designated place depending on who owns their soul. Satan's Kingdom is not limited to this planet and his fallen angels; they/he will take you to their underground and use you as their slaves, or if you choose, Christ will set you free from them. There are underground bases that belong to the satans and the fallen angels that are on Mars and the Moon and possibly other planets in our solar system. There have been all kinds of stories and speculations that, in the 1970s, groups of selected scientists were abducted and taken to work in underground laboratories inside Mars and inside the moon, never to be returned to the earth's surface.

There are also scores of stories, which include eyewitness testimonies, that many earth humans (both children and adults, including scientists and engineers) have been abducted and held hostage in the underground laboratories of Dulce, New Mexico, and remote places underground in Nevada. Many are being experimented on and used in various alien-human hybrid experiments, which are ordered and orchestrated by Draconian aliens operating within Satan's hierarchy.[2]

The Zohar talks about Death Stars, Dark Stars, and cosmological negativity in our galactic neighborhood. This concept is mentioned in great detail in the Zohar, along with the ancient apocryphal text, the *Book of Enoch,* which was never canonized into the Bible by the Church Fathers because it did not fit into their church agenda in 325 AD.

Enoch was the first known man of the Bible to ascend to God. He was taken off the earth for three hundred years and returned with scrolls, which were later suppressed by both the Jewish Pharisees/Sanhedrin and the Catholic Church, in spite of the fact that Enoch's scrolls were read by Jews during the times of Christ and considered the Word of God. The disciples quoted from the *Books of Enoch*. Christ Himself quoted Enoch's words as well.

Enoch was Methuselah's father and Noah's grandfather. He was the earliest of our forefathers, bigger in stature than Abraham, yet rejected by the church fathers because his story was too "alien" for them and, as previously stated, did not fit into their agenda of manipulation and control because the Catholic church was hijacked by a religious spirit, aka a fallen angel, who was in direct conflict with the Almighty Creator God. They are exposed in the *Book of Enoch*.

The main reason Enoch's Books was deemed heresy and taken out of the Old Testament was because the Sanhedrin, at that time, were so threatened by the passages that accurately predicted the life and mission of Jesus Christ (Yahshua). It was the Jewish scribes who first rejected the *Books of Enoch* because he accurately predicted Jesus Christ and was the first to coin the phrase "Son of Man."

> "And he sat on the throne of his glory, and the sum of judgment was given unto the **Son of Man**, and he caused the sinners to pass away and be destroyed from off the face of the earth, and those who have led the world astray."
>
> (Enoch 69:27)

> "And he (the angel) came to me and greeted me with His voice, and said unto me: 'This is the **Son of Man** who is born unto righteousness, and righteousness abides over him, and the righteousness of the **Head of Days** forsakes him not.' And he said unto me: 'He proclaims unto thee peace in the name of the world to come; for from hence has proceeded peace since the creation of the world, and so shall it be unto thee forever and forever and ever. And all shall walk in his ways since

righteousness never forsakes him: With him will be their dwelling places, and with him their heritage, and they shall not be separated from him forever and ever and ever. And so there shall be length of days with that **Son of Man**, and the righteous shall have peace and an upright way in the name of the **Lord of Spirits** forever and ever."

(Enoch 71:14-16)

Fragments of the *Book of Enoch*, written in Aramaic, were discovered in Qumran Cave 4, showing that it was among the other copies of scripture hidden away there. The Sanhedrin at Yavneh rejected it in 90 AD, and while many church fathers quoted from it, the council of Laodicea, in about 363-364 AD, rejected it; after which time, it disappeared from view. It resurfaced in around 1733 AD and again in 1912 when the R.H. Charles edition was published.[1] In fact, the Coptic Bible, contained the *Book of Enoch,* as the Coptic Christians never submitted to Rome's editing of the Bible canon, and still retains Enoch's writings to this day.

The other reason Enoch's books were rejected by the Church fathers may have been due to its accurate astronomy. Enoch, being a frequent flyer, describes in page after page the paths of the sun, moon, annual cycles, and heavenly statistics. "Paths of the sun and moon," "their stately orbits," "courses of the luminaries" and "revolve in their circular chariots" are only a few quotes of Enochian wisdom.

"And I saw in the heaven running in the world, above those portals in which revolve the stars that never set."

(Enoch 75:8)

Only from space are there stars that never set. Remember, the church, during the time of ecumenical editing, condemned accurate astronomy. (Ask Galileo) The church fathers, aka the *religious spirits*, wanted the masses to think that the Earth was flat, did not move, and was at the center of all things.

The Old Testament prophet Isaiah wrote in 740BCE that the earth was a circle, not flat, in chapter 40:22.

"God sits above the circle of the earth. The people below seem like grasshoppers to him! He spreads out the heavens like a curtain and makes his tent from them." (NLT)

Clearly to have known such detailed astronomical and scientific knowledge, so long before humankind was even aware of the facts that the earth was round and rotated around the sun, suggests that the both Enoch and Isaiah had known this because they both were taken up in God's starships, which gave them first-hand knowledge. Those scientists who dared to propose such a theory during the Middle Ages were persecuted and executed by the Catholic Church, who deemed any such knowledge as heresy by their *religious spiritual stronghold* of denial of 'who' God really is. Thank goodness that today we know better. Or do we?

I just cannot believe my eyes, when I witness people arguing on the internet and Facebook about whether or not the earth is flat or a sphere. Today we have multiple astronauts who have actually been in space, travelled around the entire circumference of the earth many times, and have countless photographs and videos of the earth as a big round sphere, which makes it really hard for the flat earthers to argue their point, but they do nevertheless. Religious spirit, or just a deaf and dumb spirit of stubbornness that blinds them to truth?

Enoch talks extensively about how the heavens became corrupted due to the sin of both angels and man. This is why there is a promise from the Lord to recreate the heavens and the earth in Isaiah 65:17 and Revelation 21:1. This is why the Lord is the Cosmic Christ, Messiah, and Savior of the entire Cosmos.

On the following pages, I will attempt to explain and discern the origins of this Cosmic Drama, and how it affects every earth human today, the state of our planet, and our present religious and belief systems, and who the gods that created them are.

NOTES:

1. R.H. Charles, *The Books of Enoch*, 1912
2. Valerian, Val. *Matrix I and Matrix II*, Leading Edge Research 1994.
3. Dr. James Hurtak, *The Keys of Enoch,* p.55, The Academy For Future Science, Los Gatos, CA, 1977.

CHAPTER TWO

ANCIENT TECHNOLOGY & BIBLICAL ASTRONAUTS

"The gods have come down to us in human form!"
(Acts 14:11, NIV)

"Do not forget to show hospitality to *aliens* (strangers),
For by so doing some people have shown hospitality
To angels (extraterrestrial messengers) without knowing it."
(Hebrews 13:2, NIV)

There have been a handful of authors who have interpreted Bible scriptures to relate to actual technology, spaceships, and a host of technological devices that were present and used in ancient days, and they were all recorded in the Bible. David Childress writes in his book *Technology of the Gods* that the Bible talks about TV monitors and PA speakers (loud voices). Each time the Lord spoke in a very loud voice, He was actually using a PA speaker, so all those on the land could hear Him. He also makes references to microwaves.

G. Cope Schellhorn in his book *Extraterrestrials in Biblical Prophecy* gives hundreds of scriptures which all refer to spaceships and extraterrestrial technology. Ann Madden Jones in her book *The Yahweh Encounters: Bible Astronauts, Ark Radiations and Temple Electronics* gives probably the most detailed descriptions of the Lord's technology all written in the Holy Scriptures.

NASA engineer Josef F. Blumrich, who was inspired by Erich Von Däniken's work, picked up the Bible and turned to the Book of Ezekiel. He was intent on disputing Von Däniken's claims; his investigation was published in his book *The Spaceships of Ezekiel* where Blumrich became convinced that the Book of Ezekiel was, in fact, a very accurate literal description of four spaceship landings. Although it was described using the limited language of that day by the prophet Ezekiel, it proved extraterrestrial contact with ancient man. In the Old Testament, the characteristics of the Ark of the Covenant and the Urim and Thummim are identified, suggesting high technology, perhaps from alien origins.

There were several works in the late 1950s and early 1960s that broke ground in this field; Morris K. Jessup, a UFO investigator, published *The UFO and the Bible* in the 1950s. Then B. Le Poer Trench came out with *The Sky People* in 1960, which speculated that the biblical angels acted very much like astronauts. The same ideas were reiterated by Barry H. Downing's courageous book *The Bible and Flying Saucers* in 1968. Another

NASA scientist, Maurice Chatelain, wrote *Our Ancestors Came from Outer Space* in 1977. His research confirmed that we have been visited by extraterrestrials in the distant past. Then the Reverend Virginia F. Brasington published her insightful work *Flying Saucers in the Bible* in 1982. All of these writings have inspired many to look at biblical scriptures in a different light.

Some of the most recent influential and pioneering works were done by the late Archeoastronomer Zecharia Sitchin's *The Earth Chronicles*, which consists of three books, *The 12th Planet* (1976), *The Stairway to Heaven* (1980), and *The Wars of Gods and Men* (1985). Sitchin's brilliant gifts gave him the ability to interpret and translate the ancient Sumerian-Babylonian tablets by deciphering the pictographic, cuneiform, and Semitic terminology for space crafts. Sitchin also revealed that the Sumerian-Babylonian planet called Nibiru (aka Marduk), which makes a 3,600 year orbit around our sun (*The 12th Planet*) corresponds to St. John's Wormwood of the Book of Revelation Chapter 8.

In the Revelation of Christ given to St. John, we find a most intriguing prophecy often used to suggest that some kind of heavenly body will crash into the earth and do great damage. The prophecy describes this as a "great star" named Wormwood. The word itself means "bitterness." Many believe this to be the planet/mother ship known as Nibiru, or as Sitchin calls it, the *Twelfth Planet*.

> "And the third angel sounded, and there fell **a great star** from heaven, burning as it were a lamp, and it fell upon the third part of the rivers, and upon the fountains of waters; and the name of the star is called Wormwood: and many men died of the waters, because they were made bitter."
>
> (Revelation 8:10-11, KJV)

Sitchin goes into great detail, stating that each time Nibiru (aka Marduk) passed by Earth; it literally wreaked havoc on the earth in the form of disastrous earth changes that caused floods, tidal waves, earthquakes, and hurricanes, which have altered the land masses and the water.

Today a planet, thought to be over four times the mass of Jupiter, has arrived in our solar system, along with four moons, which have been photographed, videographed, and tracked all around the world. It can be seen approximately one hour before sunrise and appears in the sky as a very bright star, and looks like a sun just before sunrise, as it appears to rise before the sun. It has been videotaped from the Wormwood Observatory in Hawaii, in Russia, and in Ireland as two suns rising.

However, about an hour after sunrise, our sun's light obliterates the light from this planet, which looks like another sun, and it disappears from natural view. At the Neumayer Station in Antarctica, they have a 24/7 live video of the horizon, which is probably one of the best videos that show this huge planetary mass rising before the sun, which looks like a planet, a shadowy planet. It looks similar to when the moon, when it is new, when there is a smoky glow on the dark portion of the crescent moon, which is

CHAPTER TWO: Ancient Technology & Biblical Astronauts

actually light from the sun being reflected off the earth. This video, which is up on YouTube, reveals that this is not a sun, or a mini-solar system, as some have postulated, but it is, in fact, a planet with moons. It is so close to the sun that it reflects the light of the sun and shines like a sun around sunrise.

This planet is what the ancient Sumerians called Nibiru, and the book of Revelation calls Wormwood. Since the appearance of this planet in our solar system, millions of species of fish, from all around the world, have been turning up dead; thousands of birds have been dropping from the sky, and whales and dolphins en masse have been beaching themselves to death. No coincidences, but responses to the electro-magnetic pull that this huge planet is having in our celestial neighborhood.

According to the ancient records, Nibiru is supposed to complete its orbit around the sun once every 3,600 years, and it is supposed to pass the earth twice, once on its way around the sun and lastly on its way back away from the sun on its elliptical orbit back into the vastness of space, millions of miles out from Pluto.

I wrote about the Annunaki in more detail along with other corroborating research on them in Book One, *Who's Who In The Cosmic Zoo.?* See, pp 110-119. These beings said in the records they left behind, that they were coming back to earth.

Nibiru is here. It's been in our solar system and has been tracked since the 1950s. Back in the 1950s there were articles on it in scattered newspapers, when modern day Astronomers began to track it. Then Zecharia Sitchin in the 1960s started putting his research together, which led to his series of books, *The Earth Chronicles*, and his research on Nibiru in his signature book, *The Tenth Planet*, which is what Sitchin called it, because it was the planet other astronomers didn't count in our solar system.

The general consensus among researchers of Nibiru, is that when it passes the earth for the 2nd time, will be much worse than the 1st, as the ancients depicted Nibiru as a planet with wings, this is due to what orbits around it, and how it pulls into its field all kinds of space debris. This is why they associate wormwood with Nibiru, as most Bible scholars agree that Wormwood's description behaves like a comet, and will come out of Nibiru when it passes.

As a result of Sitchin's interpretation of the Sumerian Cuneiform tablets, many now believe that Nibiru is home to the Annunaki, who are giant reptilian humanoid beings, with advanced technologies, and that this being or fallen Angel known as Wormwood, is among them and that is how it falls to earth. Most scientists, however, are convinced that Wormwood, is not a being, but a devastating Asteroid.

The planet Nibiru is one of four planets that orbit a brown dwarf star called 'Nemesis', which is considered to be our sun's evil twin. Nibiru also has its own moons, which can be seen before sunrise at the Wormwood Observatory in Hawaii. Therefore, it is no coincidence that astronomers in Hawaii named their observatory telescope "Wormwood" which is located on Mt. Mauna Kea, to track Nibiru. If you google Wormwood, you'll also find that it is now called, Project Wormwood in Australia and by other government sources.

What people need to do is understand the past orbital passings of Nibiru in order to understand its future passing of the earth. It carries what appears to be two tails in its path, which also looks like wings. This is a path of meteors, comets and asteroids, some of which are bound to hit the earth in its passing. Nemesis has already been classified as a Brown Dwarf Star by Astronomers who are tracking this, and this is a star that is clouded brown, so Astronomers need to use special filters to track it, because it no longer shines bright on its own, without the reflection of our sun. Secondly, dwarf stars are known for magnetically pulling into its energy field all kinds of space junk, which explains why its passing the earth has caused all kinds of comets, fireballs to hit the earth which has increased since 2001.

On its path towards the Sun when it passed the earth the 1st time, there has been an increase in fireballs seen all around the world, coupled by dramatic earth changes. The 9.0 Chilean quake was one, which literally shortened time by close to a minute as it literally knocked the earth from its axis. These types of quakes will continue until the pole shift is completed. Climate changes which have been markedly dramatic have increased during this planet's 1st passing by earth around the sun.

The hard scientific evidence that Nibiru, aka Planet X, along with its large mysterious non-visible to the naked eye Brown Dwarf star Nemesis, is in fact, real and orbiting the remote edges of our solar system, tugging on the mantle of the earth, and creating all kinds of bizarre landmass abnormalities which many do not know how to explain. Unusual events such as giant sinkholes, extreme weather oddities, a fast floating and more or less continuously displaced magnetic north pole, the ability to see the Northern Light, Aurora Borealis in Montana and Colorado, are deviations of the Earth's normal wobbles.

World leaders have their knickers in a twist over 'global warming' and 'climate change', but those insiders in the know, know that this is something beyond our control, and they do know about the orbit of Nemesis and its giant planet, Nibiru.

Immanuel Velikovsky postulated in his book, Earth In Upheaval, that it caused the 'Great Flood' and also appeared at the time of the 'Exodus' of the Jews from Egypt as he researched the 3600 Year Cycles which details Velikovsky's hypothesis, all of which have now been proved by today's scientists.[1]

The jury is out on the exact timing of Nibiru's 2nd passing, which could be anywhere from 2-40 years from now. There is so much disinformation and disagreement these days from astronomers on how long it will take to pass by earth on its second time around. What makes sense to me, is that after it completes its orbit around the sun, it will pick up speed, as it moves away from the sun, and this is when all the damage happens on earth, historically and what is to come.

When Nibiru passed the earth, it will be just as close as the moon, but remember it's four times the size of Jupiter, so it's going to look huge from our perspective, bigger than our supermoons. It will cause earthquakes and tidal waves that has more to do with the way the waters on earth settle based on the earth's poles and its axis. However, the

CHAPTER TWO: Ancient Technology & Biblical Astronauts

passing of this giant planet is going to complete the pole shift on earth, with a final earthquake. It's interesting that this is predicted in the Old Testament, in the book of Isaiah.

> "Behold, the LORD makes the earth empty, and makes it waste, and <u>turns it upside down</u>, and scatters abroad the inhabitants thereof.
>
> And it shall come to pass, [that] he who flees from the noise of the fear shall fall into the pit; and he that cometh up out of the midst of the pit shall be taken in the snare: for the windows from on high are open, and the foundations of the earth do shake.
>
> The earth is utterly broken down, the earth is clean dissolved, and <u>the earth is moved exceedingly</u>. The earth shall reel to and fro like a drunkard, and shall be removed like a cottage; and the transgression thereof shall be heavy upon it; and it shall fall, and not rise again.
>
> And it shall come to pass in that day, [that] <u>the LORD (YAHUAH) shall punish the host of the high ones</u> [that are] on high (Archons, the Rulers of the Darkness of this Present World, Negative ETs and Aliens), and the kings of the earth upon the earth. And they shall be gathered together, [as] prisoners are gathered in the pit, and shall be shut up in the prison, and after many days shall they be visited.
>
> Then the moon shall be confounded, and the sun ashamed, when the LORD (YAHUAH) of hosts shall reign in mount Zion, and in Jerusalem, and before his ancients gloriously."
>
> (Isaiah 24:1, 18-23-KJV)

Isaiah's prophecy actually lines up with Revelation Prophecy. This will happen at the 6th seal, when the Lord returns to Zion.

> "And I beheld when he had opened the sixth seal, and, lo, there was a great earthquake; and the sun became black as sackcloth of hair, and the moon became as blood;"
>
> (Revelation 6:12)

Pole shifts are when the earth rotates 180 degrees and literally goes "upside down" as the scripture tells us. We know this has happened before.

Many of the dire 'Terrible Day of the Lord' predictions in Bible Prophecies for the End of the Age, coincide and can be explained by the passing of Nibiru. It's very presence in our solar neighborhood, will disrupt the natural order of the earth, sun and moon, which explains all the scriptures that predict the moon will turn red, and the sun will not give its light, as written in Joel 2:31 and Matthew 24:29, Acts 2:20, are caused by comets and asteroid and all the space junk and dust they inevitably kick up as Nibiru passes by Earth.

MOVING STARS

In the Bible, the terminology for "stars" also corresponds to spaceships, as we see the ships in the sky as glowing stars. Many today, who have witnessed UFOs, see them as moving stars. The Magi, who followed the Star of Bethlehem that guided them to the exact location of the birth of Jesus Christ over 2,000 years ago, were in fact following a spaceship (c. 6 BCE–c. 30 CE).

Many have postulated that, in 7BC, the planets Jupiter and Saturn were in a conjunction, which would create a brighter light in the sky than if they were orbiting the earth separately. However, Jupiter and Saturn are planets; their lights are only seen at night, and their movement is rather slow, too slow to be moving across the desert to actually lead the wise men to the exact location of the birth place of Jesus Christ of Nazareth. They were clearly led by a spaceship with a glowing light.

In recent years, some UFO and Bible researchers have suggested that the "star" was actually a spaceship from another world, thus raising the controversial question of whether the Holy Bible contains references to UFOs and alien visitors. Provoking even greater controversy are those researchers who make reference to the Christian Apocrypha, books banned by church censorship from services and religious reading that claim that Jesus was brought to Earth *in* the Star of Bethlehem, which is described in the ancient texts as being "winged with various colored rays shooting out from behind it." (II Kings 2:11–12, 6:17; Psalms 68:17; and Habakkuk 3:8, Ezekiel 1:4, 13, 14, 20, 21, 24, Ezekiel 10:1)

DIVINE PREGNANCIES

Many are expected to believe in Mary's virgin birth by, but the Bible tells us that Mary was visited by one of the archangels, Gabriel, who told her she was chosen to give birth to the Messiah. Many wonder, how can this be? As Mary herself argued with Gabriel because she was truly a virgin and had never been with any man, including her betrothed, Joseph. Yet, this phenomenon was really nothing new in biblical literature, as Sarah, Rachel, Rebecca, Hannah, Gehazi, and Elizabeth were barren (not necessarily virgins, though), so yes the Virgin Mary and these six others were all made pregnant by the Lord's "divine interventions."

In my opinion, these miracle births were all done through in vitro fertilizations which involves "technology," aka genetic engineering. Those who received the in vitro fertilizations may not have all been virgins, but all the barren women were all visited by angels and given divine pregnancies. Sarah and Rachel birthed the forefathers of the

Jewish race. Genetic engineering and in-vitro fertilization are nothing new, and the fact that both the book of Genesis and the Sumerian tablets make reference to humans being made from clay indicates that perhaps this "clay" was what the original test tubes were made out of, and not the refined glass that we use today.

The fact that Genesis said that Eve came from Adam's rib, may also have been a way of describing genetic engineering, as Eve was made from Adam's genetics, not his literal rib. The word *rib* was used to describe the "genetic material" that came from Adam's own body. Perhaps genetic material was taken from the skin over Adam's rib, hence the record in scripture.

Genesis 1:26 (KJV) states, "And God (Elohim) said, Let us make man in our image, after our likeness." The word for God here is Elohim, which is plural for the children of El, who are the children of God. The Elohim are a type of pantheon or council of gods. The literal translation for Elohim is "gods." The word for God used here is not Yahuah, which is the Supreme God, but *the gods* (in Hebrew plural form). This implies that Adam and Eve were not created by Yahuah, but by Yahuah's children, the Elohim. The rest of the sentence uses the Hebrew vernacular for plural. The word *our* is used twice, which indicates that this was a group of beings who decided to repopulate the Earth with their new human model, the "Evadamic" race (i.e., the Adams and the Eves).

Sumerian-Babylonian tablets recorded in great detail (see *Genesis Revisited*) as Sitchin describes that the gods mixed DNA and were literally "geneticists," who helped to create early man and the early races. Not all races were able to progenate, and as I mentioned already, there were several accounts in Bible literature where the women were barren and yet were given pregnancies and carried the DNA of the Elohim (the gods).

In the case of Jesus of Nazareth, his mission was unique, and his DNA came directly from the God of Israel, his father, YHVH, Yahuah. As Jesus would often say, "I and the Father are One." Not only spiritually, but genetically. His blood was divine, as it had a divine purpose — to atone for the sins of humankind.

DIVINE SPACESHIPS

The examples of spaceships leading the ancient Israelites are abundant in the Bible. In the Exodus out of the enslavement of Egypt, Moses followed a fire by day and a light by night. This was one of the spaceships of the Lord, who literally led them for forty years, wandering through the wilderness over hundreds of miles between Egypt and Israel. How did they know where they were going? Moses said to the Lord he was not the right person to lead them, but the Lord said to just trust him.

The fire that led them by night to give them light and the light or cloud that led them by day along with the manna they were fed to keep them alive, nourished, and strengthened were distributed by the Lord's messengers (i.e., extraterrestrial astronauts, angels of God) from the Lord's spaceships that watched over them.

> "And the Lord went before them by day in a pillar of a cloud,
> To lead them away; and by night in a pillar of fire,
> To give them light; to go by day and night."
>
> (Exodus 13:21, KJV)

These objects in the sky were clearly spacecraft when you consider "clouds (or smoke) by day and fire by night." Rocket thrusters could create billowing smoke in sunlight, and at night, the flames from the propulsion systems would be what was visible to those on the ground as a pillar of fire. These chariots in the air could have easily parted the waters of the Red Sea with force fields, a type of technology that Moses and the Israelites had no reference to.

> "And the children of Israel went into the midst of the sea upon dry ground: and the waters were a wall (on either side) unto them on their right hand, and on their left. And the Egyptians pursued, and went in after them to the midst of the sea, even all Pharaoh's horses, his chariots, and his horsemen."
>
> (Exodus 14:22, KJV)

Technology can create miracles. Think of this, if our ancestors saw a television set 500 years ago and viewed other people on it or even themselves, they would automatically think it was magic or some kind of miracle. Just as all the technology that ancient earth humans had little or no reference to thought. It is easy to conclude something is magic, when you don't understand how it is done. Yet all magic has its own technology, if you understand it. We live in an age of knowledge and technology now, and that technology is expanding at an unprecedented rate. Yet there is so much technology that we still do not understand because we just don't have the knowledge or the brain power to comprehend it, but that doesn't mean it's magic.

DIVINE ENCOUNTERS

The Bible is full of evidence of visitations by ancient astronauts and extraterrestrials, who the Bible refers to as angels aka messengers of God. Enoch, Noah, Moses, Elijah, Jacob, Isaiah, Ezekiel, Daniel, Zechariah, Jesus, Paul, and St. John all had contact with extraterrestrials. In addition to their contacts and "Divine Interventions," many described their space craft in great detail. Many of these early prophets and writers had no earlier reference for what they were seeing. Their descriptions were simplistic. Over the years their meanings were understood as "symbolic" of some supernatural mystery.

The supernatural mystery has been revealed; the Bible in great detail is in fact the original "record" and "evidence" that our ancestors had interaction with extraterrestrials and ancient astronauts. Many of them did not readily understand the powers that befell their very eyes. Their descriptions were simplistic, such as the cherubim were seen as

CHAPTER TWO: Ancient Technology & Biblical Astronauts

wielding a fiery sword. This was their terminology for what we would call today a "laser" weapon.

The radiation that came from the space craft was dangerous, which is why Moses commanded the Israelites to stay at the bottom of Mt. Sinai when he went up to the top of the mountain to meet with the Lord and receive the tablets which were the Ten Commandments. Moses entered into the Lord's spaceship and came out transformed and white. The radiation from these ships were tremendous, and many died as a result of negligence and ignorance and simply not following instructions.

The Hebrew language is very specific in the book of Exodus Chapter 34 on the practicalities of what actually took place. In Hebrew, the word *Yared*, which means "to descend" was used to say, "Yahuah descended in the cloud to the Mt. Sinai." The Lord Yahuah gave strict instructions to Moses — to meet him at the top of the mountain, to make sure he came alone, and didn't let the animals graze too close to the mountain because He knew that the radiation would kill them. After Moses left the Lord Yahuah with the tablets, the scripture tells us, his face was radiant, so much so, that he had to put a veil on it because his own brother didn't recognize him.

Von Däniken's ancient astronaut theory states that aliens and extraterrestrials visited the earth in the past and became gods to mankind. The archeological evidence is certainly overwhelming enough to rewrite our present history books, but what is the whole story? Who were these ancient ETs that set themselves up as gods? And why?

Because the ancient earth humans who wrote the scriptures were godly men and were devoted to their faith, they related what they saw to both God and angels. Von Däniken claims in his ancient astronaut theory that our ancestors were so ignorant of what they saw, that they created "gods" out of the extraterrestrials, the ancient astronauts that visited them quite often during ancient times.

While this theory may be correct, there is also another side to it, and that is that many of these visitations were by the fallen angels and the two hundred fallen sons of the Elohim, who were ousted out of the high heavens, all immortals, that were cursed by the Almighty Creator God to inhabit lower worlds and have dominion over lower planets because of their sins of rebellion and their sexual lust for earth women.

Remember, that Lucifer led the rebellion and managed to persuade one-third of heavens angels (extraterrestrial warriors and messengers) to follow him on his quest to become God. These beings clearly had a god complex, and therefore set themselves up as gods to be worshipped by the ignorant earth humans, flailing their powers and their technology, completely intimidating earth humans, so naturally earth humans followed in fear and worshipped them as gods.

Von Däniken says that it was our ancestors who made gods of them, but I am saying, that these fallen angels, aka the satans (adversaries/rebels), set themselves up as gods to be worshipped by earth humans in order to enslave them and steal the worship away from the Lord by turning them against the Supreme Creator God, just as they continue to do today. This is the crux of all spiritual warfare on earth.

These extraterrestrials or ancient astronauts not only enjoyed their "god" status among earth humans, but fed off the fear and worship of earth humans. Suffice it to say, these were extraterrestrials with "wannabe" god complexes, and they continue to be to this day, as they masquerade as ascended masters, space brothers and gods.

The Book of Enoch speaks of much destruction, chaos, and corruption on Earth, as well as among the angels. Like the book of Genesis, Enoch mentions "giants" and "the Watchers." There were "the satans" — the "Sons of Heaven," "angels of punishment," "instruments of Satan," and Michael, Raphael, Gabriel, and Phenuel (who were then considered to be the Archangels).

The word "God" is never mentioned, only the Lord is referred to over and over again as the "Lord of Spirits," and plural gods (Elohim) or angels (Malachim, which translates to heaven's messengers). Enoch was taken to the mountaintops where the Lord and his messengers (extraterrestrials) resided. He observed things that no primitive man could understand. The fallen angels "corrupted the sons of man." These were the ones who, along with their technology, played "God" and decided the fate of the children on Earth.

The most amazing example of an extraterrestrial contact in the Old Testament is in the Book of Ezekiel. Chapter 1 clearly describes the landing of a spacecraft. Joseph Blumrich's book *The Spaceships of Ezekiel* analyzes the book of Ezekiel as a description of a space vehicle. Blumrich was a NASA engineer and designer of the Saturn V rocket. His son told him, after reading Erich Von Däniken's book *The Chariot of the Gods* that the prophet Ezekiel described a spaceship landing.

Blumrich was confident that he could disprove that concept because of his technical skills in this field. He assumed that the ancient text could not possibly portray an actual space craft. The NASA engineer wrote that he was never so surprised when he actually read the Book of Ezekiel. The ancient words did, indeed, conform to a realistic vehicle.

In the beginning of the book of Ezekiel, the prophet writes of the approach of four faces from above. In reality, the "four" referred to the four landing legs of the craft. Blumrich was shocked when he read the Old Testament report of "straight legs" of "burnished brass" with "round feet." The NASA engineer designed the metallic, straight legs and round footpads of the lunar lander. The famous quote from Ezekiel is "a wheel within a wheel." Once the lander touched down, Ezekiel saw wheels. This is the exact chronology of what would occur with a modern vehicle. The UFO landed, transformed into a wheeled rover, then rolled along the ground. Ezekiel was only familiar with wheels from simple carts that moved in one direction. But the prophet described wheels that moved in all directions, which was completely *alien* to Ezekiel. Blumrich then wrote a letter to Erich Von Däniken admitting he was right.

WHO WAS EZEKIEL?

So who was Ezekiel, and why do his words resonate with us today? Ezekiel's name in Hebrew means, "God Will Strengthen," which is pronounced Yehezkiel. He lived

CHAPTER TWO: Ancient Technology & Biblical Astronauts

2,600 years ago in ancient Babylon, which today is called Iraq. Ezekiel lived in Babylon, but he was not a Babylonian. He was an Israelite and had been brought to Babylon against his will. Babylon was the most modern and sophisticated city in Ezekiel's world at that time. He lived in the capital city of an international empire, an empire that crushed other nations, an empire that had swallowed up countries on every side, including ancient Israel.

The Lord Yahuah was angry at the Israelites because they had turned their backs on the Lord, through idolatry and immorality, so the Lord gave them up to their enemies and took His hand of protection off them. The Babylonians invaded Israel, destroyed the Holy Temple of Solomon, and killed every Israelite they could, except for the ones that they took back to Babylon to be their slaves. The Lord allowed this to happen to punish the Israelites for their disobedience. The Israelites became captives and sat by the rivers of Babylon and cried out to the Lord.

Ezekiel was an Israelite priest and prophet. One day, in approximately 593 BCE, when Ezekiel was walking along the river Chebar, he suddenly heard a noise. He looked up and saw, coming out of the north, zigzagging in right angles as it flew across the sky, a pulsating cloud with a brightness around it, with a fire flashing up and coming down to the land in front of him. Ezekiel tried in his own words to describe the incredible vehicle he had seen. He began by writing that the first thing he saw was a strange cloud and then a weird vehicle. (See my section on the *Cloud Ships* in my next chapter on *The Mother Ships of the Lord*).

> "And I looked, and, behold, a whirlwind came out of the north, a great cloud, and a fire enfolding itself, and a brightness was about it...."
>
> (Ezekiel 1:4, KJV)

For years, the biblical scholars who read his words called this strange vehicle a "chariot." In Hebrew, the word for chariot is "Merkavah," but Ezekiel called it the "Glory of God." Ezekiel describes the Merkavah as being made up of three parts. The bottom part was made of four identical figures.

> "And this was their appearance; they had the likeness of a man. And every one had four faces, and every one had four wings. And their feet were straight feet; and the sole of their feet was like the sole of a calf's foot: and they sparkled like the color of burnished brass. And they had the hands of a man under their wings on their four sides; and they four had their faces and their winds. Their wings were joined one to another; they turned not when they went; they went every one straight forward (there were four figures that were joined together) ... and their wings were stretched upward; two wings of every one were joined one to another, and two covered their bodies."
>
> (Ezekiel 1:5-11, KJV)

LIVING CREATURES?

Ezekiel describes the middle part of the Merkavah as being a firmament on top of the heads of the four-winged figures. Ezekiel did not tell us the shape of the firmament. He said they had the "likeness" of man, but he didn't say they were a man, which could indicate robotic beings. He is describing a very sophisticated space vehicle. That these "living creatures" were always coordinated with each other, as to when to let down their wings when they landed and when to pick them up when they took off. Ezekiel describes them as "living creatures" because he does not have the word for robot. Based on their actions, they appeared to be alive to Ezekiel, but to him, they were "creatures" not men, and not angels.

Even the human-like beings, which disembarked from the wheels, were seen as "alive" to Ezekiel because they were in control of their machines. Remember, in ancient times, anything that could move all by itself was considered to be alive.

Ann Madden Jones, author of *The Yahweh Encounters, Bible Astronauts, Ark Radiations and Temple Electronics,* claims that the cherubim were robots, which Ezekiel called "living creatures." Jones says the only difference between the cherubim and seraphim are their number of blades (wings).

> "And over the heads of the living creature there was the likeness of a firmament (a roof), like the color of the terrible ice, (the color of the terrible ice scholars interpret as the color of brushed metal) stretched forth over their heads above. And under the firmament were their wings comfortable the one to the other; this one of them had two which covered, and that one of them had two which covered, their bodies."
> (Ezekiel 1:22- 23, JPS Tenakh 1917)

The word used in the original Hebrew, "Rakia," implies that the shape was dome-like. Ezekiel describes wheels that are placed one next to each of the four figures.

> "The appearance of the wheels and their work was like unto the color of a beryl: (Beryl is a gemstone that is believed to be the modern pale green topaz) and they four had one likeness: and their appearance and their work was as it were a wheel in the middle of a wheel ... And when the living creatures went, the wheels went by them: and when the living creatures were lifted up from the earth, the wheels were lifted up."
> (Ezekiel 1:16, 19, KJV)

Ezekiel describes the top part as having a seat ... and on the seat is a man. Ezekiel does not tell us how large the man is in relation to the Merkavah on which he rides. Usually translated as "throne," the original Hebrew word *keysay* means "seat." A light is above and around the seated man. Below his waist is a bright rainbow light.

CHAPTER TWO: Ancient Technology & Biblical Astronauts

"And above the firmament that was over their heads was the likeness of a throne, as the appearance of a sapphire stone: and upon the likeness of the throne was the likeness as the appearance of a man above on it. And I saw as the color of amber, as the appearance of fire round about within it, from the appearance of his loins even upward, and from the appearance of his loins even upward, and from the appearance of his loins even downward, I saw as it were the appearance of fire, and it had brightness round about. As the appearance of the bow that is in the cloud in the day of rain, so was the appearance of the brightness round about. This was the appearance of the likeness of the glory of the LORD. And when I saw it, I fell on my face, and I heard a voice of one that spoke."

(Ezekiel 1:26-28, KJV)

"....like the appearance of lamps: it went up and down among the living creatures; and the fire was bright, and out of the fire went forth lightning."

(Ezekiel 1:13, KJV)

Lamps moving up and down among "living creatures" (robots) with bright fire and lightning? Sounds like something very high-tech to me.

EZEKIEL'S VISION OF THE DRY BONES

"I was carried off in the Merkavah, and I was then set down in the middle of a valley which was full of bones, and I walked around and around and there were many bones and they were very dry."

"Then [the Lord] said to me: "Son of man, these bones are the people of Israel. They say, 'Our bones are dried up and our hope is gone; we are cut off.' Therefore prophesy and say to them: This is what the Sovereign LORD says: 'My people, I am going to open your graves and bring you up from them; I will bring you back to the land of Israel. Then you, my people, will know that I am the LORD, when I open your graves and bring you up from them. I will put my Spirit in you and you will live, and I will settle you in your own land. Then you will know that I the LORD have spoken, and I have done it, declares the LORD.'

(Ezekiel 37:11-14, NIV)

Ezekiel was shown that the Lord intended to bring the Israelites back to the Land of Israel and restore them. He promised to reincarnate them, through his own words, "open your graves... and you will live," and to put flesh on their dry bones. This prophesy that the Lord Yahuah gave to Ezekiel over 1,800 years ago was fulfilled in 1948 when Israel became a state apportioned to the Jewish people after two-thirds of all the Jews in the world were exterminated in the Nazi Holocaust between the years 1933-1948.

"...and say to them, 'This is what the Sovereign LORD says: I will take the Israelites out of the nations where they have gone. I will gather them from all around and bring them back into their own land.... They will live in the land I gave to my servant Jacob, the land where your ancestors lived. They and their children and their children's children will live there forever...'"

(Ezekiel 37:21, 25, NIV)

Today, the State of Israel, is made up of the *diaspora* of Jews from all over the world. *Diaspora* means Jews living outside of Israel. Jews from every nation of the world continue to make *Aliyah* (Hebrew for "ascending") to the promised land of Israel. Israel today is the world's biggest melting pot of nationalities and cultures. The only common denominator is being of Jewish descent.

All the prophets of the Bible point to the future of Israel in one way or another. From the prophetic timeline of the rebirth of Israel (1948) to the return of Israel's Messiah (Yahshua HaMashiach/The Lord Jesus Christ) at the end of this timeline, with the downloading of the New Jerusalem (City of Peace) from the heavens during Christ's millennial reign on Earth, all Bible prophecies points to Israel.

WHO WAS ENOCH?

Enoch was Methuselah's father and Noah's grandfather. His books, Enoch I and Enoch 2, should have been included in the Old Testament. As I've mentioned earlier, *The Book of Enoch*[2] was edited out of the Bible by the Ecumenical Council for its controversies. However they remain intact to this day, in the Coptic Christian Bible. Enoch, like Ezekiel, was taken on many flights by the extraterrestrial angels and witnessed great horrors and incredible beauty. Enoch repeatedly describes "...a whirlwind [that] carried me off from the earth..." (Enoch 39:3).

There are numerous references to whirlwinds which "spirited" Enoch away into the sky. In fact, this term is used by Elijah, Isaiah, Daniel, Jeremiah, King David, Habakkuk, Zechariah, Nahum, and Amos and is mentioned in the Book of Job four times.

Whirlwinds are the high technological power of being taken up into a spacecraft. The word *whirlwind* shows up thirty three times in the Old Testament. Enoch writes, "The angels "showed me all the hidden things" and "mine eyes saw all the secret things of heaven." Enoch saw views that "no man shall see." In Enoch 33:4, Enoch states: "I saw a great and glorious device."

"And thence I went <u>over</u> the summits of the earth, and passed <u>above</u> the Erythraean Sea, and went far from it, and passed <u>over</u> the angel Zoltiel."

(Enoch 32:2)

CHAPTER TWO: Ancient Technology & Biblical Astronauts

Could the 'angel' Zoltiel actually be another ship? Ships that come out of Mother ships are also known as 'messengers', the literal meaning of the word, "malach" in Hebrew, means messenger, but it mostly translated into modern day English Bibles as the word, 'angel'.

The Erythraean Sea was an ancient geographical term which was comprised of what we know today as the Red Sea, the Persian Gulf, and the Arabian Sea. Clearly Enoch's report was of his travels above the earth and into outer space.

> "I looked and saw a lofty throne: its appearance was as crystal and the wheels thereof as the shining sun...from underneath the throne came streams of flaming fire so great that I could not look thereon. The vision caused me to fly and lifted me upward and bore me into heaven."
>
> (1 Enoch 14:18-19)

In this scripture, Enoch mentions crystals and wheels. The throne itself could actually be a vehicle where the extraterrestrial angels sat, and underneath them were fires that generated from the rocket thrusters. He mentions that the flaming fire was so intense that he couldn't look at it.

This reminds me of people who are literally "blinded by the light" of spaceships. Later, down the timeline, the Bible records this happening to Saul who was intent on persecuting all the Jews who believed in Jesus Christ as their Messiah. Saul was "blinded by the light" on the road to Damascus after having a close encounter with the Lord's vehicle, which precipitated his conversion and transformation into the apostle Paul, who was healed three days later of his blindness by repenting of his sin and acknowledging that Jesus was truly the *Shaliach* (the sent one from God).

(Acts 22:6-13 NIV) tells us:

"About noon as I came near Damascus, <u>suddenly a bright light from heaven flashed around me.</u> (Specifically this scripture says the bright light came from heaven and flashed around him. This rules out that this light emanated from the Lord Jesus Christ Himself alone, but was a flashing light, which came from above. This describes some type of starship.)

"I fell to the ground and heard a voice say to me, 'Saul! Saul! Why do you persecute me?' Who are you, Lord?" (In Hebrew, the word for Lord, which is 'Adonai' also means 'Sir') I asked.

"'I am Jesus of Nazareth, whom you are persecuting,' He replied. My companions saw the light, but they did not understand the voice of him who was speaking to me." (This is because the voice was being projected from the starship, they didn't actually "see" the Lord, but heard His voice, as He identified Himself.)

"'What shall I do, Lord?' I asked. 'Get up,' the Lord said, 'and go into Damascus. There you will be told all that you have been assigned to do. My companions led me by the hand into Damascus, because <u>the brilliance of the light had blinded me</u>. A man named Ananias came to see me. He was a devout observer of the law and highly respected by all the Jews living there. He stood beside me and said, 'Brother Saul, receive your sight!' And at that very moment I was able to see him"

Enoch makes numerous references to *portals* or *windows* where Earthly and celestial views appeared. In Enoch 33:2-3, he states, "...I saw the portals of the heaven open. And I saw how the stars of heaven come forth." Enoch writes about these portals as pathways to different stars. These portals could very well be what scientists call wormholes today. The terms "stars of heaven" is a term used frequently in both the Old and New Testament, which relates to starships and to angels (extraterrestrials) who travel. Enoch is referring to the portals and wormholes that starships use to travel through one dimension of space to another.

Today, when people witness UFOs and spaceships, often they see them zip up into the upper stratosphere of Earth, and disappear into outer space and become what looks like a "star of heaven." Today, you can watch the sky at night, and watch dozens of satellites move across the earth in the upper stratospheres, which appears as a moving star. This vernacular, "stars of heaven," relates to starships, which move through the heavens.

Physical stars are known as "fixed stars." They move, perhaps, one iota of a centimeter in fifty years, if that. But both the ancient scriptures of Enoch and the Bible use this phrase multiple times to describe beings that actually fall from heaven, which, in my opinion relate, to fallen ETs (i.e. fallen angels) and their fallen starships.

Jesus prophesied of this very event happening in the last days: "And the **stars of heaven** shall fall, and the powers that are in **heaven** shall be shaken" (Mark 13:25 KJV). Sounds like cosmic warfare to me and end times ... real *Star Wars*. Here, Jesus is not only relating to these fallen angels falling but to the very powers that hold them in place being brought down and shaken at their foundation. I believe that here He is referring to the powers and principalities, rulers of the darkness, and spiritual wickedness in the heavens that are mentioned in Ephesians 6:12.

Then, more prophecy foresees the dragon's tail causing one-third of the stars of heaven to be cast down to earth. "His tail swept down a third of the **stars of heaven** and cast them to the earth" (Revelation 12:4 NLT). This relates to the final days, when those who have followed Lucifer in his rebellion against God end up being defeated in the final battle that takes place on Earth.

The Bible goes on to tell us that these stars of heaven were worshipped as gods. "Then God turned away from them and abandoned them to serve the **stars of heaven** as their gods! (Acts 7:42 NLT). The Lord took his protection off his people, for following other gods. "I ...Am a Jealous God" (Exodus 20:5, NIV).

CHAPTER TWO: Ancient Technology & Biblical Astronauts

In the Old Testament, Deuteronomy 17:3 (NET) warns against "… [S]erving other gods and worshipping them — the sun, moon, or any other heavenly bodies which I have not permitted you to worship." This caused the Lord Yahuah to take His protection off his people for following after other gods, or **stars of heaven**, aka extraterrestrials in their starships. In my opinion, these fallen stars of heaven belong to Lucifer/Satan's kingdom of darkness, aka the Draconian Empire.

Lucifer began this rebellion by saying: "You said in your heart, 'I will ascend to **heaven**; above the **stars** of God I will set my throne on high; I will sit on the mount of assembly in the far reaches…" (Isaiah 14:13 ESV). Lucifer's leadership in heaven before his fall managed to persuade one-third of heaven's angels (extraterrestrials) to follow him, and they, too, lost their place in the heavens and fell.

As the book of Jude tells us: "The angels which kept not their first estate." (They did not keep their original positions of authority but abandoned their own home. Another term used for first estate is principality)." "These he has kept in darkness, bound with everlasting chains for judgment on the great Day." (Jude 1:6 NIV)

We also have reference to these morning **stars of heaven** being **falling stars** (Jude 6). And why should there be "shooting stars," falling stars, "wandering stars" (Jude 13), or in a word, ruined stars? Falling stars all turned into fallen angels, aka satans (Hebrew for adversary), also known as devils.

> "For we wrestle not against flesh and blood, but against principalities, against powers, against the rulers of the darkness of this world, against spiritual wickedness in high places."
>
> (Ephesians 6:12, KJV)

These are the fallen stars of heaven, the fallen princes, and the fallen principalities, who have become the rulers of the darkness of this world and who serve as the spiritual wickedness in the heavens, in their UFOs (counterfeit light technology).

> "When the morning stars sang together, and all the 'sons of God' (Bene HaElohim) shouted for joy?"
>
> (Job 38:7, KJV)

The comparison of a prince, a monarch, or an angel, with a star is common. "How you have fallen from heaven, morning star, son of the dawn! You have been cast down to the earth, you who once laid low the nations!" (Isaiah 14:12, NIV).

The expression "the morning stars" is used on account of the beauty of the principal star, which, at certain seasons of the year, leads on the morning; however, for the most part, it is used and applied throughout scripture naturally to those angelic beings (extraterrestrials) that are of distinguished glory and hold rank in heaven. Because it refers to the angels (extraterrestrials), it seems that this interpretation is necessitated in order to correspond with the phrase "sons of God" in Job 38:7. In today's Bibles, the words "the sons of God" (Hebrew: Bene HaElohim) has been replaced with "angels"; nevertheless, both are extraterrestrials and resemble God because they were created by Him.

Another translation was the word "Lucifer," which was the Latin translation for the Hebrew "Heylel," a name of rebuke given to him by the Lord Yahuah. I will get more into the meanings of these names later in this book.

TECHNOLOGY OF THE ARK

All through Exodus, the Lord God demands, "I am the Lord," and "I will be to you a God: and you shall know that I am the Lord, your God." In Exodus 15:3 (KJV), there is a reference: "The Lord *is* a man of war." There has been a constant battle going on in the heavens since Lucifer's rebellion. The Almighty Creator God did not destroy one-third of the fallen angels and "the satans"; instead, he allowed them dominion over lower worlds, Earth being one of them. The fact that the Lord says He is a man of war reveals his stature in the heavens as a warrior against evil.

There is a warning in Exodus to "go not up into the mount, or touch the border of it: whosoever touches the mount shall be surely put to death...." "And Mount Sinai was completely in smoke, because the Lord descended upon it in fire ... and the whole mount quaked greatly." (Exodus 19:12, 18, KJ2000) Clearly the reason they were told not to go up to the top of Mt. Sinai was because that is where the Lord's starship had landed, and the radiation levels were too high for earth humans to withstand, so they were told to keep their distance for their own good.

In Exodus, Moses was given instructions on building the Ark of the Covenant. The inventor Nikola Tesla wrote in *The Wall of Light* that Moses had to have been a skilled electrical engineer. (Moses obviously had an ingenious inventor guiding him — the Lord) The Ark, Tesla concluded, was a very powerful "condenser." It created intense vibrations that could smash solid stone. The Israelites carted the device into battle and won wars with it.

> "And when the Ark of the Covenant of the Lord came into the camp, all Israel shouted with a great shout...."
>
> (1 Samuel 4:5, KJV)

> "Woe to us! Who shall deliver us out of the hand of these mighty Gods (Elohim)? These are the Gods (Elohim) that smote the Egyptians with all the plagues in the wilderness."
>
> (1 Samuel 4:8, KJV)

Uzzah ignored warnings about not touching the Ark, so when he touched the Ark, he was electrocuted! "Uzzah put forth his hand to the ark of God, and took hold of it; for the oxen shook it. And the anger of the Lord was kindled against Uzzah; and God smote him there for his error; and there he died by the ark of God."

Another man attempted to place it back on the ox-drawn cart and died. They had no concept of high-voltage. "And David was afraid of the Lord that day" (2 Samuel 6:6-9, ESV). This was a powerful piece of technology.

Ann Madden Jones asserts, in *The Yahweh Encounters,* that the reason that over fifty thousand men died from being exposed to the Ark was due to the intense radiation that emanated from inside it. In addition, the reason priests needed to be sanctified (protected) was actually because they were better equipped with the knowledge to take care of the ark, and how to prevent it from harming others, but they knew how to use it to defeat their enemies nonetheless.

When the Philistines stole the ark from the Israelites, they thought they were cursed by God because thousands of them died, and those who survived were smitten with emerods. Many Bible translations, use the word *tumors* for emerods, but the Darby Bible and the Duoay-Reims Bible translate *emerods* to mean the modern-day word *hemorrhoids*. The Hebrew word is *techorim,* which also translates to *strongholds*. It is true that hemorrhoids are a type of tumor. The Hebrew word *techorim,* is translated in Yiddish as *tuchcus,* which means anus.

And at the end of chapter 5 verse 9 in1 Samuel, it actually says, specifically where the emerods were smitten — "in their secret parts." Well, anyone who knows about hemorrhoids knows them to be in an extraordinary hidden part of the body (i.e. the anus). Needless to say, the Philistines were scared and quickly made arrangements to return the Ark to the Israelites, so as to save the rest of Ashdod.

Word got out that this was a device to be feared. Yet, Jones believes the Ark caused the tumors, or swellings, due to the radiation. The Philistines were eager to get rid of it, knowing of its dangers. When they brought it to Ekron, the Ekronites all freaked out, thinking they brought it there to slay them.

First Samuel 5:10-12 tells that there was a deadly destruction in the city that day, and that the hand of the Lord was heavy upon them, and those who didn't die were smitten with emerods (hemorrhoids or tumors). A new cart was then made for the ark. When they finally returned it to the Israelites, the Israelites were so happy to see it and have it back that they used the wood from the cart to build a fire to offer a sacrifice to God, and then did themselves in, by opening up the ark and looking at the mercy seat. 1 Samuel 6:19 (NAS) says that 50,070 men died:

> "He struck down some of the men of Beth-shemesh because they had looked into the ark of the LORD (Yahuah). He struck down of all the people, 50,070 men, and the people mourned because the LORD (Yahuah) had struck the people with a great slaughter."

Perhaps this is why they called it the mercy seat? Because they prayed that the Lord would have mercy upon them, since the power of this thing was awesome. The Bible says that the Lord slaughtered them. But did He? Or was it just the negligence and disobedience of his people, who were given strict instructions about how to use the Ark, for their own good, but instead, ignored the Lord's "safety precautions" and did themselves in. In my opinion, this is what happens when you give what seems like twenty-second century technology to ancient primitive man.

Just look at today's modern world. How many people still do not know how to use technology safely? This, no doubt, taught them all a hard lesson as to how powerful and holy this piece of technology was. Today, people continue their search for the lost Ark of the Covenant, but knowing history, it is understandable why this piece of technology is being hidden and kept from today's earth humans. Some researchers have postulated that there were two devices — one was sent to Ethiopia, and the other is still hidden under the temple in Jerusalem. Suffice it to say, that God is protecting earth humans from it and from it getting into the wrong hands.

The fact that 1 Samuel 5-6 tells us how these ancient people looked at this powerful piece of technology, and ended up fearing God because of its dangers, as well as blaming God for the accidents it caused, was primarily due to their obvious negligence. Equally, this same reaction to powerful technology can, likewise, be said for all those who receive benefits and, due to their misunderstanding of the technology, praise God for the miracles they receive when, all along, it was merely advanced technology at work that they simply did not understand.

Point is, it goes both ways. The Lord can be blamed and praised for something that the ancients had no understanding nor reference to. True, He deserves praise for His Amazing Light technology. The stories of what happened in 1 Samuel regarding the Ark was likened to giving a child the keys to a Ferrari; a child would have no idea what to do with it or how powerful it was. Technology is dangerous in the hands of the ignorant and immature.

Even in today's age of technology, similar stuff continues to happen when earth humans encounter advanced technology. So many people are fooled by holographic technology, so much so, that they believe they are seeing visions of angels, Mother Mary, Jesus, etc., when what they are seeing are holographic projections done through technology.

This was precisely what happened during the so-called visions at Fatima, which were all witnessed by innocent young children. Let's get this straight. Both sides use technology. The only difference is that the kingdom of darkness counterfeits everything they can, everything that the Lord first created out of Light.

The other difference is that the fallen angels (aka Satan and his army of grays) use the counterfeit technology to deceive and project false beliefs and false expectations in humans, to manipulate their emotions and beliefs, whereas the Kingdom of Heaven and

CHAPTER TWO: Ancient Technology & Biblical Astronauts

the heavenly hosts (armies of heaven) do not misuse the technology to harm innocents. This is an important discernment.

This Fatima, like apparitions also known as "Marian" apparitions, have become a modern-day phenomenon, increasing significantly around the world, year by year.

Investigators have been teaming up with various Catholic theologians who are worried and concerned by the impact that today's Marian apparitions are having on millions of Catholics worldwide. Even in the Arab world, sightings of Mary are being heralded and causing significant excitement. What is happening?[3]

Firstly, let's keep in mind, that these so-called goddess apparitions are not Mary, but a projection of an image of her. They are being reported from Japan to Africa, from Korea to Australia, from Iraq to Israel, and from Egypt to Syria.

This type of holographic technology has the ability to bring a third of the world's population under its influence and ultimate control. The fact that the so-called Three Secrets of Fatima have not been fully revealed by the Vatican till now is significant in terms of how the Catholic Church will end up "spinning" this, as a valid explanation around the world.[2]

It's important to note that several Asians worship goddesses known as Kwan Yin, Kwanon, and Tara; she is also known as Devi or Shakti in Hinduism; Gaia is the modern New Age name for the Earth Goddess, and Venus and Ashtar are the names of the ancient pagan Goddess. Each country has their own version of their "vision" of the Virgin Mary apparitions.

There is a plethora of books and articles published regarding the all too "coincidental" resemblances between Marian apparitions and the UFO phenomena. This has led many researchers to conclude that these sightings are coming from the same source, and that many are the same events with a few variances between them.

My conclusion after researching Fatima, is that these holographic projections were manipulations done by reptoid/Sauroid beings, aka Grays, in order to implant humans with religious spirits and spiritual limitation devices. I explain how these work, later in this book.

THE LORD'S FLEET OF SPACESHIPS

"...and they saw the God of Israel. There was under his feet as it were a <u>pavement of sapphire stone, like the very heaven for clearness</u>."

(Exodus 24:10, ESV)

This clearly describes the Lord's spacecraft. The use of the precious stones is repeated in both the *Books of Enoch*, as well as the Book of Revelation. When I read this passage, I had a vision of a clear blue floor, lighted up, similar to what they can do now in movies and TV sets with that blue light. The fact that the writer describes it as pavement made of sapphire stone could be literal, or it could also be so technologically advanced that that was the only description that came to his mind was to describe it as pavement made of sapphire stone, clear as the sky itself, like the very heavens, for clarity implies it reflected light.

If it really was paved with sapphires, it wouldn't have been so clear, as sapphires would vary from stone to stone, and there would be interruption in clarity, unless there was some kind of technologically advanced way of taking a bunch of real sapphires and blending them together so that they could create a clear floor with the type of clarity that Moses, the writer, describes. Then again, there are water sapphires, and today's laboratory sapphires are preferred in the jewelry world for their perfect clarity.

The use of precious stones is used in Revelation: "And the foundations of the wall of the city were garnished with all manner of precious stones. The first foundation was jasper; the second, sapphire; the third, a chalcedony; the fourth, an emerald; the fifth, sardonyx; the sixth, sardius; the seventh chrysolite; the eighth, beryl; the ninth, a topaz; the tenth, a chrysoprasus; the eleventh, a jacinth; the twelfth, an amethyst" (Revelation 21:19-20, KJV). It is clear that what John describes is the wall of the holy city, the New Jerusalem, which is a huge mother ship scheduled to descend from the heavens upon the old Jerusalem after the Lord's return.

The following passage is from the *Book of Enoch*, where Enoch is swept up in a whirlwind (by one of the Lord's spaceships) and is shown a fleet of spacecraft and is told by his extraterrestrial angel guide that all this power belongs to the chosen one, the Messiah, who will reign on earth. Enoch repeatedly calls the Almighty Creator, the Lord of Spirits, and the Elect One is his Messiah King (Mashiach Nagid). (Emphasis and commentary are mine):

> "After that period, in the place where I had seen every secret sight, I was snatched up in a whirlwind, and carried off westwards. There my eyes beheld the secrets of heaven, and all which existed on earth; <u>a mountain of iron, a mountain of copper, a mountain of silver, a mountain of gold, a mountain of fluid metal, and a mountain of lead</u>."

These were spaceships, which looked like mountains to Enoch. Probably mother ships, one in each precious metal and one that he describes as "fluid metal."

> "And I inquired of the angel [the extraterrestrial's guide and space traveler] who went with me, saying, what are these things, which in secret I behold? He said, all these things which you behold shall be for the dominion of the Messiah that he may command, and be powerful upon earth."

This proves that all of these motherships were under the command of the Commander, Yahshua HaMashiach, (the Lord Jesus Christ). As I've been saying throughout this book, He is the Cosmic Christ; His mission as Savior is not limited to planet Earth.

CHAPTER TWO: Ancient Technology & Biblical Astronauts

> "And that angel of peace answered me, saying, Wait but a short time, and you shall understand, and every secret thing shall be revealed to you, which the Lord of spirits [this is the Almighty Creator Lord] has decreed. Those mountains which you have seen, the mountain of iron, the mountain of copper, the mountain of silver, the mountain of gold, the mountain of fluid metal, and the mountain of lead, all these in the presence of the Elect One shall be like a honeycomb before the fire, and like water descending from above upon these mountains; and shall become debilitated before his feet. In those days men shall not be saved by gold and by silver. <u>Nor shall they have it in their power to secure themselves, and to fly</u>."

This is revealing, because this ET angel is telling Enoch that silver and gold cannot save humans, and in the end days, they will not be able to save themselves or feel secure, and that humans will not be able to fly. Today, we fly in airplanes, and a select few fly in rocket ships. But perhaps this ET angel was referring to something more sophisticated, like not having the capability to fly in spaceships. This again proves that we need a Savior. We are not capable of saving or rescuing ourselves from the coming events on planet Earth.

> "There shall be neither iron for wars, nor a coat of mail for the breast. Copper shall be useless; useless also that which neither rusts nor consumes away; and lead shall not be coveted. All these things shall be rejected, and perish from off the earth, when the Elect One shall appear in the presence of the Lord of spirits."
>
> (Enoch 51:1-10)

The Elect One, the Messiah, was known as Yahushua when He walked the earth in the flesh, later became known as the Lord and Savior Jesus Christ. The Lord of Spirits is the Almighty Creator, also addressed by Jesus as the Heavenly Father and the giver of the Holy Spirit.

BIBLICAL ALIEN GODS

The Old Testament contains some of the best evidence of UFOs because of its accurate accounts of direct involvement with extraterrestrials and alien beings. If Abraham's, Isaiah's, Ezekiel's, Elijah's and Moses' experiences happened today, they would definitely be perceived completely different outside the context of religion.

The Old Testament Bible is most definitely the best source for examining the deceptive sinister aliens' involvement along with their treacherous agendas for humankind in the ancient world. These biblical aliens clearly masqueraded as gods to the ancients, and through so many translations, mis-translations, and outright obfuscations of the names of gods within the Hebrew Bible, this historical fact was covered up to many believers, and as a researcher and a believer, I would have to conclude, this was done on purpose.

> "It is time for the truth to be brought out in open Congressional hearings. Behind the scenes, high-ranking Air Force officers are soberly concerned about UFOs. But through official secrecy and ridicule, citizens are led to believe the unknown flying objects are nonsense. To hide the facts, the Air Force has silenced its personnel."
>
> (Admiral R.H. Hillenkoetter,
> Director of CIA, quoted from
> New York Times, February 28, 1960, p. L30)

What we can perceive through the Old Testament, are rare insights into how reptilian aliens controlled the ancient desert people known as the Hebrews or Israelites, by imposing all kinds of laws and rules that nobody was able to fully follow perfectly, which were recorded in Leviticus, Deuteronomy and Numbers. These rules and laws that had nothing whatsoever to do, with the true God of the universe, which is later proven down the timeline, when another extraterrestrial god arrives, who teaches that the fulfillment of all the laws is Grace and Love. Love for your Creator and love for your neighbor is really all that matters in the end.

There were many different types of alien breeding experiments that were done with several different generations of 'chosen people.' Wandering around in the wilderness for forty years in the desert resulted in a new generation fed with 'manna' from heaven, which actually came out of a manna machine from the spaceship that led them.

It is generally agreed upon by most Biblical scholars, that the wandering pattern was done deliberately to weed out the old attitudes and negative habit patterns of these Israelites, who had slave-victim mentality from Egypt, before they were brought into the 'promised land' to populate it with a new generation of Israelites. Scripture tells us, that they not only wandered through the desert, but they ended up walking around in circles.

As I've concluded in Book One, *Who's Who In The Cosmic Zoo?* that the biblical fall and curse of Adam and Eve, who I called the Evadamic race, their offspring became the outcome of genetic engineering to downgrade these beings, by intentionally disabling ten of the twelve strands of DNA, which today's scientists refer to as 'junk DNA', in order to give them just enough intelligence to follow orders and become slaves to the serpent race of alien gods. Adam and Eve were made in the image and likeness of the Elohim, who were gods.

The Elohim were actually a group of gods, as the original Hebrew text describes, because Hebrew is a very specific language, and the scripture about the creation of humankind is all written in the plural tense of Hebrew linguistics.

> "And God (Elohim) said, Let <u>us</u> make man in <u>our</u> image, after <u>our</u> likeness:"
>
> (Genesis 1:26)

CHAPTER TWO: Ancient Technology & Biblical Astronauts

I laid out my argument that after Adam and Eve fell and were cursed for listening to the Serpent in the Garden, that it gave the Serpent, who we know as Satan, spiritual legal ground to use them as slaves, because they essentially lost their authority to him through being deceived by him, which in effect gave him back his authority that he lost before the first floods (Genesis 1:1) which was the destruction of the ancient civilization of Atlantis.

The half-truth, which becomes today's growing mass deception amongst UFO/Alien researchers, is the Annunaki Reptilian Overlords created humans. Well, as the saying goes, 'be careful when you get a hold of half-truths, that you don't get hold of the wrong half.' It's true that satan and his host of insidious reptilian aliens, who were recorded as the Annunaki geneticists, *re-created* humans to serve them as their slaves. This is the origin and roots of all slavery on earth, and every slave race, beginning with the Sumerians, the ancient Israelites, and the African slave trade, can all be traced back to this historical event. Essentially this is the story the Sumerian Cuneiform tablets as well as the Enuma Elish tell us. Enuma Elish - The Epic of Creation:

"When Marduk heard the word of the gods, his heart prompted him and he devised a cunning plan. He said,

"My blood will I take and bone will I fashion. I will make man that man may.[..] I will create man who shall inhabit the earth.. That *the service of the gods* may be established…And that their shrines may be built."[6]

This proves that the genetic manipulations was to *serve* these extraterrestrial gods, for their purpose, as servants to them, i.e., slaves. This also proves that shrines, temples and places of worship, were built intentionally so these ET gods would be worshipped, and steal the worship away from the God of gods, the Creator of Heaven and Earth, who created them.

As humans have evolved, so have these gods who were in rebellion towards their Father.

The other half of the truth is that the Elohim, who were the gods that the God of gods created, placed the Evadamic race on earth, who were created in their image, which was the image and likeness of God. They were originally made perfect and walked the earth in their glory bodies, whose offspring were later downgraded by the satans, i.e., the reptilian Annunaki geneticists.

Researchers need to connect the dots here, and understand what came first.

In the Sumerian Cuneiform tablets, essentially there were two main gods who argued over the human race. One was Enki, the other Enlil. Enki was the compassionate, merciful one, Enlil wanted to destroy humans. Sounds familiar? In the Old Testament, these two archetypal extraterrestrial gods, are depicted through satan and Yahuah. Enlil later became known as Baal and later, Allah, all other names of satan, aka 'HaSatan', which is Hebrew for the adversary or enemy.

However, through today's English bible translations, it's nearly impossible to tell them all apart, except through deciphering the original Hebrew, the truth is revealed through the names of the cast of characters throughout the Biblical stories, which I present to you within this book.

NOTES:

1. Immanuel Velikovsky, *Earth in Upheaval*, 1955, Doubleday and Company, Inc., Garden City, New York.
2. Charles, R. H. (trans.). *The Book of Enoch.* 1917 < http://www.sacred-texts.com/bib/boe>.
3. *Marian Apparitions - Angel of Light or Messenger of Deception?* 2009- 2014 Rema Marketing http://www.fatimarevelations.com
4. Blumrich, Josef F., *The Spaceships of Ezekiel* (New York, NY: Bantam Press, 1974).
5. Ann Madden Jones, *Yahweh Encounters*, Bible Astronauts, Ark Radiations and Temple Electronics, Sandbird Publishing, North Carolina, 1995.
6. Robert Sepehr, *Species With Amnesia: Our Forgotten History*, Atlantean Gardens, Encino, CA, 2015

CHAPTER THREE

ANCIENT ASTRONAUT THEORY

"Two possibilities exist: either we are alone in the
universe, or we are not. Both are equally terrifying."

~Arthur C. Clarke

The ancient astronaut theory by Eric Von Däniken[1] says that the gods were not gods at all, but flesh and blood extraterrestrials that came to harvest the earth for resources, mate with earth women, and experiment with DNA and genetic engineering. Zecharia Sitchin also wrote about the genetic engineering from the ancient Sumerian gods called the Annunaki, in his book *Genesis Revisited*.[2]

While I agree with Von Däniken to the point that the ancient gods were, in fact, extraterrestrials; as I've already stated, many of these extraterrestrials had god complexes because they followed Lucifer's rebellion against the Almighty Creator God. These fallen sons of heaven set up earth-based religions, so they can be worshipped by earth humans. (See my chapter on *Aliens and Religion* in Book Four).

Karen Armstrong, in *Fields of Blood*, which is about gods and life in ancient Mesopotamia, said, "What role did religion play in this damaging oppression?" (Here she was referring to the dominated peasant underclass.) "All political communities develop ideologies that ground their institutions in the natural order as they perceive it[3]. The Sumerians knew how fragile their groundbreaking urban experiment was. Their mud-brick buildings needed constant maintenance; the Tigris and Euphrates frequently broke their banks and ruined the crops; torrential rains turned the soil into a sea of mud; and terrifying storms damaged property and killed livestock.

But the aristocrats had begun to study astronomy and discovered regular patterns in the movement of the heavenly bodies. They marveled at the way the different elements of the natural world worked together to create a stable universe, and they concluded that the cosmos itself must be a kind of state in which everything had its allotted function."

She goes on to say, "The cosmic state, they believed was managed by gods who were inseparable from the natural forces and nothing like the 'God' worshipped by Jews, Christians, and Muslims today. These deities could not control events but were bound by the same laws as humans, animals, and plants. There was no vast ontological gap between human and divine; Gilgamesh, for example, was one-third human, two-thirds divine.[4] The Annunaki, the higher gods, were the aristocrats' celestial alter-egos, the most complete and effective selves, differing from human only in that they were immortal."

Many of these gods subsequently entered into agreements with Lucifer/Satan, the god of this world, and therefore became part of the dark cabal of powers, principalities, and rulers of cosmic evil in heavenly places on Earth. (See my chapter on *Contracts and Agreements* in Book Four). Subsequently some of these ET/gods created karma with earth humans and have had to work their way out of their Faustian Contracts, and they belonged to the Office of Satan, which is still going on to this day.

However, some of them turned back to the Cosmic Christ and are now part of the Christ Alliance of Federation of Stars and Planets, or the Office of Christ in the Heavens, (i.e. also known on Earth and in the Bible as the Kingdom of Heaven), and they acknowledge His authority in Heaven and on Earth.

Today there are hours of video footage taken by NASA and the Russian Space Station, which shows numerous UFOs flying around the earth; some are shown in actual combat mode, in various skirmishes with one another. One video shows in excess of fifty spacecraft which looks like diamonds "patrolling" the earth from space, which was captured on film by the Russian cosmonauts. This proves what the ancient texts talk about, with respect to those who are sent to "police" the planet and be the "watchers." (See *Books of Enoch* and Genesis Chapter 6.)

The police force is different from the watchers. The ET police force is ordered by the Elohim (the council of gods) under the direction of the Creator. They are benevolent toward earth humans; they are protecting Earth from being invaded by the alien dark forces who wish to infiltrate the planet and exploit earth humans for nefarious purposes. Some people call them angels and archangels. (See, *Who's Who In The Cosmic Zoo?* Book Three: *Who Are the Angels?*)

THE WINGS OF ANGELS OR AIRPLANES?

In Hebrew, the word for wing is *kanaph* (singular) and wings is *kanaphim* (plural). According to Strong's concordance, the word for wing, wings, or winged is mentioned ninety times in the Bible.

The KJV translates the Hebrew word *kanaph* as "borders" in Numbers 15:38. According to *Brown-Driver-Briggs' Hebrew Dictionary*, the Hebrew word *kanaph* means:
1. Wing, extremity, edge, winged, border, corner, shirt wing, 1a. Wing, 1b. Extremity,
   1b1 skirt, corner (or garment).

The Hebrew word for the English word *wings* in Malachi 4:2 includes the following meanings: edges, the extremities, or the wings of a garment. It is what the woman with the issue of blood was referring to, when she said, "If I may but touch (the wing of) his garment, I shall be whole" (Matthew 9:21, KJV).

The garment Jesus wore is known as a *tallit*, which simply means a cloak. The corner of his garment is where the *tzitzit* are located, with the tassels that are tied in knots and attached to two corners of the *tallit*. These corners are called *kanaphim* which in Hebrew means "wings." This is where the healing verse comes from, the word to touch

CHAPTER THREE: Ancient Astronaut Theory

his wing or being under the wings of the shadow of the Almighty (Psalm 91), all using *kanaphim*, the Hebrew word for wings.

However, technologically speaking, the very same word is used to describe the "wings of an airplane." This same word *kanaphim* is used for the wings of an airplane in Hebrew, which is *hakanaphim shel matose*.

ON THE WINGS OF EAGLES

There are many scriptures that make reference to the wings of an eagle. Let's look at Exodus 19:4, when God is speaking of his protective care over the nation of Israel, "… I bore you on eagles' wings …" The Hebrew word for "to bear" is *nacah*, and its primary root means "to lift." This is exactly what the parent eagle does to help its young in flight. What if the Israelites were truly born on the Lord's starship and later planted on the earth? Could this be the reason why they were considered different?

> "But they that wait on the LORD (Yahuah) shall renew their strength; they shall mount up with wings as eagles; they shall run, and not be weary; and they shall walk, and not faint."
>
> (Isaiah 40:31, KJV)

Many biblical scholars read this and think it is a metaphor. But what if it's not entirely metaphorical, but literal? What if the Lord is speaking of lifting His people up into His spacecraft that has a power similar to that of an eagle? The eagle's diving speed can exceed 100 mph. At this speed, the eagle's eyesight must be perfect in order to know exactly when to pull out of a dive. Its eyes are designed to spot a rabbit or fish from up to one mile away.

The eagle also has remarkably designed wings, each covered by over 12,000 feathers. Aircraft designers are still trying to copy the eagle's engineering marvel. Besides the ability to climb to 10,000 feet within minutes, the parent eagle also assists its young in flight. As it flies alongside the eaglet, whirlpools of air formed by its primary feathers provide the eaglet with additional lift. Needless to say, eagles, like other birds, are amazing miniature natural "airplanes."

When angels are illustrated with wings, perhaps this means that it's because they arrived in a vehicle that had wings, similar to an airplane or a bird. Similarly, when the Lord uses the metaphor "wings as eagles," perhaps He is referring to the same thing, describing the wherewithal and ability of flight.

EZEKIEL'S WHEELS WITHIN WHEELS

Ezekiel's account of the fiery wheels encountered by the River Chebar is believed, by some, to be a vision, but others, including myself, believe it to be a close encounter.

The book of Ezekiel records a total of seven close encounters. Ezekiel was what we would call "a frequent flyer" today.

Author and researcher R. Cedric Leonard, PhD.[3] wrote a revealing essay on Atlantic Quest[3] on *The Wheels of Ezekiel,* and interpreted some of the ancient and unusual Hebrew words that Ezekiel used to describe his experience. What I love about Leonard's essay is how he proves, through the Hebrew language, that Ezekiel encountered Divine spacecraft and was taken up and down by the Lord's extraterrestrial pilots. But more importantly, he goes into great detail about who the beings were that Ezekiel encountered, who Ezekiel called "cherubim" (pronounced "kerubim" in Hebrew). I am reprinting portions of the essay, *The Wheels of Ezekiel* here with Dr. Leonard's kind permission:

"Certainly nothing in normal experience could be compared to the occurrence he describes:

> 'And I looked, and, behold, a whirlwind came out of the north, a great cloud, and a fire infolding itself, and a brightness was about it, and out of the midst thereof as the color of amber, out of the midst of the fire.'"

(Ezekiel 1:4, KJV)

This was Ezekiel's first sight of the unidentified flying object that was approaching him from the north. We can better understand his description of this event by taking a close look at his choice of words.

The Hebrew word *se'ahra* is translated "whirlwind" in the King James Version. The word *se'ahra* is rare, and describes a very unusual, or peculiar, type of storm." It is also used to describe sandstorms that happen in the desert also known as a *humsin*, which translates to "hot wind."

When I lived in Israel, humsins happened a few times a year. As a teenager, I didn't understand why they were happening, and just thought it was a weather event. But after studying and researching UFOs for over thirty years now, I am convinced that some of the humsins that took place in the Negev were caused by space craft landing and taking off through ancient portals that still exist and are in use today in the Negev. In fact, at night, when all the dust settled and we could see all the stars clearly, we would watch what we thought were spaceships (UFOs) crossing the sky.

The whirlwind or *se'ahra* are caused from the sheer power of their engines, which is enough to send and create these unusual whirlwinds of sandstorms that can extend for miles into the Israeli dessert. This is what I believe Ezekiel was referring to when he used the word *se'ahra* to describe this type of whirlwind.

One thing we know is that in the desserts of Israel, there are no traditional tornadoes, but there are sandstorms. I have personally witnessed half a dozen sandstorms over the three years that I spent in Israel in the Negev, on days where there was not a cloud in the sky. These whirlwinds did not come from a funnel cloud as traditional tornadoes do, but

CHAPTER THREE: Ancient Astronaut Theory

these sandstorms came literally out of nowhere, causing zero visibility for a couple of hours until the sand settled.

When God spoke to Job "out of the whirlwind" (Job 38:1), the same word *se'ahra* was used to describe this type of whirlwind.

Ezekiel mentions "a great cloud," an *anan gadol*. The word *anan* can mean a weather cloud, but, in the Hebrew Scriptures, it almost always refers to the "shining presence of deity." (See my section on the cloudships in the next chapter "The Mother Ships of the Lord.") Cloud-cloaking spacecraft is the Lord's signature space technology.

Dr. Leonard points out that, in the following sentence, Ezekiel's choice of words are very explicit: "The cloud is encircled by flashing strobe lights! Here he used an ancient and unusual Hebrew word: מִתְהַלֶּכֶת *mithaleqcheth*, which means "flashing forth continually." In the Greek, the word *exastrapton* also means "flashing out" like a modern strobe light. This is not a reference to natural lightning, and this is no ordinary cloud.[3]

The next three words are *venogah lo savev*, which translates to "touching itself around." Even the King James Version has the alternate reading in the margin: "Hebrew— catching itself" like "chasing lights." This conveys the image of flashing, strobe-like lights, turning upon themselves in a circle, like one sees in spaceships and modern day UFOs. This was not lightning, as the word for lightning is used much later in the text, this was a rare and unusual event, and Ezekiel was terrified.

The Holy Bible in Modern English translated it this way:

> "Then I looked, and saw a raging wind from the north driving a great cloud, and whirling fire flashing around it, with the gleam of polished brass [or electrum] in the center of the fire."
>
> (Ezekiel 1:4 HBME-1900)

This is because early translators rendered the Hebrew *chashmal* as "amber," but today most scholars translate it as "gleaming bronze"— the ancient Greek and Latin versions have "electrum." Electrum is a natural alloy of gold and silver, having a high reflectivity factor that is truly beautiful to behold. Either rendition indicates that very shiny metal is visible within this luminous cloud.[1]

In verse 13, the "whirling lamps" image is reinforced once more. "As for the likeness of the living creatures, their appearance was like burning coals of fire [i.e., glowing], and there was an appearance of lamps *continuously circling* among the living creatures" (Ezekiel 1:13, cf. KJV-II translation).

Notice the italics. Most translations fail to convey the meaning of the Hebrew text at this point. Instead of lamps which were "going up and down," as in the King James translation, the Hebrew text has *mithehalaqat*, a word meaning "circling continuously" (closely akin to *mitheleqachat*). The Greek (LXX) has *sustrephomenon*, that is, lamps which appear to be "revolving" or "rotating." This is a description of some type of advanced technology, particularly in Ezekiel's time.[1]

So many translators missed so many facets of this relatively accurate description. Most modern versions, including the New International Version (NIV), have "going back and forth." Which is it: going back and forth, or up and down? Our most ancient texts clearly read "continuously circling."

The following sentence says "that and the fire was bright, and out of the fire went forth lightning" (Ezekiel 1:13b, KJV). Did lightning come out of the fire? This sounds like what someone would see when witnessing a spacecraft, and the boost of the rocket causes fire and sparks, which Ezekiel described as lightning coming out of the fire. The lightning certainly wasn't coming out of the sky here but out of the fire itself. Then in verse 14, he says, "And the living creatures ran and returned as the appearance of a flash of lightning."[3]

The cherubim themselves were moving so fast, that they appeared in a flash of lightning. The New International Version translates it as:

"The creatures sped back and forth like flashes of lightning."

This gives you a better visual of their energy and how their movements themselves were likened to flashes of lightning.

Dr. Leonard goes on to say that the appearance of gleaming metal, along with revolving lamps, within this luminous cloud certainly puts an entirely different light on the event. Ezekiel clearly indicates that these vehicles land, take off, hover, and even fly in formation as they zip to and fro in all directions. They are able to do so without needing to bank and turn as airplanes or birds do (verses 14, 17). As they flash through the sky, they are — like the mighty flying machines (Vimanas) of the Hindu epics — accompanied by a thunderous roar."[3]

Back in 2000-2005, the cable TV series *Farscape* illustrated the concept of a "living spaceship," that was affectionately called Moya, which was a Leviathan living ship. Moya was a sentient being. The ship communicated with its inhabitants and "felt" its way through space. Through the inception of science-fiction, we can relate to abstract and advanced technological concepts that we have not achieved yet on earth, like Ezekiel's concept of "living ships" powered by living creatures.

LET DOWN THEIR WINGS

Finally, as they land on Earth, they "let down their wings"— a curious statement from our UFO-oriented standpoint, unless we realize that these "wings" could conceivably be metal stairways as seen from the side. Again, the word for wings in this verse is *kanaphim*. "Such 'gangplanks' might be lowered smoothly until they touched the ground, giving him the impression that the cherubim had 'let down their wings.'"[1] This could also be what Jacob experienced (Genesis 28) when he called it "the ladder to heaven," which was as Leonard puts it, just a type of "gangplank" or stairway to come and go into the spacecraft.

CHAPTER THREE: Ancient Astronaut Theory

Dr. Leonard postulates that "it would seem natural that after these vehicles had landed and the glowing cloud of supercharged plasma had dissipated and the fiery exhausts and rotating lights had ceased, that Ezekiel could better evaluate the physical appearance of the craft and their occupants."[3]

The climax of this event is when Ezekiel saw the "appearance of a throne" above the machine, and one sitting upon it having the "appearance of a man." Notice the repetition of the word "appearance" (Hebrew *eth*, "image"). Was this a projection of the ship's commander?

Next, Ezekiel does what almost everyone in the Bible does when they are confronted with one of these awesome extraterrestrial "angels"; he falls on his face in fear and worship. Dr. Leonard believes it was more than significant when Ezekiel fell on his face in awe of this being (verse 28), because he was sharply commanded to stand up (Ezekiel 2:1). Leonard rightly points out, "If this was a vision of God himself, why wouldn't Ezekiel be permitted to worship?"[5]

These extraterrestrial angels are on assignment from the Lord; they know the protocol, and they do not want to be worshipped. (See my chapter *Angel Protocol* in Book Three of *Who's Who In the Cosmic Zoo?*) The same thing happens each and every time Ezekiel prostrates himself. However, once back on his feet, he was given a message to be delivered to his fellow captives in Babylon. Then a startling thing happens:

"Then the spirit took me up, and I heard behind me a voice of a great rushing (*as the glory of the Lord rose from its place*) ... So the spirit lifted me up, and took me away, and I went in bitterness, in the heat of my spirit; but the hand of the Lord was heavy upon me" (Ezekiel 3:12, 14, KJV).[5]

Apparently as he was taken up simultaneously, the whole dazzling affair, whirling lights and all, arose majestically into the sky! As he was being carried aloft, he heard a thunderous roar (which he imagined was caused by the clapping of mighty wings). The King James Version uses the mild term "rushing," but my rabbinical consultants claim that the Hebrew words imply a thunderous roar, such as an earthquake or a tremendous waterfall.

The "spirit" or "wind" (*ruach*) mentioned here (as well as in verse 4 above) is the same powerful force which had lifted the prophet Elijah into the sky during the incident recorded in 2 Kings 2:11. In that particular case, the means of conveyance was described as a "chariot of fire." Is this much different?

It is also important to note that the Hebrew word used for wind or spirit is *ruach*; however, in these verses it is not making reference to the Holy Spirit, which in Hebrew is *ruach kodesh*. In this case, the word *ruach* means "wind," but, of course, the ancients called the wind "spirit," so the two words are interchangeable in Hebrew.

In the New International Version, it reads: "Then the Spirit lifted me up, and I heard behind me a loud rumbling sound." This clearly implies that this is not the Holy Spirit, but the Lord's technology. A loud, rumbling sound is what you hear when a spaceship takes off. The King James Version translates it as the sound of a great voice rushing.[3] We know of no such voice on Earth that can make that sound.

Then Ezekiel talks about the sound of the "wings" of the living creatures (robots) in verse 13: "The sound of the wings of the living creatures brushing against each other and the sound of the wheels beside them, a loud rumbling sound." Ezekiel is describing the sound of the technology of this space chariot. Then he says, in verse 14, "The Spirit then lifted me up and took me away, and I went in bitterness and in the anger of my spirit, with the strong hand of the Lord upon me." He was taken up in the Lord's spacecraft and describes it as not being his will, but the Lord's.

Dr. Leonard goes on to analyze, and reveal "that in Hebrew, the difference between the above passages is only one letter! Since the original Hebrew text had no vowels, a scribal error was made at some point, which substituted a Hebrew letter K for an original M, making the text to read *baruk* (blessed) instead of *berum*(as arose). Most biblical scholars believe this to have happened (with good reason) and have restored the original meaning to the text (*Peake's Commentary on the Bible*)".

A very similar phrase is later used (Ezekiel 11:23), which was helpful to scholars in spotting this error (*The Interpreter's Bible*). Before this was corrected, the meaning was so incoherent that the King James translators had to insert the English word 'saying' just to make any sense of it."[3]

> "Then the cherubim lifted up their wings with the wheels beside them, and the glory of the God of Israel hovered over them. The glory of the LORD *went up* from the midst of the city and stood over the mountain which is east of the city."

Both the Holman Christian Bible and the Net Bible translate verse 23 as "rose up." "The glory of the LORD *rose up* from the middle of the city and stood on the mountain, east of the city."

> "Then I arose, and went forth unto the plain: and behold, the glory of the Lord stood there, as the glory which I saw by the river Chebar: and I fell on my face."
> (Ezekiel 3:23, KJV)

> "Then the Spirit lifted me up, and I heard a great rumbling sound behind me, blessed be the glory of the Lord from his place."
> (Ezekiel 3:12, KJV)

Restored to: "As the glory of the Lord *rose* from its place."

Again more "lost in translation" shenanigans. The fact that this happened, in my opinion, was to subtly obscure its original meaning and confuse the reader. Just as the Masoretes did by changing the name of the Lord, from Yahuwah to Jehovah. (See my

CHAPTER THREE: Ancient Astronaut Theory

chapter *Who Is Yahweh and Jehovah?*) It's clear from the scriptures that the *glory of the Lord* was the presence of Him within His magnificent starship. The scripture describes God's glory descending, hovering, and leaving the city of Jerusalem (Ezekiel 11).

Once again, he is brought to his feet (no worship here), and another message is given him. During these encounters, he is always addressed as "son of man," which is the equivalent of "human" or "earthling." The phrase "the glory of the Lord stood there" indicates that he could see it while he was yet far off, and remained there as he approached. Does this sound like a vision?

Then the prophet was taken to Jerusalem aboard the craft. This time the text states explicitly that "the Spirit lifted me up between the earth and the heaven and brought me *in the visions of God* to Jerusalem" (Ezekiel 8:3, ESV). It couldn't be any clearer. Moreover, since he was a captive in Babylonia, he could not have traveled to Jerusalem on his own (a trip of several months by caravan).

Eventually, all four craft returned. By now Ezekiel is referring to them as cherubs (to be discussed shortly). Someone within hearing distance must have seen the craft also because Ezekiel records hearing someone cry out, "O galgal," (i.e. "spinning thing," or wheel) (Ezekiel 10:13). This is the equivalent of yelling "flying saucer!" upon seeing a modern UFO. Later, another lift-off is described, this time in downtown Jerusalem:

> "Then did the cherubims *lift up their wings*, and the wheels beside them; and the glory of the God of Israel was over them above. *And the glory of the Lord went up from the midst of the city*, and stood upon the mountain which is on the east side of the city."
>
> (Ezekiel 11:22-23, KJV)

The "glory of the Lord" is a term used repeatedly during these encounters and so-called visions. Psalm 119 says, "The heavens declare the Glory of the Lord." Besides the innumerable universes and galaxies of stars that He created, the "glory of the Lord" is His amazing, powerful starships full of light, awe, and wonder.

Leonard concludes, after consulting numerous Bible commentaries that make reference to Ezekiel's vision as a chariot, that there are only two possibilities: Either Ezekiel encountered mechanized aircraft and their occupants, or he received *visions* of mechanized aircraft and their occupants — take your pick.

In my opinion, Ezekiel was not having visions or hallucinations; he encountered the commander of the ship, had a total of four encounters, was taken up and down, and brought into a temple, which was not Solomon's temple (but a temple in the sky), and was given messages to relay to his people, which still resonate with us today.

It says that it took Ezekiel seven days to recover from his experiences. Being swept up in these fantastic spaceships can cause a person's head to spin and make him or her *think* that he or she is seeing visions, because the experience is so *out of this world*. I would imagine him having to pinch himself, and he must have wondered to himself several times, if he had been dreaming. This is the reason he chose to use the word *vision* because, after being taken up, it was like a *vision* to him, and he had nothing else to relate it to in his world.

Imagine having his experience validated by a NASA engineer 2,600 years later? Most scholars today who have looked into the book of Ezekiel, including Josef F. Blumrich in his book *The Spaceships of Ezekiel*, concluded that Ezekiel had actually physically encountered extraterrestrial messengers of the Lord and was taken up in their spacecraft and was given messages to relay back to those on earth.

In fact, Blumrich, who is a NASA engineer, recreated test models of the spaceships in the wind tunnels of NASA's Langley Research Center during the late 1960s and published the sketches in his book. What was so interesting about Blumrich's work was that he was intent on discrediting Erich von Däniken's theory postulated in his groundbreaking bestseller, *Chariots of the Gods*, where he claimed that Ezekiel had had encounters with spaceships, yet in the end, Blumrich wrote confirmed it in his conclusion of *The Spaceships of Ezekiel*, stating:

> "With these conclusions, I had to declare defeat; I wrote to Erich von Däniken, explaining that my attempt to refute his theory had resulted in a structural and analytical confirmation of a major part of his hypothesis. Determining the form, dimensions and functional capabilities of what Ezekiel saw makes understandable a number of passages in his text that are otherwise meaningless; it also aids considerably in separating the prophetic or visionary parts of Ezekiel's book from those concerning encounters with spaceships. (I confined my study to the latter.) Being an engineer, I am not qualified to investigate the non-engineering portions."

WHO OR WHAT ARE THE CHERUBIM?

Ezekiel references the cherubim who *let down their wings* and *lift up their wings*. They were living creatures that operated these spacecraft. We've already established that their wings were the spaceship's ladders or gangplanks, and not actual bird wings. What I liked so much about Leonard's essay was his explicit interpretation of the term *cherubim* in reference to these machines.

Leonard postulates that the answer is extremely simple. "All four vehicles (which Ezekiel referred to as 'living creatures') bore insignias on them which denoted their universal or 'star ship' status—the four cardinal signs of the zodiac. I believe biblical theologians have been mistaken when they have attempted to put the four faces mentioned on the human-like occupants who stood outside the craft once they had landed."

The four faces of the "cherubim" are simply the four "signs" at the cardinal points of the heavens: Leo (the Lion), Taurus (the bull), Aquarius (the man), and Scorpio (which the Chaldeans often represented as an eagle). If one looks at a circle depicting the twelve

CHAPTER THREE: Ancient Astronaut Theory

signs of the zodiac, takes a perfect cross, and rotates it until one of the arms is pointing at any one of the four named signs (Aquarius, for instance), the three remaining arms will point to the other three (Leo, Taurus, and Scorpio).

This is a sensible way of representing this region of the universe. We have now apparently identified the mysterious four faces of the so-called "living creatures." The question remains, why did Ezekiel refer to the craft bearing these zodiacal faces as "cherubim" (Hebrew plural of cherub, pronounced 'kerub' or 'kerubim')?

According to Leonard, "the word 'cherub' has no etymology in the Hebrew language." Both the word and the concept is Babylonian, not Hebrew, according to *Les Religions de Babylonie et Assyrie* by E. Dhorme. Cherubs were early mythological creatures believed by the Babylonians to possess awesome and terrifying power (in the same class with griffins and sphinxes). The winged bull is often depicted with the head of a man and the tail of a lion."[3]

The similar sphinx is usually (but not always) depicted with a human head, sometimes with an eagle's wings, and a lion's body. Cherubs were usually placed at the entrances of temples or other sacred places as protectors of those holy precincts. It should be remembered that the earliest mention of cherubim in the Bible were those guarding the entrance to the Garden of Eden.

Those cherubim, were described as guardians with fiery swords, which is another way of saying they held laser guns or sabers as someone from *Star Wars* would.

Also, it is important to note that these sphinx statutes are found, not only in the Egyptian desert on planet Earth, but also on Mars and the moon; only the head of the sphinx is facing to the sky, as opposed to the Egyptian sphinx facing toward the eastern horizon. What seems like no coincidence is that the meaning of the word Cairo, where the Sphinx and the Giza Pyramids are, comes from the Arabic name "al Qahir," which means the planet Mars.

Researchers have confirmed that the Sphinx, when first discovered, was painted red, while half of it was buried in the rocks and sand. Egyptian temples and hieroglyphs all paint the planet Mars red. Could there be an ancient connection between the sphinx and the three pyramids in Cairo and the sphinx and the pyramids on Mars? Also, if Cairo was named after the planet Mars, then could we deduce that the sphinx and the pyramids were built on Earth after they were first established on Mars and that Cairo was connected to Mars? Perhaps a dedicated space port to Mars?

Since Ezekiel was in Babylon (Chaldea) and sculpted representations of these four cardinal zodiacal signs could be seen on every hand, it is only natural that Ezekiel would use the common terminology heard day after day in the vicinities of Babylon to describe such images.

Ezekiel's wheels represent an aerial vehicle, a celestial car, a "divine chariot," the function of which is transportation! Many rabbis and biblical scholars consider Ezekiel's wheel to be a chariot.

Ezekiel witnessed even more spacecraft technology. Technology was not understood by the ancients. Anything that was done through technology was considered to be a "miracle." Today, we have many kinds of technology. Yes, 2,000 years ago, much of that was a mystery. Ezekiel was taken up into a mother ship and wrote about seeing visions on a wall (Ezekiel 8:1-4, 7-8, 10).

Today we call that television, or computer/video screens, yet the ancients had no reference for such technology, so they used spiritual vernacular, and called them "visions." Ezekiel witnessed these "visions" on the wall of the spacecraft, as he watched the Israelites in the temple of Jerusalem worshipping the idols of Ishtar (Astarte/Ashtarte), which he called "the image of jealousy" because this made the Lord Yahuah angry.

Not only did the Israelites receive harsh punishment from the Lord Yahuah for their idolatry, which essentially was betraying Lord Yahuah, a sin that reoccurred several times throughout Old Testament history, but more importantly, this technology proves, that the Lord has his eyes and ears on all of us, watching what goes on, on Earth.

Imagine this, that all of our deeds and behaviors are being recorded and viewed in the heavens on TV monitors inside spacecraft. But if this was done during the seventh century BC, how much more will it be done in post-millennium times? This concept was illustrated in the 1991 movie *Defending Your Life,* written by Albert Brooks and starring Meryl Streep. There is nothing new under the sun. You, all the rest of earth humans, and I are a reality show for ETs to monitor.

THE LORD'S AERONAUTICS

> "The LORD (Yahuah) said, 'Go out and stand on the mountain in the presence of the LORD (Yahuah), for the LORD (Yahuah) is about to pass by.' Then a great and powerful wind tore the mountains apart and shattered the rocks before the LORD, but the LORD (Yahuah) was not in the wind. After the wind there was an earthquake, but the LORD Yahuah was not in the earthquake."
>
> (1 Kings 19:11, NIV)

Those very words — "for the Lord is about to pass by" — clearly indicates that His ship was passing by. And what was the cause and effect of when the Lord's ship passed by the mountain? A great and powerful wind tore the mountain apart and shattered its rocks. What can do that to a specific spot? The scripture doesn't say there were other areas that were damaged, only the mountain top. It's obvious if it was some type of wind storm that damage would have been done beyond the mountain top, but scripture makes no mention of that.

It is obvious that this great and powerful wind that had the power to shatter rocks and tear the mountain top apart was done by the passing of the Lord's spaceship. Then the scripture tells us that "his passing caused the earth to quake as well." Both times, the

CHAPTER THREE: Ancient Astronaut Theory

passage tells us that the Lord was not in the wind, nor in the earthquake. So where was He? He was tucked away safely in his spaceship.

By the way, it's important to mention, that each time English Bibles write the word, LORD, it is a substitute for the Hebrew word YHVH (Tetragrammaton), which spells out the name of the Lord, which is pronounced Yahuwah. (See my chapter on *The Tetragrammaton.*)

Detailed descriptions of Yahuah's own spaceships in both the Old and New Testaments indicate that there was a lot of technology going on, such as the burning bush, Mt. Sinai, Urim and Thumim, the Ark of the Covenant, Jacob's ladder, Ezekiel's wheels within wheels, and the numerous contacts by angels, hosts of heavens, and commanders (as in Joshua) were all part of the Lord Yahuah's technology.

Many Christian believers will use the argument "that God can do anything and He doesn't need technology." Yet, the Almighty Creator God created technology which will be proven one day, at the second coming of Christ along with His hundreds of thousands of hosts of heaven (extraterrestrial armies) at his side.

There are many forms of technology, and the Creator Father created it all. After all, He created the heavens. "The Heavens declare the glory of God" (Psalm 19:1, KJV). God's glory is not limited to the beautiful stars and galaxies, but His amazing, powerful, larger than life starships, which navigate throughout the heavens, in the Kingdom of Heaven.

> "He lays the beams of his chambers on the waters; he makes the *clouds* his chariot; he rides on the wings of the wind."
>
> (Psalm 104:3, ESV)

This technology was stolen by the fallen angels. They counterfeited it and mimicked it, which brings us to today's clunky UFOs. The Almighty Creator God uses the technology of light and love; the dark side is void of light and love, so they compensate with "clunky" technology. Math is the language of the universe. The Almighty Creator created both math and science, and for as much as we know today, the connection between science and spirit is still a mystery to us, but that, is a type of technology.

There are many forms of technology. It is not all clunky. Genetic engineering is not clunky, and the fact that both the book of Genesis and the Sumerian tablets make reference to humans being made from clay indicates that perhaps this "clay" was what the original test tubes were made out of and not the refined glass that we use today. The fact that Genesis 2:21 said that Eve came from Adam's rib may also have been a way of describing genetic engineering, as Eve was made from Adam's genetics, not his literal rib. The word *rib* was used to describe that it came from his own body, perhaps even made reference to a simple skin graft from Adam's body in the region of his body that covered his rib.

Elijah's Journey Into Heaven

Ezekiel was not the only prophet taken up into the heavens by a "whirlwind" and a "chariot of fire." Elijah, according to the Books of Kings, defended the worship of Yahuah over the fallen angel (ET) pseudo-god Baal. Elijah lived at a time of both spiritual tyranny and terror. Ahab, the king of Israel, had forsaken the God of Israel, yielding to his wicked wife, Jezebel, who not only had the Lord's prophets murdered, but had banished the worship of the Creator God and replaced it with Baal worship. Baal worship continues today in the form of one of the world's major religions, but we'll leave that for my later chapter on *Who Is Allah?*

Elijah's name in Hebrew, *Eliyahu*, means "Yahuah is God" or "Yahuah is my strength." He was called Elijah the Tishbite, and he lived in Gilead. There is no genealogy, and no character development of Elijah to be found in the Bible. He just showed up one day and bluntly told Ahab, the King of Israel, "As the Lord God of Israel lives, before whom I stand, there shall be neither dew nor rain these years, except at my word" (1 Kings 17:1, ESV). And then he left, and in no way was he intimidated.

Elijah raised the dead, brought fire down from the sky (by way of Yahuah's technology), and ascended into heaven in one of the Lord's spaceships. In the Book of Malachi, Elijah's return is prophesied "before the coming of the great and terrible day of the Lord," making him a harbinger of the Messiah, along with the eschatology in various faiths that revere the Hebrew Bible. Elijah appears in the Talmud, Mishnah, the New Testament, and the Quran. In the New Testament, both Jesus and John the Baptist are compared with Elijah; some even believed them to be the reincarnation of Elijah. Elijah shows up again with Moses during the Transfiguration of Jesus at Mount Hermon.

> "When the LORD (Yahuah) was about to take Elijah up to heaven in a whirlwind, Elijah and Elisha were traveling from Gilgal."
>
> (2 Kings 2:1, NLT)

> "And it came to pass, as they still went on, and talked, that, behold, there appeared a chariot of fire, and horses of fire, and parted them both asunder; and Elijah went up by a whirlwind into heaven."
>
> (2 Kings 2:11, KJV)

Chariots of Fire

Whirlwinds seem to be the way everyone is taken up. This is the power of a spaceship, which can reach down with the power of "wind" and lift a person up through the air and into the spaceship, which the Bible repeatedly refers to as "chariots of fire." There are no physical earthly chariots made of fire, let alone horses of fire, especially in biblical times. Chariots of fire are otherworldly. They came from the heavens and were

CHAPTER THREE: Ancient Astronaut Theory

called chariots because that was the lexicon used in that day to describe a vehicle. Yet they are described as "fire," which is their way of explaining what they saw, which was the technology of the spaceship that apparently glowed and looked like it was on fire.

Just as our rocket ships take off with fire and come into the earth's atmosphere "on fire," Merkabahs glow with fire, they can transport (chariot) people, and even though this particular scripture doesn't mention the clouds, the pattern in the Bible of these "wheels within wheels" and "chariots of fire" all seemed to be "cloaked" in clouds, which is probably why Elijah and Ezekiel both described it as a "whirlwind."

> "As they were walking along and talking, suddenly a chariot of fire appeared, drawn by horses of fire. It drove between the two men, separating them, and Elijah was carried by a whirlwind into heaven. Elisha saw it and cried out, 'My father! My father! I see the chariots and charioteers of Israel!' And as they disappeared from sight, Elisha tore his clothes in distress. Elisha picked up Elijah's cloak, which had fallen when he was taken up. Then Elisha returned to the bank of the Jordan River. He struck the water with Elijah's cloak and cried out, 'Where is the LORD, the God of Elijah?' Then the river divided, and Elisha went across. When the group of prophets from Jericho saw from a distance what happened, they exclaimed, 'Elijah's spirit rests upon Elisha!' And they went to meet him and bowed to the ground before him."
>
> (2 Kings 2:11-15, NLT)

Drawn by horses of fire? Since when do horses produce fire? These were certainly no ordinary horses. Could it possibly be "horsepower," such as the way we describe our automobiles today, with "horsepower" engines, a type of technology that seems to increase and improve with time? This was a way of describing the power of these spaceships. There aren't any real flesh and blood horses on fire coming out of heaven. These are metaphors to describe the horsepower these space vehicles are capable of which was beyond Elijah's and Ezekiel's imagination and anything that they could relate to in their days.

In 2 Kings 2:11-12 and 6:17, Psalm 68:17, and Habakkuk 3:8, the Old Testament writers describe a cosmic craft identified as a "chariot of fire" powered by engines called "horses of fire" with "charioteers" (pilots). The chariot's lift-off is described as a "whirlwind." In 2 Kings, it is written: "And it came to pass, when the Lord would take up Elijah into heaven by a whirlwind, that Elijah went with Elisha from Gilgal…and…behold, there appeared a chariot of fire, and horses of fire, and parted them both asunder; and Elijah went up by a whirlwind into heaven…"

The word *whirlwind* is used in the book of Ezekiel, as well, to describe the power thrusters of the spacecraft that caused the lift-off.

In the following verses, we learn that Elijah's cloak has special powers, which was passed to Elisha. When he cried out in frustration and hit Elijah's cloak on the water, something miraculous happened — the river divided. The only other time that happened was when Moses was leading the Israelites out of Egypt and parted the Red Sea with his magical staff. So many of us think when reading these stories, well, God can do anything, right? But how does He empower a simple cloak to divide a river or a simple staff to part a sea? Technology.

While the group of prophets exclaimed that Elijah's spirit rested on Elisha, Elijah had not died; Elisha certainly was not the reincarnation of Elijah. I question how could Elijah's spirit be split into two while Elijah was taking a trip in one of the Lord's spacecraft? In my opinion, while power and leadership may, in fact, have been transferred over to Elisha in Elijah's absence, the cloak parting the river was not done by Elijah's spirit, but by the Lord, who empowered both the cloak and transported Elijah.

> "Perhaps the Spirit of the LORD (Yahuah) has picked him up and set him down on some mountain or in some valley."
>
> (2 Kings 2:16, NIV)

Sounds like teleportation. We have movies like *Star Trek* to relate to, when we see people beamed up, de-molecularized, and re-molecularized in a different location. Perhaps something like this happened to Elijah as he was being teleported from one location on Earth to another? Again, in the following verse, Elijah was given special powers to beat Ahab to Jezreel.

> "The power of the LORD came on Elijah and, tucking his cloak into his belt, he ran ahead of Ahab all the way to Jezreel."
>
> (1 Kings 18:46, NIV)

I'm going to quote Joe Kovacs, from his book *Shocked By the Bible,* from his section, titled "Air Jesus" which is his comment on the above scripture:

> "At least one other time, Elijah got somewhere in a hurry, but it was not by airlifting. Instead, God gave him the ability to run with superhuman speed…The story sounds like something out of a Road Runner cartoon or a comic book. Elijah, boosted by a jolt of God's own turbo power, was able to run faster than a speeding chariot!"[6]

Now let's ask ourselves, how could Elijah have run so fast and beat King Ahab to Jezreel? Before this happened, the story tells us that Elijah was praying for rain on a perfectly clear day. As soon as he saw a tiny puff of cloud over the sea, he immediately told his servant to tell King Ahab to get in his chariot and head for Jezreel. Then there were dark clouds and a severe thunderstorm, which apparently rained heavily on Ahab and his real flesh and blood horse and chariot on the road to Jezreel, but Elijah gets a boost and beats him there in the pouring rain.

CHAPTER THREE: Ancient Astronaut Theory

How? Well, the scripture tells us, he tucked his magic cloak into his "belt," and ran ahead of Ahab. Some may say that his belt was a type of jet pack that enabled him to literally fly to Jezreel, only hovering just above the ground, which is why the scripture uses the word *ran*. But the only other scripture that talks about Elijah's belt is in 2 Kings 1:8 when Elijah is first introduced as "Elijah was a hairy man, and he wore a leather belt around his waist." His belt was nothing unusual, unlike his cloak. Today we have jet packs that can attach to one's back and cause the person to take off, hovering just above ground, but not high into the upper atmosphere as to fly away, unless you're parachuting from an airplane, which was not the case here.

There was obviously another way that Elijah travelled so fast to Jezreel, beating Ahab there in the pouring rain. The scripture specifically says that "the power of the Lord" came upon Elijah. It does not say "the Spirit of the Lord"; instead, it uses the word *power*. This involves some kind of technology that was beyond Elijah's capability, as well as all the capabilities of everyone else in those days, and even today. There are portals all around our planet. The Lord took him through a portal (a dimensional doorway), and he ended up in Jezreel all dry and way ahead of Ahab.

Perhaps the reason it was recorded that Elijah ran is because he literally went through the portals and dimensional doorways as quickly as one does when falling down a slide or being vacuumed into a vortex and spewed out on the other side. For lack of a better word, the writer of the book of Kings wrote that he ran because he moved so quickly, but in reality Elijah was transported through these hidden doorways by the power of the Lord.

FIRE FROM HEAVEN

After three years and six months, there had been no rain, and there was a great famine. Elijah arranged a meeting with King Ahab and had the king assemble 450 prophets of Baal and 400 prophets of Asherah (Ishtar), all commissioned and supported by Jezebel. At this gathering, Elijah confronted Ahab and the people of Israel for abandoning the Lord. He built an altar of stones, placed a sacrificial bull on the altar, and had four barrels of water emptied three times all over the sacrifice. In 1 Kings 18, Elijah was praying to the Lord to prove to him that He was indeed the Lord God of Israel. This is what happened:

> "Immediately the fire of the Lord flashed down from heaven and burned up the young bull, the wood, the stones, and the dust. It even licked up all the water in the trench! And when all the people saw it, they fell face down on the ground and cried out, "The LORD (Yahuah) — He is God! Yes, the LORD (Yahuah) is God!"
>
> (1 Kings 18: 38-39, NLT)

Fire flashing down from heaven happens through technology. From his spaceship that was hidden in the upper atmosphere, watching and listening to the prayers of His prophets, He immediately answered Elijah's prayer with fire from heaven, which was some type of laser, being directed at that particular spot, perhaps even focused on the young bull.

When the fire of God fell and consumed the sacrifice, the wood, the stones, and the water, all those assembled fell on their faces, saying, *"The Lord. He is God! The Lord. He is God!"* Elijah then had every pagan prophet executed. Then Elijah announced to Ahab that it would rain. That evening, it poured.

Here's my take on the Lord's technology. We see through a variety of scriptures that technology was used during biblical times. This technology did not come from anyone on Earth, but from the Lord in heaven. I am reminded of the scriptures: "A day is like a thousand years unto the Lord and a thousand years is like a day" (2 Peter 3:8; Psalm 90:4). This describes time travel. If a millennium is but one day to the Lord, then that would mean that the way we count time on Earth is way slower than where the Lord is.

With that said, our development and evolution happens gradually, as we only began the age of technology at the turn of the twentieth century, and look at where we are today, only a hundred years later, in the twenty-first century? Where I'm going with this is, even though we have advanced exponentially in the past century, we're still not at the level of where the Lord is or even where the lord of darkness is with respect to the vast amount of technological space vehicles that permeate the heavens.

While the Lord's technology was so over the top advanced for the biblical prophets, which it still is to us today, in spite of us now being deeply immersed in the age of technology. In today's world, when people witness UFOs, they use modern "techno" language to describe it, something that Elijah and Ezekiel didn't have back in their day. We can relate to TV monitors, computers, microwaves, and lasers. Although, in spite of where we're at, we still can't fathom the level of technology of the Lord's spaceships, which have been described with sapphire floors and walls of crystals, and precious gemstones, and wheels within wheels being empowered by the heads of living creatures (robots?).

Yes, there were many miracles throughout the Bible that were done through the agency of the Holy Spirit. Elijah was anointed, after delivering his message to Ahab. The Lord told Elijah to hide himself by a brook called Cherith where he could get water. The Lord directed ravens to bring Elijah bread and meat every morning and evening until the stream dried up. After a time, the Lord told Elijah to go to Zarephath, where a widow would provide accommodations for him. According to the Lord's revelation to Elijah, there was a miraculous unending supply of oil and meals for Elijah, the widow, and her son. When her son became sick and died, Elijah again believed the Lord and obeyed His revelation, and raised the boy from death.

No doubt Elijah had the anointing of the Holy Spirit. The only other time in the Bible where someone raised the dead was through Yahshua HaMashiach, Jesus Christ.

CHAPTER THREE: Ancient Astronaut Theory

Jesus also multiplied two fish and five loaves of bread to feed five thousand people. This was the same type of miracle that Elijah experienced with food and oil, and the Maccabees experienced it in the Book of Esther, when their lamps burned brightly for eight days, on one day's worth of oil, known as Hanukkah. Yes, this was the Holy Spirit at work.

However, one could argue that even the Lord's technology is empowered by His Holy Spirit. I have no problem with that. There is the supernatural, and there is technology, and often they can be perceived as being one and the same, and often they do intertwine and empower one another.

"'Not by might nor by power, but by my Spirit,' says the LORD Almighty."
(Zechariah 4:6, NIV)

There is the inner "technology" of the Spirit, which is all about having an intimate relationship with the Living God, and those who are sanctified to Him experience His anointing and can, indeed, perform all kinds of miracles through the power of His Spirit. In Hebrew, the name Elijah "Eliyahu" means "God is Yahuah" or "Yahuah is my strength." No doubt, his life certainly exhibited the strength and power of the Lord Yahuah.

Let's be real for a moment here, if Elijah was caught up in a whirlwind, as the scripture says, and disappeared from human sight when he was transported miles away to another location on the earth, without any visible signs of fleshly damage, after being vacuumed up into the upper atmosphere because, as a flesh and blood human, he could easily dehydrate, or experience altitude sickness, but this didn't happen to Elijah. At least, there is no record of it in the scriptures. Elijah was a flesh and blood earth human; he was not superhuman nor was he a demi-god. The only explanation is that technology played a part in his disappearance and his teleportations which landed him safely at his next location intact, and obviously kept him in a special environment which provided for all of his human needs, thus keeping him alive and well.

Only a few men in the Bible have ever been taken up in the air and relocated to another place on earth. Elijah and Phillip in Acts 8:39-40, and it is my opinion that Yahshua Jesus walked through portals around the planet during his "missing years" (ages 13-30) that were not recorded in the canonized version of the Bible. This explains all the accounts of Him showing up in India, North America, South America, Europe, and other locations.

There is no record of Elijah's death in the Bible; he was taken from the earth by the Lord. He "ascended" into the heavens by the power of Yahuah. He is prophesied to return during the tribulation period, also known as the time of Jacob's troubles. To this day, Jews all over the world, honor Elijah with a full glass of wine during the Passover Seders every year, while they say the prayers for Elijah to return. This ritual is always done by opening up the front door, with the belief that he will, one day, just walk through it, sit down, and sup and drink. No doubt he will return the same way he left. As is the promise with Jesus:

> "Then they gathered around him and asked him, 'Lord, are you at this time going to restore the kingdom to Israel?' He said to them: 'It is not for you to know the times or dates the Father has set by his own authority. But you will receive power when the Holy Spirit comes on you; and you will be my witnesses in Jerusalem, and in all Judea and Samaria, and to the ends of the earth.' After he said this, he was taken up before their very eyes, and a *cloud* hid him from their sight. They were looking intently up into the sky as he was going, when suddenly two men dressed in white stood beside them. 'Men of Galilee,' they said, 'why do you stand here looking into the sky? This same Jesus, who has been taken from you into heaven, will come back in the same way you have seen him go into heaven.'"
>
> (Acts 1:6-11, NIV)

Here the cloud cloaks the technology of the Lord. The fact that the scripture describes that the disciples watch as He was ascending, as He was going up into the sky, indicates that he was being taken up in His Father's (Yahuah's) starship. He didn't just instantly disappear or walk into another dimension. The only thing that happened "suddenly" was the appearance of two men dressed in white. I believe the two men dressed in white were angels (extraterrestrial messengers on assignment) to distract the disciples from watching the entire event. They were also sent to guide them and help them through their immediate transition to living without Jesus. Their answer to them is what is most revealing: "The same way he left, he will return."

This tells me He will return in His father's starship, and according to Revelation, there will be thousands of them, maybe millions of them (i.e. hosts of heaven, aka celestial armies) to accompany Him upon His great return. This will be to finish the final battle with Satan and his armies of alien UFOs.

THE TRUTH IS STRANGER THAN SCIENCE FICTION

A recent UK survey in 2012 reveals why the subject of UFOs, ETs, aliens, gods, and angels are on the minds of today's earth humans, as well as how easy it is to confuse ETs, aliens, gods, and angels. More than 33 million UK citizens believe in extraterrestrial life, compared to just over 27 million — less than half the UK population — who believe in God. The survey, conducted by Opinion Matters, revealed the following statistics among those surveyed:
- Fifty-two percent believe UFO evidence has been covered up because widespread knowledge of their existence would threaten government stability;
- Forty-four percent believe in God; one in ten people reported seeing a UFO;
- Twenty percent of respondents believe UFOs have landed on Earth.

CHAPTER THREE: Ancient Astronaut Theory

- As far as Americans go, a recent study done by the National Geographic Channel[7] for their new show, *Chasing UFOs,* concluded that more than a third of people in the United States believe aliens exist — and more than 10 percent of the population believe they have seen an alien ship in the sky.
- They found that 80 million Americans, approximately 36 percent are certain alien spaceships exist;
- Of those who believe, 79 percent are convinced the White House has kept information about other life forms a secret;
- Fifty-five percent believe there are real-life Men in Black-style agents who threaten people who spot UFOs.

What if they were to learn the truth behind what they are seeing, and can earth humans really believe in extraterrestrial life without believing in God? What if they were to learn who is behind these UFOs, who the aliens are, and who the Supreme Creator God is? If there was more *discernment* of UFOs, along with the understanding of them being separated into belonging to two kingdoms, the kingdom of darkness and the Kingdom of Heaven, which is essentially the Divine Government known as the Kingdom of God, then perhaps these types of surveys would include more specific questions, as people would be answering based on some real knowledge, rather than just blind belief.

"My people are destroyed for lack of knowledge," says the Lord.

(Hosea 4:6, KJV)

Yet, the truth of the matter is understanding who created the extraterrestrials and angels, and the cosmic drama that later ensued is imperative. The truth is truly stranger than science fiction. The Bible, along with the exo-biblical books that were rejected by the Roman Emperors between 525 AD-560 AD, is the best evidence we have for the basis and understanding of this cosmic drama and ongoing spiritual battle over each and every earth human.

The understanding of how the splinter groups, hierarchies of pseudo-gods, dark aliens, and fallen angels, which created demonic intelligences, being the purpose of this book, is the ability to *discern* between the Lord's spaceships made up of faithful ETs and angels verses the fallen ETs and their counterfeit UFO technology. This clash of two kingdoms is scheduled on the prophetic calendar to culminate in a final battle planned to occur both on and above the earth at the end of this present age, in a real life *Star Wars.* According to the end of the prophetic timeline, we are told how this will end:

"The seventh angel sounded his trumpet, and there were loud voices in heaven, which said: 'The kingdom of the world has become the kingdom of our Lord and of his Christ, and he will reign forever and ever.'"

(Revelation 11:15, NLV)

In the following chapters, I will prove to you that throughout the Bible, particularly in the Old Testament, the words, Hosts of Heaven, in Hebrew literally mean "armies of heaven." The following passage from the end of the Bible, in the book of Revelation, which outlines the prophetic timeline and scheduled events, as well as *how* it will end, reiterates that the Lord is not only the King of Kings and Lord of Lords, but the commander of the armies of heaven. Remember, how this cosmic drama began, with one-third of heaven's angels (extraterrestrials messengers and sons of heaven) rebelled against their Creator God by following in Lucifer's rebellion.

What's important to keep in mind, is that two-thirds remained faithful, those of which make up the armies of heaven, and will follow the Lord to the final battle on earth to complete this drama.

> "His eyes were as a flame of fire, and on his head were many crowns; and he had a name written, that no man knew, but He himself. And he was clothed with a garment dipped in blood: and his name is called **THE WORD OF GOD**.
>
> And **<u>the armies which were in heaven</u>** followed him upon white horses (i.e. metaphors for space vehicles, starships), clothed in fine linen, white and clean.
>
> And out of his mouth goeth a sharp sword (the Spoken Word of God), that with it He should smite the nations: and He shall rule them with a rod of iron: and He treadeth the winepress of the fierceness and wrath of Almighty God.
>
> And He hath on His venture and on His thigh a name written, **KING OF KINGS, AND LORD OF LORDS**."
>
> (Revelation 19:12-16 KJV)

Suffice it to say, that the Bible is a historical record of extraterrestrial interactions with humans. But more than that fact, it also reveals how both gods and angels come and go with technology. There are so many words that most readers just accept as metaphorical, or even poetic, but are actual technological terms written by men thousands of years ago, who had little to no reference for witnessing such incredible acts which were often termed as miracles.

Fire from heaven, burning bushes that don't spread, chariots of fire, horses coming out of the heavens are just a few descriptions for the Lord's space technology. When Yahshua Jesus used words like "as lightning flashes from the east to west," to be a description for His return to earth, we know, in today's high-tech age, that is descriptive for the technology of spaceships, which often flash like lightning coming in and out of the earth's atmosphere, and just appear as "lightning."

> "For as the lightning flashes in the east and shines in the west, so it will be when the Son of Man comes."
>
> (Matthew 24:27, NLT)

NOTES:

1. Von Däniken, Erich, *Chariots of the Gods* (New York, NY: Bantam Books, 1969).
2. Sitchin, Zecharia, *The Earth Chronicles*: Sitchin, Zecharia, *Genesis Revisited* (Santa Fe, NM: Bear, 1991).
3. Gilbert, *Compassionate Mind,* pp. 170-171
4. Walter Burkert, *Homo Necans: The Anthropology of Greek Sacrificial Ritual,* trans. Peter Bing (Berkley, Los Angeles, and London, 1983), pp. 16-22
5. R. Cedric Leonard, PhD., *The Wheels of Ezekiel, A Possible Relationship To The UFO Phenomenon,* quotes used with permission. March, 2002. http://www.atlantisquest.com/Ezekiel.html
6. Joe Kovacs, *Shocked By the Bible,* Thomas Nelson, Nashville, Tennessee, 2008, p.67
7. UK Study, National Geographic Channel, *Chasing UFOs,* June 26, 2012

CHAPTER FOUR

MOTHER SHIPS OF THE LORD

"Then I saw 'a new heaven and a new earth,'
For the first heaven and the first earth had passed away, and there was no longer any sea.
I saw the Holy City, the New Jerusalem,
Coming down out of heaven from God,
Prepared as a bride beautifully dressed for her husband.
And I heard a loud voice from the throne saying,
'Look! God's dwelling place is now among the people,
And he will dwell with them. They will be his people,
And God himself will be with them and be their God.
He will wipe every tear from their eyes.
There will be no more death or mourning or crying or pain,
for the old order of things has passed away.'"

(Revelation 21:1-4, NIV)

And if that's not enough to convince you that the New Jerusalem, the Holy City, is a huge mother ship, read this passage:

"One of the seven angels who had the seven bowls full of the seven last plagues came and said to me, "Come, I will show you the bride, the wife of the Lamb." And he carried me away in the Spirit to a mountain great and high, and showed me the Holy City, Jerusalem, *coming down out of heaven from God.* It shone with the glory of God, and its brilliance was like that of a very precious jewel, like a jasper, clear as crystal. *It had a great, high wall with twelve gates, and with twelve angels at the gates.* On the gates were written the names of the twelve tribes of Israel. There were three gates on the east, three on the north, three on the south and three on the west. *The wall of the city had twelve foundations,* and on them were the names of the twelve apostles of the Lamb."

(Revelation 21:9-14, NIV)

Of course the angel that showed this to St. John, took him on a spaceship to the mountain and introduced him to the "Mother ship," the Holy City, The New Jerusalem coming down "out of heaven" from God, also known as the "Heavenly Jerusalem." In Hebrew, the word *Jerusalem* means "city of peace." The twelve gates are indicative of a huge mother ship. Again, all the space crafts described in the Bible seem to have similar descriptions, and that is being made of precious gemstones, crystals, and gold.

> "The angel who talked with me had a measuring rod of gold to measure the city, its gates and its walls. The city was laid out like a square, as long as it was wide. He measured the city with the rod and found it to be 12,000 stadia in length, (which is about 1,400 miles = approximately 2,200 kilometers) and as wide and high as it is long. The angel measured the wall using human measurement, and it was 144 cubits thick (or high) (which is about 200 feet = approx. 65 meters). The wall was made of jasper, and the city of pure gold, as pure as glass. The foundations of the city walls were decorated with every kind of precious stone. The first foundation was jasper, the second sapphire, the third agate, the fourth emerald, the fifth onyx, the sixth ruby, the seventh chrysolite, the eighth beryl, the ninth topaz, the tenth turquoise, the eleventh jacinth, and the twelfth amethyst. The twelve gates were twelve pearls, each gate made of a single pearl. The great street of the city was of gold, as pure as transparent glass."
>
> (Revelation 21:15-21, NIV)

Something so fantastic, so glorious, most earth humans could not even imagine such a thing! Yet St. John described what he saw, this holy city was made in heaven, and exists somewhere, ready to be downloaded, to descend to earth, after the final cosmic war between the satans, the fallen angels, and the Lord Jesus Christ and his celestial army is fought and won.

Then John asks, where is the temple of God?

> "I did not see a temple in the city, because the Lord God Almighty and the Lamb are its temple. The city does not need the sun or the moon to shine on it, <u>for the glory of God gives it light, and the Lamb is its lamp</u>. The nations will walk by its light, and the kings of the earth will bring their splendor into it. On no day will its gates ever be shut, for there will be no night there. The glory and honor of the nations will be brought into it. Nothing impure will ever enter it, nor will anyone who does what is shameful or deceitful, but only those whose names are written in the Lamb's book of life."
>
> (Revelation 21:22-27, NIV)

The concept of a city in the sky is not new in ancient texts as the Mahabharata speaks repeatedly of "cities in the sky," this was the way the ancients described "mother ships" which are huge, and are literal cities in their own right. Think about this. How can a city, the New Jerusalem in this case, come down from Heaven and land on the earth to dwell with man? It can if it's a huge mother ship.

> "See, I will create a new heavens and a new earth. The former things will not be remembered, nor will they come to mind."
>
> (Isaiah 65:17, NIV)

CHAPTER FOUR: Mother Ships Of The Lord

Revelation 21 also promises a "New Heaven and New Earth," but how will the Lord pull this off? This will be done with massive mother ships and advanced technology beyond our imaginations. These are the Ultraterrestrials, those who can tractor beam planets from one star system into another. The promise of a new heaven indicates that the old heavens will pass away, the cosmic evil will be defeated and new stars will be laid out as the old death stars will be obliterated. The promise of a new earth, and particularly the New Jerusalem, the Holy City of God, will be downloaded from heaven onto the new earth. When that time comes, we will all understand who we are in the vast Kingdom of God. Hope to see you there!

Yet, how can earth humans be allowed into the Kingdom of Heaven when they are at war and in a rebellious state with the King of the Kingdom? The answer is, they can't. This is what the spiritual warfare is about on earth. Those who believe in the Divine Plan of Salvation through the Lord Jesus Christ (Yahshua HaMashiach) will be saved and given the keys to the kingdom, and those who are on the side of the satans and the deceitful fallen angels will not be allowed into the Kingdom of God, for they will be defeated along with their "spirit guides," who people will soon learn are nothing but fallen angels masquerading as angels of light, phony ascended masters, and pseudo-extraterrestrial gods.

Moses, like Enoch and Ezekiel, was taken up in the Lord's spacecraft. He describes seeing the earth from space. He describes it as round, and how could he know that, when in ancient times, the common thought form was that the earth was flat. He also describes, as the backdrop from the depths of the earth, the multitudes of space, just as Enoch had described when he was taken and shown portals (pathways) of stars.

THE LAW OF READINESS

Many may ask, why haven't we seen this before? Many who have read the Bible over and over again year after year, never see the true meaning of these scriptures or completely ignore their simplicity and, in many respects, very clear descriptions of the Lord's space crafts and His coming and going as He rides through the heavens with His *clouds* back and forth to earth. One reason is because our level of consciousness was not ready to "see" it. Another reason is it's only the Holy Spirit who can reveal the Logos (written Word of God) to you. Without it, the true meaning of the scriptures is blocked, and you may just as well be reading any other book, as it will not come alive to you without the help of Rhema, which is the revelation that can only come from the Holy Spirit. While there is much truth to this, the level of consciousness also has a lot to do with the *Law of Readiness* which states that things happen in their appointed times, when people are ready to receive them.

Today, more people believe in UFOs than religion. The sightings of UFOs are all over the globe and their appearances have been amped up since the 1940s. There is not a single nation on Earth that has not been visited by UFOs. The big question remains, who are they?

Clearly not everyone will be able to handle these revelations, as the greatest chasm on our planet today is the struggle between the old and the new, darkness and light. The powers and the principalities of this world work to keep the truth from earth humans as it is in their best interest to manipulate with ignorance as ignorant earth humans are much easier to control and deceive. This is the reason for the Truth Embargo, the sixty-five-plus year-long cover-up policy that the US government has held to keep what they know from its citizens. They say it's for the purpose of national security.

While this may be justified on many levels, as WWII had more to do with alien technology than most people realize, which led us into the years of the Cold War, which was all about the secret technology that the United States and the Soviet Union were compiling from making deals with aliens. Remember the lords of darkness have their technologies. The US government may never come clean as to its vast records of UFOs because of secret agreements made between them and certain alien groups for technology, but these dealings have created the extraterrestrial military industrial complex (EMIC), which is the foundation for much of America's technologies.

Our task now is to learn how to discern between the ships of darkness and the ships of light, between the fallen angels and God's Faithful Angels of Light, who belong to and serve the Office of the Christ. Earth and earth humans are caught in the middle of these crossroads and crosshairs between this ancient cosmic battle of good and evil, light and darkness, the Satans and the Christed Ones. While much of this information may come as a shock to some, it is far better to be prepared before the final battle is fought in the sky for all the world to see, as earth humans witness a real live *Star Wars* right before their very eyes, where many may die of shock or be paralyzed in fear, while others will know that their dreams are coming true and the coming Kingdom of God is near.

> "In those days people will seek death but will not find it. They will long to die, but death will flee from them!"
>
> (Revelation 9:6, NLT)

It is clear that the writers of biblical times were at a disadvantage in describing sophisticated spacecraft. We see the world as we are, not as it actually is. For lack of a better term, they resorted to their own known word for a vehicle of transportation, which was "chariot"; therefore, horses came out of heaven on "cloudy" chariots. The cloudy chariot was found in the writings of Moses, King David, Daniel, Matthew, Paul, and John.

CHAPTER FOUR: Mother Ships Of The Lord

THE CLOUD SHIPS

> "The LORD wraps himself in light as with a garment; he stretches out the heavens like a tent and *lays the beams* of his *upper chambers* on their waters. He makes the *clouds* his chariot and rides on the wings of the wind."
>
> (Psalm 104:2-3, NIV)

Beautiful language, but is this just poetic metaphors, or was King David being literal about the Almighty Lord? In my opinion, there are no accidents in the Word of God. You will see, from the following scriptures, how this repetitive theme and word, describing the Lord coming and going with the clouds, on the clouds, and using the clouds as his chariot. A chariot is a vehicle of transportation. The cloudships are His starships.

In this verse, King David states that the Almighty Creator Lord not only created the heavens and stretched them like a tent, or a curtain, as the King James Version describes it, but that He made the "clouds" his vehicle of transport and uses them to "ride on the wings of the wind." Spaceships ride on the wings of the winds. He tells us that the Lord literally wraps Himself in Light, as one would wrap a garment around oneself. This is why the Lord's ships are always described as "clouds."

Not only do they cloak the actual starship (space chariot) underneath, but they emanate such light around the vehicle reflecting the divine beings that travels within them.

> **"Who are these that fly along like clouds, like doves to their nests?** Surely the islands look to me; in the lead are the ships of Tarshish, bringing your children from afar...."
>
> (Isaiah 60:8, NIV)

Since the early 1990s, I have been collecting pictures of cloud ships. These are cloud formations that look exactly like space crafts. They are disk shaped; some disks are shaped with crowns; others are the size of a large mother ship. All are cloaked in clouds. Some argue these are just clouds, but many are isolated in the sky, almost always above mountaintops, without other clouds to support it as a weather system. The fact that these cloud ships are mentioned in the Bible numerous times has made me think twice about the cloud ships I have witnessed myself, and the pictures I've been collecting all these years from all over the world.

It is apparent, by how many Bible scriptures refer to the Lord coming with the clouds, that the word for *cloud* was the Bible writers' word for spaceships. The word for *cloud* in Hebrew is "Anan" or clouds "ananim" (plural). However, the Hebrew meant "a covering" because clouds cover the sky. This was purely metaphorical.

The word "clouds" is used as a symbol of the Divine presence, indicating the splendor of that glory which it conceals. But this was not purely metaphorical, but literal,

75

as in the case of a spaceship cloaked in a cloud, a true covering from the harshness of space. There are 167 passages that refer to clouds in the Old Testament alone. The books of Exodus, Numbers, Job, and the Psalms testify to the divine presence *in* the form of clouds and *within* the clouds. A *bright cloud* is symbolic for the Divine presence known as the Shekinah glory (Exodus 29: 42).

Could this glory mean the cloudy presence that always surrounds His starships?

While a "cloud without rain" has become a Hebrew saying for someone who does not keep his promise (Isaiah 25:5), there have been many clouds without rain; that denotes more than just a metaphorical saying. Clouds that appeared after the rains have passed, clouds on a sunny day — these were literal spaceships cloaked in clouds. They were covered to conceal their presence. Clouds that spoke with a loud voice, which was done through some type of technological public announcement system.

> "Sing to God, sing in praise of his name,
> **Extol him <u>who rides on the CLOUDS.</u>**"
>
> (Psalm 68:4, NIV)

> **"The chariots of God are tens of thousands**
> **And thousands of thousands;**
> The Lord has come from Sinai into his sanctuary.
> **When you ascended on high,**
> You took many captives;
> You received gifts from people,
> Even from the rebellious—
> That you, LORD God, might dwell there."
>
> (Psalm 68:17-18, NIV)

> "Sing to God, you kingdoms of the earth, sing praise to the Lord,
> **<u>To him who rides across the highest heavens</u>, the ancient heavens, who thunders with a mighty voice.**"
>
> (Psalm 68:32-33, NIV)

> **"You are dressed in a robe of light.**
> **You stretch out the starry curtain of the heavens;**
> **You lay out the rafters of your home in the rain clouds. .**
> **You make <u>THE CLOUDS YOUR CHARIOT;</u>**
> **<u>You ride upon the wings of the wind.</u>**"
>
> (Psalms 104:2-3, NLT)

"Yahuah came down upon Sinai <u>in a cloud and the cloud filled the court</u> around the tabernacle in the wilderness so that Moses could not enter it at the dedication of the temple also the cloud 'filled the house of the Lord.' It's possible that the temple was a

CHAPTER FOUR: Mother Ships Of The Lord

space port for the Lord's throne which was his starship. Thus in like manner when Christ comes the second time, he is described as coming 'with the clouds.'"

"Look, he is coming *with* the clouds of heaven, and every eye will see him, even those who pierced him; and all the peoples of the earth will mourn because of him. So shall it be! Amen."

(Revelation 1:7 NIV)

This scripture was first prophesied by the prophet Zechariah:

"And I will pour out on the house of David and the inhabitants of Jerusalem a spirit of grace and supplication. They will look on me, the one they have pierced, and they will mourn for him as one mourns for an only child, and grieve bitterly for him as one grieves for a firstborn son. On that day the weeping in Jerusalem will be as great as the weeping of Hadad Rimmon in the plain of Megiddo."

(Zechariah 12:10-11, NIV)

THE CLOUDS OF HEAVEN

"In my vision at night I looked, and there before me was one like a son of man, **coming with the clouds of heaven**. He approached the Ancient of Days and was led into his presence."

(Daniel 7:13, NIV)

Here both the prophets Daniel and St. John describe the Lord as coming *with* the clouds. He doesn't say he's coming *through* the clouds, as one might think someone entering into the earth's atmosphere would need to first pass through the vast cloud system of the earth, but it says, He is coming *with* the clouds. "The clouds" were an ancient metaphor for the Lord's starships. They were cloaked in clouds, and when St. John saw this vision, he saw what many of the ancients saw, which were ships cloaked in clouds; hence, the word stuck and came to mean that the ships were then called "clouds." "Every eye will see Him" implies that not only will people of the Earth actually see the massive fleet of starships arriving all around the Earth skies, but without a doubt, this event will be televised all over the world.

"I looked, and I saw a windstorm coming out of the north—**an immense cloud with flashing lightning and surrounded by brilliant light.** The center of the fire looked like glowing metal."

(Ezekiel 1:4, NIV)

Ezekiel had all kinds of experiences on the Lord's starships. He begins his book with a very vivid description of a starships that he described as an "immense cloud with brilliant light, and glowing metal." Have you ever seen a cloud that has glowing metal?

This clearly speaks of technology. This is not just any lightning cloud. How does one ride on a "swift" cloud? These are not metaphors. They are descriptions of how the Lord travelled to Earth. His starships glowed and looked like clouds, moving clouds, very fast moving clouds:

> "An oracle concerning Egypt: Behold, **the LORD (Yahuah) is riding on a swift cloud** and comes to Egypt; and the idols of Egypt tremble at his presence, and the hearts of the Egyptians melt within them."
>
> (Isaiah 19:1, ESV)

> "I AM," said Jesus. "And you will see the Son of Man sitting at the right hand of the Mighty One and **coming *on* the clouds of heaven**."
>
> (Mark 14:62, NIV)

Here the apostle says, the Lord will return *on* the clouds of heaven. Again, this describes coming out of heaven on some type of starship or vehicle which floats through the skies, like clouds. Again, this is another description of the ships.

> "**For the Lord himself shall descend from heaven with a shout, with the voice of the archangel, and with the trump of God: and the dead in Christ shall rise first: Then we which are alive and remain shall be caught up together with them in the clouds, to meet the Lord in the air: and so shall we ever be with the Lord.**"
>
> (1 Thessalonians 4:17, KJV)

1 Thessalonians 4:17 is the scripture that Christians believe to be the "rapture," also known as "the Harvest or Gathering." This happens before the Lord Jesus Christ returns for all the world to see (Matthew 24:30). This occurs before the final *Star Wars* battle over the earth, known as Armageddon. The rapture happens in stealth. This is not for the whole world to see, but the world will know that nearly half the people of the earth will mysteriously disappear all at once.

The scripture says, after He raises the dead in Christ, those who remain alive will be caught up *in the clouds* to meet the Lord *in the air*. The Lord meets his believers in the air, *inside* the Lord's spaceships. I would imagine literally thousands of mother ships that arrive with angels (extraterrestrial messengers) to ensure that each and every soul, both living and those that have died, ascends to their proper place in the mother ships to be taken out of this third dimension of Earth, translated into immortal, incorporeal bodies, and transported through stargates and portals to the third heaven where Jesus lives.

Jesus Himself gave us many clues and signs as to when this mysterious disappearance would occur. In the following scriptures, the secret clue that Jesus gives is the ratio of 2:1, which is essentially 50 percent. For more details on my conclusions about this event along with all my research and discussion, please see my chapter on *Ascension or Rapture?* in Book Three: *Who Are The Angels?*

CHAPTER FOUR: Mother Ships Of The Lord

The following scriptures relate to this mysterious disappearance:

"Then shall two be in the field; the one shall be taken, and the other left. Two women shall be grinding at the mill; the one shall be taken, and the other left."

(Matthew 24:40-41, KJV)

"Two women shall be grinding together; the one shall be taken, and the other left. Two men shall be in the field; the one shall be taken, and the other left."

(Luke 17:35-36, KJV)

The following scripture relates to the Second Coming, when the whole world will see Him with all the Hosts of Heaven (the Celestial Army) in the sky, *on* the clouds of the sky, which are His vast fleet of starships. This will happen at the time of the battle of Armageddon, when Jesus and His angels (extraterrestrial messengers) defeat Lucifer/Satan's kingdom:

"At that time the sign of the Son of Man will appear in heaven, and all the tribes of the earth will mourn. They will see the Son of Man coming <u>on the clouds</u> of heaven, with power and great glory."

(Matthew 24:30, Berean Study Bible)

"But I say to all of you: From now on you will see the Son of Man sitting at the right hand of the Mighty One and coming <u>on the clouds</u> of heaven."

(Matthew 26:64, NIV)

This is probably one of the most revealing scriptures, as it plainly says that the Lord makes the clouds his chariot and then rides on the wings of the wind. The clouds here are another word for the starships of the Lord, as is the word "chariot."

"He makes <u>the clouds his chariot</u> and rides on the wings of the wind. He makes winds his messengers (angels), flames of fire his servants."

(Psalm 104:3-4, NIV)

"To him that rides on the <u>heavens (clouds) of heavens</u>, which were of old; see, he does send out his voice, and that a mighty voice."

(Psalm 68:33, AKJV)

This passage clearly indicates that they were sheltered by the cloud ship that appeared and then disappeared:

"As the men were leaving Jesus, Peter said to him, 'Master, it is good for us to be here. Let us put up three shelters—one for you, one for Moses and one for Elijah.' (He did not know what he was saying.) While he was speaking, *a cloud appeared*

79

and enveloped them, and they were afraid as *they entered the cloud*. A voice came from *the cloud,* saying, 'This is my Son, whom I have chosen; listen to him.' When the voice had spoken, they found that Jesus was alone. The disciples kept this to themselves, and did not tell anyone at that time what they had seen."

(Luke 9:33-36, NIV)

Of course the disciples were shocked and scared because of what they had seen. It was enough for them to preach the gospel, now they had witnessed the Lord's spaceship, and they were terrified.

"See, the Name of the LORD comes from afar, with burning anger and dense <u>clouds</u> of smoke; his lips are full of wrath, and his tongue is a consuming fire."

(Isaiah 30:27, NIV)

The Lord is coming from afar, meaning coming from someplace in the heavens; the clouds of smoke are what surrounds the starships. Again, this is why the ancients described the Lord's ships as clouds, because the ships created clouds of smoke around them. This scripture describes it exactly as "clouds of smoke."

"Who are these that fly along *like* <u>clouds</u>,
Like doves to their nests?"
Or KJV:
"What are these that fly *as a* <u>cloud</u>,
And as doves to their windows?"

(Isaiah 60:8)

Here the prophet Isaiah writes with such specificity, that there are starships flying along *like* clouds or *as* a cloud. It is clear that, when the ancients saw the starships of the Lord, they all described them as clouds because the starships of the Lord were all cloaked in clouds. Not once did they describe them as silvery metallic disk-shaped objects. This is a *major* discernment today when we see UFOs in our skies, in being able to tell *who is who*. The Lord's starships look much different than the ships of the dark forces, which are never described as clouds or as being cloaked in clouds. Perhaps this is because they do not have the technology, as they are not resonant with the vibrations of Love and Light, which is the "glory of God."

Another discernment on the difference between spaceships: while Satan can easily fool earth humans, and masquerade as an angel of light, he cannot fool the Lord and His Hosts (armies of Heaven). There are certain levels of technology and its use that require a vibrational match to get through the upper dimensions of Heaven; you have to be "of the Light," and you have to carry the spirit of Love. No matter what, Lucifer/Satan and his fallen ET angels cannot fake that because their spirits are in rebellion to this.

CHAPTER FOUR: Mother Ships Of The Lord

"There are those who *rebel* against the light, who do not know its ways or stay in its paths."

(Job 24:13, NIV)

Love is humble. Satan has never humbled himself to God. He is the unrepentant one, along with one-third of Heaven's ETs, also known as fallen angels. Where did they fall from? They fell from the upper heavens, the higher dimensions, which is pure Love and Light, and all the technology that goes with that because it is the technology of Light. They no longer have access to the upper heavens. (Jude 1:6)

"In majesty he rides <u>*through the* clouds</u>.... There is no one like the God of Jeshurun (Israel), <u>who rides across the heavens to help you and on the clouds in his majesty (glory)</u>."

(Deuteronomy 33:26, NIV)

Jeshurun is a poetic name for Israel. Here the scripture reveals again that the Lord rides through the clouds coming on the heavens, riding across the heaven, and showing his glory in his starships.

"He mounted the cherubim and flew;
He soared on the wings of the wind."

(2 Samuel 22:11, NIV)

Moses frequently mentioned the presence of the cloud chariots: "The Lord *descended* in the <u>cloud</u>"; "The Lord *came down* in a <u>cloud</u>"; "The Lord went before them by day in a pillar of <u>cloud</u> to lead them the way and by night in a pillar of fire."

The prophet Daniel was another one who described the use of a <u>cloudy</u> chariot for cosmic transportation: "In my vision at night I looked, and there before me was one like a son of man, coming *with* the <u>clouds of heaven</u>…"

(Daniel 7:13, NIV)

"The <u>cloud</u> of the LORD hovered over the Tabernacle during the day, and at night <u>fire glowed</u> *inside* the <u>cloud</u> so the whole family of Israel could see it. This continued throughout all their journeys."

(Exodus 40:38, NLT)

The "cloud," the pillar of, was the glory-cloud which indicated God's presence leading the ransomed people through the wilderness. This pillar preceded the people as they marched, resting on the ark. By night it became a pillar of fire. This is obviously *not* a natural phenomenon. Clouds do not become "pillars of fire" by night. Exodus 40:38 clearly describes a spaceship, not a weather event.

> "He guided them with the <u>cloud</u> by day and with <u>Light from the fire</u> all night."
>
> (Psalm 78:14, NIV)

The starship of the Lord was like a moving cloud to the Israelites, and at night, he guided them with the light from the fire from the starship. Could this language be any clearer? Sometimes things are so simple, that its true meaning is obscured because we assume the writers of the Bible all talked in metaphors. But I believe the writers wrote exactly what they saw. What kind of cloud moves through the day to guide people? Why would people follow a moving cloud unless it was a guide? These weren't rain clouds or cumulus clouds, these were starships that were cloaked in clouds, or looked like clouds, that moved and guided them from one place of the vast open-space desert to another.

Where does a "light from the fire" come from? Certainly rainclouds do not produce light from a fire, unless it was lightning all the time, in which case the writers would have described it as lightning, but they did not. This was obviously the Lord's technology, in the form of a spaceship that cloaked itself by a cloud during the day and glowed like fire at night as a "night light" to guide His people, the Israelites, through the deserts of the wilderness. This was a starship that had the appearance of a flame of fire beneath it, which was most likely a glowing globe.

> "Then a <u>cloud</u> overshadowed them, and a voice from <u>the cloud</u> said, "This is my dearly loved Son. Listen to him."
>
> (Mark 9:7, NLT)

The cloud that overshadowed them was one of the Lord's starships. The voice came out of the ship on a microphone/PA system and spoke to them.

> "He spoke to them from the **pillar of a cloud**; they kept his statutes and the decrees he gave them."
>
> (Psalm 99:7, NIV)

This verse clearly indicates that the *pillar of a cloud* was a spaceship.

> "These are the commandments the Lord proclaimed in a <u>loud voice</u> to your whole assembly there on the mountain from **out of the fire, the cloud** and the deep darkness; and he added nothing more. Then he wrote them on two stone tablets and gave them to me. When you heard the <u>voice out of the darkness, while the mountain was ablaze with fire,</u> all the leading men of your tribes and your elders came to me. And you said, "The LORD our God has shown us his glory and his majesty, and we have <u>heard his voice from the fire</u>. Today we have seen that a person can live even if God speaks with them. But now, why should we die? This great fire will consume us, and we will die if we hear the voice of the LORD our God any longer. For what mortal man has ever heard the voice of the living God speaking out of fire, as we have, and survived?"
>
> (Deuteronomy 5:22-26 NIV)

CHAPTER FOUR: Mother Ships Of The Lord

These scriptures reveal that the Lord spoke to them in a loud voice from the mountain out of the fire. This is a description of a spaceship, which landed on the top of the mountain, in a blaze of fire, and cloaked in a cloud. The loud voice was some kind of PA system, by speaking through a microphone, so everyone could hear it and hear it loud and clear. The voice came out of the darkness by using this technology while the mountain was ablaze with fire from the landing of the spaceship.

> "A **cloud then snatched me up**, and the wind raised me above the surface of the earth, placing me at the extremity of the heavens."
>
> (1 Enoch 39:3)

Since when do "clouds" snatch people up into the heavens? This verse comes from the *Book of Enoch*, Enoch was taken up and shown many things in the heavens, including the ten heavens. In Hebrew there are several words for clouds: *anan*, *shakhan*, and *araphel*. But the word itself also means "covering." Again this is the signature pattern of the Lord's spaceships, as they were always cloaked and covered in clouds.

The "wind" raised him above the surface of the earth. That's no ordinary wind, but the power of a flying saucer/spacecraft, with the gust of its engines, could do that.

JESUS TAKEN UP INTO HEAVEN

The Prophesy of the Lord Jesus Christ leaving and coming back the second time is described as "coming in the clouds:"

> "After he said this, he was taken up before their very eyes, and a **cloud hid him** from their sight. They were **looking intently up into the sky** *as he was going*, when suddenly two men dressed in white stood beside them. "Men of Galilee," they said, "why do you stand here looking into the sky? This same Jesus, who has been taken from you into heaven, **will come back in the same way you have seen him go into heaven.**"
>
> (Acts 1:9-11, NIV)

This was when Jesus said good-bye to his disciples and ascended into heaven **into a cloud**. The cloud that received him was the Lord's spaceship that took him up. The cloud cloaking, which is the Lord's *signature* spacecraft, hid Jesus from the disciples, so they couldn't actually see Him enter the craft. This is why they continued to stare into the sky "as he was going." They watched him as the cloud ship took him up into the heavens. The two men dressed in white, who were extraterrestrial messengers sent to oversee the ascension, came to divert their attention. They asked them, "Why are you looking at the sky?" Well, why not? Who wouldn't be staring at the sky if a cloud came and scooped up their best friend? What is revealing is that they tell them that He will return the same way they witnessed Him going into heaven, on the clouds. As it says in Matthew 24:30, "They will see the Son of Man coming *on* the clouds of the sky, with power and great glory."

Bible prophecy reveals to us that, when the Lord returns to Earth, He will instill fear into His enemies and the enemies of His people.

> "A prophecy against Egypt: See, the **LORD rides on a swift cloud** and is coming to Egypt. The idols of Egypt tremble before him, and the hearts of the Egyptians melt with fear."
>
> (Isaiah 19:1 NIV)

In each instance, He travels with and on a "cloud," a "swift cloud," as Isaiah describes; it's so fast that it causes fear in the hearts of men. Again, these are no ordinary "storm" clouds, they are spaceships, chariots of fire, cloaked in the glory of the Lord, which appears as a swift moving cloud.

Again we have reference to the Lord returning "with" the clouds of heaven, and we are told every eye will see him. This may be due to the fact that we live in an age where everyone has access to television, the Internet, and camera phones. Or it could be such a huge event, with such an enormous fleet of cloudships, that the entire planet is surrounded by the "clouds of heaven," with the Lord as their commander.

> "'Look, he is **coming with the clouds**,' and 'every eye will see him, even those who pierced him'; and all peoples on earth 'will mourn because of him.' So shall it be! Amen."
>
> (Revelation 1:7, NIV)

> "In my vision at night I looked, and there before me was one like a son of man, **coming with the clouds of heaven**. He approached the Ancient of Days and was led into his presence."
>
> (Daniel 7:13, NIV)

> "Then will appear the sign of the Son of Man in heaven.
> And then all the peoples of the earth will mourn when they see
> **The Son of Man coming on the clouds of heaven,**
> **With power and great glory.**"
>
> (Matthew 24:30, NIV)

> "At that time people will see **the Son of Man coming in clouds with great power and glory.**"
>
> (Mark 13:26, NIV)

CHAPTER FOUR: Mother Ships Of The Lord

THE COSMIC POLICE

In Zechariah 6:1–7, four cosmic pilots are dispatched in as many chariots (spacecraft), which come out from between two mountains. The prophet Zechariah is informed that each charioteer had flight orders to go to a different part of the country. According to the scripture, the four extraterrestrial astronauts had been ordered to "walk to and fro through the earth." The Con-fraternity Version of the Bible reports that the orders were to "Go patrol the Earth."

> "Now I lifted up my eyes again and looked, and behold, four chariots were coming forth from between the two mountains; and the mountains were bronze mountains."
>
> (Zechariah 6:1, NAS)

Now, how can Earth mountains be "bronze"? I believe what Zechariah saw were *mother ships* that were made of bronze, and the four chariots were space craft coming out of them.

> "With the first chariot were red horses, with the second chariot black horses, with the third chariot white horses, and with the fourth chariot strong dappled horses. Then I spoke and said to the angel who was speaking with me, "What are these, my lord?" The angel replied to me, "These are the *four spirits* of heaven, going forth after standing before the Lord of all the earth, with one of which the black horses are going forth to the north country; and the white ones go forth after them, while the dappled ones go forth to the south country. "When the strong ones went out, they were eager to go to patrol the earth." And He said, "Go, patrol the earth." So they patrolled the earth.
>
> (Zechariah 6:2-7, NAS)

"Go patrol the earth!" This clearly states that these so-called horses that came out of the chariots (space craft) were *spirits* that were ordered to be the police force to guard the earth and the spirit realm.

However, another explanation is that the word *horses* was used to describe small space vehicles coming out of the mother ship (i.e., chariot), which was sent to patrol the earth like police guards.

There are several cross references peppered throughout the Bible that correspond to Zechariah 6:1-7; Daniel 7:2-3, 8:22, 11:4-5; Zechariah 1:8-10, 6:5 8; Revelation 6:2, 4, 5, 8; Jeremiah 1:14-15, 4:6, 6:1, 25:9, 46:10, 49:36; Ezekiel 1:4, 37:9; Isaiah 43:6; Matthew 24:31.

> "As they were going along and talking, behold, there appeared a *chariot of fire* and *horses of fire* which separated the two of them. And Elijah went up by a whirlwind to heaven."
>
> (2 Kings 2:11, NAS)

85

Fire has long been a pseudonym for spirit. The horses of fire were the spirits sent to patrol the earth. Elijah went up into the space craft; the whirlwind is how the ship lifts a person off the surface of the earth. This has been illustrated many times in Hollywood movies.

> **"The chariots of God are myriads,**
> **Thousands upon thousands;**
> **The Lord is among them as at Sinai, in holiness."**
>
> (Psalm 68:17, NAS)

The spacecraft (chariots) are innumerable. There are countless starships that belong to the Lord which stretches across the heavens. The starships are the "Glory of God" filled with gold, precious jewels, and the love and light Shekinah Glory presence of the Almighty. These are His "fleet" of spaceships that are under His command. This includes many different stars systems and groupings. (See my Cosmic Drama Chart pp. 90-91, in Book One, of *Who's Who In The Cosmic Zoo?* for further elucidation as to who belongs to who.) He is truly the Lord of Hosts. Hosts are his Celestial Army. (See my chapter on *Celestial Warriors* in Book Three – *Who Are The Angels?*)

Jesus said, "In my Father's house there are **many mansions** (or abodes, in Hebrew levels)" (John 14:2, Berean Literal). As I've written in my chapters on The Divine Law of Salvation and The Word of God in the Stars (Book Five – *The Heavens*) that the word *mansions* is actually a celestial term, for celestial houses, (i.e. star systems). What I found very interesting was that in the Vedic literature, the word *mansion* is used as a description for spaceships. These are otherwise known as Vimana and also called "flying cities," which are, otherwise, known today as "mother ships."

The Vedic epic, the *Ramayana*, refers to the Vimana as "the Aerial Mansion of Ravana." The following is a translation by Swami Tapasyananda, from his book *Sunkarakandam of Srimad Valmiki Ramayan*[1]:

> "That heroic son of the Wind-god Sawa in the middle of that residential quarter **the great aerial mansion-vehicle** called *Puspaka-Vimana*, decorated with pearls and diamonds, and featured with artistic windows made of refined gold.
>
> Constructed as it was by Visvakarma himself, none could gauge its power nor effect its destruction. It was built with the intention that it should be superior to all similar constructions. It was poised in the atmosphere without support. It had the capacity to go anywhere. It stood in the sky like a milestone in the path of the sun...
>
> It was the final result of the great prowess gained by austerities. It could fly in any direction that one wanted. It had chambers of remarkable beauty. Everything about it was symmetrical and unique. Knowing the intentions of the master, it could go anywhere at high speed unobstructed by anyone, including the wind itself...

CHAPTER FOUR: Mother Ships Of The Lord

It had towers of high artistic work. It had spires and domes like the peaks of mountains. It was immaculate like the autumnal moon. It was occupied by sky-ranging Rakshasas of huge proportions with faces brightened by their shining ear-pendants. It was delightful to look at like the spring season and the bunches of flowers then in bloom. It had also for protecting it numerous elementals with round and deep eyes and capable of very speedy movements.

Hanuman, the son of the Wind-god, saw in the middle of the aerial edifice a very spacious construction. That building, half a *yojana* in width and one *yojana* in length, and having several floors, was the residence of the king of the Rakshasas....

Visvakarma constructed in the heavenly region this Puspaka Vimana or aerial mansion-vehicle of attractive form, which could go everywhere and which augmented the desire nature of its occupants. Kuvera by the power of his austerities obtained from Brahma that aerial mansion which was decorated entirely with gems, and which received the homage of the resident of all the three world. It was by overcoming Kuvera that Ravana, the king of the Rakshasas, took possession of it."

In Vedic astrology, the mansions of the moon are connected to fixed stars. When Jesus spoke of His Father's House (The Heavens) having many mansions, I believe he was referring to the vastness of the Kingdom of Heaven, which is made up of many stars, many mansions, many levels, and many places of abode, including huge mother ships or "flying cities" where literally hundreds, maybe thousands of people can dwell safely. Jesus knew the hidden meaning of the word *mansion* when he said, "in my Father's house there are many mansions." He knew what he meant; only the true meaning has been obscured to us for centuries because many did not have the reference point to understand it until now. No one can fully comprehend the word of God without the revelation known as "Rhema" (Greek) which can only come from the Holy Spirit. This is why the true meaning of the *logos* (Greek for Word) has been hidden to so many for so long.

The description of the Aerial Mansion of Ravana, speaks of a mother ship, which is eight miles by eight miles in size. No wonder the scribes of the Vedas described them as "flying cities." And how about the reference to the beings whose job it was to protect the Vimana? "Elementals with round and deep eyes" sounds like today's description of a Gray alien.

In the Bible, particularly in the book of Ezekiel, he describes the Lords spaceships as divine chariots, also called the "Throne with Wheels." Ezekiel describes them as having wheels within wheels that were powered and protected by Cherubim who each had four faces and four wings, had the face of a lion, an ox, an eagle, and a man. Completely different than the Vimana spacecraft, but obvious similarities, in that they could both fly and both had beings protecting them and powering them.

NOTES:

1. Swami Tapasyananda, *Sunkarakandam of Srimad Valmiki Ramayan, The Ramayana,* Published by The President, Sri Ramakrishna Math Printing Press, Mylapori, Chennai, India, 2006. pp.46-48

CHAPTER FIVE

COSMIC WARFARE ON EARTH

> "There is no neutral ground in the universe.
> Every square inch and every split second
> Is claimed by God and countered by Satan."
>
> ~ C. S. Lewis

The Bible is full of passages relating to extraterrestrial visitations. Some researchers believe that it speaks of "gods" from other worlds who may have prompted the destruction of Sodom and Gomorrah, suggesting that the two cities were devastated by an ancient nuclear blast. But which god? Let's discern:

The Genesis story of the destruction of Sodom and Gomorrah is not a mystery when you plug in the idea of modern technology. How do two cities, realistically, get wiped off the face of the Earth? The inhabitants of Hiroshima and Nagasaki may know the answer. Two, human angels (extraterrestrial messengers) came into town and warned people of the coming destruction.

The angels (extraterrestrial messengers) directed Lot and his family to save their lives by running to the mountain. A land mass can protect one from a nuclear blast. The cities were "consumed" with "brimstone and fire." This is a perfect description of a nuclear blast. A mushroom cloud moving vertically could be the meaning of the words in the scripture "went up as the smoke of a furnace." Lot's wife did not make it, not only because she looked back, but because she trailed "behind" the rest of her family.

Primitives seeing an atomic explosion would be more than stunned; they would tend to stop in their tracks. Not looking back is good advice to those running for their lives. The "pillar of salt" could have come from finding her body later and discovering the effects of radiation. Finally, hiding in a "cave" because of the fall-out until the land was ready for habitation is very logical. So what happened that caused this destruction?

> "Then the Lord said, "The outcry against Sodom and Gomorrah is so great and their sin so grievous that I will go down and see if what they have done is as bad as the outcry that has reached me. If not, I will know."
>
> (Genesis 18:20-21, NIV)

Here the word for Lord is Yahuah (YHVH) in Hebrew. He is speaking to Abraham about the reports He is receiving about how bad the situation has become in Sodom and Gomorrah. The scriptures tell us that there, even after the flood, the Nephilim resurfaced and walked the earth. They were abusing humans.

> "The Nephilim were on the earth in those days—and also afterward—when the sons of God went to (laid with) the daughters of men and had children by them. They were the heroes of old, men of renown."
>
> (Genesis 6:4, NIV)

We have the famous Bible story of David and the Giant Goliath, but the situation in Sodom and Gomorrah was systemic. Why were their sins so grievous to the Lord? We know that the Nephilim were lustful for sex with the lesser humans. We are told that the men of Sodom and Gomorrah wanted to have sex with other men and even with the Lord's angels (extraterrestrial messengers) who were sent on a final reconnaissance mission to redeem the righteous before they destroyed (nuked) the place. Could unbridled lust and homosexuality have been the grievous sins that caused the Lord to destroy these twin cities? Or perhaps the entire city had been given over to the lustful appetites initiated by the Nephilim? Or perhaps a bit of both?

> "The two angels (extraterrestrial messengers) arrived at Sodom in the evening, and Lot was sitting in the gateway of the city. When he saw them, he got up to meet them and bowed down with his face to the ground. 'My lords,' he said, 'please turn aside to your servant's house. You can wash your feet and spend the night and then go on your way early in the morning.' 'No,' they answered, 'we will spend the night in the square.' But he insisted so strongly that they did go with him and entered his house. He prepared a meal for them, baking bread without yeast, and they ate. Before they had gone to bed, all the men from every part of the city of Sodom—both young and old—surrounded the house. They called to Lot, <u>'Where are the men who came to you tonight? Bring them out to us so that we can have sex with them.'</u>
>
> Lot went outside to meet them and shut the door behind him and said, 'No, my friends. Don't do this wicked thing. Look, I have two daughters who have never slept with a man. Let me bring them out to you, and you can do what you like with them. But don't do anything to these men, for they have come under the protection of my roof.'
>
> 'Get out of our way,' they replied. 'This fellow came here as a foreigner, and now he wants to play the judge! We'll treat you worse than them.' They kept bringing pressure on Lot and moved forward to break down the door. But the men (angels) (extraterrestrial messengers) inside reached out and pulled Lot back into the house and shut the door.
>
> <u>Then they struck the men who were at the door of the house, young and old, with blindness so that they could not find the door.</u> (These were obviously not ordinary men.) Then the two men (angels) (extraterrestrial messengers) said to Lot, 'Do you have anyone else here—sons-in-law, sons or daughters, or anyone else in the city who belongs to you? <u>Get them out of here, because we are going to destroy</u>

CHAPTER FIVE: Cosmic Warfare On Earth

this place. The outcry to the Lord against its people is so great that he has sent us (extraterrestrial messengers) to destroy it.'"

So Lot went out and spoke to his sons-in-law, who were pledged to marry his daughter. He said, 'Hurry and get out of this place, because the LORD is about to destroy the city!' But his sons-in-law thought he was joking. With the coming of dawn, the angels urged Lot, saying, 'Hurry! Take your wife and your two daughters who are here, or you will be swept away when the city is punished.'"

(Genesis 19:1-15, NIV)

These angels (extraterrestrial messengers/celestial warriors) were commissioned by the Lord Yahuah to nuke the cities. It appears that the order had already been made because they told Lot to get out of the city, in an urgent way, because the cities was set to destruct, in the way something does when it is activated on a time bomb. There was no turning back at this point.

"Then the Lord rained down burning sulfur (nuclear fire) on Sodom and Gomorrah—from the Lord out of the heavens (from his spaceship). Thus he overthrew those cities and the entire plain, destroying all those living in the cities—and also the vegetation in the land. But Lot's wife looked back, and she became a pillar of salt (as a result of nuclear radiation). Early the next morning Abraham got up and returned to the place where he had stood before the Lord. He looked down toward Sodom and Gomorrah, toward all the land of the plain, and he saw dense smoke rising from the land, like smoke from a furnace (This is the scene of a nuclear explosion, no human on the earth at that time had that kind of power, and this came from the Lord's technology, fire from heaven)."

(Genesis 19:24-28, NIV)

"As I overthrew Sodom and Gomorrah along with their neighboring towns," declares the LORD, "so no one will live there; no people will dwell in it."

(Jeremiah 50:40, NIV)

In this passage, it is interesting that the prophet Jeremiah is saying that "God" overthrew Sodom and Gomorrah, and then says, the Lord Yahuah declared it. In the Hebrew, the word for Lord used in this passage is Yahuah. He made sure that no one could live there. To this day, nothing grows in this land, and scientists and archeologists have determined that the soil still retains radiation.

"Even as Sodom and Gomorrah, and the cities about them in like manner, giving themselves over to fornication, and going after strange flesh, are set forth for an example, suffering the vengeance of eternal fire."

(Jude 1:7 KJV)

The fact that this passage refers to them as "going after strange flesh" proves that there was something more than human beings existing in Sodom and Gomorrah. This story created the word *sodomy*. This word is also used in "sodomy laws" to describe sexual "crimes against nature" consisting of anal sex with both humans and animals, either homosexual or heterosexual, which is translated to mean the same thing in several languages.

Another possible scenario, which dovetails into end time prophecy, is that the Lord Yahuah focused a nuclear weapon upon the area known as Sodom and Gomorrah, because it was an ancient Annunaki[2] space base, who created the Nephilim that brought debauchery upon the land. (See *Annunaki* in Book One of *Who's Who In The Cosmic Zoo?*) The area was nuked, not just over sexual immorality, but over the beings that caused it and are expected to return to earth to engage in a final battle with their Creator, in the end time battle of all battles, known as Armageddon.

While this story may not be two groups fighting with "cosmic warfare" but more like "cosmic punishment," it still qualifies as warfare because of the use of high-tech weapons from space, or fire from heaven. It does, however, come under the category of spiritual warfare because the Lord Yahuah would no longer tolerate these types of abuses from the Nephilim corrupting earth humans with their lasciviousness and immoralities.

Other ancient texts that describe flying machines, advanced technology, and awesome weapons wielded by the gods were the sacred Hindu hymns, the *Rig-Veda*, which constitutes some of the oldest known religious documents. This impressive poetry tells of the achievements of the Hindu pantheon of gods, many of whom were Nephilim. One passage tells of Indra, a space god-being, who was honored when his name was turned into "India." Indra, who became known as the "fort destroyer" because of his exploits in war, was said to travel through the skies in a flying machine called the *Vimana*. This craft was equipped with awesome weapons capable of destroying a city, similar to the same technology that the extraterrestrial angels of Yahuah used on destroying Sodom and Gomorrah. The effect of these weapons seems to have been like that of laser beams or some type of nuclear device.

Another ancient Indian text, the *Mahabharata*,[1] describes forty-six different types of weapons, some of which could destroy entire cities, that could put people to sleep (a type of nerve gas), and some that were very high-tech and could only be what we know today as air-to-ground missiles. The text talks about Vishnu having a type of "guided weapon that destroyed everything that moved," which today we call heat-seeking missiles. Flaming swords are mentioned in both the *Mahabharata* and in the book of Genesis; today we would call them laser guns or sabers from *Star Wars*, and the most deadly weapon of all, known as the "Ramastra," was never to be used because it could destroy the entire planet by fire. Today we call those WMDs (weapons of mass destruction) and nuclear bombs.

CHAPTER FIVE: Cosmic Warfare On Earth

The *Mahabharata* tells of an attack on an enemy army:

"It was as if the elements had been unfurled. The sun spun around in the heavens. The world shuddered in fever, 'scorched' by the terrible heat of this weapon. Elephants burst into flames…The rivers boiled. Animals crumpled to the ground and died. The armies of the enemy were mowed down when the raging elements reached them. Forests collapsed in splintered rows. Horses and chariots were burned up….The corpses of the fallen were mutilated by the terrible heat so that they looked other than human."[1]

Only nuclear radiation can create that kind of power and heat to deform humans. This explains why many Hindu gods and goddesses are multi-armed, which may have been the result of radiation poisoning.

Anyone reading these texts can deduce that these ancient aliens, who later became known as gods, brought advanced technology in the form of weaponry and cosmic warfare to Earth, technology that was far beyond earth humans at that time, which even today, we have not completely caught up with, although we're getting close, but this proves that what we know today is nothing new, and even more distressing, it proves that the knowledge we do have that has created technological advances in today's military industrial complex comes from the influence and perhaps even actual agreements with aliens today.[2] (See Book One of *Who's Who in the Cosmic Zoo of Aliens and ETs*)

It is also important to note that these alien-gods were punished by the Almighty Creator God for defiling humankind. The *Books of Enoch* tell us that the fallen sons of heaven were punished for teaching humans how to warfare. Warfare is the history of planet earth, and with respect to today's present dilemmas, these ancient aliens have a lot to answer for, for turning planet earth into a warzone.

"And He will imprison those angels, who have shown unrighteousness, in that burning valley which my grandfather Enoch had formerly shown to me in the west among the mountains of gold and silver and iron and soft metal and tin. And I saw that valley in which there was a great convulsion and a convulsion of the waters. And when all this took place, for that fiery molten metal and from the convulsion thereof in that place, there was produced a smell of sulphur, and it was connected with those waters, and that valley of the angels who had led astray (humankind) burned beneath that land. And through its valley proceed streams of fire, where these angels are punished who had led astray those who dwell upon the earth"[3] (God's Promise to Noah: Places of Punishment of the Angels and of the Kings, *Book of Enoch* LXVII: 67:4-7).

Noah speaks of "mountains of gold and silver and iron and soft metal and tin." These are description of spaceships. The "fiery molten metal" burned and produced a smell of sulphur. This is describing a place *inside* the earth, which smells of sulphur. Sounds like the pit of hell.

Many old traditions speak of a war between the forces of light and darkness that raged in humankind's prehistory. These ancient texts tell us of rival extraterrestrial forces that fought for dominance over prehistoric Earth. According to some traditions, the Sons of Light vanquished certain Dark Magicians who sought to enslave developing humankind, yet it is blatantly obvious that many of them are still at it again today. Enslaving humans has certainly been a recurring theme for planet Earth for millennia.

Whatever may have caused such violent conflicts, physical evidence exists on Earth indicating that advanced beings exercised the power of formidable energy. There are accounts of sand being melted into glass in certain desert areas, of hill forts with vitrified portions of stone walls, such as in Ireland, and of the remains of ancient cities that had been destroyed by what appears to have been extreme heat, such as in Israel at the site of Sodom and Gomorrah, which today still emits radioactive energy, indicating a type of nuclear blast, far beyond that which could have been scorched by the torches of primitive human armies. Even conventionally trained archaeologists, who have encountered such anomalous finds, have admitted that none of these catastrophes have been caused by volcanoes, by lightning, by crashing comets, or by conflagrations set by humankind.

There is no question in my mind that our earth has been involved in Cosmic Wars between light and dark forces over the control of humanity and the control of planet Earth itself, which is, let's face it, rich in all kinds of natural resources. These beings, who we have affectionately been calling "angels," are, in fact, extraterrestrials and alien beings who have been fighting over planet Earth and humankind for as long as human beings existed here.

They are not finished, and what our planet is facing today with "daily" reports of UFO sightings all over the globe, alien abductions, animal mutilations, crop circles, and all kinds of other paranormal anomalies is that humankind is being fought over again. This time, as we live in the "Age of Knowledge," our present-day task is to learn discernment over *who* these beings are, where they come from, and what their intentions for earth humans are. Understanding the past allows us to have some insight and, hopefully, wisdom in proceeding with our futures.

The growing field of Exopolitics is still in its embryonic stages. It is, nevertheless, imperative that those investigators and researchers delve into the alien presence on planet Earth and incorporate an understanding of the past, *spiritually speaking*, and of what the ancient texts were trying to tell us. It is particularly important to learn the lessons from the downfalls and punishments. Many of the texts are actually letters to the future, to us, which is relevant to our present day and our very near future. As Yahshua predicted in Luke 17:26 (KJV 2000):

> "And as it was in the days of Noah,
> So shall it be also in the days of the Son of Man."

CHAPTER FIVE: Cosmic Warfare On Earth

The emergence of the Nephilim was what brought about the Flood of Noah. Our current experiences with alien involvement is biblically relevant today. The same type of activities that brought about the great deluge of floods upon the earth are happening again on planet Earth. The abominations that brought desolation by the Creator God were essentially the lack of respect for the laws of creation and for Him.

The rebellious ET gods created Nephilim monster hybrids and cross bred everything between humans and animals, and had sex with both humans and animals, and ate of their flesh, which lowered the vitality of God's creation and sabotaged their ability to engage in a "spiritual relationship" with the Creator God. They mixed all kinds of genetics together, human and animal, which created more Nephilim (rejects); afterward, these human/animal/alien hybrids then became mythologized into culture.

Today, the same type of hybridization and cloning is taking place in the scientific community. There are all kinds of hybrid experiments going on, including those done by aliens in the hybridization program, which is the purpose of the abductions — to obtain human DNA, human ova, and human sperm, and combine it with alien DNA to produce the new Nephilim. These hybrids are different than the hybrid Nephilim of the past; in that, they are not giants, but they have the appearance of looking human; however, underneath they are programmed with alien DNA and implants, which could be compared to the Borg on *Star Trek*, except that the implants are *inside* the body and cannot be seen by the naked eye.

Today our food supply is faced with dangerous GMOs (genetically modified organisms). We are in an age where scientists have learned how to clone animals and humans for all kinds of purposes; some of this knowledge is being used nefariously against humanity.

We are also in an age where our governments have firsthand knowledge of the alien presence on Earth and have entered into legal agreements with them in exchange for technology, which is proving to be a type of Faustian Contract, ensuing the gradual enslavement of its citizens through the economic crisis we find ourselves in, because of the obscene amount of money spent on the black budgets and the Extra-Terrestrial Military Industrial Complex, as well as the compromised food supply and stronghold of the pharmaceutical industry, which literally has a stranglehold on most citizens and controls the inflated and broken health care system. Even many of our elected politicians have found themselves powerless in the face of these larger forces, which have proven to be greater than themselves and our community.

As a community, we must learn to discern between the forces. Even though our level of technology is growing exponentially, we are still years behind the capabilities of what these alien groups can produce to deceive, hypnotize, and essentially put humans under a "spell." With that said, we must learn to discern spiritually, which is totally within our present state of human capability, if not technologically.

In ancient times, when people witnessed technological feats done by alien and extraterrestrial beings, they described them as "miracles," yet many of these so-called miracles were essentially advanced levels of technology that our ancestors had no reference to, nor could they understand intellectually or psychologically. In today's present world of growing technology and knowledge, most should, by now, have the ability to discern between techno-wizardry and bona fide "miracles."

NOTES:

1. *Mahabharata.* Sacred Texts. Ca. 400 BCE <http://www.sacred-texts.com/hin/maha/index.htm>.
2. Ella LeBain, Book One of *Who's Who in the Cosmic Zoo of Aliens and ETs,* Tate Publishing, 2013
3. Charles, R. H. (trans.). *The Book of Enoch.* 1917 <http://www.sacred-texts.com/bib/boe>.

CHAPTER SIX

THE BEASTS OF THE SEA AND EARTH

> "And four great beasts were coming up from the sea,
> Different from one another."
>
> (Daniel 7:3, NAS)

One of the most life changing encounters I've had was in 1994, when I witnessed a huge metallic disk-shaped craft emerge out of the Gulf of Mexico off the shores of Indian Rocks Beach where I used to live, while engaging in my nightly ritual of watching the sunset. It was probably an hour after sunset; the horizon had very little light left; it had turned a light purple, but the rest of the sky had already gone dark and all the stars were out. It was a very clear night. I almost couldn't believe my eyes, but I watched this huge gunmetal-silver metallic ship, probably two to three hundred feet in diameter emerge out of the ocean. It was wet and foaming with seawater as it ascended into the sky. It did this slowly until it got high enough to thrust into space. I watched as it became a light among the stars and disappeared as if it had gone into a portal in the sky and was gone.

Later on that same night, I learned that our local MUFON (Mutual UFO Network) had received over 350 calls as there were others who had witnessed this sighting as well. Well, as they say with life-changing experiences, they alter and change your life forever. This caused me to dig deeper into UFO research as it completely altered my perception of reality.

One of the things that I found out was that these encounters were called USOs (Underwater Submerged Objects), which have been seen all over the world by hundreds of eyewitnesses. This meant that UFOs must've had bases under the oceans and waters of the world. So I later looked into what the Bible had to say about this, if any, and this is what I found:

> "The dragon stood on the shore of the sea. And I saw a beast **coming out of the sea**. It had ten horns and seven heads, with ten crowns on its horns, and on each head a blasphemous name."
>
> (Revelation 13:1, NIV)

This passage indicates that the dragon controls the beast coming out of the sea. Here the ten horns and seven heads describe a hierarchical power structure of mechanical fleet of ships emerging from the ocean. Horns are symbolic of power, and heads represent authorities. Each had a blasphemous name because they were of the hierarchy of fallen angels who are at war against the Creator. They emerge with a vengeance.

I believe what St. John saw in his vision, and what he described, at that time, had no reference to what he saw. These were mechanical beings, which was why he called them "a beast." To him, it was a creature like no other. Yet what creature has ten horns and seven heads with ten crowns on each of his horns? Could this be a Nephilim monster, a remnant from ancient times, when the alien gods (Annunaki) were mixing genetics and creating all sorts of mutations? Or, perhaps it is nothing organic, but certainly something technological. At that time, St. John the Divine had no other way to describe it. I believe what he saw was a fleet, a grouping of mechanical ships, not one single entity.

> "Daniel said, "I was looking in my vision by night, and behold, the four winds of heaven were stirring up the great sea."
>
> (Daniel 7:2, NAS)

Each time the prophets write of the "four winds of heaven," they are describing space craft that literally whipped up the winds. In this passage, Daniel is referring to four space craft that were hovering over the great sea and causing the waters to stir.

> "And four great beasts were coming up from the sea, different from one another."
>
> (Daniel 7:3, NAS)

In this passage, Daniel tells us that he saw four great beasts emerge out of the sea. These are four separate ships. He describes these ships as beasts because he had no other reference to say they were underwater submerged objects, and because as we learn from Daniel's other descriptions they were all metallic in nature, made from iron and bronze, which clearly describes a piece of technology. Sometimes metallic spaceships can look really scary, especially if they are the spaceships that belong to the dark forces, who live inside the earth. He tells us they were all different from one another.

THE BEAST OUT OF THE EARTH

> "Then I saw another beast, come up out of the earth. He had two horns like those of a lamb, but he spoke with the voice of a dragon."
>
> (Revelation 13:11, NLT)

"Spoke with the voice of a dragon"? What is he referring to? Do dragons speak? If so, then perhaps these are alien Draconian beings. St. John is comparing this beast to a dragon.[1] (See, Book One *Who's Who In The Cosmic Zoo?*' chapter on Draconians, pp.154-182)

> "These great beasts, which are four in number, are four kings who will arise from the earth."
>
> (Daniel 7:17, NAS)

CHAPTER SIX: The Beasts Of The Sea And Earth

St. John of the Revelation sees beasts coming out of the earth. Daniel also tells us they will arise from the earth. Sounds like actual physical beings who live inside the earth and will surface in the last days before the Messiah returns for the final battle.

Admiral Richard B. Byrd's Flight Log: Base Camp Arctic (2/19/47): Admiral Byrd in February and March of 1947 flew his plane inside a hole in the North Pole and claimed to see strange crafts flying inside the earth, as well as a city inside the earth and strange creatures, including a mammoth, which has been extinct for millennia. He reported that several men approached him, whom he described as tall with blond hair, against a backdrop of a city with shimmering, pulsating lights with all the hues and color of a rainbow. The origin of his flight log is controversial, as no one can authenticate its true source. It is especially controversial when one considers that this log diary was written in the year 1947 in the months of February and March, under circumstances that evidently defied anyone's imagination and credibility, for those times as well as our present day. His log deals with the origin of UFOs, as well as the Hollow Earth, or Agartha, as the admiral described. See, chapter on Aghartians, Agarthans, Agharians, pp. 98-105, in Book One of *Who's Who In The Cosmic Zoo?*

The fact that beings live inside the earth is nothing new, as this has been cross referenced in the Bible. The *Books of Enoch* details that, after the great war in heaven between the fallen angels, the Sons of God (Elohim), the archangel Michael, and his angels, the result was the satans and his fallen angels were cast inside the earth. The Bible tells us of a time reserved for the last days when they will be allowed to emerge from inside the earth and be returned to the earth's surface to wreak havoc on the unbelieving earth humans, as the Lord promises to use them to punish the unbelievers.

> "And the dragon stood on the sand of the seashore. Then I saw a beast coming up out of the sea, having ten horns and seven heads, and on his horns were ten diadems, and on his heads were blasphemous names."
>
> (Revelation 13:1, NAS)

Again, this beast or mother ship is seen coming out of the ocean waters. The horns, heads, and ten diadems (crowns) may, in fact, be a fleet of spacecraft. There are many UFOs that appear to have a crown on top of a disk-shaped craft. The blasphemous names indicate that the fleet comes from the satans and the fallen angels who have been at war with the Creator and would be the only ones who would advertise what St. John is describing as "blasphemous names." Later on in this book, I go over the names of God and the counterfeit names that Lucifer/Satan has created and has used. It is possible that one of these blasphemous names are one of the names of God, as the Satan's whole agenda from the beginning of his fall was to be God and to steal the worship from the Creator and have it all to himself.

CAST DOWN TO EARTH

God has always, and will always, possess mind and power superior to His creation. Using His superior power, God brought other spirit-composed beings into existence. These spirit beings, called angels, were each created with free moral agency. They had minds with which to reason and make choices. Among the spirit beings brought into existence were three mighty archangels — Michael, Gabriel and Lucifer. Sometime after the creation of the angelic realm, God created the physical universe. Lucifer, as one of God's mightiest spiritual creations, was given great position and authority. But, after an unrevealed amount of time, Lucifer grew vain and dissatisfied with what God had given him. He wanted more.

Through smooth lies and crafty deceit, he planted the bitter seeds of discontent, and these seeds grew until a third of the angels were convinced that they should join Lucifer in rebelling against the very God that had given them life. Together they mounted an attack on God's heavenly throne. War raged in the universe. When the great battle was over, Lucifer, now called Satan, and his angels, now classified as demons, were cast out of the high heaven and sent down to the earth.

> "The beast that you saw was, and is not, and is about to come up out of the abyss and go to destruction. And those who dwell on the earth, whose name has not been written in the book of life from the foundation of the world, will wonder when they see the beast, that he was and is not and will come."
>
> (Revelation 17:8, NAS)

Again the beast here is described to come out from inside the abyss, which is *inside* the earth. His purpose is to wreak havoc and destruction on the unbelievers and the apostate.

In the end-time prophecy recorded by John in the book of Revelation, the Abyss plays a large part in the events leading up to the return of the Messiah. During the period of the "seven trumpets," when God's wrath is poured out on an unrepentant mankind, the Abyss is opened at the sounding of the fifth trumpet:

> "The fifth angel sounded his trumpet, and I saw a star that had fallen from the sky to the earth. The star was given the key to the shaft of the Abyss. When he opened the Abyss, smoke rose from it like the smoke from a gigantic furnace. The sun and sky were darkened by the smoke from the Abyss. And out of the smoke locusts came down upon the earth and were given power like that of scorpions of the earth. <u>They were told not to harm the grass of the earth or any plant or tree, but only those people who did not have the seal of God on their foreheads. They were not allowed to kill them but only to torture them for five months</u>. And the agony they suffered was like that of the sting of a scorpion when it strikes. <u>During those days people

CHAPTER SIX: The Beasts Of The Sea And Earth

<u>will seek death but will not find it; they will long to die, but death will elude them</u>. The locusts looked like horses prepared for battle. On their heads they wore something like crowns of gold, and their faces resembled human faces. Their hair was like women's hair, and their teeth were like lions 'teeth. They had breastplates like breastplates of iron, and the sound of their wings was like the thundering of many horses and chariots rushing into battle. They had tails with stingers, like scorpions, and in their tails they had power to torment people for five months."

(Revelation 9:1-10, NIV)

Clearly this description is of alien beings coming out from inside the earth. After having been housed in space craft, they've been sent to wreak havoc on the unbelievers. St. John describes them as alien; they had crowns of gold and faces that looked like human faces, with breastplates of iron (yet another reference to iron in the Bible), which describes the metallic craft they were travelling through the sky with. The sound of their wings (in Hebrew the word for *wings* is used in aeronautics as the same word for *extenders*). These were not bird wings or feathered wings, but extenders of some type of aircraft that sounded like the thundering of many horses. Horsepower? Today, for many years, we have been comparing the cylinders of the engines of cars to horsepower, which is a term used widely to describe the power of the technology.

They had the ability to sting like a scorpion. This would be from some kind of laser technology, which also had the ability to torment people. Today our military has technology that, when measured on a frequency, can be used to torment, to cripple, or to cause sickness. What St. John was describing here was an elaborate alien technology being released from the Abyss from inside Earth.

"The unlocking of the Abyss releases a horde of fallen angels and depraved demons upon mankind. God uses them as an instrument of His wrath for five months; they are allowed to torment those on the earth who don't have God's seal on their foreheads."

(Revelation 7:2-8)

In his commentary on Revelation 9:1, 3, Daniel H. Stern[2] writes: "The star is not Satan (despite Isaiah 14:12, Luke 10:17), but an angel, who still has the key at 20:1. The Abyss is not *She'ol* (as at Romans 10:7), but a place where demonic beings are imprisoned (vv. 2-11, 11:7, 17:8, 20:2- In the Apocrypha, God is called, 'You who close and seal the Abyss with your fearful and glorious name.'" (Prayer of Manasseh 3)

Demonic monsters are released which fly *like* locusts (Exodus 10:12-20; Joel 1:4, 2:4-14) and sting like scorpions (Ezekiel 2:6, Luke 11:12).[2]

Locusts may not be the organic kind as we see them in our world, but when the scriptures say "which fly *like* locusts and sting *like* scorpions," the writer is making a comparison to the organic creatures. These creatures are not organic; they are robotic mechanically cloned robots, similar to something depicted in the 2005 Steven Spielberg film *War of the Worlds*. Both these descriptions, along with the description of the Beast coming out of the sea, with iron feet and bronze, are all descriptions of machines and technological robotic beings.

It is also important to note that the origin of the word *robot* is a Czech word, which means "compulsory labor" or "drudgery."

WHO IS THE KING OF THE ABYSS?

In Revelation 9:11, a mysterious character is introduced into the story. He is released from the Abyss, along with the multitude of angels and demons, and is identified as their king or ruler:

> "They had as *king* over them *the angel of the Abyss*, whose name in Hebrew is *Abaddon*, and in Greek *Apollyon* (that is, Destroyer)."
>
> (Revelation 9:11 NIV)

Abaddon/Apollyon (literally translates to "Destroyer" in Hebrew/Greek) is the fallen "angelic" ruler of the Abyss. He is the highest-ranking evil angel now confined in the Abyss. Although not specifically mentioned by these names anywhere else in the Bible, Abaddon plays a major role in the events at the end of this current age. His Hebrew name is *Abaddon*. In the New Testament, *Apollyon* (Greek) is called the "angel of the bottomless pit." *Apollyon*, in early Christian literature, is also a name for the Devil. He is identified as an angel of death — *"hideous to behold, with scales like a fish, wings like a dragon, bear's feet, a scorpion's tail and a lion's mouth."* This sounds like the description of a draconian-reptilian-alien hybrid being (i.e., Nephilim).

The Abyss was created for the satans and the fallen angels, not for human souls. However, it is their agenda to pull as many human souls as possible down with them and keep them away from the Creator. This is the battle every single earth human faces in their lives on planet Earth.

After the release of the angels and demons from the Abyss, another group of evil spirits will be released onto the earth:

> "Then the sixth angel blew his trumpet, and I heard a voice speaking from the four horns of the gold altar that stands in the presence of God. And the voice said to the sixth angel who held the trumpet, "Release the four angels who are bound at the great Euphrates River." Then the four angels who had been prepared for the hour and day and month and year *were turned loose to kill one-third of all people on earth*. I heard the size of their army, which was 200 hundred million mounted troops.

CHAPTER SIX: The Beasts Of The Sea And Earth

> And in my vision, I saw the horses and the riders sitting on them. The riders wore armor that was fiery red and dark blue and yellow. The horses had heads like lions, and fire and smoke and burning sulfur billowed from their mouths. One-third of all the people on earth were killed by these three plagues — by the fire and smoke and burning sulfur that came from the mouths of the horses. Their power was in their mouths and in their tails. For their tails had heads like snakes, with the power to injure people.
>
> But the people who did not die in these plagues still refused to repent of their evil deeds and turn to God. They continued to worship demons and idols made of gold, silver, bronze, stone, and wood—idols that can neither see nor hear nor walk."
>
> (Revelation 9:13-20, NLT)

This scripture tells us that to further punish those who will not obey the Lord and instead follow after the false spirits, God authorizes the release of four powerful angels who have been held for just this occasion. Their mission is the destruction of one-third of humankind. To accomplish this feat, they are given an army of 200 million evil spirits. Just as Jesus Christ and his angelic army later ride white horses (Revelation 19:11, 14), these demons also ride "horses." Fire, smoke, and brimstone issue from the mouths of their horses, and with these plagues, possibly a billion and a half people are killed. I got news for you. These are no ordinary horses, but space craft emitting fire, smoke, and sulfur. Sulfur is abundant inside the earth. In fact, many report that, during encounters with Gray aliens, they smell of sulphur.

The remnant of the one-third is a repetitive theme throughout earth's history. I believe it began with the one-third of heaven's angels that followed Lucifer's rebellion. One-third seems to be a remnant. Two-thirds of the Jewish people in Europe were persecuted in the Holocaust. There were about 9.5 million Jews in Europe before the Holocaust; afterward, about 3 million. Approximately two-thirds of European Jews were murdered by the Nazis, leaving approximately a one third remnant who survived.

Both Abaddon, the imprisoned spirit currently ruling over the Abyss, and the four angels now "bound at the great river Euphrates" appear to be high-ranking and powerful angels. They will be released temporarily to fulfill their part of God's plan at the end of the age. Some Christians believe that this fallen angel, Apollyon, will be the one empowering the man known as the Antichrist with all kinds of powers, wonders, and miracles, having at his disposal the command of their UFOs. Who will work together as the trinity of Hell with Satan and the Beast?[3]

Jesus Christ states that the fate of Satan and the fallen angels is to go into the everlasting lake of fire which has been prepared for them:

> "Then he will say to those on the left, 'Depart from me, you who are cursed, into the eternal fire prepared for the devil and his angels."
>
> (Matthew 25:41, NIV)

Only Satan and his angels are mentioned here by Christ as going into the lake of fire. The demons have a different fate awaiting them. During the millennial reign of Christ, these unclean spirits will be restricted to the destroyed and uninhabited land of Babylon, which is today's Iraq, as well as the entire region of ancient Mesopotamia, Sumeria, Persia (today's Iran) and Akkadia. This was the ancient stronghold of the Annunaki, which are destined to be overthrown again, along with their descendants upon the earth.

> "Babylon, the jewel of kingdoms, the pride and glory of the Babylonians, will be overthrown by God just like Sodom and Gomorrah. She will never be inhabited or lived in through all generations; there no nomads will pitch their tents, there no shepherds will rest their flocks. But desert creatures will lie there, jackals will fill her houses; there the owls will dwell, and there the wild goats will leap about. Hyenas will inhabit her strongholds, jackals her luxurious palaces. Her time is at hand, and her days will not be prolonged."
>
> (Isaiah 13:19-22, NIV)

> "Babylon will become a heap of ruins, haunted by jackals, an object of horror and hissing, without inhabitants."
>
> (Jeremiah 51:37 NAS)

> "And he cried out with a mighty voice, saying, "Fallen, fallen is Babylon the great! She has become a dwelling place of demons, a haunt for every unclean spirit, a haunt for every unclean bird, a haunt for every unclean and detestable beast."
>
> (Revelation 18:2 ESV)

NOTES:

1. Ella LeBain, *Book One, Who's Who In The Cosmic Zoo?,* Tate Publishing, 2013
2. Daniel H. Stern, *Jewish New Testament Commentary,* pp. 815-16
3. Tom Horn, *Apollyon Rising 2012, The Lost Symbol Found And The Final Mystery of the Great Seal Revealed,* Defender Books, Crane, MO. 2009

CHAPTER SEVEN

DISCERNMENT OF GODS, ANGELS & DEMONS

> "Human beings are under the control of a strange force
> That bends them in absurd ways, forcing them to play a role
> In a bizarre game of deception."
> ~ Dr. Jacques Vallée, *Messengers of Deception*

There are way too many gods to mention here, and this is not going to be an A-Z on all the gods. For more elucidation on the gods, please see my next chapter on *Who Are the Gods?* and *The God of this World,* as well as *The Cosmic Christ.* For the most part I'm going to be addressing the "major" players in this Cosmic Drama that earth humans find themselves caught up in.

WHO OR WHAT IS GOD?

Is God a "who" or a "what"? Firstly let's define the meaning of the word *god*. God is not a name; it is a title. Today, *god* is defined as something or someone who is worshipped.

There are so many versions of god. We need to discern which god? Who answers the call when you call out to God? There are many who believe in Source or Spirit, but do they know which "source" and which "spirit" they are talking to? Is it specifically the Holy Spirit, who only comes through faith in Jesus Christ, or the spirit of the god of this world?

Then there are those who believe in a supreme being, they won't call it God or use any other name. Again we need to ask ourselves, which Supreme Being answers? Today, many New Agers believe in the Universe or Multiverse; they replace those words with God and believe the Universe will provide for them, or create synchronicity or serendipity. But the universe is a vast place, so "who" exactly is in charge of answering their prayers? The universe is a very broad term.

There are many beings who have a god complex. They want to be like god, so they pretend to be, and many are fooled by them. Some of those gods demanded worship and all kinds of sacrifices to appease them in the past, who literally put the fear of god into our ancient ancestors, creating all kinds of myths, legends and religions for them. But were they real gods or just pretend gods?

The ancient astronaut theory explains that those who came from the heavens to Earth were all extraterrestrials, not gods. They believe it was our ancestors who turned them into gods because they were technologically more advanced than them. If so, who were they? And why were they pretending to be gods? Perhaps they wanted to be worshipped as a god, so they masqueraded as a god to the ancient humans? Or perhaps they were in rebellion to a much higher god and wanted to steal His worship from earth humans?

Then we have agnostics, who don't believe in any religion, but they do not deny the existence of God and heaven but are skeptical that one cannot know for certain whether or not they exist. Atheists, on the other hand, believe there is no God, but what they are really saying is, "I don't know God." They believe in themselves and tend to lean more toward secularism; they, too, come under one of the gods, whether they realize it or not. One thing we do know for sure is disbelief may keep miracles away, but it doesn't negate the reality of God. New Agers tend to believe in a universal force, spirit, and one's "divine nature," so who then answers their prayers?

The Bible talks about more than one god. There is the Almighty Creator God named Yahuah and his son Yahshua, aka Jesus Christ, and there are the Elohim, who are gods, also known as sons of the God. They are often confused with their own sons, who were called "Bene HaElohim" translates to, sons of the gods, and then there is Lucifer/Satan, who is called "the god of this world" (2 Corinthians 4:4) and the "prince of the powers of the air" (Ephesians 2:2). He is also called the one who deceives the world (Revelation 12:9). So when a person doesn't realize there is more than one god that runs this world and just cries out to "God," and prays to have his or her prayer answered, you can be sure that a god will answer, but not necessarily the Most High God.

So many people ask this question: If God is Love than how come He allows suffering in the world? The short answer is that most of the suffering comes from the god of this world, Lucifer/Satan. The rest comes from being under the curses that were put into "legal" motion a long time ago, which gets passed down generationally and through various ancestral lines. (See my chapter in Book Four: *Covenants* chapters on *Cosmic Karma and Ancient Curses*). Satan and his fallen angels have major god complexes. They will answer prayers to those who don't know the difference, lulling them into a false sense of security, and willfully playing the role of god to the undiscerning mind and spirit.

Essentially, there are two major sides in discerning the gods. 1) Those who are aligned and contracted with the god of this world, who is Lucifer/Satan; and 2) Those who have remained faithful to their Creator God, the Lord Almighty, and His Christ. For deeper understanding on this, please refer to and read my chapter on Contracts and Agreements in Book Four – *Covenants* of *Who's Who In The Cosmic Zoo?*). After all the research I've done, this is my conclusion.

CHAPTER SEVEN: Discernment Of Gods, Angels & Demons

THE NEW AGE DILEMMA

Have you ever been deceived, betrayed, put your trust and faith into someone or something only to be sorely disappointed and heartbroken? It's amazing how many so-called spirit guides are masquerading alien(demon)(non-human intelligences) and fallen angels, who attach themselves to humans, telling them that they are space brothers, or "Ascended Masters," St. Germaine, or "Archangel Michael," Gabriel, Uriel, "Pleaidians," etc. only to be total imposters, literally disguised as them. They very cleverly guide you with just enough truth, which is always inevitably mixed with false information in order to obscure to the undiscerning soul. How often do these spirit guides mislead humans?

If these were true, the Masters and Archangels that serve the Most High Lord God of Truth, Love, and Light would never mislead, deceive, insert, or manipulate their own agenda. However, fallen angels would, and this is their modus operandi, as they have been in an ongoing battle with the Almighty Creator God since they rebelled along with Lucifer and were ousted out of heaven and then castigated to live inside the earth and in the lower heavens for millennia. And what's more shocking is that they've been deceiving humans for millennia

The reason that channeling is so popular is because these fallen angels/demons tell people what they want to hear, peppered with the "love and light" and just enough truth sandwiched between the lies, which goes unnoticed and are swallowed hook, line, and sinker by those listening and reading it because it "feels" good or fits into their present political agendas.

Many people who have fallen away from the church and strayed from their childhood religions became disenchanted with religion, so they are "open" and searching for alternative answers, and this search is satisfied by a variety of New Age remedies, philosophies, and channeling sessions.

There is absolutely no discernment, and whenever someone questions it, they are branded as being negative because they like to tailor their messages to make others feel good about themselves. These are false belief systems, which are designed to hypnotize their believers into a false sense of being when, in reality, these are highly skilled deceptive spirits that are out to lure as many unsuspecting and undiscerning humans away from the very spiritual reality that every human soul inevitably faces. This also causes the recipient to get energetically "hooked in" to their spirit, causing deceptive influences to cloud their minds from knowing and seeing the truth. These are called "counterfeits," and they are also known as "counterfeit spirits."

Dr. Jacques Vallée cites the extensive research of Bertrand Meheust:

> "The symbolic display seen by the abductees is identical to the type of initiation ritual or astral voyage that is imbedded in the [occult] traditions of every culture...the structure of abduction stories is identical to that of occult initiation

rituals...the UFO beings of today belong to the same class of manifestation as the [occult] entities that were described in centuries past."[1]

THE DIVINE FEMININE AND THE FALSE GODDESS

There are so many goddesses, but the idea of a Divine Feminine may be more of an ideal than a reality. The goddess archetype falls into several key groupings: the mother/matriarch; the seductress/sex object; the nurturer/healer; the abductress/victim; the hunter/warrior; and the judge/the blind-folded justice goddess, and the list goes on.

Many of these archetypes come from actual women who made their marks on the world in the past. Likewise, when there were dark and evil queens that ruled, they, too, made their mark spiritually on their descendants and the generations that followed. Their fallen spirit caused a spiritual stronghold of evil, bringing generational curses upon future generations.

The souls' energy of all the evil queens belongs to Satan to use, abuse, manipulate, and control as Satan sees fit to promote his agenda throughout millennia, and he employs a network of lesser demons, known as evil spirits, to carry out his malfeasance and malevolent intent. He will use the spiritual stronghold/archetype to his advantage, which is tailored to fit into each culture and time line of earth.

The goddess was worshipped for centuries in the ancient world, but when evil queens took over, it created a rift and confusion among goddess worshippers, regardless of gender. This spiritual stronghold/evil queen archetype, which is traditionally portrayed in Disney stories and movies, is still very much a force to be reckoned with in today's world. The source of this ancient archetype is the evil Queen of Judah, Jezebel, her successor daughter Athaliah and fallen angel Ashteroth (Ishtar) aka Innana, the Goddess of the Annunaki. Their spirits are still at work in today's churches, temples, and New Age circles. Jezebel's motis operandi was to destroy the true prophets of God. She is judged in Revelation 2:20-26.

Jezebel's character was wicked, controlling, sexually immoral, murderous, and demonic. Yet her relentless pursuit of Elijah drove him to wrestle with depression and suicidal thoughts. She presides over Islam, due to their ancient connection to Baal worship (See my chapter "Who Is Allah?") In every congregation or assembly, there are those who want to control, manipulate, and subvert God's men and women. In the end, Jezebel was defeated by God (Yahuah) through Elijah, followed by a great contest where the Lord sent fire from heaven (technological laser weapons from His starship) specifically targeting the destruction of the prophets of Baal. (1 Kings 18)

Here's how this story in the Bible relates to present times. When King Ahab consulted with Jezebel, she was a prophetess and served a foreign spirit named Ashtoreth (Ishtar). One of her noted traits was her ability to teach and train people for prophetic ministry. She still has a large following today. She is a seducing goddess that will hijack every generation when given the chance. Jezebel is a false prophetess and teacher,

CHAPTER SEVEN: Discernment Of Gods, Angels & Demons

cunning, deceptive, and controlling. Following the prophets of Jezebel can get you killed. That's what happened to Ahab (1 Kings 22:5-6).

Syria and Israel were at peace with each other, but King Ahab wanted to expand his kingdom. He sought a confederacy with King Jehoshaphat of Judah to aid him in the invasion. Ahab told Jehoshaphat, "Everything the king of Syria has is ours for the taking." Jehoshaphat was not convinced. He wanted a confirmation from Yahuah, so he asked for prophets to prophesy to him. Ahab said there was one other prophet they could ask. His name was Micaiah, but King Ahab didn't like him because he never prophesied anything good. Ahab preferred the agreeable smooth sayings from Jezebel's prophets. In spite of the fact that Micaiah was the "unliked" prophet, he listened and obeyed the Lord and God of Israel, Yahuah.

"Then the king of Israel gathered the prophets together, about four hundred men, and said to them, 'shall I go to battle against Ramoth-gilead, or shall I refrain?' And they said, 'Go up, for the Lord will give it into the hand of the king'" (1 Kings 22: 6, ESV). But he didn't say which king.

Ahab ignored the prophecy of Micaiah and followed the prophets of Jezebel. His army was defeated, and he lost his life (1 Kings 22:37). Self-will, pride, idolatry, and covetousness were the sins of Ahab. He followed the advice of false prophets because he liked what they said, which got him killed. What the Lord did was put "lying spirits" into the false prophets of Jezebel and Ahab. He wanted to confuse them for their disobedience, for choosing to follow false prophets and not listening to God. The Lord continues to do the same today in churches, temples, and New Age circles. People will pay to listen to what they want to hear but will continue to reject what they don't want to hear, in spite of it being the truth.

The spirits of Jezebel and Ashtoreth, who is a fallen angel, are still alive today, as are many other fallen angels, which I will discuss later in this book in more detail. The fallen angels are the demonic influences which are plaguing the New Age field with a vengeance. They are seducing so many people left and right by enticing them with a plethora of channellings and stories about ascension, space brothers, and disinformation about who we are, who they are, and where they come from. Yes, these beings are real, but they are not of the "light," as they pretend to be. There are so many people who would prefer to believe their fluffy, feel good, love and light prophesies, than the real truth. Hence, the New Age dilemma.

> "I wondered if I might not be in the grip of demons, if they were not making me suffer for their own purposes, or simply for their enjoyment."
> ~ Whitley Strieber, *Transformation*, p. 172

In today's Christian churches, the Jezebel spirit will always be found close to someone who carries the ELIJAH spirit, which is also known as the Elijah Mantel. These are the true prophets of Yahuah, the anointed ones. Messianic Jews who the Lord raises up and anoints to fulfil the great commission, are always attacked by those who carry the Jezebel spirit. This is rooted in a spirit of jealousy towards them, because of their popularity and their 'fruits', which are leading thousands of both Jews and Gentiles into the Kingdom through Yeshua. This is an important spiritual discernment, when you see Christians who marginalize Messianic Jews. They are clearly threatened by their knowledge and their anointing. This is the Jezebel spirit working through them to suppress the spirit of God. The *religious spirit* can work in partnership with the Jezebel spirit, which is a controlling dominating and manipulative spirit, which can be deadly. This spirit networks together with witchcraft, which is all about control, and is always the spirit behind controllers.

> "Religion is regarded by the common people as true, by the wise as false, and by the rulers as useful."
>
> (Seneca 4BC-65AD)

Remember from Book One of *Who's Who In The Cosmic Zoo*, pp.362-381, I went over the prime objective of the demonic *religious spirit*, (mindset) which is to have the church "maintain an outward from of Godliness", while denying the power of the Holy Spirit. When the Holy Spirit moves through anointed leaders, they deny Him with a spirit of unbelief, arrogance and haughtiness. This is why the body of Christ, is so disconnected through the spirit of strife. Christians do not seek deliverance from these spirits, nor are most of them even aware of the battle they face with them.

> "But know this, that in the last days perilous times will come: For men will be lovers of themselves, lovers of money, boasters, proud, blasphemers, disobedient to parents, unthankful, unholy, unloving, unforgiving, slanderers, without self-control, brutal, despisers of good, traitors, headstrong, haughty, lovers of pleasure rather than lovers of God, *having a form of godliness but denying its power*. And from such people turn away!"
>
> (2 Timothy 3:1-5)

So how does one *discern* and recognize religious spirits? Religious spirits tend to persecute others, usually the true believers, which is all done in the name of God. They criticize others constantly, and manipulate others in joining them. They are controlling, legalistic, and rigid. They are unforgiving. They have the accusing spirit, as I called out in Book One, as one of the seven principalities of Satan. The religious spirit is a murdering spirit, it is sent from the satans, to steal, kill and destroy God energy within humans.

> "For we war not against flesh and blood, but against powers, *principalities*, rulers of the darkness of this present world, and spiritual wickedness in the heavens."
>
> (Ephesians 6:12)

CHAPTER SEVEN: Discernment Of Gods, Angels & Demons

The seven principalities of satan's personality and spirit are: 1. Accusing Spirits (the blame game, critical spirits), 2. Bitterness (Anger, Unforgiveness, Unloving Spirits, murder), 3. Self-loathing, self-pity (suicide), 4. Jealousy (murder), 5. Rejection (that includes rejection of others, and being rejected), 6. Fear (all types of paranoia, anxiety, neurosis), 7. Occult (witchcraft, false beliefs, religious spirits, cults, phamakia which is Greek for sorcery). All of humanity's emotional, psychological and medical problems stem from these Archetypal Demon Spirits, which rules over lesser demons, which each of these represent.

Lies create mental illnesses. Lies create confusion. Lies create betrayals. Lies create heartbreak. When choose to hold onto the lies they've been told and choose to believe, because it's more comfortable than the truth, this becomes the spiritual legal ground justification for the entry of demons. Demons cause illness, both mental and physical. All illness originates in the spirit, then the mind, and finally manifests into the body.

When the spirit of error is repented of, i.e., sins, iniquities, transgressions, the spirit of Grace is poured out on those who repent to the Lord, the Holy Spirit, which is the deposit left for the Kingdom of Christ, then moves miracles in that person's life. Forgiveness creates miracles. When people repent, they receive forgiveness. Forgiveness of sins leads to healings. In most cases, healing is a gradual miracle.

Religious spirits war against the supernatural miracle working power of the Holy Spirit to perform miracle healings, raising the dead, both spiritually and physically, and deliverance of demons. There is so much puffed up pride, which is self-righteousness, which comes from the spirit of pride, not from God, because they have no real personal *relationship* with God, just a religious agenda they want followed, with them in control. This is not limited to atheism, which too, has a *religious* agenda, to exclude God from life, and replace it with secularism and science. All of these spirits are rooted in the spirit of unbelief, which is the haughty spirit. This spirit then produces and networks with the spirit of mockery, towards all that they do not understand, or are simply ignorant of. They are afraid, (the spirit of fear), of what they don't know, and therefore reject it as heresy, because of pride steals the *teachable spirit* from them, which comes from humility and humbleness, the exact opposite spirit to pride.

As you can glean from my words, you can see what the *twisted serpent* looks like, and acts like, when it has its tentacles into humans. These evil spirits are the root causes of each and every human problem. From wars to illness.

The Leviathan spirit mentioned in Job 41 is actually a major ruler of the darkness of this present world, listed in Ephesians 6:12. While Job 41 describes a giant dragon serpent that lives inside the earth, this 'being' generates spirits, and lesser serpents that emanate from this chief demon spirit. This is how the spirit realm is classified.

As I proved in Book One of *Who's Who In The Cosmic Zoo?*, that the kingdom of darkness is run as a hierarchy, which is likened to the compartmentalization of the military. This hierarchy includes, Fallen Angels, i.e., aliens, demons (Grays) and evil spirits. Similar, all on the same side of evil, but in terms of *discernment* they play individual roles, and can also be measured by the strength of their influences on human minds and spirits. Suffice it to say, it is safe to call them demons or evil spirits, but sometimes, casting out a 'spirit' is not enough to deliver a person from their powers, the 'stronghold' must be defeated that holds the spirits in place.

The Leviathan spirit is held in place through pride, but its chief purpose is to twist the truth, create miscommunications, misunderstandings and strife. It's the homewrecking spirit, because it's behind perfectly good and happy marriages which end in divorce, because the husband and wife can't repent of pride. The only way to defeat this evil spirit, is through humility in Christ. This is the spiritual battle. Evil must be defeated through Good. The stronghold of Pride is brought down through humbling. This is why the scriptures says, 'Pride cometh before the fall." (Proverbs 16:18)

When humans are able to calm down and cultivate a contrite spirit, the Holy Spirit can take over and win the battle. I am not suggesting that people need to repent to their abusers, what I am saying, is that people need to repent to God. When this happens, battles resolve supernaturally.

Leviathan orders lesser demons to cause religious spirits to infiltrate churches, temples, mosques, and all new age cults. The religious spirit influences people to become suspicious of every move of the Holy Spirit. They watch, they even study, but they do not believe it. The spread doubt. They adopt the attitude, that if God didn't do it before, according to their limited understanding of what happened in the past, then God cannot do it again. They claim God is not allowed to do anything they don't understand. They put God in a box, creating all kinds of limiting beliefs within their minds and spread lies through their rhetoric, for out of the abundance of the heart, the mouth speaks. (Matthew 12:34)

Those heavily burdened by religious spirits, forget that the devil copies God. The Lord God Yahuah *never* copies the satans. These extremist types will not join any group outside of theirs, and will reject you for not thinking like them. They think, 'we have all the truth', which is common cultic thinking. They will defile anyone who is not like them. This is their agenda and the characteristics of demonic religious spirits, which seek to destroy people's faith of the true Living God who is the spirit of Love and Grace.

DISCERNING THE SPIRITS

There are six types of demonic pneuma spirits that are mentioned in the New Testament. All of them were cast out by Jesus; they are called Demonic (which is a Greek word that means, "intelligences") Pneuma (is Greek for 'Breath' or 'spirit') Spirits:
1. *Pneuma poneron*, an evil spirit. "And the evil spirit answered and said, Jesus I know, and Paul I know; but who are you." (Acts 19:15, KJV)
2. *Pneuma python*, a python spirit or spirit of divination. "And it came to pass, as we went to prayer, a certain damsel possessed with a spirit of divination met us, which brought her masters much gain by soothsaying…" (Acts 16:16, KJV)

CHAPTER SEVEN: Discernment Of Gods, Angels & Demons

3. *Pneumata plana*, a seducing spirit or spirit of error. "Now the Spirit speaks expressly, that in the latter times some shall depart from the faith, giving heed to <u>deceitful spirits</u>, and doctrines of demons…" (1 Timothy 4:1, KJ2000)
4. *Pneuma astheneias*, the spirit of infirmity. "And, behold, there was a woman which had a spirit of infirmity eighteen years, and was bowed together, and could in no wise lift up herself." (Luke 13:11, KJV)
5. *Pneuma alalon*, a dumb spirit, one without speech. "And one of the multitude answered and said, Master, I have brought unto thee my son, which hath a dumb spirit." (Mark 9:17, KJV)
6. *Pneuma akathartos*, an unclean spirit. "And there was in their synagogue a man with an unclean spirit; and he cried out." (Mark 1:23, KJV)

I remember when I started waking up to all of this when I joined ISCNI (Institute for Study of Contact with "Non-Human Intelligences"), back in 1994, ("non-human intelligences" are also known as "demons"), their motto was the "temporary suspension of unbelief" in order to enter into a discussion about aliens and abduction stories. ISCNI was during the early stages of Internet groups, and it was at a time of my life, when I used to see grey aliens all the time.

I saw them coming through my computer screen while awake and, in my dreams, shape-shifting as my stepmother and stepsisters, tormenting me, telling me in my ear and via telepathy that if anyone asks you who your guides are, tell them you're with the Pleaidians. I just never bought into that completely, something never felt right or complete in my gut about that.

So I began to research, investigate, and twenty five years later, I am finally ready to share my research with the public. I later realized that they were using the term "Pleaidians" as a cover, because at the time *Bringers of the Dawn* was a popular New Age best seller, channeled by Barbara Marciniak, and everyone thought, the Pleaidians are "light beings" so let's all follow them. However, the gray aliens have the ability to masquerade as angels of light. "And no wonder, for Satan himself masquerades as an angel of light." (2 Corinthians 11:14, NIV) And there are many "experiencers" as well as New Agers that have been fooled by them.

Firstly, the Pleiades is a very big place; it is known as the seven sisters, because of its star formation, but in actuality there are hundreds of stars, which we cannot see. Even so, that many stars would have dozens of planetary systems, and when someone says, "I'm from the Pleiades," it's like having someone tell you that they're from America. The United States has fifty states, all different, not all united, and certainly not all Americans are the same. In fact the United States is known for its diversity. So why would a Pleaidian be any different? How can we discern if a being is really who he or she say he or she is? If they whisper something in your ear, why readily accept it, without any test or ID? Today, you can't even ask a question on your bank account without going through a series of questions to validate your identity. Shouldn't we, as earth humans, accept the same vetting process when it comes to ETs, aliens, gods, and angels?

From the early 1990s, we were given channelers who claim to be channeling the Pleaidians. One of the most famous UFO sightings case happened in Switzerland in the 1970s with Billy Myer who was visited by a blond woman who claimed she was a Pleaidian. She told him her name was *Semjaze*. Yet, isn't it a coincidence that *Semjaze* is one of the fallen angels named in the Book of Enoch that was bound to the earth? Not just any fallen angel. In fact, *Semjaze* was the highest ranking fallen angel, a commander and a chief of the two hundred fallen angels (Bene HaElohim) (1 Enoch 9:7).

Humans are so vulnerable to being duped; we have been lied to about our true history; plus so many religions have gotten in the way of telling us the truth. As a result, humans lack the foundation and the information to discern entities. If an alien appears before you who obviously has more advanced technology than anything you've ever seen or imagined, even the technology to appear as a spiritual being, and that alien tells you he or she is from the Pleiades or any other place for that matter, why don't humans question that alien?

Do we say, "Aw, I don't think so. Prove it. Show me your papers?" Most humans are so mesmerized and hypnotized by the encounter, they don't know what questions to ask, let alone what to think? Let's face it. Humans are not equipped to deal with aliens, as their technology and their ability to manipulate how we see them is far beyond our capabilities. Plus, we do not understand the role they play from the past and where they stand within this Cosmic Drama/Conflict between the Creator God and all the other so-called gods that we are essentially left powerless and vulnerable in the face of their many exploitations, hypnosis, hypnogoguery, and seemingly magical appearances and disappearances.

New Agers need to know that they have the right to fire their so-called spirit guides. Just because a spirit guide attaches to you doesn't mean it's got your ultimate best interest at heart. Many of them are fallen angels and demons in disguise who are working against the Creator to misguide you. Of course they will tell you lots of relevant information to get you hooked, and they will fill your head with all kinds of knowledge to keep you depending on them for answers. In fact, many of them give you psychic powers, through implantation which keeps you dependent on them, but in the end, they will inevitably deceive, betray, and leave you for dead, as you lose your precious soul to them and are held back from the coming Kingdom of Heaven because, for years, you listened to the wrong spirit guides.

There is only one person who has the power and authority over the aliens/demons/fallen angels, and that is the Lord Yahushua, also known today as Jesus Christ.

CHAPTER SEVEN: Discernment Of Gods, Angels & Demons

"Wherefore God also hath highly exalted him, and given him a name which is above every name: That at the name of Jesus every knee should bow, of things in heaven, and things in earth, <u>and things under the earth</u> And that every tongue should confess that Jesus Christ *is* Lord to the glory of God the Father.

(Philippians 2:9-11, KJV)

"For he hath put all things under his feet."

(1 Corinthians 15:27, KJV)

Here's a Discernment:
"For He (Yahuah) will command His angels concerning you to guard you in all your ways."

(Psalm 91:11, NIV)

The key here is the Lord's appointment. Angels were created *before* humans to serve God; they submit to His authority, His commands alone. They are not ordered around by humans. God's Holy Angels do not submit to other gods or human commands. God's Angels are assigned by the Lord to individuals, through their "faith" in God. History/scripture tells us that angels do not want to be worshipped; they are messengers serving the Lord and His Kingdom. I'll be going over these rules of engagement in more detail, in my chapter "Angel Protocol," which is in Book Three *Who Are the Angels?*

Suffice it to say, when you're in a personal relationship with the Creator through His Messiah and you pray directly to the Lord, your prayers are heard by His angels, who are empowered by His Holy Spirit to answer prayers. Many prayers are answered by His angels, who have the authority to do so in His name, and are specifically assigned to carry out God's will and the needs and requests of His believers, according to His will.

But when people pray directly to angels and avoid the Lord, they open a legal spiritual doorway for the counterfeit angels (i.e., fallen angels) to show up in their place because of the sin of idolatry. And you can bet your bottom dollar, they do!

There are, however, what is known as "assignments," which happens either when someone invokes a spirit through a magical ritual, ceremony, or spoken word spell on behalf of someone else, or by that same person, which causes fallen angel demons to be assigned to a particular person to hold them in some kind of bondage, torment, or to block their lives from moving forward in a number of areas. In the supernatural realm, this is known as an assignment or a curse. This is not done by angels of God, but by fallen angel demons, gray aliens (i.e., evil spirits).

These beings will hold the person in fear and anxiety, and claim "legal authority" based on either a generational sin/curse that the soul is under. The only way to break this kind of assignment is through turning to the authority and power of the Lord Jesus Christ who alone can break the generational curse through repentance for both yours and ancestral sin through the power of the blood of Christ. Jesus Christ is the only authority under heaven and Earth that these beings will submit to. This is essentially what the spiritual warfare is about over human souls.

> "I became entirely given over to extreme dread. The fear was so powerful that it seemed to make my personality completely evaporate ... 'Whitley' ceased to exist. What was left was a body and a state of raw fear so great that it swept about me like a thick, suffocating curtain, turning paralysis into a condition that seemed close to death...I died and a wild animal appeared in my place."
> ~ Whitley Strieber,[2] *Communion*

Lucifer/Satan is known as the "prince of the powers of the air." Wherein, in the past, you walked according to the course of this world, according to the prince of the power of the air, the spirit [commander of the unseen realms] that now works in the children of disobedience (Ephesians 2:2). G.H. Pember wrote in *Earth's Earliest Ages and Their Connection with Modern Spiritualism and Theosophy*:

> "[The occultist] is brought into intelligent communication with the spirits of the air, and can receive any knowledge which they possess, or any false impression they choose to impart...the demons seem permitted to do various wonders at their request."[3]

IMPOSTER ARCHANGELS

Archangel Michael is very popular. Many New Agers believe all they need to do is call on Archangel Michael to protect them from evil and negativity. New Agers rarely call on Jesus Christ, but they prefer to call on this particular prince for peace and protection. Archangel Michael is probably one of the highest ranking Archangels (Princes) that the Bible tells us is put in charge of protecting Israel. Yes, Archangel Michael does protect God's people, but those people need to first be in a covenant with God.

When you invoke Archangel Michael without belief in the Lord, a being who answers to Archangel Michael answers, but you end up getting the imposter Michael, the fallen angel. Yes, he masquerades as a light being causing the undiscerning to believe that he's real. However, this faith then becomes a type of Faustian Contract (a deal with the devil). Here's where human ignorance opens up a gateway for demons/aliens/fallen angels; when they sidestep Christ, thinking they can pray to angels, saints, and so-called ascended masters, and that's what they get, only the counterfeit thereof.

> "In the last days, many will follow the doctrines of demons."
> (1 Timothy 1:4)

CHAPTER SEVEN: Discernment Of Gods, Angels & Demons

Let's analyze the word 'demon', which comes from the Greek word 'daemon' which translates to 'intelligences', i.e., non-human intelligences, i.e., 'alien' intelligences, pretending to be extra-terrestrial intelligences, angels, ascended masters and space commanders.

Being betrayed because your desire to want to believe something or someone is true, only to be let down with the truth that they were not who you thought they were is a common experience many earth humans have experienced in their personal and business lives. Most people living today can recall that experience. We've all, at one time, been bamboozled, bought the "line," took the bait, got hooked into buying into something that later turns out to be a false path. But what about the emotional, psychological and often financial investments people put into these channels and these beings, only to find out later that they have been sorely misguided.

> "The UFO manifestations seem to be, by and large, merely minor variations of the age-old demonological phenomenon…"
>
> ~John A. Keel, *UFOs: Operation Trojan Horse* [4]

> "Why were my visitors so secretive, hiding themselves behind my consciousness. I could only conclude that they were using me and did not want me to know why…What if they were dangerous? Then I was terribly dangerous because I was playing a role in acclimatizing people to them."
>
> ~ Whitley Strieber, *Transformation* [5]

In some New Age channeling circles, it's been said that the so-called space commander Sananda is the "space" name for Jesus Christ. This is a lie. There is no written Word in any of the scriptures that supports this notion. Sananda is *not* the space name of Jesus Christ! Sananda is a derivative of Satan. He is a false Christ (i.e. antichrist) Jesus said:

> "For many will come in my name, claiming, 'I am the Messiah,' and will deceive many."
>
> (Matthew 24:5, NIV)

> "For false Christs and false prophets will appear and perform great signs and wonders, so as to lead astray, if possible, even the elect."
>
> (Matthew 24:24, ESV)

Sananda belongs to the Ashtar Command. The word *Ashtar* comes from the goddess Ashtarte or Ashtaroth, Ishtar, which is where Easter comes from. (See *Ashtarians* in Book One p.127.) [6] Ashtaroth was a fallen angel/false goddess who demanded worship in the form of eggs, cakes, and all kinds of idolatries, which many were severely punished for in the past from the Lord Yahuah in the Old Testament. This is part of the history of the Nephilim who tried to usurp God's creation (i.e. humans and animals), and the very reason for the great deluge was to wipe out all their abominations, i.e., hybrids through mating with earth women and animals. (See, "Giants, Nephilim, Annunaki" in Book One of *Who's Who In The Cosmic Zoo?*).

The Ashtar Command aka fallen angels (another deception and manipulation to lead humans astray) named their mother ships after the four main Archangels. When humans invoke Archangel Michael, Gabriel, Raphael, or Uriel (without believing in and respecting the authority of the Lord Jesus Christ) they end up contacting these fallen angels who are *masquerading* by using the names of God's Holy Angels. This is why there has been a wave of channelers who claim to channel Archangel Michael. But if you really discern their material, no two channelers say exactly the same thing, and almost all of their material is full of fluffy love and light stuff with a little bit of truth and conspiracy theories sandwiched between lies.

The love and light stuff is exactly what they know hooks humans into believing and thinking they are communicating with ascended beings and so-called extraterrestrials who supposedly love them. This is the biggest deception of all, as these fallen angels are waging war against the Most High God over humans. If they can steal as many human minds as they can away from the Creator, then they win souls for the underworld.

New Agers have this thing about calling on the "Light," which is a very vague and open term. This opens them up to deceptive forces. In healing circles, it is known that calling on white light attracts the opposite, which are vampiric spirits that drain energy. In fact, sending white light to those they feel are doing things that are dark or evil only feeds them and magnifies the bad behavior. New Agers do a lot of playing with different color light energies, but many are ignorant as to how they are being manipulated by dark forces. Remember, "And no wonder, for Satan himself masquerades as an angel of light." (2 Corinthians 11:14, NIV)

> "One theory which can no longer be taken very seriously is that UFOs are interstellar spaceships."
> ~ Arthur C. Clarke, *New York Times Book Review*, July 25, 1975

> "UFO behavior is more akin to magic than to physics as we know it... the modern UFOnauts and the demons of past days are probably identical."
> ~Dr. Pierre Guerin, FSR Vol. 25, No. 1, p. 13-14

> "The 'medical examination' to which abductees are said to be subjected, often accompanied by sadistic sexual manipulation, is reminiscent of the medieval tales of encounters with demons. It makes no sense in a sophisticated or technical framework: any intelligent being equipped with the scientific marvels that UFOs possess would be in a position to achieve any of these alleged scientific objectives in a shorter time and with fewer risks."
> ~ Dr. Jacques Vallée, *Confrontations*[7]

CHAPTER SEVEN: Discernment Of Gods, Angels & Demons

"I felt an absolutely indescribable sense of menace. It was hell on earth to be there [in the presence of the entities], and yet I couldn't move, couldn't cry out, couldn't get away. I'd lay as still as death, suffering inner agonies. Whatever was there seemed so monstrously ugly, so filthy and dark and sinister. Of course they were demons. They had to be. And they were here and I couldn't get away."

~ Whitley Strieber, *Transformation*[8]

Without discernment from the Lord of Lords, New Agers and many Ufologists are being misled, albeit on a path of deception that is leading them away from the very thing they desire, to be part of the 5th dimension, which is the coming Kingdom of Heaven governed by the Kingdom of God on earth. But how can anyone be given entry into the Kingdom of Heaven when they have rejected the King of the Kingdom?

THE CHRISTIAN DILEMMA

"There are those who *rebel* against the light, who do not know its ways or stay in its paths."

(Job 24:13, NIV)

"I Am the Light of the World."

(John 8:12, NIV)

"I have come into the world as a light, so that whoever believes in me may not remain in darkness."

(John 12:46, ESV)

Besides New Agers being misled by the lying wonders of the fallen extraterrestrials and Satan's hierarchy, Christians are also not immune to these deceptions. And as the scripture warns that many of these deceptions will deceive even the elect (Mathew 24:24).

What about spiritual witchcraft in the church? Witchcraft is a form of mind control; only, it is done through the intervention of demonic spirits. According to the Bible, all witchcraft falls into the same category, which is considered rebellion to the Lord. Whether it's outright black masses, which is the worship of Lucifer/Satan, or what is known as white witchcraft, which is goddess oriented or the most deceptive kind, which is hidden within Christian churches, which comes from the leadership's desire for control and their self-centered ego drives, in the form of stubbornness, and the attachment of the *religious spirit*. This makes it a perfect spiritual "legal" opportunity for the demonic to piggy back on these pastors through their own weaknesses and create a space of spiritual witchcraft to control the rest of the members of the church. This crosses all denominations, as these demonic spirits are no respecter of churches.

> "For *rebellion* is as the sin of witchcraft (divination), and stubbornness (insubordination) is as iniquity and idolatry..."
>
> (1 Samuel 15:23, KJV)

> "Do not practice divination or sorcery."
>
> (Deuteronomy 18:10)

> "The nations you will dispossess listen to those who practice sorcery or divination. But as for you, the LORD (Yahuah) your God has not permitted you to do so."
>
> (Deuteronomy 18:14, NIV)

The definition of witchcraft: Wanting to be a spiritual "mover and shaker" without submitting to God, but following spirits, demonic influences, and false gods. Believing in Satan's so-called "secrets," otherwise known as occult. Witchcraft is rebellion coupled with a desire to "stay in the game," by being a spiritual player.

"You belong to your father, the devil, and you want to carry out your father's desire... When he lies, he speaks his native language, for he is a liar and the father of lies. Yet because I tell the truth, you do not believe me!" (John 8:44-45, NIV)

On earth, all supernatural power comes, ultimately, from either God or Satan. God gives power to those who believe the truth. To approach God, truth is the cost of entry. But it is the opposite with Satan, whose very nature is deception. Satan gives power to those who believe the lie. Believing the lie is the cost of entry to access Satan's power. Witchcraft bolsters up the lie with mystery, pseudo-science, ancient knowledge, New Age knowledge, and the promise of power over others. The more absurd the lie, the better. The lie acts as a distracter. Is witchcraft real? Yes, most definitely.

Even though Satan is usually the furthest thing from most people's mind, the "father of lies" honors the self-delusion inherent in witchcraft by occasionally releasing power, through the employ of demon spirits who can perform supernatural miracles for those who have rebelled against God and yet still want to be spiritually effective. By this means, *real* power can be exerted to achieve health, beauty, enchantment, supernatural sensitivity, "insight" through drugs and experiences, oracles and visions, and the like.

When you dabble, you are empowered to believe through the demons released (i.e., "spirit guides"). This is also known as trafficking. It's all spiritually legal, if you're in rebellion toward the Lord. Remember, Lucifer started the rebellion, so he and all of his demonic fallen angels need is your willingness to rebel against the authority of the Creator Lord as well, and — Bingo! — They are there with you, empowering you, and making you believers of their deceptions and manipulations of the paranormal. This goes for Christians and non-Christians alike.

CHAPTER SEVEN: Discernment Of Gods, Angels & Demons

SYMPTOMS OF TRAFFICKING

When someone is under the spell of trafficking or witchcraft, he becomes increasingly disoriented or confused; he might even become clumsy. Satan wants to cloud your vision, thus stopping you from reaching your destiny in God. The individual under attack cannot connect with his spiritual vision; his motivation is either gone or lacking.

When one is targeted by curses, he will feel emotionally drained or debilitated. Those who have been the object of spiritual curses will carry a darkness, a cloud, in their countenance. The back of their neck is tight; a band of oppression forms around their head and manifests as a headache. The person might assume he is sick, but it is not the flu. It is witchcraft.

Often the curses released from witchcraft and trafficking will arouse a number of inordinate fears that plague the mind. The theater of the individual's imagination will be targeted: at center stage, grotesque images will flash across the mind. The individual will be further drained by lack of deep or restful sleep.

When curses are aimed at a congregation, interchurch relationships will experience constant problems, distracting the body of Christ from its primary focus and calling. Irritation levels will be high, and patience will be low. People will be more likely to complain about one another. Gossip and backbiting will increase disproportionately. Rebellion against church leaders will seem justified, and the temptation to withdraw from fellowship will be strong. These are the spiritual forces behind the apostasy, or falling away.

We need to discern for ourselves spiritually and ask, do we trust in God or in our favorite "distracter"? Will we follow the counterfeit's seductive siren song to spiritual power and become His possession, or will we follow the Holy Spirit into truth?

Some simple questions to ask in discerning witchcraft: Is it based on the truth or an outright lie? Is it the "power of suggestion" or God's power? Are we blind in not seeing how similar it is to traditional witchcraft? Is it born out of waiting upon the Lord in faith or out of impatience? Who is in control? Who gets the glory? In whom, or in what, are we trusting?

> "And they caused their sons and their daughters to pass through the fire, and used divination and enchantments, and sold themselves to do evil in the sight of the LORD, to provoke him to anger."
>
> (2 Kings 17:17, KJV)

> "Christianity is so entangled with the world that millions never guess how radically they have missed the New Testament pattern. Compromise is everywhere. The world is whitewashed just enough to pass inspection by blind men posing as believers..."
>
> ~A.W. Tozer

THE COUNTERFEIT SPIRIT

While some are deeply entrenched in witchcraft under a "Christian" banner, others see through this and are so disgusted that they are suspicious of the real gifts of the Holy Spirit. We need to be careful not to be spiritual prostitutes or to become so polarized that we become spiritually frigid.

> "Who is wise? Let them realize these things. Who is discerning? Let them understand. The ways of the Lord are right; the righteous walk in them, but *the rebellious* stumble in them."
>
> (Hosea 14:9, NIV)

What about the gift of speaking in tongues? There are denominations in Christian churches, known as Pentecostal Churches or Charismatic Churches, where they encourage and believe in speaking in tongues. Can this gift be counterfeited by the Dark Angel? Apparently so.

What does the Scripture say about speaking in tongues? Are these tongues discernable languages? Or just gibberish? What was the purpose of Pentecost when the Holy Ghost filled the believers with the ability to speak in other tongues?

> "And suddenly there came a sound from heaven as of a rushing mighty wind, and it filled all the house where they were sitting. "And there appeared unto them cloven tongues like as of fire, and it sat upon each of them. "And they were all filled with the Holy Ghost, and began to speak with other tongues, as the Spirit gave them utterance."
>
> (Acts 2:2-4, KJV)

> "And these signs shall follow them that believe; in my name shall they cast out devils; they shall speak with new tongues; "They shall take up serpents; and if they drink any deadly thing, it shall not hurt them; they shall lay hands on the sick, and they shall recover…
>
> "And they went forth, and preached everywhere, the Lord working with them, and confirming the word with signs following. Amen."
>
> (Mark 16:17, 18, 20, KJ2000)

The purpose of speaking in other tongues was so that they could go out to other cultures and nations and be the spokesperson for God to speak to them in their own language. These were actual languages that were known to man.

> "And when the day of Pentecost was fully come, they were all with one accord in one place. And suddenly there came a sound from heaven as of a rushing mighty wind, and it filled all the house where they were sitting. And there appeared unto

them **cloven tongues like as of fire**, and it sat upon each of them. And they were **all filled with the Holy Ghost**, and began to speak with other tongues, as the Spirit gave them utterance. And there were dwelling at Jerusalem Jews, devout men, out of **every nation under heaven**. Now when this was noised abroad, the multitude came together, and were confounded, because **every man heard them speak in his own language**.

And they were all amazed and marveled, saying one to another, Behold, are not all these which speak **Galileans**? And how hear we **every man in our own tongue**, wherein we were born? Parthians, and Medes, and Elamites, and the dwellers in Mesopotamia, and in Judea, and Cappadocia, in Pontus, and Asia, Phrygia, and Pamphylia, in Egypt, and in the parts of Libya about Cyrene, and strangers of Rome, Jews and proselytes, Cretes and Arabians, **we do hear them speak in our tongues the wonderful works of God**."

(Acts 2:1-11, KJV)

Notice that the tongues of fire that sat upon each of them was **cloven**. Cloven tongues would symbolize the **ability to speak in more than one tongue or language.**[1]

In Acts 2:6, it says: "Every man heard them speak in his own language." This shows they spoke a **known** language, **not an unknown tongue**. Acts 2:5-11 tells us that every nation under heaven was represented there at Jerusalem at that time. The disciples were Galileans (Acts 2:7) and couldn't speak other languages. The Lord performed a miracle by pouring out His Holy Spirit to enable them to speak in other languages so as to present the good news message to the whole world.

The Holy Spirit, assuming the form of "tongues of fire," rested upon those assembled. This was a gift bestowed on the disciples, which enabled them to fluently speak languages they had not known or ever been acquainted with. The disciples were told to preach among other nations, and they would receive power to speak other tongues. The Holy Spirit did for them that which they could not have accomplished for themselves in a lifetime. They were able to proclaim the truths of the gospel abroad, speaking with accuracy the languages of those for whom they were encountering. This was the gift of speaking of tongues.

THE LANGUAGE OF ANGELS OR FALLEN ANGELS?

The difference today, in many churches, is that believers mistakenly believe that the gift of speaking in tongues is to have some "secret prayer language" that really amounts to gibberish, that some believe is the language of angels. Angels? Or Fallen Angels? They are taken over by a spirit, who they believe is the Holy Spirit, but nobody, including themselves, can discern or understand their language or gibberish. They pray this indiscernible gibberish over people when they lay hands on them, and unbeknownst to them, they are the messengers of spiritual witchcraft within the church.

They mistakenly believe they have the "anointing" of the Holy Spirit when, in reality, they are the vehicles of a counterfeit spirit that is there to sabotage the works of the Lord within the body of believers. This creates a "cult" environment because the *religious spirit* accompanies it which holds this counterfeit spirit in place, along with the strongholds of pride and stubbornness, which also piggy backs on the spirit of unbelief, which always has the ***deaf and dumb spirit*** attached to it as well. Yet when anyone points this out to them, they deny it fervently in disbelief, and one may even be accused of blaspheming the Holy Spirit, but the truth of the matter is that it is ***not*** the Holy Spirit producing this form of gibberish, so the Holy Spirit cannot be blasphemed.

"Where the spirit of the Lord is, there is Freedom."

(2 Corinthians 3:17, HCS)

"By their fruit, you will recognize them."

(Matthew 7:16, 20, NIV)

What fruits do these counterfeit tongues product? Illness, conflict, accidents, and even divorce. How can it be the Holy Spirit then, if people speaking in unknown tongues produce the fruits of death and destruction? The Holy Spirit is all about the *dunamis* power, which is the resurrecting power of the Lord Jesus Christ, the fruits of which are deliverance, healing, wholeness, power and life.

When you confront these types of tongue-speaking Christians, they not only deny it, but they typically fear addressing Satan and are so afraid of him, that they refuse to even say the name Satan, but instead just refer to him as "the enemy." Fear is not a fruit of the Holy Spirit.

"For God has not given us the spirit of fear, but of power, and of love and of a sound mind."

(2 Timothy 1:17, KJ2000)

No true spirit-filled church can ignore the power that accompanies the Holy Spirit which is to cast out demons, do spiritual warfare, heal the sick, and anoint with power from heaven above. Confronting Satan is not only a command, but a God-given authority to bind and loose anything on earth that will be done in heaven. (Matthew 16:19; 18:18)

It is interesting to note and oddly coincidental, that one of the primary manifestations of demonic possession (listed in books on exorcisms by the Catholic Church) is the presence of speaking in foreign languages.

"For false Christs and false prophets will appear and perform great signs and wonders, so as to lead astray, if possible, even the elect."

(Mathew 24:24, ESV)

CHAPTER SEVEN: Discernment Of Gods, Angels & Demons

There is little difference between those who "channel" false prophets, (i.e. fallen angel demons, counterfeit spirits) in the New Age circles or in the Christian churches, and they are all being sabotaged by the same source. In the New Age, people call it "channeling." They may make all kinds of sounds and groans along with speaking in other accents, which to most people sounds like an actor putting on a voice. Many who speak in tongues in charismatic churches sound like it is "put on" or faked for the purpose of a "show," which again is the *religious spirit* at work. (See, my chapters on the Religious Spirit in Book One, and UFO Religions in Book Three – *Who Are the Angels?* for more information.)

What is prophesied to come in the last days of these end times, are the people of God, i.e., the redeemed, awakened and repentant souls, will be alive on the earth when celestial glory and a repetition of the persecutions of the past are blended. Angels will be in constant communication between heaven and earth. Angels are messengers of the Kingdom of Heaven, these are God's extraterrestrial messengers, guardians and warriors who have access to move back and forth between heaven and earth.

Meanwhile, satan, who is surrounded by evil angels, aliens and demons, will claim to be God. He will work miracles of all kinds, to deceive, if possible, the very elect. (Matthew 24:24) The battle between good and evil will manifest in the end times, where God's people will not find their safety in working miracles through Christ, for Satan will counterfeit the miracles that will be manifested. Ephesians 6:12, which describes what many believers think is just a 'spiritual battle', will manifest on earth, through alien technologies that will deceive even the elect.

This is exactly what the end-time mass deception will be about, people will emerge pretending to be Christ Himself, and claiming the title while stealing worship, which belongs to the world's Redeemer. They will perform miracles of healing and will profess to have revelations from heaven contradicting the testimony of the Scriptures. This is already taking place in multiple New Age circles.

As the crowning act in this great drama of deception, Satan himself will personate Christ. He will counterfeit the life of Yeshua, deceive the Jews and only one quarter of the world. The, rest of the world will oppose this final Antichrist, which the Bible calls the Great Tribulation, aka the time of Jacob's Troubles. This messiah figure will appear to show up on the timeline as an economic genius, and step in to save a failing global economy from World War Three. He is prophesied to rescue Israel from her enemies with a Seven Year Peace Treaty that will last only three and one half years, then all hell breaks loose on Jews, Christians and all those who fight against this alien-transhuman, Messiah figure.

This is the strong delusion that is prophesied in the book of Daniel. Only the second coming of the true Yeshua/Jesus Christ will defeat this final deceiver at the final battle of Armageddon, which takes place over the ancient space portal of Jerusalem.

"For the day is near, the day of the LORD is near-- a day of *clouds*, a time of doom for the nations."

(Ezekiel 30:30

"When I snuff you out, I will cover the heavens and darken their stars; I will cover the sun with a ***cloud***, and the moon will not give its light."

(Ezekiel 32:7)

This scripture is NOT talking about rain clouds. This is a different type of celestial event.

"Alas for that day! For the day of the LORD (Yahuah) is near; it will come like destruction from the Almighty."

(Joel 1:15)

"I will display wonders in the sky and on the earth, Blood, fire and columns of smoke. The sun will be turned into darkness and the moon into blood before the great and awesome day of the LORD (Yahuah) comes. And it will come about that whoever calls on the *name* of the LORD (Yahuah) will be delivered;"

(Joel 2:30-32)

"The day of the LORD is near for all nations. As you have done, it will be done to you; your deeds will return upon your own head."

(Obadiah 1:15)

"The great day of the LORD is near-- near and coming quickly. The cry on the day of the LORD is bitter; *the Mighty Warrior* shouts his battle cry."

(Zephaniah 1:14)

CHAPTER SEVEN: Discernment Of Gods, Angels & Demons

NOTES:

1. Dr. Jacques Vallee citing the extensive research of Bertrand Meheust [*Science-Fiction et Soucoupes Volantes* (Paris, 1978); *Soucoupes Volantes et Folklore* (Paris, 1985)], in *Confrontations*, p. 146, 159-161
2. Whitley Strieber, *Communion: A True Story,* Beech Tree Books, New York; First Edition (1987)
3. G.H. Pember, *Earth's Earliest Ages and Their Connection with Modern Spiritualism, Theosophy and Buddhism*: Kregel Publications; 3rd edition (1982) (1605)
4. John A. Keel, *Why UFOs: Operation Trojan Horse,* Manor Books (1976)
5. Whitley Strieber, *Transformation: The Breakthrough,* Beech; First Edition (1988)
6. Ella LeBain, Book One *Who's Who in the Cosmic Zoo of Aliens and ETs, Third Edition,* pp.127-133. Tate Publishing, 2013
7. Dr. Jacques Vallée, *Confrontations: A Scientists Search For Alien Contact*, Anomalist Books (January 2, 2008)
8. Whitley Strieber, *Transformation: The Breakthrough,* Beech; First Edition (1988)

CHAPTER EIGHT

WHO ARE THE GODS?

"I saw gods ascending out of the earth."
(1 Samuel 28:13, KJV)

"The LORD will be terrible to them:
For <u>He will famish all the gods of the earth</u>;
And men shall worship Him,
Everyone from his place, even all the coasts of the nations."
(Zephaniah 2:11, KJ2000)

"The Lord of hosts, the God of Israel, says: Behold,
<u>I will punish ... the gods.</u>"
(Jeremiah 46:25, KJ2000)

"In that day, <u>the LORD will punish the gods in the heavens
And the proud rulers of the nations on earth</u>.
They will be herded together like prisoners bound in a dungeon;
They will be shut up in prison and be punished after many days."
(Isaiah 24:21-22, NIV)

"You shall have no other gods before Me."
(The First of the 10 Commandments)
(Exodus 20:3; Deuteronomy 5:7, NIV)

Famish all the gods? That means he'll starve them of their power, which they originally got from Him. Punish the gods? What did they do? So just "who" are these ancient gods that the Almighty Creator Lord will cut off? And why? Before we begin on this journey of discernment, it's important to note, that there are gods with a small "g" and the Almighty God (the one with the big 'G') who has the power to punish the lesser gods with a small "g."

"For all the gods of the peoples are idols; but the Lord (Yahuah) made the Heavens."

(Psalm 96:5, KJV)

Lies create mental illness, whether it's believing in one's own lies they tell themselves to stay in their comfort levels or believing in the lies told to them by their family, church, or temple. Satan is the still the father of all lies and his finger pokes around every pie. Whether its false gods creating false religions which creates false belief systems, they are nevertheless all based on the distortion and often the perversion of the truth. Even if the truth is sandwiched between two lies, they are still lies.

This is why it's been said that a lie can travel halfway around the world before the truth gets its boots on. Hitler was known for saying, "If you repeat a lie often enough, people will believe it as truth." Hypnosis using lies, false information, becomes believed as truth, no matter what you try to tell people otherwise. This is how a mass deception takes place.

There are those who believe in God but don't really know "WHO" He is. Others claim there is no god only because their perception is distorted due to spiritual blindness because what they are really saying is "I don't know God."

Then there are those who are convinced "they" are God. While we are all made in the "image and likeness" of the gods (Elohim), we hold within our DNA "god sparks," but not everyone who thinks they are god lives "godly" lives. In fact, many who are convinced they are god have made "ungodly" soul ties to the fallen "sons" of heaven who were all brought down from following Lucifer/Heylel into his rebellion against the Creator "God of gods" and His faithful Son and Messiah of the Heavens and the Earth. The fallen sons were extraterrestrials to planet Earth. They still are.

First, let's take a look at the ancient relationship between the gods and the Creator Lord. The Old Testament is essentially one long cosmic drama between the Creator and his disappointment with the fallen sons, the Nephilim they created and the gods that exalted themselves and entered into Faustian contracts with Lucifer/Satan upon the earth. These fallen extraterrestrial angels all had god complexes, and they thrived on getting humans to worship them. They masqueraded as being bigger gods than they actually were, but they often fell short in their ability to save humankind when being prayed to and given offerings. They did succeed in deceiving most earth humans of their power and in manipulating earth humans to sacrifice to them and in holding earth humans as slaves while keeping them in bondage to all forms of religious practices.

> "Who is like you, O Lord (Yahuah), <u>among the gods</u>? Who is like you, majestic in holiness, awesome in glorious deeds, doing wonders?"
>
> (Exodus 15:11, ESV)

Erich von Däniken, the grandfather of the ancient astronaut theory, writes in his ground breaking bestseller, *Chariots of the Gods?*:

> "While the spaceship disappears again into the mists of the universe our friends will talk about the miracle—" The gods were here!" ...they will make a record of what happened: uncanny, weird, and miraculous. Then their texts will relate — and drawings will show—that gods in golden clothes were there in a flying boat that landed with a tremendous din. They will write about chariots which the gods drove

CHAPTER EIGHT: Who Are The Gods?

over land and sea, and of terrifying weapons that were like lightning, and they will recount that the gods promised to return. They will hammer and chisel in the rock pictures of what they had seen: shapeless giants with helmets and rods on their heads, carrying boxes in front of their chests; balls on which indefinable beings sit and ride through the air; staves from which rays are shot out as if from a sun."[1]

Von Däniken[1] has said that his first book, *Chariots of the Gods?,* asks more questions than gives answers. Let's discern here, who these so-called gods were that were visiting and creating life forms on planet Earth.

Von Däniken talks about these gods that were depicted in various ancient hieroglyphs with alien-like appearances that were human-like creatures with the heads of lions, bulls, and falcons, which he viewed as evidence of aliens genetically modifying humans and animals to create transgenic life forms, i.e., hybrids. (See my chapters on the various types of Hybrids in Book One, of *Who's Who In The Cosmic Zoo?*)

These depictions that Von Däniken wrote about was the proof of the existence of the Nephilim who were the human/animal/alien hybrids. There have been many types of Nephilim throughout history because there has been many attempts to create super strong and super intelligent beings. The Bible scriptures, along with the *Books of Enoch*, tells us that these Nephilim were an abomination to the Almighty Creator God and were destroyed off the face of the earth more than once through floods and fire.

"I claim that our forefathers received visits from the universe in the remote past, even though I do not yet know who these extraterrestrial intelligences were or from which planet they came. I nevertheless proclaim that these "strangers" annihilated part of mankind existing at the time and produced a new, perhaps the first, Homo sapiens."[1]

Many of these experiments which were initiated by the fallen sons and fallen ETs of heaven, (i.e., the gods) are continuing today, through the alien abductions of earth humans to harvest human DNA to create a new race of Nephilim to take over the earth and replace earth humans.

There has been a race war between these gods and the Creator God since the beginning of this timeline on Earth, with the goal to intercept the coming "seed" from the Creator God to save humanity.

Thomas R. Horn[2], writes in his book, *Nephilim Stargates: The Year 2012 and the Return of the Watchers:*

"One theory says when the protoevangelium was given (promise that the seed of the woman would produce a child who would crush the serpent's head), supernatural beings, perhaps aliens or fallen angels, appeared from heaven and performed genetic alterations on human DNA to intercept, pollute, and cut off the birth line of the Messiah. As Pharaoh destroyed the Hebrew children so that the deliverer might not be born, as Herod sought baby Jesus in order to have him killed, as the dragon of Revelation 12 waits to destroy the seed of the woman as soon as it is born, so too some believe Satan wanted to stop the promised seed by sending supernatural beings to alter the human race."[2]

In fact, according to Professor I.D.E. Thomas[3] in his book, *The Omega Conspiracy: Satan's Last Assault on God's Kingdom,* Satan (as opposed to aliens) was trying to produce a race of mutant warriors to exterminate the Jewish race and, worse, to genetically alter creation from the image of God to one of Satan's own. Satan's agenda and plot to corrupt the image and likeness of God in humans continues on today through the advent of pharmaceuticals, genetically modified foods, and implant technology to completely distort and pervert the innate divine intelligence that is within human DNA. Satan is altering human DNA.

Thomas[3] postulated that this was the reason the Sumerians, who brought with them a pantheon of deities, preceded the Hebrew culture, and why subsequent religions also adopted similar ideas of powerful beings, like Zeus, Apollo, Osiris, Isis, visited Earth, and used earth women to incubate their half-human children. All of these gods were in rebellion to their Creator God and had contracted with the god of this world, Lucifer/Satan, in order to have free access to the earth to carry out these plans. This was the original "cosmic conspiracy" against humanity.

WHO ARE THE CREATOR GODS?

There are many scriptures in the Bible where "the gods" are mentioned. In fact they show up in the scriptures before Yahuah does, in Genesis 1 it is stated that the gods — the Elohim — created humans in their image. The words in the Hebrew for god, is Elohim, which is plural for "gods." The entire sentence uses the plurality possessive participles in Hebrew, in the words, "us," "our," "their," and "they."

> "Let us make man in our image, after our likeness… So the gods [Elohim] created man in their own image according to their likeness … male and female they created them."
>
> (Genesis 1:26-27)

Yahuah (YHVH) is not mentioned once in the entire Genesis story of creation. Every English Bible has the word Elohim mistranslated. It should read "the gods," not God (singular). The Hebrew is very specific as to when something is singular or plural or masculine or feminine. The word *Elohim,* is masculine plural.

This proves that the Elohim (the gods) were the original creator gods, according the Bible. Now the next question is, who are the Elohim? How many gods make up the

CHAPTER EIGHT: Who Are The Gods?

Elohim? As I've mentioned in Book One, the Elohim, also known as the ELs, are the original sons of God. I go into more detail in my next chapter, *Who Are The Biblical God(s)?*

In Genesis 2 we are introduced to Yahuah Elohim, who is not just one of the gods, but the Most High God of the Elohim. We later learn He is also called "El Elyon," which translates to God Almighty. Yahuah, being the god of the Elohim, who first created Adam and then Eve, forbids them to eat from the Tree of Knowledge of Good and Evil. After they are influenced and deceived by the serpent, they are ousted from Eden and Yahuah Elohim said: "Behold, the man (the human) has become as one of us, to know good and evil and now lest he put forth his hand and take also of the tree of life and eat and live forever." (Genesis 3:22, ASV)

After that, everyone was cursed. This declaration from Yahuah has begun the entire 5,774 year journey humanity finds itself on, which is to find the path toward salvation from the curses through the Divine Plan of Salvation through Yahshua, and the promise to eat of the Tree of Life and live forever, which is promised to all those who put their faith in Him.

When it comes to the Elohim, unfortunately there isn't any text in both Biblical and Apocryphal that tells us exactly how many Elohim (gods) there are. But we can see their character throughout the Biblical stories and how they have been mistaken for the Lord Yahuah, and even Satan himself at times, which I go into more detail about in later chapters.

The Sumerian tablets, however, have their own version of the Creation story Archeoastronomer Zecharia Sitchin, who interpreted these tablets, said these beings were known as Annunaki, and Nephilim. Their creation story, speaks of two competing brother gods named Enki and Enlil who fought over control of humans and even claimed to create humans in a test tube. As you read on, I will be connecting the dots to these so-called gods, and how they play into the entire story, and where these gods stand in relation to the Almighty and his Elohim.

IDOLATRY

"Because of your detestable idols, **I WILL PUNISH YOU LIKE I HAVE NEVER PUNISHED ANYONE BEFORE OR EVER WILL AGAIN.**"

(Ezekiel 5:9, NLT)

Throughout the history of the Bible, we learn what continues to repeat itself are the sins and consequences of idolatry. The Israelites lost their lives, their land, and even their identity because they chose to worship and sacrifice to other gods, other than Yahuah. The first commandment is very clear, and it's the first commandment for a very good reason.

"THOU SHALT HAVE NO OTHER GODS BEFORE ME."

(Exodus 20:3, KJV)

Even though the Bible is quite clear that there are other gods, it is also glaringly clear that it is wise to stick with only one of them. The command in Exodus 20:3 may even be interpreted as a "non-competition clause."

More relevant passages, such as:

"Who is like unto thee, O LORD (Yahuah), among the **gods** (BaElim)?"

(Exodus 15:11, KJV)

"Now I know that the LORD (Yahuah) is greater than all the other **gods**(HaElohim)…"

(Exodus 18:11, NIV)

"Thou shalt have no other **gods** (Elohim) before me."

(Exodus 20:3, KJV)

"Thou shalt not revile **the gods** (Elohim) or curse the ruler …"

(Exodus 22:28, KJV)

"…make no mention of the **name of other gods** (Elohim), neither let it be heard out of thy mouth."

(Exodus 23:13, KJV)

In Book One, I concluded, in my response to the Ancient Astronaut Theory, who postulate that the gods of the past, weren't actually gods at all, but extraterrestrials, which I agree with them on this fact, however, as I've stated, that while the Ancient Astronaut Theory assumes that it was our ancestors who mistook these extraterrestrials beings as gods, I, however, believe that those extraterrestrials set themselves up as 'gods' on earth, did so deliberately in order to harvest the energy from humans, whether that was 'soul' energy in the form of worship and fear, or actual blood sacrifices, which was prevalent in the ancient world all around the world in various cultures, not just the lands of the Bible. This is why I find the following scripture so interesting, from the prophet Jeremiah, who literally questions if people can make up their own gods?

"Lord, you are my strength and fortress, my refuge in the day of trouble! Nations from around the world will come to you and say, "Our ancestors left us a foolish heritage, for they worshiped worthless idols. Can people make their own gods? These are not real gods at all!"

CHAPTER EIGHT: Who Are The Gods?

"The Lord says, "Now I will show them my power; now I will show them my might. At last they will know and understand that I am the Lord.""

(Jeremiah 16:19-21)

For the benefit of my readers who enjoy revelatory research and Bible study, there is a large number of other examples in Exodus 12:12; 20:5; 22:20; 22:28; 23.24; 23:32-33 and 34:14-16, in Numbers 25:2 and 33:4, in Deuteronomy 4:28; 5:7; 6:14; 7:4; 7:16; 7.25; 8:19; 10:17; 11:16; 11:28; 12:2-3; 12:30-31; 13:2; 13:6-7; 13:13; 17:3; 18:20; 20:18; 20:26; 28:24; 28:64; 29:18; 29:26; 30:17; 31:16; 31:18; 31:20; 32:16-17 and 32:37 as well as in many more passages in Joshua, Judges, 1Samuel, 2Samuel, 1Kings, 2Kings, 1Chronicles, 2Chronicles, Ezra, Psalms, Isaiah, Jeremiah, Daniel, Hosea, Nahum und Zephaniah, obviously too many to print here.

"I will praise you, O LORD (Yahuah), with all my heart; **before the "gods" (Elohim)** I will sing your praise. I will bow down toward your holy temple and will praise your name for your love and your faithfulness, for you have exalted above all things your name and your word."

(Psalm 138:1-2)

It is blatantly obvious, that the same word used for the "gods" consistently throughout the Hebrew text is Elohim. Yet, it is often mis-translated to be GOD (singular), misleading many Bible readers to determine that these passages related to the Most High God, who is YHVH (Yahuah/El-Elyon) and not the Elohim. (For more elucidation and discernment on who are the Elohim, see chapter, *Who Are the Biblical God(s)*).

There is a difference between the Elohim and the Bene Elohim. When the Bene Elohim are mentioned in the Hebrew text, Elohim and "the sons of God" are correctly translated, "the sons of the gods." The text makes a difference between them and humans. They were definitely not humans. Genesis 6:2 and 6:4 mentions the "sons of God" in Genesis 6:2 and 6:4:

"That the sons of HaElohim (the gods) saw the daughters of men that they were fair; and they took them wives of all which they chose... There were giants/tyrants (Nephilim) in the earth in those days; and also after that, when the sons of HaElohim (the gods) came in unto the daughters of men, and they bare children to them, the same became mighty men which were of old, men of renown."

Were they half-gods? And the "giants" who were born from them, were they maybe quarter-gods? We know that the word Nephilim comes from the Hebrew root word *Naphal*, which means "to fall," a word also used to describe rejects. These beings were genetic anomalies, seen as monsters, tyrants. They were cannibals, bloodthirsty for human blood, full of lust and rebellion toward the Creator. They were cursed, and the very reason Yahuah ordered the floods to destroy all life on earth, not once but twice. (See, my section on Giants and Nephilim in Book One of *Who's Who In the Cosmic Zoo?*)

The sons of God were fallen ETs who became demonic partners with Satan. How do we know this? It is written,

> "The Sons of the gods (Bene HaElohim) came to present themselves before the Lord (Yahuah) and Satan was among them."
>
> (Job 1:6 and Job 2:1)

NOTES:

1. Von Däniken, Eric. *Chariots of the Gods?* 1968. Econ-Verlag (Germany), Putnam (USA), p. 26, p. 10
2. Thomas R. Horn, *Nephilim Stargates: The Year 2012 and the Return of the Watchers,* 2012. Defender Publishing, Crane, MO. p.25 (used with permission)
3. Professor I.D.E. Thomas, *The Omega Conspiracy: Satan's Last Assault on God's Kingdom.*

CHAPTER NINE

THE RETURN OF THE GODS

> "Then the sign of the Son of Man will appear in heaven,
> And then all the tribes of the earth will mourn,
> And they will see the Son of Man
> **Coming in the clouds** of heaven,
> With power and great glory.
> And he will send his angels with a great sound of trumpet call,
> And they will gather together his elect
> From the four winds,
> **From the ends of the heavens, to the end thereof**."
>
> (Matthew 24: 30-31, Berean)

Many are expecting the gods to return, but which gods? And why now? Are they gathering their forces for a Divine Appointment over the Earth?

It is also important to note that the return of the flying gods of mythology is a very big part of end times prophecies mentioned in the Bible. The "ancient gods" (Quetzalcoatl, Zeus, Apollo, Demeter, Osiris, Isis, Astarte, Nimrod, etc.) are viewed as going to war with the Creator God (Yahuah, the Elohim, and Jesus Christ) in the last days.

Let's also not forget, that all these ancient gods who are at war with their Creator God followed Lucifer/Satan, "that old serpent, called the Devil" (Reptilian/Draconians), who is the god of this world that led them into their rebellion. His destiny, according to Bible prophesy, is to be thrown into the Lake of Fire along with all of his army of angels.

These are the gods and goddesses of ancient Egypt, Persia, Greece, Rome, the Annunaki, the Nephilim, the Hindu gods and goddesses, all the alien gods, and the so-called ET gods that New Agers worship, invoke, and idolize. Many of these are fallen angels (rebel ETs) who have aligned with Lucifer/Satan. (See my chapter on "Contracts and Agreements" in *Covenants:* Book Four of *Who's Who In the Cosmic Zoo?*)

> "And I saw a beast rising out of the sea, with ten horns and seven heads, with ten diadems on its horns and blasphemous names on its heads. And the beast that I saw was like a leopard; its feet were like a bear's, and its mouth was like a lion's mouth. And to it the dragon gave his power and his throne and great authority. One of its heads seemed to have a mortal wound, but its mortal wound was healed, and the whole earth marveled as they followed the beast. And they worshiped the dragon, for he had given his authority to the beast, and they worshiped the beast, saying,

"Who is like the beast, and who can fight against it?" And the beast was given a mouth uttering haughty and blasphemous words, and it was allowed to exercise authority for forty-two months."

(Revelation 13:1-18)

This is why there is so much deception in these "end times," which brings us close to the end of this timeline. However, those gods and goddesses, who have repented of their rebellion and have turned back to the Creator God and have aligned themselves with the cosmic alliances of Christ, may be part of the handful of deities that are saved by the Creator in the end. There are also gods that remained faithful to the Creator in their works and good deeds toward humankind. There are references to early works that have prayers for the fallen angels of Heaven. See, Book Three: *Who Are The Angels?*

The Creator is full of Grace, and many will be saved who serve Him. Remember, the ratio is 2:1; only one-third of heaven's angels (ETs) followed Lucifer's rebellion. The other two-thirds remained faithful. The dark forces are outnumbered 2:1.

According to Horn[1], "Earliest histories from around the world speak of significant involvement by 'super intelligences' involved in the origin of the species with promises by this Creator to return someday. Secular and religious Ufologists point to the universal documentation of such history as a record of 'heavenly beings' visiting earth and engaging in a process leading to hominid creation and the first civilizations. When the Sumerians first appeared, following the event described above, they brought with them a pantheon of sky deities, the first written language, and a superior knowledge of the cosmos. Post-Sumerian myth held that powerful beings with names like 'Zeus' and 'Apollo' visited the earth, intermarried with women, and fathered half-human children."

In 1986, Christian college professor I.D.E. Thomas[2] combines this mythos with modern Ufology, claiming that a race of anti-God warriors were approaching the earth from "out there" and were bringing with them end-times delusion and Armageddon.

According to Professor I.D.E. Thomas[2], the rise in recent UFO and abduction activity may already indicate the return of the Watchers, the lesser "fallen angels," (i.e. demons), as we approach the end of the age and the coming of Armageddon. Thomas thinks that Genesis and other ancient texts are records of these fallen angels acting in accord with Satan. Horn says, we may find out sooner than we think, as unexplained phenomenon are occurring all around us and reports of "beings" moving through portals (i.e., UFOnauts) are coming in with regular frequency. Whoever or whatever these beings are, the reality of their activity can no longer be doubted.

> "More and more we are finding that mythology in general though greatly contorted very often has some historic base. And the interesting thing is that one myth, which occurs over and over again in many parts of the world, that says somewhere a long time ago supernatural beings had sexual [relations] with natural women and produced a special breed of people."
>
> ~ Francis A. Schaeffer

CHAPTER NINE: The Return of the Gods

THE HINDU GODS

Many of the Hindu gods are Nephilim. They were the result of genetic experiments that were done during the times of Atlantis, which began when the sons of God mated with earth women and produced giant offspring with supernatural powers. They didn't stop with the earth women; they mated with animals as well, which is where we get all the myths of satyrs, centaurs, flying horses, mermaids, elephant men, and all kinds of other monstrosities and genetic anomalies.

The Hindu gods' epic is found in the Vedic literatures, known as the *Vedas* and the *Mahabharata*, which tells the stories of these gods and goddesses who fought in Vimanas (space crafts), also called flying cities in the air, over the earth and over earth humans. Some valiantly battled against monsters who wanted to devour humankind. Yet others battled against each other.

There are stories of many of these gods and goddesses and how they became hybridized gods, such as Ganeesha, who is said to have battled against the dark forces. After his head was severed, the gods cured him by putting an elephant head on him, so he could continue the battle, which he won. Then there is the Hanuman, a Hindu monkey god, who was supposed to be an incarnation of the Lord Shiva. He had the head of a baboon and the body of a man.

Most of the Hindu gods are multi-armed; this is the result of the Nephilim experiments and offspring, which brought on the wrath of the Creator God and destroyed the Nephilim off the face of the earth through a great deluge, not once but twice.

Even though many of the Hindu gods are Nephilim, some have done courageous and noble deeds on behalf of humankind. They are not all aligned with Lucifer, as when the Creator God promised to impoverish the gods, many feared losing their power, as it is written "The fear of the Lord is the beginning of wisdom" (Psalm 111:10). These gods feared the Creator God and many followed Him and helped humanity.

They aligned with the office of Christ in the heavens for protection. Some of them were behind the formation of Buddhism, because they knew that Hinduism was taken over by the demonic religious spirits and the spirits of self-exaltation, which is considered rebellion to the Creator God.

> "I will praise you, O LORD, with all my heart; **before the "gods"** I will sing your praise."
>
> (Psalm 138:1)

King David knew of these other gods, but chose to stay faithful to his Lord Yahuah.

Jesus is known in India as "Issa" and, according to the Buddhist scriptures, spent seventeen years in India from the ages of 13-30. According to the Buddhist scriptures, Jesus rebuked the Brahmin priests for exalting themselves and for worshipping empty idols and fallen gods (Nephilim).[3]

Many of these Nephilim pleaded with the Creator to allow them to serve Him, so they had to perform good deeds to earth humans who turned them into gods. Some of them, however, were behind the creation of Buddhism because they needed to correct the spiritual rebellion in Hinduism. This is why, during Jesus's stay in India, he took refuge in Buddhist temples because the Hindu priests were mad at Him for rebuking them, so they plotted to kill Him.[3] However, His appointed time for death was later in Jerusalem. Jesus came to give up His life willingly at an appointed time, which is why he managed to dodge a few assassination attempts along the way.

It's important to remember that, while all this was going on, Lucifer/Satan was already developing and scheming ways to take over Buddhism and sidetrack it. Every religion has been infiltrated by his demonic fallen angel spirits and *religious spirits*. Earth is a battlefield. The spiritual battle really is fought in heavenly places just as Ephesians 6:12 says: "For our struggle is not against flesh and blood, but against the principalities (rulers, i.e., princes, archdemons), against the powers, against the world forces of this darkness, against the spiritual forces of wickedness in the heavenly places. (1st and 2nd heaven—realm of UFOs)."

Jesus was Jewish. Out of Judaism came Christianity, just as out of Hinduism, Buddhism was born. But Buddhism was derailed when Lucifer took over and called himself "Buddha" and inserted the belief system that "you are god." Buddhism, then, became the path of enlightenment which, essentially speaking, is what Lucifer is known as — the god of enlightenment. In rebellion against the Creator, nevertheless, so many fall into his spiritual web of deceit. They don't know that his agenda is to keep earth humans away from their Savior. There are many different sects of Buddhism, including the New Age form of Buddhism, which falls right into Lucifer's trap, obscuring many from the truth.

The Buddhist scriptures[3] recognize Jesus as a Saint, whom they call Bodhisattva, which is a Master. He is the Master because He is the Savior of the world and the Cosmos. Even when the Buddhists die, they go to meet their maker; they are not "god." Jesus rebuked the excessive chanting because it opens the door for demonic spirits, as do all rhythmic rituals like drumming. (Matthew 6:7). Eventually it opens a gateway through to another dimension and in comes a spirit, which many mistakenly believe to be a deceased ancestor or another deity, but actually it's a fallen angel demon. Discernment is called for here.

BUDDHA PROPHESIED JESUS

Buddhists believe that living through the eight-fold path, which is about right action, right thought, etc., essentially doing "merit," which is their way to better one's life. They know that people have sin, so each person tries to do "merit" to cover over his sins. But they know that their sins are too great.

CHAPTER NINE: The Return of the Gods

This is especially difficult on poor people because they know that, to do "merit," one needs money. The way to get money is to be a powerful person, but many powerful people steal and are not just. Often they are corrupt and abuse their power. Money received by doing sin to others is not acceptable merit money. So sin continues because no one is able to have enough merit to take away sin... unless someone is so perfect He could have enough merit for Himself and others.

It is interesting that in the Buddhist Scriptures of Cambodia, there is a prophecy regarding a "Holy One" (who) would come, one who would lead people away from the old way and introduce a new way.

> When Buddha was travelling and living in this world, there was an old Brahman priest who wore white robes who asked the Buddha, "How will all men and all Brahman continue in their merit-making so as to escape the results of sin?"
>
> The Buddha answered, "Even though all of you give alms according to the 5 precepts, the 8 precepts, the 10 precepts, or the 227 precepts for 9 trillion years and you raise your hands and offer yourselves as a burnt offering, or you pray 5 times a day, you will still not escape the results of your sins. If you do this every day, your merit gained will only be equal to the smallest strand of hair of an unborn infant extremely small. You shall not enter heaven's doors."
>
> The old Brahman priest asked further, "What are we all to do to be saved?"
>
> The Buddha answered the old Brahman priest, "The results of sin and karma are very great, heavier than the sky, thicker than the earth, and so high that it would be like an angel dusting the corner-posts of the temple compound with a cloth post that are 18 inches high dusting them one time per year - until the posts were worn down to the ground. When the posts are worn down, that's how long it would take to end your sins."
>
> The Buddha said further, "I have given up my high position and entered the priesthood. I considered that even though I am good, I would have only a very small amount of merit at the end of the year. If I was given this same amount of merit for 100,000 epochs and live 10 more lifetimes, I would not be saved from sin's results even once."
>
> The old Brahman priest asked further, "So what should we all do?"
>
> The Buddha answered, "Keep on making merit and look for another Holy One who will come and help the world and all of you in the future."
>
> Then the old Brahman priest asked, "What will the characteristics of the Holy One be like?"
>
> The Buddha answered him, "The Holy One who will keep the world in the future will be like this: in the palms of his hands and in the flat of his feet will be the design of a disc, in the side will be a stab wound; and his forehead will have many marks like scars. This Holy One will be the golden boat who will carry you over the cycle of rebirths all the way to the highest heaven (Nirvana). Do not look

for salvation the old way; there is no salvation in it for sure. Quit the old way. And there will be a new spirit like the light of a lightning bug in all of your hearts and you will be victorious over all your enemies. Nobody will be able to destroy you. If you die, you will not come back to be born in this world again. You will go to the highest heaven (Nirvana)."[4]

A man born in Thailand and who trained as a Buddhist priest told how he read that the Buddha stated in writings the priest read during his studies, that he, the Buddha was not God, and you would know God had come among us when you saw a man walking on water. This, too, happened with Jesus Christ (Matthew 14:22-32; Mark 6:48-50; John 6:16-21). That priest from Thailand decided to follow Jesus Christ and came to live in New Zealand and led many to become followers of Jesus Christ. He died at an advanced age in 2004, and was delighted to go to heaven with Jesus Christ.

Buddha was correct about the uselessness of trying to earn merit. It is impossible. The Holy One Buddha said would come has come. About five hundred years after Buddha left this world, the prophecy was fulfilled. When Jesus Christ died on the cross to take away human sin, each hand and foot was pierced with a large nail leaving a disc shape (John 20:20); his side was pierced with a spear (John 19:34); and his forehead had many marks on it from the crown of thorns the Romans put on him (John 19:2).

Jesus Christ opened up a new way of faith to relate to God so that the old ways of merit could be left behind. Through Jesus Christ alone, one can find perfect assurance that the highest heaven is opened by God's grace. One cannot be a Christian without verbally confessing the deity of Jesus the Christ. One cannot even pray to God, let alone have sin remitted by Him, without approaching Him through Jesus Christ (John 14:6, 13; 15:16; 16:23-24; Romans 5:2, and Ephesians 2:18.)

I know Muslims and Mormons, Christian Scientists, Jehovah Witnesses, Unitarians, Scientologists, Jews, Roman Catholics, Buddhists, Hindus, Seventh-Day Adventists, Wiccans, New Agers, and many others will not want to hear this, but the Bible declares that Jesus was the final revelation of God to man (Hebrews 1:1-3). There have been no others.

While many in New Age circles now wholeheartedly believe and accept the theories postulated by both Eric von Däniken and Zecharia Sitchin that ancient alien visitations from the heavens came to Earth to breed with humankind, which is why ancient man worshipped these ETs as gods, both Von Däniken and Sitchin believe that these ancient astronauts were the creators of life on Earth. While this theory does have some validity, it still does not solve the problem of the origin of life. If the ancient astronauts had a hand in creating or genetically manipulating humankind, then WHO created the ancient astronauts?

This is why it says, the Almighty Creator God, the "God of gods," will *famish* the gods. He created them, and he will starve them of their power due to their rebellion. This Cosmic Drama is not just about us; even the ancient ET gods need to reconcile with their

Creator, as many have sinned against Him. Many have already been bound. As we read in the *Books of Enoch*, there were punishments, destructions, great floods to obliterate their obscene creations, and genetic mutations. But not all were destroyed. Some stayed in rebellion, yet others witnessed the power of God and were humbled, and have tried to reconcile with Him.

Because they sinned against earth humans, they became karmically indebted to Earth itself. They wanted to clear themselves and pleaded with the Creator to give them another chance, so they accepted assignments in heaven to be benevolent to earth humans and planet Earth as atonement. Many need to work out their own salvation and evolution through us to essentially pay back or undo the mistakes they make.

"Let all the idolaters in my nation be confounded and **let all the gods worship the Lord**."

(Psalm 97:7)

"They went off and worshiped other gods and bowed down to them, **gods they did not know, gods he had not given them**. And the anger of the LORD was kindled against this land, to bring upon it all the **curses** that are written in this book."

(Deuteronomy 29:27)

THE EGYPTIAN GODS

There is a huge blind spot in New Age circles about Egyptian gods and goddesses. Many are fascinated and even obsessed with ancient Egypt and believe these ancient gods and goddesses to be deities and extraterrestrials who they believe can still be invoked today through magical rituals and tapping into ancient stargates. What is behind the mystery schools is the way of the occult, which is magic, which is how these ancient Egyptian gods were invoked and worshipped.

There are several blind spots here, one is the misunderstanding of the actual history of ancient Egypt, which was known as a polytheistic empire. Except for the brief time of pharaoh Akhenaton, who was the only pharaoh of ancient Egypt to insert the idea of monotheism into the akashic record of Egypt, that when he died, so did his legacy of monotheism, and Egyptians went back to worshipping the many different gods and goddesses, i.e., extraterrestrials, Nephilim and fallen angels, in their polytheistic way.

These gods and goddesses were Nephilim remnants from the first flood, known as the flood of Lucifer, or the sinking of Atlantis. They inherited the land of Khem, which today is known as Egypt. Khem is where we derived the word *chemistry* from, because that is essentially what they were involved in, as inheritors of Atlantis.

The Sun-god Osiris and his consort, Isis, together with Ra-Atum, were regarded by the ancient Egyptians as the supreme rulers of a Golden Age of plenty called *Zep Tepi* or the "First Time." Their kingdom ended abruptly when Osiris was murdered by his evil brother, Seth, also known as Typhon.

The childless Isis searched for the dismembered body of Osiris, which she then reassembled and resuscitated through magic (i.e., genetic engineering) long enough to conceive a son named Horus. Horus was believed to be the reincarnation of Osiris, and the new husband of Isis, whose destiny it was to repossess the Kingdom of Osiris from the control of Seth. Horus had the head of a falcon and the body of a human. He was Nephilim.

The mythology of Isis, Osiris and Horus are the stories of how these ancient Nephilim, from the original Luciferian rebellion, developed on Earth. Many of these Egyptian gods and goddesses that were half-human and half-animal were all Nephilim. Because they had supernatural powers and supernatural strength, notwithstanding being bloodthirsty for human blood, these Nephilim gods were worshipped and appeased by earth humans and turned into deities. Sekhmet was such a goddess, as stories abound of her lust for human blood, appeasing her only through wine and magical rituals.

Sabik, the god that is half-crocodile and half-human, is also a Nephilim. He was worshipped in the temples. The Egyptians actually sat around and did astrological charts of crocodiles to appease his spirit. Anubis, the god who has the head of a dog and the body of a man, another Nephilim, was also worshipped and revered as a guardian. Today all of these gods and goddesses are worshipped in the form of idolatry. They have been made into dead statutes. And all of them have fallen and come under the judgment of the Creator God and from the likes of history have already received their punishment through the fall of their kingdom.

> "You shall not make for yourself an idol in the form of anything in heaven above or on the earth beneath or in the waters below." (The Second of the 10 Commandments)
>
> (Exodus 20:4; Deuteronomy 5:8)

> "But those who trust in idols, who say to images, 'You are our gods,' will be turned back in utter shame."
>
> (Isaiah 42:17)

> "All who make idols are nothing, and the things they treasure are worthless. Those who would speak up for them are blind; they are ignorant, to their own shame."
>
> (Isaiah 44:9)

> "They worshiped their idols, which became a snare to them."
>
> (Psalm 78:58)

> "Everyone is senseless and without knowledge; every goldsmith is shamed by his idols. His images are a fraud; they have no breath in them."
>
> (Jeremiah 10:14)

CHAPTER NINE: The Return of the Gods

"Of what value is an idol, since a man has carved it? Or an image that teaches lies? For he who makes it trusts in his own creation; he makes idols that cannot speak. Woe to him who says to wood, 'Come to life!' Or to lifeless stone, 'Wake up!' Can it give guidance? It is covered with gold and silver; there is no breath in it." (The Lord's answer to Habakkuk 2:18)

"And again, when God brings his firstborn into the world, he says, "Let all God's angels (extraterrestrials) worship him."

(Hebrews 1:6)

"Has any nation ever traded its gods for new ones, even though they are not gods at all? Yet my people have exchanged their glorious God for worthless idols!"

(Jeremiah 2:11)

"But why not call on these gods you have made? When trouble comes, let them save you if they can! For you have as many gods as there are towns in Judah."

(Jeremiah 2:28)

"I will punish her for the days she burned incense to the Baals; she decked herself with rings and jewelry, and went after her lovers, but me she forgot," declares the LORD."

(Hosea 2:13)

"The LORD of Heaven's Armies, the God of Israel, says: "I will punish Amon, the god of Thebes, and all the other gods of Egypt. I will punish its rulers and Pharaoh, too, and all who trust in him."

(Jeremiah 46:25)

"God is spirit, and his worshipers must worship in the Spirit and in truth."

(John 4:24)

"Therefore behold, days are coming when I will punish the idols of Babylon; and her whole land will be put to shame and all her slain will fall in her midst."

(Jeremiah 51:47)

"Do any of the worthless idols of the nations bring rain? Do the skies themselves send down showers? No, it is you, LORD our God. Therefore our hope is in you, for you are the one who does all this

(Jeremiah 14:22)

The other blind spot about those who follow after ancient Egypt is the fact that it held many people in bondage as slaves to their empires. This went on for hundreds of years. It was not just the Israelites, as the book of Exodus tells us, but also Egyptian people themselves. The pharaohs ruled through alien bloodlines, through a hierarchy of priests and scribes, and the common folk were slaves to them.

They appeased the many Nephilim gods of the past through magic, which today is misunderstood as being an "advanced" ancient civilization, which history tells us fell because of its rebellion, idolatry, and cruelty. History repeats itself, as today modern Egyptians overthrew their own government led by President Mubarak, who also treated his people with cruelty, arrogance, and injustice.

History repeats itself again at the end of this age. New Agers are being used ignorantly to open up portals and gateways to invite these ancient gods back; however, they do not know all the implications and consequences that go with it, especially because they are unaware of the history of when it happened before.

As a result, these ancient Nephilim gods are invited to return through these ancient portals to take their place in the end times "mother of all wars" against the Almighty Creator God and his two-thirds of extraterrestrials in the heavens, led by their King, Captain, and Commander, the Lord Jesus Christ (Yahshua HaMashiach) when he returns to defeat the kingdom of darkness at the end of this timeline.

> "Then the Lord said to me, "There is a conspiracy among the people of Judah and those who live in Jerusalem. They have returned to the sins of their forefathers, who refused to listen to my words. <u>They have followed other gods to serve them</u>. Both the house of Israel and the house of Judah have broken the covenant I made with their forefathers. Therefore this is what the Lord says: '<u>I will bring on them a disaster they cannot escape. Although they cry out to me, I will not listen to them</u>. The towns of Judah and the people of Jerusalem will go and cry out to the gods to whom they burn incense, but they will not help them at all when disaster strikes. You have as many gods as you have towns, O Judah; and the altars you have set up to burn incense to that shameful god Baal are as many as the streets of Jerusalem.'"
> (Jeremiah 11:9-13)

The god, Baal, is part of the Hierarchy of Satan, Baal was also a title, meaning Lord. He has been known as the Lord of the flies, but more specifically the "Lord that flies," (i.e., in UFOs) or the lord of those that "fly" or that flit about in the atmosphere, which UFOs do. He is also known as Beelzebub, and is known as one of the chief of demons.

Baalbamoth is known as the lord of the aerial regions.[1] When you delineate all of his names, they are all under the curse of the Creator, and what is even more dangerous is when earth humans invoke and worship them under his various names. It has, in the past, brought down the wrath of God and will again in the future. What happens is that the Creator God turns His back on His people and allows them to suffer at the hands of their enemies. The end-times scenario that is being set up on earth, is that these ancient gods are scheduled to return and battle with the Almighty Creator God.

CHAPTER NINE: The Return of the Gods

"The Lord Almighty, who planted you, has <u>decreed disaster for you</u>, because the house of Israel and the house of Judah have done evil and provoked me to anger by burning incense to Baal."

(Jeremiah 11:17)

All of the deities of the past that were invoked through portals, worshipped, and appeased by earth humans are all under the curse of the Almighty Creator God. The main reason is that earth humans have turned their back on their Creator. When a human dies, they go back to the Creator of their soul to be judged. These gods and deities did not create their spirits, and therefore cannot save them. Idolatry is a huge iniquity when it comes to the judgments of God.

Earth humans were created to have intimacy with their Creator, to be in a personal relationship, to lean on Him, and in turn, He promises to cover and protect them. Protect them from what? Protect them from all the evil influences and the hierarchy of demons, fallen ET angels, and rebellious gods. However, when earth humans turn against their Creator God, all hell literally breaks loose.

Thomas R. Horn[1], writes in his book *Nephilim Stargates: The Year 2012 and the Return of the Watchers* about the "Father of Nephilim and the Son of Perdition": (emphasis mine)

"The book of Revelation details what follows the rise of Antichrist, culminating in cataclysmic war called Armageddon, a time during which **God Almighty judges the "gods" who come through portals**, including, we would assume, so-called Zeus, Apollo, Demeter, Isis, and others.

However, futile, <u>the *gods* will retaliate</u>, and a war of indescribable intensity will occur. It will be fought on land and sea, in the heavens above, and in the earth below, in the physical and spiritual worlds. It will include "Michael and his angels [fighting] against the dragon; and the dragon [fighting] and his angels" (Rev. 12.7). Some humans will join the battle against God, calling on "idols of gold, and silver, and brass, and stone, and of wood" (Rev.9.20) to convene their power against the Christian God, even uniting with "unclean spirits like frogs...the spirits of *devils* [the frog goddesses Heket] Working miracles, which go forth unto the kings of the earth...to gather them to the battle of that great day... [To] a place called in the Hebrew tongue Armageddon ["Mount Megiddo"] (Rev. 16.13-14, 16).

There, in the valley of Megiddo, the omnipotent Christ will utterly repel the forces of darkness and destroy the New World army. Blood will flow like rivers, and the fowl of the air will "eat the flesh of the mighty, and drink the blood of the princes of the earth" (Ezek.39.18). Besides Armageddon, battles will be fought in the Valley of Jehoshaphat and in the city of Jerusalem. Yet, the battle of Armageddon is the event that culminates the hostility between God Almighty and the lower gods that traverse portals."[1]

Over three thousand years ago, Satan and his "god" spirits, (extraterrestrials) challenged Yahuah at Megiddo. They lost. On Mount Carmel, overlooking the Valley of Armageddon, the prophets of Baal dared the Hebrew God to answer by fire. He did, and according to Revelation 19:19-21; 20:11-12, 15 he will do it again. What is this fire from Heaven? It's a nuclear pulse from the celestial armies of heaven, through their heavenly "chariots." Today we call them spaceships.

So where does this leave us now? We are living in a time of "Grace." However, the window of Grace may close at any minute, when the Lord redeems his believers from the face of the earth and allows the kingdom of darkness to reign for the time known as "Jacob's troubles," otherwise known as the seven-year tribulation, a time apportioned on the time line for the punishment of the unbelieving world, a time where literally all hell breaks loose on earth, a time where the forces of darkness reigns.

All that God is asking for is for people to turn to Him and to repent from their errant lifestyles, unbeliefs, idolatry, immorality, and bad attitudes, otherwise known as "sin."

Remember the words of Jesus, "I have not come to call the righteous, but sinners to repentance."

(Luke 5:32)

It's been said many times, that when one person returns to the Lord and repents, literally hundreds of thousands of heaven's angels rejoice. The problem with most people, especially those who have invested so much into their religions and belief systems, is that they are empowered by believing in their lies and cannot discern the truth and, through their stubbornness, will perish. This is particularly true for New Agers, who are sadly being used as pawns of the Luciferian/Satanic end times scheme to use them to invoke ancient gods and goddesses in order to open up the portals and "legally" bring them in.

Many New Agers are fascinated by ancient gods and goddesses, so much so that they have essentially begun a new religion around it. The lure of ancient knowledge titillates their egos, in their quest for enlightenment. But for many, it is too late to learn that their quest for enlightenment is part of one of the many schemes and agendas of the god of this world, who is Lucifer/Satan, whose name literally means "rebel of light," also known as "rebel light bearer." This is a mass deception to lure them down a garden path that will lead to not only their destruction, but the destruction of the world. 1 Timothy 4:1 tells us that, in the last days, many will follow after the doctrines of demons who will deceive the world. The demons are made of a hierarchy of fallen angels who have become evil spirits of the earth. They masquerade as light beings to the uninitiated and unaware.

Lucifer, Leviathan, and Beelzebub are known as the trinity of evil and are often invoked through the Black Mass. Leviathan is the great dragon of the sea. (See my chapter on Leviathan pp. 304-306, in Book One of *Who's Who In The Cosmic Zoo?*). Revelation's prophetic timeline tells us of the final conflict between God and this Dragon

CHAPTER NINE: The Return of the Gods

to complete their "unfinished business," which is scheduled to occur at the end of our timeline. In fact the prophet Isaiah said it first:

> "Behold, the Lord is coming out of his dwelling to punish the people of the earth for their sins. The earth will disclose the bloodshed upon her; she will conceal her slain no longer. In that day, the Lord will punish with his sword, his fierce, great and powerful sword, Leviathan the gliding serpent, Leviathan the coiling serpent; he will slay the monster of the sea.
>
> (Isaiah 26:21-27:1)

Besides all the idolatry, the pharaohs of ancient Egypt set up their empires through using humans as slaves. This is the other blind spot of many New Agers — Egypt used slaves for hard labor, held thousands of people in bondage, not just the Israelites, but a variety of different tribes and peoples that were clumped in together with the Israelites. I remember talking to the talk show host of *Metaphysically Speaking*, who took pride in Egyptian objects, idols, and jewelry that she owned. She insisted that "Egypt never had slaves." This is called denial or believing in your own lies. History records it differently. Denial is not a river in Egypt.

> "'This is what the Sovereign LORD says:
> "'I will destroy the idols and put an end to the images in Memphis.
> (Bible in Basic English Translation says:
> I will put an end to the false gods in Noph (Memphis))
> No longer will there be a prince in Egypt, and I will spread fear throughout the land."
>
> (Ezekiel 30:13)

Horn writes, "The Egyptians originally migrated from the biblical land of Shinar, which means 'the Land of the Watchers.' The Egyptians called it *Ta Neter*— the land of the Watchers, 'from which the gods came into Egypt.' "[1]

"According to the Dead Sea Scrolls, only two hundred of this larger group of powerful beings called 'Watchers' departed from the higher Heavens and sinned. Thus, Enoch refers to the Watchers in the High Heavens as separate from the ones on Earth. The fallen class of Watchers are considered by some to be the same creature who in the Book of Jude are called the 'Angels which kept not their first estate, but left their own habitation... [and are] reserved in everlasting chains under darkness unto the judgment of the great day.'" (Jude 1:6)[1]

Remember, the Jews came out of the tribe of Judah, the Israelites were the rest of the other eleven tribes. The Old Testament book of Exodus tells the story of the 400 year bondage of the Israelites to the Egyptians. What is interesting is how the Creator God chose to free them and lead them back to the land of Israel. The Creator God Yahuah judged Egypt by plaguing them with their own gods' power, exhibiting a total defeat of Egypt's gods by the true God of Israel.

1. The Nile was turned to **Blood**. This was a judgment humiliation against the Egyptian god of the Nile.

2. **Frogs** appeared everywhere. This was a judgment and humiliation against the goddess Heqt (Heket) who is represented as a frog and worshipped as a god who helped in childbirth. Egyptians worshipped the frog as a female goddess because frogs were common around the Nile, because they reproduced rapidly, and because as amphibians they are part of two worlds, creatures of both land and water. The Lord threatened a plague of *frogs* for a specific reason. The Egyptian goddess Heqt was always pictured with the head of a frog, a Nephilim. For this reason frogs were considered sacred and could not be killed. God showed the Egyptians the foolishness of a frog-god!

It is interesting that frogs are mentioned in Revelation 16:13: "Then I saw three evil spirits that looked like frogs; they came out of the mouth of the dragon, out of the mouth of the beast and out of the mouth of the false prophet."

3. The plague of **Lice** was an irritation to the neurotically hygienic Egyptians.

4. **Beetles** were sacred to the Egyptians and considered divine. They were a symbol of their solar deity, the sun god Ra.

5. **The Death of all Livestock** was another plague because the Egyptians worshipped the sacred bull Apis. Again this was to humiliate this false god and to all those who worshipped it in folly.

6. **Boils** also known as **pestilence**, was sent on all males and animals. Egypt had a hoard of sacred animals.

7. **Hail** destroyed the crops with which they thanked their gods for.

8. **Locusts** were sent to destroy their crops, as well.

9. **Darkness** was sent as an insult to the sun god Ra.

10. **Death to the Firstborn** was a judgment against Satan himself. The Angel of Death was not an Egyptian god. This symbolized that the Son of God would break death's hold not only on Israel, but the entire world. This was the meaning of the "Passover," which was the commandment to the Israelites in Exodus 12:7-14:

> "And they shall take the *blood*, and put it on the two side posts and on the lintel, upon the house where in they shall eat the flesh on that night...with your loins girded, your shoes on your feet, and your staff in your hand; and ye shall eat it in haste: it is Yahuah's Passover. **<u>Against all the gods of Egypt I will execute judgments</u>**: I AM Yahuah. And the *blood* shall be to you for a token...And this day shall be unto you for a memorial, and you shall keep it as a feast by an ordinance forever."

CHAPTER NINE: The Return of the Gods

Jesus Christ was the final Passover lamb. Through the ***blood*** of Yahshua HaMashiach aka Jesus Christ, all the gods of this world are defeated and their works are destroyed.

We can say that the slavery of ancient Egypt is a mockup of the way the kingdoms of this world have been set up. The Annunaki gods tampered with DNA to create a race of human beings to be used as slaves to the Annunaki, as workers to mine the earth for gold and other natural resources. They were adamant about keeping a boundary between the earth humans and them, as these so-called gods created all kinds of religious protocols that were set up to maintain their secrecy and supremacy over earth humans. Priests and pharaohs were used to represent them to the earth humans. There was little to no interaction between these gods and the common folk. This was the mock-up of many of the world's religions.

Today many find themselves as slaves to a state, a nation, a religion, to a servitude, or to some type of psycho-spiritual bondage. Even America, the home of the brave and the land of the free, is not free. Freedom comes with a price. Jesus said, "I've come to set the captives free... I have bought you for a price." That price was His life and His blood, which was paid as atonement for the sins and curses of humankind.

THE GREEK AND PAGAN GODS

Remember the movies, *The Clash of the Titans*. The original film was made in 1981. Then in 2010 Hollywood did a remake, with all the special effects and techno-wizardry. Mythology is only a version of history put into a melodramatic story, which for millennia, could not be related to because the Greek gods, i.e., the Titans, were so sensational, supernatural, and otherworldly that earth humans had to create and imagine a fairy tale myth to understand their stories. But the truth of the matter is that Greek mythology is no fairy tale; it really happened.

These were the fallen sons of heaven, the Watchers, the Titans, the Nephilim, who, at one time, did in fact rule the earth, walk the earth, and mated and lusted after earth women. They made all kinds of deals with humans, creating demi-gods, and fought with each other over power and dominion over the earth and earth humans.

Zeus was also known as Lucifer, whose lust for power and control, and his ability to shape shift into animals and appear as a mortal man, still precedes him. The only difference between the Greek gods and the Roman "pagan" gods was the fact that the Romans, who essentially took over the Greek Empire, changed their gods' names into Roman names. They are the same gods.

Zeus became Jupiter. Poseidon became Neptune. Aphrodite became Venus. Demeter became Ceres. Eros became Cupid (Amor). Asclepius became Aesculapius. Artemis became Diana. Satyr became Faun. Hera became Juno. Phosphorus became Lucifer. Ares became Mars. Hermes became Mercury. Athena became Minerva. Persephone became Proserpina. Cronus became Saturn. Helios became Sol. Hypnos became Somnus. Gaia became Tellus. Hecate became Trivia. Odysseus became Ulysses. Hestia became Vesta. Hephaestus became Vulcan. Apollo remained Apollo.

These pagan gods were then venerated and worshipped throughout the Roman Empire, and Pergamum became known as the seat of Satan. Pergamum's altar of Zeus was then excavated and moved in the nineteenth century to Berlin and Nuremberg. The Nazis carried on various forms of pagan worship to gain power during WWII. Many of these gods are still influencing modern-day society.

Asclepius was known as the god of healing whose symbol was a snake wrapped around a pole. Today this is known as the Caduceus staff, which is the universal symbol of the medical profession and the AMA (American Medical Association).

Can false gods create healings, miracles, and produce signs and wonders? Yes, because they are empowered by the god of this world, Lucifer/Satan, to do so. It is to counterfeit the healings, and signs from the Holy Spirit.

> "The coming of the lawless one will be accompanied by the power of Satan. He will use every kind of power, including miraculous signs, lying wonders, and every type of evil to deceive those who are dying, those who refused to love the truth that would save them."
>
> (2 Thessalonians 2:9-10)

As I detail, in my chapter "Contracts and Agreements" of Book Four: *Covenants*, all of these gods had to be in some kind of cosmic contract with the god of this world, who was/is Lucifer/Satan, in order to have free reign, build a kingdom, and have earth humans fear and worship them. In entering into these Faustian contracts, these gods then sealed their part in Lucifer's rebellion against their Creator God, who made them immortal and gave them supernatural powers.

These are the gods that the Lord promises to famish, because of their rebellion toward him and because they irresponsibly influenced all kinds of immorality to earth humans. When you read their stories in the various mythologies, it is one long drama over power and control, uncontrollable lusts, jealousy, murder, magic/witchcraft, and revenge between these gods, often with earth humans as the innocent target of their many rages. Zeus was especially known and feared for his cruelty.

> **"....keep yourself from idols."**
>
> (1 John 5:21)

THE MAYAN AND INCAN GODS

Viracocha is known as the great creator god in the pre-Inca and Inca mythology in the Andes region of South America. He was called "Kukulkan" to the Mayans and "Quetzalcoatl" to the Aztecs. We can see from all the legends that this is one and the

CHAPTER NINE: The Return of the Gods

same god, which just goes by different names according to the different tribes and cultures that he visited.

Viracocha was one of the most important deities in the Inca pantheon and seen as the creator of all things. Viracocha was believed to have created the universe, sun, moon, stars, time, and civilization itself. The myth of Viracocha spreads throughout South America and beyond. This ancient mystical God, who by local legend rose from the middle of Lake Titicaca to create mankind, was and is still today respected.

One legend says Viracocha had two sons, Imahmana Viracocha and Tocapo Virachocha. After the Great Flood and the Creation, Viracocha sent his sons to visit the tribes to the Northeast and Northwest to determine if they still obeyed his commandments. Viracocha himself traveled north. Eventually, Viracocha, Tocapo, and Imahmana arrived at Cuzco (in modern day Peru) and the Pacific seacoast where they walked across the water until they disappeared in their spaceships. This is why he was named Viracocha, which literally means "Sea Foam."

Quetzalcoatl is known as the feathered "serpent," who the Mayans claim to be their god. They projected his return after the solar eclipse of the galactic center on December 21, 2012. Is it now 2015, and no one has reported seeing him yet. This is the god that they sacrificed live humans, including women and children, in order to appease this blood thirsty "reptilian" god. Yet we need to remember that Viracocha and Kukulkan are names for the same god. In my opinion, the return of this reptilian god is not exactly something we should all celebrate; instead, we should be extremely wary of, discerning of, and suspicious of it, especially if he will be demanding more live human sacrifices and human blood to appease him.

Quetzalcoatl, known as the god of civilization, was identified with the planet Venus and with the wind; according to the Mayans, he represented the forces of good and light pitted against those of evil and darkness, which were challenged by Tezcatlipoca, the ancient deity of the Toltec in Mexico. These gods fought for supremacy, as both were "warrior" gods. Both were identified with the night sky, the moon, and the stars, and associated with the forces of evil and destruction because they travelled from out of the sky in their spaceships. Tezcatlipoca shared dominion over humanity with Quetzalcoatl, who was deemed as the god of light and good. This kept their followers in the bondage to duality.

In the Valley of Mexico, from the north, toward the end of the twelfth century, they linked Tezcatlipoca with the worship of the war god Huitzilopotchtli and applied it to some of their ranking priests. The famous Temple of Quetzalcoatl at Teotihuacán, which was once thought to be the great religious center of the Toltec, is now held to be the relic of an earlier civilization and is now regarded by some authorities as having been consecrated to a different god. Some scholars believe that the gods who built these ancient temples had to be giants. As I've already gone over in my chapter on the giants and Nephilim in Book One of *Who's Who In The Cosmic Zoo*, these were all considered to be fallen sons of heaven, who mixed their DNA with both earth humans and animals, creating the abominations that brought down the wrath of the Almighty Creator God, which are known as Nephilim.[5]

The Nephilim were destroyed in two separate floods, as well as by nuclear fire from heaven, during the destruction of Sodom and Gomorrah. The fact that the Mayan people mysteriously disappeared in the ninth century could be because they were consumed by their own god and/or abducted off the planet for future food and experimentation. The rest, scholars say, were assimilated throughout southern Mexico and were conquered by the Spanish conquistadors.

Spanish chroniclers from the sixteenth century claimed that when the conquistadors, led by Francisco Pizarro, first encountered the Inca's, they were greeted as gods or Viracochas because their lighter skin resembled their God Viracocha. This story was first reported by Pedro Cieza de León (1553) and later by Pedro Sarmiento de Gamboa.

Similar accounts by Spanish chroniclers (e.g. Juan de Betanzos) describe Viracocha as a "White God," often with a beard. These accounts confirm that he may have been one of the original two hundred fallen sons of heaven, *Bene HaElohim*, who sinned by mixing their DNA with earth human women and created Transgenics, monsters and giants.

The Spanish chroniclers also explained that Tiahuanaco had been constructed by a race of giants called "Huaris" before *Chamak-pacha,* the "period of darkness," and that these giants were created by Viracocha, who were Nephilim. Pedro Sarmiento de Gamboa wrote in *Acosta, Hint of the New World* that: "Viracocha created animals and a race of giants. These beings enraged the Lord, and he turned them into stone. Then he flooded the earth till everything was under water and all life extinguished."

It is possible that Quetzalcoatl may have in fact been one of Virachocha's sons or Nephilim because he was known to have bird wings and was reptilian in nature, hence the need for live human blood sacrifices to appease him. Yet over time, all of their names became interchangeable among the legends within the tribes and cultures of the Mayans, Incans, Aztecs, and Toltecs.

The Qquichuas expected the return of Viracocha, not merely as an earthly ruler to govern their nation, but as a god, who by his divine power, would call the dead to life. Precisely as in ancient Egypt, the literal belief in the resurrection of the body led to the custom of preserving the corpses with meticulous care.

All of these gods may even be one and the same but just go by different names or were sons of the original fallen sons of heaven responsible for creating Nephilim on Earth and have all come under the wrath of the Creator Lord for it.

WHY WILL THE GODS BE PUNISHED?

As we started this chapter with this question, it is only fitting to end it with an answer. The gods of the earth broke the laws of creation; they rebelled against the Almighty Creator God, who they once enjoyed intimate contact with. After all, they received all their supernatural strength and powers from Him. Yet in their rebellion, they

CHAPTER NINE: The Return of the Gods

went their own way and misused their powers. They mated with earth women, which was their original sin. They created the Nephilim and all sorts of monsters, along with biochemical weapons that consumed earth humans. They sinned against the laws of Creation, using genetic engineering to create hybrids and Transgenics that were used as weapons against humanity.

Some of the watchers involved in this are already being punished and held in a prison in the fifth heaven (see Book Five: *The Heavens*); others were castigated into demonic reptilian creatures and bound inside the inner earth. Those who escaped punishment at that time set themselves up as gods of the earth. They held earth humans in all sorts of bondages. They lied to them by misleading them into thinking that they were the only ticket in the universe. And what was really immoral to the Creator was that they taught earth humans how to make war. As a result of this, they started the constant pattern of warring on the earth.

Some of these Transgenics still exist on earth today. This is why there is a list of unclean animals that all are commanded to avoid by the Almighty Creator Lord. They are not fit for human consumption because of the origin of these species. One in particular is the pig. Pigs were created by mixing human blood with an animal similar to humans. This is why Aborigines traditionally call white people "long pig," which comes from the pigs' Nephilim roots.

Now the pig is coming full circle as it is being used today in transgenic experiments with humans because scientists discovered the similarity between human blood and pig blood. What a coincidence! The reason the Almighty Creator Lord commanded humans not to eat pig flesh in Leviticus 11:7, 8 and Deuteronomy 14:8 is because it was a form of cannibalism, due to its human transgenic origins.

Today modern science has caught up with the ancient laws and discovered that pig meat causes cancer, which is why all cancer patients are immediately ordered off pork upon entering into cancer treatment. Is it any wonder that this scripture is written within the long prophetic chapter that the prophet Isaiah wrote on the coming Judgment Day of the Lord?

> "Those who consecrate and purify themselves to go into the gardens, following the one in the midst of those who eat the flesh of pigs and rats and other abominable things--they will meet their end together," declares the LORD."
>
> (Isaiah 66:17)

In addition to perverting the laws of nature and creation, these fallen ET gods created earth religions after themselves, so earth humans would fear and worship them and offer all kinds of sacrifices (some actual live human sacrifices) to appease them. (See Book Three – *Who Are the Angels?* Chapter - Aliens and Religion for more discernment) in doing so, they misled humans away from the path of salvation through the Creator. They kept the truth of the cosmos from them by distorting some truths and editing it to meet their needs, which was to appease their god complexes. They failed to direct their followers to seek and worship the Almighty Creator God, who is the Creator of all of humankind's souls and spirits, the very Creator that created them, who they were in a type of teenage rebellion with, insisting on doing their own thing in their own way.

In this way, they are guilty of the iniquity written in the scriptures of idolatry, which caused the Almighty Lord to punish humanity several times for following these pseudo-gods and their idols, which caused the Lord to eventually turn His back on those earth humans who succumbed to following these gods, instead of the Creator God, until the Divine plan of Salvation was fulfilled through Christ, and the price was paid back to the Creator in the form of his innocent blood to be the covering for all of humankind's sins and their resultant curses.

It is through Christ that we are made right with the Almighty Creator. That was the plan established at the beginning of creation in Genesis 3:15, which has been written in the Heavens long before the scriptures were written (see Book Five – *The Heaven*, Chapter on The Word of God as Written in the Stars). This was the plan of salvation for all humans held in bondage by the dark lord and his principalities of darkness who have infiltrated throughout the cosmos. The Almighty Creator of the heavens and the earth is the only one who has the power to punish the lesser gods. While these gods are extraterrestrial in nature, the Bible is full of passages concerning them and calling them "gods" with a small "g." Yet it also distinguishes them from their Creator God, the God of gods.

"For the Lord is the great God, the great King above all gods."

(Psalm 95:4)

"Among the gods there is none like you, O Lord; no deeds can compare with yours."

(Psalm 86:8)

DEEP ROOTED SPIRITUAL WOUNDS

The gods are responsible for the deep psychological and psycho-spiritual damage that earth humans suffered when they set up all kinds of temples and interacted with the priests, who were their intermediaries, and then suddenly left the earth. This created deep seated abandonment issues in earth humans, who are still struggling with this to this day in their DNA. When the gods left the planet, it created doubt, as many lost faith because they never returned when they said they were returning. So much so, the very civilizations they started ended up crumbling and disbanding and many were overthrown by other groups. Psychologically speaking, the wounding created a loss of faith and trust in the Divine and/or in the Universe.

CHAPTER NINE: The Return of the Gods

Many people today suffer from this spiritual wounding and struggle with their faith which is something greater than themselves. In my opinion, this is a combination of genetic inheritance, past life recall, and ancestral curses caused by idolatry, in following these pseudo-gods. There is a deep seated sense of betrayal and victimization caused by the abandonment of these gods, which, through psychological transference, is projected onto the Creator God and the Universe. With some of these people, the wounds are so deep that they now choose to live a life of atheism. Others, however, stubbornly adhere to the traditions of their ancestors, in spite of the fact that their tribes and cultures were overturned as a result of their errant beliefs, yet they continue in a religion of superstition ruled by demon spirits masquerading as their ancestors and so-called star gods.

At the core of this wound is the fear of being hurt and rejected again by these gods. Coupled with the core belief in the injustice, inequity, and victimization of the Universe, to the point where they question the existence of any god. This feeling of being forsaken was mirrored and taken on the cross by Jesus Christ, who took the sins and curses of humankind to the cross, so that humankind may be redeemed through his final blood sacrifice to the Creator God, when in his final empathy of humanity cried out, "My god, why have you forsaken me?" (Psalm 22:1; Matthew 27:46).

In my opinion, the feeling of being forsaken by the gods created more karma than when the gods created the Nephilim, who were later destroyed. Because of their abandonment, deep wounds inevitably have left their mark on humankind. This is why true healing is found by repenting and turning to the Almighty Creator Lord of all souls through Jesus Christ.

Those cultures and religions that believe that these gods are returning to save them are still living in the victim consciousness that these very gods created in their psyches. These gods cannot save them, and if they could, they would have already. The stark truth is accepting the fact that many of the gods (ancient ETs) are scheduled to be brought down along with the god of this world and all who are responsible for these mass deceptions and psycho-spiritual abuses toward humanity. Only the power of Christ can save a soul from the false beliefs in these pseudo-gods and their lifeless, empty idols.

These so-called gods, who are really only ancient extraterrestrials and aliens, are evolving through their many interactions with earth humans. Some were severely punished; others were limited and quarantined. Meanwhile, others were allowed second chances to prove themselves worthy of being sons and daughters of heaven, through how they interact with the "lower species" which would be us. Remember the original human blueprint that humans were created in the image and likeness of the Elohim, entails twelve strands of DNA, yet earth humans only have two.

Earth humans are considered lower species, but because we were given souls from the Creator of all souls, a plan of salvation was etched into the heavens and scripture for earth humans. Salvation from what? Salvation from oppression from the abuses of the higher species of humans, i.e., rogue extraterrestrials, many of whom have sold out to the cosmic rebel, Lucifer/Satan, in various legal contracts and agreements to come and go from Earth at various times along the time line. As a result, this was the root cause of idolatry and belief in "magic" from outer space, set up by these pseudo-gods in deep antiquity, whose records and evidence are found etched in stone around the planet.

Spiritually speaking, idolatry sets a person up for demonic oppression and demonic possession. This happens from the false belief that worshipping a pseudo-extraterrestrial god in the form of a statute, burning incense, and candles to it, opens up a portal for demonic influences to come through. Why? Because it is a belief in a lie, and spiritually speaking, this gives "legal ground" for demonic intelligence, who are under the control of Lucifer/Satan hierarchy to have dominion in the spirit of an earth human. This has been the crux of the spiritual battle since deep antiquity.

There are countless stories of people who become sick with mysterious illnesses that are resistant to modern medicine and even most prayers. Yet when they remove the idols of these pseudo-gods from their homes, they are miraculously healed of their illnesses. Others were plagued with legal problems, social problems, and family trouble. This is because each and every statute comes with a demonic spirit attachment.

In my first novel, *CinderElla's Shadow*, which is based on my true life stories, I will prove that any involvement with these pseudo-gods in the form of idolatry brings nothing but suffering. I went through a living nightmare, hell on earth battle. After spending twenty-five years in the fields of New Age religions and Metaphysics, I invoked several of these gods for help, who not only failed to deliver me, but actually made my troubles worse, until I was so broken that I turned back to the Lord Jesus Christ who, in His Mercy, answered my cry for help and delivered me from the powers of darkness that had enveloped me. I then rid myself of every idol, i.e., New Age brick-a-brack from my home, repented of my ignorance, waywardness, and idolatry, and the Lord in His faithfulness restored my peace and my health, and has given me the strength to complete this manuscript.

Many falsely believe that these statutes represent their ancestors, who are, at all times, "watching them" from the afterlife, such as the false beliefs of Easter Island. But the truth is that these idols have no power in and of themselves. Neither do empty skulls with photos of dead ancestors. However, the false belief that they do is what ensnares the earth human, and then the powers of darkness are allowed to take over.

The real watchers are the fallen angel demons watching humans, so they can entangle them in their spiritual battle against the Creator Lord and His Christ. Because all idolatry falls under the curse and judgment of the Almighty Creator God, then worshipping and believing in idols and the pseudo-gods that they represent legally opens the door for this demonic stronghold, which only creates more suffering in humankind.

We must learn from history. All the battles of the past were over what these pseudo-gods did and how they defiled humankind. They raped earth women, used humans as slaves, demanded the blood of virgins and children, and defiled the spirits and souls of humankind by creating false beliefs and false religions, only to abandon them, leaving many without hope and the legacy of deceptive beliefs.

CHAPTER NINE: The Return of the Gods

That these gods left the legacy of their promise to return is yet another deception to humankind as to their true intentions. One must wonder and ask, why are they returning? It is not to save humans, but to fulfill a cosmic appointment to fight the final battle against their Creator God. Today we have all kinds of researchers trying to unearth what these gods left behind. The fascination has created a new form of worship because of their enormous techno-wizardry in creating huge megaliths, temples to venerate themselves, and flawless statutes of themselves at a time when humankind had not yet developed the tools to erect such monuments, nor did we have that ability, understanding, or technology at our disposal then or today.

Many are connecting the dots that these ancient structures were created by extraterrestrials, as there is no earthly or logical explanation for them, back then, or even today. True, they were extraterrestrials. Yes, they left behind their legacies, not only in stoned ruins, lost civilizations, and fallen empires, but also in the broken psyches of earth humans, who are still trying to understand what happened in deep antiquity that is somehow connected to what is happening today. This is why understanding history is so important because it tends to repeat itself. I am repeating this theme for the purpose of emphasis.

That is the reason the Almighty Creator sent Christ to save, heal, and deliver humankind from the trappings and woundedness that these pseudo gods created. Deception by otherworldly beings is nothing new. This is the original cosmic conspiracy, which will culminate with the world's worst and most vile form of deceptions at the end of this timeline.

> "The coming of the lawless one will be accompanied by the power of Satan. He will use every kind of power, including miraculous signs, lying wonders, and every type of evil to deceive those who are dying, those who refused to love the truth that would save them."
>
> (2 Thessalonians 2:10)

As far as I know, the only God who promises to return to earth to save humans from the god of this world and all of his pseudo-gods and their deceptions is the Lord Jesus Christ. His prophesies are detailed throughout all the books of the Bible, as well as the *Books of Enoch*, in a way no other god has detailed. While the New Age is all agog with the trappings of the Mayan Calendar and pseudo-gods and so-called mythological deities, the Bible scriptures reveal a much more detailed accounting of the end of this timeline that cannot be ignored because it affects the whole world, and the entire cosmos.

One theme that seems consistent throughout the scriptures is the consequences of following and worshiping other gods other than the Supreme Creator. This has been a major stumbling block for humanity since human beings were created with a soul. Many New Agers, as well as those Ufologists ascribe to the ancient alien theory, believe that the gods of ancient mythology created humankind. While there are many theories with respect to the Sumerian tablets, ancient Egyptian hieroglyphs, and Bible scriptures, only the Lord of all Spirits can breathe a soul into the human being. Spiritually speaking, this is why historically, disaster came upon all those civilizations and groups of people who chose to ignore the Creator and instead were seduced by extraterrestrials pseudo-gods from space.

We have historical accounts of ancient empires crumbling, whole civilizations disappearing and dispersing because of worshipping extraterrestrials and believing they were gods. While it is true that many of these extraterrestrials did indeed have "god complexes," they played upon the ignorance of earth humans and even schemed to set up religions so that they could continue to receive the worship of earth humans, by instilling fear into them. These ancient aliens were all in rebellion to the Most High, the very Creator God who created them.

Spiritually speaking, their quest has been likened to an adolescent who rebels against their parents in their quest for independence and experimentation. For this reason, is why many of these ancient aliens were not completely destroyed. Many were given second chances to redeem themselves, others were punished and held in a variety of celestial prisons. [NIV translation, emphasis and comments mine]

> "For if God did not spare angels (extraterrestrial messengers) when they sinned, but sent them to hell, putting them into gloomy dungeons to be held for judgment; if he did not spare the ancient world when he brought the flood on its ungodly people, but protected Noah, a preacher of righteousness, and seven others; if he condemned the cities of Sodom and Gomorrah by burning them to ashes, and made them an example of what is going to happen to the ungodly; and if he rescued Lot, a righteous man, who was distressed by the filthy lives of lawless men (for that righteous man, living among them day after day, was tormented in his righteous soul by the lawless deeds he saw and heard)--if this is so, then the Lord knows how to rescue godly men from trials and to hold the unrighteous for the day of judgment, while continuing their punishment. This is especially true of those who follow the corrupt desire of the sinful nature and despise authority. Bold and arrogant, these men are not afraid to slander celestial beings; yet even angels (extraterrestrial messengers), although they are stronger and more powerful, do not bring slanderous accusations against such beings in the presence of the Lord. But these men blaspheme in matters they do not understand. They are like brute beasts, creatures of instinct, born only to be caught and destroyed, and like beasts they too will perish. They will be paid back with harm for the harm they have done."
>
> (2 Peter 2:4-13)

Here, the forty-fourth chapter of Jeremiah reveals the mind of the Lord and what became of the Jews living in Egypt for worshipping these false gods. If the Lord is the same, yesterday, today and tomorrow, how much more will today's world endure of His

CHAPTER NINE: The Return of the Gods

wrath for the rebellion of idolatry? What so many unbelievers in this world fail to understand is the ultimate and supreme power of the Creator, the Most High God, the Almighty YHVH (Yahuah). History consistently repeats itself mainly because humans fail to learn from their lessons, or because they forget.

Think of today's headlines all around the world, as you read these words of judgment on worshipping false gods. It's so ironic that New Agers flock to Egypt in their beliefs that they may connect with the "magic" of the ancient world, yet completely deny what happened there. "There is nothing new under the sun," couldn't ring more true today.

The following passages comes from the New International Version, the emphasis, commentary in the parentheses are mine for the purpose of connecting this message to today's most popular New Age gods and goddesses:

DISASTER BECAUSE OF IDOLATRY

"This word came to Jeremiah concerning all the Jews living in Lower Egypt--in Migdol, Tahpanhes and Memphis--and in Upper Egypt: "This is what the LORD Almighty, the God of Israel, says:

"You saw the great disaster I brought on Jerusalem and on all the towns of Judah. Today they lie deserted and in ruins because of the evil they have done. They provoked me to anger by burning incense and by worshiping other gods that neither they nor you nor your fathers ever knew. Again and again I sent my servants the prophets, who said, 'Do not do this detestable thing that I hate!' But they did not listen or pay attention; they did not turn from their wickedness or stop burning incense to other gods. Therefore, my fierce anger was poured out; it raged against the towns of Judah and the streets of Jerusalem and made them the desolate ruins they are today."

"Now this is what the LORD God Almighty, the God of Israel, says:

"Why bring such great disaster on yourselves by cutting off the men and women, the children and infants, from Judah and so leave yourselves without a remnant? Why provoke me to anger with what your hands have made, burning incense to other gods in Egypt, where you have come to live? You will destroy yourselves and make yourselves an object of cursing and reproach among all the nations on earth. Have you forgotten the wickedness committed by your fathers and by the kings and queens of Judah and the wickedness committed by you and your wives in the land of Judah and the streets of Jerusalem? To this day they have not humbled themselves or shown reverence, nor have they followed my law and the decrees I set before you and your fathers."

"Therefore, this is what the LORD Almighty, the God of Israel, says:

"I am determined to bring disaster on you and to destroy all Judah. I will take away the remnant of Judah who were determined to go to Egypt to settle there.

They will all perish in Egypt; they will fall by the sword or die from famine. From the least to the greatest, they will die by sword or famine. They will become an object of cursing and horror, of condemnation and reproach. I will punish those who live in Egypt with the sword, famine and plague, as I punished Jerusalem. None of the remnant of Judah who have gone to live in Egypt will escape or survive to return to the land of Judah, to which they long to return and live; none will return except a few fugitives."

(Jeremiah 44:1-26)

Then the people rebelled, and told Jeremiah, that they were going to continue to do as they pleased, and burn incense to the Queen of Heaven and give offerings to her. Jeremiah warned them again, and they remained stubborn. Then, the word of Yahuah came through:

"But hear the word of the LORD, all Jews living in Egypt: 'I swear by my great name,' says the LORD, 'that no one from Judah living anywhere in Egypt will ever again invoke my name or swear, "As surely as the Sovereign LORD lives." For I am watching over them for harm, not for good; the Jews in Egypt will perish by sword and famine until they are all destroyed. Those who escape the sword and return to the land of Judah from Egypt will be very few. Then the whole remnant of Judah who came to live in Egypt will know whose word will stand--mine or theirs." 'This will be the sign to you that I will punish you in this place,' declares the LORD, 'so that you will know that my threats of harm against you will surely stand.' This is what the LORD says: 'I am going to hand Pharaoh Hophra king of Egypt over to his enemies who seek his life, just as I handed Zedekiah king of Judah over to Nebuchadnezzar king of Babylon, the enemy who was seeking his life.'"

(Jeremiah 44:26-40)

We know that that the rest is history. The Lord Yahuah kept his word, and the great Egyptian empire was destroyed, as well as Judea. The Judeans were scattered. It's important to learn this lesson from history, to prevent ourselves from suffering the same wrath by repeating the same mistake. These are precarious times we live in.

The prophets speak of a time of God's wrath being poured out on all those who rebel against Him. Yet, the scriptures also promise, that His believers are not appointed to wrath, and are saved from this time period, which is known as the great tribulation, otherwise known as the time of Jacob's troubles.

"For God did not appoint us to suffer wrath,
But to receive salvation through our Lord Jesus Christ."

(1 Thessalonians 5:9)

CHAPTER NINE: The Return of the Gods

NOTES:

1. Thomas R. Horn, *Nephilim Stargates: The Year 2012 and the Return of the Watchers, 2012.* Defender Publishing, Crane, MO. pp., 26, 27, 146, 163,.201, 202 (used with permission)
2. Professor I.D.E. Thomas, *The Omega Conspiracy: Satan's Last Assault on God's Kingdom,* 2008, Anomalos Publishing House, Crane 65633
3. Nicholas Notovich, *The Unknown Life of Christ. The Lost Years of Jesus: The Life of Saint Issa,* 1894, India, http://reluctant-messenger.com/issa.htm
4. This article was first printed on http://www.jubilee.org.nz/articles/buddha-prophesied-jesus/ and is being used here with permission. Permission was granted to copy these Buddhist Scriptures from Wat Phra Sing in ChiangMai Province. The person who gave permission was Phra Sriwisutthiwong in Bangkok. It is guaranteed that there is no error in transmission, which is in the book of the district headman, the religious encyclopedia volume 23, book #29. This inquiry was made on October 13, 1954 AD, (Buddhist era 2497)) Phra Sriwisutthiwong is the Deputy Abbot and Director of Wat Pho Museum, Wat Pho Temple, Thailand.
5. Ella LeBain, Book One *Who's Who in the Cosmic Zoo of Aliens and ETs, Third Edition,* pp.326-329. Tate Publishing, 2013.

CHAPTER TEN

GODS OR ETS? – WHAT'S NEXT?

"Life's riddles are answered in the movies."
~ Steve Martin, *Grand Canyon*

ARE FALSE GODS JUST EXTRATERRESTRIALS?

There are some in the field of Ufology and New Age circles who believe we need to cultivate a relationship with the "benevolent extraterrestrials" in order to save humanity from the malevolent ones. As I've stated in my introductory chapter on Exopolitics in Book One of *Who's Who In the Cosmic Zoo?*, this is a dangerous path to take. There is no way that earth humans have evolved their spirits to be able to discern correctly between the benevolent and malevolent ETs and aliens. How can they tell who is who?

While yes, some of the malevolent ones may be obvious, it's the ones that are not so obvious, the ones who claim to be of the "light," the ones who make all kinds of promises to earth humans through various channels, the ones who stake their claim to fame as the space brothers who have come to save us ... these are the ones that earth humans need to be most suspicious of because Lucifer, the leader of the Cosmic rebellion against the Creator God, was once the "Light Bearer." To this day, he still masquerades as an angel of light.

I am reminded of the TV mini-series, *V,* which is about a group of good-looking human-looking extraterrestrials who land on Earth, make contact with earth humans, and appear to be kind and benevolent. This, of course, is only their outer covering. When they peel off their skin, they are reptilian lizard beings with malevolent intentions. All the earth humans were duped.

Let's not forget that Lucifer's hierarchy consists of fallen extraterrestrial angels, who have the same motis operandi — to deceive earth humans and mislead them away from the Creator's Divine plan of Salvation and the path of Christ. They may appear to be angels of light, as they masquerade as ascended masters, space brothers and "star gods," but underneath they have evil intentions toward earth humans. Many of them have reptilian bodies and natures; they have the powers to shape shift and project themselves as human when they walk among us. This is why I believe, Stephen Hawking, the famous physicist, said in 2010, not to make contact with aliens. He warns that alien life might try to conquer and colonize Earth.

Until every single ET and alien starts showing their "ID" to all the earth humans they contact, as every traveler on earth is compelled to do so when traveling from country to country in the form of a passport or driver's license, then no earth human should have any business trying to make contact with any extraterrestrial unless they know without a doubt "who" they are, where they come from, and what exactly is their agenda for earth humans and planet Earth. Just think of how many earth humans have been duped by their ruse of empty promises to lift groups off the planet, which never happened.

Let us never forget all the doomsday cults that were born out of deception and wishful thinking. Heaven's Gate, comes to mind, where their leader Applegate was convinced they were going to hitch a ride on a space craft as comet Hale Bopp passed the earth, and convinced all of his followers to commit suicide in order to "get on board." Suicide is self-murder which is influenced by demonic spirits. Sadly, this group did not make their ride.

Perhaps this is one of the main reasons for the UFO cover-up. Maybe the official denial from military ranks is because they genuinely feel that the alien presence on earth is way too shocking for most earth humans to handle. The truth is definitely stranger than fiction. So they deal with it within their own ranks and feel that only "qualified" people should interact with them. Yet without spiritual discernment, they, too, can make the wrong judgment when it comes to dealing with aliens, as was the case when the US Military made a deal with a group of Grays, only to be betrayed and have the whole thing blow up in their face, literally, in what was known as the "Dulce Wars" in their underground facilities. (See my section on the Dulce Wars, pp. 185-203 in Book One of *Who's Who In The Cosmic Zoo?*)

As a result of the exopolitical landscape between the US Military and various groups of aliens, they have created what Stephen Basset[1] has called a "Truth Embargo." When we understand the seriousness of the situation and how threatening and dangerous it is to earth humans, one can understand why the military makes those decisions to keep the truth from the public in order to uphold National Security measures, by protecting society. The "inconvenient" truth that pervades the US Military in preventing full disclosure about the alien presence on earth is to their embarrassment because they entered into an agreement with the wrong group of aliens.

While I have no way to prove this for sure, just based on accounts from a variety of whistleblowers, I would imagine that a faction of the US Military in charge of making these decisions probably felt strong-armed and perhaps even bullied by these aliens as well as being lured in by the attractive exchange for advanced technology.

The Elite on this planet have, for thousands of years, been appeasing the Reptilian Overlords of this planet which is what all the secret societies have been formed to venerate, such as the Order of the Dragon, the Order of the Seraphim, and the Order of the Snake, and various other serpent and Luciferian cults that make up the foundation of the Illuminati and the power elite on this planet. As you've read in Book One in *Who's Who in the Alien and ET Zoo,* the Reptilians are controlled by Satan.

When Lucifer became Satan after rebelling against the Almighty Creator, he was cursed into the beast, i.e., the dragon, the reptilian form. This is why he controls a hierarchy of Draconian Reptilian overlords, princes, and warriors, which believe that

CHAPTER TEN: Gods Or ETs? — What's Next?

planet Earth belongs to them because Earth was once given to Lucifer as a kingdom, and as the story goes, after Adam and Eve succumbed to his seductions, he continued to rule the earth albeit in a constant cosmic drama with the Almighty Creator God over the creation of earth humans.

The "illumined" ones, aka the Illuminati, are aware of this, and this is why the worship and appeasement of these Reptilian Overlords is the basis of all mystery schools and their source for gaining power and control on earth, but this all comes with a price, and that is their very souls. Unraveling and disclosing all of this is way too much for the US Military and the shadow governments of this world to bear, so with each new appointed president, it is easier for them to continue the pattern of "official denial" than it is to have any government of transparency for the people and by the people, which is in reality, nothing more than an American ideal.

Ufologists have said over and over again that, once the "official" announcement is made that we have been contacted by aliens and ETs, it will alter the foundations of society as we know it, particularly religions. So, in the meantime, the information trickles down from a variety of whistleblowers, investigators, researchers, and contactees, which is disseminated to the public and put on the market place in the form of books, documentaries, and Hollywood films for all those interested. My contribution is to encourage *spiritual discernment*, to encourage earth humans to seek the Creator God first and foremost, and allow Him to guide and protect us.

I want to promote the understanding that, first and foremost, this is a spiritual battle which trickles down into both the material and non-material worlds. That when we align ourselves on the side of the victor and the only one who has ultimate authority over all the aliens, ETs, gods, and angels, then we, as a human society are in good hands.

Sadly, there is so much unbelief in the world that the scriptures tell us creates a "deaf and dumb" spirit which causes earth humans' ears and eyes to be closed spiritually and creates a spiritual "muteness" when it comes to understanding spiritual and inter-dimensional realms. As a result of this spiritual condition, earth humans as a society turn first toward science and proving this in the realm of the scientific before turning to God for answers.

Fortunately, we are living in a time where science and spirit are merging with one another, and ancient laws are catching up with modern science in many ways, from food laws to the laws of interacting with the spirit realm, which has all been written down in the Bible thousands of years ago, all for good reasons. We are reminded that there is nothing new under the sun.

The Bible tells us that the Almighty Creator Lord God will punish the gods, that he will "famish" the gods by starving them of their powers for misleading earth humans down the wrong paths. This is something every earth human should take seriously. Yes, many have invested their lives and all of their money and their spirits into the worship of many of these gods, but where will it take them? Unfortunately many earth humans are bound by pride and stubbornness, and the false belief that they have the right to follow any religion they want to. While on an earth level, this may be true, what if they are being misled?

Well, yes, "Everything is permissible" — but not everything is beneficial. "Everything is permissible"—but not "everything is constructive" (1 Corinthians 10:23). We must use wisdom. "If anyone lacks wisdom, he should ask God, who gives generously to all without finding fault, and it will be given to him" (James 1:5). We must seek the guidance from the Almighty Creator God Himself. It is only through Him that we can learn discernment and even be given the gift of discernment (1 Corinthians 12:10).

In my opinion, the only way out of this dilemma is for humanity to repent and seek to renew their personal relationship with the Almighty Creator God, and He will guide humanity with wisdom, and discernment, and He will protect earth humans from the deleterious and deceptive influences of the pseudo-gods.

> "You are my witnesses," declares the LORD, "and my servant whom I have chosen, so that you may know and believe me and understand that I am he. **Before me no god was formed, nor will there be one after me**. I, even I, am the LORD, and apart from me there is no savior. I have revealed and saved and proclaimed-- I, and not some foreign god among you. You are my witnesses," declares the LORD (Yahuah), "that I am God. Yes, and from ancient days I am he. No one can deliver you out of my hand. **When I act, who can reverse it**?"
>
> (Isaiah 43:10-13)

These are powerful words. This is why it says "the fear of the Lord is the beginning of wisdom." He has allowed all these dramas with these pseudo-gods to take place, to reveal His true power in the end, and to test to see how many people will love Him willingly, and how many will be seduced by the empty promises from these ancient aliens pretending to be gods.

(Emphasis and commentary in brackets are mine):

> "The Spirit clearly says that in later times some will abandon the faith and follow deceiving spirits and things taught by demons."
>
> (1 Timothy 4:1)

> "They are demonic spirits who work miracles and go out to all the rulers of the world to gather them for battle against the Lord on that great judgment day of God the Almighty."
>
> (Revelation 16:14)

> "And he performed great and miraculous signs, even causing fire to come down from heaven to earth in full view of men."
>
> (Revelation 13:13)

CHAPTER TEN: Gods Or ETs? — What's Next?

Fire coming down from heaven happens from spaceships and UFOs. It's a modern day *Star Wars*.

"They [**the gods of this world**] will make war against the Lamb (Jesus Christ), but the Lamb will overcome them because he is Lord of lords and King of kings--and with him will be his called, chosen and faithful followers."

(Revelation 17:14)

"Then I saw the beast and the kings of the earth and their armies gathered together to make war against the rider on the horse [**Jesus Christ**] and his [**celestial**] army."

(Revelation 20:8)

"So if the Son sets you free, you will be free indeed."

(John 8:36)

NOTES:

1. Steven Basset, http://www.paradigmresearchgroup.org

CHAPTER ELEVEN

WHO ARE THE BIBLICAL GOD(S)?

"Mother is the name for God
In the lips and hearts of little children."
~William Makepeace Thackeray

So much gets lost in translation. Today's Bibles use the word LORD and God to describe the voice of God. But when you read the original Hebrew, we see that those words for LORD and God are not always the same. Both the word LORD and God are not names, but merely titles.

It is clear that there are many names for God. However, in the Hebrew/Aramaic language, it is very specific, with respect to singular, plural, masculine, or feminine participles. Through Hebrew, we can delineate the many names of the God of the Bible. The Bible is an historical record of the many interventions and interactions from multiple gods. They are definitely not all one and the same. Suffice it to say, the Bible describes a cast of characters of one Creator God of gods and the gods that He inevitably created and called his sons.

ELOHIM

אלוהים

In Genesis 1:1, Psalm 19:1, the Hebrew word, Elohim is used, which means "gods." Elohim is mentioned over 2,500 times in the Old Testament. Aware of the plurality of this Hebrew word, many Christians believe that the Elohim refers to the trinity, which describes the Father, Son, and Holy Spirit. Nowhere in the Hebrew Bible is there a Hebrew word for trinity, which is Shelosh; Shelishiyah (שילוש; שלישיה).

A trinity implies three separate beings acting as one. Just as unity implies two separate beings acting as one. However, the Elohim is more than just a trinity or a unity; it implies a group of "ELs" which in Hebrew is translated as God. Why would Hebrew use a plural word to describe one god while there are many other words in Hebrew that do in fact describe the Almighty as one? The Hebrew word "Elohim" is not that word.

The *Bene Elohim* translates from Hebrew to the *Sons of the God(s)*, which is only mentioned twice. The Elohim are extraterrestrial deities, in the true sense of the word. They do not reside on this planet, but are sent to intervene in the affairs of humanity. They are part of the Human Vine of Extraterrestrials. They are also considered *Ultraterrestials* in that they are beyond the limitations of most extraterrestrials, and have the power to be both inter-dimensional, and obviously extraterrestrial, but can travel and create with mere thoughts, words, and decrees.

The Hebrew Scriptures are clear that the Elohim are a *council of gods*. Hebrew is a very specific language, and the word Elohim is in its masculine plural form. Elohim is plural for "Gods" or "Magistrates" and is the word used to describe a pantheon of Canaanite Gods, who are the children of "EL."

> "And God (Elohim) said, Let us make man in our image after our likeness...So God (Elohim) created man in his own image, in the image of God (Elohim) created he him; male and female created he them."
>
> (Genesis 1:26, 27)

In the original Hebrew, the word for God is Elohim, which we've already established is plural or "uniplural" because it is a collective noun. Hebrew is very specific when it comes to the cohortative verb mood, as well as singular, plural, masculine, and feminine nouns. The specific use of the words "us" and "our" indicates that "they" are speaking as a collective group, which concludes that early man (Adam and Eve, known as the Evadamic man or Evadamic vine) was not created by one singular god, but by a group of gods known as the Elohim.

Yes, the Bible does delineate the difference between the Elohim and El-Elyon, who is the Almighty Creator Father God who created the Elohim, as the Elohim are considered children of the Father God (El-Elyon), which means God Almighty. This is why the Elohim represent the Creator Father, which is why, in verse 27, the object pronouns shift to "he" when they collectively say, "in the image of God (Elohim) created he him; male and female created he them." Suffice it to say, that man was created in the image of the Creator Father, by the Elohim, who were also created by that same image, likeness, and DNA.

The scriptural facts are that Yahuah (YHVH) is the Most High God of the Elohim:

> "For YAHUAH (the LORD) your God is the God (Elohei) of gods (Elohim) and Lord of lords (Adonai HaAdonim), the great God (EL), mighty and awesome, who shows no partiality and accepts no bribes."
>
> (Deuteronomy 10:17)

THE YHWH CODE

The mapping of the genetic code, known as DNA, is probably the most important scientific breakthrough of the new millennium.

CHAPTER ELEVEN: Who Are The Biblical God(s)?

"Mapping the chemical sequences for human DNA — the chemical 'letters' that make up the recipe of human life — is a breakthrough that is expected to revolutionize the practice of medicine by paving the way for new drugs and medical therapies."[1]

A direct link can easily be found between the building blocks of life and the Creator of the universe. Mankind is fearfully and wonderfully made (Psalm 139:14), equipped with a hidden code within the cell of every life. This code is the alphabet of DNA that spells out the Creator's name and man's purpose.

Geneticists discovered a "map" of four DNA bases that carry the ability to sustain life. These bases, known as chromosomes, are paired differently for each person. Human DNA contains twenty-three pairs of chromosomes, made up of hydrogen, nitrogen, oxygen, carbon, and their acidic counterparts. Programmed within these elements is an amazing blueprint of life that proves the Creator has put His own unique stamp upon every person. This stamp is actually His *name* as revealed to Moses thousands of years ago. It is the very secret in our DNA.

At the burning bush the Almighty revealed his character as the great "I AM." His name is called the Tetragrammaton of the Hebrew letters yod, hey, uau, hey. "I AM WHO I AM. This is what you are to say to the Israelites: I AM has sent me to you." The Almighty said to Moses, "Say to the Israelites, Y H W H, (pronounced Yahuah), the mighty one of our forefathers." "This is my name forever, the name by which I am to be remembered from generation to generation." (Exodus 3:14-15)

The Almighty has given us His name as a sign of His existence and an avenue of communication. However, translators hid His Hebrew name in English Bibles. In the Scriptures, the sacred name of YHWH is used whenever the English words "LORD" or "GOD" appear in all capital letters. Yahuah (YHWH) is used almost 7,000 times throughout the Bible as the unique name of the Almighty One of Israel.

After all, we are told, in Genesis 1:26 that we are made in the image and likeness of God. When comparing this four-lettered name to the four elements that make up human DNA, therein lies an ancient secret of creation.

Rabbi Daniel Rendelman[1] writes in the *YHWH Codes,* "The key to translating the code of DNA into a meaningful language is to apply the discovery that converts elements to letters. Based upon their matching values of atomic mass, hydrogen becomes the Hebrew letter Yod (Y), nitrogen becomes the letter Hey (H), oxygen becomes the letter Wav (V or W), and carbon becomes Gimel (G). These substitutions now reveal that the ancient form of YHWH's name, YHWH, exists as the literal chemistry of our genetic code."

"When we substitute modern elements for all four letters of YHWH's ancient name, we see a result that, at first blush, may be unexpected. Replacing the final H in YHWH with its chemical equivalent of nitrogen, YHWH's name becomes the elements hydrogen, nitrogen, oxygen, and nitrogen (HNON) — all colorless, odourless, and invisible gases! In other words, replacing 100 percent of YHWH's personal name with the elements of this world creates a substance that is an intangible, yet very real form of creation! This is

173

not to suggest that YHWH is simply a wispy gas made of invisible elements. Rather, it's through the very name that YHWH divulged to Moses over three millennia ago that our world and the foundation of life itself became possible. YHWH tells us that in the form of hydrogen, the single most abundant element of the universe, He is a part of all that has ever been, is, and will be."

> "Hear, O Israel: The LORD (YAHUAH) our God, the LORD (YAHUAH) is one." (Unity)
>
> (Deuteronomy 6:4)

This essentially means, that everything that moves, lives, and has breath obtains its essence in the pure spirit state of Yahuah, God Almighty. This is why the scripture says, "Let everything that has breath, praise the LORD (Yahuah)."

> (Psalm 150:6)

For this very scientific reason, there is no room for atheism. Atheists say that there is no God. But what they are really saying is, "I don't know God." Now we know that God exists, because God exists within the very cellular structure of our DNA. This is why there is no excuse for atheism. "Because that which may be known about God is manifest within them, because God has made it plain to them. For since the creation of the world God's invisible qualities—His eternal power and divine nature—have been clearly seen throughout His creation, being understood from what has been made, so that people are without excuse."

> (Romans 1:19-20)

THE ELOHIM ARE NOT YHVH (YAHUAH)

The Elohim are the Mighty Ones of God, who are ruled by Yahuah, El Elyon, who is the Almighty Creator God.

The word *Elohim* is used as a plural verb in 1 Samuel 28:13: "The witch of Endor tells Saul that she sees 'gods' (Elohim) coming up (*olim*, plural verb) out of the earth."

The Elohim are the sons of the Most High. The word *Elohim* occurs more than 2,500 times in the Hebrew Bible, with meanings ranging from "god" in a general sense (as in Exodus 12:12, where it describes "the gods of Egypt"), to a specific god (e.g., 1 Kings 11:33, where it describes Chemosh "the god of Moab", or the frequent references to Yahuah as the "Elohim" of Israel), to demons, seraphim, and other supernatural beings, to the spirits of the dead brought up at the behest of King Saul in 1 Samuel 28:13, and even to kings and prophets (e.g., Exodus 4:16).

According to the famous medieval rabbinic scholar Maimonides, the Elohim occupy the seventh rank of ten in the Jewish angelic hierarchy. Maimonides said: "I must premise that every Hebrew knows that the term Elohim is a homonym, and denotes God, angels, judges, and the rulers of countries."

Yahushua (Jesus Christ) was the only begotten son, meaning the only one who came into flesh and was the most highly favored (beloved) son, who was One with the Father Yahuah. Nevertheless, the Elohim play many roles in scripture. Sometimes they show up as creators, and other times, they test humans. The elohim (with a small "e") have been used to describe pagan gods. One must take into account the context in which the word *Elohim* is used in scripture. The Elohim have often been mistaken and misinterpreted to be "the Lord." The Lord is Yahuah, who is the Lord God and Creator of the Elohim (gods).

In the following verses, Elohim was translated as God singular, in the King James Version, even though it was accompanied by plural verbs and other plural grammatical terms.

"...and there he built an altar and called the place El-bethel, because there the gods (HaElohim) had revealed (plural verb) himself (should be, 'themselves') to him when he fled from his brother."

(Genesis 35:7)

Here the Hebrew verb "revealed" is plural, hence: "the-gods were revealed." A NET Bible note claims that the Authorized Version wrongly translates: "God appeared unto him." This is one of several instances where the Bible uses plural verbs with the word Elohim.

Elohim is not one of God's names, but the word means "gods." Within the Elohim are a council of gods. Each of these gods have individual names. But they are all known as sons of the Most High God El-Elyon, El Shaddai, also known as Yahuah.

THE DIVINE COUNCIL OF ELOHIM

Psalm 82:1, "Elohim presides in the great assembly; and gives judgment among the "gods" (Elohim), or "Elohim has taken its place in the divine council."

In the Hebrew, both words for God are Elohim. Specifically what the Hebrew implies is that the gods (Elohim) take congregation of the mighty God, in the midst of judges and rulers as gods. This clearly implies that the Elohim are a council of gods who all answer to the Almighty God and are in exopolitical appointments as judges and rulers within the Divine Council. Again, the word Elohim does not mean a singular God, and this verse clearly distinguishes them from the Almighty God, to whom they all answer to.

Yet, all English Bibles, translate the word *Elohim* as God, singular, misleading many to think that, when the Elohim show up in Bible history, it is referred to the Lord Most High. Clearly this is not the case with Hebrew scripture. It is the Most High God,

(Yahuah, El Elyon) who is speaking in various Bible stories, when they are clearly two entirely different spiritual entities, one being subject to the other. The Elohim are not Yahuah, the Almighty God, but they are gods with a small "g." This discernment is lost in most English translations.

However, it is very revealing that the various translations of Psalm 82:1 indicates that the Elohim are a council of gods, which make up the congregation of gods, who all stand before and answer to the Most High God, who is Yahuah (YHVH). They are clearly NOT the Most High God, and therefore are not GOD or LORD in the capital sense. Yet, the singular word "God" is mis-translated for the Hebrew word Elohim, which is clearly plural.

> Psalm 82:1: "God (Elohim) presides in the great assembly; he gives judgment among the "gods": (NIV)
>
> "God (Elohim) presides over heaven's court; he (they) pronounces judgment on the heavenly beings: (NLT)
>
> "God (Elohim) has taken his (their) place in the divine council; in the midst of the gods he holds judgment: (ESV)
>
> "God (Elohim) stands in the congregation of the mighty; he judges among the gods." (KJV)

But in verse 6 of the Psalm, it gets more specific about who exactly are the *Elohim*. The Most High God says to the other members of the council, "You [plural] are *Elohim* (gods)." "I have said you are gods and all of you are children of the most High." Psalm 82 is evidence of a scene of "the gods" meeting together in Divine Council, standing in judgment against the wicked and upholding the orphaned, the fatherless, and the weak. The Elohim stand in the council of El. "Among the Elohim He (El Elyon) pronounces judgment." Here *Elohim* means gods and specifically states that they are sons and children of the Most High, which in Hebrew is Elyon (Yahuah). Various translations:

> "I said, 'You are "gods"; you are all sons of the Most High. (Elyon)' (NIV)
>
> "I say, 'You are gods; you are all children of the Most High. (NLT)
>
> "I have said, you are gods; and all of you are children of the Most High. (KJV)

Let's not forget Yahshua's argument reiterating this Psalm (82) in John 10:34-36 "And then, in answer to the charge of blasphemy, Jesus replies 'Is it not written in your Torah (Psalm 82).' 'I said ye are gods? If he called them gods unto the word of God came, the Scripture cannot be broken.' Now what is the force of this quotation 'I said ye are gods?' It is from the Asaph Psalm which begins 'Elohim hath taken His place in the mighty assembly. In the midst of the Elohim He is judging.'"

Elohim is always plural in Hebrew. The singular version is El. El would be translated as "God," yet Elohim are always mistranslated as "God" as well, completely ignoring the

CHAPTER ELEVEN: Who Are The Biblical God(s)?

specificity of the Hebrew language, which is always either singular, plural, masculine or feminine.

Psalm 82 illustrates a scene of the gods meeting together in divine council as a congregation standing before Elyon. Among the Elohim, he pronounces judgment. Yahshua argues concerning this Psalm (82) in John 10:34-36 in an answer to the charge of blasphemy. "Yahshua replies 'Is it not written in your Torah (Psalm 82).' 'I said you are gods? If he called them gods unto the word of God came the Scripture cannot be broken.' "Now what is the force of this quotation: "I said you are gods?" It is from the Asaph Psalm which begins: Elohim hath taken His place in the mighty assembly. In the midst of the Elohim, He is judging.' "What about the one whom the Father set apart as his very own and sent into the world? Why then do you accuse me of blasphemy because I said, 'I am God's Son?'"

Another example is Psalm 8:5 where "Yet you have made him a little lower than the Elohim." The Septuagint reads this as "gods" and then later corrected the translation to "angels," which is an inaccurate translation, as the word for *angels* in Hebrew is "malachim," not Elohim. Then this reading is taken up by the New Testament in Hebrews 2:9. "But we see him who for a little while was made lower than the angels, namely Yahshua/Jesus." The following version of Psalm 8:5 comes from the NIV, the bracket comments and emphasis is mine.

> "What is man (mortals) that you are mindful of him, the son of man (Messiah) that you care for him? You made him (the son of man) a little lower than the heavenly beings (Elohim; i.e., gods) and crowned him with glory and honor."

In the original Hebrew, the word used is "MayElohim." The prefix, "May" can mean "from," or "more than," in this case, the word "ma'at, "which means "little," is ahead of it. So in this tense, it is a little (or less than) from the Elohim (gods), only to be exalted above them later. This Psalm is prophetic of the life of Yahshua, who lowered himself into the "son of man," and temporarily was lower than the Elohim, in order for the rest of humanity to be saved through him. The Hebrew never uses the word angels (malachim).

"This shows that the Son is far greater than the angels, just as the name God gave him is greater than their names." (Hebrews 1:4)

The words of Joshua sets the record straight in distinguishing the Elohim from the Almighty YAHUAH:

> "And if it seem evil unto you to serve YAHUAH, choose you this day whom ye will serve; whether the Elohim (Mighty gods) which your fathers served that [were] on the other side of the flood, or the Elohim of the Amorites, in whose land ye dwell: but as for me and my house, we will serve our heavenly Father YAHUAH."
>
> (Joshua 24:15)

Many Christians argue that Jesus was God's "only" begotten son. Well, let's define the word *begotten*. Begotten is the past participle of the word *beget*, which means to produce or bring into being. Out of all of God's sons, Yahshua/Jesus was the only one who came into the flesh as an earthly human being. Yahshua is clearly the Lord's most favoured of all His sons. He is given His full inheritance, which is His power and authority over all creation. More on that later. But according to scripture, there are other sons of God.

In ancient Hebrew, the highest god was called "El Elyon," who was believed to have had seventy sons. These sons were known as the Elohim. Then the Elohim had sons, who were called the "Bene HaElohim". The Bene Elohim are the Sons of the Elohim or the Sons of the Gods. The phrase "Bene HaElohim," has an exact parallel in Ugaritic and Phoenician texts, referring to the council of the gods. According to the *Books of Enoch*, two hundred of these "Bene HaElohim" came to earth to mate with the daughters of men, the early humans that the Elohim created. The Bene HaElohim were later described as a band of angels (malachim) who fell from heaven, i.e., fallen malachim (angels).

> "And so it happened, one the bnei a'am (sons of man) multiplied, beautiful and wholesome daughters were born. So the malachim (A band of Angels; referred to as "The Watchers") children of the skies (Bene HaElohim), saw them and lusted for them." "They decided to leave heaven and make earth their home....
>
> In all, they were 200, those who descended upon the summit of Mount Hermon in the days of Jared. They called it Mount Hermon because they had sworn and bound themselves by mutual vows upon it."
>
> They had twenty leaders. Their leader's name was Semyaza. Their sexual relationship with women produced a genetic offspring, the Nephilim, who were part-human and part- angelic. The Nephilim considered themselves to be a superior race and turned against the humans, launching a holocaust against mankind."
>
> (*Book of Enoch*, Chapter 6)

The Bene HaElohim are mentioned three times in the Hebrew Scriptures:

> "And it came to pass, when men began to multiply on the face of the earth, and daughters were born to them, that the sons of God (*Bene HaElohim*) saw the daughters of men that they were fair; and they took them wives of all that they chose."
>
> (Genesis 6:1-2)

> "Now there was a day when the *Benei HaElohim* came to present themselves before Yahuah, and Satan came also among them."
>
> (Job 1:6)

CHAPTER ELEVEN: Who Are The Biblical God(s)?

"Again there was a day when the *Benei HaElohim* came to present themselves before the Yahuah, and Satan came also among them to present himself before the *Yahuah*."

(Job 2:1)

In both of these cases, the *Bene HaElohim* are described as separate from *Yahuah*, and presenting themselves before Him, as in a conference or royal court. The *Book of Jubilees* and *Book of Enoch* are factually consistent with Genesis and with each other.

One of the most fascinating and controversial passages in the Bible is Genesis 6:1-4. These *Bene Elohim* were sons of the Elohim who had turned away from God, and decided to make earth their home and live among the humans.

The *Book of Enoch* tells us that there were two hundred of them and that they had twenty leaders. Their offspring were called Nephilim. They were giants who turned out to be an abomination to the Lord. They were the reason the floods of Noah came upon the earth to destroy them and their wicked deeds. "They were the heroes of old, men of renown" (Genesis 6:4).

According to the *Books of Enoch*, the Nephilim made war against the humans and intended to completely wipe out the human race so only their race would inherit the earth. The Lord Yahuah intervened and stopped the Nephilim and all of their violence and evil that had come upon the earth by bringing the Floods.

THE NAMES OF THE GOD OF ISRAEL

"Therefore my people shall know my name; therefore in that day I am the One who is speaking, 'Here I am'."

(Isaiah 52:6)

"If you will not hear, and if you will not lay it to heart, to give glory to my name, said Yahuah, the LORD of hosts, I will even send a curse on you, and I will curse your blessings: yes, I have cursed them already, because you do not lay it to heart."

(Malachi 2:2)

The following are the many other names of God (Yahuah) in the Bible, names which describe His specific characteristics and attributes:

Aleim - sometimes seen as an alternative transliteration of Elohim.

Some have asked, where is the word "Father God" in the Old Testament? The Hebrew words "Avinu Malkeinu" literally translate to "Our Father, our King."

Abi/Avi - My Father
Abi Yah - My Father Yah

Adonai - The rabbinic substitute for the Tetragrammaton. Malachi 1:6, meaning "Lord," a reference to the Lordship (authority) of God. The correct translation of Adonai is Yahuah. Zeroah Adonai - Arm of God.

Adon Olam - "Master of the World"

Avinu Malkeinu - "Our Father, our King"

Boreh - "the Creator"

El - means "God" singular (Genesis 33:20, 46:3)

El Abhir - Mighty One.

El Elohe Yisrael - "El the god of Israel" (Genesis 33:20)

El Berith - Covenant Keeper

Elah - This is another name that is translated as Yahuah (God). It is used seventy times in the Hebrew Scriptures. It is combined with other words to make a different attribute of Yahuah is emphasized.

Elah Shemaya - The God of Heaven, "His throne is in heaven, He rules over the heavenly hosts." (Ezra 7:23)

Elah Shemaya Varah - The God of Heaven and Earth, (Ezra 5:11)

Elah Yisrael - The God of Israel, (Ezra 5:1)

Elah Yerushaliyem - The God of Jerusalem, (Ezra 7:19). He is forever bound to Jerusalem. It is the apple of His eye, His eternal capital, and future center of the universe.

El Chaiyai - The God of My Life, (Psalm 42:9). He is the strength of my life.

El Chanun - The Gracious God (Jonah 4:2). His nature is gracious, even when we do not deserve it.

El Chesed - God of Loving-kindness.

El Chuwl - The God Who Created You and Gave You Birth and Life, (Deuteronomy 32:18; Psalm 139:13-8).

El Dayot - The God of all Knowledge, "Whatever knowledge man has comes from Him, He is the source of all knowledge. (1 Samuel 2:3). He is revealed as the "I Am That I Am" whose depth of knowledge is unsearchable. He knows all, and in Him, all deeds are weighed and judged. (Romans 11:33-36),

El Ehad - The One (Malachi 2:10). Echad means "oneness" and implies compound unity.

Ha' el Elohe Akiba - "El, the god of your father" (Genesis 46:3)

El-Elyon - meaning "The Most High God;" Elyon means 'Supreme' God. (Genesis 14:17-20, Isaiah 14:13-14) Elyon signifies power and position. He is the lifter of our heads, our Most High Yahuah.

El-Gibbor - The Mighty God, God the Hero, God the Strongest One, or God the Warrior. He is the mighty warrior and the strongest force in the universe. (Isaiah 9:6)

El-Abhir - The Most Powerful

El-Ha Gadol - The Great God. Gadol means He is big and large. He is larger than any circumstance, bigger than any problem. (Deuteronomy 10:17)

CHAPTER ELEVEN: Who Are The Biblical God(s)?

El Ha Kadosh - The Holy God. El Ha Kadosh the holy one, pure and righteous, undefiled in any way. (Isaiah 5:16)

El Ha Kavod - The God of Glory. At the hand of El Ha Kavod the world is beautiful and glorious, and He is glorious. (Psalm 29:3)

El Ha Ne'eman - The Faithful God. El Ha Ne' eman is faithful to all that trust and obey Him. He is the keeper of his covenant with us, and performs His word. (Deuteronomy 7:9).

El HaShamayim - The God of the Heavens. El HaShamayim rules over the heavenly realm. (Psalms 136:26). Melech Ha Olam means He is King of the universe, (Daniel 2:8).

El Kana - The Jealous God. El Kana is extremely protective toward His beloved children, and forbids us to share out affections with other pagan "gods". (Deuteronomy 4:24). His very name El Kana is jealous (Exodus 34:14). El Kana commands us 44 times in the Torah (Law) to avoid any form of idolatry. El Kana, who is jealous for your beloved affection.

El Lahai - The God Who Lives.

El Ma'ownah - The Mighty God of Our Refuge. In El Ma'ownah we find refuge and help. (Deuteronomy 33:27).

El Maowz Dal - The God Who is a Defense to the Helpless, (Isaiah 25:4). El Maowz Dal lifts us up, and gives victory to the helpless. (Exodus 2:23-25).

El Maowz Ebyowne - The God Who is a Defense to the Needy, (Isaiah 25:4). El Maowz Ebyown is the defense to the poor and needy, those in want, and to those who are subject to oppression and abuse. (Exodus 23:6).

El Nasa - The Forgiving God - Yahuah (Psalms 99:8). El Nasa reveals Himself as forgiving, compassionate and merciful, particularly through the embodiment of His Son Yahshua HaMashiach (Jesus Christ). Not to be associated with America's NASA, the space agency, although it's an interesting coincidence that the Hebrew word sounds the same as the space agency's abbreviation.

El-Olam - "The Everlasting God" (Isaiah 40:28-31), The God of Eternity, or the Mighty God Yahuah of the Universe, (Genesis 21:33). El Olam is King and ruler of eternity, He is eternal, the maker of time, and the universe. El Olam is without beginning and end.

El Palet - The God who Delivers.

El-Roi - "Living God who Sees", or "The Strong One Who Sees". His eyes are on those who believe and obey Him, and upon all things done in secret and in darkness. He discerns and knows the very thoughts and intents of our heart. Nothing escapes El Roi's sight. (Genesis 16:13)

El Sali - The God of My Rock (Psalms 42:10). El Sali is my rock, He is the firm foundation.

El Simchat Gili - The God Yahuah, Who is the Joy of My Exaltation (Psalm 43:4). El Simchat Gili is my joy, and He removes sorrow. His presence fills us with perfect joy, and we exalt Him.

El-Shaddai - meaning "Under the Mighty Wing of Almighty," or "The Great Almighty Breast" 'Shad' means breast or nurturer in Hebrew, El Shaddai also means the "Almighty Nurturer". Shaddaim is the Hebrew word for breasts. (Genesis 17:1, Psalm 91:1) El Shaddai is like a nursing mother nourishing His children. He is all sufficient for us.

El Tzakik - The God of Righteousness. He is Holy and Righteous. (Isaiah 45:21)

El Yahshuati - Yahuah, the God of My Salvation. He is the source of my salvation (Isaiah 12:2). This is where the name of the Son comes from. Yahshua HaMashiach, aka, Jesus Christ the Messiah/Savior.

Elohei is the singular form of Elohim, meaning God. Elohim meaning 'gods'. Elohai explains the different attributes of the Creator Yahuah Emphasized. The Most High God rules over all the Elohim. The name Yahuah always follows or precedes these descriptions, defining which these attributes belong to.

Elohei Avraham, Elohei Yitzchak ve Elohei Ya'aqov - "God of Abraham, God of Isaac and God of Jacob"

Elohei Bashamayim - God in Heaven (Deuteronomy 4:39), Ruler of the Heavens. He is Yahuah, there is no other.

Elohei Chasdi - Yahuah, God of My Kindness, (Psalms 59:10)

Elohei Elohim - Yahuah of the Gods (Deuteronomy 10:17). He is supreme Yahuah, the God of all gods.

Elohei Gelah Raz - Yahuah, the Revealer of Secret Things, (Daniel 2:22, 28, 47).

Elohei Ha Ruchot Le Kol Basar - Yahuah, the Lord God Of the Spirits of all Flesh, (Numbers 16:22). Ruach HaKodesh is the Holy Spirit which is His Spirit.

Elohei Kedem - The Eternal Yahuah Of The Beginning (Deuteronomy 33:27).

Elohei Kol Basar - Yahuah Of All Flesh (Jeremiah 32:27).

Elohei Marom - Yahuah of Heights (Micah 6:6).

Elohei Mauzi - Yahuah of My Strength (Psalms 109:1).

Elohei Mikarov - Yahuah Who Is Near (Jeremiah 23:23).

Elohei Mishpat - Yahuah of Justice (Isaiah 30:18).

Elohei Olam Zerovot - The Everlasting Arms (Deuteronomy 33:27).

Elohei Selichot - Yahuah, God of Forgiveness (Nehemiah 9:17).

Elohei Tehilati - Yahuah, God of My Praise (Psalms 109:1).

Elohei Tzur - Yahuah, God of Rock (2 Samuel 22:27). He is our rock and our foundation.

Elohei Tzevaot - Yahuah, the God of Hosts, or the God of Armies. (2 Samuel 5:10). He is the mighty warrior and the Commander in Chief of the armies of Heaven, and earth.

Elohei Yachal - Yahuah of Hope (Romans 15:13).

CHAPTER ELEVEN: Who Are The Biblical God(s)?

Elohei Yishi - Yahuah, God of My Salvation (Psalms 18:47, 25:5). The words Yishi and Yahshua come from the same root, meaning salvation and deliverance. He is our deliverer, Yahuah, who saves us through YAHUAHshua (Jesus Christ).

Ehyeh-Asher-Ehyeh - Exodus 3:14 is the first three responses given to Moses when he asks for God's name. The Tetragrammaton itself derives from the same root. After the destruction of the Second Temple, there remained no trace of knowledge as to the correct pronunciation of the Name (see Tetragrammaton). The Rabbinical authorities and commentators, however, agree as to its interpretation, that it denotes the eternal and everlasting existence of God, and that it is a composition of היה הוה יהיה (meaning "a Being of the Past, the Present, and the Future").

The name Ehyeh (היה) denotes His potency in the immediate future, and is part of YHVH. The phrase "ehyeh-asher-ehyeh" (Exodus 3:14) is interpreted by some authorities as "I will be because I will be," using the second part as a gloss and referring to God's promise: "Certainly I will be [ehyeh] with thee" (Exodus 3:12). The King James Bible translates the Hebrew as I AM THAT I AM and uses it as the proper name of God. However the literal Hebrew translation is "I will be what I will be" or "I will be because I will be" or "I will be that I will be" or in the book of Revelation 1:4, 1:8, 4:8: "I am The Existing One."

I AM THAT I AM: the Almighty I AM Presence, Latin, *ego sum qui sum*, "I Am Who I Am" (Exodus 3:14, John 8:58). The word ego comes from the Latin, but in this sense in Hebrew, it refers to the Higher Self, which is God, not the lower ego that English refers to as the personality.

Immanuel - "God is with us" (Matthew 1:23)

Ancient of Days - (Daniel 7:9)

Emet - "Truth"

The Elect One - Meshiach (Messiah) also known as the Anointed One

Ein Sof - "endless, infinite", Kabbalistic name of God

HaKadosh, Baruch Hu - "The Holy One, Blessed be He"

Kadosh Israel - "Holy One of Israel"

Melech HaMelachim - "The King of kings" or Melech Malchei HaMelachim "The King, King of Kings," to express superiority to the earthly rulers title.

Magen Avraham - "Shield of Abraham"

Ribono shel 'Olam - "Master of the World"

Roeh Yisrael—"Shepherd of Israel"

Tzur Israel—"Rock of Israel"

HaShem - means The Name" - (Leviticus 24:11) it was common Jewish practice to restrict the use of the word "Adonai" to prayer only, but Jews were not to utter any of the names of God in conversation, so they refer to Him as "HaShem."

HaMakom - "The Omnipresent" literally Hebrew for "The Place." Used in traditional expression of condolence in Hebrew; e.g., "The Omnipresent One will comfort among the mourners"

Adoshem - Basically combining the first two syllables of the word "Adonai" with the last syllable of the word Hashem. This was discouraged by the leading rabbinical authorities as it took a few hundred years for it to become obsolete.

Shekhinah – "Eternal Light" of God which is the feminine presence or manifestation of God who descends to "dwell" among humankind. It has been used as the "Shekhinah Glory" shines down on the Torah, (the Law of God) and is the presence of God that comes upon a man and a woman when they get married. It is sometimes seen as a white light with a very uplifting, joyful and healing presence.

The Lord of Spirits - This term was first penned by Enoch in his scrolls. It refers to the Almighty Creator of all souls and spirits. It is the Father of all spirits. He has given all authority in heaven and on earth to his anointed one, Yahshua, which is why the demons tremble at the name of Jesus (Yahshua). The *Books of Enoch* tell us about the ten heavens. (See Book Five: *The Heavens,* of *Who's Who In The Cosmic Zoo?*)

Enoch wrote about the un-nameable God in the upper heavens, the One who oversees all. In fact, in Revelation 19:12, it tells us when the Lord returns with all of his crowns, there will be a name that no one knows but Himself: "His eyes are like blazing fire, and on his head are many crowns. He has a name written on him that no one knows but He Himself."

NOTES:

1. Rabbi Daniel Rendelman, *The YHWH Code*, Emet Ministries, http://www.emetministries.com

CHAPTER TWELVE

THE TETRAGRAMMATON

"My people will know my name."

(Isaiah 52:6)

There are four Hebrew consonants (YHVH יהוה) called the Tetragrammaton. Suffice it to say, that this Holy Name of the God of Israel has been mispronounced, mis-transliterated, and basterdized to the point of creating three completely different names which have gone on to become counterfeit gods. The ancient Aramaic-Hebrew correct pronunciation of the name (YHVH יהוה) is "YAHUAH"! Pronounced YaHuWah.

"The name of the LORD (YAHUAH) is a strong tower; the righteous man runs into it and is safe."

(Proverbs 18:10)

So why all the confusion and controversy over the name? And why all the changes over time?

I'll get right to the point, to the ultimate reason the Sacred Holy Name of God (YHVH יהוה) has been changed so many times. It is because it is and has been Satan's goal to be worshipped and to steal worship from the Most High God. He hates YAHUAH (YHVH יהוה), and he is not thrilled about humans either because humans were given souls and the chance to have the Kingdom of Heaven through Yahshua, which Satan lost. He is insanely jealous that YHVH יהוה favored humans over the angels.

Therefore, Satan's plan has been from the beginning to get humans to worship him and not YHVH יהוה, and essentially "steal" from humans the opportunity to inherit the Kingdom. He does this in very sneaky ways, and altering the Holy Name of God and creating a couple of counterfeits for himself is one of his plans. Satan does not care how you worship him: yahweh, yahveh, yahovah, jehovah, ahayah, allah, Elohim, god, etc. Anytime we call the Father by any name other than יהוה YAHUAH, Satan is pleased. The god of this world (Satan) loves to deceive and counterfeit the Lord.

But many will say that it doesn't matter what pronunciation you use or what language you speak; if you're heart belongs to the Lord, then He still hears prayers. Because of the fact that His name has had so much historical theft and deliberate counterfeiting, creating confusion, mistranslation, and outright avoidance of even saying the name, as is the case with most Jews, suffice it to say, there is much Grace upon this issue for those who are believers and worship the Lord in spirit and in truth. So what happened historically to create such controversy of the sacred name?

WHY YAHUAH? WHY NOT YAHWEH OR JEHOVAH?

After the Jewish exile from Israel and Judea (Sixth Century B.C.), and especially from the third century BC on, Jews ceased to use the name YAHUAH for two reasons. As Judaism became a universal religion through its proselytizing in the Greco-Roman world, the more common noun Elohim, meaning "Mighty gods" tended to replace YAHUAH (YHVH יהוה) to demonstrate the universal sovereignty of Israel's God (*descriptive character*) over all others. At the same time, the divine name was increasingly regarded as too sacred to be uttered; it was thus replaced vocally in the synagogue ritual by the Hebrew word Adonai ("My Lord"), which was translated as Kyrios ("Lord") in the Septuagint, the Greek version of the Old Testament.

Jewish scholars, known as the Masoretes, worked to reproduce the original text of the Hebrew Bible during the sixth to the tenth centuries A.D., by adding vowels to the name YHVH יהוה. This is how the artificial/counterfeit name Jehovah pronounced, YeHoVaH in Hebrew, came into being. Although after the Renaissance and Reformation periods, Christian scholars used the term Jehovah for YHVH. In spite of that, in the nineteenth and twentieth centuries, some biblical scholars continued to use the form YAHUAH.

Early Christian writers, such as Clement of Alexandria in the second century, had used the form YAHUAH, and this correct pronunciation of the Tetragrammaton was never really lost. Other Greek transcriptions also indicated that YHVH should be pronounced Yahoo-ah. The pronouncement of Yahoo-ah really sounds like Yahoo-wah, then gradually truncated to Yahweh, and another counterfeit god was born. Yes, pronunciation matters here.

The word *Jehovah* appears five times in the 1611 *King James Version* (Genesis 22:14; Exodus 6:3; Exodus 17:15; Psalms 83:18; Isaiah 12:2; 26:4) As Harper's Bible Dictionary (copyright 1985 p. 1,036) explains: "Its (i.e. the word 'Jehovah') appearance in the 1611 *King James Version* was the result of the translators' ignorance of the Hebrew language and customs."

Many scholars believe that the most proper meaning of YAHUAH-Asher-YAHUAH is 'I was, I am, and I Always Will Be." In 1 Samuel, "God" is known by the name YAHUAH Tzevaot or "The Lord of Hosts" (Lord of Celestial Armies). The hosts also refer to the heavenly court, which is made up of all of heavens extraterrestrials also called

CHAPTER TWELVE: The Tetragrammaton

angels on earth, who have remained faithful to their Creator Lord YAHUAH, the Almighty, including the Elohim. As I've noted previously, the word *Tzevaot* means "armies."

It is also interesting to note that, in spite of the fact that the transliteration "Jehovah" has been used for some time, neither the Hebrew, nor the Greek up to this day ever had the letter "J." The Hebrew language has only twenty-two letters, consisting only of consonants. Vowels were added mainly to help the language to be relearned. This was done by monks. Many of whom were not Hebrew speaking.

I believe the confusion and the many mispronunciations and mis-transliterations come from the misunderstanding of the letter ו **Vav** or **Uau**. In Hebrew, this letter can be used in three different ways: 1) as an "uau" which has an "oo" sound, which is the correct pronunciation of Yah-oo-ah (Yahuah); 2) as a "vav," which has a "v" sound, which is where the word Yahveh came from, which was later mispronounced as Yahweh; or 3) as an "O" which is a long "o" sound, hence the rendering Yahovah/Jehovah.

The name YHWH (YAHUAH) appears in the original Hebrew manuscripts 6,823 times. Almost every translation on Earth, including the King James Bible, takes out the Creator's personal name and replaces it with the name Lord, a generic title that means Baal or Master. In English versions of the Scriptures, His Name is commonly substituted with the title "LORD" written in all caps as well as the word "God" written in small caps. "The LORD" and "God" are not translations of His Name, but are merely titles.

They are substitutions of His True Hebrew Name YAHUAH, due to superstition and over-reverence, it has been replaced with the meaningless title LORD, which means Baal or Master. This constitutes as a breach of the first and the third Commandments; the first commandment forbids to have any other gods before YAHUAH. The third commandment strictly forbids using YAHUAH's name in vain. "In vain" literally means to change, falsify, or make common.

Obviously, all this was Satan's handiwork. Not only was this done with the name of YAHUAH (YHVH יהוה), but also His Son's name or directly transliterated YAHUSHUA יהושע, has been changed into a Greek hybrid of Jesus, which is a poor transliteration from the Greek IE-Zeus. This is the poor Greek transliteration of the name you find in most English bibles. As mentioned earlier, even the original 1611 King James Bible never once used the name Jesus, but Ieseus.

The English transliteration of Yahshua would be the equivalent to Joshua. Because the letter "J" did not exist, in any language until the sixteenth century. The Greek transliteration name "Jesus" clearly changes the name of the Messiah and fulfills the Messiah's own prediction of his true name not being accepted, but that most people would accept another name, hence, the modern English name Jesus. The fact of the matter is that when the Messiah walked the earth in the flesh, nobody called him Jesus.

There are nearly one hundred times in the Hebrew Tanach (Old Testament) where the personal name of the Messiah, YAHUSHUA is personified in the Holy Scriptures, but due to the fact that most translators do not recognize the true Hebrew name of the

Messiah as YAHUSHUA, they do not translate these references about the Messiah into the English language, which is clearly lost in translation.

Conspiracy? Or just plain ignorance? So what are we now to think? It's hard to dispute the fact that substitutes have been made; some are so far removed from the original, thereby creating several counterfeits to the "Holiness" and "Sacredness" of HIS Majestic Name, the Almighty Creator God. YAHUAH is his name!

יהוה = YAHUAH

"This is My Name forever, and this is My remembrance to all generations."
(Exodus 3:15)

Many people worship without knowing their Father's true name and, through mispronunciations, end up unintentionally invoking and worshipping a counterfeit god, who is one of the satans (Hebrew for "adversaries"). The Heavenly Father is seeking those who worship Him in spirit and truth (John 4:23). The truth is that His Name is NOT Lord or God. These names are titles, and tell what He is, but they are not names. His name is not Yahweh, Yahveh, or Jehovah, the Father's Name is יהוה YAHUAH.

"And it shall be that everyone who calls on the Name of יהוה Yahuah, shall be saved." (Joel 2:32, Acts 2:21; Romans 10:13)

He is the Sovereign Creator of the universe, Maker of all things. YAHUAH means 'I WAS, I AM, I WILL BE.' YAHUAH is forever present in all three tenses: past, present, and future. YAHUAH is Self-Existent! (Psalm 68:4, Isaiah 12:2, 38:11).

There is an easy and simple way to know, pronounce, and remember the Father's name. Most people know how to pronounce the name of the Tribe of Judah which in Hebrew is YAHUDAH (yod, he, vav, daleth, he). The only difference between the spelling for the name of YAHUDAH and the Father's name of YAHUAH is one letter, the D (daleth). So if you remove the letter D from the name YAHUDAH you have the proper pronunciation for the Father's name of YAHUAH. Here is how the Hebrew root (*shoresh*) is built along with their correct corresponding pronunciations:

יה = YAH
יהו = YAHU
יהוה = YAHUAH
יהודה = YAHUDAH

CHAPTER TWELVE: The Tetragrammaton

Everyone knows the word *Halleluyah*, which in Hebrew simply means "Praises to Yah," which is truncated for Yahuah. In poetry the name of Yahuah is abbreviated as Yah.

Here is another major false belief that was born out of fear, superstition, false humility, and satanic interference. Jews have a tradition to avoid saying the name of God. Instead, as I've already mentioned, Jews refer to Him as *HaShem* which means "the name" or *Adonai* which means "Lord." They won't even write out the entire word, God, but instead write "G-d." God is not a name; it is a title and function. So let's measure this tradition against scripture ... more importantly, the Jewish scripture. What is the LORD commanding his people to do?

YAHUAH commands us to CALL upon His Name, to make His Name known, and to *not* wipe out or forget His Name (Isaiah 12:4; Psalm 105:1,3; Exodus 9:16; Ezekiel 39:7; Deuteronomy 12:3,4; Jeremiah 23:27; Psalm 44:20).

The following scriptures contain the original name, (that has since been replaced with the titles LORD and God):

"Moreover YAHUAH said to Moses, 'Thus you shall say to the children of Israel: YAHUAH the God of your fathers, the God of Abraham, the God of Isaac, and the God of Jacob, has sent me to you. This is My name forever, and this is My Memorial Name to all generations.'"

(Exodus 3:15)

His Name is Memorial. The original Hebrew text used the word "my memorial name." This means it is to be remembered for ever. One thing about the Lord — He has been consistent throughout the scriptures in telling His people "who" He is and "what" is His name? This is why, for those scriptures where His name does not appear, but the words are used for God, this is not Him talking, but a counterfeit and an adversary.

Abraham thought it was the Lord who told Him to go sacrifice his miracle child Isaac. Yet, according to the scripture, the Lord YAHUAH is never mentioned in the Genesis story, only the words "a voice," and later the words, Elohim, which is NOT the name of the Lord, but a group of mighty gods, that answer to the Lord YAHUAH.

At the end of the story, an angel (extraterrestrial messenger) was sent from YAHUAH to prevent Abraham from harming his son. Abraham thought he was being tested by the Lord YAHUAH, yet this was clearly not YAHUAH testing him, but the adversary within the Elohim. We know this from reading the scriptures in Job 1 and Job 2 when the Elohim appear before the Lord Yahuah and HaSatan was among them.

How many of us mistake the actions and tests of our lives as coming from the Most High, when in reality we are being tested by His chief adversary, the chief adversary of our souls, who are the satans, i.e., the devil masquerading as god? We must learn to discern the voice and actions of the Lord, from the voice and actions of HaSatan (the adversary of our souls).

Many people mistakenly believe that the story of Jacob wrestling with an angel was actually the Lord Jesus Christ. I go into great detail in my chapter on Angel Protocol in Book Three of *Who's Who In The Cosmic Zoo?* proving that this was not the Lord, based purely on the "Word" of scriptures and its original meanings in Hebrew. We must learn to discern the difference between the Lord's angels, Satan's angels, and an actual encounter with the Lord Himself.

In this story, the angel (or a man as he is described) refuses to tell Jacob what his name is after Jacob asks him his name. This is NOT, the character of YAHUAH, nor Yahushua! Both the Father and the Son consistently throughout scripture reveal their name to those humans they encounter. They even give authorization to USE their name, to heal the sick, cast out demons, and raise the dead, in the same way a Father gives a son a blank check.

His name endures forever!

> "HIS NAME ENDURES FOREVER! Your name O YAHUAH, endures forever. Your fame, O YAHUAH, throughout all generations."
>
> (Psalms 135:13)

> HIS NAME IS A MEMORABLE NAME! "That is, YAHUAH Father of hosts. YAHUAH is His memorable name."
>
> (Hosea 12:5)

We are told to CALL UPON HIS NAME in order to be saved and delivered. Of course, HaSatan knows this and tricks humans into calling on one of his names, instead of the Holy name of god, in order to interfere, and even steal away their salvation and deliverance from him!

> "And it shall come to pass that whoever calls on the name of YAHUAH shall be saved. For in Mount Zion and in Jerusalem there shall be deliverance, as YAHUAH has said, among the remnant whom YAHUAH calls."
>
> (Joel 2:32)

Reiterated in the New Testament:

> "And it shall come to pass that whoever calls on the name of YAHUAH (YAHUSHUA) shall be saved."
>
> (Acts 2:21)

> "For "whoever calls on the name of YAHUAH (YAHUSHUA) shall be saved."
>
> (Romans 10:13)

CHAPTER TWELVE: The Tetragrammaton

Both translations use the word LORD, but it is HIS NAME that is above all other names, not his title.

We are told to PRAISE HIS NAME! If we do not know His name, then how can we properly praise His name or him? Of course, this is another one of HaSatan's tricks. If we praise the wrong name, then he steals the worship from the Most High God and sucks it up himself, deceiving many heartfelt believers in the process. This is why congregations have to get His name straight. If they are praising a counterfeit god with a false name, they are essentially invoking the presence of the satans into their midst, whose sole purpose is to steal, kill, and destroy (John 10:10).

This is why churches are thwarted, stunted, and in bondage to all kinds of demonic strongholds. Worship is one of the major weapons in spiritual warfare. Let's not forget that Lucifer was once the worship leader in Heaven. He guarded the throne of Yahuah and led the angels in worship of Him until He decided, one day, that He wanted it for himself. This is why the satans (i.e., demonic) cannot stand it when people worship the Lord, but they can stand it when people are tricked into worshiping their leader, who is Satan, who wears many masks and answers to many names.

"From the rising of the sun to its going down YAHUAH's name is to be praised."
(Psalms 113:3)

We are told to GLORY IN HIS HOLY NAME, not shrink away from it. Say it, seek it, praise it. "Glory in His Holy Name; Let the hearts of those rejoice who seek YAHUAH!" (Psalms 105:3)

The Scriptures tell us that ALL THE NATIONS will GLORIIFY HIS NAME. Imagine that! "ALL THE NATIONS whom You have made shall come and worship before You, O Sovereign Lord, and shall glorify Your Name! (Psalms 86:9)

We are told to DECLARE HIS NAME! "To declare the Name of YAHUAH in Zion, And His praise in Jerusalem, When the peoples are gathered together, and the kingdoms, to serve YAHUAH. (Psalms 102:21)

"I will DECLARE YOUR NAME to My brethren; In the midst of the assembly I will praise You." (Psalms 22:22)

We are told to WALK IN HIS NAME! "For all people walk everyone in the name of his god, but we will walk in the Name of YAHUAH our Father forever and ever." (Micah 4:5)

We are encouraged to RUN TO HIS NAME! "The Name of YAHUAH is a strong tower: The righteous run to it and are safe." (Proverbs 18:10)

We are told to SING TO HIS NAME! "All the earth shall worship You and sing praises to You; they shall sing praises to Your Name." (Psalms 66:4)

We are told to GIVE THANKS TO HIS HOLY NAME! "Save us, O YAHUAH our Father, and gather us from among the Gentiles, to give thanks to Your Holy Name, to triumph in your praise." (Psalms 106:47)

We are encouraged to EXALT HIS NAME! "Oh, magnify YAHUAH with me, and let us exalt His Name together." (Psalms 34:3)

We are told to BLESS HIS NAME! "Sing to YAHUAH Bless His Name: Blessed be the name of YAHUAH!" (Psalms 96:2) And Job said: "Naked I came from my mother's womb, And naked shall I return there. YAHUAH gave, and YAHUAH has taken away Blessed be the name of YAHUAH" (Job 1:21)

We are admonished to WAIT UPON HIS NAME! "I will praise You forever, Because You have done it; And in the presence of your saints I will wait on Your Name, for it is good." (Psalms 52:9)

We are told to REMEMBER HIS NAME! "Some trust in chariots, and some in horses; but we will remember the Name of YAHUAH our Father." (Psalms 20:7)

We are told to seek His Name, "Fill their faces with shame, that they may seek Your Name, Oh YAHUAH." (Psalms 83:16)

We are told to KNOW HIS NAME! Not some other counterfeit name attached to a false god and satanic fallen angel masquerader seeking to steal souls. We must know exactly "who" we are putting our trust in. "And those who know Your Name will put their trust in You; For You, YAHUAH, have not forsaken those who seek You." (Psalms 9:10)

We are told to MEDITATE ON HIS NAME! Then those who feared YAHUAH spoke to one another, And YAHUAH listened and heard them; so a book of remembrance was written before Him for those who fear YAHUAH and who Meditate on His Name." (Malachi 3:16)

We are admonished to FEAR HIS NAME! "But to you who fear My Name the Sun of Righteousness shall arise with healing in His wings; and you shall go out like calves released from the stall." (Malachi 4:2) The Sun of Righteousness is the Son of YAHUAH, YAHUAZADEK, which is the future name of Christ, who is the Son of Righteousness, who comes with healing in His wings.

We are encouraged to TRUST IN HIS NAME! "Who among you fears YAHUAH who obeys the voice of His Servant? Who walks in darkness and has no light? Let him trust in the Name of YAHUAH and rely upon his Father." (Isaiah 50:10) This world is ruled by dark forces; many walk in darkness and don't even realize it.

Even believers, who are misled by Satan into worshipping a false god, are bound by religious spirits, who deceive them into thinking that Yahweh or Jehovah are the most high gods, but in reality, they are giving their worship over to Satan. This is supreme darkness. By their fruits, you will know them. The first fruit is freedom. "Where the spirit of the LORD is, there is freedom." (2 Corinthians 3:17)

CHAPTER TWELVE: The Tetragrammaton

We are told to SANCTIFY HIS NAME (set His Name apart)! "But when he sees his children, the work of my hands, in the midst of him, they shall sanctify my name, and sanctify the Holy One of Jacob, and shall fear the God of Israel." (Isaiah 29:23)

We are told who HIS HOLY NAME dwells with: "For thus says the High and Lofty One Who inhabits eternity, whose Name is Holy: "I dwell in the high and holy place, but also with him who has a contrite and humble spirit, to revive the spirit of the humble, and to revive the heart of the contrite (repentant) ones." (Isaiah 57:15)

We are told HIS NAME IS EXCELLENT and above the heavens! "O YAHUAH, our Sovereign, how excellent is Your Name in all the earth, who have set your glory above the heavens! (Psalms 8:1)

HIS NAME IS MAJESTIC! "And He shall stand and feed His flock in the strength of YAHUAH, in the majesty of the Name of YAHUAH His God; and they shall abide, for now He shall be great to the ends of the earth." (Micah 5:4)

HIS NAME IS HOLY AND AWESOME! "He has sent redemption to His people; He has commanded His covenant forever: Holy and awesome is His Name." (Psalm 111:9)

In the book of Malachi, chapter two, we learn how Yahuah cursed the Priests of Israel for no longer esteeming His name. They stopped speaking His name; they stopped uttering it on their lips, and this broke the special anointing they once enjoyed from Yahuah. They became compromised with a *religious spirit,* succumbing to spiritual pride, and they stopped teaching His name to the people of Israel. In fact, the Israelites were told a lie — that they should never utter the sacred name of God, lest they be struck with a curse and die.

Turns out, according to the scriptures, it was the priests who were held responsible for this curse, not the people of Israel, but because they believed the lie, they suffered the fellowship between themselves and their Creator, causing them to be lost in the wilderness, literally walking around in circles in search of the promised land. If the people of Israel would have continued to keep the commandments from the LORD to praise, worship, and memorialize His name, they wouldn't have spent so much time in confusion. They were later tagged in history as the "Wandering Jews."

Here is what the LORD Yahuah had to say about that when He warned His Priests through the prophet Malachi:

> "And now, O you priests, this commandment is for you. If you will not hear, and if you will not lay it to heart, to give glory to my name, said the LORD of hosts, I will even send a curse on you, and I will curse your blessings: yes, I have cursed them already, because you do not lay it to heart."
>
> (Malachi 2:1-2)

While the LORD Yahuah does not want you to take His name in vain, it is glaringly clear and obvious throughout scriptures that He very much wants His children to use His name whenever they are in need, so that the blessings of His holy name may be rained down upon them. He commands his children to praise his name, think his name, sing to his name, memorialize his name, and most definitely use His name for every spiritual, emotional, and physical need.

The curse of the priests of Israel was later manifested in spiritual blindness when the Sanhedrin and the Pharisees conspired to crucify Yahshua, simply because they were threatened by His power to save, deliver, heal, and work miracles throughout the land of Israel, without going through them, the high priests, first. It's clear to any historian that this was a case of jealousy and sabotage. The spirit behind the jealous and bitter high priests was, no doubt, satanic and caused by a spiritual assignment upon them, aka the Lord's curse on them, opening up the spiritual legal ground, creating a portal for satan to work through them, which everyone agrees is what happened, historically speaking.

THE PERSONALITY OF YAHUAH

YHVH Tzevaot - The name YHVH (Ya-hu-wah) and the title of God (*Elohe*) and Lord (*Adonai*) frequently occur with the word *tzevaot* or *sabaoth* ("hosts" or "armies) such as YHVH (Yahuah) *Elohe Tzevaot* ("YHVH the God of Hosts"), *Elohe Tzevaot* ("The God of Hosts"), *Adonai* YHVH *Tzevaot* ("Lord YHVH of Hosts") and, most frequently, YHVH (Yahuah) Tzevaot ("YHVH of Hosts").

As I previously stated, the Tetragrammaton YHVH (Yahuah) is used close to 7,000 times in the Hebrew Scriptures to describe the personality of YHVH (Yahuah), His characteristics, and all of His attributes. Here are some of them:

Yahuah-Attiyk Yomeen - meaning "The Ancient of Days" (Daniel 7:9, 13, 22).

Yahuah-Bara - meaning "Yahuah Creator God" or "Lord of Creation" (Isaiah 40:28).

Yahuah-Kether - meaning "Yahuah Our Hiding Place" (Psalm 32:7)

Yahuah-Elohim - meaning "Lord Yahuah" or "God of the Elohim" (Genesis 2:4). This proves that the Hebrew words — Elohim and Yahuah — are distinctly different. In English translations, both words are translated as God. Yet, only Yahuah is the Lord and God. The Elohim are the sons of God and plural "gods." Genesis 2:4 makes it clear that Yahuah is the God of the Elohim. Yahuah is the Lord of the gods.

"Hear O Israel Yahuah Elohaynu, Yahuah Echad." Hear O Israel, Yahuah is our God, Yahuah is One. (Deuteronomy 6:4)

Yahuah-Erek Appayim - meaning "Yahuah, The Lord of Long Suffering" (Psalm 86:15).

Yahuah-Ishi - meaning "Yahuah, Our Husband" "In that day," declares the Yahuah (Lord), "you will call me 'my husband'; you will no longer call me 'my master' (Hosea 2:16). "As a young man marries a maiden, so will your sons marry you; as a bridegroom rejoices over his bride, so will your God rejoice over you." (Isaiah 62:5) "Jesus said, at

CHAPTER TWELVE: The Tetragrammaton

midnight the cry rang out: 'Here's the bridegroom! Come out to meet him!'" (Matthew 25:6) The Bridegroom is the Lord coming for His Bride, who are His faithful believers.

Yahuah-Ga'al - meaning "Yahuah Our Redeemer" (Isaiah 49:26). "I will make your oppressors eat their own flesh; they will be drunk on their own blood, as with wine. Then all of mankind will know that I, Yahuah, am your Savior, your Redeemer, and the Mighty One of Jacob."

Yahuah-Gibor - meaning "Yahuah the Hero" or "Yahuah the Warrior" (Zephaniah 3:17). Yahuah Elohe Gibor, means, 'Yahuah our God who is our Hero/Warrior'.

Yahuah-Gmolah - meaning "The God of Recompense" (Jeremiah 51:6).

Yahuah-Hazak - meaning "The Lord of My Strength" (Isaiah 40:31).

Yahuah-Ha Adonim - meaning "Yahuah, Lord of Lords" (Deuteronomy 10:17), Yahuah is the Lord over all the powers in the universe.

Yahuah-Hatikvahti - meaning "Yahuah is My Hope" or "The Lord is My Hope" (Psalm 71:5).

Yahuah HaMoshiah - means "Yahuah the Deliverer" (1 Samuel 14:39).

Yahuah-Hesed - meaning "Yahuah, The Lord of Lovingkindness" or "The Lord of Love" or "Yahuah, the Merciful One." "Yahuah (The Lord) is compassionate and gracious, slow to anger, abounding in love" (Psalm 103:8). "Return to the Lord (Yahuah) your God, for he is gracious and compassionate, slow to anger and abounding in loving-kindness, and he relents from sending calamity." (Joel 2:3)

Yahuah-Maccaddishem - meaning "Yahuah, The Lord who sanctifies" (Exodus 31:13).

Yahuah-Magen - meaning "Yahuah, The Lord is My Shield" (Psalm 3:3)

Yahuah-Melek Ka'avode - meaning "Yahuah, The King of Glory" (Psalms 24:9, 10).

Yahuah-M'kadesh - meaning "Yahuah Who Makes Us Holy" (Ezekiel 37:28). Any holiness we have comes from Him, which comes from our closeness to Yahuah M'kadesh. All are sanctified and made holy through Yahushua HaMashiach, known today as The Lord Jesus Christ.

Yahuah Moshiah - means "Yahuah the Deliverer". (1 Samuel 10:19); Yahuah Yahushua, "Yahuah Saves and Delivers" (1 Samuel 17:47; Psalm 37:40)

Yahuah-Natsar - meaning "Yahuah Who Preserves Us From Trouble" (Psalms 32:7). Petition Yahuah Natsar over your children to keep them from troubles in life. Call Him in your time of trouble.

Yahuah-Nissi - meaning "Yahuah is My Miracle" or "Yahuah is My Banner" (Exodus 17:15).

Yahuah-Ori - meaning "Yahuah Is My Light" or "The Lord is My Light" (Psalms 27:1): "Yahuah is my light and my salvation. Whom shall I fear? He is the stronghold of my life, of whom shall I be afraid? He is always with us, and lights the path before us with His illuminating glory."

Yahuah-O'saynu - meaning "Yahuah Our Maker" (Psalms 95:6).

Yahuah-Ra'ah - meaning "Yahuah Our Shepherd" (Psalms 23:1). He watches over us. He is the good shepherd.

Yahuah-Rab - meaning "Yahuah, The One Who Abounds" (Psalm 103:8).

Yahuah-Rapha - meaning "The Lord Yahuah is our healer" (Exodus 15:26).

Yahuah-Umarim Roshi - meaning "Yahuah, The One Who Lifts My Head" (Psalms 3:3).

Yahuah-Shalom - meaning "Yahuah, The Lord is My Peace" (Judges 6:24, 2 Thessalonians 3:16).

Yahuah-Shammah - meaning "Yahuah, The Lord Who is Ever Present, He is always there" (Ezekiel 48:35).

Yahuah-Shaphat - meaning "Yahuah, The Lord Is Our Judge" (Isaiah 33:22). Yahuah is our Judge and Lawgiver. "There is only one Lawgiver and Judge, the one who is able to save and destroy." (James 4:12)

Yahuah Shuah - meaning, "Yahuah the Savior", Yahuah Hoshiah, Yahuah Saves, truncated, YAHUSHUA, YAHSHUA, YESHUA (Psalm 20:6); in English, Jesus Christ.

Yahuah-Tsidkenu - meaning "Yahuah, The Lord is our Righteousness" (Jeremiah 23:6).

Yahuah-Tzevaoth - meaning "Yahuah, The Lord of Hosts" (Isaiah 6:1-3) or "The Lord of the Armies" (1 Samuel 1:11). He is the Supreme Commander and Chief of the Celestial Armies.

Yahuah-Yireh (Jireh) - meaning "The Lord will Provide" (Genesis 22:13-14). He knows all that we need and provides.

Yahuah Yahshuati - means, "Yahuah is the God who saves me" or "Yahuah, my salvation" (Psalm 88:1). Yahuah walked the earth in the flesh and blood body of His son, who was named "Yahushua," which means, Yahuah Saves, or Yahuah the Savior, also known as Jesus Christ.

Yahuah-Pele Yoetz - meaning "Yahuah, The Wonderful Counselor." "For unto us a child is born unto us a son is given and the government shall be upon his shoulder and his name shall be called Wonderful Counselor, the mighty God, the everlasting Father, and the Prince of Peace." (Isaiah 9:6)

THE NAME YAH

Yah - 'Jah' יה is composed of the first two letters of the Tetragrammaton YHVH, it is used in praise, as in the expression "Halleluyah," which means Praise Yah or Praise the Lord. (Psalm 68:4). Yah is the shortened form of YHVH and has the same meaning as Yahuah (YHVH). Yah is used approximately forty times in the Hebrew Scriptures. Yah appears mainly in the book of Psalms. "Jerusalem is built as a city that is compact together, to which the tribes of Yah (the Lord Yahuah) go up" (Psalms 122:3-4).

CHAPTER TWELVE: The Tetragrammaton

HIS NAME IS YAH! (Psalms 68:4) This is where we get the praise word "Hallelujah" which in Hebrew means "Praise to Yah" or "Praise the Lord." Yah יה is shortened from YAHUAH יהוה.

> "Sing to the Gods (Elohim), sing praises to His name; EXTOL HIM <u>who *rides* on the clouds</u> (on the heavens), BY HIS NAME YAH יה, and rejoice before Him."
>
> (Psalms 68:4)

What I love about this scripture is that it reveals that YAH rides on the clouds of heavens. This is not just poetic or metaphorical, but a literal Word of God (See my chapter Mother ships of the Lord).

> "Let the heavens praise your wonders, O LORD (YAHUAH), your faithfulness in the assembly of the holy ones! For who in the skies can be compared to the LORD (YAHUAH)? Who among the heavenly beings is like the LORD (YAHUAH), a God greatly to be feared in the council of the holy ones, and awesome above all who are around him? O LORD (YAHUAH) God of hosts, who is mighty as you are, O LORD (YAHUAH), with your faithfulness all around you?"
>
> (Psalm 89:5-8)

Every Semitic language scholar, if honest, must admit the miracle of the global preservation of the word *Halleluyah*. In all tongues, the whole world knows how "Halleluyah" is pronounced! They may not know what it means, but they know how to say it. I submit this miracle as Evidence #1 to the doctrine of the obvious...

HalleluYAH means "Praise Yah". **Hallelu,** in this context, means to "praise" ecstatically, and is a second-person imperative masculine plural form of the Hebrew root verb *hallal*. From this, we know that what follows this word is the SUBJECT of the praise, which is YAH, a truncation and poetic form of YAHuah. **Yah** is a shortened form of **YAHUAH**, the name for the Creator.

Nowhere, in any language, in any culture that I know of, is HalleluYAH pronounced "Hallelu-YEH." While scholars and proponents of the pronunciation Yehovah/Jehovah may offer all kinds of complex excuses to explain away the obvious, truth is, the obvious remains, the name of the Creator begins with **YAH**(YAHuaH), not YEH (Yehovah) and the evidence is in the word to Praise Yahuah, HalleluYAH! Nearly almost every honest language scholar admits this, as well as the timeless, unaffected way it is pronounced throughout generations, in all languages around the world through today.[2]

He is true to His name, which means I was, I Am, and I always will be.

> "I AM the LORD (YAHUAH), and I change not."
>
> (Malachi 3:6)

What is intriguing and most interesting about the Bible is that nearly all of the Prophets carry a part of **YAHUAH's** Name within their Names. Every one of their names "testifies" to *who* YAHUAH is to us, who believe in and call on His Name.

It's important to note that the correct "title" for the Creator in Hebrew is "Eloah" and not the pagan title "God." Eloah is Creator (a title), whose name is YAHUAH.

YAHUAH'S NAME WITHIN THE PROPHETS

Bible Name	Phonetic Pronunciation	Meaning in Hebrew
Aaron	AHaron	YAHUAH is Exalted
Abiathar	EbYAHtaar	The Father YAHUAH of Abundance
Adam	AHdam	YAHUAH's Mankind
Ahaziah	AchazYAHU	Seized by YAHUAH
Ahaz	AHchaaz	YAHUAH is the Possesor
Amariah	AmarYAHU	Promise of YAHUAH
Amaziah	AmatsYAHU	Strength of YAHUAH
Amos	AHmoce	YAHUAH is Strong
Asahiah	AsaYAH	The Maker is YAHUAH
Azariah	AzarYAHU	The Helper is YAHUAH
Benaiah	BenaYAHU	The Builder is YAHUAH
Benjamin	BinYAHmiyn	Son of YAHUAH's Right Hand (prophesies the Savior)
Berechiah	BerekYAHU	The Blessing of YAHUAH
Dalaiah	DelaYAHU	Lifted by YAHUAH
Daniel	DaniYAHel	The decision is YAHUAH's
Eliashib	ElYAHshiyb	Eloah YAHUAH will Restore
Elioenai	ElYAHehnay	Toward Eloah YAHUAH are my eyes
Elkanah	ElqanAH	YAHUAH Eloah has Obtained
Ezekiel	YAHchezqel	YAHUAH the Righteous One
Ezra	EzrAH	Our help is YAHUAH
Gedaliah	GedalYAHU	Great is YAHUAH
Habakkuk	ChabakUuk	Embrace YAHUAH
Haggai	ChaggaYAH	YAHUAH is Celebrated or the Celebration is YAHUAH
Hananiah	ChananYAHU	Favor from YAHUAH
Hannah	ChanAH	Favor of YAHUAH
Hezekiah	YAHchizqiYAHU	Strengthened of YAHUAH
Hilkiah	ChilqiYAHU	Portion of YAHUAH
Hizkiah	YechizqiYAHU	Stengthened of YAHUAH
Hodaiah	HowdavYAHU	Majesty of YAHUAH

CHAPTER TWELVE: The Tetragrammaton

Hosea	**HosheAH**	The Deliver is YAHUAH
Isaiah	**Yesha' YAHU**	YAHUAH is salvation
James	**YAHcob**	YAHUAH rises up
Jecamiah	**YaqamYAHU**	The Riser is YAHUAH
Jehoshaphat	**YAHUshaphat**	YAHUAH is Judge
Jehoiakim	**YAHUyaqiym**	YAHUAH will Raise
Jeremiah	**YirmeYAHU**	The Resurrection Rising is YAHUAH
Jeroham	**YAHrocham**	YAHUAH is Compassionate
Jesiah	**YishshiYAHU**	The Lender is YAHUAH
Jesus	**YAHUshua**	YAHUAH our salvation
Joab	**YAHab**	YAHUAH Fathered
Job	**YAHshub**	YAHUAH Will Return
Joel	**YAHel**	YAHUAH is God
Joelah	**YoelAH**	The Ascender is YAHUAH
John	**YAHUchanon**	YAHUAH is Grace
Jotham	**YAHtaam**	YAHUAH is Perfect
Jonah	**YonAH**	YAHUAH provides Warmth
Jonathan	**YAHUnataan**	YAHUAH Gives
Josedech	**YAHUtsadaq**	YAHUAH Righted
Joshua	**YAHUshua**	YAHUAH is Salvation
Josiah	**YoshiYAHU**	Founded of YAHUAH
Jude	**YAHUDAH**	YAHUAH's Tribe, Genetic Bloodlines
Kolaiah	**QowlaYAHU**	Voice of YAHUAH
Luke	**LukAH**	The Light is YAHUAH
Maaseiah	**Ma' aseYAHU**	The Work of YAHUAH
Malachi	**MalakiYAH**	Messenger of YAHUAH
Mark	**MarkU**	Man of YAHUAH
Matthew	**MatithYAHU**	The Gift is YAHUAH
Micah	**MiykahYAHU**	Who is like YAHUAH
Moses	**MoshAH**	The Rescuer is YAHUAH
Nahum	**NachUm**	Comfort comes from YAHUAH
Neariah	**Ne' arYAHU**	Servant of YAHUAH
Nedabiah	**NadabYAHU**	Free Offer of YAHUAH
Nehemia	**NechemYAH**	Consoled, Comforted by YAHUAH
Noah	**NoAHch**	The Rest is YAHUAH
Obadiah	**ObadYAHU**	The Servant of YAHUAH
Pedaiah	**PedaYAHU**	Redeemed by YAHUAH
Pelatiah	**PelatYAHU**	The Deliverer is YAHUAH
Peter	**KephAH**	The Rock is YAHUAH

Reaiah	Re' aYAHU	Seen by YAHUAH
Rephaiah	RephaYAHU	The Cure is YAHUAH
Samuel	ShamAHuel	Listen to YAHUAH your Eloah
Saul	ShaUl	Ask YAHUAH
Seraiah	SeraYAH	The Prevailer is YAHUAH
Shallum	ShallUm	The Reward is YAHUAH
Shebaniah	ShebanYAHU	The Prosperer is YAHUAH
Shechaniah	ShekanYAHU	The Dweller is YAHUAH
Shemaiah	ShemaYAHU	The Listener is YAHUAH
Shephatiah	ShephatYAHU	The Vindicator is YAHUAH
Zechariah	ZacharYAHU	YAHUAH Remembers
Zedekiah	TsidqiYAHU	The Right of YAHUAH
Zephaniah	TsphanYAHU	The Secret is YAHUAH

REFERENCES:

1. Ann Spangler, *God's Word, The Names of God Bible,* Baker Publishing Group, 1995.
2. http://www.wwyd.org/Studies/Yahuwah_or_Yehovah.html
3. http://promotethetruth.com/id1.html

CHAPTER THIRTEEN

THE NAME ABOVE ALL NAMES

"Who has gone up to heaven and come down? Whose hands have gathered up the wind? Who has wrapped up the waters in a cloak? Who has established all the ends of the earth? **What is His name, and what is the name of his Son?** Surely you know!"

(Proverbs 30:4)

I have come in My Father's Name and you do not receive Me,
If another comes in his own name, him you would receive."

(John 5:43)

The Messiah YAHUSHUA prophesied that many would reject His true Hebrew name and accept the replacement, which is Jesus. He was right. The Messiah/Savior came in the name of His Father. YAHUSHUA is the only name that fits the Father's name YAHUAH. The Son's True Hebrew name is: **YAHUSHUA** pronounced: YA-HOO-SHOO-AH. YAHUSHUA means "YAHUAH is Salvation," which He is through His son. His son is the physical manifestation of the Father. But what if Jesus, which you will see is merely a transliteration of His Hebrew name, wasn't the other name Christ was referring to at all? What if the above verse was prophetic for the End Times?

Isn't it interesting that, in the original 1611 King James Bible, there is no one named "Jesus"! The name used for the Messiah is *Iesus Christos*. The name *Jesus* was transliterated and added in later versions, first showing up in 1769. That's seventeen centuries after he walked the earth!

"Set-apart (Holy) Father, guard them in Your Name which You have given Me, so that they might be one, as We are one."

(John 17:11-12)

The Father gave His firstborn Son His name. YAHUAH is in the name YAHUSHUA. They are One. The Son's true Hebrew name was replaced long ago with the Greek/Latin name Jesus. The letter "J" is only 500 years old. There is no "J" sound in Hebrew or Aramaic. No one called the Master "Jesus" when He walked the Earth 2000 years ago. When He appeared to Paul, He spoke in the Hebrew language (Acts 26:14-15). He could not have said, "I am Jesus," if there was no letter "J," and He spoke Hebrew (not Greek, Latin, or English). He announced His true Hebrew Name: YAHUSHUA.

Yahushua - HaMashiach- "Messiah," "Savior," truncated to "YAHSHUA" (Jesus) meaning "Salvation," aka Jesus the Christ, "The Lion of the Tribe of Judah," "the Word became Flesh."

> "In the beginning was the Word (Logos), and the Word was with God, and the Word was God. He was with God in the beginning (YAHSHUA). All things came to be through him, and without him nothing made had being. In him was life, and the life was the light of mankind. The light shines in the darkness, and the darkness has not suppressed it. The Word became a human being (the Logos became flesh) and lived with us (YAHSHUA), and we saw his Shekhinah (glory, presence), the Shekhinah of the Father's (YAHUAH) only Son, full of grace and truth."
>
> (John 1:1-5, 14)

YAHSHUA was gloriously resurrected after three days in the tomb by YHVH (YAHUAH) and can now be found sitting at His right hand. He is the "son of God" (son of YAHUAH); he is the "son of man" which points to his role as the representative of the Kingdom of "Israel" and as Messiah (Daniel 7:13-14) *Mashiach Nagid,* Messiah/King. YAHSHUA is the "sent one" (*shaliach*), the unique agent of YAHUAH (God). The Hebrew word *shaliach* comes from the same root as the Hebrew word *Mashiach*, which means Messiah/Savior.

He is the High Priest, mediating between YAHUAH and man. YAHSHUA is the "lamb of YAHUAH." He was the final sacrificial lamb, which abolished the practice of sacrificing animals for the propitiation of humankind's sins. His blood paid the final price to YAHUAH. YAHSHUA has been chosen by YAHUAH to be the King of Israel, to rule from his God-given throne, both in the Heavenly City of Jerusalem and the New Jerusalem on Earth, in the coming Messianic Kingdom during the millennial reign.

> "But one of the twenty-four elders said to me, 'Stop weeping! Look, the Lion of the tribe of Judah, the heir to David's throne, has won the victory. He is worthy to open the scroll and its seven seals."
>
> (Revelation 5:5)

The Messiah carries the fullness of His Father's name in all four Hebrew letters of YOD, HE, VAV, HE, "YAHUAH." About 169 different names of people in the Old Testament carry two or three letters of the Father's name of YAH (yod, he) or YAHU (yod, he, vav) but never ever with the fourth Hebrew letter "he." The only exception is the Messiah himself, as written in Jeremiah 23:6 and Jeremiah 33:16. There you will see the Messiah's future name of YAHUAHTZADAK (yod, he, vav, he, tsaddi, daleth, koph) with seven Hebrew letters, which is also the future name of the New Jerusalem, as also noted in Revelation 3:12. It means YAHUAH IS RIGHTEOUSNESS.

CHAPTER THIRTEEN: The Name Above All Names

יהוהצדק = YAHUAHTZADAK

If you check the New Testament Greek manuscripts, you will find the Greek name used for the Messiah as IHCOYC (iota, eta, sigma, omicron, upsilon, sigma) and other variations such as IHCOY, IHCOYN, IHCOI, depending on the grammatical structure of the sentence. It is very rare to see the name IHCOYC written out in full in the New Testament Greek manuscripts. However, in the Greek Septuagint, the only name that does match is the name for JOSHUA. It is, also, written as IHCOYC in the Old Testament Greek with its variations. In the Greek Septuagint the name IHCOYC is usually written out in full, but there are manuscripts where it is also abbreviated, just like in the New Testament Greek.

The Messiah's name in the New Testament Greek is identical to the name of JOSHUA in the Greek Septuagint. The secret is in the Hebrew name. The name of JOSHUA in the Hebrew Bible is usually written as YOD, HE, VAV, SHIN, AYIN (five letters) and pronounced as YAHUSHUA. But it is also written in its fuller form twice as YOD, HE, VAV, SHIN, VAV, AYIN (six letters) in Judges 2:7 and Deuteronomy 3:21 and is, also, pronounced as YAHUSHUA.

יהושע = YAHOSHUA
יהושוע = YAHUSHUA

The only difference between whether the second VAV is visible or not is a cosmetic one. Since Hebrew is a consonantal language, the vowels are visually put in as the reader reads the word. The second VAV is there in both cases, but in the more common occurrence, it is understood and put in while reading; while in the rare occurrence, it is there visually. In both cases, the names are identical and pronounced the same.

Even though the Messiah's name and Joshua's name are identical in the Greek, there is one major difference between the names of these two men — the fourth letter of the Father's name. Joshua only carries three letters of the Father's name as do other people in the Old Testament. <u>The Messiah carries the fullness of His Father's name</u> with all four letters. The Messiah's true name is YAHUASHUA (yod, he, vav, he, shin, vav, ayin) with seven Hebrew letters.

יהוהשוע

However, it was truncated in the original Hebrew text of the Gospel of Matthew, which exists today under glass in the British Museum, as YAHUSHUA and truncated even further as YAHSHUA. Many Messianic Jews spell it as *Yeshua*. Some of the New Testament scriptures that prove that the Messiah's name is unique:

Acts 4:12: "Salvation is found in no one else, <u>for there is no other name under heaven given to men by which we must be saved</u>."

Ephesians 1:20-21: "That power is like the working of his mighty strength, which he exerted in Christ when he raised him from the dead and <u>seated him at his right hand in the heavenly realms, far above all rule and authority, power and dominion, and every title that can be given, not only in the present age but also in the one to come</u>."

Philippians 2:9-11: "Therefore God exalted him to the highest place and **gave him the name that is above every name**, that at the name of Jesus (YAHUHshua) every knee should bow, in heaven and on earth and under the earth, and every tongue confess that Jesus Christ (YAHUHshua HaMashiach) is Lord, to the glory of God the Father."

Hebrews 1:4: "This shows that the Son is far greater than the angels, just as the name God gave him is greater than their names."

We also know that the Messiah's name is unique because there are other people in both the Old and New Testaments with the name of Jesus. In Acts 7:45 and Hebrews 4:8, the Jesus here is Joshua, the son of Nun. In Colossians 4:11, it is a Jesus called Justus. In Acts 13:6, there is Bar-Jesus, where the word *Bar* is Aramaic for son.

We are not saved through common names such as Jesus or Joshua. There are thousands of Spanish speaking people that use the name of Jesus (pronounced *HeyZeus*) as their first or last name. Also in Israel, a lot of people have the name of Yahoshua (Joshua). The Messiah's name is unique, and there is only one person with that name, and that is the Messiah Himself. There is no other name under heaven by which we can be saved.

When we call upon the Messiah using his name YAHUHSHUA, we are actually calling upon His Father because the Messiah's name carries the Father's name and means YAHUAH (the Father) is my SALVATION and DELIVERANCE.

The meaning of the root *shua* is everything that the Messiah represents — salvation, deliverance, overcoming, health, healing, help, prosperity, welfare, and well-being. This root *shua* is added to the Father's name because YAHUAHSHUA and the Father YAHUAH are one.

When we pray to YAHUAH the Father, we appeal to Him through His favored and beloved Son YAHUHSHUA, who is our High Priest after the Order of Melechitzadak, and our Passover Lamb, who became the perfect and final sacrifice, who died for the sins of humanity so that, through Him, we may have Eternal Life. This is why Yahushua said, "I am the way, the truth, and the life: no man comes to the Father, but by me" (John 14:6). He was the father Yahuah, personified in the flesh.

Many people also say that no one knows the proper pronunciation of the Father's name of YAHUAH anymore and that it has been lost, which is not true. Anyone who can read Hebrew knows it but will not pronounce it and replaces the name with other words such as Elohim (the Mighty Ones), Adonai (Lord/Master), Ha Shem (The Name), or G-D. Today's Jews are bound in so much fear and superstition that they are afraid to even spell out the word GOD; again it's only a title, not a name.

CHAPTER THIRTEEN: The Name Above All Names

The Father's Name: יהוה = YAHUAH
The Son's Name: יהושוע = YAHUHSHUA
The Chosen Royal Tribe: יהודה = YAHUDAH (Judah)

DISTORTIONS AND TRUNCATION OF THE NAME

> "In your world I have another name,
> try to understand it." ~ Aslan
> C.S. Lewis, *The Voyage of the Dawn Treader*

Jesus, Yehushua, Yahshua, Yahoshua, Iahushuah, Yahusha, Yahuahshua...the list could go on and on. All of these names are used by various "Messianic" groups as the Messiah's name. How do we know which one is correct? We have evidence in scripture that will leave no doubt as to what the Messiah's true name is.

The first issue is with the name "Jesus." Anyone familiar with the Hebrew or Greek scriptures knows that the letter "J" didn't exist in the Messiah's day. A perfect example of this can be found in the original 1611 King James Bible:

> "The booke of the generation of *Iesus* Christ, the sonne of Dauid, the sonne of Abraham."
>
> (Matthew 1:1 KJV-1611)

Through time and the evolution of language and syntax, there have been many types of truncations and abbreviations which have led to inevitable distortions and mistransliterations of the name of the Father and His Messiah Son. With the hybrid forms of Jehovah, Yahweh, Yahvah, and Jesus, we can see that the distortions evolved over time because the value of the letters of the alphabet have changed.

The letter **J** developed from the Roman letter **I** during the Middle Ages, and, at one time, was the same letter. The same can be said for the letters **U** and **W,** which both derived from the Roman letter **V,** which originally carried an **"oo"** or **"uu"** sound. Even the name for the letter **W** still carries the old value of **double UU** or, as it is called in French, **double VV**. So back in the Middle Ages, all three of these variations would have been pronounced as YAHUAH. The name Yahuah was preserved by believers, passed down to their generations.

Yahshua (YOD, SHIN, VAV, AYIN) is a truncated form of YAHUshua. In Hebrew, properly translated to and pronounced as YAHSHUA, meaning YAH is SALVATION. This is the Hebrew equivalent of the English name Jesus.

ישוע = YAHSHUA

All the different forms, variations, and substitutes can be traced back in time. Again, the word **God** is Teutonic and was used to worship stones and other pagan objects.

Lord is old English and comes from two words meaning "loaf" and "guardian," essentially "guardian of the loaf."

Amen is an Egyptian god, whose name literally means "hidden" and was used in conjunction with other Egyptian deities, such as "Amen-Ra," for example. However, the Hebrew word *amen* literally means "so be it." Therefore, saying "so be it" is an agreement to a prayer, instead of the word "amen." They are essentially one and the same. The word *amen* is in both the Old and New Testaments and in Revelation. The Messiah is, also, called "the Amen." Believers need to use the Father's name and the Messiah's name when praying so that there is no confusion as to who is being invoked in prayer.

When it comes to the name of God and the many counterfeit names of the god of this world and all of his fallen angel counterparts, ignorance is definitely not bliss. False teachings come from the counterfeit names, misleading many through counterfeit spirits and holding congregations and churches and whole denominations in bondage to spiritual witchcraft. "My people perish because of lack of knowledge" (Hosea 4:6).

JESUS = English, transliterated from the Latin.
IESOUS = Latin, transliterated from the Greek.
IHCOYC = Greek, poor transliteration of the Hebrew name Joshua.
KYRIOU = Greek, name for YHVH, or LORD.

Joshua - YOD, HE, VAV, SHIN, VAV, AYIN = Hebrew, properly translated to and pronounced in English as YAHUSHUA, the fullest form of the Hebrew name of Joshua and means YAHU is Salvation.

יהושוע = YAHUSHUA

The Name Above All Names: Joshua and Jesus are both common names, but the Messiah's name is a name above all other names. His life was anything but common. This is expressed in His name. YOD, HE, VAV, HE, SHIN, VAV, AYIN = Hebrew, properly translated to and pronounced in English as YAHUHSHUA. This is the full Hebrew name of the Messiah after his resurrection from the dead, and it means YAHUAH is SALVATION.

יהוהשוע = YAHUAHSHUA

The only tribe of Israel to carry the Father's name is the tribe of YAHUDAH (Judah). Judah was the fourth son of Jacob, who became the royal tribe of the Israelites, bearing the line of the kings of Israel, including the Messiah, YAHUAHSHUA.

CHAPTER THIRTEEN: The Name Above All Names

יהודה = YAHUDAH

The "dalet" ד added means the "door." Yahushua said that He is the "Door" to the Father (John 10:7-9). I am come in my Father's name (John 5:43).

The name of the members of the tribe of YAHUDAH is called YAHUDI.

יהודי = YAHUDI

The Messiah was born through the tribe of YAHUDAH and was called a YAHUDI. The Messiah carries the name of His Heavenly Father in his present name of YAHUHSHUA, as well as in his future name of YAHUAHTZADAQ.

The Messiah is our High Priest after the Order of Melechitzadaq which, from the Hebrew, means "The King of Righteousness."

There are about 169 people in the Hebrew Old Testament who have a part of our Heavenly Father's name of YAH or YAHU as part of their name. Here are some examples:

Isaiah = YESHAYAHU, which means Salvation of YAHU and is the Messiah's present name spelled backward less one letter.

Zedekiah = TZEDAKYAHU, which means Righteousness of YAHU and is the Messiah's future name spelled backward less one letter.

Joshua, Jehoshua, Jehoshuah = YAHUSHUA, which means YAHU is Salvation and was one of the nicknames of the Messiah while he was alive on this Earth.

JEHOZADAK, JOSEDECH = YAHUTSADAQ, which means YAHU is Righteousness, which is the Messiah's future name, less one letter.

ELIJAH = ELIYAHU, which means My Mighty One is YAHU.

JOSEPH = YAHUCEPH, which means YAHU will Add.

Originally people in the Old Testament used the full form of YAHU in their own names, but they later started to shorten it to YAH (yod, he) or YU (yod, vav). An example of the use of YU in a name is in the name of Joseph, which now is written as the shorter form YUCEPH. The fuller form of Joseph used to be YAHUCEPH.

As you can see, translating the Hebrew names into the English or any other language, for that matter, can create many variations for the same name, but in the Hebrew, the names are consistent.

To further illustrate this, take an Israeli telephone book in English and check the names of people who carry the name YAHU as part of their own name. You will find YAHU translated as Yahu, Yahoo, Iahu, Iahou, Iahoo, etc. but the Hebrew would still be the same three letters of YOD, HE, VAV. Is it any wonder that Yahoo, since 1997, with its e-mail service and search engine, has been a popular Internet sensation with over 300 million users worldwide? Perhaps there's something in the name.

If His name in the form of the "Tetragrammaton" appears close to 7000 times in the original texts of the Bible, then why would the Almighty inspire the writers to write His name in His original language, if we're not supposed to use His Name? There are no scriptures in the Bible, which indicate that it is forbidden to use His name; in fact, it is just the opposite.

Yes, it is forbidden to use His name in VAIN. So here we have to understand what "in vain" means. And according to the dictionary, that means we should not use it in a "conceited, worthless, unavailingly, empty, or useless way." His name should not be used flippantly or irreverently. Nor should it be made common. This was most likely the reason why the Jews in the Greco-Roman times did not use it — for fear that the heathen convert would give less reverence to it. They obviously wanted to protect it from being misused in common day cussing, swearing, and cursing, as they have done up till now with the name of Jesus, and the title "God."

The reason His name has become bastardized and changed into completely different counterfeit gods is due to his adversary, "HaSatan" (the devil), who also goes by many names, (see, my chapters on The God of This World, and The Satans). This is the main reason behind the hiding of His Holy Name (Kodesh HaShem). Even when Messiah (YAHUHshua HaMashiach) (Jesus Christ) was here on Earth, HaSatan (aka the god of this world) tempted YAHUHshua, telling him that, "if" he worshipped him (Satan), he could give YAHUHshua all the kingdoms of this world. YAHUHshua rebuked HaSatan with the word of His Father (YAHUAH) and said, "You shall worship YAHUAH your God, and only Him will you serve."

The very fact that Satan will do anything to get people to worship him is the number one cause of the fragmentation of religions on Earth. Plus, he is the cause of all the confusion over who the real Creator God is and what His true name is. HaSatan works through fear, which he put into the early Jews, which is why they made the decision to cease pronouncing the true name of the Lord and, instead, substitute it for the word *Adonai*, which means "Lord" or "HaShem," which means "the Name." Then over the centuries, he (Satan) used monks and the Masoretes to misplace the vowels (which, by the way, were never there in the first place) within the Hebrew Torah and literally replace the Holy Name of YHVH (YAHUAH) with the false/counterfeit name of Jehovah.

All of this name changing is the devil's handiwork, not the Lord's. This is where the old saying "the devil's in the details" comes from, but then again, so is Truth and Discernment! It has been established through the scriptures that the Lord desires for His people to speak His name, call on His name, and use His name for His glory.

"I am YAHUAH, that is my name! I will not give my glory to another, or my praise to idols." (Isaiah 42:8)

"LORD" is not a name; it's a title. Everyone uses the same title for pagan gods and idols. This is why Isaiah states that "YAHUAH" told him: "I will not give my glory to another, or my praise to idols."

CHAPTER THIRTEEN: The Name Above All Names

The prophets spoke on His behalf when they said:

"'I will make known my holy name among my people Israel. I will no longer let my holy name be profaned, and the nations will know that I YAHUAH am the Holy One in Israel."

(Ezekiel 39:7)

"And I will sanctify my great name, which was profaned among the heathen, which you have profaned in the middle of them; And the nations shall know that my name is YAHUAH, said the Lord YAHUAH, when I shall be sanctified in you before their eyes."

(Ezekiel 36:23)

IN THE NAME OF

When we use the phrase "in the name of," it is likened to a proxy in legal terms. This means that one has all the authority and legal rights to act on behalf of the one that they are standing proxy for or for one that they come in the name of. It is important to understand this in order to understand what Christ meant when he said:

"I have come in the name of My Father, and you do not receive Me. If another comes in his own name, him you will receive."

(John 5:43)

Many in the Sacred Name Movement believe that this verse relates to the false Jesus. We know that the Messiah was never called Jesus when He walked the Earth, but many agree that Jesus is his English name, and as many people have different names in different languages, what difference does it make if someone addresses him in their own language and not the Lord's original language? However, when people start to make changes due to misunderstandings and misinterpretations of the original Hebrew language, then we have a problem.

There is such a stronghold of a falsehood within the Sacred Name Movement because they think that they have to use the Lord's Hebrew name in order to be accepted and truly saved by Him. But based on the proof of millions all around the world, through the miracles of the Holy Spirit, we know this is not the case. The name *Jesus* has a lot of power it in. Demons flee; the dead are raised, and the sick are healed.

John 5:43 speaks to another Christ, not the one that nearly three billion people worship and put their faith in, but the false Christ, the counterfeit Christ, the one who deceives even the elect in the end times. We know, from Bible prophecy, that the antichrist will blaspheme one of the names of God. Being that his role will be to deceive people and make them believe that he is their savior, it will most likely be one of the names for the son, as we already have the false names for the father being worshipped.

There is a group of people in the Sacred Name Movement that believe that Yahusha is the correct pronunciation and name of the Messiah. They are not basing this on what is actually written in the Hebrew scriptures, particularly the original manuscript of the Book of Matthew, written in Hebrew, now preserved under glass in the British Museum for all the world to see, which clearly shows that the Son of God was called *Yahushua*, and truncated to *Yahshua*, which is also spelled *Yeshua* in Hebrew.

Yeshua was not only written into the scriptures, but was literally written in stone. The ancient Messianic Temple near the Jewish settlement in Hebron, Israel, which dates back to the third and fourth centuries, has the name *Yeshua* written into the stone artifacts, and on the temple floor in Hebrew. Not Yahusha!

The Hebrew language truncates both, the name of the Father and the name of the Son, affectionately for poetic reasons, for song, and for the sake of writing in scriptures. Yahuah is often referred to in scripture as Yah, even the letter Yod, which is an abbreviation for the sacred name.

Jesus is the English transliteration from Yeshua. Yeshua is truncated from Yahushua. Linguistically, Yeshua turns into Jesus. In Hebrew, this is done often with the LORD'S names in the Old Testament. It's considered poetic to use "affectionate" nicknames. Jesus is one of them. The Holy Spirit responds to the name Jesus with signs, wonders, and miracles. There is much grace over the name confusion. God's grace is sufficient here.

I already explained it above. Linguistically speaking, Yeshua turns into Jesus. The word *Jesus* is derived from Yeshua. It is the English version of Yeshua and comes directly from the Greek name Iesus. The "I" was changed to a "J" in English the 1700s.

This is how the transliteration of Yahshua into Jesus came about:

Yah	**sh**	**ua**	Hebrew
Ie	**s**	**ous**	Greek
Ie	**so**	**Us**	Latin
Je	**s**	**Us**	English

His Hebrew name is Yeshua. Some people believe that Yeshua may be spelled in different ways (i.e., Yahshua, as I prefer). There are many in the Hebrew Roots Movement who believe it is impossible for His name to be Jesus, because of the missing letter "J," which does not exist in the Hebrew alphabet, and it never did. It was the Jesuits who created the name "Jesus" (Society of Jesus).

"Jesus" is an English name which comes from the Greek "Iesous" (via Latin). Truth be told, the way Jesus came about was from the original Hebrew name, Yahshua. Yeshua was transliterated as Yesus (Iesous). Hence, linguistically there is nothing wrong with saying it as Jesus. Contrary to the popular belief in the Hebrew Roots Movement, the name Jesus is NOT derived from the name of the pagan god Zeus. As you can see,

CHAPTER THIRTEEN: The Name Above All Names

linguistically speaking, Jesus used to be Iesous pronounced Yesoos. The letter "y" became a "j" in English.

However, there is a false belief among a minority of Messianics (which is the reason Messianics are affectionately referred to as "messy antics") that the name the Messiah was called was not Yahushua, but Yahusha. They completely based their beliefs on a linguistic misunderstanding written in the Strong's Concordance, which has misled many to the incorrect interpretation of the Hebrew language.

Even the Jewish rabbis, who are believers in the Messiah Yeshua, will prove that Yahushua, Yeshua, or Yahshua are all correct versions and pronunciations of the Messiah's name when He walked the Earth.

I have researched this intensely and could not find one single Jewish scholar or Messianic Jew who has grown up with the Hebrew language, or any Israeli believer whose mother tongue is Hebrew to corroborate this falsehood — that a single Hebrew text records the Messiah's name as "Yahusha." In fact, they all insist that the name Messiah was called, based on the Hebrew scripture, *Yahushua* and was shortened to *Yeshua*. Some spell it Yahshua in English, which I have done in this book for phonetic clarity; others Yeshua, but it's still the same ending, which is "shua," which means salvation.

I have also read all the websites written and copied by those who insist it is Yahusha, and not a single one of them is Jewish, knows Hebrew, or has grown up understanding the Hebrew language. Instead, they're basing their beliefs on what appears to be a mistake and a gross misinterpretation of the Hebrew "root" language in the Strong's Concordance, a book written by James Strong, LL.D., S.T.D., who is a Gentile, not a Jew. I have even heard someone defend it to the point where they actually said that the Strong's Concordance was Holy Spirit inspired. Really? Then why does it contradict the original language in the Old Testament? I thought the Holy Spirit knew all languages perfectly? After all the Holy Spirit is the giver of the gift of tongues, is He not?

Here is where the "devil is in the details":

They claim that the Savior's name is derived from Yasha: Strong's Hebrew word #3467, not from #7769 shua. Old Testament #07769 shuwa' pronounced {shoo'-ah} from #07768, which Strong's Concordance incorrectly writes means - 1) to cry, cry for help, cry out 2) opulence; 2a) meaning dubious. They claim that only the suffix "sha" means deliverance and salvation. According to them, the suffix "shua" means to cry out for salvation.

This is absolutely and utterly incorrect! In fact, according to classical Biblical Hebrew, just the opposite is true! The word *Yahushua* literally translates to "**Yahuah is Our Salvation.**" The Son comes in the Father's name, and He is the Savior. The ending letters *Shin, Vav, Ayin* makes the suffix "shua." This is the very Hebrew root word for salvation and deliverance. "Sha" is a <u>derivative</u> of that root, not the root itself.

The Hebrew language is based on "root" words and all participles, whether they be singular, plural, masculine, or feminine. All derivatives come from the root word, not the other way around. How do I know this? I was educated in Hebrew in Israel and matriculated in Hebrew. This movement is teaching a misunderstanding and falsehood. Not a single Jew or Israeli who knows Hebrew agrees with. Doesn't that tell you something?

The other issue I have with this mis-translation is that it is too closely spelled to the derogatory name that the unbelieving Jews give to Jesus, whose name they spit upon, after centuries of being persecuted in his name.

Today, all non-believing Jews use the Jewish/Yiddish word for Jesus, which is "Yeshu," which comes from a Talmudic acronym for "Yimach Shmo V'Zichro" which means "May his name and memory be obliterated." "Yeshu" is a derogatory name, and when Jews invoke it, they are essentially saying, "May his name be erased from history," as if he never existed, as if all that he did never happened. This is due to all the persecution done to Jews in the name of Jesus. This is why the End Times prophesies all culminate with the Jews in Israel, Jerusalem in particular. More on that later.

Strong's Concordance's grossly misinterprets claims that the Messiah is not crying out to Himself or to God. Claiming this makes Him look weak. This is simply a misunderstanding and a misinterpretation of the Hebrew language, which has consequently perpetrated a falsehood (lie) among many unknowing and innocent believers, who are now convinced that this is the truth, simply because it says so in the Strong's Concordance, as if Strong's Concordance is the ultimate authority on the Hebrew language? Which it is not!

"By their fruits, you shall know them."

(Matthew 7:20)

The fruits I have encountered with each and every person who adamantly adheres to this falsehood and name distortion is a stronghold of the fruits of the *religious spirit*, which is to reject others for not complying with their misunderstanding. When telling them the correct Hebrew from the Jewish perspective, they simply delete you. I searched for just one Jewish believer that adheres to this crazy belief, throughout a rather large group of believers on Facebook, and out of 5,000 people, I couldn't find a single one!

I even asked all the Messianic Jewish rabbis in the state of Colorado, and all of them agreed that Yahushua was the Messiah's Hebrew name, truncated to Yeshua. Not one of them agrees with this distortion of Yahusha. Also, included in the leaders I consulted with were Christian Messianic pastors, who have studied the Hebrew language and the source of the sacred names, and they, too, agreed — Messiah's name was Yeshua.

The fruit of the spirit is love, peace, tolerance, acceptance, understanding, patience, and long-suffering. That is the spirit of Christ, which is manifested on Earth living *inside* the believers. The *religious spirit* wars against the Holy Spirit. This is why religion is so deceptive, and while the devil's in the details, the truth is in the hidden details missing in translations.

CHAPTER THIRTEEN: The Name Above All Names

"For this reason God sends them a powerful delusion so that they will believe the lie."

(2 Thessalonians 2:11)

This is a precursor to the counterfeit messiah that will emerge at the end of times, the one who will take one of the names of the Messiah, distort it, blaspheme it, and use it for Himself. The tabernacle of God is His saints, the true believers of the Lord and Savior, who have invited Him to live inside their hearts. This is the true tabernacle of God.

"Do you not know that your bodies are temples of the Holy Spirit, who is in you, whom you have received from God?"

(1 Corinthians 6:19)

"There was given to him a mouth speaking arrogant words and blasphemies, and authority to act for forty-two months was given to him. And he opened his mouth in blasphemies against God, <u>to blaspheme His name</u> and <u>His tabernacle</u>, that is, those who dwell in heaven. It was also given to him to make war with the saints and to overcome them, and authority over every tribe and people and tongue and nation was given to him.

(Revelation 13:5-7)

There is something to be said for this, as there is a strong religious movement among a number of Christian churches that preach replacement theology and are the most Anti-Semitic people on the planet. This is not of truth, nor is it godly for a so-called believer to hate Jews and despise Jewish input, especially regarding their own language. This is precisely why so many Jews are turned off from Christians and feel that many are stealing their identity, while hating them in the process. There is a word for people who do that; it's called "jealousy."

"The thief comes only to steal and kill and destroy. I came that they may have life and have it abundantly."

(John 10:10)

WHAT'S IN A NAME?

"Who has gone up to heaven and come down? Whose hands have gathered up the wind? Who has wrapped up the waters in a cloak? Who has established all the ends of the earth? What is his name, and what is the name of his Son? Surely you know!"

(Proverbs 30:4 – NIV)

Does the name we use for the Lord and Savior matter? Does it matter to Him? What about the name of the Father? Does it matter if people mispronounce it or mistranslate it?

For instance, YHWH is the phrase I WAS, I AM, I EXIST whereas HA YAH is the phrase I AM. To those whose language is English, HA YAH and YHWH and YEHOSHUA are tainted by the English cultural perception of "naming," but to the ancient Hebrews these are more than what we esteem as "names," but rather declarations: I AM, HE IS, I AM IS SALVATION.

One of the predictions in the Old Testament (or signs to look for), made way before Messiah's coming, was that His name would be called *salvation*. It's like a pun or a double meaning. He would be named *Salvation*, and his name would mean "salvation for the world."

The Hebrew pronunciation of the name Jesus is Yahushua/Yeshua.

"The whole earth will acknowledge the LORD (YAHUAH) and return to him. All the families of the nations will bow down before him."

(Psalm 22:27)

He says, "You will do more than restore the people of Israel to me. I will make you a light to the Gentiles, and you will bring my salvation (Yeshua) to the ends of the earth."

(Isaiah 49:6)

"Many nations will join themselves to the Lord (Yahuah) on that day, and they, too, will be my people. I will live among you, and you will know that the Lord of Heaven's Armies sent me to you."

(Zechariah 2:11)

"But my name is honored by people of other nations from morning till night. All around the world they offer sweet incense and pure offerings in honor of my name. For my name is great among the nations," says the Lord of Heaven's Armies."

(Malachi 1:11)

COUNTERFEIT NAMES LEADS TO COUNTERFEIT MESSIAHS

We know that the Antichrist will be accepted by Israel at first and will be worshipped as a peacemaker. The book of Daniel tells us he is the only one to succeed in a peace treaty between Israel and her enemies (Daniel 9). There is no way Jews and Israel will accept a Muslim, which some claim is the Mahdi, or the name Jesus Christ. It is too Christian for them; that's how Jews think. All Jewish believers call him Yeshua and Yahushua anyway. Not a single Jewish believer, nor anyone in the entire organization of Jews for Jesus around the world, Beit Sar Shalom, which is in Israel, agrees with this false name of Yahusha; it sounds too much like Yeshu to them. All the Hebrew-English New Testaments have the name Yeshua written in Hebrew in them.

CHAPTER THIRTEEN: The Name Above All Names

It's not clear which of the names the counterfeit Messiah/Antichrist will claim as his own. It may be one of the counterfeit names of the Father that was deliberately created. Nobody knows. But John 5:43 speaks and relates to that future prophetic event, Yeshua is not referring to a mere transliteration of His name, which is Jesus. Christ is merely a title, which means the anointed one or Messiah. Remember the Lord created all the languages at the Tower of Babel. He understands all languages. I believe Yeshua was speaking specifically to the Jews here, it was prophetic because He foreknew that another Jew would counterfeit Him. It is my conclusion that John 5:43 does not relate to the transliteration of the name, "Jesus," but of another name that the Jewish Counterfeit Messiah, aka the Final Antichrist, will claim as his own.

There is a vast difference between using a "transliteration" of the names and a "mistranslation" of the names. The mistranslations have created deliberate counterfeits, which have become intentional deceptions. These would be, names of the Father, i.e., Jehovah, Jahve, and Yahweh. Yahweh isn't just a mistranslation; it is the name of the first Nephilim recorded in the Gnostic Gospels, who is a giant being with the head of a lion and body of a dragon. This being is written about extensively in Pistis Sophia, which were the Gnostic Gospels, written during the time of Christ. They were rejected by the Catholic Church because they did not fit into Rome's agenda. They are historical records, nonetheless.

There are other counterfeit made-up names, like Jesus Sananda, his alleged space name, but I exposed this one in my first book; this was part of the ruse by the Ashtar Command, a cover for Ashtoreth, who is still the enemy of the Lord. Then there is Matreiya, another counterfeit name.

There is much grace on the name confusions, and there is absolutely no issue with the Lord using His name in other languages. These are merely transliterations, but outright deceptions create counterfeit spirits and are spirits of error. Those who continue to perpetuate these will reap the fruit of deception.

The greatest proof of the accuracy of Yeshua vs Yahusha is from the Septuagint LXX (the seventy), thus called because of seventy rabbis who translated the Old Testament into Greek, which was widely used and quoted. Since the Jews themselves translated this version, it is unbiased and establishes some common word usage and understanding.

The name Yeshua is used twenty-nine times in the Tenakh (not Yahusha), and the rabbis transliterated the name into Yay-soos, the very same name in the Greek New Covenant, later transliterated into Jesus. Simply put, Jesus is a translation of yay-soos which actually proves what the actual name of Messiah is — Yeshua. This can be proved by cross referencing the Greek Septuagint Bible with Hebrew Bible verses 1 Chronicles 24:9; 2 Chronicles 31:15; Ezra 2:2,6, 36, 40; Nehemiah 7:11, 39, 43. Yet, in spite of the truth and facts there, Gentile Hebrew Roots Cultists continue to infiltrate the Internet with this mis-translation and refuse to correct themselves.

The name Jesus is only about 500 years old, and Yaysoos is just a translation. I happen to believe the New Covenant was originally written in Hebrew, not Greek anyway, which can be proved by the ancient Hebrew scrolls of Matthew that currently sit in the British Museum.

Yeshua came from the tribe of Judah, the bloodline of King David. However, the counterfeit Messiah will come from the tribe of Joseph, a tribe that is not mentioned in the book of Revelation as the twelve surviving tribes of Israel, who each have gates named after them in the Grand Mothership/Heavenly City/the New Jerusalem. Instead, Joseph's portion was doubled, and his sons Manasseh and Ephraim took his place.

Hebrew is also a poetic language. There is poetry in all the Psalms, and the Lord is given many names in the Old Testament. He answers to each and every one of them. But if you are invoking one of the counterfeit names, which were deliberately born out of a schemed mass deception upon the Gentiles, then you are being fooled by a different spirit. This deceiving spirit is the spirit of religion, aka the religious spirit, which is one of satan's chief demons over the religions of the world.

Names do matter. From a spiritual standpoint, if you call one entity by the name of another, the other gets whatever energy. This may come as a shock to some modern day Christians, but there were Christians around 300 years before the biblical Christ. They were the cult of Serapis, an Egyptian cult led by Serapis Christus, who was Ptolemy I. He was a general left in Egypt after Alexander conquered it. He shares the same bloodline as Cleopatra.

Many historians believe Serapis was a made-up god, a composite god. Simply put, Serapis (Sarapis, Zaparrus) was an invented god. He was a composite of several Egyptian and Hellenistic deities who were introduced to the world at the beginning of the Ptolemaic (Greek) Period in Egypt, during the reign of Ptolemy I, though his legacy lasted well into the Roman period. Thus, he was meant to form a bridge between the Greek and Egyptian religion in a New Age in which their respective gods were brought face to face with each other, so that both Egyptians and Greeks could find union in a specific supreme entity.

Linguistically, the god's name is a fusion of Osiris and the bull Apis, which, by the Greek period, might be said to have represented the essence of the Egyptian religion. In fact, a cult of this combination god, named Osirapis (or Userhapi, Asar-Hapi), had existed in Egypt prior to the rule of the Ptolemies.[3]

A "name" is not merely a flash label to which we answer, as "names" have been reduced to in our time. The "names" of ancient times were actually phrases of declarations attributing a trait or significance concerning the one so named.

Then again, there is the space name that is very popular, which is Sananda. Jesus Sananda is an imposter, but compelling to many. Turns out he is a projection from the Ashtar Command, a group of so-called space brothers. I connect the dots to the ancient goddess Ashtoreth/Astarte in Book One of *Who's Who In The Cosmic Zoo?*, who was one of the Lord's chief enemies in the Old Testament.

CHAPTER THIRTEEN: The Name Above All Names

Even though the Catholics projected a different Jesus, the Lord wants to save Catholics, so while the religion itself is completely unbiblical to Yeshua's religion and central message, it is the Holy Spirit who is working through the Age of the Gentiles. God's plan, in pouring out His Grace and Favor through the Holy Spirit to the Gentiles, was to make the Jews jealous of their blessings, so the Jews would see "who" their true Messiah is. There's power in the names of God. There's also power in the counterfeit names. So how do you tell the difference? By their spiritual fruits.

Those who use the counterfeits are in bondage from the religious spirit, and the spirit of error. It creates a type of spiritual pride and stubbornness that blinds them from their error, and why it is such error.

The Catholic Jesus projects the crucified, nailed to the cross Jesus. This is an act of voodoo. The power of Jesus is in His Resurrection. He is the Risen Christ. He is alive. The everlasting one. He is real, and He is revealing Himself to people all the time. If you follow Him, He will direct you in all truth.

Jews are deathly afraid of idolatry. This is the reason most Jews reject Jesus. They fear that worshipping Jesus is idolatry. Suffice it to say, this is blind spot created by all the persecution. The Jews need to learn to trust Christians again, which is why there are so many well intentioned and well-funded Christian organizations that serve as outreaches or bridges to Jews.

Let me be clear, nowhere in the Bible does it suggest that Gentiles should convert to Judaism or that Jews should convert Christianity. Jews are prophesied and destined to know "who" their Messiah is, who Yeshua is. When a Jew accepts Yeshua, they are not becoming Christian; they are becoming completed Jews.

When you call on one of the names of God, it's important to realize that every name represents a "spirit." In the spirit world, NAMES DO MATTER. The story of Jesus is coincidentally similar to other deities throughout history, which I go over in my chapter: The Christmas Gods. The power of prayer is the same power as "magic," and in those realms, you must call the entity by its proper name, or you don't get the result you are looking for.

"And whenever those possessed by evil spirits caught sight of him, the spirits would throw them to the ground in front of him shrieking, 'You are the Son of God!'"

(Mark 3:11- NLT)

Demons tremble in the name of Yeshua/Jesus. It doesn't matter if you use His name in another language, the spirit world recognizes His name. The spiritual realm, also, recognizes who His true followers are, and who is just a "Christian in Name only." You can't fool the spirits, but you can take authority over them in the power of the Name Above All Names, provided your life belongs to the Messiah and you have repented of the lies of this world.

I communicated with a Hebrew Roots Cultist over their ongoing stance that Jesus is just a made-up name, I told them that the proof is in the pudding. I am a witness to miracle healings, the resuscitation of the dead, and deliverance of the demonic, all happening in response to the name of Jesus. I told them demons tremble in the name of Jesus, and I was quickly "unfriended." I knew that the demon known as the "religious spirit," trembled at the name and knew "who" I was in the spirit realm as well, and "who" I belonged to, and totally exposed itself as such — a demon called the "spirit of religion" aka the "religious spirit."

Quibbling about the same name in different languages detracts us from worshipping the One Whose Name is I AM in every language. You may speak His name in whichever language you choose. The objection is the attempt to "correct" others by insisting that the name is invalid in any other language other than Hebrew, which is what goes on within the Hebrew Roots Cult, who refuse to accept anyone who does not address Messiah by His Hebrew name.

Discerning the Spirit Behind HRM

The Hebrew Roots Movement (HRM) is a movement run by Gentiles. Let me be clear, according to the Scripture, Christians are not required to convert to Judaism, nor are they expected to speak Hebrew, or even speak the Lord's name in Hebrew. This is not an expectation or requirement laid out in any scripture. However, there is a movement that relies on the Strong's Concordance for its knowledge of Hebrew (which is deeply flawed), and then the followers of this movement think they can dictate to Jews or other Christians that they have to speak Hebrew, follow all the Jewish holidays, and keep Mosaic Law.

The Lord's plan has always been very clear, even when the prophet Jeremiah walked the Earth:

> "But this shall be the covenant that I will make with the house of Israel; after those days, said the LORD (YAHUAH), I will put my law in their inward parts, and write it in their hearts; and will be their God, and they shall be my people."
>
> (Jeremiah 31:33)

Going back to the Old Covenant, going back under the law, is not only regressive from the New Covenant, which is the law of Grace, it causes much strife and consternation between believers. This movement, while it is passionate for following the Lord and the Bible, are being misled by a "spirit of religion," aka religious spirit (Revelation 3).

Again, I want you to think about the outpouring of the Holy Spirit in countries like Madagascar, Mozambique, Burma, India, Pakistan and China, all places that are illiterate in the Bible, because in most of these nations, it is illegal to even own a Bible, yet in spite

CHAPTER THIRTEEN: The Name Above All Names

of their illiteracy and ignorance of the "Words of God," they are coming to the Lord in the thousands, because of the signs, wonders and miracles happening to them through the revival and outpouring of the Spirit of Grace.

Most of these people are "poor in spirit," which evokes God's Grace and Mercy, and the type of signs, wonders, and miracles happening in their communities are likened to the times of Pentecost mentioned in the Book of Acts. Supernatural happenings, such as miraculous and instantaneous healings, raising of their dead, deliverance from the demonic, and a love and worship of Jesus Christ. Many of these people are given dreams and visions of Christ, which they are accepting as miracles and are coming to salvation, nonetheless. They are being provided for, which is a miracle to them.

Remember, Ephesians 2:8, 9: "For by grace are you saved through faith; and that not of yourselves: it is the gift of God: Not of works, lest any man should boast."

Only on planet Earth, which is the planet where anything goes, every vain imagination that exists gets played out on Earth's stage. From the utterly bizarre to the most wickedly evil, distorted perverted stuff goes on daily on our beautiful blue-green planet.

Only on planet Earth, can you be rejected for having a relationship with the Lord, the Creator God, who happens to answer to a variety of names, and yes, in case most believers haven't figured this out yet, God speaks ALL languages.

When I was growing up, due to my cruel and bitter stepmother, I had to leave home, at the age of fifteen and a half, to complete my high school and college education in Israel. I graduated in 1979 at Sde Boker, Negev, Israel, which is when and where I met the Lord who appeared to me in a vision in the Negev Desert at Sde Boker. It was unforgettable.

Then when I returned home to both my Jewish and Catholic families and friends, and shared my discovery with them, with such passion and excitement, they rejected me. That was thirty-five years ago, not much has changed with them, but a lot has changed with me.

Only Messianic Jews can understand what many go through with their Jewish families and friends. I know I'm not alone; it's a spiritual condition, a syndrome, a mental disorder that affects so many non-believing Jews. On one hand, Jews are wounded through so much persecution, that a "persecutory spirit" is attached to them, and they continue to perpetuate the same evil spirit that wounded them onto others. They lack spiritual discernment, as well.

When I accepted Christ, my ignorant Jewish stepsister responded with "Why don't you just become a nun and join a convent?" They mistakenly think that everyone who knows Jesus must be a Catholic. Even though my mother's family are Italian Catholics, when I told them I saw Jesus, and started speaking the Word to them, they, too, turned their backs on me because I wasn't speaking Catholicism but Freedom through the Living God. Their implants were spluttering. They couldn't relate to having a relationship to

Jesus without having to go through a priest and all the other empty ritualistic bureaucracies Catholics are in bondage to.

It's not about religion, yet everyone makes it about religion. I have had a relationship with the Lord all these years, even when I became disenchanted by the Church, which led me to spend twenty-five years in and around New Age circles, because that is where the Love and Light was, and that is also where Christians go when they are driven out of the Church through the religious spirit. What most Christians fail to realize is, while they are judging New Agers, the New Agers are disenchanted Christians. Almost everyone I met along the way came out of one Christian church or another.

I have spent thirty-five years, living, and being raised by the Lord, "outside the tribe." I know "who" God is. I know Him because of His faithfulness and loving-kindness to me. I know Him as my Savior, my Deliverer, my Protector, my Provider, my Healer and my closest friend. I know Him because it is only through the Lord, that I am still here. The stuff I've lived and survived through as an "orphan child" can fill several books. But suffice it to say, that I am no longer an "orphan child," I have been adopted by the King of Heaven. He knows my name, and I know His name.

> "The LORD watches over the foreigner and sustains the orphan and the widow, but he frustrates the ways of the wicked."
>
> (Psalm 146:9)

> "The LORD is a father of the fatherless, a defender of widows, is God in His holy habitation. God sets the solitary in families;"
>
> (Psalm 68:5-6)

It is only because He has proven Himself to me, as God of gods, that I write these books, because through my journey and research, I came face to face with the oppression of Gray aliens, Reptilian Lizard men, Giants, Blue Amphibian Frog men, and a bunch of different demonic entities and occult spirits, that no other god or person could liberate me from. How come the church leaders never talk about that? Then I meet so many other people who have had similar experiences, who also questioned their faith and their religion because no one ever addresses these very real issues happening across the board, all over the planet.

This was the cause of my spiritual train wreck, while calling on every other so-called god and goddess that New Agers worship to free me from these aliens, in the end, it was only when I returned to the Lord Jesus Christ/Yeshua HaMashiach in heartfelt repentance that I was freed and my eyes were opened. The outcome is this book series, which details all my research. My testimony which includes my contacts, abductions, experiences, and visions are all documented in my sixth book, *CinderElla's Shadow,* which will be released after this book series is completely edited and published.

CHAPTER THIRTEEN: The Name Above All Names

I share this now, because I want my readers to know who I am and why I put these books together, I am a witness to the power and intervention of the Lord Yeshua/Jesus the Christ. Unlike what religion teaches (that you need a savior to save you from the afterlife), the truth of the matter is that salvation is needed now, while you're still alive. Humanity needs a Savior from the huge cast of characters of extraterrestrials, aliens, gods, and angels, who are clearly NOT representing humanities' best interest. See Book One of *Who's Who In The Cosmic Zoo?* for an A-Z compendium of just "who" the ETs and aliens are.

Yahushua/Yahshua/Yeshua/Jesus — His name means Savior. His name describes everything He is. Yes, there are His original Hebrew/Aramaic names, but His name exists in ALL languages. It doesn't matter what language you speak His name in, He will answer to it. There are, however, some mistranslations, but mistranslations are not transliterations. And those who understand language, along with God, understand that it doesn't matter.

However, to some fanatical funda-"mental" religious Hebrew Roots Movement people, they are literally bent out of shape, over the different versions of God's names. In their funda- "mental" minds, it has to be their way or the highway. Many of them stumble onto knowledge of the true name and try to create a new religion out of it. That is regressive. Leaving the New Covenant of Grace out of the picture is most definitely NOT the will of God.

This is evidence of the presence of a demon, a very big demon, in fact it is put in place on planet Earth as a power, a principality that is literally being "ruled" by the dark forces, (Ephesians 6:12), and that is the arch-demon spirit of Religion. Revelation 3 describes this as a type of end time church, which is judged by their spirit of religion, aka the religious spirit. Believers of any kind, should never forget that it was this spirit of religion that conspired to have Yeshua crucified.

This spirit is responsible for division and discord among brethren. It partners with the spirit of rejection, and is a persecutory spiritual stronghold that holds millions of people in bondage to the darkness of confusion and the spirit of unbelief of "who" the Lord truly is.

Only on planet Earth, can you be persecuted for being a Jew who accepts Yeshua (Jesus), by Gentile Christians, who have essentially converted to the religion of Judaism, as the Hebrew Roots Cult, who persecute and reject both Christians and Jews who accept the name Jesus. It's the nuttiest twisted delusionary deception that Gentiles have adopted.

Gentiles, who are not Jewish, are now rejecting Christians becoming Jewish, including actual Messianic Jews (Jewish Christians). They even call themselves "Messianics," even though they are not Jewish. And you wonder why so many people leave the church and join the New Agers, who, generally speaking, accept just about everyone. They are much more inclusive than so-called Christians. However, New Agers have other "blind spots," which I will get into later. The HRM so-called Christians, including Jehovah's Witnesses, who reject other believers, do not represent Christ. They are filled with stolen knowledge that has been distorted; some of it deliberately implanted by ancient Jewish priests (Masoretes) who did so to protect their religion and their covenant with God regarding His sacred name. See, my chapter on *Who Is Jehovah?*

News alert: God understands this; He was there; He witnessed History. Believe me. He understands way more than you give Him credit for. He allows for all the errors, all the mistakes, all the battles over Him, His scrolls, His Words, His Angels, His Messengers, His Children, and His followers. That is why He created Grace. Grace covers a multitude of sins, errors, mistakes, and battles.

JEALOUSY OF JEWS & GENTILES

Messianic Jews are the most persecuted bunch of Jews and Christians. They get it from all sides. A Jew who walks with Yahshua is a completed Jew. Israel needs to recognize that. The word "Jew" comes from the tribe of Judah. Yahshua/Jesus came from the tribe of Judah. Believing in Him completes any Jew and grafts in every Gentile unto Him. The Hebrew Roots Movement is antithetical to real Messianic Jews around the world. Jews for Jesus© is a worldwide evangelical organization made up of completed Jews who believe it's their duty to evangelize the rest of the Jewish world.

The Hebrew Roots Movement, for the most part, is made up of misguided Gentiles, who have been deceived over the true name of Messiah, and refuse to listen to Jews, because of the rampant jealousy and antisemitism running through them. Yes, antisemitism is rooted in jealousy.

Jealousy is an evil spirit that wants to put another's lights out. The root of antisemitism is jealousy that the Lord God Yahuah chose the tribe of Judah to represent Him and do His will on Earth. No matter how much Jews contribute to the world in the way of discoveries, inventions, new technologies in science, medicine, military intelligence, innovation, humanitarianism, economic growth, oh and let's not forget the Messiah, the world continues to hate Jews even more for their accomplishments. This hate is rooted in jealousy of Jewish genetics, which is extraterrestrial DNA.

The irony here is that it was the Lord's plan, from the beginning, to give His Gospel (the good news of God's salvation) to the Gentiles to make the Jews jealous. Yet, Gentiles are jealous of Jews?

> And so I ask, "They have not stumbled so as to fall, have they?" Of course not! On the contrary, because of their stumbling (Israel), <u>salvation has come to the Gentiles to make the Jews jealous</u>."
>
> (Romans 11:11)

Jealousy rears its ugly head in many ways, as a spirit, this usually manifests itself as deliberately ignoring those whom they are jealous of, to the point of persecution. I have witnessed this type of anti-Semitism inside so-called Christian churches. This went on in

CHAPTER THIRTEEN: The Name Above All Names

Rome during the formation of Catholicism, when Constantine decreed to delete all things "Jewish" from the Bible canon, and from the religion of Rome, lest they be a "Judaizer" and be anathema to Rome (See, Constantine's Creed).

Truthfully, when a Jew accepts Jesus (Yeshua) as his or her Lord and Savior, he or she doesn't stop being Jewish, no more than a black person stops being black when he or she accepts Jesus. There are two kinds of Judaism — one is genetic; the other, religious. Remember all the Jews who were singled out by the Nazis in Germany to be exterminated in gas chambers because they were one-fourth or one-eighth Jewish? They died because of their genetics. The Holocaust was about the genocide of a race of people. The other kind of Judaism is the Jewish religion, which ironically, many Jews do not even follow anymore, except for annual holidays like Rosh Hashanah and Passover, if that. Secular Jews do not identify with the Jewish religion. Many are Buddhists, New Agers, or even atheists. Yet they are still Jews by genetics. See my point?

A Jew who accepts Jesus as his or her Messiah, both scientifically and in God's eyes, remains a Jew; however, according to God's covenants, they are now a "Completed Jew."

Ironically, there are many Gentile Christians who become "Messianic," and essentially convert to following Judaism.

> "Jesus spoke to them, saying, "I am the light of the world. Whoever follows me will not walk in darkness, but will have the light of life."
>
> (John 8:12)

As a result of all that went on during the Dark Ages, the forces of darkness were in full gear in oppressing humanity with dark religious spirits, which were the influences behind the Crusades. Yes, working through both sides. This spirit exists today and can stretch itself into many forms, from the self-righteous do-gooder who wants to please God, to the extremism expressed through the Muslim Jihadists; the religious spirit is an unloving spirit.

Unloving spirits include jealous spirits, who cannot stand what another is, or another has, so it must put out its light. This is the spirit behind hatred, racism, anti-Semitism, and it partners with bitterness spirits, spirits who keep people in bondage to grudges, resentments, and pride. These are the spirits behind all the dissension, all the discord. The religious spirit is overseer of so much of that, as most wars on planet Earth have been fought over differences in religions.

What's truly ironic, is the Hebrew Roots movement is run by Gentiles. Please don't be fooled by their name. They are not "Hebrews." They are not Jews by birth, nor by religion, although they think they are now, but they follow a different religion than most Jews and the majority of the world's Christians. They are a hybrid of Gentile Christians, and while they have some truth particularly about how the Catholic Church perverted Christianity and rejected and persecuted the Jews, they are bound by a legalistic spirit of religion.

Many of the Hebrew Roots Movement people are well-meaning, self-righteous Christians, who believe that they've essentially converted to Judaism. They have gone back to preaching the law, following the Torah, observing all the Jewish holidays, including the Sabbath. This is all fine and good, and Jews welcome them in celebrations, but they are not that much different to the Seventh Day Adventists who also keep dietary laws and the Sabbath.

Through confusion and misunderstanding they have adopted a lie, which is, if you're not speaking the savior's Hebrew name in Hebrew, then you're false. This is a lie. This is the religious spirit at work, creating division and discord.

You want to know how to anger someone in the Hebrew Roots movement? Tell them or post that demon's tremble in the name of Jesus Christ. And watch them run …This is revealing of "what spirit" is behind them. They are not expressing Christ's spirit, which is a spirit of kindness, compassion, understanding and peace. Yeshua is Jesus Christ.

On a purely spiritual level, which is where this author is coming from, the spirit behind rejections and persecutions for believing differently from one another is a demon spirit, yes, a big old fallen angel, who overseas this spiritual stronghold known as the "spirit of religion." To those who know Christ spiritually, know that all power has been given to Him. Demons flee and tremble at His Breath and His Word, let alone His name. Demons know what He's called.

Those who are not experiencing victory over the demonic must first overcome the subtleties of the demonic within their own flawed theologies. The demon known as the religious spirit wars against the Holy Spirit, which is the Spirit of Christ. Demons recognize "who" carries the Spirit of Christ in them, which is not dependent on whether believers use any version of His name, they have accessed His Spirit within them, because His Grace and His Invitation is to ALL of humanity to accept His Free Gift of Salvation, regardless of religion, religious upbringing, Bible knowledge, or cultural backgrounds.

I have witnessed demons flee when the presence of Christ shows up. He doesn't even need to say anything, He can look at them, and they know where to go. It's really not a whole big drama as so many people turn it into, which ends up giving more glory to the devil, than it does Christ. Deliverance can happen in a moment. It doesn't take people years to get saved, and it shouldn't take people years to get delivered either, if they are truly being guided by the Spirit of Christ.

Spiritually speaking, it will prove in the end, to be humanity's only answer and protection, because the dark forces have already been spoiled and exposed (Colossians 2:15), and they are prophesied to lose the final battle against Him at the end of this timeline. That's the positive timeline overlapping this present one, which is the coming Kingdom. Heaven is coming to Earth. It will arrive after much chaos and destruction; yes, the wrath of God will come before the Kingdom comes, and you can count on that.

CHAPTER THIRTEEN: The Name Above All Names

"And having spoiled principalities and powers, he (Yeshua) made a show of them openly, triumphing over them in it."

(Colossians 2:15)

Remember, the very spirit that conspired to crucify Christ was the spirit of religion. The religious spirit is still alive and thwarting believers today, turning them into funda-"mentalists," judgmental hypocrites, filling them with spiritual pride. This spirit actually is the antithesis of "who" Christ is. The religious spirit was the enemy of Christ. He rebuked it. He taught against it. He emphasized the importance of following the spirit of the law, not the letter of the law.

Discernment: Funda-"mentalism" is a mental disorder influenced by the demon of the religious spirit. It is void of the spirit of love, kindness, understanding and wisdom, which comes from the Spirit of Christ. Being passionate for the truth of the Gospel, which was sent to free the captives (those who are in bondage to demons, aliens, evils spirits), heal the sick, taking care of the poor and needy, is a different spirit than fundamentalism. The fundamentalist wants you to do things their way; the passionate believer wants to fulfill the will of God for humanity, which is healing and liberation.

The Lord's Divine Will and Plan was to write His laws on the hearts of humans. This means, that when people accept the Lord into their hearts and lives, He guides them in all truth and righteousness through their inner spirits, their inner men (i.e., their hearts). Many call this a "conscience," which gives you that nagging feeling that you erred, and causes you to become aware of it, so you can give it back to the Lord for forgiveness, healing, and correction.

The religious spirit is NOT a loving spirit. People who are bound by this spirit and its inherent funda-"mentalism" do not have the "fruits" of the Holy Spirit in their lives. They think it's all about their effort, their fleshly acts, and their so-called good deeds, which are all self-righteousness, and while they are doing so, they also preach to others that they need to do the same, showing no mercy for others' conditions or beliefs.

The evidence of the spirit of Christ, which is the Holy Spirit in a person, is the spirit of love, mercy, kindness, goodness, understanding, compassion, forgiveness, tolerance, patience, long-suffering, and gentleness (See, Galatians 5:22).

When people become rigid in their mindsets, believing that it must be the way they see it, with no wiggle room, this is the spirit of fundamentalism, which is held in place by the spiritual stronghold called the religious spirit. This is a spiritual stronghold that comes from the Serpent race and forces of darkness.

Religious spirits also are spirits of doubt and unbelief of a haughty spirit. These spirits cause the religious person to rely on works for salvation instead of what God has already done for them through His Grace through Yeshua's blood. The religious spirit, is saying, that's not enough, we need to follow religious traditions and laws, in order to have salvation. But when Yeshua walked the earth, this battle manifested between the

Pharisees, Seducees, Sandherin, who were the religious priests and elite, and Yeshua/Jesus. See, Concluding Words on Yeshua's Eight Woes to Religious spirits.

These folks are the first ones that point fingers at others. They are the first ones that attack the very ones walking with the Lord, in spirit and in truth, that they are false teachers or false prophets, which in psychology is called "projection", which is to obfuscate their own error, so they kick up some dust, reject the ones who are actually producing good fruits in the Spirit, through healings, miracles, signs and wonders, and insist they are false, when they are the ones doing the Will of God..

Isaiah 5:20: "Woe to them that call evil good, and good evil; that put darkness for light, and light for darkness; that put bitter for sweet, and sweet for bitter!"

This is the work of the twisted serpent, the Leviathan Spirit aka spiritual pride, who twists communications, in order to deceive and create confusions and strife within the body of Christ.

Again, those who "know" the Lord know "who" He is. They know His healing touch and liberating peace in their lives. No doctrine of man, nor man's misinterpretation or the bastardization of the Word, can separate them from their "intimate" relationship with the Lord. And "no weapon forged against you will prevail, and you will refute every tongue that accuses you. This is the heritage of the servants of the LORD, and this is their vindication from me," declares the LORD" (Isaiah 54:17).

The other offense of the Hebrew Roots Movement is toward Jews. Many prominent, true Messianic Jewish rabbis do believe in Yeshua, yet they continue to practice Judaism. They are deeply offended by those of the Hebrew Roots Movement because they feel that they have "stolen" their identity, something the Hebrew Roots Movement is completely insensitive and unaware of. Jews have suffered through centuries of persecution to preserve their identities as Jews, and these Gentiles come along, steal parts of their identity, and replace them with their distortions, bastardizations, misinterpretations, and misunderstanding of the language. I have witnessed this again and again, both in assemblies who profess to be Messianic, which have otherwise proven to be "messy antics" instead.

Back in 2011 in Denver, Colorado, a Gentile messianic minister calling himself a rabbi, who leads a messianic church and dresses like a Jew in a Tallit, was parading a Torah around. While he was doing this, the Tallit and its Kanafim were being dragged on the floor. This sent the entire Messianic Jewish Community into a tailspin, creating quite a stir in not only South Denver, but throughout the entire Internet community. This is the kind of stuff that even Jewish believers in Yeshua find offensive and anti-Semitic.

Replacement theology is not the Will of God. The time of the Gentiles will come to an end. It was God's will to pour out His Spirit upon ALL flesh in the End Times, so that they will all be saved. It is God's will to give the Gentiles His Holy Spirit which was done originally to make the unbelieving, stubborn, stiff-necked Jews jealous, so that they would seek Him for the same.

When the time of the Gentiles comes to an end, then all Jews will come to salvation.

CHAPTER THIRTEEN: The Name Above All Names

> "For comes now the Day of the LORD (YAHUAH), **the day of clouds**! The time of the Gentiles is fulfilled (A time of doom for the nations).
>
> (Ezekiel 30:3)

A day of *clouds*! Each time this word appears in Hebrew, it is not describing rain clouds, but the Lord's starships, which are cloaked in clouds.

In the meantime, those who are creating their future in the coming Kingdom in the Age to come, understand that it's not about **what** you know, but absolutely about **who** you know, and in order to be a part of the Kingdom of Heaven, you really have to know the King of Heaven, who is Yahshua, Jesus.

I speak as a witness to the power of the name. I have witnessed deliverance in the name of Jesus, I have witnessed the resurrection of the dead in the name of Jesus, and I have witnessed healing miracles in the name of Jesus. Jesus is Yeshua; they are the same person.

People have to understand something here; this a big discernment. There is a vast difference between the "letter of the law," and the "spirit of the law." Those who adhere to the "letter of the law" in their treatment and dealings with others, without a spirit of love, are nothing but an expression of their quest for self-righteousness, which is the manifestation of the religious spirit.

Remember God is greater than all the errors of humanity. He has provided a Divine plan to cover all errors, and all mistakes, and that is through the spiritual gateway of Jesus Christ.

> "**I AM THE GATE**; whoever enters through me will be saved. They will come in and go out, and find pasture."
>
> (John 10:9, NIV)

Satan, the Prince of the Powers of the Air, is the leader of fleets of UFOs, aka the god of this present world. He oversees all these arch-demons. He directs them through a militaristic hierarchy, and they carry out his agenda through their commands over lesser demons, which are individually "assigned" to individuals, groups, and churches.

Satan's overall agenda is to steal energies from humans, kill humans, (that includes influencing humans to kill each other), and to destroy life on planet Earth.

> "The thief comes not, but for to steal, and to kill, and to destroy: **I AM** come that they might have life, and that they might have it more abundantly."
>
> (John 10:10, NKJV)

But the good news is, spiritually speaking, that Christ has overcome and spoiled all principalities and powers for His intervention on our timeline. The believer only needs to accept and access His Spiritual victory, which is available to ALL humans. I think everyone can agree that Christ's appearance has, in fact, caused a number of factors to come together, to change the counting of time, by changing our calendar. We started counting in AD after Christ, and when we refer to the times before Christ, we write BC. Surely any historian can see something significant occurred on our timeline, when and after Yeshua walked the Earth.

THE NEW AGE CHRISTIAN

This title may be an oxymoron to some and offensive to others; for others, this might resonate, and they might identify as such. So many Christians judge New Agers, but what they fail to realize is that New Agers were all once part of a Christian church community, whether they were raised Catholic or within some other Christian denomination. They left the church looking for power, understanding and love, elements that many churches have lost.

If more churches taught that there's power in Christ to heal every sickness, power over every demon, alien, and evil spirit, and that they are loved more than they can imagine or feel, I bet those people wouldn't leave Christianity. There is nothing "new" about New Age; it's all Old Age stuff recycled. Most of it is paganism under a new name. As I've written about and exposed it in Book One,*Who's Who In The Cosmic Zoo?* For example, the Ashtar Command is just a disguise for the ancient pagan Goddess Astarte, Ishtar, Isis etc.

Most New Agers focus on one ancient mythology or another, whether it's the fascination with Egyptology, Atlantis, the ancient Mayan calendars, or Native American beliefs, Ancient Greece and Roman paganism; it's all old age stuff recycled into what many call the New Age. King Solomon said, "The thing that has been, it is that which shall be; and that which is done is that which shall be done: and there is no new thing under the sun."

(Ecclesiastes 1:9)

The religious spirit has taken over most Christian churches; they have exchanged supernatural power for political gain and 501c status, and in order to hold onto their 501c status, they appease political correctness by not preaching the entire Gospel. They preach only that which titillates the ears, giving way to doctrines of demons, which may be popular and bring them lots of money, but bears little fruit of the Spirit of Christ. They end up being puffed with the spirit of religion and judgmentalism of others, because others sin differently than they do.

> "Now the Holy Spirit tells us clearly that in the last times some will turn away from the true faith; they will follow deceptive spirits and teachings that come from demons."

(1 Timothy 4:1)

CHAPTER THIRTEEN: The Name Above All Names

Their judgments do nothing to further the Kingdom of Christ on Earth; in fact, they are responsible for more damage, both psychological and physical harm than New Agers and Jews are. Christianity has spent past centuries persecuting Jews; now they persecute New Agers, too, when they should be embracing them because Christ died for them, too. There is very little outreach to New Agers in the Christian community. In fact, if you've been a New Ager anything, churchgoers treat you like you've just stepped off the planet Xercon. Such hypocrisy, such ignorance, such misunderstanding. If Christians have outreaches to Muslims and Hindus, then they should have outreaches to New Agers, too. God loves New Agers; Jesus died to save them, too.

Most New Agers came out of the church. Christians reading this book must realize that. These are people who were raised in one Christian denomination or another. They left the church because they felt disenchanted and discerned what was missing, which is the love, grace, understanding, and forgiveness. That is the very essence of the Gospel, i.e., the good news.

Most New Agers leave the church to pursue a spiritual path because they grew disillusioned with the church. They feel that they don't belong because they believe in love, light, and grace, which the church has traded for ritual, works, and judgmentalism. It's a spiritual thing. Most New Agers do not believe that Christians are spiritual because they've never met one who is. This is the reason the New Age movement began. Christians need to acknowledge that fact.

Instead they turn into "light workers" as New Agers because they experienced the limitation of their spirits within Christian churches. For every Christian who left the church and turned to New Age beliefs and practices, the church bears some responsibility for them. They are called to share the love, power, and grace of Jesus Christ with a dying world and that includes New Agers. Yet New Agers are treated with more judgment and coldness than Muslims, who chant death to all infidels and are actively beheading Christians on Earth now.

New Agers do not engage in spreading such negativities. Most New Agers seek to spread love, truth, and light. That's typically the New Age mantra and dogma. Many New Agers lack spiritual discernment because they fail to discern that the demonic realm masquerades as light beings, space brothers, and ascended masters. Many New Agers are misguided. They see Buddhas as spirit guides, deceased loved ones as spirit guides, but in actuality, these spirit guides are nothing but demons masquerading as such. The church should be teaching this, which is no wonder why these people all strayed.

Many New Agers are confused; they lack spiritual grounding and are plugged into counterfeits who serve the Kingdom of Darkness. They trade their souls for healing powers, which can come from both sides, and their quest for secret knowledge, which is occult, and comes with occult spirits, which is witchcraft. The word *witchcraft* is about control. It doesn't matter which side is using it, whether it's outright black magic or white magic (i.e., Wicca, or spiritual witchcraft used in churches, like Catholicism), it's all about control, which networks with the spirit of religion. Christianity has its fair share of "charismatic witches."

New Agers are no better off when it comes to the attachment of the religious spirits. They all create the same kind of ritualistic bondages, along with the same kind of false beliefs that one color or one particular crystal or New Age bric-a-brac will heal or energize them, when what many lack is the direct connection to the Lord, who is the King of the Kingdom of Heaven and the One who has the power to heal them permanently.

I have witnessed New Agers put their faith into things like Reiki, which literally invokes the Japanese names of demon spirits for healing, which is never permanent, because what the recipient is essentially doing is trading the spirit of sickness for belief in demon spirits to heal them. This is nothing but a Faustian contract. It creates more harm than good in the end for the recipient.

The anointing of the Holy Spirit to heal is far more powerful than Reiki. Reiki doesn't raise the dead, the Holy Spirit does. Reiki can't cast out demons; the Holy Spirit frees the soul and the mind. Reiki may relax some, but this is part of the spell; the healing is never permanent, and the recipient is forever on the quest for healing. The Holy Spirit heals life-threatening illnesses and restores people in both body, mind, and spirit. I have never seen Reiki compare to what the Holy Spirit can do, proving that Reiki is a false reality.

Tapping into the Living Waters, which comes from a personal relationship with the Living God who alone has all the power over every spirit, which is why one of His names is Lord of Spirits (see the Book of Enoch), is really the only true path to freedom from sickness, pain, and despair, that New Agers are seeking.

Many are agog over those who channel so-called ETs, ancient deceased gods or goddesses, or angels, and are "hooked" on the information they get, but this, too, is nothing but a parlor game for the demonic realm, which is the original "spiritual conspiracy." A medium is used to channel a deceased loved one, and a demon shows up in his place, deceiving both the medium and the bereaved.

"And no wonder, for Satan himself masquerades as an angel of light."
(2 Corinthians 11:14)

This is the premise for my dissertation. New Agers need to wake up to the spiritual conspiracy. Most of what they channel is NOT of the highest good; instead it is a masquerade of fallen angels, demonic intelligences (i.e. aliens and evil spirits who act, speak and appear as anything they want to project, better than the best actor or actress on earth can do). It's their job; it's what they do. They are assigned to deceive humans. This is what the spiritual battle is all about.

So it's a shame that so many turn to all kinds of hoodoo and voodoo, which enables spiritual mischief making, when what almost every New Ager I have ever met and

CHAPTER THIRTEEN: The Name Above All Names

spoken to wants is peace, love, joy and healing, which can only be permanently secured by and through the Lord of Lords, who is Yeshua/Jesus the Christ.

This has nothing to do with religion, but everything to do with relationship, and a willingness to repent (i.e. turn from spiritual arrogance and pride), which networks with the Archonic strongholds of religious spirits.

The irony and hypocrisy of New Agers, is that the religious spirit is what drove them out of the Church as many have been wounded by religion, only to essentially meet the same spirit in a different form within New Age circles. It's still the same legalistic spirit that demands works for earning their place in heaven, which is something no one can do. It's already been established, in the heavens and on Earth, that the spiritual gateway is the Son of God. His completed works on the Cross saved all of humankind from the strongholds and bondages of the god of this world, who are the satanic aliens, reptilians, the archons, who are the rulers of darkness behind most of the world's religions. One could say that, spiritually speaking, the New Age Christian has jumped out of the frying pan of the lukewarm church and into the fires of New Age deceptions.

The spirit of Christ differs from "Christ Consciousness." The word "Christ" comes from the Greek and means "the anointed one" or Messiah. To suggest that one believes in Christ consciousness opens the door to all kinds of counterfeit Christs and counterfeit Messiahs. It is not specific. Therefore, this belief gives spiritual legal ground to the forces of deception to play within the minds of New Agers, who think themselves more spiritual than others because they embrace Christ consciousness, which is what most New Agers believe and subscribe to, but this type of broad thinking leaves them open to all kinds of counterfeit spirits. The only way to discern the counterfeit is to know the original, and that is the person and name of Yeshua/Jesus, through His Holy Spirit.

The thing that turns most New Agers off of Christ are Christian judgments, and the fact that the Holy Spirit's job is to convict people of their sins, in order to cause them to come to repentance, which, in turn, releases oceans of God's grace to be poured out on them. Many are afraid of this kind of spiritual transformation because it can be uncomfortable to face one's issues, and New Agers don't like to feel guilt and shame. The Holy Spirit conviction is about love, so the individual can feel forgiveness from the grace of God. It is not about keeping a person in the spirit of guilt and shame, which is exactly what was nailed to the Cross of Calvary.

One thing I want to mention, to connect the dots in the minds of my readers, whether they be New Agers, Christians, Jews or atheists, is that the expected 5th Dimension coming to Earth, which is widely predicted in New Age circles, is really the coming Kingdom of Heaven through the Millennial Reign of Christ on Earth (See, Revelation 20:4-6). Once you see that, it all makes sense, and you can call it for what it is, which has been written down both in the heavenly scrolls and on Earth and planned from the foundation of the world. The real "New Age" is the age to come, which is the Golden Age, aka the processional Age of Aquarius, aka the Millennial Reign of Christ in the coming New Jerusalem, the heavenly city (huge mothership) that lands on Earth where

Yeshua/Jesus sits on a throne and rules over all the Earth and the Heavens from the new Earth.

Yes, when Christ shows up, the vibration of everything changes. His very presence heals sickness and scatters demons. His reign on Earth will, in effect, raise the vibration and experience of this planet into what New Agers call the 5th Dimension. This is when heaven comes to Earth (See, Revelation 20, 21, 22).

The question remains, "who" gets to be there? Whose name is written in the Book of Life? The answer lies in not "what" we know, but "who" we know. The answer lies in our personal relationship to the only One who Saves: Yeshua/Jesus, whose very name means, Salvation.

A relationship begins by inviting His spirit to live and dwell inside of you, which begins to clean you up from the inside out. It does not guide you to worship stuff outside of yourself, because the well is full from the inside. The spirit of Christ, aka the Holy Spirit, transforms your mind daily through His Spirit and through His Living Word. This is not putting on Christ consciousness, but actually becoming the mind of Christ, through the transformation of one's heart, aka inner man, aka inner spirit and soul through a living relationship. In order to "think" like Christ, we need to invite His Spirit to inhabit in us, which clears the space of any other spiritual dweller.

In Book Three: *Who Are The Angels?*, I go into more detail discerning and proving all the different New Age and occult practices that are actually invocations to fallen angels, who masquerade as ascended masters, space brothers, extraterrestrials and angels..

NOTES:

1. http://faithlenders.weebly.com/uploads/5/5/3/7/5537776/constantines_creed.pdf
2. http://www.compellingtruth.org/Jesus-sabbath.html#ixzz3g5qEOpZg
3. http://www.touregypt.net/featurestories/serapis.htm

CHAPTER FOURTEEN

WHO IS THE GOD OF GODS?

"There are more idols in the world than there are realities."
~ Friedrich Nietzsche

As I've already established, Yahweh is the <u>incorrect</u> pronunciation of YHVH, there is no "W" sound in the Hebrew language, יהוה YAHUAH is the name of the Hebrew God of Israel, so to create a new vibration or sound that simply does not and has never existed in the Hebrew/Aramaic language is a false interpretation. Hebrew/Aramaic is the spoken language of YAHUAH. The Masoretic text (the alleged Rabbinical authorities on the Hebrew lexicon) say (YAHUAH) is pronounced *Yehovah* or *Yahveh* (depending on where you place the vowels). In English, this is pronounced *Jehovah*.

When it comes to the names of gods, vibration and pronunciation mean everything. Imagine this: What if a small group of Jewish scholars rewrote the Old Testament by putting vowels (known as nikkudot) where there have never been any? Putting a few dots here and a line there can not only change the meaning of a word, it can change the entire name to mean a completely different word and god.

You may wonder, why would they do that? I believe that the Masoretes, unbeknownst to them, were guided by a sinister hand, the hand of the adversary of YHVH, whose job it is to deceive, steal, kill, and destroy. A few dots here and a line there, and — Voilà! — a new god is born by causing many to mispronounce the true name of God. The devil is in these details and/or mistakes. Ignorance is not bliss; it is the doorway to darkness. This is a plot straight out of the pit of hell. To this day, we have well-meaning churches, whole religions, and well intentioned congregations that are praying to a counterfeit god. Read on and I will prove to you how this happened and why.

GOD IS A FOUR LETTER WORD

The name Yahweh is actually a misinterpretation of the consonants יהוה YHVH made up of the Hebrew/Aramaic letters, Yud, Hay, Vav, Hay. However, many incorrectly spell it now as, Yahweh. In written Hebrew, the vowels are, if at all written, marked with diacritics (additional signs), which is never or only rarely done with YHWH. However, according to the Masoretic Text, they place the vowels to read the word/name: YeHoVaH. When this word/name is translated into English, it always reads as LORD in capital letters for emphasis.

Why did they choose those particular vowels, you may ask? Because it was a reminder to them and all Jews not to say the sacred name of God; instead, we use the word "Adonai," meaning Lord or Master, so they placed the vowels of the word Adonai on the Tetragrammaton YHVH, and centuries later, Gentiles who were unaware of what the Levitic Preisthood, a group Masoretes Priests, did after learning to read Hebrew and why, read the word Yahovah, which later became Jehovah in English.

The Masoretes deliberately did this, by taking the vowels from the Hebrew word, Elohim, and placing them over the word YHVH to remind Jews not to utter the sacred name, and instead say the word for god in its plurality — Elohim. Instead Jews said Adonai, which means LORD, which has similar vowels, and since then, it stuck. The other reason, and perhaps just as equally motivating for the Masoretes was to prevent Gentiles from saying the proper sacred name of God, so they obscured the true pronunciation when adding vowels to the entire Torah and Old Testament Scriptures between 750-1000AD. The Masoretic text is the official Hebrew version of the Old Testament in the world today, endorsed by the Rabbinical Council in Jerusalem, Israel.

As previously stated, there is no "W" sound in the Hebrew language; however, in ancient Aramaic, the "vav" was mispronounced "waw," which is where the use of the Yahweh came from. Consequently, a double "vv" was misinterpreted as a "w." Yahweh and Yehovah (Jehovah) are actually two different gods.

Dr. Selwyn Stevens claimed in his article "Gods or God: How Many & Who?"that, because the Hebrew name for God was written Y H W H, or J H V H, in the Hebrew language only, consonants are used, vowels were unknown, and adding them was only guessing. "The name 'Jehovah' was invented by a Catholic monk, Raymundus Martini, in 1270 AD. He simply added some vowels. This doesn't devalue the name Jehovah, but the fact remains that it wasn't in the Hebrew Scriptures."[1]

I have researched this intensely, and haven't found anything to prove or disprove this. However, as I have mentioned, the Masoretic Text includes all the vowels and writes YHVH as *Yehovah, not Yahweh, or Yahveh.*

For example, we know that the reason the *Books of Enoch* were rejected from the canon was because both the Catholic scholars and Jewish priests were threatened by Enoch's detailed prophesies of the Son of Man and his specific mission in the flesh which came true over 2000 years ago. We know that Enoch's scriptures were considered the "Word of God" by the Jews and the early Christians.

In fact, much of the New Testament gospels written by the Jewish disciples quoted Enoch, including Jesus Himself. Enoch was the first to coin the phrase "Son of Man." Suffice it to say, both the Jewish scholars and the Catholic Church Fathers conferred with one another on coming up with the canonized version of the scriptures we know today as the Holy Bible during the course of their seven ecumenical councils from 325 AD to 787 AD.

What I believe has happened over time is that the letter "V" or in Hebrew "Vav" was written twice. The German rationalist Heinrich Ewald (1803-1875) was the first to popularize the form Jahve, followed by E. W. Hengstenberg (1802-1869) promoting Jahveh, which later became Yahweh. Oyvey Yahveh!

CHAPTER FOURTEEN: Who Is The GOD of Gods?

Because there is no "W" sound in the Hebrew language, these German scholars failed to see that even when you put two Vs together, it still doesn't make a "W" sound in Hebrew. This is a false interpretation and, in my opinion, created a completely different vibration which, in turn, created a different being which comes from the fallen angels. (See, Book Three: *Who Are The Angels?* Chapters: Fallen Angels and Watchers.)

When it comes to language, pronunciation is key in conveying the proper understanding, and when it comes to names, pronunciation is key in invoking the right person, especially a deity.

THE MASORETIC CONTROVERSY

The Hebraic Roots Bible takes the original Hebrew and Aramaic Peshitta manuscripts and replaces all that was lost in transliteration from the Masoretic texts and the many mis-transliterations that arose from them. Don Esposito of the Congregation of YHVH in Jerusalem has replaced all the inaccuracies of the titles of 'Lord' and 'God' with the original Hebrew and Aramaic names of God. While I must commend him on his exhaustive and well-intentioned research, the only thing I disagree with is the fact that he replaces YHVH with the mispronunciation Yahweh. As I've stated (and will continue to expound upon in this chapter), Yahweh is a mistranslation and a gross mispronunciation of the original Hebrew/Aramaic YHVH. It is on this major detail that the well-intentioned Hebraic Roots Bible misses the mark.[2]

However, I do agree with the author when he asserts that the Hebrew Masoretic text of the Tanach or Old Covenant, which is maybe one of the oldest and overall most reliable source of scripture that we have to date, the 'lying pen of the scribes' has not kept the Masoretic text without fault. There has been several areas where the translators of the Masoretic text purposely changed scripture to fit their own theology." This is where the devil is definitely in the details.

Esposito checked and referenced each discrepancy with the Masoretic text with, at least, two other witnesses of written ancient scriptures, which were the Septuagint Greek translation from the second century B.C., and the Dead Sea Scrolls, written between the first and second century B.C. The following is a list of some of the scribal errors of the Masoretic text, which I researched from the Hebraic Bible that I have expounded and commented on:

1. The personal name of YHVH (YAHUAH) was changed 113 times to Adonai in the Masoretic Text from the original Hebrew manuscripts.

2. The Masoretic text[3] takes the word for *pierced* in Psalm 22:16 (The Psalm of the Crucifixion) *kaaru* and changes the last letter from a *vav* to a *yod*. The change of letter changes the meaning from "pierced my hands and feet" to "lion," "as a lion they are at

235

my hands and feet." The Septuagint used the word *pierced* from the original Hebrew *karu*, not *kaari*.

The Masoretic text[3] says: "For dogs have compassed me: the assembly of the wicked have enclosed me *watching* my hands and my feet *as though I were a lion*." They have changed the words from pierced to watching, and added the word "lion." Plus the fact that in the Masoretic text, this verse is listed as verse 17, whereas every other version of the Bible lists this as verse 16, and they do translate it as "piercing my hands and feet" (NIV, NLV, ESV, KJV, AKJV, ASV, GWV, ERV, etc.).

According to the Dead Sea Scrolls dated about 100 BCE, the Hebrew Word in verse 16 is *kaaru* (pierced) and not *lion*. Not only that, but the Aramaic Peshitta also agrees with the Septuagint. "And You appoint Me to the dust of death; for dogs have encircled Me; a band of spoilers have hemmed Me in, piercing My hands and My feet."

3. In Isaiah 53, the Masoretic text[3] is missing a key word in verse 11. After the word "see," there should be another word "light" qualifying what the Suffering Servant sees. But the missing word LIGHT is found in the Septuagint and the Dead Sea Scrolls.

After researching all the various Bible translations, only the NIV seems to have it right: "After the suffering of his soul, he will see the light [of life] and be satisfied; by his knowledge my righteous servant will justify many, and he will bear their iniquities."

4. In the Masoretic text[3], both Exodus 1:5 "The descendants of Jacob numbered seventy in all; Joseph was already in Egypt." and Genesis 46:27 states: "With the two sons who had been born to Joseph in Egypt, the members of Jacob's family, which went to Egypt, were seventy in all." But both the Septuagint and Dead Sea Scrolls say seventy-five souls. Perhaps they miscounted, Joseph's family? Who were at that time five? Joseph was always the oddball, in spite of the fact that his sons received the double portion of land.

5. In Genesis 10:24, the Masoretic text[3] is missing generations. The New Testament in Luke 3:36 inserts Canaan, as does the Septuagint and the Dead Sea Scrolls, leaving three biblical witnesses. Now why would the Masoretic writers delete a whole generation? Did they have an agenda to discount certain "key" descendants from the bloodline?

6. In Deuteronomy 32:8, the Masoretic text[3] uses the term "children of Israel." The Septuagint uses the term "Cherubs Of Elohim," as do the Dead Sea Scrolls.

"When the Most High gave the nations their inheritance, when he divided all mankind, he set up boundaries for the peoples according to the number of the sons of Israel" (NIV). According to Barnes Notes on the Bible, "Some texts of the Greek

CHAPTER FOURTEEN: Who Is The GOD of Gods?

version have 'according to the number of the Angels of God'; following apparently not a different reading, but the Jewish notion that the nations of the earth are seventy in number (compare Genesis 10:1 note), and that each has its own guardian Angel (compare Ecclesiastes 17:17). This was possibly suggested by an apprehension that the literal rendering might prove invidious to the many Gentiles who would read the Greek version."

In Hebrew, the word for *Cherubs* is Cheruvim, pronounced Keruveem, who were later mistaken for angels in the Septuagint. Yet the word for *angels* in Hebrew is Malachim. The Cheruvim were a completely different type of being. They were not angels, but more like technological anomalies, similar to robots.

7. In Isaiah 61:1, the Masoretic text[3] does not contain the phrase "recovery of sight to the blind." Yet the Septuagint version of Isaiah 61:1 does include these words, as Luke 4:18 does:

"The Spirit of the Lord is on me, because he has anointed me to preach good news to the poor. He has sent me to proclaim freedom for the prisoners and recovery of sight for the blind, to release the oppressed,"

8. In Psalm 40:6, the Masoretic text[3] has purposely changed the phrase "a BODY you have prepared for me", as properly quoted again in Hebrews 10:5, and verified by the Dead Sea Scrolls to the phrase "you have opened up my ears."[3]

According to Clarke's Commentary on the Bible:

'A body hast thou prepared me' - The quotation of this and the two following verses by the apostle, Hebrews 10:5, etc., is taken from the Septuagint, with scarcely any variety of reading: but, although the general meaning is the same, they are widely different in verbal expression in the Hebrew. David's words are (oznayim caritha li), which we translate, My ears hast thou opened;"

The NIV translates it as: "Sacrifice and offering you did not desire, but my ears you have pierced; burnt offerings and sin offerings you did not require." Which is far from the original meaning: "a body has thou prepared for me." Nowhere in both the Old and New Testament does it say that Yahshua had his ears pierced, but his hands and feet. So the NIV doesn't even make sense here.[4]

There are so many places where the meanings have been changed due to mistranslations, in what appears to be a deliberate altering of the original texts to fit a particular agenda of the time, which was to suppress the rise of Christianity, particularly among the remaining Jewish community.

In the 1972 film *The Ruling Class,* starring Peter O'toole, he pronounced the true name of יהוה as YAHUAH. The filmmakers researched it to make sure they got it right. It was purposeful, proving that the name of YAHUAH was always preserved by certain tribes of Jews and passed down verbally through generations in spite of the Masoretic Cover-Up.[5]

Also important to note, that the Native American Cherokee tribes used the name 'Yahuah' as their name for Great Spirit. This is evidenced in the 1986 film, *Gone To Texas,* staring Sam Shepherd. The movie is based on documented fact of the great historical figure Sam Houston, who spent his early life amongst Cherokee Indians. Sam Houston led the "Texas Revolution," and was a Major in the "Revolutionary War." He became the first President of Texas, and Houston, Texas was named after him. What was not readily known, was that he knew the ancient Name of the Great Spirit that was worshipped by the Cherokee. That name is none other then the One true God of Israel. This is evidenced by the film, which was based on historical fact.[6]

There is much speculation that the Cherokee were one of the lost tribes of Israel. I go into this in more detail in Book Four: *Covenants.* Be that as it may, both the Cherokee and Jewish tribes have preserved the spoken sacred name of the God of Israel, who is Yahuah.

"For my thoughts are not your thoughts, nor are your ways my ways," declares the LORD (YAHUAH). For just as the heavens are higher than the earth, so are my ways higher than your ways, and my thoughts than your thoughts."

(Isaiah 55:8, 9-ISV)

"The LORD says, "I will rescue those who love me. I will protect those who trust in my name."

(Psalm 91:14-NLT)

NOTES:

1. Selwyn Stevens, M.C.R., Ph.D., *God or Gods: How Many and Who?* http://jubileeresources.org/?page_id=608
2. *The Hebraic Roots Bible,* http://www.coyhwh.com/en/bibleDownloadPDF.php Don Esposito, http://thekeytoredemption.blogspot.com/2009/05/who-is-don-esposito.html
3. *The Holy Scriptures: A Jewish Bible According To The Masoretic Text – Hebrew and English.* Sinai Publishing House, 72 Allenby Rd., Tel-Aviv, Israel. 1977.
4. Adam Clark, Bible Commentary, Published 1810-1826. http://www.preteristarchive.com/Books/1810_clarke_commentary.html
5. *The Ruling Class,* 1972 United Artists film, Directed by Peter Medak, screenplay by Peter Barnes.
6. *Gone To Texas,* 1986, Directed by Peter Levin, screenplay by John Binder, story by Frank Dobbs and John Binder, CBS Television Movies.

CHAPTER FIFTEEN

WHO IS YAHWEH?

"If the Holy Spirit was withdrawn from the church today, ninety five percent of what we do would go on and no one would know the difference. If the Holy Spirit had been withdrawn from the New Testament church, ninety five percent of what they did would stop, and everybody would know the difference."

Dr. A.W. Tozer

In the ancient Sumerian myths, both Enki and Enlil were sons of the Most High God "El Elyon." These two brothers, Enlil and Enki fought over humanity. Enki was known as the compassionate god, and Enlil was known as the punishing and cruel god. The Sumerian tablets tell a story that predates or, some say, coincides with the early Bible story of Creation.

In comparison to the Sumerian text with Bible scriptures, Enki represented Yahuah, and Enlil was Yahweh or Satan (John 1:6). Enlil later became Allah. (See my chapter on *Who Is Allah?*) These gods are often confused and treated as one god; in reality, they are two completely different, separate gods.

Some theologians have said that they are one god with two sides, like the pagan god Janus, who is known as the two-faced god. But according to the Hebrew text, this is only conjecture. In my opinion, when Yahuah speaks in the Old Testament, his name is recorded as YHVH. When Yahweh speaks, he has often come through as the Elohim, such as in the famous story of when Abraham was tested to sacrifice his son Isaac.

This is where the argument that HaSatan, a name which just means "the adversary" in Hebrew, represents a real son of the Most High God, who fell from grace and lost his lofty position in Heaven in rebellion against his Creator. There are conflicting views on whether Lucifer (which is the Latin for the Hebrew name, Heylel, who became Satan) was actually an Archangel or Cherub. Ezekiel 28:16 states:

> "Through your widespread trade you were filled with violence, and you sinned. So I drove you in disgrace from the mount of God, and I expelled you, O guardian cherub, from among the fiery stones." (the fiery stones are the planets in our solar system)

Or was HaSatan an actual son of God, one of the Elohim, as the book of Job relates to:

"Again there was a day when the sons of Elohim (gods) came to present themselves before Yahuah, and HaSatan came also among them to present himself before Yahuah."

(Job 1:6; 2:1)

This scripture implies that HaSatan was one of the sons of God. He was once considered to be a god, but rebelled against the Most High. It's important to note that this fallen son is not alone. He persuaded others in his rebellion against the Almighty, who are all known as the satans. They all don many names and disguises, but their agenda is the same — to wage war against the Most High and his saints.

Unfortunately, in today's churches, most pastors know that Satan is the enemy; they call him the "devil," but very few understand who is really is, and how many names he has, and how many satans there really are. This type of ignorance allows the enemy (the satans) to infiltrate through false names of YHVH and false doctrines. When fighting in any battle, particularly spiritual warfare, the first rule of thumb is to "know thy enemy." One of Satan's biggest lies is to purport that he doesn't exist. In actuality, he exists under many different names and disguises.

The name Lucifer was coined by the Latin Vulgate Bible, which is the Latin name for the interpretation of the Hebrew word, Heylel. This word, Lucifer, was inserted in the place for Heylel by Jerome, who was commissioned by Pope Damasus I in 382 to rewrite the Bible in Latin for the Catholic Church.

The only place where Heylel/Lucifer is found is in Isaiah 14:12. It reads, "How art thou fallen from heaven, O Lucifer (Heylel), son of the morning!"

The word Lucifer comes from the Hebrew word Heylel which means *shining one* (Young's Concordance), *morning star* (Strong's Exhaustive Concordance), *bright star or splendid star* (Gesenius' Hebrew-Chaldee Lexicon). Whether it's Heylel or Lucifer, both have become HaSatan (Hebrew meaning "the adversary" or "the rebel"), and he is not alone. (For more information about the many names of the satans, see my chapters on the God of this World, and The Office of Satan.)

Some theologians have said that they are one god with two sides, like the pagan god Janus, who is known as the two-faced god. But according to the Hebrew text, this is only conjecture. In my opinion, when Yahuah speaks in the Old Testament, his name is recorded as YHVH. When Yahweh speaks, he has often come through as the Elohim, such as in the famous story of when Abraham was tested to sacrifice his son Isaac. Recounted in the twenty-second chapter of Genesis, Abraham said he heard a voice, who he called "Lord" tell him to sacrifice his son Isaac, who was his miracle child, promised to him by the Lord Yahuah.

Afterward, Abraham gears up his wood on his donkey, along with two men and his son Isaac, and they all head toward Mount Moriah to perform the burnt sacrifice. All the while, young Isaac is thinking they will be sacrificing an animal. The poor young boy has no idea that he is the one to be offered in the fire. Then, they arrive, and as Abraham begins to perform the deed, an angel of the Lord Yahuah specifically utters the words "malach Yahuah." He speaks to him, not once, but twice, and tells Abraham not to harm his son, and then delivers a message from Yahuah to Abraham.

Why would YHVH, who clearly has decreed it a sin to sacrifice a child, test Abraham to do the very thing he forbids? We know from the book of Job 1.12 that the

CHAPTER FIFTEEN: Who Is Yahweh?

Lord Yahuah does not test, but Satan does. While God allows these kinds of tests, as He did in the case of Job, He is not the cause of them because He never tempts anyone to do evil (James 1:13. 1 Corinthians. 10:13). In the entire story in Genesis, not once, is the name of YHVH (Yahuah) mentioned.

In the Genesis story of Abraham in chapter 22, Abraham hears a voice that he assumes is the Lord's, telling him to sacrifice his son Isaac. Remember the Lord is Yahuah. The Elohim is plural for gods or the mighty ones of God. The Elohim is not the Trinity. The voice that Abraham first heard came from the Ha-Elohim (Hebrew for "the gods"), who tested Abraham. I have heard some people even say that this was Satan, which very well could have been because Satan is the tempter. The Lord does not tempt.

Satan is also known as the counterfeit god. He pretends to be god, and it is possible that the biblical writer of Genesis did not know the difference between the two at that time. But the scripture says nothing about him. It does use the words "VeHa-Elohim Nisah," which literally translates to "and the gods tested Abraham."

In my opinion, this was Yahweh/Satan, who acted as an "adversary" or "tempter" which is what the office of the satans do. It specifically says throughout both the Old and New Testaments that the Lord does not test.

> "Let no one say when he is tempted, "I am being tempted by God," for God cannot be tempted with evil, and he himself tempts no one."
>
> (James 1:13)

> "Do not put the LORD Yahuah your God to the test."
>
> (Exodus 17:2, 7; Deuteronomy 6:16; Deuteronomy 33:8; Luke 4:12, Matthew 4:7)

Many Christians believe that the Elohim are the Trinity, as I've mentioned before, but there is absolutely nothing in the Hebrew Scriptures to support this. If the Elohim are the Trinity, which consists of the Father, The Son, and the Holy Spirit, then what are they doing testing humans?

The truth of the matter is the Elohim do NOT represent the Trinity, nor do they represent the Most High God, Yahuah, but the Elohim are god(s), children, i.e., sons of God, and Lucifer/Satan in his many forms and counterfeit names was one of them. Modern Jewish thought believes the Elohim is the Universe. For discernment purposes, the term *universe* is too broad of a term to describe any one god or being.

Now doesn't it seem contradictory that the Lord Yahuah Himself has decreed to the children of Israel that sacrificing children is forbidden, so why would He, the Lord Yahuah, tempt or test Abraham in the manner described in Genesis?

> "And you shall not let any of your children pass through the fire to Molech, neither shall you profane the name of your God: I am YAHUAH (the LORD)."
>
> (Leviticus 18:21)

> "For when you offer your gifts, when you make your sons to pass through the fire, you pollute yourselves with all your idols, even to this day: and shall I be inquired of by you, O house of Israel? As I live, said YAHUAH (the Lord GOD), I will not be inquired of by you."
>
> (Ezekiel 20:31)

The answer is that it was not the Lord Yahuah who tested Abraham, but one of the gods of the Elohim, which was his counterfeit, Yahweh/satan. In the Hebrew, we have two distinct voices here, which are often confused as being the same voice, or the same god, and this is simply not the case. The voice of the Elohim (this could be "one" of them, yet the scripture records it as a plurality), and the voice of the angel of the Lord Yahuah, delivering a message from Yahuah. But Yahuah Himself does not speak at all during this entire episode.

It's also important to note, the word, HaElohim, is consistently used throughout the Genesis story, which literally means "the gods." After the angel of Yahuah saves Isaac from being killed, a ram shows up caught in the bush thistles, and they sacrifice the ram in the place of Isaac. Then Abraham declares the place, *Yahuah Yireh*, which means "Yahuah provides."

Was there jealousy among the gods? You betcha! They fought for ultimate rulership and worship of earth humans. Yahuah decided to wipe out humanity and start all over again. Acts like these are not done alone, but only through the Most High, the Almighty "El Elyon."

The true creator god, the prime creator, was Yahuah, also called "El Elyon." He obviously created a number of secondary gods as his "sons" who became known as gods and deities of which Yahweh (Enlil) and Heylel (Lucifer/HaSatan) are.

Yahweh had a consort named Asherah who was a goddess. Her name is mentioned forty times in the Old Testament, but it is almost always translated as "grove" or "tree." This is because her symbol was a tree and an upright wooden pole. So when the Old Testament states that it is forbidden to plant a tree at the altar of Yahuah, what it's referring to is that it is forbidden to place a symbol of Asherah there, known as an Asherah pole or tree (Deuteronomy 16:21). Yahuah did not want any other gods before Him, and that included the consorts of his sons.

Both Enki, Enlil, and Yahweh are not the prime creators, however, they have produced certain creations.

The *Books of Enoch* are probably the best of the ancient texts that spells this out, when Enoch is taken up by an angel of the Lord and shown the ten different heavens. (See, Book Five, *The Heavens*, for the entire story.) Enoch is shown the throne rooms of the Lord of Lords and King of Kings, the Father of Yahshua, who is Yahuah, and then yet another higher level throne room where the Most High God abides, who has a totally unpronounceable name. This proves the heavenly hierarchy of creators with the Almighty Prime Creator above the rest.

CHAPTER FIFTEEN: Who Is Yahweh?

To parallel to the Sumerian creation story known as "Enuma Elish," which tells us of a pair of creator gods, known as Apsû and Ti'âmat, who are also known to the ancient Sumerians, Acadians, and Assyrians as the male and female side of the prime creator because they created a number of deities, from which further deity races arose. This race of gods became known as the Annunaki, after its leader named Anu. They separated themselves off from the two prime creators and wanted to live and act without them. "Enûma Elish" tells about a murder of the highest gods. The Annunaki are told to have killed first Apsû and then Ti'âmat! How is it possible to kill the prime creators? The answer is ... it isn't possible. Apsû and Ti'âmat were not prime creators, but created beings that were given the status of deities and gods.

The murder symbolizes that they turned away from them and didn't want to have anything to do with them, as if they were dead — that was their fall, their plunge out of the divine light into a relative darkness. The Annunaki became fallen deities. The one who is said to have murdered Ti'âmat is Marduk, who also became the lord of the Earth, is also known as Satan.

Marduk is another one of HaSatan's names. (See, my chapters "The God of This World" and "The Office of Satan.")[1] The Annunaki then came under his rule, through a contract with him, (see Book Four – *Covenants,* my chapter on *Contracts and Agreements* for how this works) and allowed to create new human beings on Earth by means of genetic manipulation, as a slave race to the gods, and from their slave race, became descendants of today's earth humans and their various races. The Annunaki are fallen extraterrestrials who are believed to return to Earth in the last days of this age to team up with Satan against his war with the Faithful Elohim and the King of their army, Jesus Christ, aka Yahushua HaMashiach.

YAHWEH, THE COUNTERFEIT GOD

Yahweh and Yahuah are not the same god as many mistakenly think. Many will slough it off and say it's just a mispronunciation, but to the gods, pronunciation is everything because it identifies their signature "vibration," so if Lucifer/Satan can get humans mispronouncing the name of god, then that is a perfect opportunity for Lucifer/Satan and his hierarchy of fallen angel gods to step in and become that vibration by pretending to be that god, by deceiving earth humans into worshipping the counterfeit.

Remember when it comes to counterfeit money, most people cannot tell the difference between the real thing and the counterfeit, but it must be discerned under a lens of a special ultraviolet light, where it exposes the subtle differences, in addition to the fact, that one needs to know the original before identifying its counterfeit. Both the devil and the truth are in the details.

Yahweh Yaldabaoth, curiously, is also known as *Yaldabaoth Demiurge* and there is reference by none other than Jesus himself in John 8:44, that it is this serpent-dragon-god which is subsequently worshipped by a faction of the Jews, calling all those who follow him, children of the devil.

My readers may wonder, how can this be? We need to remember that, in ancient Jewish history during the times of animal sacrifices done by the High Priests of Israel, the priest would put a blood sacrifice on the altar for the atonement of the sins of the people. Then he would offer another sacrificial slain goat and place it in the desert for Beelzebub because they feared him and believed it would appease him; that's how superstitious they were. They believed Beelzebub had magical powers. They even accused Jesus of doing miracles by Beelzebub.

The High Priests were known as the Cohanes, which meant "priesthood" in Hebrew. They were the only ones allowed to perform these rituals. They also appeased another devil called Azazel, who was a Nephilim, half-goat, half-reptile. Leviticus 16:8, 10, 26 all describe the protocol for preparing the "scapegoat" sacrifice for Azazel, which was sent by one of the priests into the wilderness.

Why on Earth would the Jewish priests need to prepare two goats — one for their sins, and one for Azazel? Because they were terrified that this serpent goat demon would eat them. Yahweh was another Nephilim, who was just as terrifying as Beelzebub and Azazel, and the Jewish priests couldn't always tell the difference between them, except that they knew that they had better sacrifice to one of them to protect themselves from being eaten and attacked by them.

Historically speaking, the Israelites were rebuked and punished many times for worshipping and sacrificing to false gods which was part of their habit pattern. In this case, it was a destructive false dragon-god, who is, as it were, a manifestation of Satan! A serpent-dragon god named Yahweh! Jesus confronted the High Priests, i.e., Sanhedrin, who ended up sending Jesus to be crucified, becoming the ultimate and final blood sacrifice for all. Only carnivorous reptilian dragon are bloodthirsty.

YAHWEH, THE DRAGON

Most Gnostic texts agree that the *Yahweh Yaldabaoth* lion-serpent-dragon was created by an unauthorized act of creation by Sophia; subsequently, this creature arrogantly plotted and schemed to spoil the divine plan to create a physical planet that would be a divine example of God's power. The *Yaldabaoth* lion-serpent is, as it were, a freak of divinity. It has great power, but it is not an "official" creation. This hybrid being is a Nephilim. *Yahweh Yaldabaoth* is frighteningly powerful, but very distorted. This lion-serpent is accredited with basically throwing a monkey wrench into the works and has been called the "ghost in the machine" in the matrix of Creation.

The *Yaldabaoth* lion-serpent-dragon has become known as the "*Demiurge*." It was written into commentaries and books by Plato, most notably in his work known as *Timaeus*, and this is yet another reason why the Nag Hammadi authors kept Plato's writings in their archives. Plato's works seem to suggest that the unseen, ether-like matter

CHAPTER FIFTEEN: Who Is Yahweh?

in the cosmos is pure and god-like, while the physical planets and us, humankind, have been created by the Demiurge, and therefore we are evil.

So why did the lion-serpent become known as a Demiurge? It is a curious term. It means (in a kind of derogatory way) someone who works in public, like a brick-layer, or mason (Greek; demiourgós, or Latinized; demiurgus, meaning "artisan" or "craftsman"). The Demiurge lion-serpent is therefore able to construct beings and planets just like God, but does it in a nuts 'n' bolts way, rather than being able to manifest Creation from light as God does.[2]

This is how Nephilim are created, through a pseudo process that combines genetic manipulation and the hybridization of more than one species with another. Mixing the DNA of angels (extraterrestrials) with that of an animal, in this case, combining the DNA of a lion, a dragon and a man to create this being called *Yahweh Yaldabaoth*, which was so fearsome and awesome, it caused a group of Jewish priests to worship it and appease it for fear of being eaten by it. This was the original 'Yahweh.'

"A veil exists between the world above, and the realms that are below; and shadow came into being beneath the veil. Some of the shadow became matter, and was projected apart. And what Sophia [Pistis Sophia] created became a product in the matter, like an aborted fetus [Nephilim]. ...It assumed a plastic shape molded out of shadow, and became an arrogant beast resembling a lion. It was androgynous, because it was from matter that it derived (synthetic, as opposed to spiritual 'matter')"[3]

No wonder why many get this god confused with the God of Israel (Yahuah). This *Yahweh* was and still is cruel to mankind. Then came Yahshua who taught a truth, which *Yahweh* didn't want mankind to know. This *Yahweh Yaldabaoth*, who belongs to the Office of Satan, played a part in having Yahshua killed, and later infiltrated Christianity to have a Church established, which twisted and falsified Christianity with an artificial dogma that actually serves Annunaki/Nephilim interests.

That is why Catholicism combines Mithraism and Paganism, and only replaced Mithras with Jesus Christ, and the Pagan goddesses with Mother Mary. They still maintained their idolatries, through their false beliefs in praying to saints and priests instead of directly to the Lord. This satanic spirit/religious principality continues to infiltrate both Christian and Messianic churches today, mainly through one's ignorance and mispronunciation of the word YHVH-Yud, Hay, Vav, Hay, i.e., Yahveh, Yahweh, or Yehovah, Jehovah. This is only a slight difference, but it makes all the difference in the two beings. Like any counterfeit, however, the devil is always in the details.

YHVH (Yahuah) is the name of God that the Israelites would never pronounce because it was so sacred that no one was allowed to pronounce it, except the High Priests, but when the High Priests stopped pronouncing God's name, they were sent a curse from the Lord (Micah 2:2). Instead they would call Him "HaShem," which literally translates as "The Name" or they would call Him "Adonai," which is the word for Lord.

This is the name of the God of Israel, who gave them the Hebrew language, so it is clear that His name cannot have a pronunciation of a letter and sound that doesn't even exist in His own language, which would be Hebrew or Ancient Aramaic. Arabic has a "w" sound, but the Old Testament is written in Hebrew, not Arabic. Therefore, Yahweh is not the true name of the God of Israel, nor the correct pronunciation of YHVH. Yahuah is the correct pronunciation because the original texts did not have vowels in it, hence the speculation.

In Hebrew, pronunciation is important because of the nature of the Hebrew language, all words come from a shoresh, meaning "root," which is like a tree. The three or four letters that make up the root is then used to create dozens of offshoots from that same root word, changing the meanings, yet staying close to the original meaning of the root, whether it be used as a singular, plural, masculine, feminine, adjective, verb or noun, can all come from the original root, with variations in vowels, prefixes, and suffixes.

However, the fact that there might be two gods, one being the true god and one being the counterfeit god interacting with humankind in the Bible is not only a possibility, based on language, but in my opinion, is clearly a fact! We're talking about the Most High God here, so, of course, someone is going to, out of jealousy, want to copy and counterfeit Him? In my opinion, this is where the misnomer Yahweh comes from, who is one of the satans. It is such a subtle difference in the vibration of the sound of the name, but it is enough to invoke an entirely different entity.

This explains why, in the Bible, it appears that there are two gods at times, one who is compassionate and long suffering toward his people, and one who seems cruel, and acts out of jealousy and tests humans. This parallels the Sumerian tablets, where there were two gods, both brothers, Enki and Enlil. Enki was the compassionate god to humans, while Enlil wanted to destroy humans. In the Old Testament, there is clearly two different gods involved in the Bible stories. Suffice it to say, it's all hidden in the original Hebrew, which is often lost in the English translations.

As in the story of Abraham and Isaac, this is clearly a time where he was tested by one god, who could have been Yahweh, (who was really Satan pretending to be God) while Yahuah, who wouldn't let Abraham kill his gifted child Isaac, sent one of his angels to save him. Satan (the false Yahweh) has the power to mimic the voice of God in the mind of Abraham, where Abraham couldn't tell the difference between the two voices.

Abraham said he heard a voice, who he called "Lord" tell him to sacrifice his son Isaac, who was his miracle child, promised to him by the Lord Yahuah. In obedience and faith to God, he takes Isaac to a rock and is prepared to kill him with a knife and burn him on the altar until he hears a voice that he also thought was the Lord's (which was actually an angel from Yahuah) telling him to stop, that he shouldn't hurt or sacrifice his son.

Why would Yahuah, who clearly has decreed it a sin to sacrifice a child, test Abraham to do the very thing He forbids? We know from the book of Job 1.12 that the

CHAPTER FIFTEEN: Who Is Yahweh?

Lord Yahuah does not test, but Satan does. While God allows these kinds of tests (as He did in the case of Job), He is not the cause of them because He never tempts anyone to do evil (James 1:13, 1 Corinthians. 10:13). In the entire story in Genesis, not once, is the name of Yahuah mentioned.

How many of us, go through the same thing in our lives, thinking we are being told something from God, when in fact it is the counterfeit god, who is Satan masquerading as some angel of light, ascended master, or extraterrestrial? How many criminals say, "God told me to do it," when, in reality, they followed the voice of Satan (the god of this world), who tricked them into thinking it was the Most High God. How often does the Lord YHVH get blamed for the actions and manipulations of Satan?

The creation of the word "Yahweh", is not only biblically unsound; it, also, borders on creating an entity which is a counterfeit and fraud of the God of the Bible. The God named Yahweh" is not referring to the Lord of the Bible, YHVH (Yahuah). It is influenced by Satan and his hierarchy of fallen angels, who have been at war with the Lord of the Bible, i.e., Yahuah.

Once people started believing the lie that the Lord's name was Yahovah or Yahweh, Satan succeeded in his evil plan to steal souls and worship away from the Lord Yahuah.

As a result, since the name Yahweh was coined, many jumped on the bandwagon, creating Yahweh cults, which are contrary to the very words of the God of the Bible, who is consistent with His anger toward idolatry and the worship of other gods. Not only that, there are many well-intentioned Bible believers who have been influenced by this false god, aka the Yahweh spirit, and have distorted their interpretation of the Bible as a result.

But this is planet Earth, and this is what has gone on for millennia, the creation of false gods, false religions, and the confusion resulting from countless cults created by fallen angels in their plan to get humans away from the truth and an intimate relationship with their Creator.

When Hengstenberg decided the Tetragrammaton YHVH was Yahweh, he was influenced by the spirit of this serpent-dragon, which was formed by Lucifer/Satan, who wanted to be like god, so he became Yahweh as one of his many masquerades. If you ever go into a Yahweh cult/church, the people are not free, there's all kinds of bondage. The sermons are the hell and brimstone judgmental stuff; there is little tolerance for those whose lifestyles are not in agreement with theirs; there is little "Christ Love," who loves all sinners. There is illness and bondage of all kinds and the church are bound by *religious spirits*, which are entities that thwart the power of the Holy Spirit. The Holy Spirit, sent by the Father and the Son Jesus Christ that comes to set the captives free.

Yahweh cults are not free; they are bound by legalism which are *religious spirits* and the spirits of judgment, which are all part of Satan's realm. All erected by using, invoking, and worshipping the name Yahweh. As subtle as it may be, it's a counterfeit spirit and not the true name of the Creator God. I heard a pastor of a Yahweh cult say that it's not about the pronunciation, but the intention. This is a deception and a misunderstanding of the God of the Old Testament. Pronunciation is everything when it comes to the sacred name of God. Precisely the very reason the Masoretes Priests went to such great trouble to conceal the true pronunciation.

> "And now, you priests, this warning is for you. If you do not listen, and if you do not resolve to honor my name," says the Lord Almighty, "I will send a curse on you, and I will curse your blessings. Yes, I have already cursed them, because you have not resolved to honor me.
>
> (Malachi 2:1-2)

Remember in ancient times, the High Priests were appointed and anointed to be the judge between the people and God. If they spoke to the wrong god, the people perished. They had to know the true name and correct pronunciation to bring down His blessings upon their people. When the priesthood stopped using the correct pronunciation, and then refused to even say or utter the sacred name, the Malachi prophecy came true, as the Jews went through such horrific persecution just for being Jewish.

Spiritually speaking, one has to ask, were these historical persecutions of the Jewish people somehow linked to the ancient Levitical Priesthood's sins and mistakes?

To this day, there is a deeply rooted superstition in Jews to avoid saying the name of the Lord, nor would they even spell out the word God, but instead write G-d.

All this in spite of the abundance of the Lord Yahuah's commands to speak His name, honor His name, praise His name, sing to His name, call on His name in times of trouble, etc.

How can you be sure when you do need the Lord and you pray to a false name, that He, the Lord Almighty, will answer you? Perhaps this is the reason why there are so many unanswered prayers? If Satan has already established/blasphemed God's names as his own, and a believer prays to one of these names ignorantly, you can be sure Satan will hear it, and a spiritual battle will pursue over that believer's life.

From my observations, when we address and worship the Lord by His true name, we get His attention, and we know by faith that He hears us, and He is true to His Word and true to Himself.

> **"Since no man is excluded from calling upon God, the gate of salvation is open to all. There is nothing else to hinder us from entering, but our own unbelief."**
>
> ~John Calvin

YAHWEH THE GOLDEN CALF

James Michener writes in *The Source*: "In fact, when the average citizen...prostrated himself before Yahweh he could scarcely have explained which god he was worshiping, for El had passed into Baal and he into El-Shaddai and all into Yahweh."[4]

CHAPTER FIFTEEN: Who Is Yahweh?

It was explicitly stated in the Book of Numbers that God (*Elohim*) had "the horns of the wild ox" (Numbers 24:8). The "wild ox" here is, the primeval beast known as the aurochs, a giant, untamed bison that was deemed more dangerous than a lion in ancient times. And His throne was guarded by human-headed bulls called cherubim. In fact, bulls were set up as golden images of Yahweh in the two rival temples of the ten northern tribes of Israel (1 Kings 12:28-29).

Aaron made a golden image of a male calf in order that the people might worship Yahweh under this form (Exodus 32:4). After the division of the kingdom, Jeroboam set up two golden calves in his kingdom, one at Bethel and one at Dan because he was afraid his people would abandon him if they continued to worship in Jerusalem (1 Kings 12:29). While it wasn't his intention to create a new pagan religion, as the bull images were supposed to represent Yahweh, but were rejected by the Almighty Yahuah as the images were regarded as common idols (1 Kings 12:30, Hosea 12:11).

YAHWEH CULTS

It is important to keep in mind, that in the realms of magic and occultic practices, pronunciation is everything. The wrong pronunciation could cause a spell to backfire and invoke the wrong spirit. Likewise, because of this misunderstanding and lack of discernment of how the name YHVH is pronounced, there are numerous Yahweh cults that come under the guise of Christianity. Many of them are considered "Messianic"; others come from Ethiopia.

I visited a Messianic Church where the members believed in Yahshua as their Savior, but worshipped Yahweh. The Bible says, "By their fruits you will know them." The pastor preached Hell and damnation. He was a legalist and judged people for their lifestyles, had no compassion on those who had to break the commandment "Honor thy Father and Mother" because of physical and sexual abuse from their parents, and preached that children needed to submit to their parents, regardless of various abuses. I was so uncomfortable listening to him that I couldn't return.

The pastor was tied up in all kinds of bondage. He was suffering from a medical condition and in severe pain, which he shared with the whole church; others in the church were also suffering with one affliction or another. There was no freedom and certainly no compassion. He even said it didn't matter that the name of God was mispronounced because it was the intention that counted. The road to hell is paved with good intentions. Ignorance is definitely not bliss! No wonder so many Messianic churches are called "Messy-antics."

When people worship Yahweh, they are essentially invoking the presence of this counterfeit god into their lives and into their house of worship. *Yahweh Yaldabaoth* is under the hierarchy of Lucifer/Satan. His presence is always felt with a heaviness, a dark cloud, and manifests as all kinds of physical afflictions, illness, frustration with finances, and blocks the congregation from growing in the grace and power of Christ. He essentially comes to clip the wings of the most fervent and zealous believers, which manifests as some kind of self-conflict within themselves, like migraines, sinus infections, and a weakened immune system. Why? Because one part of them is calling on Yahshua (Jesus Christ), yet they are giving their worship to a counterfeit god, Yahweh, which creates a false belief system that opens the door to various demonic strongholds. This is called, spiritual witchcraft.

Many believers believe in laying hands on the sick and commanding demons to go in the name of Jesus. These acts of faith get thwarted because the believer is in effect practicing idolatry, even though they are unaware. Because they are calling out to Yahweh, giving various demons a "legal right" to be there, whether in the lives of the believer or in the place of worship itself. They can only be fully cast out through repentance. If the congregation does not repent, rebuking these demons essentially becomes an act of futility.

Hosea 4:6 says, "My people perish because of lack of knowledge." Knowledge is power. Many churches are crippled because they are afraid of knowledge. This is the reason for the end-times apostasy, which essentially created the New Age Movement, which as I've been saying throughout this book, was created by disenchanted Christians, who left the church because they were searching for power and found it in the occult. (See my chapter, The New Age Christian.)

Invoking Yahweh is spiritual witchcraft. Most Christians do not realize that the spirit of witchcraft can exist as well as be nurtured in Christian churches. Invoking Yahweh through worship, essentially puts them under a spell, *Yahweh Yaldabaoth's* spell. Unfortunately, coupled with the *religious spirit,* who always accompanies the counterfeit spirit, creates a layer of spiritual pride and fundamentalism, which blinds these so-called believers from seeing and learning the truth. There is just as much denial in Christian churches about the supernatural as there is in the world.

Have they lost their salvation? No, salvation comes through confessing Christ and happens in a moment through a decision. But deliverance and true liberation can only come through repentance. While demons can't steal a person's salvation away, they can, steal their joy, their health and well-being, their success, and their abundance away while living in the flesh. So many of these types of churches literally get "stuck" at the cross. They get saved, but deliverance from all bondages is an entirely different story. Many fail to see that true power lies on the other side of the cross.

> "For rebellion is as the sin of witchcraft,
> And stubbornness is as iniquity and idolatry."
>
> (1 Samuel 15:23-KJV)

The Barna Group who routinely audits Christian churches recently said, "The problem facing the Christian church is not that they lack a complete set of beliefs; the problem is that they have a full slate of beliefs in mind, which they think are consistent with Biblical teachings, and that they are neither open to being proven wrong nor learning new insights.

It may well be that spiritual evaluation is so uncommon because people fear that the results might suggest the need for different growth strategies or for more aggressive approach in the growth process. No matter what the underlying reason is, the bottom line among both the clergy and the laypeople was indifference toward their acknowledged lack of evaluation."

There are so many false beliefs in the church, stemming from the corruption of the formation of the Catholic Church, which has influenced all the Christian denominations through the centuries. Most churches focus on bringing people to the cross, people getting saved, but then they are stuck at the cross. The quintessential message of Christ is in the *Dunamis* power of His resurrection, and the fact that Jesus Christ overcame the cross of Calvary and Death itself.

Most churches fail to get beyond the cross to live on the other side of the cross, which is where all the power lies. This is the very reason the Catholic Church continues, to this day, to worship a crucified Christ. In every Catholic Church, there is a crucifix with a dead Jesus nailed to the cross. This is voodoo. In voodoo, when they "nail" anyone down, it is done for the purpose of binding its power. Yet in spite of the many offshoot denominations that emerged from the Catholic Church, who do not worship the crucifix, their doctrines are nevertheless stuck at the cross, and spiritually speaking, they are stunted.

> "Is it faith to understand nothing, and merely submit your convictions implicitly to the church?"
>
> ~ John Calvin

Many people believe it's all about what's in your heart. If your heart loves the Lord, then that's all that counts. If you're sincere about your faith, then surely that's what matters. Yet what if you're sincerely wrong about who you are worshipping? After all is said and done, it is not about man's traditions, but what the Lord wants. After all, He is the one who is to be worshipped. So what if you're sincere in your heart about your love and worship, yet you miss the mark, literally, and worship the wrong god? This is why the scripture says, "The heart is deceitful above all things, and desperately wicked: who can know it?" (Jeremiah 17:9). We can whole heartedly believe something, and be sincere, but in the same way, can be whole heartedly and sincerely wrong about it.

> "The great enemy of the truth is very often not the lie, deliberate, contrived and dishonest, but the myth, persistent, persuasive and unrealistic."
>
> ~ President John F. Kennedy

Where the spirit of the Lord is, there is freedom.
Jesus said, "I have come to set the captives free."

(Isaiah 61:1; Luke 4:18)

The good news is that we are living in a time of grace. No matter what the error, sin, or condition, if anybody accepts and believes in the Messiah of Grace, who is Yahshua HaMashiach, aka the Lord Jesus Christ, he will be saved through grace by faith. Anyone can have all that the Lord of Grace wants to pour out on His faithful children; persistence prayer does pay off, and as Jesus promised, ask and it will be answered, knock and it will be opened, seek and you will find (Matthew 7:7).

During the writing and researching of this chapter, I would stop and pray about it, asking the Lord to show me truth. I agonized over what I was shown here because so many people are ignorant and do not take the time to research the history, so they end up believing lies that others have told. I was comforted by the Lord, who told me that there is much grace on this topic of the mispronunciation of the Father's name, and even His name, Yahshua, Yeshua, Jesus. "Where sin (error) abounds, Grace increases even more." (Romans 5:20)

So I am conveying this to all my readers, who may have experienced this in your church, not to beat yourself up over it, but to become empowered with the knowledge of the truth here. However, if you want your walk with the Lord to become more fulfilling, or if you are seeking healing that you still have not received, think about the name you worship in church songs. Is it Yahweh? Or is it Jehovah? Know this. You are always safe worshipping the name Jesus, aka Yahshua/Yeshua.

After I completed my "hit" piece on Yahweh, I heard the Holy Spirit tell me as I was going to bed one night, "Jehovah is also a counterfeit spirit." I realized that is why Jehovah Witnesses are a false belief system. Not only do they ignore worshipping the "King of the Kingdom" who is Jesus Christ, in their "Kingdom Halls," but that they do not speak to Christ, but to Jehovah. Everything is Jehovah, in spite of the fact that they do believe that Christ is the Savior. (See my chapter, Who Is Jehovah?)[1]

GNOSTIC YAHWEH

In ancient Aramaic the letter "Vav" was translated into English as a "W," which is where the pronunciation of the "w" sound comes from. Pronouncing the Tetragrammaton YHVH, as "Yah<u>v</u>eh" or "Yahweh" creates a separate vibratory frequency and another counterfeit god (i.e. Yahweh was born), which is the name of *Yahweh Yaldabaoth Demiurge*, "Yahweh" for short, who was one of the serpent dragon gods worshipped by the Israelites in Old Testament times in one of their many rebellions and disobediences toward the Lord. Idolatry got the Israelites punished many times.

Satan knew that if he could get the Israelites to worship another god, then the Lord would turn his back on them and give them up to their enemies. This is why many today believe the god of the Old Testament was cruel and aligned with Satan because Satan came through and counterfeited him in his age-long rebellion and battle against YHVH (Yahuah). Along the way, the Israelites and the Jews woke up to this discrepancy about

CHAPTER FIFTEEN: Who Is Yahweh?

the name of the Lord and stopped pronouncing it for fear that they would mispronounce it, get it wrong, and invoke and/or worship the wrong god.

Today, Jews still refuse to utter the name spelled out nearly 7,000 times in the Old Testament, which is YAHUAH, and instead say "Adonai," which means Lord, or "HaShem" which, in Hebrew, means "the name." Both are titles, not names.

> "Now therefore what have I here," declares the LORD Yahuah, "seeing that my people are taken away for nothing? Their rulers wail," declares the LORD Yahuah, "and continually all the day my name is despised."
>
> (Isaiah 52:5)

Most English translations insert the word LORD in all caps everywhere the name YAHUAH (YHVH) appears in the Old Testament. I have replaced the true name in the above verse, for the edification of my readers.

Early Christianity had two mainstreams: the Paulinian and the Gnostic Christians. Saul had persecuted Christians until he converted and became Paul. The year of his conversion is estimated to be between 33AD and 35AD. Paulinian Christianity began to develop after that. Who were the Christians that Paul persecuted? They were the so-called Christian Jews, otherwise known as "Messianic Jews." This concept refers to groups among the earliest Christians, who were Jews, who still believed and practiced Jewish customs and traditions, just like Yahshua and his disciples themselves.

Out of these Christian Jews emerged a movement known as Gnostic Christians. *Gnosis* means knowledge in Greek. Gnostics were involved in the knowledge of spiritual mysteries. Because of Paul's radical views, he came into conflict with these two original already established groups of Christianity.

One of Paul's views had to do with his suppression of women having power and authority. This goes against traditional Judaism, as Jewish sects such as the Essenes and the Gnostics all supported female teachers. The Book of Judges tells the story of the prophetess Deborah, whose actions and decisions brought forty years of peace to Israel. In fact when the Elohim created man and woman, it specifically says they were originally created equal.

It's certainly not news that this controversy has perpetuated throughout the last two thousand years, with various persecutions and suppression of the feminine side of humanity. The *Book of Thekla* tells the story of the first female minister who insisted on doing baptisms herself. She came into direct conflict with Paul over these issues, and he had her sent to the lions to be eaten. It turned out the lions were not able to eat her, as all the female lions surrounded her and protected her from the male lions, which was done in the eyes of the multitudes in the coliseum.

Thekla's story, similar if not identical to Daniel's testimony in the lion's den, was written as one of the gospels within the times of the Book of Acts, but was later rejected from the Bible canon by the Catholic Church priests because Paul's agenda and words about the suppression of women fit their political and spiritual agenda of the time. The point is that the Gnostics were in direct rebellion with Paul's views, and this is why in their writings, they put a feminine spin on the being they called *Yahweh Yaldabaoth*.

It's important to keep in mind that Paulinian Christianity did not emerge out of the original Church, nor with Paul, who never knew Jesus Christ personally when he walked in the flesh. Paul had a conversion experience over three decades after Christ's ascension, when Christ appeared to him on the road to Damascus and asked him (then Saul) why he was persecuting him (Acts 9:4). After which time, a modified version of Christianity began that distanced itself from the Christianity that was close to Jesus from the beginning.

For the Gnostics, the creator of this world wasn't the true prime creator, but a demiurge, a "craftsman," a fallen angel, who also has an evil side. One really needs to ask oneself, what did they know two thousand years ago, that we have lost now? While the real *God*, the true prime creator, the one who Jesus called "father" is unrestrictedly good, they believed an imperfect demiurge created an imperfect world. Created? Or Interfered?

There are many passages that show that the Gnostics identified this imperfect demiurge "god" with the god of the Old Testament, who they also called Yaldabaoth, who wanted to keep humans in a state of ignorance in a material world and who punished their attempts to achieve knowledge and insight, (i.e., those who "eat from the tree of knowledge."). The Gnostics believed the demiurge was a lesser god who wanted to be the only one. The text *The Apocrypha of John* (also called *The Secret Book of John*) states:

> "He is impious in his madness, she who dwells in him. For he said, 'I am *God* and no other god exists except me', since he is ignorant of the place from which his strength had come."
>
> (Exodus 20:23 and Deuteronomy 5:7)

WHO IS YAHWEH YALDABAOTH?

We first learn of who *Yahweh Yaldabaoth* truly is through the *Apocrypha of John*, also known as the Gnostic writings, or the Nag Hammadi Texts. *Yahweh Yaldabaoth* is the mythic god/ Demiurge who came from the Gnostic Goddess Sophia (wisdom) who had a son named *Yaldabaoth* who many confuse and mistakenly believe to be identical with the jealous god of the Old Testament.

The difference being that this *Demiurge/Yaldabaoth* is the "blind God" who created the manifest universe and entrapped the human spirit inside physical vessels. *Yaldabaoth*, being blind, believes that he created himself out of nothing but in fact is the offspring of Wisdom (Sophia). This story reflects more or less the narrative in the Matrix films and even the *Truman Show*.

CHAPTER FIFTEEN: Who Is Yahweh?

"And when she saw (the consequences of) her desire, it changed into a form of a lion-faced serpent. And its eyes were like lightning fires which flash. She cast it away from her, outside that place, that no one of the immortal ones might see it, for she had created it in ignorance. And she surrounded it with a luminous cloud, and she placed a throne in the middle of the cloud that no one might see it except the Holy Spirit who is called the mother of the living. And she called his name Yaldabaoth.

"This is the first archon who took a great power from his mother. And he removed himself from her and moved away from the places in which he was born. He became strong and created for himself other eons with a flame of luminous fire which (still) exists now. And he joined with his arrogance which is in him and begot authorities for himself...And he shared his fire with them, but he did not send forth from the power of the light which he had taken from his mother, for he is ignorant darkness.

"And when the light had mixed with the darkness, it caused the darkness to shine. And when the darkness had mixed with the light, it darkened the light and it became neither light nor dark, but it became dim.

"Now the archon who is weak has three names. The first name is Yaldabaoth, the second is Saklas, and the third is Samael. And he is impious in his arrogance which is in him. For he said, 'I am God and there is no other God beside me,' for he is ignorant of his strength, the place from which he had come."[2]

"After the natural structure of the immortal beings had completely developed out of the infinite, a likeness then emanated from Pistis (Faith); it is called Sophia (Wisdom). It exercised volition and became a product resembling the primeval light. And immediately her will manifested itself as a likeness of heaven, having an unimaginable magnitude; it was between the immortal beings and those things that came into being after them, like [...]: she (Sophia) functioned as a veil dividing mankind from the things above."[3]

The rest of the text goes on to explain how creation was divided between the immortals and the mortal. The following passages are revealing as to how the counterfeit god *Yahweh Yaldabaoth* came into being:

"And when Pistis Sophia desired to cause the thing that had no spirit to be formed into a likeness and to rule over matter and over all her forces, there appeared for the first time a ruler, out of the waters, lion-like in appearance, androgynous, having great authority within him, and ignorant of whence he had come into being. Now when Pistis Sophia saw him moving about in the depth of the waters, she said to him, "Child, pass through to here,' whose equivalent is 'yalda baoth' ..."

255

In Hebrew, *Yalda*, means child, and *baoth*, (pronounced 'buy-oat') means "come here," or "pass through here."

"...Now when the heavens had consolidated themselves along with their forces and all their administration, the prime parent became insolent. And he was honored by all the army of angels. And all the gods and their angels gave blessing and honor to him. And for his part, he was delighted and continually boasted, saying to them, 'I have no need of anyone.' He said, 'It is I who am God, and there is no other one that exists apart from me.' And when he said this, he sinned against all the immortal beings who give answer. And they laid it to his charge.

Then when Pistis saw the impiety of the chief ruler, she was filled with anger. She was invisible.

"She said, 'You are mistaken, Samael,' (that means 'blind god'). 'There is an immortal man of light who has been in existence before you, and who will appear among your modeled forms; he will trample you to scorn, just as potter's clay is pounded. And you will descend to your mother, the abyss, along with those that belong to you. For at the consummation of your (pl.) works, the entire defect that has become visible out of the truth will be abolished, and it will cease to be, and will be like what has never been.'"[5]

It is blatantly obvious to most scholars that Pistis was referring to Jesus Christ, who was sent to destroy the works of Satan. It is also interesting to note, that Samael is known as the angel (or demon) of death and is one of the chief satans in Satan's hierarchy. This proves how Lucifer and all of his fallen angels and fallen sons from heaven sought to counterfeit god through intense jealousy, competition, and rage through mimicking the Lord in their attempt to oust the King of Heaven and become god.

This was Lucifer's original quest, which was to exalt himself above the Creator God and become god himself and suck up all the worship from the servants of heaven and all of the created beings, i.e., earth humans. This is why, to this day, he fights over the worship of earth humans by masquerading as different gods, in different languages, different cultures, creating all kinds of different religions, cults and diversions from worshiping the one true Creator God of Heaven and Earth.

This is also why Satan absolutely hates it and literally "falls to pieces, when people worship the true name of God, whenever the Israelite praised God, their enemies fell, and the Lord gave them the victory. This is why Satan's battle against believers is to thwart their worship through infiltrating worship music worship leaders and 'words' in worship songs. Worshipping and praising God is a spiritual weapon of warfare against the enemy's strongholds."

Because of the Gnostic texts, many scholars have equated YHVH, the God of the Old Testament with *Yahweh Yaldabaoth*, but is this true and accurate or is this a false

CHAPTER FIFTEEN: Who Is Yahweh?

belief, which has perpetuated itself into a spiritual and religious counterfeit over time? Let's discern.

Many have been turned off from religion because Yaldabaoth falsely believes himself to be the only god in the entire cosmos. Were the Gnostics correct in identifying *Yaldabaoth* with Yahuah of the Old Testament, someone the Gnostics believe also suffers from cosmic egotism. But is it cosmic egotism, or is Yahuah the true God, and Yahweh Yaldabaoth, the counterfeit? Let's not forget that the Gnostics were in rebellion against the Jews and the God of the Jews, who is Yahuah, so there was a hidden agenda in all of their writings.

Was *Yaldabaoth* (Samael) created blind, or was that a curse for his disobedience and for following Lucifer's rebellion? The fact that he was blind meant that he couldn't perceive the *Pleroma* (galactic core) or recognize Sophia (Wisdom), the cosmic current that surged from the core and produced him in the first place. How many people today suffer from this same curse? Not necessarily physical blindness, but spiritual blindness? There are many who simply cannot perceive the Creator of their very souls and instead mistakenly follow after whichever god or goddess has their attention at the time, kind of like the flavor of the month.

Because *Yaldabaoth* became filled with pride, a pattern after Lucifer, and bloated with grandiosity, he caused Sophia (Wisdom) to feel shame and want to hide him from the sight of the *Pleromic Aeons* (the galactic core and higher immortals):

> "She cast him away from her radiance, so that no one among the immortal ones might see him... She joined a luminous cloud (spaceship) with him, and placed a throne in the middle of the cloud."[5]

The throne in the cloud is a repetitive theme in the Bible. Yahuah's throne was *within* the cloud. The cloud covered His spaceship, which was also called his throne. Yahuah cloaked his throne with a cloud.

> "He holds back (covers in secrecy) the face of his throne, and spreads his *cloud* upon it."
>
> (Job 26:9)

> "For the day is near, the day of the LORD is near-- a day of *clouds*, a time of doom for the nations."
>
> (Ezekiel 30:3)

NOTES:

1. Ella LeBain, *Who Is God?*, chapters *The God of This World* and *The Office of Satan, Who Is Yahweh?*
2. Chris Everard, *Feed Your Mind Magazine*, 2009.p.28
3. The *Hypostasis of the Archons,* Nag Hammadi Library; emphasis and commentary is mine.
4. James A. Michener, *The Source*, Random House, 1965, p. 205
5. *Apocryphon John* BG 38, 1-10

CHAPTER SIXTEEN

WHO WERE THE ARCHONS?

"For we do not wrestle against flesh and blood, but against the rulers, against the authorities, against the cosmic powers over this present darkness, against the spiritual forces of evil in the heavenly places.

(Ephesians 6:12)

The Gnostics believed that the Aeon Sophia is the cosmic current that produced the Archons i.e., spiritual wickedness in the heavens. We have already identified that the Archons are the invisible rulers of the darkness, which Ephesians 6:12 refers to. These are the fallen gods and fallen sons of heaven who have aligned with Lucifer/Satan in their war against the Creator. Yet because they were created immortal, they have not died, just transformed after falling from their once lofty positions in the heavens from the Kingdom of God, Light, and Love and into the kingdom of darkness.

Yaldabaoth then becomes the leader of the Archons and pretends to be the creator of the cosmos. While they have the power to create, they are not the Prime Creator, but created beings. They have evolved with technology because they have lost their ability to create through the power of love, which was taken from them when they fell from their once lofty positions in the high heavens when they shared intimacy with the Most High Creator. They were cursed, so they resorted to technology to create.

Yaldabaoth, the Lord of the Archons, originates nothing. He only copies the model of the *Pleroma* (galactic core). The Gnostic teachings have repeatedly emphasized that the Archons are "imitators" who cannot produce anything original, yet they arrogantly claim they can.

The Lord Archon is called *antimimon pneuma*, which means "counterfeit spirit."[1] The words *antimimon pneuma* occurs several times throughout the text. The cosmos he produces is nothing but a "simulation" which is described by the Coptic term *hal*. The truth of the matter is that the vast planetary system of the Archons are actually a "virtual reality projection" which is a counterfeit simulation of a higher dimensional pattern.

This is why Enoch was taken into the Ten Heavens, and was shown where the boundaries are between the higher dimensional beings and the fallen ones. (See, Book Five: The Heavens of *Who's Who In The Cosmic Zoo?*) Once these fallen gods and angels lost their position in the higher heavens, they had to find alternative ways to peruse the lower heavens as "gods," so they used various types of technologies to project themselves as gods and simulated other dimensional realms, which humans call heaven, to deceive the mortals.

THE VIRTUAL HEAVENS

Today, on Earth, we have and use many of these kinds of technologies. Holographic technology can project images into the heavens and into any space to appear to be seeing a three- dimensional figure, or even a vision. This type of technology has already been used on earth humans as a form of trickery in getting ignorant and immature earth humans into believing that they were seeing visions of the Virgin Mary, Archangel Michael, and other religious figures, as in the famous documented case of the children of Fatima, Portugal in 1917.

I am reminded of the 1998 movie *The Truman Show,* which chronicles the life of a man who is initially unaware that he is living in a simulated "constructed" reality television show that is being broadcast 24/7 to billions of people across the globe. Once Truman becomes suspicious of his "perceived" reality, he embarks on a quest to discover the truth about his life. Through this film, one really needs to ask, how much does art imitate life? How many of us realize that planet Earth is within a type of simulation within the vastness of the cosmos? What if our perception of the heavens, in present "scientific" terms is nothing but a simulation of yet a much higher cosmic model?

The main cosmological texts in the Nag Hammadi Library, *The Apocrypha of John,* and *On the Origin of the World and the Hypostasis of the Archons,*[2] all describe how the solar system comes from an inorganic simulation of the living pattern of the eternal Aeons. The main premise is that the Archons are imitating and counterfeiting the creation from the Prime Creator.

The Archonic mock-up of a planetary system is always portrayed by spherical shapes composed of hoops, which is what planet Earth and our solar system represents. But how do we know that this archetype reflects divine design or is an imitation of divine design, not reflecting the living reality of the entire cosmos? Our solar system is a singular star, whereas most solar systems are either binary or triple stars. Perhaps ours is not a direct reflection of other star systems?

We know that, through the lens of science, which measures the planets in miles and measures stars in light years, that the paradigm has been busted when learning of the many different types of extraterrestrials interacting with earth governments. Space travel, time travel, and the concept of bending space allows for portals and wormholes to appear. Passages to travel to and from can mean moving from one space to another in a matter of minutes compared to the old paradigm of moving through space in light years. For instance, if a distant star is 102 light years away from earth, and a portal is available which opens up through the bending of space, then one can travel that path in minutes verses years.

In fact, in September of 2011, physicists working at CERN in Geneva did an experiment which busts Einstein's original theory that there is nothing faster than the speed of light. For years, we were saying that the only thing faster than the speed of light

CHAPTER SIXTEEN: Who Were The Archons?

was "thoughts"; however, these physicists found that there is something even faster called *neutrinos*.

According to Einstein's 1905 special theory of relativity, the speed of light — 186,282 miles per second (299,792 kilometers per second) — has long been considered a cosmic speed limit. A collaborative team between France's National Institute for Nuclear and Particle Physics Research and Italy's Gran Sasso National Laboratory, fired a neutrino beam 454 miles (730 kilometers) underground from Geneva to Italy. They found it traveled sixty nanoseconds faster than light. That's sixty billionths of a second, a time no human brain could register.

Another paradigm broken. Of course, physicists are arguing about whether there was human error in this experiment, and have not accepted this yet, as theoretical physicist and science show host Michio Kaku wrote in *The Wall Street Journal* in September 23, 2011:

> "According to relativity, as you approach the speed of light, time slows down, you get heavier, and you also get flatter (all of which have been measured in the lab). But if you go faster than light, then the impossible happens. Time goes backward. You are lighter than nothing, and you have negative width. Since this is ridiculous, you cannot go faster than light, said Einstein."

> "This is quite a shake-up," Alvaro de Rujula, a theorist at CERN, told the *New York Times*. "The correct attitude is to ask oneself what went wrong." Kaku writes in *The Journal* that his "gut reaction" is "that this is a false alarm." He cites past examples in which physicists claimed to have disproved relativity only to have found simple errors in their experiments.[3]

Perhaps scientists' resistance to throwing out relativity would mean more work for scientists who would literally need to re-write the book on modern physics. Michael Lemonick at *Time* said it would be "a complete upending of modern physics. The implications could be huge. Particles that move faster than light are essentially moving backwards in time, which could make the phrase *cause and effect* obsolete." And Kaku said in the *Journal*, "Modern physics is based on two theories, relativity and the quantum theory, so half of modern physics would have to be replaced by a new theory. My own field, string theory, is no exception. Personally, I would have to revise all my theories because relativity is built into string theory from the very beginning."

The fact that these paradigms are morphing and busting all the time should cause everyone to ponder and question their present view of reality on Earth, especially with relation to the heavens, as well as who god is. We know that heaven is separated by dimensions. There could be an infinite amount of dimensional doorways throughout the cosmos. (See, Book Five: *The Heavens* in *Who's Who In The Cosmic Zoo?*)

IS YAHWEH ANNUNAKI?

In *Divine Encounters,* Zecharia Sitchin questions who Yahweh is. His argument is somehow biased to prove that Yahweh wasn't an Annunaki, but that he was the "god" of the Annunaki. Is there a difference? Jan Erik Sigdell, in his paper "Is Yahweh An Annunaki?"[4] argues that Sitchin's reasoning can also be seen to demonstrate that Yahweh is Marduk, and that is something he certainly wants to deny. Marduk is another name for Satan. "Thus one can actually set up the hypothesis that Yahweh is an Annunaki! And that he, during their physical absence from the Earth, is a kind of 'governor' of the Annunaki. This fits into what is stated above about his abominable cruelty, on one side, and on the other side, the violent nutrition of the Annunaki with our life energies."

If it was Yahweh, who insisted on blood sacrifices, then one really needs to look into why the blood of humans and animals was so important to this god. If this was a creator of souls, why would he need blood to satisfy him? This only proves that Yahweh and all the Reptilian Annunaki are not creator gods, but bloodthirsty space Draconians who feed off the *life force* from the blood of humans and animals and continue to do so today.

As I've mentioned several times in this book, the Almighty Creator cursed the fallen sons and fallen angels (extraterrestrials) for following in Lucifer's rebellion against him. They were cursed into serpent bodies and bodies that can no longer procreate naturally. This is the reason they turn to the technology of genetic manipulation and continue this practice today through the abduction of earth humans, cattle, and various animal mutilations to obtain blood, DNA, sperm, and ovum for their genetic experiments.

LIFEFORCE IS IN THE BLOOD

Their "harvest" of life energies from both humans and animals reveals the cruel practice of living sacrifice. "For the life of the flesh is in the blood: and I have given it to you on the altar to make an atonement for your souls: for it is the blood that makes an atonement for the soul." (Leviticus 17:11)

The Lord speaks in Leviticus 17:14, saying, "because the life of every creature is its blood. That is why I have said to the Israelites, 'You must not eat the blood of any creature, because the life of every creature is its blood; anyone who eats it must be cut off.' "While the meat is of no use to the "gods," that is why they are commanded not to eat or drink the blood but to offer it as a sacrifice because of the invisible life force it holds. Since this life energy is contained in the blood, this also explains the command for the cruel practice of letting an animal bleed to death that is maintained in certain cultures. It is for this practice that Yahshua (Jesus Christ) bled to death on the cross, so that through his lifeforce in His Divine Blood, all of humanity can be saved from these bloodthirsty reptilian gods.

CHAPTER SIXTEEN: Who Were The Archons?

There is speculation amongst researchers, that the Mercy Seat was underground at Golgotha, and when the earth split open during an earthquake at the time of Yeshua's death, that His blood went down through a crack in the earth, and fell onto the Mercy Seat on the Ark of the Covenant.

The Reptilian Annunaki want to claim that they are our creators! The reptilians are not our creators. However, they may have genetically manipulated our DNA for their purposes of downgrading us to create a slave race to serve them; they are not the prime creators, but more specifically the interferers. Only the Almighty Creator, the Lord of all Spirits, has the power to create souls and give them life. It is this very life force that the Reptilian Archonic Annunaki are after. Hence the battle of our souls, our minds, our bodies, and our very existence on planet Earth.

ANNUNAKI IN THE BIBLE

The Bible talks about a giant race of people called in Hebrew, the Anakim, who are the sons of Anak. They were descendants of the Nephilim, who were created when the "sons of the gods (Elohim)" descended to the Earth and mated with the "daughters of man" (Genesis 6:4).

The "Anakim" and "Anak" are mentioned in the following scriptures: Numbers 13:22; 13:28; 13:33, Deuteronomy 1:28; 2:10-11; 2:21, 9:2, Joshua 11:21-22; 14:12; 14:15; 15:13-14; 21:11, Judges 1:20. The Anakim are the offspring of the Annunaki (in their three-dimensional form) resulting from their sexual involvement with humans of the Earth.

The Bible tells us that the twin cities Sodom and Gomorrah were destroyed by fire from heaven, which was a targeted nuclear explosion. The land, to this day shows the effects of radiation. According to Jude 1:7, this happened because of their sexual perversions and homosexuality, and Genesis 18:20 says, their sin was so grievous they had to be destroyed. Besides the sins of sexual perversions, these twin cities were also populated with Nephilim, (Annunaki) who were supposed to be destroyed and wiped off the face of the earth during the floods of Noah. To this day, archeologists have unearthed skeletal bones from giants throughout the land of Israel.

While the Nephilim were given to all kinds of perversions and lusts of the flesh, including cannibalism, they were an abomination to Yahuah. In my opinion, these Nephilim remnants, or Annunaki, returned to this land after the floods through a space portal. Jeremiah 49:18 tells us that Yahuah destroyed them, so no man could ever live or dwell there again. "As Sodom and Gomorrah were overthrown, along with their neighboring towns," says Yahuah, "so no one will live there; no man will dwell in it." This is interesting because, to this day, it is still barren, next to the Dead Sea, and nothing grows there.

The question is, who ordered the hit? Was it Yahweh, the counterfeit god of the Annunaki? Or was it Yahuah, the Creator God of Israel? According to the Bible, it clearly says it was Yahuah. Remember, Yahweh and Yahuah are not the same beings, even though many misinterpret and mispronounce the name of Yahuah to be Yahweh. Sitchin claims, according to his interpretation of the clay tablets, that the reason these twin cities were hit was because there was an operating space base there that directed space traffic with Nibiru.

If that is true, then it proves that there was and has always been a conflict between these two gods over who occupies the land and over what humans do. Perhaps Yahuah wanted to destroy Yahweh's base and put an end to his space traffic? It is my opinion and belief that these gods continue to fight to this day over the ancient space portals established in the land of Israel, which is why Israel is the location for the return of these ancient gods to complete their unfinished business over the earth, earth humans, and over who controls Jerusalem in the final "space" battle known as Armageddon.

It is no coincidence that the Annunaki left the earth and gave up their three-dimension presence on Earth after Sodom and Gomorrah got nuked.

Are All "Gods" Extraterrestrials?

Many authors believe that all of the gods are, in fact, extraterrestrials. In the true sense of the word, they are because they come from "beyond the earth." The true Almighty Creator God, however, isn't, in that sense, an extraterrestrial because He is beyond that concept and is everywhere and is in every created being and every creation, both on the earth, inside the earth, and beyond the earth. The Holy Spirit, which comes from the Almighty Creator exists here on Earth and is considered to be the last bastion of grace to a fallen world.

However, the fact that some of his creations were regarded as "gods," when they came from somewhere else to visit the Earth, is quite another matter.

Who Are The Annunaki?

(See, Book One *Who's Who In The Cosmic Zoo?* Chapter – Annunaki, pp.110-119)[5]

Zechariah Sitchin authored nearly a dozen books based on his translations of the Sumerian texts, which tells us about Nibiru, a planet that behaves like a comet, which moves in a rather long-stretched elliptical orbit around our solar system and passes the earth approximately every 3,600 years. Sitchin claims that Nibiru is the home of the Annunaki. If this planet is so far away from the sun for approximately 3,000 years, it must therefore be frozen. So one would ask, how can anything live in such a world? This is why Nibiru behaves more like a comet than a planet.

In Revelation 8, we learn of a star that falls from the sky and crashes into the waters of the earth. Many Bible scholars refer to this as a comet. Perhaps this great star or comet is Nibiru.

CHAPTER SIXTEEN: Who Were The Archons?

"The third angel sounded his trumpet, and a great star, blazing like a torch, fell from the sky on a third of the rivers and on the springs of water-- the name of the star is Wormwood. A third of the waters turned bitter, and many people died from the waters that had become bitter.

(Revelation 8:10-11)

According to the Acadian Dictionary, the word *Nibiru* (also transliterated *Neberu, Nebiru*) is a term which means "crossing" or "point of transition," especially of rivers, i.e. river crossings or ferry-boats. Interesting that this very ancient Acadian/Sumerian word "Nibiru" relates to rivers. In my mind, it is no coincidence that St. John's Revelation specifically says this great star falls from the sky and turns one-third of the earth's rivers and waters bitter.

Another train of thought is that every time the Bible scriptures make reference to "stars" falling from heaven, it is referring to fallen angels, also known as sons of God. In Luke 10:18 is when Yahshua tells us, "I saw Satan fall like a bolt of lightning out of heaven."

Satan is also referred to as the morning star or star of the dawn in Isaiah 14:12. Revelation 1:9 also makes reference to a star falling from Heaven: "and the fifth angel sounded and I saw a star fall from heaven to the earth and to him was given the key of the bottomless pit."

This star is specifically referred to as a "him," meaning a celestial being, an angel, an extraterrestrial, or a son of the Elohim. With that said, Wormwood and Nibiru could very well be one and the same — a celestial being in charge of this celestial object, i.e., comet, planet, or starship. The fact that the Annunaki came under the curse of the Almighty Creator God is revealed in the fact that their so-called home planet Nibiru may, in fact, be the Wormwood of Revelation, which may be the celestial object heading for earth in the final days.

After the last galactic war over our solar system, the explosions not only caused the planet between Mars and Jupiter, also known as Maldek or Rahab to explode into thousands of pieces, making up today's asteroid belt, but it also caused moons to be displaced from Saturn and thrown out of orbit, which is what we call today as Pluto and Charon, as well as knocking the planet Uranus off its side, and destroying the earth's two moons.

It is my opinion that Nibiru was then thrown out of orbit into its unusual elliptical path that takes 3,600 Earth years to rotate around the sun. This was due to the fact that both the Annunaki and Nibiru were cursed for abusing the laws of creation and for joining in Lucifer's rebellion against the Almighty Creator God. This is why the Annunaki have left our planet and transferred their creation over to Lucifer/Satan in a contractual agreement.

The Annunaki created the first "slave race" and are the authors of slavery on planet earth. This continues to this day. Whether it be the trafficking of sex slaves or other types of human abuses, the Annunaki sowed these seeds. Just as Lucifer was cursed into the serpent body, so were the Annunaki, which is why they are said to be reptilian in nature and have the ability to be multidimensional.

Earth humans are only three-dimensional (i.e., we can only perceive three space dimensions and think only three-dimensionally). As I've been saying throughout this book, our DNA was manipulated and downgraded from its original blueprint which was the image of the Elohim, who are ultraterrestrial humans who hold all twelve strands of Human DNA.

Adam and Eve were created in their glory bodies, which are also referred to as the Evadamic race, were originally made perfect with all twelve strands of DNA. After the fall in Eden, they lost their rights over the earth to Lucifer, who gave power to the Annunaki gods when they came to Earth. The Annunaki knew they couldn't control humans that were made like the Elohim, so they literally clipped and disabled ten of the original twelve strands of the human DNA, through genetic manipulation, thereby creating a race of beings that had just enough intelligence to follow orders, do heavy chores, and follow their directions to mine the earth for gold and other natural resources. Sitchin goes on about this in great detail in his series of books, *The Earth Chronicles,* as well as *Genesis Revisited,* [6] which focuses on his interpretation of the Sumerian creation myths, as written in the cuneiform tablets.

The Annunaki deliberately manipulated earth humans' DNA so that we could not perceive them, unless they appeared in their three-dimensional form. Reptilian gods are known to shapeshift, and these Annunaki giants are no exceptions. (See, Book One *Who's Who In The Cosmic Zoo?* Chapter – Reptilians, Giants & Annunaki) [5]

Others, who have postulated their three-dimensional bodies, appear only when Nibiru is closer to the sun, as they are depicted in their clay tablets and other stone carvings and statutes. However, when Nibiru is far from the sun, they go into a state of hibernation and act in other dimensions, invisible to earth humans; nevertheless, their invisible influence from other dimensions, as the Archons, or rulers of the darkness, as Ephesians 6:12 states that, along with their manipulation of politics, science, and international affairs through the veil of secret societies and various bloodlines, they seeded on the earth continues to this day.

As all reptilians and dark entities do, they need life energy. Because they have been cursed by the Almighty Creator, their access to higher dimensions to receive life energy has been cut off to them, so instead they steal it from earth humans and milk people to death, just as humans keep cattle for food. The only difference is that most earth humans are totally oblivious and unaware that this is happening, whereas cows do have awareness they are being milked.

They continue this charade and collude with the dark forces or "satans" of this world because they are separated from their divine roots because they killed their prime creators and because of a power struggle over their manipulation of human DNA. Because they are under the curse from the Almighty Creator, their prime energy source, they are in effect a dying race of extraterrestrials. They thrive on war, violence, brutality, trauma, and bloodshed. The reason being that, when earth humans die through a trauma or tragedy, resulting in a violent death, the body is still full of life energy and the energy released at the time of death is harvested by the Annunaki, as opposed to someone who dies a slow death through illness or old age.

Apparently these ET gods enjoy watching us become warlike and provoked to violence, similar to when kids play war games on a computer. This is why they manipulated the human DNA by putting aggression and fear in our genes, which to them are effective ways to control and manipulate earth humans. When earth humans feel fear and rage and act on it, it's a way of giving our power away, and unconsciously we release our life force to them. These dark beings thrive on these emotions from earth humans, which is why earth's history has been in a constant state of war, conflict and struggle for millennia.

In *Bringers of the Dawn,* Barbara Marciniak[7] describes the Annunaki as "lizzies," which is her nickname for "lizards" because they are reptilian. The Annunaki have, to this day, been an invisible, behind-the-scene influence, through secret societies like the Illuminati, through certain Masonic orders and lodges. Only those at the very top of the pyramid know about the Annunaki connection, but the masses, including many of the members of these secret societies are kept in the darkness of ignorance.

NOTES:

1. Apocryphon John III, 36:17, *The Apocryphon of John,*
   http://www.gnosis.org/naghamm/apocjn.html
2. Nag Hammadi Library, *The Apocryphon of John, On The Origin of the World* and *The Hypostasis of the Archons, The Complete Nag Hammadi Library*
   http://www.gnosis.org/naghamm/nhlalpha.html
3. Michio Kaku, *The Wall Street Journal,* September 23, 2011
4. Jan Erik Sigdell, *Is Yahweh An Annunaki?*
   http://www.christian-reincarnation.com/YahAn.htm
5. Ella LeBain, *Who's Who In The Cosmic Zoo? Book One – Third Edition,* Chapter – *Annunaki* pp. 110-119, Tate Publishing & Enterprises, LLC. 2013
6. Zecharia Sitchin, *The Earth Chronicles, Genesis Revisited,* Avon Books, NY, NY. 1990
7. Barbara Marciniak, *Bringers Of The Dawn,* Bear & Company (December 1, 1992)

CHAPTER SEVENTEEN

WHO IS JEHOVAH?

"I am the LORD, and there is no other, besides me there is no God;
I equip you, though you do not know me,"

(Isaiah 45:5 ESV)

"Beloved, do not believe every spirit, but test the spirits to see whether they are from God, for many false prophets have gone out into the world."

(1 John 4:1 ESV)

We've already gone over how Yahweh was formed and replaced the true name of YHVH which is Yahuah, but Jehovah is another counterfeit god, invented between the third and sixth centuries through the Jewish scholars, the Masoretes, who essentially took the Torah, the entire Old Testament Hebrew/Aramaic scriptures, and placed vowels in the purely vowel-less Hebrew script, creating an entirely new lexicon, particularly when it comes to the Holy Name of the Tetragrammaton. They created the name יְהֹוָה YeHoVaH, otherwise known as Jehovah in English, by placing vowels under the Yud and above and below the OO of UU also called the Vav.

What many people today reading this text are not aware of is why this was deliberately done by the Masoretes Jews in Babylon from 750AD-1000AD. As I've mentioned earlier, they deliberately were protecting the sacred name from being uttered by the Gentiles, and in so doing, were inevitably used by Satan to create a new name for himself.

The editors of the *Brown-Driver-Briggs Lexicon* wrote that YHVH interpreted as "Yehovah" occurs 6,518 times in the Masoretic Text and that it is read as "Adonai" or "Elohim".[1]

JEHOVAH - THE COUNTERFEIT GOD

In my research, I discovered that that the counterfeit god Jehovah is not just the creator of another cult, i.e., *Jehovah Witnesses,* but an integral part of the belief system of Free Masonry. In the Ancient & Accepted or Scottish Rite of Free Masonry, which operates in British Commonwealth countries, the secret password of the 18th, 30th, 31st, 32nd, and 33rd degree of the Knight of the Ninth Arch of Solomon or Enoch Degree, its secret password is JEHOVAH. The penalty of its blasphemous use is having one's body given to the beasts of the forest as prey, which is connected with revelations from the Kabbalah in this and subsequent degrees.

When the Jews regarded it as too holy to pronounce, it opened up the door for those who did not, and then the mis-pronunciation set in. After the third century, it was mis-transliterated as YHWH (Yahweh) and JHVH (Jehovah). This then became known as the mystic number four, which was often symbolized to represent the Deity in Freemasonry, and was worshipped and deified as *JeHoVaH*, It was a tradition that it was pronounced in the following seven different ways: *Juha, Jeva, Jova, Jevo, Jeveh, Johe*, and *Jehovah*. In all these words the *j* is to be pronounced as *y*, the *a* as *ah*, the *e* as *a*, and the *v* as *w*. This is where the mispronunciations and mis-transliterations came in. As there is no *"w"* sound in the Hebrew language. As I've stated earlier, the letter VAV in the original Aramaic/Hebrew is the sound "OO" or "UU". Somehow the double UU became misinterpreted as a W, and then a V.

The triangle has, in all ages and in all religions, been deemed a symbol of the Deity. The Egyptians, the Greeks, and the other nations of antiquity considered this figure, with its three sides, as a symbol of the creative energy displayed in the active and passive, or male and female, principles, and their product, the world; the Christians referred it to their dogma of the trinity as a manifestation of the Supreme God, and the Jews and the primitive masons to the three periods of existence included it in the signification of the Tetragrammaton—the past, the present, and the future.

The three symbols of the Deity which are to be found in the Masonic system express a different attribute. The letter *G* is the symbol of the self-existent Jehovah. The *All-Seeing Eye* is the symbol of the omnipresent God. The *triangle* is the symbol of the Supreme Architect of the Universe—the Creator, and when surrounded by rays of glory, it becomes a symbol of the Architect and Bestower of Light.

The names of God were intended to communicate the knowledge of God himself. So if the name was changed, mispronounced, and mis-translated, then the knowledge of God Himself would be lost, and another god, who competes and is adversarial with the Most High, would take His place. This is how counterfeits are formed. Counterfeits are based on lies and mis-communications. Yet the lies are so pervasive and convincing that people believe them to be truth.

To both the Masons and the Jehovah's Witnesses, the name of God, however, expressed is a symbol of DIVINE TRUTH, which is the incessant labor of every Mason and Jehovah's Witness to seek. When a Free Mason reaches the 33rd degree after years of secret oaths and rituals, it is then revealed to them — that the god they were serving and worshipping is none other than Lucifer himself. The letter *G* is the symbol of the self-existent Jehovah (who is really Lucifer). The *All-Seeing Eye* is the symbol of Horus, and within the *triangle*, which represents the pyramid, symbolizes the god of this world, who is Lucifer, in his many forms, disguises and counterfeit names masquerading as the Supreme Architect of the Universe.

It is interesting to note that the name Jehovah did not exist in any ancient text prior to the third through sixth centuries, when the Masoretes were used to create this, and in so doing, a false god was created. There is an old saying that, by the time the TRUTH gets its boots on, a lie has spreads halfway around the world. The Catholic Church took on this false name and literally etched it into the stone in their cathedrals. The word "Jehovah" is displayed in the Old Catholic St. Martinskirche in Olten, Switzerland, 1521.

According to various research compiled by Wikipedia on the origin of the name Jehovah, "Jehovists" claim that vowel signs are necessary for reading and understanding Hebrew, because modern Hebrew is written without vowel points. However, the original Torah scrolls do not and never have included vowel points, and ancient Hebrew was written without vowel signs. The Dead Sea Scrolls, which were discovered in 1946, and are believed to date back from 400 BC to 70 AD, include texts from the Torah and Pentateuch and from other parts of the Old Testament Hebrew Bible, which have all provided documentary evidence that the original Hebrew texts were, in fact, written without vowel points. Menahem Mansoor's *The Dead Sea Scrolls: A College Textbook and a Study Guide* claims the vowel points found in printed Hebrew Bibles were devised in the ninth and tenth centuries.[2]

When יהוה precedes or follows *Adonai*, the Masoretes placed the vowel points of *Elohim* into the Tetragrammaton, producing a different vocalization of the Tetragrammaton יְהֹוָה, which was read as *Elohim,* but pronounced "yehovie."

This is the Hebrew word *Elohim* -אֱלֹהִים- now even to someone who doesn't know how to read Hebrew, I ask you, does this אֱלֹהִים look anything like this יהוה or how about if we add the same vowels from the word *Elohim* — יְהֹוָה, would that make a difference? I don't think so. According to the Jewish Encyclopedia, the form יְהֹוָה (*Jehovah*) has been characterized by some as a "hybrid form", and even "a philological impossibility."

The word *Elohim* is an entirely different word used separately in the Hebrew texts from יהוה, and as I've said several times before, it is a "plural" Hebrew word for *gods* or *Mighty Ones*. It is not the name of the god, but a group of gods, or sons of god. (See, *Who's Who In the Cosmic Zoo? Book One* – Chapter, Els, Elohim, pp.204.)[3]

The argument that vowel points are necessary for learning to read Hebrew is refuted by the fact that the Samaritan text of the Bible is read without them and that several other Semitic languages, kindred to Hebrew, are written without any indications of the vowels. The books used in synagogue worship have always been without vowel points, which, unlike the letters, have thus never been treated as sacred. In addition to the fact that, in Israel today, Modern Hebrew is in newspapers, television, and even road signs, all written without vowels.

Jehovah was never used in the LXX, the Samaritan Pentateuch, the Apocrypha, or in the New Testament. Early Christian writers, such as Clement of Alexandria in the 2nd century, had used a form like Yahuweh (pronounced YAHUWAH) as this pronunciation of the Tetragrammaton was never really lost. There is evidence that the Greek church fathers showed the forms Jabe (Yave) and Jâo (Yahu) to be traditional, as well as the shortened Hebrew forms of the words Jah (Yah) (see Psalm 68:4, for example) and Jahu (in proper names).

APPENDIX OF SUPPORTING EVIDENCE:

"**Jehovah,** name of the God of the Hebrew people as *erroneously transliterated* from the Masoretic Hebrew text. The word consists of the consonants *JHVH-* or *JHWH*, with the vowels of a separate word, Adonai (Lord). What its original vowels were is a matter of speculation, for because of an interpretation of such texts as Exodus 20:7 and Leviticus 24:11, the name came to be regarded as too sacred for expression; the scribes, in reading aloud, substituted 'Lord' ...The evidence of the Greek church fathers shows the forms Jabe and Jâo to be traditional, as well as the shortened Hebrew forms of the words Jah (see Psalm 68:4, for example) and Jahu (in proper names). It indicates that the name was originally spoken Jaweh or Yahwe (often spelled Yahweh in modern usage)."[4]

"**Jehova,** *An artificial form of the name of Yahueh* which is obtained by using the consonants of the word Yahweh with the vowels of Adonai, which means "My Lord." Due to reverence for the Bible text the Jews would not make a correction even where there was an obvious error. Since to read the error as written would itself sound ridiculous they distinguished between kethibh, the text as written, and qere, what was to be read."[5]

Jehovah, (Heb. *yehowah*) A name of god, devised... by *artificially combining* the consonants of the name Yehuah (JHWH: held by the Jews to be unutterable), and the vowels of the substitute name Adonai ("The Lord").[6]

"**Jehovah,** *a hybrid form for the divine name which originated in the mistaken idea* that the consonants of Tetragrammaton, YHWH (really pronounced 'Yahweh'), were to be read with the vowel points found with them in the MT, which really gives the vowels which are to be read with the substituted word *'dny*, (Adonai, 'Lord'). The proper vowels for the latter word are a-o-a, but since the first consonant in *YHWH* is not a guttural, the vowel *e* is placed under it (to be read after it) instead of the vowel *a*; thus, by combining these vowels with the consonants of the Tetragrammaton, the mongrel form, 'Yehowah,' came into being, which with the English consonant *j* in place of *y* and with the German pronunciation of *was v*, produced in turn the quaint form of 'Jehovah.'"[7]

The name Jehovah was "erroneously transliterated from the Masoretic Hebrew text." (Saul Lieberman, M.A., D.H.L., Ph.D. Late Distinguished Service Professor of Talmud and Rector of the Rabbinical School, Jewish Theological Seminary of America. Author of *Greek in Jewish Palestine* and *Hellenism in Jewish Palestine*.)

CHAPTER SEVENTEEN: Who Is Jehovah?

"In the Old Testament various names for God are used, Elohim most commonly. The four-letter form YHWH is the most celebrated; the Hebrews considered it ineffable and in reading substituted the name Adonai [my Lord]. The reconstruction Jehovah was based on a mistake, and the form Yahweh is not now regarded as reliable."[8]

"Jehovah, name of the God of the Hebrew people as erroneously transliterated from the Masoretic Hebrew text."[9]

"It was The Masoretes, who from about the 6th to the 10th century worked to reproduce the original text of the Hebrew Bible, replaced the vowels of the name YHWH with the vowel signs of the Hebrew words Adonai or Elohim. Thus, the *artificial* name Jehovah (YeHoWaH) came into being."[10]

"Jehovah: English transliteration of the Divine name, based on a misunderstanding of the Hebrew text, which should probably be read Yahweh."[11]

"... commonly represented in modern translations by the form "Jehovah", which, however is a philological impossibility."[12]

"Jehovah: A mispronunciation (introduced by Christian theologians, but most entirely disregarded by the Jews) of the Hebrew "YHWH," the (ineffable) name of God (the Tetragrammaton or 'Shem ha-Meforash"). This pronunciation is grammatically impossible.[13]

"The form Jehovah is of late medieval origin; it is a combination of the consonants of the Divine Name and the vowels attached to it by the Masoretes but belonging to an entirely different word. The sound of **Y** is represented by **J** and the sound of **W** by **V**, as in Latin. The word 'Jehovah' does not accurately represent any form of the Name ever used in Hebrew..."[14]

"The pronunciation *Jehovah* was unknown until 1520, when it was introduced by Galatinus; but was contested by Le Mercier, J. Drusius, against grammatical and historical propriety." Rotherham continues his analysis of this ghost word: "Erroneously written and pronounced *Jehovah*, which is merely a combination of the sacred Tetragrammaton and the vowel in the Hebrew word for Lord, substituted by the Jews for YHWH, because they shrank from pronouncing The Name...To give the name YHWH the vowels of the word for Lord (Heb. Adonai) and pronounce it *Jehovah*, is about as hybrid a combination as it would be to spell the name *Germany* with the vowels in the name *Portugal* –viz., *Gormuna*."[15]

"The name itself was considered by the Hebrews as too holy to utter so the world "Lord" (Heb. *Adonai*) was substituted when the text was read."[16]

"Jews thought the name YAHUAH was too holy to pronounce. By the 200s B.C., they were using the word Adonai as a respectful substitute when reading from the scriptures."[17]

The term Jehovah, is *an* **Erroneous Hybrid** *form for the divine name which originated in the mistaken idea* that the consonants of Tetragrammaton, YHWH (really pronounced "Yah-oo-ah"), were to be read with the vowel points found with them in the MT, which really gives the vowels which are to be read with the substituted word *'dny*, (Adonai, "Lord"). The proper vowels for the latter word are a-o-a, but since the first consonant in *YHWH* is not a guttural, the vowel *e* is placed under it (to be read after it) instead of the vowel *a*; thus, by combining these vowels with the consonants of the Tetragrammaton, the mongrel form, "Yehowah," came into being, which with the English consonant *j* in place of *y* and with the German pronunciation of *was v*, produced in turn the quaint form of "Jehovah." Even the Jews today such as Saul Lieberman, M.A., D.H.L., Ph.D. Late Distinguished Service Professor of Talmud and Rector of the Rabbinical School, Jewish Theological Seminary of America. Author of *Greek in Jewish Palestine* and *Hellenism in Jewish Palestine,* admit the name Jehovah was: "ERRONEOUSLY TRANSLITERATED from the Masoretic Hebrew text."

JEHOVAH WITNESSES-FALSE DOCTRINES

As a result of this deception and deviation from the original name of YHVH YAHUAH, a cult called, *Jehovah Witnesses* were formed, which built an entire false doctrine around this counterfeit name and false god. Those who belong to this cult are bound by demonic strongholds, known as "The Spirit of Watchtower Deception." Other demonic spirits which hold *Jehovah Witnesses* in bondage are, the spirits of Antichrist, the spirit of Unbelief which manifests as the deaf and dumb spirit, which acts as a spiritual gatekeeper, preventing *Jehovah Witnesses* from hearing truth. Other demonic strongholds are the spirit of Error, the demon of False Doctrine, Confusion, Legalism, Hardness, Harshness, Guilt, Fear of Watchtower Authorities, and Fear of Armageddon.

Even so-called believers, who do not belong to the cult of *Jehovah Witnesses* but who mistakenly believe that the name of YHVH is pronounced Jehovah, say it and worship it. They are being deceived and bound by these spiritual strongholds, which all come from the hierarchy of satans.

CHAPTER SEVENTEEN: Who Is Jehovah?

NOTES:

1. Francis Brown, R. Driver, and Charles Briggs, *The Brown-Driver-Briggs Hebrew and English Lexicon,* Hendrickson Pub; Complete and Unabridged, fully searchable, with Strong Numbers and interactive Index edition (September 1, 1994)
2. Menahem Mansoor, *The Dead Sea Scrolls: A College Textbook and a Study Guide,* Eerdmans; First American Edition (1964)
3. Ella LeBain, *Who's Who In The Cosmic Zoo? Book One – Third Edition,* Chapter – Els – Elohim, pp.204-205, Tate Publishing & Enterprises, 2013.
4. Scott Thomas - Editor, *Funk & Wagnalls New Encyclopedia, 2000 Yearbook, 1999 Events,* Funk & Wagnalls, 2000
5. The Catholic Church, *The New World Dictionary-Concordance to the New American Bible*, p. 295. World Publishing (1970)
6. David Noel Freedman, Astrid B. Beck, Allen C. Myers, Editors *Eerdmans Dictionary of the Bible*, p. 682, William B. Eerdmans Publishing Company (October 23, 2000)
7. Louis F. Hartman, Bijbels Woordenboek (Translator), *Encyclopedic Dictionary of the Bible*, p. 1110, McGraw-Hill; 2nd Revised edition (1963)
8. *The Concise Columbia Electronic Encyclopedia*, Third Edition, Columbia University Press Houghton Mifflin; 3 Sub edition (October 12, 1994)
9. *Encarta Online Encyclopedia*, Microsoft, 2000
10. Philip W. Goetz, Robert McHenry, Dale Hoiberg, Editors, *Encyclopedia Britannica*, 15th Edition, 1999-2000
11. Cecil Roth, *The Concise Jewish Encyclopedia*, p. 277. Plume (April 1, 1980)
12. Isidore Singer, *The Jewish Encyclopedia*, vol. 9: p. 160, Ktav Publishing House; 1st edition (1901)
13. Ibid, vol. 7: p. 87
14. American Standard Version, Preface to the *Revised Standard Version* of the Bible (2nd Ed., 1971) p. 6-7, Thomas Nelson & Sons, NY.
15. Joseph Rotherham, Editor, *The Emphasized Bible*, p.24-25. Kregel Classics (June 30, 1959)
16. Paul Achtemeier, *Harper's Bible Dictionary*, p. 1,036. 1985 Harpercollins; First Edition (October 1985)
17. *World Book Encyclopedia* World Book Inc (November 2002)

CHAPTER EIGHTEEN

LIKE FATHER, LIKE SON

"I and the Father are one."

(John 10:30)

"No one who denies the Son has the Father;
Whoever acknowledges the Son has the Father also."

(1 John 2:23)

"You will travel far, my little Kal-El. But we will never leave you, even in the face of our death. The richness of our lives shall be yours. All that I have, all that I've learned, everything I feel, all this, and more, I bequeath you, my son. You will carry me inside you, all the days of your life. You will make my strength your own, and see my life through your eyes, as your life will be seen through mine. The son becomes the father, and the father the son. This is all I can send you, Kal-El." Jor-El (bidding his son farewell, as Lara looks on), *Superman*[1]

WHOM DID JESUS PRAY TO?

While Jesus Christ walked the earth in his three-dimensional flesh and blood body, he spoke often about his Father in Heaven, and regularly prayed to Him. Jesus presents his Heavenly Father as a god of universal love, justice, and mercy. So who was He?

"Then they asked him, "Where is your father?" "You do not know me or my Father," Jesus replied. "If you knew me, you would know my Father also."

(John 8:19)

The Bible tells us that all power in both heaven and Earth has been transferred over to Jesus. "Then Jesus came to them and said, "All authority in heaven and on earth has been given to me" (Matthew 28:18). So who authorized and gave Jesus all this power and authority?

It is written: "As surely as I live, says the Lord, 'every knee will bow before me; every tongue will confess and give praise to God'" (Romans 14:11). This is what his father Yahuah said through his prophet Isaiah approximately 500 years before the birth of Jesus:

"Turn to me and be saved, all you ends of the earth; for I am God, and there is no other. I have sworn by myself, the word is gone out of my mouth in righteousness, and shall not return, that to me every knee shall bow, every tongue shall swear. Only in Yahuah, it is said of me, is righteousness and strength; even to him shall men come; and all they that were incensed against him shall be put to shame."

(Isaiah 45:22-24)

It is clear that Yahuah, is the father of Yahshua (Jesus). "I and the Father are One." (John 10:30) They are one both spiritually and genetically, as it was Yahuah's Divine blood that ran through the body of Yahshua. It was important to use Mary as the vessel to carry him because she was a direct descendant of King David and of the root of Jesse. His father was Yahuah, and Mary was impregnated with his seed, in order to fulfill the Divine mission of Yahshua Jesus to be the final blood sacrifice for all of humanity because he carried incorruptible blood. That means that his blood could not have died, could not be misused or abused as in the case of the many murders of innocent children, adults, and animals whose blood was drained to appease these reptilian gods. The blood of Jesus has more power than all the blood sacrifices combined. While this is a mystery to many, both unbelievers and even some believers, His blood was willingly shed to "buy back" the souls of all the humans kept in bondage by the blood thirsty reptilian gods, i.e., the Annunaki, Lucifer/Satan, and all the satans and fallen angels who have fallen into Draconian bodies.

"You were bought at a price; do not become slaves of men."

(1 Corinthians 7:23)

This is why at the name of Yahshua (Jesus Christ), demons (aliens) tremble and flee, and those who are under the "blood" of Yahshua are covered as if to have an invisible wall around them. Just as the Israelites were told to do in Egypt by placing lamb's blood on their doorposts, so that the angel of death would "Passover" them and they would be saved. It is only through the Divine shed blood of Yahshua (the Lamb of God) that humans find freedom and salvation from the god(s) of this world.

"All things have been committed to me by my Father. No one knows the Son except the Father, and no one knows the Father except the Son and those to whom the Son chooses to reveal him."

(Matthew 11:27)

It is the Father Yahuah, El Elyon, the Almighty and Most High God, who gives authorization to Yahshua (Jesus). This is why it says, "That at the name of Jesus every knee should bow, in heaven and on earth and under the earth, and every tongue confess that Jesus Christ is Lord, to the glory of God the Father (Yahuah/El Elyon)." (Philippians 2:10-11)

Yahushua was the name that Jesus had while he walked in the flesh. As I've already proved, the name of the Father is in the name of the Son, fulfilling His very words:

CHAPTER EIGHTEEN: Like Father, Like Son

"Don't you believe that I am in the Father, and that the Father is in me? The words I say to you are not just my own. Rather, it is the Father, living in me, who is doing his work." (John 14:10)

"Yet a time is coming and has now come when the true worshipers will worship the Father in spirit and truth, for they are the kind of worshipers the Father seeks."

(John 4:23)

WHO ARE THE CHILDREN OF ABRAHAM?

"To the Jews who had believed him, Jesus said, "If you hold to my teaching, you are really my disciples. Then you will know the truth, and the truth will set you free." They answered him, "We are Abraham's descendants and have never been slaves of anyone. How can you say that we shall be set free?"

(John 8:31-33)

Isn't it interesting that they didn't even realize they were being held in bondage? They deny that they've never been slaves of anyone, yet the political situation at that time, clearly indicates that they were slaves of the heavy handed Roman Empire and under their rule. Not to mention that Abraham's descendants, the Israelites were also in bondage as slaves to Egypt until the Exodus. So their denial or the lies they tell themselves was flagrant, even for those days. In many respects, not much has changed, as Jews as well as Gentiles today deny their need for a savior from the bondage they are held in, within the system of this world, and their worldly powers, principalities, rulers of the darkness and spiritual wickedness ruling the heavens (Ephesians 6:12).

"Jesus replied, "I tell you the truth, everyone who sins is a slave to sin. Now a slave has no permanent place in the family, but a son belongs to it forever. So if the Son sets you free, you will be free indeed. I know you are Abraham's descendants. Yet you are ready to kill me, because you have no room for my word. I am telling you what I have seen in the Father's presence, and you do what you have heard from your father." "Abraham is our father," they answered. "If you were Abraham's children," said Jesus, "then you would do the things Abraham did. As it is, you are determined to kill me, a man who has told you the truth that I heard from God. Abraham did not do such things. You are doing the things your own father does." "We are not illegitimate children," they protested. "The only Father we have is God himself." (v. 8:34-41)

First of all, Abraham is not a god. He is a created being, who became the father of a race of Israelites and Semites, within which was birthed the twelve tribes of Israel, and the Jews came from the tribe of Judah. Abraham is also the father of the Arab race, through the birth of his son Ishmael. So claiming to be a child of Abraham does not define anyone here as which god they serve. Yahshua convicts them of their denials. Yet they continue to claim that God is their father.

The question is, which god? This is not only the question of their day, but the age old question which still permeates today. How many people in this world believe in God, but do not know which god they are believing in and serving? This is the purpose of this book — to shed discernment between the god of this world and his many fallen and false gods who have all kinds of evil agendas to keep earth humans in bondage, and the God who created the Heavens and the Earth, the Almighty Creator of souls, who created a Divine Plan of Salvation for all humans. To put it succinctly, the children of Abraham are the ones who serve the God of Abraham, Isaac, and Jacob.

WHO ARE THE CHILDREN OF THE DEVIL?

> "Jesus said to them, "If God were your Father, you would love me, for I came from God and now am here. I have not come on my own; but he sent me. Why is my language not clear to you? Because you are unable to hear what I say. You belong to your father, the devil, and you want to carry out your father's desire. He was a murderer from the beginning, not holding to the truth, for there is no truth in him. When he lies, he speaks his native language, for he is a liar and the father of lies. Yet because I tell the truth, you do not believe me! Can any of you prove me guilty of sin? If I am telling the truth, why don't you believe me? He who belongs to God hears what God says. The reason you do not hear is that you do not belong to God." (v. 8:42-47)

In my opinion, Jesus is referring to Yahuah, the Father. Now, when you read Book Five, my final book in this series, *The Heavens,* you will see that, when Enoch was taken up throughout the ten heavens, he encountered the throne rooms in the third heaven, which is where the Lord Jesus Christ rules; then in the seventh heaven, he encountered another throne, where his Father, who in Hebrew is called "Aravat," which means the Father of Creation rules from, who is known as YHWH in the Old Testament, translated into English is Yahuah. However, when Enoch was taken into the tenth and highest heaven, he also described another throne where the Most High God sits, which is called "Aravoth," who is the Creator Father of all the gods, the eternal one, also known as the "ineffable one."

The Hebrew Bible calls him "El Elyon," which means the Almighty Creator of all gods or "Most High." The prime creator was Yahuah, also known as "El Elyon." He has obviously created a number of creator gods/deities as his "sons" i.e., Elohim.

Spiritually speaking, the children of the devil, however, are all those in rebellion to the Father of Creation. They follow the god(s) of this world in all their many forms and masquerades. From ancient gods and goddesses to the outright worship of Lucifer and Satan himself (in all his forms) to all those who profess atheism, who deny the existence

CHAPTER EIGHTEEN: Like Father, Like Son

of a creator, to those who believe in themselves and science above Spirit, to those who deny the existence of any god, including the existence of the devil himself — these are the children of the devil. However, the Bible tells us that Satan has a genetic 'seed' in Genesis 3:15 and Matthew 13:24-30. This is an actual serpent race 'alien' bloodline that exists in humankind on earth. This is the root cause of all racism on earth. Satan's seed is at enmity with God's seed. This is the basis of all ancient and present day spiritual battles between various tribes and races.

I think it's interesting to note for my readers, the origin of the word *devil*. It is actually two words that have been truncated into one, which is derived from the Germanic language, combining the word *da* which means "the," and the word *evil*, which is the same in English, and the word *devil* was formed. So who exactly is the devil? (See my chapters here on The God of This World, and The Office of Satan)

THE HOLY TRINITY: ONE GOD OR THREE?

The word's Holy Trinity does not appear in the Holy Scriptures, but is a phrase that was coined by the formation of the Catholic Church and has been adopted as Christian doctrine. For many this is a mystery, how three individuals gods can be seen as one, but just as a braid, which are three strands that are intertwined to make one cord, or a married couple who becomes "one" flesh, and one spirit in the union of marriage, we can see how individual entities can merge together as partners.

"Hear, O Israel: the Lord our God, the Lord is one!" (Deuteronomy 6:4). Let's go into the original Hebrew: Shema (Hear) Yisrael (Israel) Yahuah (YHVH) Eloheinu (is our god) Yahuah (YHVH) Echad (one). The Hebrew term *Echad* means one. It does not always mean "absolute unity," and it frequently denotes composite unity.

When the Jewish commentary, the Zohar, looks at this verse, it asks why the name of God is mentioned three times. It then answers by saying that the first Yahuah is the Father above. The second is the stem of Jesse, who has come through the family line of Jesse and David, and the third one is the Spirit below, and these three are one. Christians agree with this understanding.

The Father, the Son, and the Holy Spirit are one in unity but separate in personality and wills. If Jesus didn't pray to the separate personality of the Father then, who did He pray to? He couldn't pray to Himself as He could then be accused of not knowing His own mind or will. Jesus said, "No one can come to me unless the Father who sent me draws him." (John 6:44) They work as a partnership. "Jesus also said, "I am the way and the truth and the life. No one comes to the Father except through me." (John 14:6). You can't even get to the Father, unless you go through Him. That's the protocol. "Therefore I tell you that no one who is speaking by the Spirit of God says, "Jesus be cursed," and no one can say, "Jesus is Lord," except by the Holy Spirit." (1 Corinthians 12:3)

It is obvious that they all work together with one mind, in one spirit, with one purpose, yet each having individual roles.

Dr. Selwyn Stevens claimed in his article, "Gods or God: How Many & Who?": "So the Father, the Son and the Holy Spirit are one God who are shown in three separate persons. One of the stumbling blocks to understanding this mystery is our use of the term 'Person.' We usually mean a separate distinct individual. Jesus said He only did the things the Father told Him to, and then He did them in the power of the Holy Spirit. Jesus never acted alone. He prayed to the Father many times. He asked the Father to send the Holy Spirit. In Gethsemane Jesus submitted to the will of the Father. Jesus wasn't play-acting for the sake of others. He was addressing and submitting to another person. There is a false and anti-Biblical view that Jesus is also the Father. The prayer in Gethsemane proves that wrong."[2]

So who is the father? The father is YHVH pronounced Yahuah.

So who is the Son? The son is the physical flesh and blood manifestation of YHVH, called Emmanuel which is Hebrew for, "God is With Us" and Yahshua (Savior) aka Jesus Christ.

> "He is the <u>image</u> of the invisible God, the firstborn over all creation. For by him all things were created: things in heaven and on earth, visible and invisible, whether thrones or powers or rulers or authorities; all things were created by him and for him. He is before all things, and in him all things hold together. And he is the head of the body, the church; he is the beginning and the firstborn from among the dead, so that in everything he might have the supremacy. For God was pleased to have all his fullness dwell in him, and through him to reconcile to himself all things, whether things on earth or things in heaven, by making peace through his blood, shed on the cross."
>
> (Colossians 1:15-20)

Are all these one god? They are in unity, but in order to have unity, there needs to be more than one being. Yahuah is the father of Yahshua (Jesus) being the son of God, who carries the divine blood of El Elyon, fulfilling his mission to be the final blood sacrifice, a price that was needed to be paid in flesh and blood, to free all humans from the bondage of the god of this world, who is Lucifer/Satan.

I AM A JEALOUS GOD

The thought of jealousy usually evokes all kinds of strong feelings in people — from the emotions we feel when someone we love and trust betrays us, to the crazy passions of a jealous lover which leads to murder and abuse. To think that there is a "jealous" side to God pushes most people's comfort levels, as well as misunderstanding. Let's discern.

Yahuah was not only *Jealous* but *Zealous*, "...for you do not bow yourselves to another god - for Yahuah, whose name [is] Zealous, is a zealous God." (Exodus 34:14) In Hebrew the same root word is used for *jealous* and *zealous*, "qannah" being jealous and "qanno" is zealous. (1 King 19:14) This is what the LORD Almighty says: "I am very jealous 'qinneti' for Zion; I am burning with jealousy 'qinneti' for her." (Zechariah 8:2) Yahuah was known as "El Qannah," the Jealous/Zealous God.

Jealous and Zealous not only sound alike, but have roots in similar meanings. It is all about passion. There are two kinds of jealousy — the jealousy that comes from love, compassion, and commitment, which is a possessive/protective type of expression of love, such as the kind of love parents feels for their children, and what a husband feels for his wife, and then there is the dark side of jealousy, which takes the passion and possessive/protection over the edge, and says, if I can't have/possess this person, then nobody can, which leads to murder, competition, and bitterness. Spiritually, it is important to discern the difference. Just as all emotions (energies in motion) were initially created by the Creator God, the counterfeit dark lord takes all of them and imitates them by perverting and distorting them.

Zechariah 8:2 says, the Lord is jealous for Zion, what kind of jealousy is this? What many people miss when they initially read this, particularly those who are reading these passages from a purely intellectual standpoint, is the spiritual message behind it. As I've been saying throughout these books, is that, without the revelation of the Holy Spirit, the Bible scriptures are only words on a page. What many people miss, including the ancient Israelites, is that the God of Israel wanted a personal intimate relationship with his people. The word *Bride* is mentioned thirty-one times in the scriptures, most of which relates to the "spiritual covenant" between the Lord and his people. His people are his Bride and He is the Bridegroom. In fact, as poetic as the love story in the book of the Song of Solomon is, it is a metaphor for the Lord and his Bride. The book of Revelation completes this when the Bridegroom returns to collect his Bride for the wedding feast in Heaven.

> "I saw the Holy City, the new Jerusalem, coming down out of heaven from God, prepared as a bride beautifully dressed for her husband."
>
> (Revelation 21:2)

The jealousy the Lord speaks of comes from having a passionate "covenant" with His people. Love is not something that can be forced; it must come of a person's free will; otherwise it is not love. This is why humans were made with freewill, the freedom to choose whether they want to be in a personal, intimate with their Creator, or not, as the case may be. The entire scripture really sums this up in the end with the Harvest of His Angels, (see, Book Three – *Who Are The Angels?* Chapter— The Harvest of Angels) who, at the end of this timeline, will separate the lovers from the rebels and salvation will come to all those who love the Lord, and those who remain in rebellion will perish.

Paul writes in 2 Corinthians 11, "I am jealous for you with a godly jealousy. I promised you to one husband, to Christ, so that I might present you as a pure virgin to him." Again the distinction between a godly jealousy (a protective love) and the jealousy of the world.

As all marriages are covenants and agreements, the Lord does not take His covenant with His people lightly. His love is purposed in a covenant, out of His love, out of His purposes. He sees His people from the heart of a shepherd. In the past, the Kings were the shepherds to their people. Ezekiel call these shepherd to task, in chapter 34, by rebuking them because they were put into power by God and they abused their power because they ignored the needs of the flock. They hoarded the wealth for themselves. They did not take care of the widows and the orphans, which brought down the Lord's punishment on them. The Lord empowers leaders to look after the weak. Lord can exalt individuals, as well as bring them down when they fail in their God-given duties to shepherd God's flock. It's a recurring pattern throughout the Bible, as well as in our planet's history.

SHEPHERDS AND THEIR SHEEP

> "The word of the Lord came to me: 'Son of man, prophesy against the shepherds of Israel; prophesy and say to them: 'this is what the Sovereign Lord says: 'Woe to the shepherds of Israel who only take care of themselves! Should not shepherds take care of the flock? You eat the curds, clothe yourselves with the wool and slaughter the choice animals, but you do not take care of the flock. You have not strengthened the weak or healed the sick or bound up the injured. You have not brought back the strays or searched for the lost. You have ruled them harshly and brutally.'"
>
> (Ezekiel 34: 1-4)

Politically speaking, Ezekiel 34 is not only a rebuke to the shepherds of Israel, but it should be a template to all the leaders of the nations of the world today. God doesn't change his heart when He empowers a leader; it is for the purpose of carrying the duties and responsibilities to take care of the rest. Think about how many leaders, kings, and dictators have been raised up and brought down because of their greed and cruelty to their flocks? In many respects, this is a template for political power and leadership, not just for Israel, but for all the nations. The Lord's "zealousy" is being expressed for his people through the prophet Ezekiel because his heart is grieved by the way the leaders of Israel are ignoring the needs of His people. This comes from a heart of love, commitment, and a type of fatherly protection.

> Jesus said, "I AM the Good Shepherd, the good shepherd lays down his life for his sheep."
>
> (John 10:11)

> "The Lord is my shepherd, I shall not be in want, The Lord takes care of me as his sheep and I shall not be without any good thing."
>
> (Psalm 23:1)

CHAPTER EIGHTEEN: Like Father, Like Son

The Lord sees His people with compassion and mercy. He sees them as tender sheep, and just as sheep are often victimized by prey, so are his people victimized "spiritually" by straying and being deceived by the empty promises of idols and pseudo gods. Yet, in spite of the sheep's nature to stray, the Lord brings them back into the flock, forgives them, and cleans them up. That is His love and "zealousy" for His people.

> Jesus said, "O Jerusalem, Jerusalem, you who kill the prophets and stone those sent to you, how often I have longed to gather your children together, as a hen gathers her chicks under her wings, but you were not willing."
>
> (Matthew 23:37)

The heart of God is unchanging toward His people. He doesn't break covenants based on emotions like humans do. Humans are subject to changing emotions, demonic oppression, and spiritual confusion. There is no confusion in God. The Lord understands how we are made, and how we are compromised living under the powers, principalities and rulers of the darkness of this world. His love is steadfast, in spite of our mistakes and the changing tides of our moods.

> "Because of the oppression of the weak and the groaning of the needy, I will now arise," says the LORD. "I will protect them from those who malign them."
>
> (Psalm 12:5)

One of the ways the Lord protects His people from those who malign them is by turning against their oppressors and destroying their strongholds.

> "'Therefore, you shepherds, hear the word of the Lord: As surely as I live, declares the Sovereign Lord, because my flock lacks a shepherd and so has been plundered and has become food for all the wild animals, and because my shepherds did not search for my flock but cared for themselves rather than for my flock, therefore, O shepherds, hear the word of the Lord: This is what the Sovereign Lord says: **I am against the shepherds and will hold them accountable for my flock. I will remove them from tending the flock so that the shepherds can no longer feed themselves. I will rescue my flock from their mouths, and it will no longer be food for them.** "'For this is what the Sovereign Lord says: I myself will search for my sheep and look after them. As a shepherd looks after his scattered flock when he is with them, so will I look after my sheep. **I will rescue them from all the places where they were scattered on a day of clouds and darkness."**
>
> (Ezekiel 34:7-12)

We see here that the Lord has a plan. While Ezekiel 34 was referring to the people of Israel, we know today that this covenant extends to all the twelve tribes of Israel, which were scattered to all the ends of the earth. We know that in 1948, the land of Israel was reborn, just as the prophet Ezekiel prophesied, in chapter 37, that the Lord would put flesh on the valley of the dry bones and breathe "His" spirit into them and cause them to live and flourish again in the land of Israel. While it may have taken nearly 2,500 years to fulfill his prophesy, nevertheless the land of Israel is now thriving with Jews and Israelites who were gathered from all ends of the earth. Even in Ezekiel 34, the Lord covenants to gather up His flock and heal them:

> "I will bring them out from the nations and gather them from the countries, and I will bring them into their own land. I will pasture them on the mountains of Israel, in the ravines and in all the settlements in the land. I will tend them in a good pasture, and the mountain heights of Israel will be their grazing land. There they will lie down in good grazing land, and there they will feed in a rich pasture on the mountains of Israel. I myself will tend my sheep and have them lie down, declares the Sovereign Lord. I will search for the lost and bring back the strays. I will bind up the injured and strengthen the weak, but the sleek and the strong I will destroy. **I will shepherd the flock with justice**." (vs. 34:13-16)

Then we see it is the Lord who appoints leaders and shepherds. In the next verses, we see the heart of the Lord over his people by giving them a faithful, just and strong leader, who is King David. He calls him a prince. He promises to save them.

> "'As for you, my flock, this is what the Sovereign Lord says: <u>I will judge between one sheep and another, and between rams and goats</u>..... "'Therefore this is what the Sovereign Lord says to them: See, myself will judge between the fat sheep and the lean sheep. Because you shove with flank and shoulder, butting all the weak sheep with your horns until you have driven them away, I will save my flock, and they will no longer be plundered. I will judge between one sheep and another. I will place over them one shepherd, my servant David, and he will tend them; he will tend them and be their shepherd. I the Lord (Yahuah) will be their God, and my servant David will be prince among them. I the Lord have spoken." (vs. 34:17, 20-24)

The promise here is that the Lord (Yahuah) will be their God, and his servant will be their prince. We have the same promise in the New Testament, through Yahshua (Jesus Christ), who is the descendant of King David, destined to take over his throne in the New Jerusalem when it is downloaded upon the earth during the Millennial Reign. All power and authority was given to Yahshua for "spiritually" defeating the kingdom of darkness on the cross. The final battle known as Armageddon is scheduled to overthrow the physical kingdom of darkness and the god of this world, who is Lucifer/Satan.

The age between the crucifixion, resurrection, and ascension, and the return of the Lord Jesus Christ with his vast celestial army bringing an end to this present world and its system is about a time period allotted to testing the faith of earth humans, during a time

CHAPTER EIGHTEEN: Like Father, Like Son

of "Grace," by giving every earth human the opportunity to be saved through faith in what the Lord has done over two thousand years and to hold fast to the spiritual victory of the cross. Then at the end of this age and this present timeline, there will be a separation between the sheep and the goats, as the Jesus Christ promises in Matthew 25:32, "All the nations will be gathered before Him, and <u>He will separate the people, one from another as a shepherd separates the sheep from the goats.</u>"

Here we have a correspondence between the will of Yahuah, and the authority given to Yahshua (Jesus) to judge and separate people, as Yahshua uses the metaphor, as a shepherd separates the sheep from the goats. As I've said earlier, the sheep are the ones who listen to the voice of God and love Him with all their heart and mind; the goats are the rebels, who may profess His name, but their hearts are with another. I have written extensively on these differences in Book Five, *The Heaven,* see, Chapters - The Word of God as Written in the Stars; The Coming Kingdom of God.

There are many who misinterpret Yahuah's actions in the Old Testament as cruel because of his warrior nature expressed the many times He protected his people from their enemies, as well as the many times He punished his own people for their disobedience and their idolatry. The idolatry was a huge trigger for Yahuah because He did not want His people to worship and follow other gods, especially because He knew "who" these so-called gods were, "where" they came from, and "what" their hidden agendas were for His people.

In many respects, his jealousy stemmed from what He knew, which most of his people were unaware of, which again came from His heart of compassion for His people. He punished them and disciplined them as a father disciplines His own children, for they were His children. True, some of their punishments were severe, but now that we've come full circle as we approach the end of this timeline, which is culminating into the final battle between the Lords Yahuah, Yahshua, and all of the Elohim against these pseudo-gods who have, for millennia, endeavored to steal the souls of his own people, we can understand, through hindsight, why Yahuah came down so hard on His people for following these other gods. (See, my chapters herein, *Who Are the Gods?* and *The God of This World.*) We are all being called to learn the lessons of history, lest we be doomed to repeat its mistakes.

> "But mark this: There will be terrible times in the last days. People will be lovers of themselves, lovers of money, boastful, proud, abusive, disobedient to their parents, ungrateful, unholy, without love, unforgiving, slanderous, without self-control, brutal, not lovers of the good, treacherous, rash, conceited, lovers of pleasure rather than lovers of God—<u>having a form of godliness but denying its power</u>. Have nothing to do with them."
>
> (2 Timothy 3:1-4)

Having a form of godliness but denying its power is the "religious spirit." I have written extensively on this in my chapter on Aliens and Religion in Book Three:*Who Are The Angels?*, and all the many ways this demon spirit manifests itself in religions and in church and temple goers of all faiths. It is a demon spirit that holds people in bondage to the legalism and traditions of religion, but blocks their spiritual power. This is the agenda of the god of this world, the Archons who are the rulers of the darkness and all the enemies of our souls who seek daily to keep earth humans from having a personal, intimate relationship with the Living God and the Creator of the souls, because of their hatred for God because that is what they lost.

These aliens and their entire demonic hierarchy hate earth humans, because the Lord has a plan of salvation for us, but not for them. So they masquerade as spiritual beings, so-called light-workers, religious leaders, in an attempt to deceive earth humans from attaining their prize. It's literally a daily battle on earth over the souls and minds of earth humans.

In terms of jealousy, the Lord is jealous for our love and our worship; the satans (the enemies and adversaries of our souls) are jealous of the Lord's love for us. Hence, the crux of the battle. The satans (the Archons, the Annunaki, the Draconian/Reptilians, the Grays, i.e., demons) fight for the control of the minds and "soul" energy of earth humans. If they can get earth humans to worship them in their many disguises, even if it's in the form of a lifeless statute, then they win the "soul" energy that comes from earth humans, which thwarts earth humans from their spiritual power that is available to them from the Lord.

Ironically, even so-called Christians in their many denominations, are thwarted from the Lord's spiritual power through His Holy Spirit because their earthly lives are in bondage to the satans in a myriad, through false beliefs, unconfessed sin, unbroken family and generational curses, religious spirits, and hypocrisy. While they may confess Jesus Christ as their savior, their minds and bodies still belong to Satan, which manifests with all kinds of mental and physical illness, poverty, and immoral lifestyles. Having a "form" of godliness, but denying its power. This spiritual condition is rampant throughout the entire of body of Christ, and most of its churches. (See my chapters in Book Three – *Who Are The Angels?* on *Aliens and Religions* for more elucidation on Christian Churches and their Denominations, Demons in the Church, The Shadow of the Church)

> "For the time will come when men will not put up with sound doctrine. Instead, to suit their own desires, <u>they will gather around them a great number of teachers to say what their **itching ears want to hear**</u>. <u>They will turn their ears away from the truth and turn aside to myths.</u>"
>
> (2 Timothy 4:3-4)

CHAPTER EIGHTEEN: Like Father, Like Son

Sounds like New Age belief systems. This is exactly what is happening at the end of this timeline. Many have become disenchanted with religion and have been damaged by its many hypocrisies (through the religious spirits and demons), so spiritually speaking, they have thrown the baby out with the bathwater and have given up on the Lord and have turned away from truth to appease their "itching" ears, to be told what they want to hear.

This trend is not limited to New Age circles, but is also prevalent within Christian churches, as pastors tailor their sermons into "feel good" messages, in order to keep their churches and their donation hats full, so as not to offend anyone. Sometimes the truth hurts. But the only thing the truth really hurts is one's pride and ego. However, the truth sets us free; it is liberating. Jesus told us to deny ourselves and take up our cross daily and follow Him (Luke 9:23). That means to put the almighty ego on the cross. Spiritually, regardless of what church, cult, or denomination, it's irrelevant, if the doctrine is teaching cheap grace and telling people only what they want to hear. That, in and of itself, is deceptive.

Turning to myths is the basis for a lot of New Age thought forms. Resurrecting ancient myths and believing them as present truths. The only thing going on there is the lack of discernment between the truth and the lie, as well as the "forgetfulness" of the lessons of history.

It amazes me how many New Agers literally worship ancient Egyptian myths, gods, and goddesses, thinking they had more power and magic, and were more advanced than most. They completely deny the many downfalls of the Egyptian Pharaohs, their many punishments from the Lord, and the fact that they held most of their people in all sorts of bondage and slavery, which, spiritually speaking, continues today through curses. Why worship something that promotes oppression and bondage?

There are valuable lessons to be learned from the histories which created these mythologies, something many New Agers today completely ignore, because following the myths is more fun than facing the truth.

When we talk about the jealousy of the Lord, we also have to remember that it literally breaks his heart and grieves His Spirit, when His children rebel against Him, turn against Him, and follow all kinds of paths of deception from the pseudo-gods. Yes, God has a heart, and many do not think about how heartbroken the Lord's spirit is over the wickedness of earth humans. The scriptures tell us in the book of Genesis 6:5-6 that He regretted making man. Yet in spite of his grief, he followed through with His word, with His covenants and promises.

He has and will continue to keep His end of His agreement and His Divine Plan of Salvation for humankind, which is not only written in the scriptures, but first written into the stars. (See Book Five *The Divine Plan of Salvation as Written in the Stars*).

This is why believers cling to the promises and the covenants from the Lord because they are unbroken and will be fulfilled not matter what passing trend or latest New Age doctrine or philosophy comes down the pike, the collective "we" are all on the Lord's timeline of Grace, until this world of duality comes to an end.

The following verses conclude the end of the Ezekiel 34 which is the promise and covenant from the Lord. While many scholars interpret these passages to relate to Israel, it specifically relates to the "house of Israel." In my opinion, the house of Israel are the entire twelve tribes of Jacob (Israel), who were scattered all over the earth, along with all of their descendants.

The tribes of Judah and Benjamin became the Jews. Yet the rest of the "ten lost tribes" are still, to this day, very much part of the "house of Israel" and still under the covenant and promises from the Lord. Many of which do not even have Jewish blood. You could be one of them, which means the Lord's promises and covenants are for you, regardless of where you live, or what religion you belong to. To the Lord, a promise is a promise, and his covenants are unbroken. The only ones who can break away from His promises are those who reject them. That is each and every one's prerogative and freewill.

> "'I will make a covenant of peace with them and rid the land of wild beasts so that they may live in the desert and sleep in the forests in safety. I will bless them and the places surrounding my hill. I will send down showers in season; there will be showers of blessing. The trees of the field will yield their fruit and the ground will yield its crops; the people will be secure in their land. They will know that I am the Lord, when I break the bars of their yoke and rescue them from the hands of those who enslaved them. They will no longer be plundered by the nations, nor will wild animals devour them. They will live in safety, and no one will make them afraid. I will provide for them a land renowned for its crops, and they will no longer be victims of famine in the land or bear the scorn of the nations. <u>Then they will know that I, the Lord their God, am with them and that they, **the house of Israel**, are my people</u>, declares the Sovereign Lord. <u>You my sheep, the sheep of my pasture, are people, and I am your God, declares the Sovereign Lord.</u>'"

(Ezekiel 34:25-31)

WHERE'S THE POWER?

Suffice it to say, that the King of the Kingdom is Jesus Christ. "Then Jesus came to his disciples and said, "<u>All authority</u> in heaven and on earth has been given to me."

(Matthew 18:18)

"For from him and through him and to him are all things. To him be the glory forever! Amen."

(Romans 11:36)

CHAPTER EIGHTEEN: Like Father, Like Son

"If anyone speaks, he should do it as one speaking the very words of God. If anyone serves, he should do it with the strength God provides, so that in all things God may be praised through Jesus Christ. To him be the glory and the power forever and ever. Amen."

(1 Peter 4:11)

"To him be the power forever and ever. Amen."

(1 Peter 4:11)

"To the only God our Savior be glory, majesty, power and authority, through Jesus Christ our Lord, before all ages, now and forevermore! Amen."

(Jude 1:25)

"I have given you authority to trample on snakes and scorpions and to overcome all the power of the enemy; nothing will harm you."

(Luke 10:19)

"When Jesus had called the Twelve together, he gave them power and authority to drive out all demons and to cure diseases, and he sent them out to preach the kingdom of God and to heal the sick."

(Luke 9:1-2)

"And all the people, both high and low, gave him their attention and exclaimed, "<u>This man is the divine power known as the Great Power</u>."

(Acts 8:10)

"Wealth and honor come from you; you are the ruler of all things. In your hands are strength and power to exalt and give strength to all."

(1 Chronicles 29:12)

"You are worthy, our Lord and God, to receive glory and honor and power, for you created all things, and by your will they were created and have their being."

(Revelation 4:11)

The only One we are called to worship is the Lord and God Jesus Christ (Yahshua, the Messiah). The ineffable name of the Father has clearly granted all power and authority to rest upon Him. It is written that the Lord Jesus Christ gathers His own into "His" Kingdom, only to present them, holy and blameless before the Father in Heaven at the end of the age. Through focusing our worship on Him, we are worshipping the effable name of the Father.

But for some strange reason, there are many Christians who believe that Jesus Christ is just an intercessor to bring us to the Father. They prefer to worship the Father above the Son. As long as they do not fall into the enemy's trap about mistakenly worshipping the wrong name because, by doing so, they give their power and worship to the wrong god. This is why it is far safer, spiritually speaking, for the body of Christ, to focus their worship on Christ alone, and His Holy Spirit, who will in turn give it over the Father in Heaven without stain or blemish. Then to exceed one's authority in prayer (and worship) and think that they can get to the Father by bypassing the Son.

We must not forget that the ancients used the names of angels to invoke them and, by doing so, abused their authority, which is why the Lord changed the names of the angels, and in doing so, confounded those who would attempt to invoke them and disobey the Lord. King Solomon made this mistake, which contributed to his downfall. (See Book Three – *Who Are The Angels?* Chapter - Angel Protocol) For this same reason, the Lord has given the name above all names in heaven and on earth which is Jesus Christ (Yahshua HaMashiach), who carries with Him the government on His shoulders.

> "For to us a child is born, to us a son is given, and the government will be on his shoulders. And he will be called Wonderful Counselor, Mighty God, Everlasting Father, Prince of Peace."
>
> (Isaiah 9:6)

> "And what is the exceeding greatness of his power to us-ward who believe, according to the working of his mighty power, which he exerted in Christ when he raised him from the dead and seated him at his right hand in the heavenly realms, <u>far above all rule and authority, power and dominion, and every title that can be given, not only in the present age but also in the one to come.</u>"
>
> (Ephesians 1:19-21)

It is clear that the ineffable name has given the name above all names all power and authority in heaven and on earth. He alone is worthy of all worship, praise, and thanksgiving. By trying to overreach one's authority in prayer, in mistakenly believing one can go over the head of the King of Kings, Lord of Lords, and God of Gods, and think they know better, to call on the name of YHVH, they are falling into the trap of the religious spirit, who attaches to believers, by getting them to believe they are more spiritual than others, in so doing, getting them to commit idol worship. The enemy is clever. He's got his finger in every pie (i.e. Christian church).

So how does one outsmart Satan's ministers? "For the weapons of our warfare are not carnal, but mighty through God to the pulling down of strong holds; Casting down arguments, and every high thing that exalts itself against the knowledge of God, and bringing into captivity every thought to the obedience of Christ;" (2 Corinthians 10:4,5) Our weapons are spiritual. So what are our weapons? Repentance, Forgiveness, and the Word of God which is the sword of the spirit.

CHAPTER EIGHTEEN: Like Father, Like Son

Can a believer use the sword of the spirit without repentance and forgiveness? They can try, but they will never completely have the victory. Remember Satan and his ministers know the word of God inside and out, too. They often quote it and create false doctrine from it. Knowing the Word of God is not enough. Just as owning a sword or a gun is not enough, you must know how to use and how to fill it with ammunition in order for it to be effective. Repentance and Forgiveness is our ammunition, because without it, the enemy has a "legal right" to attack and hold hostage. This is the nature of the Spiritual Warfare.

The Armor of God specifically says:

"Finally, be strong in the Lord and in his mighty power. Put on the full armor of God so that you can take your stand against the devil's schemes. For our struggle is not against flesh and blood, but against the rulers, against the authorities, against the powers of this dark world and against the spiritual forces of evil in the heavenly realms. Therefore put on the full armor of God, so that when the day of evil comes, you may be able to stand your ground, and after you have done everything, to stand. Stand firm then, with the belt of truth buckled around your waist, with the breastplate of righteousness in place, and with your feet fitted with the readiness that comes from the gospel of peace. In addition to all this, take up the shield of faith, with which you can extinguish all the flaming arrows of the evil one. Take the helmet of salvation and the sword of the Spirit, which is the word of God. And pray in the Spirit on all occasions with all kinds of prayers and requests. With this in mind, be alert and always keep on praying for all the saints."

(Ephesians 6:10-18)

Truth is an armor, and you better know the difference between God's truth and Satan's lies in order for that spiritual belt to protect you as armor. The breastplate of righteousness is worn to protect the heart and torso. The Bible says, "The human heart is the most deceitful of all things, and desperately wicked. Who really knows how bad it is?" (Jeremiah 17:9), the breastplate of righteousness covers up the wickedness of the heart, which can only happen through repentance and forgiveness. Forgiveness is not just some 'touchy feel good, warm, and fuzzy emotion, which couldn't be further from the truth.

Forgiveness is an act of faith and a decision of freewill, to purposely choose to forgive someone, including oneself, for mistakes, sins, and offenses. It must be confessed in order to break demon strongholds of bitterness (resentment, vindictiveness, anger, rage, hatred, ill will, revenge, etc.) Bitterness is a major principality of the dark forces, which unfortunately holds more people in bondage then the common outward sins of the flesh.

Matthew 5:25 says, "Agree with your adversary quickly, whiles you are in the way with him; lest at any time the adversary deliver you to the judge, and the judge deliver you to the officer, and you be cast into prison." This scripture has several layers to it, on the obvious legal advice when dealing with lawsuits, second, the spiritual "legal" ground that is often brought against every earth human, including believers, by the accuser (the prosecutor) of the brethren, who is Satan, who can cast a person into a spiritual prison, through demonic stronghold and all types of spiritual bondage.

This is why forgiveness is used as a weapon in the warfare, by agreeing with your adversary, yet choosing to forgive them through confession, breaks Satan's power and authority over that issue and demon stronghold in your life, and then those demons no longer have a "legal right" to be there — in your body temple or in your congregation. The rules of the spiritual battle are Satan can only oppress you, if he sees something in you that is of himself.

His personality is expressed through his seven principalities: 1) accusing spirits; 2) bitterness; 3) self-bitterness; 4) jealousy and envy; 5) rejection; 6) fears; 7) occult and pharmakia. Through repentance and forgiveness, these principalities and all of their armors and demon strongholds are brought down. This is what it means when it says, "They overcame him by the blood of the Lamb and by the word of their testimony" (Revelation 12:11). Confession is the journey of every believer. It begins through confessing Christ and continues through confession and repentance of sins, asking for forgiveness, choosing forgiveness and confessing it over others and oneself. This defeats the ministers of Satan because it gives them no right to hold on.

Repentance is a weapon, not only in deed, but in word. You can repent of a way of thinking, of a false belief system. A person can repent of all types of bitternesses through choosing forgiveness, and when doing so, the Holy Spirit cleanses the house and resides there. Even a person who has been so severely wounded can forgive the unforgiveable through choosing to, and inviting the Holy Spirit to complete its perfect work in them.

So many people think they must do it by themselves, and we all struggle with it in our own fleshy minds, but it is through confession and repentance that essentially transfers the powers of the demon stronghold to the power of the Holy Spirit to embody and surround the human vessel. This is true deliverance.

There are so many Christians out there who believe they are given authority to command and rebuke demons, and while this is scripturally true, their power is thwarted through the armors of the strongholds of any or all of the seven principalities, through unconfessed and unrepentant sins. Unconfessed sins gives the satans the right to oppress and even possess the human vessel, through all kinds of afflictions and illness.[3]

> "Give thanks to the Lord, for he is good,
> for his steadfast love endures forever.
> Give thanks to the **God of gods,**
> for his steadfast love endures forever.
> Give thanks to the **Lord of lords,**
> for his steadfast love endures forever."
>
> (Psalm 136:1-3)

NOTES:

1. Jerry Siegel, Joe Schuster, creators, *Superman, The Movie*, Warner Brothers, 1978
2. Dr. Selwyn Stevens, *Gods or God: How Many & Who?*
3. Art Mathias, *Biblical Foundations of Freedom,* Wellspring Ministries of Alaska, 2000

CHAPTER NINETEEN

WHO IS THE HOLY SPIRIT?

"Not by might, nor by power,
But by my **SPIRIT**, said the LORD of Hosts."

(Zechariah 4:6)

The 7 fold spirit of GOD:
The Spirit of the Lord shall rest upon Him,
The Spirit of wisdom and understanding,
The Spirit of counsel and might,
The Spirit of knowledge and of the fear of the Lord.
His delight is in the fear of the Lord.

(Isaiah 11:1-3)

The Holy Spirit in Creation — The Spirit is seen from the beginning as present at creation in Genesis 1:2: "The Spirit of God hovered over the face of the waters," like a bird watching over its nest, and then God "speaks" and the process continues. The Psalmist conjoins these ideas of spirit and word when he describes the creation in these terms — "By the word of the Lord were the heavens made, and all their hosts by the breath (spirit) of His mouth" (Psalm 33.6). So when God spoke, the Spirit acted. God is seen to be at work through His divine breath (Ruach Kodesh, in Hebrew the word *ruach* means *spirit*, breath or wind, *kodesh* means holy).

The Holy Spirit Empowers God's Servants for Service: In Numbers 11:25-26, the helpers appointed by Moses to assist him in his work are to receive the same "spirit" as he enjoys — "The Lord took some of the spirit that was upon him, and put it upon the seventy elders, and when the spirit rested upon them they prophesied." The activity of the Spirit is revealed in prophesying, but in this case as a sign of permanent endowment with the Spirit of wisdom. In fact we later learn that God's whole deliverance of His people is by His Spirit, the angel of His presence (Isaiah 63:7-14).

It should be noted that apart from in creation God's Spirit only works through and enters into people. He is never said to enter or fill a place, even the Tabernacle. His presence is known by His activity through people. When Moses is finally to be replaced, it is by a man "in whom is the Spirit" (Numbers 27:18), probably linking him with the seventy elders previously mentioned.

The Holy Spirit Inspires Deliverance: When Israel is in danger of being annihilated or absorbed into the surrounding nations, "the Spirit of the Lord" comes upon various leaders to enable them to deliver them from their enemies. For example, Othniel (Judges

3:9), Gideon (Judges 6:34), Jephthah (Judges 11:29), and Samson (Judges 14:6, 19; 15:14), the latter being first "stirred by the Spirit" (Judges13; 25). In all these cases, the presence of the Spirit is seen in the successful outcome of events. There is no reason to think that they experienced any special emotions that they connected with the Spirit.

The Life-giving Spirit: Ezekiel takes up the idea of this future work of the Spirit. In a vision, he sees a valley full of dry bones. Then, even though they become covered with flesh, they are still unresponsive to the prophet's message, for there is as yet no life in them (Ezekiel 37:1-10). So he is told to call on the "Spirit," likened to wind and breath (the same word in Hebrew), commanding that the Spirit breathe life into them so that they might live (v10). The result is that the lifeless corpses become a great army, ready for action. This is then likened to Israel, who are dried up spiritually, and unresponsive to God's messengers. But it is God's intention that He will "put My Spirit within you, and you will live" (v.14). Thus the dry bones will come to life by the action of the Spirit. The process we know as reincarnation.

This reviving process is explained more fully in Ezekiel 36:25-27. There the work of the Spirit is likened to the sprinkling of cleansing water. The idea of the sprinkling of water which cleanses comes from Numbers 19:17-19, where it is water made clean by use of the ashes of sacrifice. Water by itself never cleanses in the Old Testament; it is always accompanied by the Spirit of God.

"Then will I sprinkle clean (cleansed) water upon you, and you will be clean. From all your filthiness, I will cleanse you. A new heart I will give you, and a new Spirit I will put within you. I will take away the stony heart from your flesh, and I will give you a fleshy heart. I will put My Spirit within you, and cause you to walk in my statutes, and you will keep my judgments" (Ezekiel 25-27). They are thus to be cleansed by sacrifice, and given life by the Spirit. He will "pour out His Spirit" upon them (Ezekiel 39:29). This is all linked with fruitfulness and blessing, for the land will become "like the garden of Eden" (Ezekiel 36:35). "I will call for the corn and increase it, I will multiply the fruit of the tree and the increase of the field" (Ezekiel 36:29-30). From now on, there will be no more famine. Once again rain and Spirit are linked, even though Ezekiel the priest has used a priestly metaphor in vv. 25-27 rather than Isaiah's picture of abundant rain. It's a fact that the land of Israel was in a drought for 1,800 years and literally came back to life when Ezekiel's prophesy was fulfilled when the Jews returned to their homeland in May 14, 1948. Israel became a land of milk and honey, abundant with natural resources, vegetation, and industry.

The Prophecy of Joel: An added dimension to the work of the Spirit is brought out by Joel. "I will send you corn and wine and oil, and you will be satisfied with it. I will cause to come down for you the early rain and the later rain, and the floors will be full of wheat, I will restore to you the years that the locust has eaten, and you will eat in plenty and be satisfied, and it will come about afterwards that *I will pour out My Spirit on all flesh*, your sons and your daughters will prophesy, your old men will dream dreams and

CHAPTER NINETEEN: Who Is The Holy Spirit?

your young men will see visions, and also on the servants and maidservants *I will pour out My Spirit in those days*" (Joel 2:18-29).

Notice once again the close connection between the fruitful rain and the coming of the Spirit. Sadly the fact that the outpouring will be on "all flesh" does not indicate that every single person in the world will benefit. Men who will not respond to God cannot be so blessed. The point being made is that every type of person will be included — master and servant, bondman and free. None will be left out. It will not be restricted to the important and mighty, for it will be available to every class of person. Even the humblest will be able to partake, and become partakers of God's word.

So the prophets consistently point forward to a day when the Spirit will be active as never before, like abundant rain producing a harvest in the hearts of men, resulting in obedient hearts and changed lives, which has been happening since the day of Pentecost, when the Holy Spirit descended upon all believers and continues to do its miraculous work to this day.

The Holy Spirit in the Psalms: In Psalm 51, the psalmist can pray expectantly that "a new spirit" will be put within him, a "willing spirit" obedient to God (vv. 10 - 12). Such an idea is related to God's Spirit as we have seen in Ezekiel 18:31-32; 36:26 and 37:14. The righteous can thus enjoy the blessing of the Spirit in any age. He goes on to pray, "Do not take Your Holy Spirit from me" (v.11). What this means is clear from the context. It is put in parallel with "do not cast me from Your presence," which suggests that what the psalmist is afraid of is that he deserves, because of his sin, to lose the sense of the presence of God. To become as one who has been cast off. This is what his disobedience deserves, but in his repentance, he is confident that God will not do it to him and will restore him in His faithfulness.

Psalm 139:7 confirms this. "Where can I go from Your Spirit? Where can I flee from Your presence?" The answer is nowhere, for everything is under God's control (v.13). He therefore prays that God will show him any wrongdoing in his life, so that he may be led in the way everlasting (vv.23-24). Being secure in God does not make him spiritually careless.

Lastly in Psalm 143:10, the psalmist, overwhelmed by a sense of his own weakness, prays "teach me to do your will, for you are my God. Your Spirit is good. Lead me into the land of uprightness." Here we have the Spirit at work within him to lead him in the right way.

These Psalms are important because they stress the quiet work of the Spirit going on in men's hearts through all ages. They are aware that, in their weakness, they are being kept in the right way by the Spirit, and that their hope is in His working. God never deserted those who trusted in Him, or left them to struggle on their own. What, however, was lacking was the wider work of the Spirit, the "pouring out of the Spirit" which would turn the few into the many.

> "For prophecy never had its origin in the human will, but prophets, though human, spoke from God as they were carried along by the Holy Spirit."
>
> (2 Peter 1:21)

THE HOLY SPIRIT IS THE SPIRIT OF CHRIST

> "When the Counselor comes, whom I will send to you from the Father, the Spirit of truth who goes out from the Father, he will testify about me."
>
> (John 15:26)

Jesus promised to his disciples right before he ascended, that the Counselor, also known as the Comforter, would come and be with them, but only after he left them. Many can say the Holy Spirit was there all along, and to a certain extent, it was, but not to the extent that the Holy Spirit was after Christ ascended because of His promise to send the Holy Spirit in his place (John 16:7-8, 20:22), also Acts 1:5,8; Peter's own words in Acts 2:33; 1 Peter 1:12). This was His Spirit, the Mind of Christ, and the Spirit of Christ. It is through the workings of the Holy Spirit to this day, that the miracles of healing, the deliverance from the demonic, and the resurrection of the dead takes place. It is also through the fulfillment of the Holy Spirit that the word of God can turn into Rhema, which revelation of the Word. It is through the Holy Spirit that the gifts of God and Christ can be experienced.

When people in New Age circles speak of "Christ Consciousness," what they are referring to is having the mind of Christ. But it is only through the Holy Spirit indwelling that one can truly embody the "mind of Christ." Here's another discernment, in New Age circles, the dependency on "spirit guides" is prevalent. Of course, if you've been reading my book, you now know that all of these "spirit guides" are demonic intelligences masquerading around as departed loved ones, ETs, and ascended masters. All this is to seduce humans into *their* rebellion against the Creator into counterfeiting following the Holy Spirit, which is God's will for humankind. But the Holy Spirit does not push; it must be invited through one's confession of faith in Christ.

Others have also said that following the kundalini energy is the counterfeit Holy Spirit, which again is at war with Christ, because of its distortions and idolatry. The kundalini energy is connected to a serpent spirit, often seen as a python, identified by those in deliverance ministries as a python spirit. This is because those who believe in the kundalini energy believe that one end is psychic energy and the other end is sexual energy, which can be controlled. Python spirits show up when people are involved in divination, through psychic work. Psychic energy is the counterfeit of the Holy Spirit manifestation gift known as the "Word of Knowledge," which comes from the Holy Spirit, the Spirit of Truth. The counterfeit, however, comes from the spirit of lie, which is why it often misleads, seduces, and hypnotizes its followers, creating confusion and blocking the truth. In fact all the nine manifestations of the Holy Spirit are counterfeited by occult gifts.

The difference is the occult is ruled by demon spirits, and the Holy Spirit is the spirit of Truth, which comes from Christ.

Jesus is the ultimate example of being "Spirit-filled." The Holy Spirit shows up in force in every part of Jesus's mission as Messiah: Conception and Birth (Luke 1:35); Baptism (Mark 1:9-11; Luke 3:21-22; John 1:31-34); the reading at his home synagogue (Luke 4:14-21, Isaiah 61:1-2); Ministry work (Matthew 12:18); Miracles (Matthew 12:22,28); Preaching (Luke 4:18-21); Temptations (Mark 1:12, Luke 4:1-13).

The Holy Spirit does his work by making Christ present among us, and Christ can do his work on Earth only being present in his Holy Spirit.

The Trinitarian baptismal formula found in Scripture (Matthew 28:19: "in the name of the Father and of the Son, and of the Holy Spirit") dates back to the church's earliest days.

THE HOLY SPIRIT IS A LIVING PERSON

The Holy Spirit is the Spirit of Grace. Grace is something no human can earn; it is a free gift given by God Himself. Grace is about forgiveness, healing, understanding. The Holy Spirit is not a mere symbol of anything. No mere symbol is able to: communicate (speak) (Acts 13:2), intercede (step in on behalf of someone) (Romans 8:26), testify (John 15:26), guide (John 16:13), command (Acts 16:6,7), appoint (Acts 20:28), lead (Romans 8:14), reveal to someone's mind and conscience how wrong he/she was (John 16:8), seal God's promise in believers' hearts (Ephesians 1:13-14), shape the life of each person and community to Christ's (Romans 8:1-17). In the Bible, the Holy Spirit has intellect, passions, and will, and can be grieved. In short, the Spirit has a personality.

The Holy Spirit reveals the Logos (the Word of God) through Rhema (Revelation) through Scripture. Without the Spirit's work, the Bible is just dead ink and paper. Without the Spirit's wisdom and insight, science is but trickery, psychology is just self-obsession, sociology is just the workings of the rabble, language becomes merely a tool for manipulation, and religion really becomes the opiate of the masses that Marx thought it was.

WHERE THE SPIRIT IS, THERE IS FREEDOM

We are all destined, designed, and created to be free. This is the spiritual battle every earth human finds itself in. Many forge chains for ourselves and each other, corrupting our freedom till it isn't freedom anymore. Only someone who isn't bound by the mess can free us from it. That's where Christ comes in. And after Christ arose, it's where the Holy Spirit comes in. The Holy Spirit is sent from Christ to humanity, breathed on and to us by Jesus Christ Himself. The Holy Spirit enables us to be able to take part in God's work in the world.

The Holy Spirit is like a good spiritual medical team for those who have especially deep wounds. In the case of those who have been raped, those who suffer from the deeds of despotic governments, those who daily have to face their society's racisms, those on the losing end of an economic system or a political power struggle, those who are slaves to alcohol or drugs, or slaves to fear. In Jesus's own ministry, inner healing was linked to physical healing as a work of the Holy Spirit. God is concerned about the whole person, not just the inner self. We are all fractured beings; the Holy Spirit is working to restore us and make us complete.

The Holy Spirit makes God's work in the world, personal. The Truth becomes mine to spread. The Kingdom becomes my vision for living. God's hope for all becomes my hope for all. God's sorrow over peoples' situations and deeds becomes mine, too. If the Holy Spirit has me, God is not distant but up-close, very real, and personal. This new freedom isn't something we "have" or possess; it's something that has us just as the Holy Spirit does. The human spirit soars because of the Holy Spirit; otherwise, it is still bound to the ground.

Freedom becomes everything. Many will say, "Love is everything," but in my opinion freedom trumps that because there are so many broken-hearted people in the world who cannot give or receive love. They need liberation, which comes from the power of Christ and His Holy Spirit to free them to be able to give and receive love again.

Many people refer to the force of God as "Spirit," so much so that there is such a lack of discernment between God's Holy Spirit, and the "spirit" that many claim to channel. They will often refer to their channelings as "spirit" told me this, or "spirit" told me that. This is not the Holy Spirit because these people are channeling deceptive spirits, and/or deceased spirits, and those who think they are tapping into the spirit realm without the guidance of the Holy Spirit are, in fact, channeling demonic spirits, i.e., fallen angels masquerading as light beings, ascended masters, ETs, or demons pretending to be deceased loved ones.

This is not the work of the Holy Spirit, and there needs to be an important distinction through the "spirit of discernment" between God's spirit and the spirit of demons which can so cleverly trick humans into thinking they are channeling spirits of light. Discernment is a gift that comes *only* from the Holy Spirit. Think about it, if a person is in a darkened room, how can he or she see without the light? This is what the Holy Spirit provides the discerning power of light to reveal the darkness. Darkness cannot reveal nor illuminate darkness, only light can.

CHAPTER NINETEEN: Who Is The Holy Spirit?

THE ONE AND ONLY UNFORGIVEABLE SIN

After all the talk about how boundless and all-covering God's forgiving grace is, the Bible throws us a curveball. Matthew 12:31-32 speaks of one sin that will not be forgiven — the sin of blaspheming the Holy Spirit. Yet, the verse in Matthew does not say that God cannot forgive it; it says that God will *not* forgive it. One can sense that there's more to it than just the bare fact. Let's start by asking ourselves how it could possibly be that this sin and only this sin will not be forgiven. "Whoever is not with me is against me, and whoever does not gather with me scatters. And so I tell you, people will be forgiven every sin and blasphemy. But the blasphemy against the Spirit will not be forgiven. Anyone who speaks a word against the Son of Man will be forgiven, but anyone who speaks against the Holy Spirit will not be forgiven, either in this age or in the age to come." (Matthew 12:31-32)

Most people believe that the unforgiveable sin of blaspheming the Holy Spirit is to claim that the miracles that happen through the Spirit were done by demons or the devil. This is the ultimate insult to the Spirit of Grace. The Pharisees accused this of Jesus, when he cast out a "deaf and dumb" spirit from a boy (Mark 9:17-26; Luke 11:14). The Jews at that time did exorcisms by ordering the demon to name itself and then calling it by its name and commanding it to leave the person. However, a "dumb" spirit would never tell anyone its name, but Jesus knew and was able to cast it out. So the Pharisees accused Jesus of using Beelzebub's (the Prince of the Demons) help to cast out the evil spirit. Jesus responded, "And if I cast out demons by Beelzebub, by whom do your sons cast them out? Therefore they shall be your judges. But if it is by the Spirit of God that I cast out demons, then the kingdom of God has come upon you" (Matthew 12:27-28).

Jesus said, "Every kingdom divided against itself is laid waste, and no city or house divided against itself will stand; and if Satan casts out Satan, he is divided against himself; how then will his kingdom stand?" (Matthew 12:25-26). Jesus's first argument for why he is not casting out demons by Satan is that it would pit Satan's own forces against himself and tear apart his kingdom of darkness. Satan and his demons are psychologically incapable of voluntarily letting go of a person they have possessed. Only God's grace will deliver such a person. If Satan were to order a demon to strategically remove from a person, his kingdom would be torn apart by civil war. Jesus's critics are therefore ignorant of the psychology of demons.

After Jesus left the earth, he poured out His Holy Spirit in bigger ways than before upon us. So he said he would forgive those who blaspheme the son of man (Him), but not those who blaspheme the Holy Spirit. The Holy Spirit is a very important part of the Divinity of God.

FRUITS OF THE HOLY SPIRIT

Everything has a spirit that guides them. The question on the discerning mind always needs to be "Which spirit?" "By their fruits you shall know them" has been a major theme of this book. Whether it's in the realm of ETs, Aliens, Gods, Angels, or human beings, the fruits of the spirit that they are actually led by, will always manifest in the end, even in the counterfeits. One only needs to know what to look for. See my chapter on The Office of Satan for the counterfeit fruits.

> "There are nine fruits that reveals the presence of the Holy Spirit in our lives: 'But the fruit of the Spirit is love, joy, peace, patience, kindness, goodness, faithfulness, gentleness, self-control; against such things there is no law.'"
>
> (Galatians 5:22-23)

THE SPIRITUAL GIFTS OF THE HOLY SPIRIT

The manifestations of the presence of the indwelling Holy Spirit has been called "gifts" of the Spirit. But truly, those who are filled with the anointing of the Holy Spirit, i.e., the spirit and the mind of Christ can manifest all the gifts at different times, which has been known to happen to those who are truly led by the Spirit. Here is an important discernment, spiritually speaking, many New Agers often refer to their messages coming from "Spirit," but it is not the Holy Spirit, but the spirit that comes from the god of this world, which comes from the Office of Satan, which are actually demon spirits i.e., familiar spirits, divination spirits, and a variety of attachments, which are counterfeiting the manifestations of the Holy Spirit.

> "Now about the gifts of the Spirit, brothers and sisters, I do not want you to be uninformed. You know that when you were pagans, somehow or other you were influenced and led astray to mute idols. Therefore I want you to know that no one who is speaking by the Spirit of God says, "Jesus be cursed," and no one can say, "Jesus is Lord," except by the Holy Spirit. There are different kinds of gifts, but the same Spirit distributes them. There are different kinds of service, but the same Lord. There are different kinds of working, but in all of them and in everyone it is the same God at work. Now to each one the manifestation of the Spirit is given for the common good. To one there is given through the Spirit a message of wisdom, to another a message of knowledge by means of the same Spirit, to another faith by the same Spirit, to another gifts of healing by that one Spirit, to another miraculous powers, to another prophecy, to another distinguishing between spirits, to another speaking in different kinds of tongues, and to still another the interpretation of tongues. All these are the work of one and the same Spirit, and he distributes them to each one, just as he determines."
>
> (1 Corinthians 12:1-11)

CHAPTER NINETEEN: Who Is The Holy Spirit?

DISCERNING TONGUES: THE GIFT OF LANGUAGES

The gift of speaking in different tongues usually accompanies another person with the matching gift of interpreting those foreign tongues. Discernment says that, if a language is indiscernible to men on earth, it is not a language that comes from God for the purpose and edification of others on Earth; this is the work of the counterfeit spirit, not the Holy Spirit.

If a Christian is speaking in tongues that comes from a counterfeit spirit, how can that be discerned? Well, for one, the spirit cannot say that Jesus Christ came in the flesh, nor does it practice repentance before God and man.

> "Do not believe every spirit, but test the spirits to see whether they are from God, because many false prophets have gone out into the world. This is how you can recognize the Spirit of God: Every spirit that acknowledges that Jesus Christ (Yahushua HaMashiach) has come in the flesh is from God.
>
> (1 John 4:1, 2)

One may wonder, how can a Christian be filled with a counterfeit gift? The answer is demonization due to unconfessed and unrepentant sin which gives spiritual legal ground that opens the door for a demon. Many Christians desire the gift more than they desire to be close to God, the Giver of the gift, so they put more importance on receiving the gift, which opens the door to the god of this world, who masquerades as light, who will do anything to cause a Christian to stumble in their relationship to the Lord. Often this comes from ignorance, arrogance, and pride, so that they can feel "part of the group" who speaks in tongues, not knowing that these gifts can be mimicked by lying counterfeit spirits.

Another interesting manifestation of the Holy Spirit anointing and dwelling within believers, is the ability to speak other languages that are discernable on earth. One person who has never learned a language, all of sudden start speaking and understanding it. This is the work of God. The true gift of tongues is the ability to be multi-lingual in earth languages to further the Kingdom of God on earth.

The Holy Spirit wants to dwell within us; we are the temple of God, but when the temple has become defiled, we need the Holy Spirit and the Blood of Jesus to cleanse the temple of all sin, both ancestral and generational through confession, repentance, and forgiveness. When all unclean spirits have been cast out, then the anointing of the Holy Spirit can dwell, leaving no opening for the counterfeit. We are to desire to be close to God first, then the gifts of His Spirit (manifestations) comes, not the other way around.

Just as in politics, there are people who are known as RHINOs (Republicans in Name Only), but who are really Democrats undercover, who vote in Republican primaries. And so it goes in spiritual circles, there are people who are CHINOs,

(Christians in Name Only). These people are led by counterfeit spirits to infiltrate the church.

It's time to discern and call out the watered-down, so-called gospel that offers everything and calls for nothing. It's nothing but Satan's counterfeit, inspired and motivated by his evil *religious spirit*. The main recurring message through both the Old and New Testaments is, "Repent, for the Kingdom of God is near."

We need to discern between preachers and churches who preach "cheap grace," which does not call for repentance. For it is repentance that brings God's favor and grace into our lives. It's also God's grace that can lead a person to repentance. It's time to get back to the cross of grace and back to the truth. Otherwise, as America collapses in a heap of amoral ruin, the soft preachers and clown preachers (for entertainment only) of America will be largely to blame.

Only true, heartfelt repentance can bring back God's favor on a nation full of every kind of church under the sun, who have been usurped and sabotaged by the counterfeit *religious spirit,* and restore God's protection upon America again. For the most part, American churches have traded in supernatural power for political power, which ends up leaving them with neither.

Dr. Karl I. Payne[1] writes in his groundbreaking book, *Spiritual Warfare, Christians, Demonization and Deliverance,* in his chapter "Demonic Subtleties of Evil," which is about a woman who so desired the gift of speaking in tongues, but reported that each time she used it, she felt the presence of evil and felt dirty. After testing the spirit of the tongue, they both determined it was a counterfeit because she desired the gift so badly, instead of wanting to please God. Her husband, however, also had a counterfeit, but it was hidden beneath a religious spirit, wanting to be seen as godly. He focused his attention on this gift of the Holy Spirit and not on the completed word of Christ.

> "This know also, that in the last days perilous times shall come. For men shall be lovers of their own selves, covetous, boasters, proud, blasphemers, disobedient to parents, unthankful, unholy, Without natural affection, trucebreakers, false accusers, incontinent, fierce, despisers of those that are good, Traitors, heady, high-minded, lovers of pleasures more than lovers of God; **Having a form of godliness, but denying the power thereof:** from such turn away."
>
> (2 Timothy 3:1-5 - KJV)

What can we do to make sure we have the real thing? What can we do to make sure it's really the Holy Spirit? Jesus said, "I have not come to call the righteous, but sinners to repentance." (Luke 5:32). "If we confess our sins, he is faithful and just to forgive us our sins, and to cleanse us from all unrighteousness." (1 John 1:9) We are called to repent; then we are cleansed and purified. Then we can be assured that we are delivered from all counterfeit spirits and are vessels for the Holy Spirit. There are so many Christians who come to Christ, accept Him as their Savior, and believe all their sins are

CHAPTER NINETEEN: Who Is The Holy Spirit?

forgiven automatically. This is sadly not the case. The scripture says, "Work out your salvation with fear and trembling" (Philippians 2:12). We are to purify and seek holiness, not religiosity. This is precisely why Jesus promised to separate the sheep from the goats on the Final Day of Judgment in Matthew 25.

THE SHEEP AND THE GOATS

"When the Son of Man comes in his glory, and all the angels with him, he will sit on his throne in heavenly glory. All the nations will be gathered before him, and he will separate the people one from another as a shepherd separates the sheep from the goats. He will put the sheep on his right and the goats on his left. "Then the King will say to those on his right, 'Come, you who are blessed by my Father; take your inheritance, the kingdom prepared for you since the creation of the world. For I was hungry and you gave me something to eat, I was thirsty and you gave me something to drink, I was a stranger and you invited me in, I needed clothes and you clothed me, I was sick and you looked after me, I was in prison and you came to visit me.' "Then the righteous will answer him, 'Lord, when did we see you hungry and feed you, or thirsty and give you something to drink? When did we see you a stranger and invite you in, or needing clothes and clothe you? When did we see you sick or in prison and go to visit you?' "The King will reply, 'I tell you the truth, whatever you did for one of the least of these brothers of mine, you did for me.'

"Then he will say to those on his left, 'Depart from me, you who are cursed, into the eternal fire prepared for the devil and his angels. For I was hungry and you gave me nothing to eat, I was thirsty and you gave me nothing to drink, I was a stranger and you did not invite me in, I needed clothes and you did not clothe me, I was sick and in prison and you did not look after me.' "They also will answer, 'Lord, when did we see you hungry or thirsty or a stranger or needing clothes or sick or in prison, and did not help you?' "He will reply, 'I tell you the truth, whatever you did not do for one of the least of these, you did not do for me.' "Then they will go away to eternal punishment, but the righteous to eternal life."

(Matthew 25:31-46)

This is why the scripture says, "The Fear of the Lord is the beginning of Wisdom" (Proverbs 111:10). The separation of the sheep and goats should send chills down every so-called Christian's life. I believe the goats are a reference to the many Christians in name only (CHINOs). So many create all kinds of cults and churches in Christ's name, yet they are operating with a spirit of control, ego, greed, and with that comes the counterfeit spirits and the *religious spirits*, which do not come from the Holy Spirit, but from the god of this world, who is Lucifer/Satan.

Many churches have been hijacked and sabotaged because the people are filled with pride, self-aggrandizement, and are not coming to the Lord with the humility that is necessary to have complete forgiveness of sin and deliverance, which is a process done little by little, similar to peeling an onion; it is not automatic.

> "**Little by little** I will drive them out before you, until you have increased enough to take possession of the land."
>
> (Exodus 23:30)

> "The LORD your God will drive out those nations before you, **little by little**. You will not be allowed to eliminate them all at once, <u>or the wild animals will multiply around you</u>."
>
> (Deuteronomy 7:22)

There is so much wisdom in these scriptures, which relate directly to the deliverance process, and it can be a process. Demonic oppression and possession actually imprint the body with the demonic spirits, in the way of influencing a person toward habit patterns, thought forms, and ways of feeling and doing. Once those unclean spirits leave a body, then the person needs to be filled with the opposite spirit, which is the Holy Spirit. However, psychologically speaking, the individual needs healing of the mind and emotions to learn to walk with their new heart and mind, that Christ impresses into the born-again soul.

Yes, Jesus Christ died for the sins of the world; yes, Jesus Christ took on the curses of God upon Himself, so that through Him we may be freed from the curse of the law (Galatians 3:13), but it is definitely not automatic, and requires repentance and confession, not only of our own sins, but the sins of our ancestors, which are passed down from generation to generation. Then true deliverance is experienced, as God is faithful and just to forgive, wipe out all memory of sins, and deliver us from the demonic and the counterfeit spirits who hold souls (yes, even so-called Christians) in all kinds of bondages through generational curses and very cunning and subtle lies, and all that is required of us, is faith in Him.

The "Children's Bread" was the words of Christ for God's *deliverance* of His children. Who are his children? Those who believe and put their faith in his Son, who is the Messiah-King of God's Kingdom.

This is the story of the faith of a Syropheonician Woman, who was a Gentile, and how her faith caused Jesus to deliver her daughter of a demon. The *children's bread* is deliverance for those who believe.

> "And from thence he arose, and went away into the borders of Tyre and Sidon. And he entered into a house, and would have no man know it; and he could not be hid. But straightway a woman, whose little daughter had an unclean spirit, having heard of him, came and fell down at his feet. Now the woman was a Greek, a Syrophoenician by race. And she besought him that he would cast forth the demon out of her daughter.

And he said unto her, "Let the children first be filled: for it is not right to take the *children's bread* and cast it to the dogs." But she answered and saith unto him, "Yea, Lord; even the dogs under the table eat of the *children's crumbs*." And he said unto her, "For this saying go thy way; the demon is gone out of thy daughter. And she went away unto her house, and found the child laid upon the bed, and the demon gone out."

(Mark 7:24-30; Matthew 15:21-28, ASV)

NOTES:

1. Dr. Karl Payne, *Spiritual Warfare, Christians, Demonization and Deliverance,* WND Books, Washington, D.C., 2011

CHAPTER TWENTY

THE GOD OF THIS WORLD

> "To admire Satan is to give one's vote
> not only for a world of misery,
> But also for a world of lies and propaganda,
> Of wishful thinking, of incessant autobiography."
> ~ C.S. Lewis, Preface to *Paradise Lost*

LUCIFER, FALLEN ANGEL OF ENLIGHTENMENT

The Bible tells us that the god of this world is Lucifer/Satan. We call him Lucifer because this was the name the Latins gave him which first showed up on the Latin Vulgate Bible approximately four hundred years after Christ. However, the original name given to him in Hebrew was "Heylel," which literally means "bright star" or "shining one." The Latin word *Lucifer* is composed of two words: *lux,* or in the genitive form used *lucis* (meaning "light") and *ferre* (meaning "to bear" or "to bring") which meant "Light Bearer" because he was the chief cherub that protected God's throne in the highest heaven.

The term *Lucifer* in fourth century Latin became a name for Venus, especially as the morning star. Some say he was the top archangel, but the Bible clearly calls him a son and a "covering cherub." When he rebelled, he became known as "Satan," which in Hebrew is the word for the "enemy" or "adversary." He was still a created being, though of the highest rank, and was not destroyed, but lost his place in the high heavens and was brought down to the lowest depths of Earth and the first and second heavens, which is the sky around the planet and outer space.

> "How you are fallen from heaven, O shining star (Heylel), son of the morning! You have been thrown down to the earth, you who destroyed the nations of the world. For you said to yourself, 'I will ascend to heaven and set my throne above God's stars. I will preside on the mountain of the gods far away in the north. I will climb to the highest heavens and be like the Most High.' Instead, you will be brought down to the place of the dead, down to its lowest depths. Everyone there will stare at you and ask, 'Can this be the one who shook the earth and made the kingdoms of the world tremble? Is this the one who destroyed the world and made it into a wasteland? Is this the king who demolished the world's greatest cities and had no mercy on his prisoners?'"
>
> (Isaiah 14:12-17, NLT)

Contrary to popular belief, Lucifer/Satan is not bound to hell. One of his fallen angels which the Bible names, Abaddon in Hebrew, and Apollyon in Greek is the Fallen Angel in charge of the Abyss (Hell). He is scheduled to be released to the surface of the planet during the reign of the final Antichrist. Heylel/Lucifer was a son of God. Lucifer/Satan, also known as Sataniel, is still allowed audience before God, where he accuses the faithful, "And I heard a loud voice saying in heaven, Now is come salvation, and strength, and the kingdom of our God, and the power of his Christ: for the accuser of our brothers is cast down, which accused them before our God day and night" (Revelation 12:10). This is the future prophesy; it hasn't happened yet.

He has not been completely cast down yet, but that is his fate. He still roams above and within the earth. "One day the sons of God (Bene Elohim) came to present themselves before the Lord, and Satan also came with them. The Lord said to Satan, "Where have you come from?" Satan answered the Lord, "From roaming through the earth and going back and forth in it" (Job 1:6, 7). "On another day the sons of God, members of the heavenly court came again to present themselves before the LORD, and the Accuser, Satan, came with them." (Job 2:1)

However, Heylel/Lucifer was the most beautiful and powerful son/prince/cherub, He was demoted from his high position in the heavens and cast down to the lower heavens and to the earth. He is called the Prince of the Powers of the Air and is the chief intelligence behind the modern UFO phenomena. He happens to have authority over the first and second heavens (i.e., the aerial regions extending into space from Earth). In the following pages, I will discuss why he is so concerned with Earth and with earth humans.

Before we go any further, it's important to establish the fact that the reason why the Almighty Creator Lord allows him this position as the "accuser of the brethren" and to have limited access in the heavens is because the Almighty uses him to test earth humans. The book of Job probably contains the best accounts of this relationship with Satan as the role of "prosecutor," exposing the shadow parts of Job, which all began with fear. He was given authority by the Almighty to take everything away from Job, who was blessed with all kinds of wealth and abundance from the Lord, to see if he would curse God without it.

As the drama unfolds, Job passes that test, after having what we would call in modern terms, a "nervous breakdown" but in his ignorance challenges the Almighty, who responds to Job in a long dissertation, and reveals His Almighty power as the Creator of the Universe, the stars, and all of creation. In the end, He restores Job with more wealth, health, and family than he had before and a long life. The story, however, exposes the role of Satan in the lives of earth humans and reveals the scope of his power to curse and bring all kinds of trouble and illness upon humankind.

Each day on planet Earth, humans are tested and face all kinds of challenges. The Almighty is sorting out the wheat from the chaffe, so to speak, meaning he allows these tests to happen to see just who is faithful to the Creator God of their souls, and who is easily misled by every seemingly popular wind and wave of this temporary world. Who

CHAPTER TWENTY: The God Of This World

searches for the truth, and who settles for lies that feel good? Who is easily misled and who looks to the Lord for guidance?

The final test of humankind will be at the end of this timeline, when the earth's skies are filled with UFOs, and earth humans succumb to the false beliefs that the space brothers have arrived to save them. A man will be raised up on the earth, who will deceive the nations, and many will believe he is the long awaited Messiah of Israel, sent to save them from a failing economy and wars in the Middle East. This being will be the final antichrist who will wield supernatural power from aliens using UFO technology, and create such a mass delusion upon earth humans by counterfeiting the truth about ETs and aliens, and getting earth humans to join him in waging the final cosmic battle against the Creator God and all of his celestial army.

David Flynn wrote in his article, *Satan's Counterfeits: Judgment Day, UFOs, Angels & End Time Prophecy*: "Satan's plan involves deceiving humans into accepting aliens and UFOs, and a global religion based on the occult which will pave the way for antichrist. The main focus of this deception will be to convince humans that the Bible was wrong — that life evolved on other planets and that these 'alien space brothers' perhaps were the ones who created humans ... and the Bible was just a primitive misinterpretation of alien and UFO encounters.[1]

Look at the current fascination with the occult and divination in our popular culture, how aliens and UFOs have become mainstream, and how the recent discovery of fossils in Mars rock, and the images of the Cydonia region of Mars have caused many to speculate that humans are not the only intelligence in the universe. What is more insidious is the assertion that superior beings out there — aliens, or the White Brotherhood, or enlightening angels — are giving us the technology and spiritual wisdom to become gods. Humans have been vulnerable to that temptation since Eve bit the apple."

GOOD GOD, BAD GOD

I was moved to write this book because I wanted to create spiritual discernment in the minds of both spiritual and religious seekers. Ask yourself this question: When you call on "God," but don't really know who god is or which god you're calling to, guess who answers you? The god of this world. How many people have cried out in despair, "Oh, God, if you're real, please help me now"? Then after some time, your life begins to change, and you believe in a "force" or are convinced in the supernatural or paranormal. There seems to be a growing number of people today who believe in the paranormal, and who are fascinated with ghosts, vampires, aliens, and other nefarious creatures, to the point of having all kinds of "experiences." Yes, the paranormal is real, but do they ask who is behind it? The answer is the god of this world.

Even if you're an agnostic, who believes that nothing is known or can be known of the existence or nature of God or of anything beyond material phenomena, a person who claims neither faith nor disbelief in God, but believes in some "higher power" or "force," and you call out to "God," the god of this world answers. Atheists, who deny the existence of god completely and instead believe in secularism and science, are clearly under the influence of the god of this world. All those in between, who are not grounded in truth and discernment of which god they are talking to, will hear the voice of the god of this world, in its many disguises.

> "Satan, **who is the god of this world**, has blinded the minds of those who don't believe. They are unable to see the glorious light of the Good News of the Kingdom of God. They don't understand this message about the glory of Christ, who is the exact likeness of God."
>
> (2 Corinthians 4:4)

Spiritually speaking, earth humans can receive power from either the Almighty Creator or from the god of this world. Lucifer/Satan and all of his fallen angels and demonic hierarchy of evil spirit are masters of deception. They have the ability to empower earth humans with healing powers, psychic gifts, even supernatural strength, all unbeknownst to the unassuming and undiscerning earth human, who believes that their newfound healing and psychic powers come from God, a spirit guide, or an archangel. This is all a masquerade. Lucifer's demons have the ability to mimic by voice and by actions, better than the most seasoned actor anybody they choose. They can create the illusion that one is being spoken to by either their deceased loved one, or a supernatural being, archangel, ascended master, space brother, Mother Mary, or even Jesus Christ himself.

There are scores of stories of people in New Age circles who were touched by an angel, and then received miracle working powers to heal, to see visions, to see spirits, to become more psychic, all of whom have become rich and famous for doing so. I am not going to mention names because my purpose is not to expose individual false prophets; instead I want to expose the source from which these counterfeit powers come.

We are in a spiritual war that is designed to take us out. Lucifer/Satan and his forces do not care about misleading people. He will give them fame, wealth, and temporary honor in this world, if he can use them toward spreading his agenda of mass deception to mislead others, and, in the end, own their soul. Physical death is not the worst thing that can happen to a person, but the death of the soul is irrevocable. Living in this type of deception happens because the soul has lost its original connection with the Creator and is in rebellion toward His Divine Plan for Salvation through Christ Jesus.

Another big deception is that the United States of America was founded as a Christian nation. Many people say this, and believe it because the early settlers were indeed Christian. However, the truth of the matter is that the founding fathers who established the United States were not Christians, but Freemasons. George Washington, Thomas Jefferson, Benjamin Franklin, and others were all Freemasons, which is based on

CHAPTER TWENTY: The God Of This World

Luciferianism, i.e., the Illuminati, which are all "secret societies" based on taking oaths and vows to the god of this world.

These secret societies and Masonic Lodges and temples blend ancient occult wisdom with sacred geometry, ancient symbolism, with the way the gods of the past erected buildings, which is known as masonry. Washington D.C. is laid out according to Freemason symbolism which combines ancient Greek and Egyptian architecture. The founding fathers wanted to break away from the religion of the Church of England. America was not built on Christian principles but on the occult. The dollar bill holds all kinds of freemason symbolism, including the "all seeing eye" (the Egyptian eye of Horus/Apollo) within the capstone above the pyramid. The very words "in god we trust" is misleading to many, because it actually pays homage to Lucifer/Satan, who is the "god of this world."

The US Capitol building is adorned with all types of Freemasonry symbolism and idols in the form of pagan gods. In fact the Rotunda of the Capitol is decorated with pagan frescos which is focused on the *Apotheosis of George Washington*, which essentially turns George Washington into a god, surrounded by the *Frieze of American History,* along with Mesoamerican scenes called *Cortez and Montezuma at Mexican Temple,* which focuses on the Aztec Calendar. Also included on the ceiling of the Capitol Dome is the sun god Tonatiuh, with his tongue sticking out, who is in the center of the Sun Stone who is said to represent the god of present time, which like the Mayan calendar, is believed to end in 2012.

The Great Seal of the United States is actually a combination of pagan symbols invoking the ancient pagan sun gods, Apollo and Osiris, who all served and contracted with Lucifer/Satan. In fact the Bible identifies the final Antichrist with a number 666. Numbers are very important to the Illuminati and Freemasons, who repeatedly pattern certain numbers after ancient gods.

It is no coincidence that the Washington Monument, which is a replica of the Egyptian Obelisk, is exactly 6,666 inches tall. The obelisk represents Osiris' missing genital. According to Egyptian mythology, when Osiris was murdered and cut up into fourteen pieces and thrown into the Nile by his evil brother Seth, Isis recovered thirteen pieces of his body parts, but was missing his genital.

The myth says, she "magically" impregnated herself and bore Horus, which was actually a form of genetic engineering using Osiris's DNA. Since then the obelisk was erected in Egypt as a place of worship. Osiris is believed to be the resurrected god, and Osiris, Isis and Horus are the pagan gods to counterfeit the Father (Yahuah), Son (Jesus) and the Holy Spirit. Freemason and Illuminists believe that some type of combination of these ancient sun gods, Osiris and Apollo, will return to earth, and/or be resurrected to rule again.

This is why the Great Seal of the United States is symbolized by a two-headed eagle, each facing in opposite directions, which according to the Freemason belief is the blending of Apollo and Jesus Christ. The final Antichrist will be Lucifer/Satan's final curtain call to counterfeit God. He will deceive many into believing he is the Messiah, the long-awaited Christ King who has come to save the nations of the world from global collapse and bring peace on Earth. However, subtle the lie is, it is still a lie. Jesus Christ is not coming back as a blend of pagan gods, but as Himself, with all the glory of Heaven. In fact the pagan gods have historically been at war with the Almighty Creator and His Christ. This cosmic drama culminates as the final cosmic battle of Armageddon.

Suffice it to say, that the entire realm of the occult, is actually Lucifer/Satan's counterfeit of every single aspect and gift from the Creator and His Holy Spirit. Because we are living in the last days of this age and getting closer to the end of this timeline, his forces are amping up his spiritual arsenal against earth humans in trying to steal as many souls away from the Almighty as possible through the seduction of the occult, the paranormal, counterfeit New Age beliefs, and misinformation about aliens and UFOs, by creating a movement in the wrong direction, away from the Divine Plan of Salvation from Lucifer/Satan and his host of pseudo-gods.

He is actually using a combination of New Agers, occultists, and Illuminists to invoke the ancient pagan gods and open up ancient portals for their return so that they can team up with him against his final war with the Almighty Lord. In doing so, his agenda as the god of this world is to seduce and lie to his undiscerning followers and all those who are disenchanted by and through the church, including all unbelievers, to follow a New Age religion, a type of universalism, in preparation for his New World Order (*novus ordo seclorem* — as written on the dollar bill)where he will embody as the leader, the final Antichrist. His final scheme is to get the armies of the earth to team up with him against his final war with the Lord and his celestial army, by lying to the world that when the Rapture happens, that billions of people were abducted by aliens from outer space, by creating the fear of a threat from ETs and aliens, thus completing his agenda in turning as many earth humans against the Creator as possible, and sadly taking them all down with him.

The god of this world, Lucifer/Satan has a very long history with planet earth, and with his need for control and his "god complex." He will come in any form you think or believe he is. He will play on your mind, which to him is the ultimate spiritual battlefield, to either confuse your thinking about who god is, or create doubt in your mind about the nature of god, or masquerade as any ancient god or deity that appeals to you, to fit your mind's idea of god. Anything to misguide you from the truth of who the true God is, and anything to deter you off the path of having a personal intimate relationship with the Creator of your soul.

Lucifer/Satan may be the god of this world, but he is not the creator of your soul. He can send you spirits in the form of "spirit guides" that make you think you are speaking with heaven's angels, ascended masters, space brothers, and ancient gods and goddesses. All of which is a huge lie. His deception is cunning and subtle. Unlike the Almighty Creator God, he is not omnipresent, which means he cannot be in all places at the same time, as the Almighty can through his Holy Spirit. Lucifer/Satan is the original

CHAPTER TWENTY: The God Of This World

counterfeiter of the Almighty, so instead he has minions of demons, fallen ET angels, and a host of evil spirits permeate the world for him. He is not omnipotent, which is why he and his hierarchy all answer to the Lord of Hosts in Heaven and to his Christ.

Even in the Bible, the voice of Satan is mistaken as the voice of God, which has gotten lost in the translations. Consistently throughout scripture, it specifically will identify the Lord Almighty in Hebrew as YHVH, Yahuah, when the Lord Yahuah spoke, the scriptures would record it as YHVH in Hebrew letters, which many Jews would read as HaShem, which means "the name," or they would call "the Lord." Even Yahshua makes multiple appearances in the Old Testament. The Hebrew word for "Lord" is Adonai, which is also written throughout the scriptures when the Lord would speak. Another consistency would be when the Lord would send an angel to speak on His behalf, the scriptures would clearly say, "an angel of the Lord" spoke or "the commander of the Lord's Host (one of his celestial warriors)." These words are specific in the Hebrew language. That's how you know who is speaking. However, there are two stories that stand out that are translated as "God" or "Lord," but the original Hebrew does not concur.

With respect the Abraham's test of faith, this was not the voice of the Lord Yahuah. In fact, His name is not even mentioned in the story. The word used is Elohai, which means "my god" and Elohim, which is plural for the sons of God. Elohim is the word used in Genesis 1:26 when it says: "Let us make man in our image, according to our likeness." The entire participle is plural. So in the story, when Abraham was told to sacrifice his son Isaac, there is more than one voice speaking with Abraham. First the Elohim, or Elohai, then after Abraham proves himself worthy and gets his son for sacrifice, it says, an angel of the Lord cried out from Heaven to him to tell him not to harm the boy. "But the angel of the Lord called out to him from heaven, "Abraham! Abraham!" "Here I am," he replied. "Do not lay a hand on the boy," he said. "Do not do anything to him. Now I know that you fear God, because you have not withheld from me your son, your only son" (Genesis 22:17-18).

Nowhere in that entire story does the name of the Lord Yahuah (YHVH) appear. So what we need to ask is, who is Elohai? And who are these Elohim? Another problem I have with this story is that the Lord Yahuah made it clear that he does not like human sacrifice. In fact it was forbidden in the Torah (the Five Books of Moses). "Do not permit any of your children to be offered as a sacrifice to Molech, for you must not bring shame on the name of your God. I am the LORD." (Leviticus 18:21)

Molech was a Nephilim Minotaur sent from Baal/Satan. The word for the Lord here is Yahuah. Why would the Lord Yahuah test Abraham and tell him to sacrifice his son when he was clearly against sacrificing children? In my opinion, the voice Abraham heard was not the Lord Almighty, but one of the many disguises of Satan, and in the end, it was "an Angel of the Lord" that saved him. Yahuah was not involved in that story, in spite of the fact that the English translation makes you think it is God's voice. Yes, it is the voice of a "god," but not the voice of the Lord God Almighty.

Another incident where the voice of the Lord is mistaken for the voice of the god of this world is in the controversial story in the New Testament when Peter fell asleep from hunger and had a vision while lucid dreaming. It specifically says, "a voice spoke to him," but it does not say who the voice belonged to. Of course, the ancients called every voice they heard out of heaven, Lord. They consistently bowed down to angels and called them Lord. This is like calling someone "Sir." They were not "The Lord" though.

> "About noon the following day as they were on their journey and approaching the city, Peter went up on the roof to pray. He became hungry and wanted something to eat, and while the meal was being prepared, <u>he fell into a trance</u>. He saw heaven opened and something like a large sheet being let down to earth by its four corners. It contained all kinds of four-footed animals, as well as reptiles of the earth and birds of the air. <u>Then a voice told him</u>, "Get up, Peter. Kill and eat." "Surely not, Lord!" Peter replied. "I have never eaten anything impure or unclean." <u>The voice spoke to him a second time</u>, "Do not call anything impure that God has made clean." This happened three times, and immediately the sheet was taken back to heaven."
>
> (Acts 10:9-16)

Many Christians take this dream as permission to eat anything they want. This scripture is often brought up when discussing eating pork, which the Lord Yahuah clearly forbids in the Old Testament. But then the very same Christians will argue other points in the Bible and use the scripture: "I AM the Lord, and I change not." "I AM the same, yesterday, today and forever." "Heaven and Earth will pass away, but my words will never pass away."

How can this be when there are three laws both in Leviticus, Deuteronomy, and Isaiah that clearly forbids the eating of pig flesh, and a host of other animals deemed unclean and unfit for human consumption, all of which Peter saw in his vision? Let me add here an aside point that I find interesting, that modern science is catching up with ancient laws of diet. We now know that pork causes cancer. It is the first meat cancer patients are ordered to avoid during cancer therapy because it's proven to exacerbate cancer.

Could God's dietary laws be given for good sound scientific reasons? O.K. with that said, then why would the Lord Yahuah go back on his own word? The answer is, He wouldn't and He didn't. Peter was hungry. His blood sugar was low, so he fell into a light trance-like sleep state. "A voice" spoke to him while he was napping. It clearly doesn't say what voice or "whose" voice. But the voice was adamant in "tempting" Peter during his time of hunger to kill and eat unclean animals, which he never ate because he followed the Lord's laws of Kashrut (Purity), like all the Jews did. It is clear that the tempter is Satan, the god of this world, who will do anything he can to get God's people to break God's laws.

CHAPTER TWENTY: The God Of This World

THE DEVIL'S IN THE DETAILS

What many people do not realize is that spiritually speaking, there is something called "legal ground" when it comes to who controls which human on Earth. In my next book, I am going into more detail on this, with respect to healing and deliverance issues. But for now, suffice it to say, that the god of this world holds souls on earth in all kinds of "legal bondage." How is this so you might ask? And why is it legal? Well, remember the ancient adage: "As above, so below." As we have all kinds of legal loopholes and laws on earth, so it is in heaven. In fact, it started in the heavens and was then grounded on earth. There are the Almighty Creator God's laws, and there are Lucifer/Satan's laws. Because he was given access to the lower heavens, and to earth and what the Bible calls the "stones of fire" which are the planets in our solar system, which I'll discuss in more detail shortly, his dominion and kingdom is limited. He operates within certain laws, and as the scientific microcosm/macrocosm model goes, he creates laws within laws, within his own world, that includes planet Earth.

Because earth humans are given freewill, he cannot force anyone to accept him or worship him, but he can "influence" earth humans and creatures with all kinds of seductions and hypnosis. When an earth human turns away from the Creator of their soul, this gives Lucifer/Satan the "legal right" to rule and possess their minds, spirits, and bodies. One may think, Well, why not destroy the person right then and there? Well, he can't always do that legally, but he can "use" them for his own purposes, which is what is behind all the evil in the world. Sometimes that evil is outright, violent, and horrible; other times, that evil is more subtle and exists beneath the radar.

Every soul undergoes battles over who controls their soul. The human soul is the prize in this spiritual warfare, and if Satan owns your mind, he can own your soul. Most earth humans live for the "now." They are not focused on the future, particularly the future of their souls in the afterlife and in the age to come. This is part of Satan's distraction system — to keep people focused on survival issues, worldly issues, and pleasures of the flesh and ego. All are temporary and fleeting.

He controls the kingdoms on earth. How do we know this? It was written in the Bible. If you think back on all the different gods and idols set up on this planet that "demanded" worship and sacrifice, Lucifer/Satan was behind them, particularly human sacrifices. (For more information on his rulership and influence on the world's religions, please see my chapter Aliens and Religions.) He created a trade in the universe between himself and all the other rebellious fallen sons (extraterrestrials) angels, that they, too, can be "god" if they "contract" and sign an agreement with him. With that, they got their own kingdom on earth. Remember the temptation of Christ? Satan offered Christ a kingdom, but Jesus resisted, knowing that his Kingdom in Heaven was greater.

"The devil led him up to a high place and showed him in an instant all the kingdoms of the world. And he said to him, "<u>I will give you all their authority and splendor,</u>

> for it has been given to me, and I can give it to anyone I want to. So if you worship me, it will all be yours." Jesus answered, "It is written: 'Worship the Lord your God and serve him only.'"
>
> (Luke 4:5-8)

The very fact that Satan had the authority to offer kingdoms, if anyone paid homage to him, proves that he was the god of this world, and has been offering Faustian-type Contracts with every other rebellious extraterrestrial who also had a god complex and wanted to rape the earth for his or her natural resources. In exchange, they were given access to mining the planet for gold and all kinds of precious metals and gems, and as a bonus, they could conquer a tribe of humans who would fear and worship them. This has been the recurring pattern of human history since planet Earth was populated with humans.

> The Lord Yahuah said through the prophet Ezekiel, "You have defiled your sanctuaries by the multitude of your iniquities, by the iniquity of your traffic; therefore will I bring forth a fire from the middle of you, it shall devour you, and I will bring you to ashes on the earth in the sight of all them that behold you."
>
> (Ezekiel 28:18)

It is clear that his trade and his trafficking has been allowing rogue and rebellious ETs and Aliens to rape the earth, its humans, and its creatures, and by doing so, deceive cultures and nations into believing they were gods, ancient astronauts, when in reality they were fallen sons of heaven. But the Lord of Heavens had a plan, which is promised and prophesied at the end of this age, which will culminate in a *Star Wars* type of intergalactic battle between Lucifer/Satan's host of fallen ET angels and the faithful ETs (angels) who have remained aligned and serve the office of Christ in the Cosmos.

LUCIFER/SATAN'S HISTORY

The Bible describes Lucifer (aka Satan), as having had a place in heaven. Where in heaven did he dwell? What happened to this celestial being? Research suggests that Lucifer/Satan dwelt in a literal location in the heavens, which, when destroyed, left the debris we now see as asteroids and comets.

> Jesus said, "I saw Satan fall like lightning from heaven."
>
> (Luke 10:18)

When Lucifer rebelled against his Almighty Creator, he persuaded one-third of heaven's angels (extraterrestrials) to follow his rebellion against the Most High Creator with him. They fought over territory in the heavens; it was the original galactic battle, between the fallen extraterrestrials and the faithful extraterrestrial (angels) who remained

CHAPTER TWENTY: The God Of This World

loyal to the Creator. After this initial battle, many of these "fallen angels" were imprisoned in various places. During these heavenly battles, some were bound inside the earth, and some were fastened to the fifth heaven; others, including Lucifer, were denied access to the higher heavens but given free reign in the lower heavens.

Because of the satans' fallen state, they lowered their vibration and could not enjoy access into certain portals, stargates, and dimensions that require a "love" vibration to pass through, hence their limitations in interstellar travel. Ezekiel 28 describes Lucifer and his fall from the heavens. Ezekiel 28 also indicates that he ruled over the "stones of fire" which were the words for planetary spheres, i.e., planets. This includes his reign and kingdom on Earth.

> "And I destroyed you, oh covering Cherub, <u>from among the Stones of Fire</u>...thus brought a fire from your midst."
>
> (Ezekiel 28:16)

He was once called the "anointed cherub covered the throne of God" (Ezekiel 28:14). He was described as "full of wisdom, and perfect in beauty." He was the embodiment of created perfection, and apparently led the worship of the universe. He was in the "mountain of God," where God manifests His glory, and was "perfect" in his ways until "iniquity" developed in him. He became proud and conceited because of his beauty, which corrupted his wisdom because he was such a bright being and had the full blessing of the Creator. He really had it all, power, top status with the Almighty, beauty, adorned by all kinds of precious jewels, and freedom. Yet, unholy ambition and jealousy ruined him, when he led a host of angels in rebellion against the Almighty Creator God and Christ (Revelation 12:7-9). As a result he was cast out of the mountain of God (Ezekiel 28:16), and thrown down to the "ground", or earth (Isaiah 14:12).

> "'Thus says the Lord GOD:
>
> "You *were* the seal of perfection, Full of wisdom and perfect in beauty. You were in Eden, the garden of God; every precious stone was your covering: The sardius, topaz, and diamond, Beryl, onyx, and jasper, Sapphire, turquoise, and emerald with gold. The workmanship of your timbrels and pipes was prepared for you on the day you were created.
>
> **You were the anointed cherub who covers**; I established you; you were on the holy mountain of God;
>
> **YOU WALKED BACK AND FORTH IN THE MIDST OF THE STONES OF FIRE.** You were perfect in your ways from the day you were created, till iniquity was found in you. By the abundance of your trading you became filled with violence within, and you sinned; therefore I cast you as a profane thing out of the mountain of God; and I destroyed you, O covering cherub, from the midst of the fiery stones.

Your heart was lifted up because of your beauty;

You corrupted your wisdom for the sake of your splendor;

I CAST YOU TO THE GROUND, I laid you before kings that they might gaze at you.

You defiled your sanctuaries by the multitude of your iniquities, by the iniquity of your trading; therefore I brought fire from your midst; it devoured you, and I turned you to ashes upon the earth in the sight of all who saw you. All who knew you among the peoples are astonished at you; you have become a horror, and shall be no more forever."

(Ezekiel 28:13-19)

"But you [satan] said in your heart, 'I will ascend to heaven; I will raise my throne above the stars of God, and I will sit on the mount of assembly In the recesses of the north. I will ascend above the heights of the clouds;'"

(Isaiah 14:13-14)

LUCIFER, RAHAB AND THE STONES OF FIRE

David Flynn, author of *Cydonia: The Secret Chronicles of Mars,* researched that the "Stones of Fire" written about in Ezekiel 28 refer to the planets that were in Lucifer's charge. Some key points from David Flynn's research on the *Stones of Fire* and how they relate to Lucifer is being reprinted here with his permission from his website www.mt.net/~watcher/stones.html. David Flynn and I were Internet friends in 2011, which was a year before he passed away with cancer. He was a brilliant researcher, and his research is still relevant and lives on.[1]

"When Lucifer rebelled, God cast him as profane from the heights of heaven. Because of his rebellion, Lucifer/Satan was destroyed from the midst of the Stones of Fire, the planets, where he had reigned over literal physical kingdoms. Evidence of the civilization on Mars can still be seen, while another civilization of the Bene Elohim (sons of the Els, (the sons of Gods of the pantheon of Gods) was destroyed thoroughly, which was the planet Rahab, which became the asteroid belt. It is not surprising that a two-faced Sphinx has been found amongst the ruins of Mars. Lucifer was the most powerful of all the Cherubim, and the biblical description of a cherub can be illustrated by a Sphinx.[1]

The cherubim are first mentioned in the Bible in Genesis 3:24, "After He drove the man out, He placed on the east side of the Garden of Eden cherubim and a flaming sword flashing back and forth to guard the way to the tree of life." Prior to his rebellion, Satan was a cherub (Ezekiel 28:12-15).

Chapters 1 and 10 of the book of Ezekiel describe the "four living creatures" (Ezekiel 1:5) as the same beings as the cherubim (Ezekiel 10). Each had four faces; that of a man, a lion, an ox, and an eagle (Ezekiel 1:10; also 10:14); and each had four wings. In their appearance, the cherubim "had the likeness of a man" (Ezekiel 1:5). These

CHAPTER TWENTY: The God Of This World

cherubim used two of their wings for flying and the other two for covering their bodies (Ezekiel 1:6, 11, 23). Under their wings the cherubim appeared to have the form, or likeness, of a man's hand (Ezekiel 1:8; 10:7-8, 21).

When Satan and his angels rebelled, God destroyed their literal dwelling places. According to scripture, this destruction was swift and decisive. The fifth terrestrial planet, which God calls "Rahab" (boaster, pride), was obliterated. Job 26:11-13: "The pillars of heaven are stunned at His rebuke. He quiets the sea with his power, and by his understanding He shatters (*maw-khats*, dashes asunder), Rahab, by His spirit the heavens were beautiful; His hand forbids the fugitive snake."

According to authors John Milor in his book, *Aliens and the Antichrist*,[2] along with author Fenis Dake, in his book, *God's Plan For Man*,[3] both prove through scripture that angelic (extraterrestrial) civilizations existed on Earth <u>before</u> the times of Adam and Eve, which were under the rulership of the Kingdom of Lucifer. Both authors believe that there were two major floods that destroyed civilization. The first flood was known as the "Flood of Lucifer." In my opinion, this coincides with the sinking of the civilization of Atlantis, which happened approximately 12,000 years ago. Then approximately 6,000 years ago, God repopulated the Earth beginning with Adam and Eve, who were then subjected to being tested and tempted by the old King of this Earth, i.e., Lucifer/Satan, who started out as an attractive luminous bipedal, speaking serpent in the Garden of Eden, and was then cursed into a snake and made deaf and mute.[2]

The scripture prophesy in Genesis 3:15, that says, "and I will put enmity between you and the woman, and between your seed and her seed; it shall bruise your head, and you shall bruise his heel;" was the first of biblical prophecies that pointed to the flesh and blood incarnation of Jesus Christ, whose heels were bruised on the cross, but His victory over death through his resurrection bought back the keys of Death and Hades from Lucifer/Satan, the god of this world, as He crushed his "head," meaning his authority.

In the final battle of Armageddon, where Christ returns with his fleet of starships and defeats Lucifer/Satan and his darkships (UFOs) in a real life *Star Wars* battle, his powers, principalities, rulers of the darkness, and spiritual wickedness in the heavenly places will be defeated once and for all (Ephesians 6:12).

I agree with Milor that Isaiah 14:12–14 provides the first clear piece of evidence that Lucifer ruled Earth as a king before the days of Adam. This passage covers a period in Lucifer's history when he ruled, and then was defeated, so it had to be a time before Adam was created because the Lord Almighty gave Adam dominion over the Earth, not Lucifer. However, it wasn't until after Adam was created and deceived by Lucifer/Satan that he was able to regain dominion of Earth as the god of this world, but not indefinitely. We can deduce that Adam and Eve were an experiment, a test to see if created beings would be obedient to their Creator, or be seduced by its adversary. Needless to say, we all know the way that experiment turned out. They all failed, both Adam and Eve, and Lucifer. All disobeyed the Lord, and all became cursed as a result of it.

Milor goes on to say that both Isaiah 14:12–14, Ezekiel 28:11–19, and numerous other key scriptures plainly reveal that Earth's significance in the universe has to do with its history, and all the clues point to the fall of Lucifer: hell is located <u>in the center of Earth</u>; Christ came to Earth to fulfill the Divine Plan of Salvation, which was originally written into the stars (see my chapter The Word of God in the Stars in Book Five: *The Heavens*); Satan will be confined to and defeated on Earth in the future, and Christ will set up His Kingdom on the Earth for a millennium. Furthermore, Earth, of all places, is Satan's focal point because it was once the center of his kingdom, but was taken away and given to beings that are at present time, lower than the angels, which are humans.[2]

However, it is written that redeemed humans will be made <u>equal</u> to the angels and become immortal, when they enter the Kingdom of God. This is why there is such a battle over human minds, human bodies, and human souls. The root of the battle is jealousy over the status of earth humans, particularly those who align themselves with Christ.

Lucifer/Satan's battle plan has been, thus far, if he and his demonic hierarchy (fallen angels) can control earth humans, then earth humans will never find their God-given power to rule and have dominion over the Earth, which only comes through aligning with the Creator God and His Christ. However, if humans turn toward Christ, then that breaks the power and authority of the satanic realm over the rulership of Earth and our nations. These are the cosmic battles of Earth's history of humanity.

It is clear from so much of the biblical evidence that Lucifer once ruled a vast civilization that spanned the cosmos, as there is evidence on Mars and Saturn, as well. However, it appears that his seat of power for that vast civilization was centered on the Earth.

Ezekiel's prophecy is addressed to the "king of the rock," an "anointed Cherub," who is described as traveling "in the midst of the stones of fire," which literally translated is "in the midst or among the *eh-ben*, 'built stones or rocks,' 'of fire.'"

David Flynn's research reveals who built the stones.[1]

"What are they that the greatest angel created could travel up and down in their vastness? The answer is in the night sky. There can be seen God built stones reflecting the light of the sun which are the planets. Before the creation of Adam, the civilizations of angels (Bene Elohim) existed on the terrestrial planets. Throughout scripture there is a consistent reference to the first dwelling places of some of the ancient sons of God. These extraterrestrials created habitations on the Earth, Mars, 'Rahab' the Fifth Planet and the Moon."

This is why today, UFO researchers have gathered evidence through photographs taken by NASA, and their satellites, of Mars, the Moon, and even Saturn of exact pyramid replicas that we have on Earth, along with a Sphinx on Mars. Today's researchers have concluded that this is evidence of extraterrestrials or ancient astronauts. But we need to ask *who* these extraterrestrials are? *Who* put those structures on Mars, our Moon, and even Saturn? The answers are in the Bible, as we learn "who" exactly

CHAPTER TWENTY: The God Of This World

Lucifer/Satan is and was, and what the scope of his power in the "stones of fire" or his original kingdom was.

When Satan and his angels rebelled, God destroyed their literal dwelling places. According to scripture, this destruction was swift and decisive. The fifth terrestrial planet, which God calls "Rahab" (boaster, pride), was obliterated.

> "The pillars of the heavens quake, aghast at his rebuke. By his power he churned up the sea; by his wisdom he shatters Rahab to pieces. By his spirit the heavens were beautiful; His hand pierced the gliding serpent."
>
> (Job 26:11-13)

"God brought a fire out of Satan's midst, in the center of his greatest planetary kingdom. The planet Rahab exploded sending pieces of itself into the orbits of the interior terrestrial worlds. Asteroid impacts on the surface of mars rocked the planet, oceans washed over its dry land. The Martian atmosphere was blasted into space."[1]

Immanuel Velikovsky wrote *Worlds in Collision* in the 1950s proving, through mathematical theory, that there was once a huge explosion in our solar system, and that the asteroid belt was once a planet which exploded, which also caused disruption of the orbits of the other planets, causing them to be thrown out of their orbits. Pluto, for example, was once a moon of Saturn and was thrust into the outer orbits of the solar system. Uranus was tilted from this explosion, which is why its rings are going up and down, instead of horizontally, like Saturn's. In fact, the rings of Saturn may have even been created as a result of this powerful explosion of Rahab.[4]

Others have postulated that Earth, at that time, had two moons, and they were destroyed in this cosmic punishment, and the moon we have today was actually tractor beamed to us from another star system. The asteroid belt between Mars and Jupiter is actually the remains of this broken planet Rahab, also known as Maldek, and that many of the meteorites that come into Earth's atmosphere today are remnants of Rahab/Maldek.

Flynn goes on to say, "Clearly, God wrought destruction on the heads of the rebellious 'sons,' with power that cannot be imagined. Satan is described as a serpent trying to escape the judgment of God. It is symbolized by the constellation Draconis, which winds itself between the Big and Little Dipper, which represented to the ancients, the flock of the good shepherd and the stronghold of the saved." Yes, indeed it does, please see my chapter The Word of God in the Stars, Book Five: *The Heavens,* for the whole story.

On earth virtually the same catastrophes took place; cities were destroyed on Earth before there was (humankind). "I looked on the earth, and beheld it formless (laid waste) and void; and to the heavens, and they had no light. I looked on the mountains, and, behold, they quaked. And all the hills were shaken. I beheld and lo, there was no man (Adams); and all the cover of the skies had fled. I looked, and, behold, the fruitful place was a wilderness; and all its cities were broken down before the face of Yahuah, before his glowing anger. For so Yahuah has said. The whole land shall be a desolation; yet I will not make a full end." (Jeremiah 4:22-3)

Jeremiah looked into the ages before Adam and described the destruction of the earth. There were no men (descendants of Adam), yet there were cities which were destroyed by God's wrath, so who dwelt in these cities? Never in history, since the creation of Adam, has man been completely destroyed from the earth. We, ourselves, are descended from Adam. The inhabitants of these "cities" were, in fact, the angelic host, the Bene Elohim, before the rebellion.

This proves Milor's and Dake's theory that there were two major floods that destroyed the earth. And according to Plato, the first flood was the destruction of the civilization and empire known as the Atlantis.

"God has set signs and wonders in the land of Egypt, even to this day." (Jeremiah 32:20)

The three pyramids of Egypt, almost identical were also found on Mars as well as the Sphinx.[5] The only difference between the Sphinx in Egypt and the Sphinx on Mars is that the face of the Sphinx on Mars is facing upward toward space, whereas the face of the Sphinx in Egypt faces the earth's eastern horizon.

The exact words of Genesis 1:2 "and the earth was (became) formless and void", are recorded in chapter 4 verse 26 of Jeremiah. The majority of Christian scholars believe Genesis 1:2 means that the earth was created in an imperfect state. Genesis 1:1 lays the reality of creation out clearly: In the beginning God created the heavens and the earth. The next sentence, "and the earth was formless and void" is in error in most English translations. It should read, "and the earth *became* formless and void." The Hebrew word translated "was formless" in English versions of the Bible is *"toh-ho"* a verb which means, "to lay waste".[6]

"For God is not the author of confusion" (1 Corinthians 14:33). He creates order out of nothing. Lucifer/Satan, on the other hand, corrupted what God had already created in perfection. The rebellion of Lucifer/Satan plunged all creation into a state of corruption (the curse), where before it was perfect and glorified.

Lucifer/Satan's rebellion was part of the plan. "For the creation was not willingly subjected to vanity, but through Him subjecting it, on hope; that also the creation will be freed from the slavery of corruption to the freedom and the glory of the children of God." (Romans 8:20)

"For we know that the whole creation groans and travails in pain together until now." (Romans 8:22) The Almighty Lord God uses Lucifer/Satan's and his fallen rebellious extraterrestrial angels to reveal His righteousness, mercy, and Divine Plan of His Salvation and throughout history. One day, all of creation will understand this when His plan culminates here on Earth in the final battle and ending of these satans and fallen ETs, for all the world to see, when Christ returns with two-thirds of heavens faithful extraterrestrial angels, i.e., the celestial armies (Hosts of Heaven) in full glory in

CHAPTER TWENTY: The God Of This World

hundreds of thousands of spaceships. All created humans, including the descendants of Adam are central to that plan, which includes those humans on other planets in the cosmos who have been in bondage to the cosmic evil and subsequent curse from Lucifer/Satan's infiltration.

All of his angels (extraterrestrial rebels), who have were not caught in captivity in the last cosmic battle, will be judged. These are the ones who have been focused on the goings on of earth humans on the earth, but why? Because they know the plan, which is written in the ancient texts, that the redeemed humans, will end judging the angels. These are the ETs and Aliens that have been witnessed, their space vehicles continue to show up around the planet in their UFOs that hundreds of millions of earth humans have witnessed over time. These are the ones some call the "watchers" or the "visitors." They are watching earth humans to see which humans are aligned with the Almighty Creator Lord's plan, who will end up judging them in the end. Discernment is called for now, more than ever before.

These are the beings that are creating so much confusion, frustration, and fascination at the same time. These are the ones who are "seducing" the minds of earth humans into thinking that we are being visited by aliens from outer space. These are the ones masquerading as space brothers, ascended masters, space commanders, and even space saviors, the very beings Dr. Jacques Vallée discerned over thirty years ago:

> "Human beings are under the control of a strange force that bends them in absurd ways, forcing them to play a role in a bizarre game of deception."
>
> (Dr. Jacques Vallée, *Messengers of Deception*, p. 20)

WHO OR WHAT IS RAHAB?

Scripture tells us that the Lord created the heavens by his power, and through his wisdom stretched out the heavens by his understanding, then rebellion corrupted it, and parts of the heavens fell under a curse.

> "<u>You have broken Rahab in pieces</u>, as one slain: you have scattered your enemies with your mighty arm."
>
> (Psalm 89:10)

> "Awake, awake! Clothe yourself with strength, O arm of the LORD; awake, as in days gone by, as in generations of old. <u>Was it not you who cut Rahab to pieces</u>, who pierced that monster through?"
>
> (Isaiah 51:9)

Rahab was a planet in our solar system, also known as Maldek, Marduk, Tiamat, Phaeton, Lucifer, and Luna. The Bible has over a dozen references to Rahab; however, the name Rahab was also the name of a prostitute in the Old Testament book of Joshua, as well as the name of a sea monster, and a reference to Egypt. "to Egypt, whose help is utterly useless. Therefore I call her Rahab the Do-Nothing" (Isaiah 30:7). All this may have come from the fact that the planet called Rahab was once ruled over by Lucifer/Satan's kingdom and was destroyed by the Creator God Yahuah, and other beings who were also targeted for judgment by the Lord, were also given that name.

"Go and cut off Tiamat's life, and let the winds convey her blood to secret places" (The Enuma Elish).

The following is a reference from Michael Tsarion's book, *Atlantis, Alien Visitation and Genetic Manipulation*:

> "We read from various sources that approximately 50,000 years ago a certain planetary body in our own solar system was mysteriously destroyed. This body has been called Tiamat, Phaeton, Lucifer, Marduk, Maldek, Rahab, and even Luna (not connected to the name later given to the moon). It was believed to have existed between Mars and Jupiter and was referred to as the "second sun" and may have been mistaken as such, because its atmosphere was resplendent with reflections of the actual sun...
>
> Around the time of this event, the solar system, and later the Earth, was colonized by extra-terrestrial beings who were either attracted to this solar system by that conflagration or upon coming here caused the calamity themselves. Whether the disaster was natural or not, the result was that mankind on Earth experienced total and long lasting chaos and confusion.
>
> The surface of the planet Tiamat consisted mostly of great oceans. Upon its destruction, these vast saline waters entered into the Earth's atmosphere causing the first of two massive prehistoric deluges and tribulations that mankind would experience. It is thought that the alien invaders took full advantage of this predicament and moved in to bring about colonization. They met no resistance from the disoriented and weakened inhabitants of the Earth who believed their visitors were powerful gods.
>
> Some theorists, like the energetic Erich von Daniken, have also determined that there was a great intergalactic war between two (or possibly more) extraterrestrial forces in a neighboring galaxy or solar system. The result of this titanic war had enormous consequences for the Earth because, it is postulated, the losers on being pursued into our system pretended to take refuge on Tiamat. They even erected a makeshift radar-type station there to decoy their pursuers. However, the defeated ones had really taken refuge on planet Earth, not on Tiamat. Upon their arrival, they almost immediately went underground into existing caverns that through scans of the planet they knew existed. They also descended into other caverns that they themselves cut out of the living rock."[7]

Tsarion is referring here to the inner earth, which is full of myths of all kinds of people and aliens that live in this subterranean worlds. (See my chapter on Agartha in

CHAPTER TWENTY: The God Of This World

Book One: *Who's Who In The Cosmic Zoo?*) Dwarfin, Trolls, Elves, and all the Scandinavian myths of the "King who lives *under* the mountain" all relate to these beings who went *inside* the earth after this galactic war took place, and after the Earth was flooded.[8]

Tsarion also believes that the Nephilim established their main headquarters in Atlantis. Many of the indigenous tribes have records and stories of these advanced beings that visited Earth and used humans to help them mine the earth for various minerals and resources. These Nephilim were brought under God's judgment, and the civilization of Atlantis and Lucifer's kingdom on Earth were destroyed by a flood, known as Lucifer's flood.

"After Satan's kingdoms were devastated, many of the rebellious fallen angels were bound and held until the time of judgment, the Day of the Lord; the end of the age when God gathers rebel angels on earth to receive His wrath. Other factions of the rebel fallen angels continued existing with the ability to travel in the atmosphere outward from earth, space, and amongst the planets — 'the stones of fire.'"[9]

The *Book of Enoch* tells us: "And over an abyss I saw a place that had no heaven above it and no firmament of earth below it ... it was a void place, and there I saw a terrible thing: seven stars, like great burning mountains and like spirits, that petitioned me. The angel with me said: "this is the place of the consummation of heaven and earth; *it is a prison for the stars of heaven and for the host of heaven.* And the stars that roll over the fire are they who have transgressed the command of God... And He was enraged at them, and bound them till the time and the consummation of their sins *in the year of the mystery.*" (Enoch 18:13)

The Lord Yahuah questioned Job from the whirlwind (the whirlwind represents his spaceship) Job 38:4-7: "Where were you when I laid the foundations of the earth? ... or who cast its corner stone, when the morning stars sang together, and all the sons of Yahuah shouted for joy? Yahuah created the angels before he spoke the worlds into existence." Yahuah is known throughout the Bible as the Lord of Hosts. "Rule and fear are with Him. He makes peace in his high places. Is there any number to his armies?"

(Job 25:2)

"Jesus said, "This voice was for your benefit, not mine. Now is the time for judgment on this world; <u>now the prince of this world will be driven out</u>. But I, when I am lifted up from the earth, will draw all men to myself."

(John 12:30-32)

"The God of peace will soon crush Satan under your feet."

(Romans 16:20)

NOTES:

1. David Flynn, *Satan & Cherubim on Literal Planets - Stones of Fire* used with permission, http://www.mt.net/~watcher/)
2. John Milor, *Aliens and the Antichrist,* iUniverse, 2006
3. Fenis Dake, *God's Plan For Man,* Lawrenceville, Georgia: Dake Publishing Inc., 1977
4. Immanuel Velikovsky, *Worlds In Collision,* Dell; A Laurel Edition (1969)
5. David Flynn's research on *Cydonia Mars* www.mt.net/~watcher/
6. ibid, Flynn
7. Michael Tsarion, *Atlantis, Alien Visitation and Genetic Manipulation*: Angels at Work Publishing Santa Clara, California. 2002
8. Ella LeBain, *Who's Who In The Cosmic Zoo? Book One – Third Edition,* Chapter – Agartha/Agarthians p.98-p.105, Tate Publishing & Enterprises, 2013.
9. ibid, Flynn

CHAPTER TWENTY-ONE

THE OFFICE OF SATAN

"And there was WAR IN HEAVEN:
Michael fought against THE DRAGON;
And THE DRAGON fought and his angels...
And the GREAT DRAGON was cast out,
That OLD SERPENT, called the Devil, and Satan,
Which DECIEVETH the whole world."

(Revelation 12:7)

Literally, *Ha-satan* (in Hebrew "the adversary") was originally the title of an office, not the name of an angel. When Lucifer rebelled, one-third of heaven's extraterrestrial angels rebelled with him all becoming the satans (adversaries). There is more than one adversary; in fact, there are armies of them. This phrase, "the satans," was first coined in the *Books of Enoch*, who told the original story of the fall of Lucifer and the fallen sons from their high place in the heavens. We have learned that they go by many names, and that there are different ranking satans within Lucifer/Satan's hierarchy.

Suffice it to say, we can call the satans demons (which is Greek for intelligences). The satans represent all the fallen angels (impious angels) who followed Lucifer who then became known as Satan and belong to the office of Satan. You will see, by his many names and disguises, he does not work alone, although many refer to him as just Satan. However, for the sake of discernment and language, I have been referring to him and his hierarchy throughout this book, as the satans, or the office of Satan. Suffice it to say, that the Office of Satan wars against all those faithful extraterrestrial angels, who belong to the Office of Christ.

THE ORIGINAL COUNTERFEITER

Remember Lucifer was the angel of light, who is known as the "god of this world," whose purpose is to bring enlightenment to the world as the "god of enlightenment," Lucifer became Satan (the accuser/the adversary) after he rebelled against the Creator God because he wanted to "be" god himself and exalt himself above the Most High God. Lucifer has a huge "god complex." He is all about setting himself up as god and demands all kinds of worship and bondage to himself. Everything good and worthy that God has made, Lucifer/Satan and his rebel angels (ETs) have corrupted and perverted.

From the heavens themselves, to the understanding of astrology, food, sex, yoga, religion, spirituality, technology, knowledge, and history, i.e., His-story. More importantly, he wants to block/stymie/thwart earth humans from worshiping and having an intimate relationship with the Almighty Creator God and Jesus Christ. He creates all forms of idolatry to snare earth humans in, seducing them to set their hearts on anything but worshipping the Creator Lord of the Universe.

Some of the names Lucifer/Satan goes by on earth are: Sananda, Santa, Sanat Kumara, Buddha, Krishna, Matreya, Mastema, Mabus, the false prophet. Many may wonder, how can this be? Aren't these beings supposed to be "ascended masters"? Yes, that is precisely my point — Lucifer/Satan masquerades as an "angel of light." He is the one behind this mass deception on Earth. He and his fallen angels masquerade as gods, ETs, and space brothers of all kinds. See, my chapter on Aliens and Religion in Book Two – *Who Are the Angels?* for more details.

Lucifer infiltrated Buddhism to turn it into a religion that believes that you can be your own god and that, through meditation alone, you can tap into your higher self and attain "Buddhahood." Today this path has been embraced by New Agers, who mistakenly believe that they, too, will ascend and become "gods" or like god. He created this false path, along with many others. He is the original "counterfeiter."

> "Don't let anyone deceive you in any way, for [that day will not come] until the rebellion occurs and the man of lawlessness is revealed, the man doomed to destruction. He will oppose and will exalt himself over everything that is called God or is worshiped, so that <u>he sets himself up in God's temple, proclaiming himself to be God</u>."
>
> (2 Thessalonians 2:3-4)

> The temple of God are human beings. Do you not know that <u>your body is the Temple of the Living God</u> and that God's Spirit lives in you?
>
> (1 Corinthians 3:16)

The battlefield is our minds, our bodies, and ultimately our souls. We are designed to be vessels of a higher power. Yet we have freewill. It is our choice whether we choose to have the Spirit of God live within us, or the spirit of the "god" of this world, which are his demonic hierarchy of fallen angels often masquerading as angels of light. The New Age is seduced by them.

There are so many people who have lost their connection with the Living God, due to becoming despondent or disenchanted with various religions. They have doubted the Bible as being the ultimate word of God. They argue the Bible was written by men. True, it was penned by men, but inspired by the Holy Spirit. Yet at the same time, they give credence to channeled materials and channelers, who are merely human and inspired by fallen angels within Satan's hierarchy, which they deny because they have been seduced by the deceiving spirits. There is a way that seems right to a man but the end of that road leads to destruction (Proverbs 14:12).

CHAPTER TWENTY-ONE: The Office Of Satan

The Antichrist will come offering peace and worldwide prosperity. He will claim to be Jesus Christ returned. He will claim to be an Ascended Master who will appeal to the gullible and masses. Just by watching him, he will capture and attempt to enslave your mind with his hypnotic charm.

The scripture prophesy tells us that Satan comes first to deceive mankind through his False Prophet who prepares the way for the final Antichrist who comes claiming to be the "Father, Most High God." Both are liars and counterfeiters. When the real Most High comes, He will destroy both of these beasts. He comes at the war of Armageddon with hundreds of thousands of His Saints and faithful extraterrestrial angels, and He will cast both of two beasts into the Lake of Fire. However, Satan's beasts come first.

LUCIFER, FALLEN ANGELS & INTER-DIMENSIONALS

It's important to note that all of the angels, satans, fallen angels/demons all have *inter-dimensional* capabilities. That means that they can exist in more than one dimension; they can travel between dimensions, the ones that are resonant with them. The universe operates on resonance and frequency. Remember the Creator bound them to the lower heavens, so their traveling capabilities are limited, but let's not forget they have way more capabilities than we do. Earth humans are in the middle of battle, and earth humans are the prize. These beings can appear and disappear at will, they can manifest themselves in all kinds of forms, shapeshifting themselves to *appear* to be something they are not.

Ufologists are well-aware of *inter-dimensionals*; certainly not all *inter-dimensionals* have evil intent, but when we're discerning the realm of the fallen angels and how deceitful they are, we need to keep in mind that they, too, have *inter-dimensional* capabilities. Many ufologists consider extraterrestrials and *inter-dimensionals* to be mutually exclusive, as the ability to have access to other dimensions does certainly facilitate space travel.

Some entities have access to an infinite number of dimensions; some entities can materialize from hyperspace into our three-dimensional space at will. Just because an entity can manifest into our 3D space, doesn't necessarily mean that their origin comes from a 3D space. In fact many entities cannot live in our environment because there is too much radiation from the sun. They do not have the capabilities to breathe our oxygen, as their bodies are made differently. This is why so many of the ancient astronauts immortalized in stone carvings and statutes depict a type of space suite and helmet protecting them from our environment and from the harshness of space.

The entities known as the satans and fallen angel/demons originate from the inner earth, where there is sulphur, darkness, and a completely different type of environment. This is why many grays cannot exist on the surface of the planet for too long, so they move *inter-dimensionally* which seems like a form of trickery to us — now you see them, now you don't. Many of them exist primarily in the spirit world, which is where they are empowered as *principalities, powers, rulers of the darkness, and spiritual wickedness in heavenly places,* as Ephesians 6:12 states. This the crux of the cosmic/spiritual warfare that each and every earth human finds itself in the middle of.

Earth humans need to realize that the stakes in the game are real, and it is being played for keeps. Once the end of this timeline is reached, there is no turning back.

WHY DO EVIL ANGELS EXIST?

The Creator has allowed them to exist for all kinds of purposes; some have to do with the *Grand Experiment* of earth humans. These satans and fallen angel/demons are used to test earth humans, try their souls before God, and are even used to punish the wicked. Nothing in the universe is here for banality; everything has a purpose under heaven, under the Divine Order of the Creator. This is why the prophetic timeline indicates an end to these beings after the full amount of souls are harvested by the faithful angels (extraterrestrials) for the Kingdom of God in the *Grand Experiment*, and then the Creator's use of the satans and demonic fallen angels will come to an end, as promised in Revelation 20:10, "And the devil, who deceived them, was thrown into the lake of burning sulfur, where the beast and the false prophet had been thrown. They will be tormented day and night forever and ever."

"Then I continued to watch because of the boastful words the horn was speaking. I kept looking until the beast was slain and its body destroyed and thrown into the blazing fire." (Daniel 7:11)

"Then the King will say to those on his left, 'Depart from me, you who are cursed, into the eternal fire *prepared for the devil and his angels*." (Matthew 25:41)

"Then death and Hades were thrown into the lake of fire. The lake of fire is the second death." (Revelation 20:14)

"If anyone's name was not found written in the book of life, he was thrown into the lake of fire." (Revelation 20:15)

"I beheld the angels of punishment, who were dwelling *there*, and preparing every instrument of Satan. Then I inquired of the angel of peace, who proceeded with me, for whom those instruments were preparing. He said, these they are preparing for the kings and powerful ones of the earth, that thus they may perish." (Enoch 52:3-5)

"Then I inquired of the angel of peace, who proceeded with me, saying, for whom are these fetters and instruments prepared? He replied, these are prepared for the host of Azazel, that they may be delivered over and adjudged to the lowest condemnation; and that their angels may be overwhelmed with hurled stones, as the Lord of spirits has commanded.

"Michael and Gabriel, Raphael and Phanuel shall be strengthened in that day, and shall then cast them into a furnace of blazing fire, that the Lord of spirits may be avenged of them for their crimes; because they became ministers of Satan, and seduced those who dwell upon earth.

CHAPTER TWENTY-ONE: The Office Of Satan

"In those days shall punishment go forth from the Lord of spirits; and the receptacles of water which are above the heavens shall be opened, and the fountains likewise, which are under the heavens and under the earth." (Enoch 53:4-7)

Their end is scheduled to happen at the end of this timeline, which is at the end of this age. Before that time, they will have their last hurrah and precipitate a mass deception of humankind, which has already begun, through the abduction of the earth humans for various reasons, to the appearance of UFOs being witnessed all over the globe, to the growth of New Age concepts and beliefs that people are ascending and becoming gods, to the growing popular subculture of the fascination with the paranormal, ghosts, vampires, and aliens. This is all being done as part of their end-times agenda to literally pull the wool over the eyes of undiscerning earth humans.

Why does the Almighty Creator allow this deception to play itself out? Because He is testing earth humans to see if they will seek Him and His Holy Spirit for truth or follow the lies of the satans. Let's face it, in this world, lies are more popular than truth for so many reasons.

Some people prefer to believe in lies because they are afraid of the truth, and the denial is more comfortable. Others believe in lies, and invest in those lies, emotionally and financially, and their pride doesn't allow them to admit that they were misled. Yet others believe in the lies from the satans as "truth" because they do not know the difference between truth and lie, particularly when it comes to ufology, religion, and spirituality. And then there are those who have invested in the lies because it gives them power, as in the case with secret societies. An old saying states that "the road to hell is paved with good intentions," which I think comes from this Proverb 16:25. There is a way that seems right to a man, but in the end, it leads to death and destruction.

THE PRINCIPALITY OF JEALOUSY

"For we war not against flesh and blood, but against **principalities, powers, world rulers of this present darkness and spiritual hosts of wickedness in heavenly places**."
(Ephesians 6:12)

Jealousy and Envy are a Principality, so is Fear, Bitterness, Self-Bitterness, Rejection, and the Occult. All of these are Principalities (dominions), which means that these are "Princes" who are ruled by a hierarchy of Satan's Arch Fallen Angels (Archdemons), to keep earth humans in emotional, mental, psychological, spiritual, and physical bondage. These were emotions that all the fallen angels, including their band leader Lucifer, felt when they were castigated out of the high heavens, and to this day, they hold on to these wounds.

As the saying goes, "misery loves company," so it is with the Principalities of Darkness. There are armors associated with each of these principalities, which are spiritual strongholds that are held in place by demons. They all represent the "personality" of Lucifer and his fallen angels. These are the "spirits" that cause mental illness in earth humans. In fact when humans turn to Christ, Christ heals these illnesses through the deliverance of these very demons.

As far as the spiritual battle goes, when we turn to Christ, "the weapons we fight with are not the weapons of the world. On the contrary, they have divine power to demolish strongholds." (1 Corinthians 10:4) This means that Christ becomes our Commander in Chief, who leads the Celestial Army of extraterrestrial angels to fight the spiritual battle against Satan's army of fallen ET angels, over our minds, souls, and bodies.

The very fact that humans were placed above angels angered these angels. Angels were created immortal; humans are created mortal. Yet the promise to the redeemed humans is immortality and to become "like the angels." Herein lies the rub. In the end, it says that the saints (believers in Christ) will become like the angels as they will receive their full inheritance as adopted sons and daughters of God's Kingdom. Not only is that, but another part of the promise that the redeemed will end up judging the angels:

"Do you not know that we will judge angels?
How much more the things of this life!"

(1 Corinthians 6:3)

"Then the King will say to those on His right, 'Come, you who are blessed of My Father, inherit the kingdom prepared for you from the foundation of the world" (Matthew 25:34) are the righteous who have eternal life and become immortal. James said that those who love God are promised a crown of life, and he also said we are heirs of the kingdom. "Blessed is a man who perseveres under trial; for once he has been approved, he will receive the crown of life which the Lord has promised to those who love Him." (James 1:12)

Satan's fallen angels are jealous of the Lord's promise to redeem the faithful and raise them up into immortality to become like the angels of heaven. Satan and his rebel angels will not just sit by quietly and allow redeemed earth humans to take over the heavenly positions previously held by Lucifer/Satan and his fallen angels. This is why his end time plan involves the mass deception of earth humans into believing that aliens, UFOs, ancient astronauts, and star gods are returning to save humanity, along with the creation of the New World Order and a universal religion based on the occult/New Age beliefs which actually prepares the way for his created antichrist.

In fact, he will do everything he can to distort the true Rapture of the faithful from occurring. While he cannot prevent this event from occurring, as he does not have the power in heaven to do so, he can, however, lie to the remaining world that the redeemed were "abducted" by space aliens. He may also create his own "false rapture" which will be a mass abduction of earth humans. When Christ comes back to redeem His Bride (his faithful) from the earth, He will translate their bodies into immortal bodies. This is not an

CHAPTER TWENTY-ONE: The Office Of Satan

abduction but part of the Divine Plan of Salvation. Yet those abducted by aliens (fallen angels and rebel space gods) will not be translated but held in some type of bondage or even eaten by the carnivorous reptilian overlords.

"God is just: He will pay back trouble to those who trouble you and give relief to you who are troubled, and to us as well. This will happen when the *Lord Jesus is revealed from heaven in blazing fire with his powerful angels,* in flaming fire, inflicting vengeance on those who do not know God and do not obey the truth and good news of our Lord Jesus." (2 Thessalonians 1:6-8) The blazing fire is with his fleet of starships.

"He who has an ear, let him hear what the Spirit says......To him who overcomes, I will grant to eat of the tree of life which is in the Paradise of God." (Revelation 2:7)

"He who overcomes, I will make him a pillar in the temple of My God, and ***he will not go out from it anymore***; and I will write on him the name of My God, and the name of the city of My God, the new Jerusalem, which comes down out of heaven from My God, and My new name." (Revelation 3:12)

Not go out from it anymore! This means the soul will stop reincarnating, which is essentially the return of the soul to God, who then sends the soul back to Earth for another incarnation until the soul realizes the power to overcome the world comes from Christ Himself. He is then promised a new name that only the Lord Himself will authorize, thus forever changing the vibration of that soul, giving it immortal life eternal in the heavens. (See Book Five, *The Heavens* – Chapter: What Happens When You Die for further elucidation.)

THE SPIRIT OF ANTICHRIST

> "This is how you can recognize the Spirit of God: Every spirit that acknowledges that Jesus Christ has come in the flesh is from God, but every spirit that does not acknowledge Jesus is not from God. <u>This is the spirit of the antichrist</u>, which you have heard is coming and even now is already in the world."
>
> (1 John 4:2-3)

Angels are merely messengers. There are messengers from the Kingdom of God, and messengers from the kingdom of darkness who masquerade as light. They are known as the spirit of antichrist.

Only the Almighty Creator Lord of all Spirits has the authority to assign guardian angels, ministering angels, and warrior angels to anyone. Psalm 91, The Lord promises to puts "His" angels in charge of anyone *that* <u>puts their trust in Him, first and foremost</u>. The deal is, we must *first* put our trust in the Almighty Lord, than in turn, He dispatches His angels to us. Not the other way around, as most New Agers think. Trusting in angels and not knowing which realm they come from is idolatry, not to mention spiritual ignorance. What they end up getting are "counterfeit angels" that all come from Lucifer/Satan's hierarchy and dominion of fallen angels and demonic spirit, who all have the power to masquerade as angels of light. They will tell you what you want to hear, lull you into a false sense of security, tell you all sorts of lies mixed with some truths …just enough to hook you in and even give people information about the past, just to fascinate you and convince you that they are supernatural and they know you.

> "Satan, **who is the god of this world**, has blinded the minds of those who don't believe. They are unable to see the glorious light of the Good News of the Kingdom of God. They don't understand this message about the glory of Christ, who is the exact likeness of God."
>
> (2 Corinthians 4:4)

FEAR BASED OR FEAR OF THE TRUTH?

The reason why New Agers turn to spirit guides to answer their questions is because they have lost their connection with the Heavenly Father and His Holy Spirit. They are either angry at Him because religion gave them a bad rap, or they are in outright rebellion or both. Many New Agers have become disenchanted and confused about their childhood religions, so they turn to so-called angels of light for guidance, who, unbeknownst to them are lying spirits. They are amazed that these spirit guides, so-called angels, ascended masters, even archangels all talk to them and tell them all sorts of things. In fact, by accepting them, many are made psychic, so they depend on these spirits for information. These are all counterfeit gifts of the Holy Spirit, who gives the word of knowledge, words of wisdom, and revelation. However, these "spirits" do not come from the Holy Spirit, but from the spirit of antichrist in the world.

> "Many deceivers, who do not acknowledge Jesus Christ as coming in the flesh, have gone out into the world. Any such person is the deceiver and the antichrist."
>
> (2 John 1:7)

Firstly, what many New Agers do not realize is that archangels do not interact with human beings. They are princes put in charge of other angels. When angels are sent from their "office," they may announce themselves, as Gabriel, or Michael, but they are not the Archangel Gabriel or Michael, but angels who work under these mighty princes. Secondly, if you read your history, judgment came down on our ancient ancestors when they consulted "spirit guides" in the past.

> "Don't let anyone condemn you by insisting on pious self-denial or the worship of angels, saying they have had visions about these things. Their sinful minds have made them proud,"
>
> (Colossians 2:18)

CHAPTER TWENTY-ONE: The Office Of Satan

Not knowing the difference between light and darkness, good and evil, God's angels, and Satan's fallen angels, is the big dilemma most New Agers face. They ignorantly think if you call on the "light," whichever color they assign to it (which is irrelevant) that they are protected. Protected from what? The very fact that they need to protect themselves with light indicates that they know that there are demonic entities lurking in the spirit realms, which they often dismiss as "fear based." Please see my chapter "Masquerade of Angels" in Book Three – *Who Are The Angels?* for further discernment on how aliens and demons pretend to be angels of light to undiscerning earth humans.

It is unfortunate that these New Agers have spent so much time, energy, and money on lies and delusion that, when the truth is told to them, they are so threatened by it that they resist it because of pride. Nobody likes to face the fact that they've been duped, bamboozled, and betrayed, particularly by their trusted spirit guide or god, or even an archangel. But if they knew angel protocol (please see my chapter on "Angel Protocol" in Book Three – *Who Are The Angels?*), they would understand that there is a hierarchy. The truth is that, in Satan's world, demon angels are dispatched to morph into anything you want to believe they are. They know how fragile human egos are; they also know how earth humans are so easily deceived. They watch us constantly. They never sleep. They know what lulls us to sleep (spiritually speaking), and they also know all the laws of hypnosis.

I know people who are so convinced that they can just surround themselves with white light, meditate, and voilà, the spirit of the earth, who they call "Gaia" talks to them and tells them her plans for earth changes, like when she plans an earthquake, or a hurricane, etc. This is another ruse. There are lies within lies, and it almost always begins with ignorance. This false spirit, Gaia, is not creating earthquakes, nor does this spirit have control over earth and climate changes.

Firstly, let's not forget that it was the Lord Almighty who created the heavens and the earth, the waters, and the cycles of nature. The more we advance scientifically, the more we understand that climate change is governed by the cycles within the sun. Yet we have a whole religion that is centered on a lie, by guilt tripping earth humans into believe that they are the cause of "global warming." This comes from the flat earth people, along from a particular disenchanted politician who missed his calling. Remember when people were convinced that the earth was flat? Or that the earth was the center of the universe? The truth is, these false beliefs are more reflective of their level consciousness than grounded in science. Spiritually speaking, this comes from the prince of this world's culture of narcissism.

Scientists know today that climate change is caused by the sun. In fact, as our sun is getting ready to eclipse the Galactic Sun, our Sun is going through some of the worst and most intense solar storms, X class flares, and coronal mass ejections that have been recorded. Each time the sun belches one of these flares, an earthquake is felt on Earth, along with all sorts of intense storms. Yet, those who have invested in the lies of global warming continue to believe that global warming is what is causing these storms and earthquakes, which they mistakenly claim is caused by humans. Humans are not responsible for climate change; humans are responsible for pollution.

Yet along with the lies that go around the world, there are lying spirits, and those who believe in them, like those who actually believe they are channeling Gaia and believe that this so- called spirit is ruling earth changes. Lies perpetuating other lies. The truth of the matter is that the Creator is causing these changes. We're on His timeline, and He controls the sun and all the planets.

Lucifer and his fallen angel demons all masterfully masquerade as "angels of light." Most New Agers accept these disguises and believe in their dishonesties because they are comfortable. There is always a spirit of arrogance that accompanies these channelers, who think that they are above lower entities, because they believe they are "doing it right" by surrounding themselves with light, meditating in a certain position, and believing in benevolent outcomes. These are called "dead works." This all creates denial and a huge spiritual blind spot in their spirits, which actually attracts these lying spirits to them. In the spirit realm they are tagged as being easily duped, so that is why they speak to them and call their name. But what they don't realize is that their spirit guides are not who they think they are, no matter what name they claim to be.

We must remember the Prophesy about these end times: "In the last days many will... Having a form of godliness, but denying the power thereof: from such turn away." (2 Timothy 3:5) This means, appearing to be spiritual on the outside, but denying the true power, which comes from the God's Holy Spirit.

For hundreds of years, channeling, mediumship, psychic phenomenon, and the paranormal, all came under the heading of the occult. Then in the 1970s, occult bookstores changed their name to Metaphysics; then in the 1990s, metaphysics became New Age. Regardless of what you call it, all occult activities come under the dominion of the god of this world, the prince of the powers of the air, and all of his demonic fallen angel hierarchy. They have made it attractive and cool to be involved with channeling, what someone called "talking to the men upstairs." Who are these men upstairs?

New Agers think they are talking to ETs. But that's the purpose of these books, *Who's Who In The Cosmic Zoo?* Are they benevolent ETs or fallen angel demons, who are hell-bent on deceiving humankind? The men upstairs comes from the fact that Lucifer/Satan and his fallen angels actually have access to the first and second heavens. As I've mentioned before, this is why we see UFOs come and go. They are also fastened with various alien bases on the moon, Mars, and various star systems, which have been compromised by cosmic evil.

My point is, that earth humans are being deceived, and do not understand which forces they are dealing with, because of their clever masquerade and powers of belief. Some New Agers are prone to self-fulfilling prophesies. That is when they have a belief such as "ETs are here to help us, to help us advance," and then they are contacted by beings who claim to be good ETs, and without the spirit of discernment, they are duped

CHAPTER TWENTY-ONE: The Office Of Satan

into believing a lie, which they accept as truth because it fulfills their self-fulfilled prophesy that they must be good.

Here's another big stronghold: "Only good aliens, or only good ETs" can come to me because I surround myself with white light daily and because I meditate. I can only attract good spirits to me. I'm way too spiritual to attract fallen angels or demons." I call this a stronghold, because spiritually, this is an armor from one of Satan's seven principalities called the spirit of Pride, Arrogance, Narcissism and Denial. That they are so above it all, that demons wouldn't dare contact them. Again, another huge lie. As the Scriptures say, "No one is righteous — not even one." (Romans 3:10)

In ancient times, when prophets were wrong, they were stoned and killed. Thankfully in modern times, nobody adheres to those old standards. But spiritually speaking, the demonic realm knows and empowers these false prophets and takes full advantage of them. These souls are in bondage to these deceptive spirits and spirits of divination. When they are wrong, they seem to spend more time making excuses about why were wrong, then admitting the truth, that they were lied to by your fallen angel spirit guides.

They are told to just send white light, even to the fallen angels. Sending fallen angels white light is exactly what they want, your energy. It's vampiric. White light attracts the opposite to you. Dark spirits are attracted to the light, just like moths. However, when you turn to the Lord, and repent of rebellion, divination, and spiritism, He will fill you with His Holy Spirit, which reveals all truth in love to you. You will no longer need false spirit guides. You will walk in freedom.

LIVING IN THE LIGHT

> "This is the message we heard from Jesus and now declare to you: God is light, and there is no darkness in him at all. So we are lying if we say we have fellowship with God but go on living in spiritual darkness; we are not practicing the truth. But if we are living in the light, as God is in the light, then we have fellowship with each other, and the blood of Jesus, his Son, cleanses us from all sin. If we claim we have no sin, we are only fooling ourselves and not living in the truth."
>
> (1 John 1:5-8)

There is also a New Age cult that involves focusing and requesting "benevolent outcomes" through meditation and prayers to angels. False spirits will do everything they can to keep you hooked on believing a lie because they are in rebellion toward Christ and all of His Holy Angels. If they can produce lying wonders and benevolent miracle outcomes for you to keep you believing in them, they will. Their prize is your lost soul in the end. Trusting in benevolent outcomes is like believing in "wishful thinking"; it does not seal one's fate. But by bringing requests before the throne of Grace of the Lord of Lords will grant your request. Trusting in spirit guides that tell you only what you want to hear will only help your soul end up in judgment in the end. No matter how many seemingly benevolent outcomes they give you.

> "The Holy Spirit clearly says that in later times some will abandon the faith and follow deceiving spirits and things taught by demons."
>
> (1 Timothy 4:1)

Many have fallen away because of the fact that the Bible was edited during the seven ecumenical councils and feel the word of God is not complete. But the rejected books are still available today. With that said, that is no excuse to throw the baby out with the bathwater. Even though they tried to outlaw beliefs in reincarnation, it is still in the scriptures — in both the Old and New Testaments, even Jesus Christ Himself spoke of it, but without His Spirit to reveal it to you, most people miss those truths. (See, Book Five – *The Heavens,* Chapter - What Happens When You Die?) The Bible books were penned by men but inspired by the Holy Spirit. Again, the New Age counterfeit is channeling books inspired by false and deceptive spirits. That is the difference.

All truth is revealed ONLY through the agency of the HOLY SPIRIT. You can read the scriptures inside and out and know it "intellectually," but if you are in "spiritual" rebellion toward the Lord, and carry the spirit of unbelief, the truth and all of its mysteries will be hidden from you. We are called to repentance with the promise that all of our sins (errors), iniquities, and rebellions are forgiven, if we turn to the Lord Jesus Christ, who is the only one who has the power to forgive sins and deliver humans from the "power of sin." Now is the time, when you are alive. When you pass over, you will come face to face with Him and be responsible for rejecting Him, His Spirit, His Truth, and His Way, and instead choosing the path of lying spirits, who all answer to the spirit of the god of this world, who is Satan.

> "There is a way that seems right to a man, but the end of that road leads to destruction."
>
> (Proverbs 14:12)

Another major deception in New Age beliefs today is the false belief that we are becoming like gods and will ascend to heaven all by ourselves. This is stolen from the promises from the Lord in Revelations 12:11, who promises are only to all those who overcome this world and the god of this world, through the blood of the Lamb (which is Jesus Christ) and the word of their testimony, which is confessing the blood of Jesus and the name of Jesus, which are the two most powerful weapons used in this spiritual warfare again the satans. However, as counterfeits go, the New Age belief is that you can ascend and become god all by yourself. All you need to do is meditate, think good thoughts, clear your chakras, and believe in "Christ Consciousness." Herein lies the rub and the deception. Let's discern.

CHAPTER TWENTY-ONE: The Office Of Satan

I have already discerned Christ Consciousness is counterfeit. The true "mind of Christ" comes from being transformed out of the kingdom of darkness into the Kingdom of God's dear son, Jesus Christ (Colossians 1:13). Having the "mind of Christ" comes from being sanctified by the blood of Jesus and receive the "indwelling" Holy Spirit, who gives a believer the power to overcome the spirit of the world (which is Satan) through the indwelling Holy Spirit. "You overcome the world, because greater is He that lives within you, than he that is in the world" (1 John 4:4). Therein lies the spiritual warfare, which is over which spirit gets to live inside of humans, who were created to be "temples of God."

> "Do you not know that your body is a temple of the Holy Spirit, who is in you, whom you have received from God? You are not your own; you were bought at a price. Therefore honor God with your body."
>
> (1 Corinthians 6:19, 20)

> "If anyone destroys God's temple, God will destroy him; <u>for God's temple is sacred, and you are that temple</u>. Do not deceive yourselves. If any one of you thinks he is wise by the standards of this age, he should become a "fool" so that he may become wise. For the wisdom of this world is foolishness in God's sight. As it is written: "He catches the wise in their craftiness"; and again, "The Lord knows that the thoughts of the wise are futile."
>
> (1 Corinthians 3:17-20)

Being transformed by the renewing of our minds, (Romans 12:2) is a process of bringing all of our issues to Christ, through confession, repentance (turning away from the personality of Satan) through daily prayer, and believing that the blood of Christ washes away the power of sin from our lives. That is how the "mind of Christ" comes into a human vessel, as well as a new heart, which comes from the indwelling Holy Spirit. For most humans, this is a process; it doesn't happen overnight.

Christ Consciousness is a pseudo-counterfeit philosophy which is actually inspired by religious spirits sent from the god of this world. It's a form of self-righteousness, having a form of godliness but denying its power (2 Timothy 3:5), which often lacks an intimate relationship with the Living Christ, through His Holy Spirit. It's subtle because it lulls and seduces its followers into thinking they are holy and righteous and that they can be like god.

This is the very thinking that created the fall of Lucifer and his fallen angels out of the high heavens. His mark is in many of the world's religions because earth humans are in bondage to his ways, until redeemed and delivered out of his kingdom of darkness, which only Christ can do, as no matter how "holier than thou" or "spiritual" earth humans may deem themselves to be, they do not have the power to save themselves and extricate themselves out of the god of this world's influence and power without the power of Christ.

For it is by grace we are saved, through faith — this not from ourselves, it is the gift of God — it is not by our own works, so that no one can boast (Ephesians 2:8, 9). Many miss that point from God, "so that no one may boast." The so-called ascension movement, along with the Christ Consciousness movement, are both pseudo-counterfeit philosophies, which are inspired by the spirit of narcissism, which was created by Lucifer, in the false belief that that he could elevate himself above the Most High.

As history tells us, he was, instead, brought down. This is why the wisdom of scripture tells us that whoever exalts himself, will be humbled, and whoever humbles himself will be exalted. It may be a conundrum to many, but it is the standard of heaven.

This is why God chose the lowly things of this world and the despised things — and the things that are not — to nullify the things that are, so that no one may boast before him. (1 Corinthians 1:29)

THE AGE OF NARCISSISM & GODLESSNESS IN END TIMES

> "But mark this: There will be terrible times in the last days. People will be lovers of themselves, lovers of money, boastful, proud, abusive, disobedient to their parents, ungrateful, unholy, without love, unforgiving, slanderous, without self-control, brutal, not lovers of the good, treacherous, rash, conceited, lovers of pleasure rather than lovers of God—having a form of godliness but denying its power. Have nothing to do with them."
>
> (2 Timothy 3:1-5)

Narcissism is an ancient spirit that was limited to kings, pharaohs, and pseudo-gods in the ancient times; however, this spirit will expand throughout the world as an end-times spirit. It has already become part of our culture. Our present culture of narcissism is inspired by the god of this world. Everyone has a certain amount of narcissism as our DNA is coded with self-preservation.

Healthy narcissism is defined as a sense of self-worth that includes a realistic assessment of your strengths and weaknesses — you respect yourself, but you also respect others, seeing them as separate human beings who have legitimate needs and wants, including values and ideals that may be different but no less valuable than yours. But this is not the case with people diagnosed with Narcissistic Personality Disorder or NPD. Instead, they exhibit unrestrained self-preoccupation foreign to most of us. "Unhealthy narcissism is occurring when an individual excessively pursues admiration, attention, status, understanding, support, money, power control or perfection in some form."[1]

When we look into NPD, we see the very personality of Lucifer/Satan, and all those who pledge allegiance to him in the form of Faustian contracts, which are those who pay homage to him in some form or another, in exchange for power, fame, wealth and status in this world. Just think of all the dictators of the world, all the empires of the world, all the kingdoms of this world that have come and gone. All have been possessed with an unbalanced form of narcissism, creating megalomaniacs and evil dictators. This is the epitome of the defilement of the temple of God, where the human vessel is literally possessed by the personality of Lucifer/Satan.

In *The Culture of Narcissism*, Christopher Lasch identified a narcissistic culture as one in which every activity and relationship is defined by the hedonistic need to acquire symbols of wealth. It becomes like a competition to see that whoever has the most toys wins.[2]

"We know that we are children of God, and that the whole world is under the control of the evil one."

(1 John 5:19)

Spiritual Narcissism

"I have seen the most sophisticated and well-educated individuals seduced by spiritual narcissists," says Linda Martinez, Ph.D., an expert on narcissistic and borderline disorders. "But true spirituality is the opposite of narcissism. Its purpose is to work through layers of delusion to the truth. Teachers on a spiritual path focus on your issues, not themselves."

Spiritual narcissism is a like a virus in the New Age community because many are really harboring a deep-seated feeling of not being worthy, or good enough, or they are trying to fill a void in themselves from their childhoods or from broken relationships, so they deny working on themselves and mistakenly think they can heal through helping others. Helping others becomes just another kind of addiction. This kind of thinking is distorted because they will bump up against their own issues, as it inevitably will be mirrored back to them from those they attract. They use this to create and attract the drama they need to work out their unresolved inner conflicts. Spiritual narcissism is oxymoronic because the whole purpose of the spiritual path is to transcend the ego; nobody's perfect but that's the journey.

In my opinion, the condition is brought on by attachments, some from the spirit realm and some alien. These attachments keep people under a spell, thinking that they are being given special information from ascended masters, archangels, and a variety of other spirit guides, which titillates the spiritual ego, and instead they are really being manipulated by aliens, fallen angels, and other dark demonic spirits that are used to misguide and disempower others.

> "Certain men, the children of Belial, are gone out from among you, and have withdrawn the inhabitants of their city, saying, Let us go and serve other gods, which you have not known;"
>
> (Deuteronomy 13:13)

Belial is one of the fallen angels (Archdemons) that is sent into the world to influence earth humans *away* from the Almighty Creator Lord. His very name means "worthlessness." So he and his hierarchy of demonic spirits attach to anyone who feels worthless. Psychologically speaking, those with inferiority complexes, compensate with superiority complexes, and this is the most perfect match for this spirit. The spirit of Belial is used to draw people away from the Holy Spirit to serve other gods.

In Hebrew, the word, *eliyl* means "good for nothing, vain or vanity, of no value, thing of naught." Belial tries to lead men astray to follow something that is worthless, whether that be an ideology, a false belief system, or idols, which are worthless and have no value, and cannot satisfy. Think of all the New Age "brick-a-brack" on the market. It is literally a billion dollar market place — from replicas of ancient statutes to crystals, to images of angels, ascended masters, gods, and goddesses. People think, if they can surround themselves with these objects and wear its jewelry, it will make them enlightened and appear to be more spiritual to others. I know this firsthand after spending twenty-five years moving through New Age circles until I woke up to the truth. "Having a form of godliness, but denying the power thereof."

These spirits are seductive. They know how to lure people away from the truth which is in Christ. "In the end times, some shall depart from the faith, giving heed to seducing spirits, and the doctrines of devils." (1 Timothy 4:1). To seduce means "to lead away, to persuade toward disobedience or disloyalty, to lead astray by persuasion or false promises, to attract and to lure." The word *apostasy* means "to abandon one's previous loyalty, to defect." The word *apostasy* is used in the Living Bible's translation of this verse, to say, "some in the church will turn away from Christ."

It's important to note that many New Agers grew up in the church but became despondent and disenchanted because of the religion and the religious spirits. Yet because they were never delivered from these religious spirits, these very spirits followed them into the New Age, expressing the same kind of spiritual narcissism, as they do within religious circles, only it's free to anyone to become a self-proclaimed expert who says, "Look at me! Look at how spiritual I am! I am on the path of ascension, and I am becoming a god!"

The scriptures are clear that only those who have washed their robes clean in the blood of Lamb are given immortality and will become like the angels (extraterrestrial messengers) in heaven. There is a chilling scripture which are the words of Christ Himself, talking about how He will separate his sheep from the goats at the final judgment in Matthew 25. There will be those who will say that they did all kinds of things in his name, and He will turn around and tell them, "I never knew you, depart from me, you who are cursed, into the eternal fire prepared for the devil and his angels. Then they will go away to eternal punishment, but the righteous to eternal life." Then in Revelation 3:16, He will say, "...because you are lukewarm, and neither cold nor hot, I will spew you out of my mouth."

These are heavy duty words coming from the mouth of Jesus Christ, which everyone should take seriously, both Christian and non-believer alike, especially all those in between, like New Agers, who profess to accept Christ, but also follow all the other gods and goddesses, and believe themselves to be so enlightened and spiritual because of it. There is a way which seems right to a man, but the end thereof are the ways of death (Proverbs 14:12).

In the ancient times of the Old Testament, we learn that this spirit caused others to follow other gods. Please read my chapters on Who Are the Gods? And Book Four: Contracts and Agreements for further elucidation. However, suffice it to say, that the god of this world's agenda is to get earth humans off the path of finding truth and liberation from the Almighty Creator Lord, and will employ as many gods or fallen angels who masquerade as gods, as he can to keep people distracted. This was the ongoing story of the Israelites in the Old Testament, and it's the same old story in today's New Age. As the wise old Solomon said, "There is nothing new under the sun."

Every New Ager needs to ask themselves, "What if I'm being deceived? Seduced by spirits of Belial who all masquerade as angels of light?" Again, I ask, if you've invested in lies and delusions, how would you know until it is too late, especially if you believe in those lies as truth." Carl Jung, the first psychologist to coin the phrase "the shadow self," said, "The shadow is a moral problem that challenges the whole ego-personality, for no one can become conscious of the shadow without considerable moral effort."

The shadow self, which is known in psychology, is the part of us that holds onto wounds, unhealed parts, guilt, shame, blame, rejection, which are the personality traits of Lucifer/Satan. Spiritually speaking, the shadow is the portal for demonic activity. While there are New Age techniques to turn one's shadow into empowerment, without Christ, the spirits of the god of this world are at work, just transferring one demon stronghold for another. Spiritually speaking, only Christ can completely "deliver" and heal from the fragmented "psychological shadow."

Carl Jung said, "The masses of men and women in the western world compulsively avoid true, authentic psychoanalytic investigation of their natures, particularly in regards to the so-called "darker" aspects of the personality [the "Shadow" Self]. However, not dealing with the psyche at all proves systemically hazardous. A compromise is required. Hence, the proliferation of the "New Age" Philosophy and movement, together with its many permutations, riddled with ego-customized shams and gimmicks, the application of its methods serve, for the most part, to merely bolster the falling ego and its drives."

In fact, some argue that Westerners on a spiritual path are eager for a "quick fix" to ease their pain or achieve spiritual enlightenment, these are the most vulnerable to narcissistic gurus, self-proclaimed experts in the field of self-improvement, metaphysics, and spirituality. Spiritual Narcissists are emotional and energy vampires.

How often do you go to someone for help and you end up getting sucked into their dramas? Or how many spiritual gurus are motivated to help others just to further their own careers? This happens a lot in the New Age fields, as a little knowledge is a dangerous thing, and many will put out a shingle to help or teach others, when it's really all about them. They are really wolves in sheep's clothing. Spiritual discernment comes in very handy here. Even if you're confused because consciously you are hearing one thing, but subconsciously your emotional guidance system, which often shows up in your body's responses, is telling you another.

One thing to always listen to is your brain's "in the gut" feeling. If you feel like someone is trying to kick you in the stomach, then that's a sure sign that person is an energy vampire. By definition, this is witchcraft, which is all about the control of energy, particularly spiritual energy. Even though they may come in the guise of being a spiritual teacher or an energy healer, what they're really after is your energy, your power, and/or your money. Money is just a form of energy. However, if you pay someone for their services and you walk away feeling drained, tired, or get a headache, that's another sure telltale sign that the "spirit" behind that person has "trafficked" on your energy. This is spiritual narcissism at work. It's also important to note, that most people do not realize that they are doing it, but are demons working through the person's blind spot and/or unhealed shadow self.

Spiritual narcissists mistakenly believe that their issues will dissolve through helping others. Yet the law of attraction kicks in each and every time; they will attract those with the same issues that they refuse to deal with in themselves. If you shift something in yourself, then you are in a better position to assist another to shift that same thing without any residual effects. You can lead by example. However, if there are places in yourself that are blocked or hidden in darkness, then sure as day, you will attract others who will mirror that back to you. This is how the shadow self manifests.

Too many spiritual narcissists have unresolved and unintegrated shadows. This is why they resist hearing anything about healing their shadows. They are in complete denial. Spiritually speaking, there is always a dark spirit attached to their shadows, which energetically feeds off of their clients unaware. This happens through "energy transference," so how can they benefit with clarity and healing when they are going to a healing practitioner who is not clear?

Another common distortion with New Agers is that they are just about "love & light." Suggest that they have unresolved shadow issues means that they will take it as a personal attack to their "spiritual egos." For someone on the path of truth and self-actualization, one must accept the fact that even the light casts a shadow, which is sometimes greater than the shadow cast from darkness.

Another false belief system prevalent in New Age circles is that we create our own reality, that everything that happens to us, we have created. This too is spiritual

CHAPTER TWENTY-ONE: The Office Of Satan

narcissism. How does that belief system account for the actions or inactions of others? It doesn't. It's just another offshoot of the distorted thinking that we are the "center of the universe" and everything we think, say, or do comes to pass. If that were true, then many would be instantly manifesting their fantasies, both dark and light. The truth is always in the middle ground. Yes, we are responsible for our thoughts and actions, but we cannot control the thoughts or actions of others, and to think we can is spiritual narcissism or a form of tyranny.

Not only is it a false belief to think we control everything. It's arrogant to think we do. There is so much going on within the spiritual realms over the control of earth humans; spiritual battles are fought daily over our minds, our bodies, and over who we give our energy to, i.e., in the form of worship. This is the reason other gods were allowed to come to earth. Yet the history tells us that they only set up more control systems and demanded all kinds of worship through fear, particularly live human sacrifices. They fought over control of earth's real estate and resources, one of them being earth humans. They enslaved humans, abused their powers, and in spite of the fact that their empires were overthrown, New Agers today are fascinated with unearthing their lost objects and opening up portals for them by invoking these fallen gods of the past.

The ancients believed the planets were gods. That's why they are named after the gods. There is much interference, as well as many interventions. These battles will eventually all culminate very soon at the end of this present age, where the faithful extraterrestrial angels who serve the Living God within the Federation or Office of Christ will return and overthrow the forces of darkness and deception once and for all for all the world to witness.

Negative people, too often, find their way into our lives. At first they can be fun, friendly, and cool to hang out with. We may believe they want to be close friends, or that they genuinely want to help us. But they end up stealing our energy and draining and depriving us of our spiritual strength.

Discernment is a very important tool and spiritual gift we all need to get us through these changing times. It can make or break someone as to whether or not to "drink" the Kool-Aid, and the many illusions that are thrust upon humans these days. How do you know when to slough something off or when to drink it in?

Most of the time, energy vampires do their best to suck the life force right out of you; it's done subconsciously, but sometimes it's not. These are the types of people who hunt for victims to energize themselves because they have lost their connection with their Creator, who is the source of all life force. These types are actual self-proclaimed "vampire cults," who seem to have more awareness about energy cording than the "subconscious vampires," who are the proverbial drama queens (both men and women included). With chronic bad moods and rehashing of the same dramas, they always seem to be depressed or angry to the point where you may suspect they like it.

Again these people are possessed by the spirits of Lucifer/Satan, as these traits display his personality. They are conversation dominators, and they have no problem talking over your voice as they seem to happily play the role of the victim. They have no interest in you, only to talk about their problems and their issues. They are often resistant to advice because that means they need to change, and they don't want to change. What these folks really need is an exorcism. Deliverance of the demonic is their only salvation, which can only come through turning to Christ, the enemy of the god of this world, who possesses them.

Psychic and emotional vampires don't feel empathy nor do they try to comfort the people around them; instead they are agitators, finding all kinds of ways to provoke your anguish even further. While talking to them, you may even get the feeling of "phantom tentacles" reaching out from their body to yours! After spending time with them, you may wonder where your anxiety build up is coming from without being able to pinpoint the cause?

Psychic vampires can zap your energy from a distance. They do not need to interact with you verbally. This proves that they are being used as vessels for Lucifer/Satan. It's always important to remember this: "We fight not against flesh and blood, but against powers, principalities, rulers of the darkness and spiritual wickedness in the heavens."

(Ephesians 6:12)

DERIVATIVES OF LUCIFER/SATAN

The following names are known as *infernal names* of Satan, and are used to invoke him in rituals. They are also the names of his many *aliases* and *disguises* throughout human history and mythology, and many represent the names of fallen angels and demons that are under his control.

Abaddon - The Destroyer (Hebrew) - Angel of the Abyss
Adramalech - Samarian devil
Ahpuch - Mayan devil
Ahriman - Mazdean devil
Amon - Egyptian ram-headed god of life and reproduction
Apollyon - Greek synonym for Abaddon - Angel of the Abyss
Asmodeus - Hebrew devil of sensuality and luxury, originally "creature of judgment"
Astaroth - Phoenician goddess of lasciviousness, equivalent of Babylonian Ishtar
Astarte – Enemy of Yahuah during Old Testament times, aka Ishtar, today known as the Ashtar Command
Azazel - Taught man to make weapons of war (Hebrew)
Baal - the lord of the sky (UFOs)
Baalbamoth - the lord of the aerial regions. (UFOs)
Baalberith - Canaanite Lord of the covenant who was later made a devil
Balaam - Hebrew devil of avarice and greed
Baphomet - Worshipped by the Templars (by accusation) as symbolic of Satan
Bast - Egyptian goddess of pleasure represented by the cat

CHAPTER TWENTY-ONE: The Office Of Satan

Baalzebub- was the lord of those that 'fly' or flit around the atmosphere (UFOs)
Beelzebub - Lord of the Flies, taken from the symbolism of the scarab (Hebrew)
Behemoth - Hebrew personification of Lucifer in the form of an elephant or hippopotamus
Beherit - Syriac name for Satan
Belial - spirit of worthlessness, causes: idolatry, immorality, filth and godlessness
Bilé - Celtic god of Hell
Chemosh - National god of Moabites, later a devil
Cimeries - Rides a black horse and rules Africa
Dagon - Philistine avenging devil of the sea
Damballa - Voodoo serpent of God
Demogorgon - a name so terrible as to not be known to mortals
Diabolous - "Flowing downwards" (Greek)
Dracula - Romanian name for son of the devil or dragon, which would also denote a "devilish" name—Romanian isn't too clear on which meaning, if not both, is correct.
Enma-O - Japanese ruler of Hell
Euronymous - Greek Prince of Death (a misspelling, correct spelling *Eurynomos*)
Fenris - Son of Loki, depicted as a wolf
Gaia- Fallen ET/angel pseudo god, Greek mythology, Telles Mater (Roman name)
Gorgo (Gorgon) - diminutive of Demogorgon, see above
Gregoroi – Fallen Angels, rebel ETs
Guayota - guanche devil
Haborym - Hebrew synonym for Satan
Hades - Greek mythology, god of underworld, Zeus and Poseidon's brother, one of the most powerful gods
Hecate - Greek goddess of the underworld and witchcraft
Hephaestus - Greek god of fire, Zeus's son.
Hubal - The Babylonian Moon God.
Ishtar - Babylonian goddess of fertility
Jezebel – the pagan Queen of Israel who usurped the Kingdom of Judah through her marriage to King Ahab, who represents all false prophets and is the enemy of Yahuah and Yahuah's prophets.
Jupiter - Roman name for Zeus, who was Lucifer.
Leviathan - Hebrew personification of Lucifer in the form of a great sea reptile (usually it represents the Antichrist; the beast of the sea)
Lilith - Hebrew female devil, Adam's first wife who taught him lust
Loki - Norse god of trickery and deception (not actually a god, a giant instead who lives beside the gods)
Mammon - Aramaic god of wealth and profit
Mania - Etruscan goddess of Hell

Mantus - Etruscan god of Hell

Marduk - god of the city of Babylon

Mastema - Hebrew synonym for Satan; chief of the fallen angel demons

Melek Taus - Yezidi devil

Mephistopheles - he who shuns the light, q.v. Faust (Greek)

Metztli - Aztec goddess of the night

Mictian - Aztec god of death

Midgard serpent - Jörmungandr, son of Loki, depicted as a serpent

Milcom - Ammonite devil

Moloch - Phoenician and Canaanite devil (Nephilim Minotaur)

Mormo - King of the Ghouls, consort of Hecate (Greek)

Naamah - Hebrew female devil of seduction

Nergal - Babylonian god of Hades

Nihasa - American Indian devil

Nija - Polish god of the underworld

O-Yama - Japanese name for lord of death

Pan - Greek god of lust, later relegated to devildom

Pluto - Roman god of the underworld

Prosperine - Greek/Roman queen of the underworld (also spelled Persephone)

Pwcca - one of the myriad of fairy (faerie) folk

Rimmon - Syrian devil worshipped at Damascus

Sabazios - Phrygian origin, identified with Dionysos, snake worship

Saitan - Enochian equivalent of Satan

Samael - "Venom of God" (Hebrew)

Sammael - angel of death; leader of hosts of Satan's army.

Samnu - Central Asian devil

Sanat Kumara - New Age name for Satan (masquerading as an ascended master bound inside the earth. Collects data on earth humans to use to accuse them before God.

Sataniel - the fallen archangel Lucifer/Satan - Hebrew name, for the accuser of God.

Sedit - American Indian devil

Sekhmet - Egyptian goddess of vengeance

Set - Egyptian god of evil (god of disease)

Shaitan - Arabic name for Satan

Supay - Inca god of the underworld

T'an-mo - Chinese counterpart to the devil, covetousness, desire

Tchort - Russian name for Satan, "black god"

Tezcatlipoca - Aztec leopard god of darkness

Thamuz - Sumerian god who was later relegated to devildom

Tunrida - Scandinavian female devil

Typhon - Greek personification of devil

CHAPTER TWENTY-ONE: The Office Of Satan

Yaotzin - Aztec god of Hell
Yen-lo-Wang - Chinese ruler of Hell
Zeus - Lucifer-Jupiter (Roman name)

The Bible calls Satan by many different names. Each name has a slightly different meaning. Remember, that there are many "satans," which in Hebrew means adversaries or enemies. Lucifer/Satan literally has a hierarchy of satans under his dominion. There are princes (arch-demons) and lesser demons. The many other names for Satan give a fuller picture of who Satan is and what he does. It is interesting to note that there are more names for Satan in the Bible than for anyone else, except Jesus Christ.

The following list of names for Satan comes from the New King James Version of the Bible. Toward the end of this present age, Satan will leave the spirit world that he has lived in for thousands of years. He will become visible to us and will claim that he is God. The Bible calls him the Beast and Antichrist.

Abaddon

Hebrew name for Satan meaning "Destruction". "And they had as king over them the angel of the bottomless pit, whose name in Hebrew is Abaddon, but in Greek he has the name Apollyon." (Revelation 9:11)

Accuser

"Then I heard a loud voice saying in heaven, 'Now salvation, and strength, and the kingdom of our God, and the power of His Christ have come, for the accuser of our brethren, who accused them before our God day and night, has been cast down.'" (Revelation 12:10)

Adversary

"Be sober, be vigilant; because your adversary the devil walks about like a roaring lion, seeking whom he may devour." (1 Peter 5:8)

Angel of light

"And no wonder! For Satan himself transforms himself into an angel of light." (2 Corinthians 11:14)

Angel of the bottomless pit

"And they had as king over them the angel of the bottomless pit, whose name in Hebrew is Abaddon, but in Greek he has the name Apollyon." (Revelation 9:11)

Anointed covering cherub

"You were the anointed cherub who covers; I established you; you were on the holy mountain of God; you walked back and forth in the midst of fiery stones." (Ezekiel 28:14)

Antichrist

"And every spirit that does not confess that Jesus Christ has come in the flesh is not of God. And this is the spirit of the Antichrist, which you have heard was coming, and is now already in the world." (1 John 4:3)

Angel of Light

"And no wonder, for Satan himself masquerades as an angel of light." (2 Corinthians 11:14)

Apollyon

Greek name for Satan meaning "Destroyer". "And they had as king over them the angel of the bottomless pit, whose name in Hebrew is Abaddon, but in Greek he has the name Apollyon." (Revelation 9:11)

Beast

"Then a third angel followed them, saying with a loud voice, 'If anyone worships the beast and his image, and receives his mark on his forehead or on his hand, he himself shall also drink of the wine of the wrath of God, which is poured out full strength into the cup of His indignation. He shall be tormented with fire and brimstone in the presence of the holy angels and in the presence of the Lamb.'"(Revelation 14:9-10 - Who is the beast?)

Beelzebub

"Now when the Pharisees heard it they said, 'This fellow does not cast out demons except by Beelzebub, the ruler of the demons.'" (Matthew 12:24)

Belial

"And what accord has Christ with Belial? Or what part has a believer with an unbeliever?" (2 Corinthians 6:15)

Deceiver

"So the great dragon was cast out, that serpent of old, called the Devil and Satan, who deceives the whole world; he was cast to the earth, and his angels were cast out with him." (Revelation 12:9)

Devil

"He who sins is of the devil, for the devil has sinned from the beginning. For this purpose the Son of God was manifested, that He might destroy the works of the devil." (1 John 3:8)

Dragon

"So the great dragon was cast out, that serpent of old, called the Devil and Satan, who deceives the whole world; he was cast to the earth, and his angels were cast out with him." (Revelation 12:9)

"And there was war in heaven. Michael and his angels fought against the dragon, and the dragon and his angels fought back." (Revelation 12:7)

Enemy

"The enemy who sowed them is the devil, the harvest is the end of the age, and the reapers are the angels." (Matthew 13:39)

Evil one

"I do not pray that you should take them out of the world, but that you should keep them from the evil one." (John 17:15)

CHAPTER TWENTY-ONE: The Office Of Satan

Father of lies
"You are of your father the devil, and the desires of your father you want to do. He was a murderer from the beginning, and does not stand in the truth, because there is no truth in him. When he speaks a lie, he speaks from his own resources, for he is a liar and the father of it." (John 8:44)

God of this world (age)
"Whose minds the god of this world (age) has blinded, who do not believe, lest the light of the gospel of the glory of Christ, who is the image of God, should shine on them." (2 Corinthians 4:4)

Great Red Dragon
"And there appeared another wonder in heaven; and behold a great red dragon, having seven heads and ten horns, and seven crowns upon his heads. "- (Revelation 12:3)

"The great dragon was hurled down--that ancient serpent called the devil, or Satan, who leads the whole world astray. He was hurled to the earth, and his angels with him." (Revelation 12:9)

Heleyl
"How you are fallen from heaven, O Heleyl, son of the morning! How you are cut down to the ground, you who weakened the nations! For you have said in your heart: 'I will ascend into heaven, I will exalt my throne above the stars of God; I will also sit on the mount of the congregation on the farthest sides of the north; I will ascend above the heights of the clouds, I will be like the Most High.'"

(Isaiah 14:12-14)

King of Babylon
"That you will take up this proverb against the king of Babylon, and say: 'How the oppressor has ceased, the golden city ceased!'"

(Isaiah 14:4)

King of the bottomless pit
"And they had as king over them the angel of the bottomless pit, whose name in Hebrew is Abaddon, but in Greek he has the name Apollyon." (Revelation 9:11)

King of Tyre
"Son of man, take up a lamentation for the king of Tyre, and say to him, 'thus says the Lord GOD: "You were the seal of perfection, Full of wisdom and perfect in beauty."'(Ezekiel 28:12)

Lawless one
"And then the lawless one will be revealed, whom the Lord will consume with the breath of His mouth and destroy with the brightness of His coming. 9 The coming of the lawless one is according to the working of Satan, with all power, signs, and lying wonders, 10 and with all unrighteous deception among those who perish, because they did not receive the love of the truth, that they might be saved."

(2 Thessalonians 2:8-10)

Leviathan

"In that day the LORD with His severe sword, great and strong, Will punish Leviathan the fleeing serpent, Leviathan that twisted serpent; And He will slay the reptile that is in the sea." (Isaiah 27:1)

Liar

"You are of your father the devil, and the desires of your father you want to do. He was a murderer from the beginning, and does not stand in the truth, because there is no truth in him. When he speaks a lie, he speaks from his own resources, for he is a liar and the father of it." (John 8:44)

Little horn

"And out of one of them came a little horn which grew exceedingly great toward the south, toward the east, and toward the Glorious Land. And it grew up to the host of heaven; and it cast down some of the host and some of the stars to the ground, and trampled them. 11 He even exalted himself as high as the Prince of the host; and by him the daily sacrifices were taken away, and the place of His sanctuary was cast down." (Daniel 8:9-11)

Lucifer

"How you are fallen from heaven, O Lucifer, son of the morning! How you are cut down to the ground, you who weakened the nations! For you have said in your heart: 'I will ascend into heaven, I will exalt my throne above the stars of God; I will also sit on the mount of the congregation on the farthest sides of the north; I will ascend above the heights of the clouds, I will be like the Most High.'"(Isaiah 14:12-14)

Mammon

In the Bible, Mammon is personified in Luke 16:13, and Matthew 6:24, the latter verse repeating Luke 16:13. In some translations, Luke 16:9 and Luke 16:11 also personify mammon; but in others, it is translated as 'dishonest wealth' or equivalent. "No one can serve two masters, for either he will hate the one and love the other; or else he will be devoted to one and despise the other. You cannot serve both God and Mammon." (Matthew 6:24)

Man of sin

"Let no one deceive you by any means; for that Day will not come unless the falling away comes first, and the man of sin is revealed, the son of perdition, 4 who opposes and exalts himself above all that is called God or that is worshiped, so that he sits as God in the temple of God, showing himself that he is God."

(2 Thessalonians 2:3-4)

Murderer

"You are of your father the devil, and the desires of your father you want to do. He was a murderer from the beginning, and does not stand in the truth, because there is no truth in him. When he speaks a lie, he speaks from his own resources, for he is a liar and the father of it." (John 8:44)

CHAPTER TWENTY-ONE: The Office Of Satan

Power of darkness

"He has delivered us from the power of darkness and conveyed us into the kingdom of the Son of His love, 14 in whom we have redemption through His blood, the forgiveness of sins." (Colossians 1:13-14)

Prince of the power of the air

"In which you were living in the past, after the ways of this present world, doing the pleasure of prince (lord) of the power of the air, the spirit who now works in the sons of disobedience (those who go against the purpose of God)." (Ephesians 2:2)

Rahab

"By his power he churned up the sea; by his wisdom he cut Rahab to pieces." (Job 26:12)

Roaring lion

"Be sober, be vigilant; because your adversary the devil walks about like a roaring lion, seeking whom he may devour." (1 Peter 5:8)

Rulers of the darkness

"For we do not wrestle against flesh and blood, but against principalities, against powers, against the rulers of the darkness of this age, against spiritual hosts of wickedness in the heavenly places." (Ephesians 6:12)

Ruler of demons

"But some of them said, 'He casts out demons by Beelzebub, the ruler of the demons.'" (Luke 11:15)

Ruler (Prince) of this world

Jesus said, "Now is the judgment of this world; now the ruler (prince) of this world will be cast out. And when I am lifted up from the earth, I will draw all peoples to Myself."

(John 12:31-32)

Satan

And the LORD said to Satan, "I, the LORD, reject your accusations, Satan. Yes, the LORD, who has chosen Jerusalem, rebukes you." (Zechariah 3:2) "And He was there in the wilderness forty days, tempted by Satan, and was with the wild beasts; and the angels ministered to Him." (Mark 1:13)

Serpent of old

"So the great dragon was cast out, that serpent of old, called the Devil and Satan, who deceives the whole world; he was cast to the earth, and his angels were cast out with him." (Revelation 12:9)

Son of the Morning

"How you are fallen from heaven, O Day Star, son of the Morning (Dawn)! How you are cut down to the ground, you who laid the nations low! You said in your heart, "I will ascend to heaven; I will raise my throne above the stars of God; I will sit on the mount of congregation on the heights of Zaphon; I will ascend to the tops of the clouds, I will make myself like the Most High." But you are brought down to Sheol, to the depths of the Pit. Those who see you will stare at you, and ponder over you: "Is this the man who made the earth tremble, who shook kingdoms, who made the world like a desert and overthrew its cities, who would not let his prisoners go home?"

(Isaiah 14:12)

Son of perdition

"Let no one deceive you by any means; for that Day will not come unless the falling away comes first, and the man of sin is revealed, the son of perdition, who opposes and exalts himself above all that is called God or that is worshiped, so that he sits as God in the temple of God, showing himself that he is God."

(2 Thessalonians 2:3-4)

Star

"Then the fifth angel sounded: And I saw a star fallen from heaven to the earth. To him was given the key to the bottomless pit."

(Revelation 9:1)

Tempter

"Now when the tempter came to Him, he said, 'If You are the Son of God, command that these stones become bread.'"

(Matthew 4:3)

Thief

"The thief does not come except to steal, and to kill, and to destroy. I have come that they may have life, and that they may have it more abundantly."

(John 10:10)

Wicked one

"Above all, taking the shield of faith with which you will be able to quench all the fiery darts of the wicked one."

(Ephesians 6:16)

"When any one heareth the word of the kingdom, and understandeth [it] not, then cometh the wicked [one], and catcheth away that which was sown in his heart. This is he which received seed by the way side. . . . The field is the world; the good seed are the children of the kingdom; but the tares are the children of the wicked [one];"

(Matthew 13:19, 38)

NOTES:

1. Eleanor D. Payson, MS.W., *The Wizard of Oz and other Narcissists* (Julian Day Publications, 2002).
2. Christopher Latch, *The Culture of Narcissim,* W. W. Norton & Company; Revised edition (May 17, 1991)

CHAPTER TWENTY-TWO

WHO IS ALLAH?

"You shall have no other gods before me."
(Exodus 20:3; Deuteronomy 5:7)

"You shall have no alien god among you;
you shall not worship any god other than me. (YAHUAH)."
(Psalm 81:9)

In Islam, worshipping Allah as the one and only God, arrived on the scene about 600 years after Christianity. With no written Arab history before the prophet Mohammed, Allah's origins are a matter of conjecture, but Muslims regard him as one in the same with the Judeo-Christian God that spoke to Abraham, Moses, and Jesus. Contrary to Muslim claims, the word, "Allah" is never found in the Judeo-Christian Bible in either Hebrew or Greek. The closest two words we find is the Hebrew 'alah' (which means to curse, mourn or rise, and is never applied to God) and the Hebrew word, "Elah" which has been translated to either an oak or turpentine tree in Isaiah 6:13).

The following information came from Alberto Rivera, former Jesuit priest after his conversion to Protestant Christianity. It is excerpted from his book, *The Prophet*.[1] Since its publication, after several unsuccessful attempts on his life, he died suddenly from food poisoning at age sixty-one. His testimony should not be silenced. Dr. Rivera speaks to us still...

Mohammed's development is even more intriguing as told in Rivera's book, *The Prophet*:[1] "What I'm going to tell you is what I learned in secret briefings in the Vatican when I was a Jesuit priest, under oath and induction. A Jesuit cardinal named Augustine Bea showed us how desperately the Roman Catholics wanted Jerusalem at the end of the third century. Because of its religious history and its strategic location, the Holy City was considered a priceless treasure. A scheme had to be developed to make Jerusalem a Roman Catholic city.

"In their 'holy' book, the Quran, Christ is regarded as only a prophet. If the pope was His representative on earth, then he also must be a prophet of God. This caused the followers of Muhammad to fear and respect the pope as another 'holy man.'

"The pope moved quickly and issued bulls granting the Arab generals permission to invade and conquer the nations of North Africa. The Vatican helped to finance the building of these massive Islamic armies in exchange for three favors:

1. Eliminate the Jews and Christians (true believers, which they called infidels);
2. Protect the Augustinian Monks and Roman Catholics;
3. Conquer Jerusalem for 'His Holiness' in the Vatican.

In the Vatican briefing, Cardinal Bea told us this story:

'A wealthy Arabian lady who was a faithful follower of the pope played a tremendous part in this drama. She was a widow named Khadijah. She gave her wealth to the church and retired to a convent, but was given an assignment. She was to find a brilliant young man who could be used by the Vatican to create a new religion and become the messiah for the children of Ishmael. Khadijah had a cousin named Waraquah, who was also a very faithful Roman Catholic and the Vatican placed him in a critical role as Muhammad's advisor. He had tremendous influence on Muhammad.

"Under Waraquah's direction, Muhammad wrote that Abraham offered Ishmael as a sacrifice. The Bible says that Isaac was the sacrifice, but Muhammad removed Isaac's name and inserted Ishmael's name. As a result of this and Muhammad's vision, the faithful Muslims built a mosque, the Dome of the Rock, in Ishmael's honor on the site of the Jewish temple that was destroyed in 70 AD. This made Jerusalem the second most holy place in the Islam faith. How could they give such a sacred shrine to the pope without causing a revolt?

"Turkey fell and Spain and Portugal were invaded by Islamic forces. In Portugal, they called a mountain village 'Fatima' in honor of Muhammad's daughter, never dreaming it would become world famous.

"As a result, the Muslims were allowed to occupy Turkey in a 'Christian' world, and the Catholics were allowed to occupy Lebanon in the Arab world. It was also agreed that the Muslims could build mosques in Catholic countries without interference as long as Roman Catholicism could flourish Arab countries.

"Cardinal Bea told us in Vatican briefings that both the Muslims and Roman Catholics agreed to block and destroy the efforts of their common enemy, Bible-believing Christian missionaries. Through these concordats, Satan blocked the children of Ishmael from a knowledge of Scripture and the truth.

"As a result of the vision of Fatima, Pope Pius XII ordered his Nazi army to crush Russia and the Orthodox religion and make Russia Roman Catholic. A few years after he lost World War II, Pope Pius XII startled the world with his phony dancing sun vision to keep Fatima in the news. It was great religious show biz and the world swallowed it."

Biblical and historical sources trace Allah's lineage back to the Meccans' Hubal, passed down Baal from the Moabites. That Allah is the God of the Bible is problematic. Julius Wellhausen stated, "At first Allah was the title used within each individual tribe to address its tribal deity instead of its proper name. All but one had its own deity in mind which became the common expression for 'the God' (al-ilah)."

One of Islam's central principles and confessions, commonly known as the Tahlîl (meaning rejoicing or jubilation) is: â Ilâh La Illâ Allâh[2], which means, "There is no God

CHAPTER TWENTY-TWO: WHO IS ALLAH?

except 'The God.' "It is interesting to note, that the word, Allah literally means "The God" in Arabic. It really isn't a name but a title and designation; just like Adonai which in Hebrew means "The Lord."

"No God, except 'The God' does not make good literal sense; however it suggests a direct correlation to the Judeo-Christian scriptures in which Yahuah (YHVH) says, "Thou shalt have no other Gods before me" (Exodus 20:3; Deuteronomy 5:7). There is a God, whose name is Yahuah (YHVH). The name Yahuah is not a title or designation, but the name of the God of Israel, which literally translates to 'I was, I am, and I always will be."

The Hadith[3] was compiled two centuries after Mohammed's passing. Muslims use the Hadith as their prime point of reference that Allah is God. There is no reference in the ancient Hebrew or Greek writings that Allah is the name of the Judeo-Christian monotheistic God. If any such references would have existed, they in fact would have preceded all Islamic references to this claim. The monotheistic God of the Judeo – Christian bible, "Yahuah'[4] is derived from the root 'H V H' - "ה ו ה", meaning 'to exist' or 'present.' 'YHVH' (יהוה) is transliterated to 'The Self Existent One' or 'He who is.'"

That the name Yahuah is unique to the Judeo-Christian Bible is attested to by the fact that no other tribe, nation or culture ever worshipped a deity of that name. Created as the sacred name of God, it is comprised of the consonants "Y H V H" and the vowels from the Hebrew word Adonai meaning "Lord."

"And he that blasphemes the name of the LORD, he shall surely be put to death, and all the congregation shall certainly stone him: as well the stranger, as he that is born in the land, when he blasphemes the name of the LORD, shall be put to death." (Leviticus 24:16)

Muslims continue to claim that Allah is the God of the Bible, and that he is mentioned in all sacred texts. This is false; however, this may be true when relating to the texts of the Quran. This statement cannot be justified as true for any Judeo-Christian sacred texts and certainly there is no reference to Allah meaning God in the Hebrew texts, nor is there any reference in the Greek texts.

Muslims continue to argue that Allah is the same word as the Hebrew words "Eloah," "El," or "Elohim." However these words only refer to the word "God," which can infer to any of the pagan deities and idols, and not specifically to the actual name of God, which is clearly noted in the Judeo-Christian Bible as Yahuah and not Allah. It is only the Islamic contention that Allah is the only name of God, and sets him apart from all other gods.

However, for the Judeo-Christian monotheistic believers, the true name of God is engraved in stone, within the Third Commandment:

"Thou shalt not take the name of YAHUAH (the LORD) thy God in vain; for YAHUAH (the LORD) will not hold him guiltless that takes his name in vain." (Exodus 20:7)

It is important to note here, too, that the true name of the Messiah and the "Son of God," was preserved in "His" name, too. The name given to Miriam (Mary) through the Angel Gabriel, was Yahushua - which literally translated, means "YAHUAH saves."

H.A.R. Gibb[5], a renowned Middle East scholar claims that Muhammad's audience was well-acquainted with a deity persona called Allah, long before his own birth. The Prophet Mohammed, as a spiritual leader was never required to explain the existence of Allah.

There are those that argue that linguistic origin of the word Allah is purely Arabic; however Dr. Arthur Jefferey[6] contends, "The common theory is that it is formed from ilah, the common word for a God, and the article al-; thus al-ilah, the God;" becomes Allah, "God."; this theory, however, is untenable. In fact, the name is one of the words borrowed into the language in pre-Islamic times from Aramaic."

"Al-Ilah" is an Arabic compound word, structured from 'Al' (definite article), meaning 'the' and 'Ilah' meaning God, or "The God", before it was contracted to its shorter form of Allah. 'Ilah' is the Arabic masculine root for the word Allah, and 'Al Ilat is the feminine, which results in 'Allat'[7]. Arabic Lexicographical Miscellanies is well sourced reference to this argument.

In addition to numerous historical references, there is a general consensus among scholars that Allah was a pagan idol-deity, worshipped long before the Prophet Muhammad.

Dr. Arthur Jeffery[6], professor of Islamic and Middle East Studies at Columbia University, states, "The name Allah, as the Quran itself is witness, was well known in pre-Islamic Arabia. Indeed both it and its feminine form, Allat, are found not infrequently among the theophorous names in inscriptions from North Africa."

Henry Preserved Smith[4], of Harvard University states, "Allah was already known to Arabs."

Dr. Kenneth Craig[8], (former editor of *Muslim World*) commented, "The name Allah is also evident in archeological and literary remains of pre-Islamic Arabia" Dr. W. Montgomery Watt[9], professor of Arabic and Islamic Studies at Edinburgh University concluded, "In recent years I have become increasing convinced that for an adequate understanding of the career of Muhammad and the origins of Islam great importance must be attached to the existence in Mecca of belief in Allah as a 'high God.' In a sense this is a form of paganism, but is as different from paganism as commonly understood that it deserves separate treatment."

Caesar Farah[10] in his book on Islam, states, "There is no reason, therefore, to accept the idea that Allah passed to the Muslims from the Christians and the Jews" The following are a sample of historic records, showing that Allah was indeed linked to a pagan deity, preceding the birth of the Prophet Mohammed." Allah is a pre-Islamic name…corresponding to the Babylonian Bel."[11] "Allah is found…in Arabic inscriptions prior to Islam."[12] "The Arabs, before the time of Mohammed, accepted and worshipped,

CHAPTER TWENTY-TWO: WHO IS ALLAH?

after a fashion a supreme God called Allah."[13] "Allah was known to the pre-Islamic ... Arabs; he was one of the Meccan deities."[14] "The name Allah goes back before Mohammad."[15] "Abd Allah" was the name of the Prophet Mohammad's own father, and his Uncle was named "Obred Allah" thus proving that the name of Allah existed prior to the Prophet's birth.

Moshay[16] states that, "Historians like Vaqqidi have said Allah was actually the chief of the 360 Gods [one for each day of the year] being worshipped in Arabia at the time Muhammad rose to prominence. Ibn Al-Kalbi gave twenty-seven names of pre-Islamic deities. Interestingly, not many Muslims want to accept that Allah was already being worshipped at the Ka'aba in Mecca by Arab pagans before Muhammad came. Some Muslims become angry when they are confronted with this fact. But history is not on their side. Pre-Islamic literature has proved this." Allah, along with his 360 pagan-idols were worshipped at the sacred temple of Kaabah[17] in the holy city of Mecca, long before the birth of the Prophet Mohammed and the rise of Islam, by the pagan Bedouin tribes of the Arabian Peninsula.

Caesar Farah[18] also contended that, "Allah, the paramount deity of pagan Arabia, was the target of worship in varying degrees of intensity, from the southernmost tip of Arabia to the Mediterranean. To the Babylonians, he was IL (God); to the Canaanites, and later the Israelites, he was El; the South Arabians worshiped him as Ilah, and the Bedouins as al-Ilah (the deity). With Muhammad he becomes Allah, God of the Worlds, of all believers, the one and only who admits of no associates or consorts in the worship of Him. Judaic and Christian concepts of God abetted the transformation of Allah from a pagan deity to the God of all monotheists. There is no reason, therefore, to accept the idea that Allah passed to the Muslims from Christians and Jews."

The Encyclopedia of World Mythology and Legend[19] states that unlike other pagan religions, "In Arabia, the sun God was viewed as a female Goddess, and the moon as the male God." Deadmond[19] continues to note that scholars such as Alfred Guilluame claim that this moon God was called Allah. "Along with Allah, however, they worshipped a host of lesser Gods and "daughters of Al-lah." Each tribe of the Arabian Peninsula worshipped their own variety of pagan idol-deities, in the form Gods and Goddesses.

Nazir Ali[12] states, "A number of these tribes also acknowledged the existence of an unknown God, they called 'Al-Ilah', which literally means 'the God.' He was considered to be the invisible supreme deity." This moon God, 'Al- Illah' or Allah, was the God of the Quarish tribe. Together with the sun Goddess, they produced three 'Goddesses of Allah,' named 'Al-Lat,' 'Al-Uzza,' and 'Al-Manat.' 'Al-Lat' and 'Al-Uzza' are both feminine forms of Allah. These 'high-Goddesses' were perceived by the people of the desert tribes as their personal emissaries and mediators to Allah or 'Al-Illah,' the supreme God."

The daughters of Allah, along with Allah and the sun Goddess were viewed as "high" Gods, meaning they were viewed as being at the top of the pantheon of Arabian deities."[20] This quartet, the moon God and his three daughters, were the most prominent and dominant pagan idol-deities of all the Gods worshipped at the Kaabah or Beit-Allah (House of Allah).

These Goddesses represented "Al-Lat"- the sun, "Al-Uzza" - the planet Venus, and Al-Manat ~ Fortune.[21] It is interesting to note that, according to McLean, "Long before the coming of the austere patriarchal system of Islam, the Arabic people worshipped this trinity of desert goddesses who were the three facets of the one Goddess. Al-Uzza ('the mighty') represented the Virgin warrior facet; she was a desert Goddess of the morning star, who had a sanctuary in a grove of acacia trees to the south of Mecca, where she was worshipped in the form of a sacred stone. Al-Lat, whose name means simply 'Goddess,' was the Mother facet connected with the Earth and its fruits and the ruler of fecundity. She was worshipped at At-Ta' if near Mecca in the form of a great uncut block of white granite. Manat, the crone facet of the Goddess, ruled fate and death. Her principal sanctuary was located on the road between Mecca and Medina, where she was worshipped in the form of a black uncut stone."[22]

NOTES:

1. Alberto Rivera, *The Prophet*. Chick Publications, 1979.
2. Hanna Jones, 2.2 Billion: World's Muslim Population Doubles, Time News Feed, Jan. 27, 2011, Web. 2011, Web. wsfeed.time.com/2011/01/27/2-2-billion-worlds-muslim-population-doubles/) 19 August, 2013.
3. Wellhausen, Juli Reste Arabischen Heidenthums, p. 221. Book. Berlin, Druck Und Verlag Von Geroge Reimer, 1897. Printed Book from the Collection of Harvard University. Digitilizing Sponsor: Google: Web. (http://archive.org/stream/restearabischen000wellgoog#page/n7/mode/2up.) 21 August 2013.
4. Arthur Jeffery, Islam: Muhammad, and His Religion, New York: The Liberal Arts Press, 1958, p.85
5. "Hadith" Wikipedia® The Free Encyclopedia, Wikipedia.com, 26 Jan 2013, Web, August 18, 2013, Web. (http://en.wikipedia.org/wiki/Hadith) 18 August, 2013
6. "Judaism" Exposed, Abrahams Faith.Blogspot.com, Blogspot, March 30, 2011, Web, (http://abrahamsfaith.blogspot.com/2011/03/allah-god-of-ishmael-god-of-israel.html) 22 March, 2013
7. H.A.R. Gibb, Mohammedanism: An Historical Survey, New York: Mentor Books, 1955 Web, Google Books, (The Islamic Invasion – Ph. D. Dr Robert a Morey - Google Books – (http://goo.gl/HwKvGt)
8. "Arabic Lexicographical Miscellanies"; by J. Blau in the Journal of Semitic Studies, Vol. XVII, #2, 1972, pp. 173-190A

CHAPTER TWENTY-TWO: WHO IS ALLAH?

9. The Bible and Islam, or The Influence of the Old and New Testament on the Religion of Mohammed, New York, Charles Scribner's Sons, 1897, p 102
10. The Call of the Minaret, New York: Oxford University Press, 1956, p.31
11. William Montgomery Watt, Muhammad's Mecca, p.vii. Also see his article, "Belief in a High God in Pre-Islamic";, Journal of Semitic Studies, Vol. 16, 1971, pp. 35-40.
12. Islam: Beliefs and Observations, New York Barrons, 1987, p. 28
13. Encyclopedia of Religion, I:117, Washington DC, Corpus Pub, 1979
14. Encyclopedia Britannica, I:643
15. Encyclopedia of Islam, I:302, Leiden: E.J. Brill, 1913, Houtsma
16. Encyclopedia of Islam, I:406, ed. Gibb
17. Encyclopedia of World Mythology and Legend, I:41, Anthony Mercatante, New York, The Facts on File, 1983
18. G. J. O. Moshay, Who Is This Allah? 1994, pg. 138.
19. "Understanding Al-iLah – The god of Muhammad, Islam and Muslims (Part 1)", Welcome to Islam Watch, Islam Watch, 12 January, 2013, Web (http://www.islam-watch.org/authors/110-brokaan/1224-understanding-al-ilah-the-god-of-muhammad-islam-and-muslims-part-1.html)
20. Caesar E. Farrah, Ph.D., Islam: Its Beliefs and Observances [Barron's Educational Series, Inc., Sixth Edition, 2000; ISBN: 0764112058], p. 28
21. Encyclopedia of World Mythology and Legend, I:61.
22. Robert Morey, *The Islamic Invasion*, Eugene, Oregon, Harvest House Publishers, 1977, pp.50-51.

CHAPTER TWENTY-THREE

BABYLONIAN HISTORY: WHERE IT ALL BEGAN

"All the false religions come out of Babylon." ~Anonymous

The sacred and the profane are sometimes two sides of the same coin. Satan's power is still strong and pervasive, making discernment man's best remedy.

Idolatry was born in Babylon, and just like a virus, it spread in all directions, through all civilizations down through history. This is why it's been said, that all the false religions come out of Babylon. The first people to be worshiped as gods were Nimrod, his wife Semiramis, and their child Tammuz. What does Tammuz have to do with the sign of the cross? We will explore that and much more in this chapter.

We can still see that worship throughout most of the world today. Most pagans were so superstitious that they kept the same names for gods in use down through the ages, even though different names were used in different cultures, you can still see their influences today in many of the world's religions. Sadly these influences crept into the church and still are there today.

BABYLON: THE GREAT MOTHER OF PROSTITUTES AND THE ABOMINATIONS OF THE EARTH

"I saw that the woman was drunk with the blood of God's holy people, the blood of those who bore testimony to Jesus.

When I saw her, I was greatly astonished. Then the angel said to me: "Why are you astonished? I will explain to you the mystery of the woman and of the beast she rides, which has the seven heads and ten horns. The beast, which you saw, once was, now is not, and yet will come up out of the Abyss and go to its destruction. The inhabitants of the earth whose names have not been written in the book of life from the creation of the world will be astonished when they see the beast, because it once was, now is not, and yet will come."

This calls for a mind with wisdom. The seven heads are seven hills on which the woman sits. They are also seven kings. Five have fallen, one is, the other has not yet come; but when he does come, he must remain for only a little while. The beast who once was, and now is not, is an eighth king. He belongs to the seven and is going to his destruction."

The ten horns you saw are ten kings who have not yet received a kingdom, but who for one hour will receive authority as kings along with the beast. They have one purpose and will give their power and authority to the beast. They will wage war against the Lamb, but the Lamb will triumph over them because he is Lord of lords and King of kings (and God of gods)—and with him will be his called, chosen and faithful followers."

Then the angel said to me, "The waters you saw, where the prostitute sits, are peoples, multitudes, nations and languages. The beast and the ten horns you saw will hate the prostitute. They will bring her to ruin and leave her naked; they will eat her flesh and burn her with fire. For God has put it into their hearts to accomplish his purpose by agreeing to hand over to the beast their royal authority, until God's words are fulfilled. The woman you saw is the great city that rules over the kings of the earth."

(Revelation 17:1-18 NIV)

Babylon: The First "United Nations"

"And Cush begat Nimrod: he began to be a mighty one in the earth. He was a mighty hunter before the Lord: wherefore it is said, even as Nimrod the mighty hunter before the Lord. And the beginning of his kingdom was Babel."

(Genesis 10:8-10)

"And it came to pass, as they journeyed from the east, that they found a plain in the land of Shinar; and they dwelt there. And they said one to another, Go to, let us make brick, and burn them thoroughly. And they had brick for stone, and slime had they for mortar. And they said, Go to, let us build us a city and a tower, whose top may reach unto heaven; and let us make us a name, lest we be scattered abroad upon the face of the whole earth."

(Genesis 11:2-4)

"And the LORD (Yahuah) came down to see the city and the tower, which the children of men built. And the LORD said, Behold, the people is one, and they have all one language; and this they begin to do: and now nothing will be restrained from them, which they have imagined to do. Go to, let us go down, and there confound their language, that they may not understand one another's speech. So the LORD scattered them abroad from thence upon the face of all the earth: and they left off to build the city."

(Genesis 11:5-8)

After the flood, eventually all of Noah's descendants migrated to the plains of Shinar in Babylonia. The religion formed by Cush (who was also known by other various names such as the god Bel/Nebo Janus/Hermes and also known as the False Prophet) and Nimrod was the beginning of polytheism, or the worship of many gods. The first ancient empire was formed; the Chaldean Kingdom (Sumerian Kingdom). Nimrod, one of the great-grandsons of Noah was their leader, their King and the founder of Babylon.

Everyone spoke the same language and also had one religion but over the generations the truth had been distorted and astrology, ancient myths and spiritism had crept in. Idolatry and human sacrifice were among its rituals. The first astrological tower, known as a ziggurat or step pyramid, was built on the plains of Shinar in the very evil city of Babel.

The Bible tells us that God "has made of 'one blood' all nations of men for to dwell on all the face of the earth" (Acts 17:26). It appears that God had, from the beginning, intended that man multiply and fill the earth, but at Babel, the great grandson of Noah, Nimrod, organized a great rebellion. It was Satan's attempt to defy God and His authority. Nimrod claimed to have the wisdom of the world that was before the flood. He told them, "I know the truth, and I know the mysteries and the secrets." (Those secrets were about the civilization prior to the flood).

Who Was Nimrod?

Nimrod was the originator of sun worship. In ancient Nineveh Artifacts dated 2000 BC, Nimrod was deified. His name (in Hebrew "Na-ma-rood") was a derivative from the Hebrew root verb "Marad" which means "to rebel." Nimrod was born in 3,275 BC about ninety-five years after the flood waters receded. He was a descendant of Noah. His birthday was celebrated three days after the Winter Solstice, which is December 25.

Mithras, later replaced Nimrod, whose birthday was also on December 25. Yahushua Ha Mashiach, aka Jesus Christ of Nazareth was not born on December 25. The Bible record is clear that he was born at the beginning of the Feast of Tabernacles, which is also called Sukkot, and always begins at the Harvest Moon in the beginning of the Fall. So we have the celebration of the birth of Jesus changed to comport with pagan precedence.

Nimrod claimed to have the wisdom of the world that was present before the flood. He told them, "I know the truth, and I know the mysteries and the secrets." Nimrod and Semiramis revived occult practices that caused the flood in the first place. They claimed to be the wise ones.

The Nephilim, pre-flood warriors, were not totally wiped out during the flood, some of them escaped into the underworld through caverns and surfaced after the flood. There are various sources that state that Nimrod acquired the knowledge from two fallen angels, Horus and Marduk. He also had incredible magical powers given to him by those fallen angels. Nimrod set himself up as superior to God in every conceivable way.

Nimrod was a great astronomer and astrologer. He traced the circular path (Zodiac) followed by the sun in the sky during the various seasons to complete the annual solar cycle. He divided the zodiac into twelve more or less regular portions (houses) or months, to be able to forecast more accurately what could best be grown in that particular period, what influence it would have upon plants, animals, and even human beings. He claimed that each of these constellations of the zodiac controlled and guided the lives, career, health, character, behavior, marriage, and destiny of that person, who was born during its corresponding period of influence. Nimrod was influenced by one of the two hundred fallen sons of heaven, which the Book of Enoch names as Baraquiel, who taught men astrology. Nimrod's version of Astrology came from those who were in rebellion against God, and twisted the original meanings of the stars and constellations. This is why giving credence to your astrological prediction is paying tribute to Nimrod, which is idolatry to the Lord of Israel.

Astrology is God's Language; as the Bible says, that the Heavens Declare the Glory of God (Psalm 19:1). (See my chapter, The Divine Plan of Salvation as Written in the Stars, Book Five of my book series, *The Heavens*). There is a Prophetic Significance of the Twelve Signs of the Zodiac; and the heavenly scrolls reveal that The Word of God was "first" written into the stars before it was given on written scrolls to humankind. All of that knowledge was perverted when Nimrod rewrote the Zodiac by altering the meanings of the signs and counterfeited the prophesies in the stars to further his own agenda. This was part of his rebellion and the effects of which still resonate today.

Nimrod also renamed the twelve guides or satellites of the Sun, appropriating periods of influence, even his names have changed with the changes of languages, as well as the rise and fall of both Greco-Roman empires, who changed the names of the stars again and again. In spite of which, the main principles remained the same throughout these 4,000 years; however, the truth of the original prophesies have been unfortunately obscured over time. That being that the cosmos reveals the glory of God through sending a savior to deliver all of His people, to live together in His Kingdom.

The offering of human sacrifices were common rituals in Nimrod's day. Anybody who refused to accept Nimrod's teachings were tortured, and if after being tortured, one still dissented, then that person was put to death. A reign of tyranny began against the believers in the God of Noah, who was the Lord Yahuah (YHUH). Nimrod wiped out all opposition to his Anti-God teachings. He took the truth of God and perverted it, changed it into a lie. Nimrod was possessed by the fallen Lucifer/Satan, who was denied a physical body, and still is to this day, but he can possess a human.

When Shem, Nimrod's great uncle, saw what was happening, he became troubled. He knew this to be the same sin that brought the destruction of the world through the flood. He raised an army with seventy-two co-conspirators to destroy Nimrod. In the battle, Nimrod was captured and his body was hacked into pieces. Shem told his co-conspirators to each take a piece of Nimrod's body and distribute it to a city under his rule. The pieces were sent throughout the kingdom with the message to show that Nimrod was not a god, and if any were found in the same practice as Nimrod, their fate would also be the same.

The dismembering of the body of Nimrod is in contrast with Jesus Christ, at the time of the Crucifixion; the body of Jesus Christ was intact and no bones were broken at Christ's death. (Psalm 34:20; John 19:36)

CHAPTER TWENTY-THREE: BABYLONIAN HISTORY: WHERE IT ALL BEGAN

Since Nimrod was the leader of a great empire, you would expect to find other details about him in other literature. In Sumerian history, there is a story about a man named Gilgamesh who fits his description. Likewise he is mentioned by the Babylonians, the Hittites, the Assyrians, and even in Palestine. The first clay tablets naming him were found among the ruins of the temple library of the god Nabu (Biblical Nebo) and the palace library of Ashurbanipal in Nineveh. These were later titled *The Epic of Gilgamesh*. Gilgamesh was just as rebellious as Nimrod, and some records describe him as a vile, cruel man. Yet the myth says of him that he was "two-thirds god and one-third man." This qualifies him as Nephilim.

After Nimrod was killed and his body pieces disseminated throughout the kingdom, followers were frightened because they worshipped him as a god who would live forever. Now that he was clearly dead, the continuation of his religion was in question. Cush, his father, was shamed for his actions and was not able to unite the people under this Babylonian system of old again. However, this unification would be accomplished by another Babylonian character, a woman.

Josephus wrote about Nimrod: "He also said he would be revenged on God, if he should have a mind to drown the world again; for that he would build a tower too high for the waters to be able to reach! And that he would avenge himself on God for destroying their forefathers." (Antiquities of the Jews 1: iv: 2). What Josephus says here is precisely what is found in the Gilgamesh epics.

WHO IS SEMIRAMIS?

Semiramis married Cush – Noah's grandson and gave birth to Nimrod. She was also the granddaughter of Noah's wife. She was Cush's wife at the time of the tower of Babel, and the mother of Nimrod. After Cush was disgraced at the tower, Semiramis did not want to go down with her husband. She did the unthinkable— she married her own son! By marrying Nimrod, Semiramis could maintain her position of authority in Babylon, as long as her husband remained in power; however once he died, she would, once again be in danger of losing everything she had.

After Nimrod was killed, and his body parts spread throughout the kingdom of Uruk, Semiramis had every body part gathered together. Only one part could not be found. That missing part was his reproductive organ. Sound familiar? This is the identical archetypal story to the Ancient Egyptian myth of Isis, Horus, and Osiris. Semiramis claimed that Nimrod could not come back to life without it and told the people of Babylon that Nimrod had ascended to the sun and was now to be called "Baal," the sun god.

Queen Semiramis also proclaimed that Baal would be present on earth in the form of a flame, whether a candle or lamp, when used in worship. With Satan's help, Semiramis become a goddess, the daughter of the fish-goddess Atargatis (because fish weren't destroyed during the flood), and herself connected with the doves of "Ishtar or Astarte."[1]

Semiramis claimed that she was immaculately conceived. She taught that the moon was a goddess that went through a twenty-eight day cycle and ovulated when full. She further claimed that she came down from the moon in a giant moon egg that fell into the Euphrates River (sounds like a spaceship). This was to have happened at the time of the first full moon after the spring equinox.[1] Could this giant moon egg have been some kind of extraterrestrial craft?

Semiramis became known as "Ishtar" which is pronounced "Easter," and her moon egg became known as "Ishtar's egg," or as we call them today "Easter eggs." She became known as Isis, Diana, Artemis. Astarte, Cybele etc. in other cultures, as people migrated from Babel. Different names due to the differences in languages. This fallen angel being, later took form as the evil Queen Jezebel, who was married to King Ahab of Israel, and was defeated by the Lord, through the prophet Elijah. Eventually, she morphed into the 'Virgin Mary' of Catholicism, and is mentioned in the book of Revelation as the 'Whore of Babylon' in Revelation 17.

But as I've pointed out previously in my chapters on the different names of God, that even though there is a different language pronunciation, which may be based on the original god or goddess, it doesn't necessarily mean that new pronunciation is the same entity. In the office of Satan, his fallen angels assume all kinds of counterfeit names of God and God's faithful angels. (See, my chapter, The Office of Satan.)

STRIKING SIMILARITIES

While Semiramis may have been archetype or even chief principality, other characters at different times of the timeline appearing in different cultures and languages all come under this principality as the same influence by being on the same side of the hierarchy. There are striking similarities, in the name "Mary" or "Miriam" also comes from the root name, Semiramis, and was later counterfeited, as Mother Mary replaced the pagan goddesses worshipped in Rome during Mithraism, which was transformed into the Roman Catholic Church.

Semiramis soon became pregnant (father unknown) and she claimed that it was the rays of the sun-god Baal that caused her to conceive. The son that she gave birth to was named Tammuz. Tammuz, like his supposed father, became a hunter. One day Tammuz was killed by a wild pig. Semiramis told the people that Tammuz was now ascended to his father, Baal, and that the two of them would be with the worshippers in the sacred candle or lamp flame as Father, Son, and Spirit, a description, in word only, resembling the Christian Holy Trinity. Semiramis was now worshipped as the "Mother of God and Queen of Heaven."

She told the worshippers that, when Tammuz was killed by the wild pig, some of his blood fell on the stump of an evergreen tree, and the stump grew into a full new tree overnight. This made the evergreen tree sacred by the blood of Tammuz. History does not reveal if Christmas like decorations were used to adorn the tree. She also proclaimed a

CHAPTER TWENTY-THREE: BABYLONIAN HISTORY: WHERE IT ALL BEGAN

forty-day period of time of sorrow each year prior to the anniversary of the death of Tammuz. During this time, no meat was to be eaten. Worshippers were to meditate upon the sacred mysteries of Baal and Tammuz. And so Semiramis, aka Ishtar pronounced *Easter*, proclaimed a period with a striking resemblance to Christian Lent.

The initial letter of "Tam-Muz" was written in Hebrew script as an upright sign of the cross and was pronounced as "Tau". So the sign of the cross was the initial letter of the Babylonian god "Tammuz" or Bacchus or Nimrod. Babylonians had to make the sign of the "T" in front of their hearts as they worshipped. They also ate sacred cakes with the marking of a "T" or cross on the top. The sign of the cross was, therefore, used as a sacred magical symbol to ward off evil.

Every year, on the first Sunday after the first full moon after the spring equinox, a celebration was made. It was called Ishtar's Sunday. She also proclaimed that because Tammuz was killed by a pig, that a pig must be eaten on that Sunday.[2]

Isn't it interesting that pigs were forbidden food to the believers of the God of Israel (Yahuah-YHUH), yet a required food to be eaten by this Babylonian/pagan goddess. Clearly, this is a difference due to rebellion. I have mentioned this previously that there are several reasons why pigs were deemed unclean animals by Yahuah.

Firstly, because they carried disease and bacteria. Unlike cows and sheep, pigs do not sweat and release toxins; therefore, their meat carries toxins. Secondly, it is legend that pigs were a by-product of Nephilim experiments, mixing the DNA of an animal, with that of a human. It is no coincidence that to this day, the Aborigines in Australia, call white humans or "long pig." Perhaps the Creator Yahuah forbid the eating of pigs, because on some genetic level, it was considered an act of cannibalism?

Be that as it may, pigs are proven to cause cancer, which is why in today's world, cancer patients are immediately ordered off of all pig products, because it exacerbates cancer. This may be due to a mutant gene or to the very fact that pig meat is more toxic than any other meat. Pigs lick off the cancerous sores from each other, and they will virtually eat anything that they can, making them an unclean animal, unfit for human consumption.

Yet, the rebellion is so flagrant that today we have pig farms, and the marketing of pig products in spite of the medical evidence which confirms the reason Yahuah forbid the eating of pig meat. In New Testament times, they may not have had the scientific knowledge that we have today, of bacterias and cancer causing agents, yet the Creator God knew exactly why He wanted to protect his people from this unclean animal. Here we have a prime example how Biblical law has caught up with modern science, or depending on your point of view, it could be said that modern science has caught up with Biblical law.

Which makes it an enigma why so many choose to ignore the judgment written within the prophecy of the "Day of the Lord" in Isaiah, chapter 66 (The bracketed comments within the text are mine): "They that sanctify themselves, and purify themselves in the gardens behind one tree in the middle, eating swine's flesh (pig), and the abomination, and the mouse (rat), shall be consumed (destroyed) together, said the LORD (Yahuah)." (Isaiah 66:17)

While the Lord wanted to keep his peoples' bodies pure, the rebels had a completely different agenda, which was to influence humans into all sorts of defilement. They made the very things that the Lord decreed as evil to be seen as attractive and good. What happened 4,000 years ago, continues to exist today, but it is done with more marketing flare, clever hypnosis, political lobbying and various types of demonically induced sociological pressures.

"And I will put enmity between thee and the woman, and between thy (the serpent's) seed and her seed; it shall bruise thy head, and thou shalt bruise his heel."
(Genesis 3:15)

The people of Babylon were familiar with the story of what had happened in the Garden of Eden. This is why Adam's clothing was coveted for its power. While the Garden of Eden may be considered "ancient history" to us, to the Babylonians, it was more like recent history. Nevertheless, it was the goal of Semiramis to keep her authority in Babylon. She believed that should she convince the Babylonian people that her unborn son was the one who could "bruise the head" of the serpent then she would succeed in staying Queen. She wanted the people to think that this unborn child was the "promised seed spoken" of by Noah - the one that would save the world from the serpents' curse. She wanted her child to be known as the reborn Nimrod!

Legends say that her unborn child was Nimrod reincarnated. She proclaimed that she had slept with no man to get pregnant and that the child she had conceived was through the spirit of Nimrod. She told the people that it was a blessing that Nimrod had been killed, that he had died for the sins of the world and had defeated death. She claimed that her son was both "god the father" and "god the son."

The people of Babylon then looked on her as the "great mother," the virgin who had given birth to a god. But she was no virgin. She was already married to Cush and gave birth to Nimrod the first. The people now believed that Nimrod was their savior — their god incarnate and that, through his death, they were all saved from the curse in the Garden of Eden. When she died, legend has it that she turned into a dove.[2]

Semiramis and Nimrod acquired their vast and intricate knowledge from Horus and Marduk, the two fallen angels, who are hanging suspended in the underground well at Babel."[3]

BAAL WORSHIP

The Old Testament is full of accounts of Baal Worship. The Children of Israel were constantly coming in contact with sun worship. They were constantly being tempted to follow the religion of the pagans instead of the way of the LORD Yahuah. Satan

CHAPTER TWENTY-THREE: BABYLONIAN HISTORY: WHERE IT ALL BEGAN

succeeded many times in leading God's people into sin and pagan sun worship. The prophet Ezekiel was shown that the people were turning their backs on the temple of God and worshipping the sun toward the east. While Moses was on the mountain, the people below built the golden calf (called Apis by the Egyptians and was tied with their pagan sun worship) Exodus 32:5 "they rose up early on the morrow" to worship the sun.

Priests instructed the people that Baal was responsible for droughts, plagues, and other calamities. People were often worked up into great frenzies at the prospects of displeasing Baal (also known as Molech). In times of great turbulence human sacrifices, particularly children, were made. Molech was depicted as a Minotaur, half-human, half-bull, these beings are also called Nephilim. (See, Nephilim, Book One, *Who's Who In The Cosmic Zoo?*)

On Mount Carmel, it was the prophet Elijah who discredited King Ahab's belief in the power of Baal at his request "the fire of the Lord fell, and consumed the burnt sacrifice, and the wood, and the stones, and the dust, and licked up the water that was in the trench" (1 Kings 18:38). Afterwards Elijah had the people slay "the prophets of Baal," thereby assuring the survival of the worship of Yahuah in Israel.

> "And he put down the idolatrous priests, whom the kings of Judah had ordained to burn incense in the high places in the cities of Judah, and in the places round about Jerusalem; them also that burned incense unto Baal, to the sun, and to the moon, and to the planets, and to all the host of heaven."
>
> (2 Kings 23:5)

> "Then He said to me, "Son of man, have you seen what the elders of Israel are doing in the darkness, each at the shrine of his own idol? They say, 'The Lord does not see us; the Lord has forsaken the land.' " Again, he said, "You will see them doing things that are even more detestable." Then he brought me to the entrance of the north gate of the house of the Lord, and I saw women sitting there, mourning the god Tammuz. He said to me, "Do you see this, son of man? You will see things that are even more detestable than this."
>
> He then brought me into the inner court of the house of the Lord, and there at the entrance to the temple, between the portico and the altar, were about twenty-five men. With their backs toward the temple of the Lord and their faces toward the east, they were bowing down to the sun in the east.
>
> He said to me, "Have you seen this, son of man? Is it a trivial matter for the people of Judah to do the detestable things they are doing here? Must they also fill the land with violence and continually arouse my anger? Look at them putting the branch to their nose! Therefore I will deal with them in anger; I will not look on them with pity or spare them. Although they shout in my ears, I will not listen to them."
>
> (Ezekiel 8:12-18)

Satan worked many years before the conception and birth of the true Messiah, Jesus, to counterfeit through sun worship, His miraculous conception and birth. He perfected an entire false religious system based upon sun worship/Baal worship/devil worship. Satan understood exactly what God meant in Genesis 3:15. "And I will put enmity between thee and the woman, and between your seed and her seed; it shall bruise your head, and you shall bruise his heel."

The prophecy stated the seed of the woman would crush his head. God was telling the devil that Jesus is coming, that he will be born of a virgin, a first born male child, and that child will be the undoing of Satan's kingdom. This was the ancient prophecy that caused people of that time to know the redeemer would be born of a virgin.

Satan, with the help of willing men tried to stop this prophecy from happening. Nimrod, Semiramis and Tammuz were the first to be worshiped as gods. Other ways he tried to prevent a virgin birth happening were by decreasing the number of virgins in the population through the introduction of temple prostitution and fertility worship.

THERE'S NOTHING NEW UNDER THE SUN

"That which hath been is that which shall be; and that which hath been done is that which shall be done: and there is no new thing under the sun."

(Ecclesiastes 1:9)

Due to the birth of Christianity and through the preaching of the gospel by the Apostles, the Babylonian beliefs started to be challenged. Even though they had been challenged in the Old Testament by many such as Moses, Daniel, Ezekiel and Jeremiah — this challenge was on a new scale which would sweep across the world. Unfortunately there were false teachers among the early church and drip by drip the old Babylonian ways started to creep into Christendom.

Constantine was a pagan sun-worshipper who had a "Christian experience." He wanted to unite his empire, both Christian and pagan together. Constantine attempted to merge biblical beliefs concerning Christ with pagan beliefs and practices. He replaced the religion of Rome, which was Mithraism, with Catholicism. He absorbed the Mother and Child cult into Christianity. Mithras was replaced by Jesus, and the pagan goddesses were replaced by Mother Mary. It isn't hard to see from Church history that Constantine was very successful as the doctrines, rituals, and festivals of Roman Catholicism, and even elements of the Protestant Church, are based on the ancient Babylonian mysteries.

THE RETURN OF NIMROD

In A.D. 284, Emperor Diocletian divided the Empire into two legs. In A.D. 312, the Emperor Constantine relocated the capital of the empire to Byzantium, its eastern leg,

CHAPTER TWENTY-THREE: BABYLONIAN HISTORY: WHERE IT ALL BEGAN

naming it Constantinople (the "New Rome"). This eastern leg, in fact, survived the western leg by a thousand years!

There are a number of Biblical texts that strongly suggest that the coming world leader, commonly called the Antichrist, will emerge from the region of the eastern leg of the Roman Empire.

> "And beware not to lift up your eyes to heaven and see the sun and the moon and the stars, all the host of heaven, and be drawn away and WORSHIP them and serve them, those which the LORD your God has allotted to all the peoples under the heavens."
>
> (Deuteronomy 4:19)

> "Therefore, COME OUT FROM THEIR MIDST AND BE SEPARATE," says the Lord. "AND DO NOT TOUCH WHAT IS UNCLEAN; And I will welcome you."
>
> (2 Corinthians 6:17)

> "I heard another voice from heaven, saying, "Come out of her, my people, so that you will not participate in her sins and receive of her plagues;"
>
> (Revelation 18:4)

> "Declaring the end from the beginning, and from ancient times the things that are not yet done, saying, My counsel shall stand, and I will do all my pleasure"
>
> (Isaiah 46:10)

The first dictator was Nimrod. Will the last one also be Nimrod?

> "Therefore pray not you for this people, neither lift up cry nor prayer for them, neither make intercession to me: for I will not hear you. See you not what they do in the cities of Judah and in the streets of Jerusalem? The children gather wood, and the fathers kindle the fire, and the women knead their dough, to make cakes to the queen of heaven, and to pour out drink offerings to other gods, that they may provoke me to anger. Do they provoke me to anger? said the LORD: do they not provoke themselves to the confusion of their own faces?"
>
> (Jeremiah 7:16-18)

> "He said also to me, Turn you yet again, and you shall see greater abominations that they do. Then he brought me to the door of the gate of the LORD's house which was toward the north; and, behold, there sat women weeping for Tammuz. Then said he to me, 'Have you seen this, O son of man? Turn you yet again, and you shall see greater abominations than these.'"
>
> (Ezekiel 8:13-15)

Mother And Child Worship

From Babylon the mother and child worship spread throughout the whole world. In Egypt, the mother and the child were worshipped under the names of Isis and Osiris. In India, even to this day as Isi and Iswara; in Asia, as Cybele and Deoius, Astarte, Ashtoreth; in Pagan Rome as Fortuna and Jupiter-puer or Jupiter, the boy; in Greece as Ceres, the Great Mother, with the babe at her breast, or as Irene, the goddess of peace, with the boy Plutus in her arms; and even in Tibet, in China and Japan where Shing Moo, the Holy Mother in China was represented with a child in her arms. In Britain, the Druid priests worshiped the Virgo-Patitura as the "Mother of God." Other names (Roman equivalent in brackets) are Aphrodite (Venus), Artemis (Diana), Athena (Mineva), Demeter (Ceres), Geae (Terra), Hera (Juno), Hestia (Vesta), Rhea (Ops), all part of the same archetype/principality.

Christian Missionaries were surprised when they arrived in distant lands to find that a mother and child were already being devoutly worshipped, just under other names. The image of the mother and child was so firmly entrenched in the pagan mind that when the Roman Catholic Church appeared on the scene. These pagan statues and paintings were merely renamed and worshipped as the Virgin Mary and her god-incarnate son Jesus. Mary was then crowned as the Queen of Heaven and worshiped.

This is an issue with Catholicism, being the true representation of Christianity on Earth, as nowhere in the Bible does it say that anyone should worship a queen of heaven, let alone designate Mary the mother of Jesus as the queen of anything. What the Bible clearly does spell out several times is that Jesus (Yahushua HaMashiach) the Christ is the King of Kings and Lord of Lords, and that all authority in heaven and on Earth was given to Him.

> "In the beginning was the Word, and the Word was with God, and the Word was God....And the Word became flesh and dwelt among us, and we beheld His glory, the glory as of the only begotten of the Father, full of grace and truth."
>
> (John 1:1, 14)

> "And Jesus came and spoke to them, saying, "All authority has been given to Me in heaven and on earth. Go therefore and make disciples of all the nations, baptizing them in the name of the Father and of the Son and of the Holy Spirit,"
>
> (Matthew 28:18, 19)

> "[Jesus says] He who rejects Me, and does not receive My words, has that which judges him — the word that I have spoken will judge him in the last day."
>
> (John 12:48)

> "After God spoke long ago in various portions and in various ways to our ancestors through the prophets, in these last days he has spoken to us in a son, whom he

appointed heir of all things, and through whom he created the world. The Son is the radiance of his glory and the representation of his essence, and he sustains all things by his powerful word, and so when he had accomplished cleansing for sins, he sat down at the right hand of the Majesty on high. Thus he became so far better than the angels as he has inherited a name superior to theirs."

(Hebrews 1:1-4)

THE SON OF GOD AND THE "SONS OF GOD"

(Hebrews 1:1—2:18)
- God has spoken in His Son (1:1-4);
- The Son is God's "final Word" (1:1-2a);
- The Son is above all, particularly the angels (1:2b-4);
- The Son is higher than the angels (1:4-14);
- The Exhortation: Listen to Him! (2:1-4); The Son became lower than the angels to save men (2:5-18)

The term "angels" appears twelve times in the Book of Hebrews; ten of the twelve occurrences of this word occur in chapters 1 and 2 (five times in each chapter). The author begins by demonstrating that the Son is "higher than the angels" (1:1-14) and then, after a few words of exhortation (2:1-4), he tells us that the Son of God became "lower than the angels" in order to save sinful men, and having done so, He is once again exalted above all others (2:5-18). Hebrews 1 and 2, thus, sums up the person and work of Jesus Christ from beginning (Creator) to end (Heir of all things), with particular emphasis on His incarnation and saving work at Calvary.

- "For as the Father has life in Himself, so He has granted the Son to have life in Himself, and has given Him authority to execute judgment also, because He is the Son of Man." (John 5:26-27)
- "Jesus spoke these words, lifted up His eyes to heaven, and said: "Father, the hour has come. Glorify Your Son, that Your Son also may glorify You, as You have given Him authority over all flesh, that He should give eternal life to as many as You have given Him." (John 17:1-2)
- "Therefore God exalted him, and gave him the name that is above every name, that at the name of Jesus every knee should bow, in heaven and on earth and under the earth, And that every tongue should confess that Jesus Christ is Lord, to the glory of God the Father." (Philippians 2:9-11)

THE SIGN OF THE CROSS

Through Satan, Tammuz was represented by the letter T - the first letter in his name. This then became a worldwide symbol for sun worship. For thousands of years before Christ, people offered human sacrifices to Satan on crosses. When the generals went into battle, they offered thousands of sacrifices to the devil. Alexander the Great crucified over 10,000 people on crosses to the devil to celebrate his victory. When the Catholic missionaries went to South America, they were amazed that the sun worshipping natives had crosses. These peoples knew nothing about Christianity, but they had the crosses as they were the sign of Tammuz-the Sun god.

When Jesus was crucified it looked as if the Sun god was victorious over the true God. Jesus, ironically died upon the symbol of sun worship. In order to show that Satan's system of worship was superior to that of God's and to show his supremacy, Satan heaped the supreme insult upon Christ by crucifying Him upon the cross, the symbol of sun worship.

On that Friday afternoon, the sun was darkened. God placed His hand over the sun while Christ hung upon the cross. Now, the blackening of the sun by God's hand was not just an incidental thing. It had some significance to it. There was a reason why that sun was darkened. You see, the sun to the heathen was the symbol of the Devil or Sun God. So God placed His hand over the sun to show that He controlled the sun. God said, "That is as far as you can go." God darkened the sun to prove He was the creator and had power over these things!

WHY JESUS CAME FORTH FROM THE TOMB BEFORE DAYBREAK

On the first day of the week men would be worshiping the Sun, or the Devil, at sunrise while Jesus Christ was lying in the tomb. Now, to make sure of his victim, the devil had the tomb of Jesus Christ sealed with a seal. Do you know what the Latin name of that seal was? It is called "SINGLEM-SOLIS," which means "the seal of the sun" also known as the Roman seal. They placed the "Singlem-solis," the seal of the sun, also known as the Roman seal. They placed the "Singlem-solis," the seal of the sun god, on the tomb of Jesus Christ; and the Devil thought he had forever sealed the fate of his victim inside. Satan sealed Him with the seal of the sun.

But it would be a revealed, before daylight on the first day of the week, just whom was superior. Christ rested in His tomb as the Sabbath passed on. He knew that sun worshippers everywhere would worship Satan, the moment the sun rose. Before the rising of the Sun, whilst the stone was still in place, something miraculous happened. In John 20:1 it says He came forth "while it was yet dark."[4]

What distinguishes Jesus Christ from Nimrod, Osirus, and Tammuz is that, even though He became the sacrificial Lamb of God and his blood a living sacrifice for all

CHAPTER TWENTY-THREE: BABYLONIAN HISTORY: WHERE IT ALL BEGAN

humankind, not a single bone of His body was broken. Unlike Osirus, Nimrod, and Tammuz, Jesus Christ was resurrected and healed on the third day to the witness of his family and disciples and lived among them for forty days until he ascended into heaven.

Scripture tell us that He will return at the end of this age, the same way He left, in a cloud. The cloud is the lexicon for the Lord's spaceship in scripture because the ships were all cloaked with clouds. (See my chapter on The Mother Ships of the Lord; Cloud Ships)

There were principalities and powers there that morning, but Christ triumphed over them! And Jesus Christ was out of that tomb before the sun rose, and the Devil was worshipped while Christ lay in His tomb. Christ's victory was over the grave, the principalities, and everything that Satan stood for. It had been Satan's plan to make the first day of the week, the pagan day of the sun, a triumphant celebration over the defeat and death of Jesus. But he lost that opportunity when Christ broke forth from the power of the tomb before those heathen worshipers could gather to have their sun-day ceremonies. God did not allow them to triumph over the death of His Son. Satan had failed in his efforts to exalt the pagan day of sun worship.[4]

CONSTANTINE'S CREED

> "I renounce all customs, rites, legalisms, unleavened breads and sacrifices of lambs of the Hebrews, and all the other feasts of the Hebrews, sacrifices, prayers, aspirations, purifications, sanctifications, and propitiations, and fasts and new moons, and Sabbaths, and superstitions, and hymns and chants, and observances and synagogues. absolutely everything Jewish, every Law, rite and custom and if afterwards I shall wish to deny and return to Jewish superstition, or shall be found eating with Jews, or feasting with them, or secretly conversing and condemning the Christian religion instead of openly confuting them and condemning their vain faith, then let the trembling of Cain and the leprosy of Gehazi cleave to me, as well as the legal punishments to which I acknowledge myself liable. And may I be an anathema in the world to come, and may my soul be set down with Satan and the devils."[5]

Furthermore, any follower of the "Jewish Rabbi" (Rebbe Yeshua -"Jewish Messiah" (Yahushua HaMashiach) who wished to join this "holy community" was compelled to adopt a different set of rules and customs. Subsequently special creeds were drafted, to which the Christian would have to swear such as:[6]

- "I accept all customs, rites, legalism, and feasts of the Romans, sacrifices.
- Prayers, purifications with water, sanctifications by Pontificus Maximus (high priests of Rome)
- propitiations, and feasts, and the New Sabbath "Sol Dei" (day of the Sun)
- all new chants and observances, and all the foods and drinks of the Romans.

In other words, I absolutely accept everything Roman, every new law, rite and custom, of Rome, and the New Roman Religion. "Additionally, in approximately 365 AD, the Council of Laodicea wrote, in one of their canons decreed fifty-nine laws canon."[7]

Christians must not Judaize by resting on the Sabbath, but must work on that day. Rather, honoring the Lord's Day. But if any shall be found to be Judaizers, let them be anathema (against) from Christ".

Antiochus Epiphanes set up an image of Zeus in the Temple which was the Abomination of Desolation spoken of in Daniel 11. For three years, he continued to desecrate the Temple.

These were the new laws that Antiochus set up:

- Thou shall profane the Sabbath;
- Thou shall change the set times (festivals) and laws;
- Thou shall set up idols;
- Thou shall eat unclean animals
- Thou shall not circumcise;
- Thou shall forget Torah.

Three years and two months later, the Temple was taken back and rededicated. This is known as the Feast of Dedication, or Festival of Lights, or Hanukkah.

What is truly ironic is that these laws were created by an antichrist figure, Antiochus, and are exactly the same creeds Constantine later repeated, which is what many Christians are living by today, mostly through ignorance. Christians, are totally going against God's Word by living under laws created by Antiochus and Constantine, who were both antichrists.

This is why End Time Churches, as spoken of in Revelation 3, are going to come under God's judgment, because they are still allowing the ancient "fallen" Roman Empire to control their religion, by living under and still following Constantine's Creed. This is the spiritual legal ground that allows the foothold and stronghold of the demonic religious spirit, to permeate many of today's churches.

> "Therefore when you see the 'abomination of desolation, 'spoken of by Daniel the prophet, standing in the holy place" (whoever reads, let him understand). "Then let those who are in Judea flee to the mountains. Let him who is on the housetop not go down to take anything out of his house. And let him who is in the field not go back to get his clothes. But woe to those who are pregnant and to those who are nursing babies in those days! And pray that your flight may not be in winter or on the Sabbath. For then there will be great tribulation, such as has not been since the beginning of the world until this time, no, nor ever shall be. And unless those days were shortened, no flesh would be saved; but for the elect's sake those days will be shortened."
>
> (Matthew 24:15-22)

CHAPTER TWENTY-THREE: BABYLONIAN HISTORY: WHERE IT ALL BEGAN

And then I will declare to them, 'I never knew you; depart from Me, you who practice lawlessness!'

(Matthew 7:23)

"I speak in human terms because of the weakness of your flesh. For just as you presented your members as slaves of uncleanness, and of lawlessness leading to more lawlessness, so now present your members as slaves of righteousness for holiness."

(Romans 6:19)

"For the grace of God that brings salvation has appeared to all men, teaching us that, denying ungodliness and worldly lusts, we should live soberly, righteously, and godly in the present age, looking for the blessed hope and glorious appearing of our great God and Savior Jesus Christ, who gave Himself for us, that He might redeem us from every lawless deed and purify for Himself His own special people, zealous for good works."

(Titus 2:11-14)

"Whomever commits sin also commits lawlessness, and sin is lawlessness."

(1 John 3:4)

"A little while longer and the world will see Me no more, but you will see Me. Because I live, you will live also. At that day you will know that I am in My Father, and you in Me, and I in you. He who has My commandments and keeps them, it is he who loves Me. And he who loves Me will be loved by My Father, and I will love him and manifest Myself to him."

(John 14:19-21)

"And the dragon was enraged with the woman, and he went to make war with the rest of her offspring, who keep the commandments of God and have the testimony of Jesus Christ."

(Revelations 12:17)

"Let us hear the conclusion of the whole matter: Fear God, and keep his commandments: for this is the whole duty of man."

(Ecclesiastes 12:13)

"Beware lest any man spoil you through philosophy and vain deceit, after the tradition of men, after the rudiments of the world, and not after Christ."

(Colossians 2:8)

> "Then Peter and the other apostles answered and said, "We ought to obey God rather than men."
>
> (Acts 5:29)

> "But in vain they do worship me, teaching for doctrines the commandments of men."
>
> (Matthew 15:9)

FALSE BELIEFS – FALSE RELIGIONS

> "The Spirit clearly says that in later times some will abandon the faith and follow deceiving spirits and things taught by demons. Such teachings come through hypocritical liars, whose consciences have been seared as with a hot iron."
>
> (1 Timothy 4:1-2)

Besides the obvious false religions and cults out there, think about how many so-called Christian churches fall into this category? If a Christian is supposed to follow the teachings of Jesus Christ and the Holy Spirit, what if they are being deceived into thinking they are, when in fact they are following and reinforcing the beliefs of Roman Emperors, such as Constantine's Creed?

There are so many churches today, who are doing just that, in ignorance because they are unaware of their own history. Most believers understand basic history, such as what is written in the Bible. Most believers who belong to non-denominational churches also have some basic understanding of how they were formed after "breaking away" from either one of the denominations that broke away from Catholicism. But how many of them have ignorantly taken with them, the creed of Constantine?

Many of today's churches are still living under Constantine's Creed — they worship on the Sunday, they believe they can eat pork and every other unclean animal that the Lord clearly wrote in His "law books" in the Torah, that His people should stay away from. While many claim to adhere to the "Word of God" in the Holy Bible, many do not keep and honor the Feasts of the Lord, which the Lord Himself says will be celebrated even when His Kingdom comes to Earth, and all the nations of the world will celebrate the Feast of Lord throughout the year with the Lord Himself ruling from the New Jerusalem.

> "You must observe this festival to the LORD for seven days every year. This is a permanent law for you, and it must be observed in the appointed month from generation to generation."
>
> (Leviticus 23:41)

The very words "permanent law" should tell believers today that this feast is important to the Lord, and all of his believers should honor it. Yet, Constantine's Creed,

CHAPTER TWENTY-THREE: BABYLONIAN HISTORY: WHERE IT ALL BEGAN

which was clearly a war on Judaism, making any so called Judaizer anathema to Rome, has continued to permeate modern-day Christianity, in spite of the best of pastors and ministers whose hearts are on fire for God.

Same thing goes for the Sabbath. In Hebrew, all the days of the week are numbered. For example, Yom Rishone which means Day One (Sunday), all the way to Day Seven, which is Yom Shevee-ee, aka Shabbat, is what we call today Saturday. Yet the majority of Christian churches worship and meet on Sundays, not Saturday. They are still under the authority of Constantine's Creed and their continued worship of the "Sun" God on "Sunday" which was the tradition in ancient Mithraism.

Under the New Covenant, we are no longer under the law, to rest on a given day and time of the week, but believers receive their rest, peace and shalom through the person of Yeshua HaMashiach, the Lord Jesus Christ, who alone is the only One who gives the soul true peace and shalom. This is God's Wisdom at work, to put an end to the endless squabbling over the timing of the Sabbath, which has been divisive. Yeshua/Jesus, He alone is our Sabbath, and it is through Him and by Him that we take refuge and have shalom.

The true meaning of the word "shalom," in Hebrew, means "to be full," full of peace, full of abundance, and satisfied. This word is used as a greeting and salutation in modern Israel today, and it is generally interpreted as "peace," but it is the peace of God which passes all human understanding that keeps our hearts and minds in Christ Jesus. (Philippians 4:7)

NOTES:

1. Salemi, Peter. *The Plain Truth About Islam*, retrieved from - http://www.british-israel.ca/Islam.htm;
2. http://www.discerningthetimesonline.net/OriginOfCrescentandStar.html
3. DTTO - Showing You the World in Scripture (http://www.discerningthetimesonline.net/BabylonianHistoryWhereitallbegan.html)
4. DTTO - Showing You the World in Scripture - *The Harlot links with Turkey*, (http://www.discerningthetimesonline.net/BabylonianHistoryWhereitallbegan.html)
5. Tafrihul Askia Fil Ahwal Ul AMBIA, pp. 134 - 139, Vol. 1.
6. www.discerningthetimesonline.net/BabylonianHistoryWhereitallbegan.
7. Roberts, J.J.M., *The Earliest Semitic Pantheon*, Johns Hopkins University, Baltimore, 1972

CHAPTER TWENTY-FOUR

WHAT IS ISLAM?

"Definition: A religion, founded by Muhammad, whose members worship one God who is called Allah in Arabic and follow the teachings of the Quran. The word, 'Islam' means "submission to the will of God;" adherents of Islam are called Muslims."

~Dictionary.com

Be thoughtful about the "God" you choose to worship. There is the God of the Bible, Yahuah, worshipped by Christians and Jews and then there is Islam featuring a "god" of this world.

Islam is not a religion, nor should it qualify for protection under the U.S. constitution against religious persecution. It is a creation of Mohammed, whose primary motive was to raise an army to gain power over the Arab cities of Mecca and Medina. There is nothing in the Quran or about Allah resembling the Christian relationship with the Savior and the Father.

Arguing that Islam is a constitutionally protected religion is like arguing that Nazism is a constitutionally protected religion. Hitler tried to make Nazism a religion to fill that void, but failed. There are many parallels to Nazism and Islam. The Third Reich is god the father, Hitler is the son, and the Nazi party is their holy spirit. In North Korea they are called to worship Kim Jon Il as god, its totalitarianism.[1]

Muslims should not be eligible for service in the U.S. military, which would be like having Nazis in our military during WWII. They are spies and murderers.

Lie #1: Islam: The Religion of Peace? The "peace" referred to in this statement is the "peace" that will come after the entire world has been conquered by Islam and all infidels have been executed.[1]

Lie #2: Islam Never Kills "Innocent" People. Islam teaches that all infidels are guilty of apostasy. All people are born Muslim and any who are not Muslim are apostates, including children and infants. These children and infants are worthy of murder.[1]

Prominent Saudi writer Abdullah Mohammad Al Dawood urged his 97,000 Twitter followers to sexually molest all women who work as cashiers in grocery stores in order to force working women to stay at home and protect their chastity. Is this not the epitome of a radical perversion? If they want to protect women's chastity, then why is he advocating raping and molesting them? This is the fruit of radical Islam, which proves that this religion is not from the God of the Bible who is Yahuah, but the god of this world, who is Satan.

ISLAM TEACHES WIFE BEATING

Muhammad teaches male superiority over females in Quran 4:34:

> "Men are the managers of the affairs of women for that God has preferred in bounty one of them over another, and for that they have expended of their property. Righteous women are therefore obedient, guarding the secret for God's guarding. And those you fear may be rebellious admonish; banish them to their couches, and beat them. If they then obey you, look not for any way against them; God is All high, All great." (Arberry's version of the Quran, Quran, 4:34)

The Quran is clear and unmistakable. Exactly mirroring all legal systems that administer increasingly harsher penalties for continued wrongdoing, the Quran says the husband should first verbally admonish her, give her a piece of your mind by scolding and rebuking her, then ground her to the bedroom like a child, and finally, when all else fails, to beat her.

Just to illustrate this vast contrast, here in the West, when a man ignores his wife, grounds her to her room, starves her of sex, affection and attention, this behavior is recognized as a form of passive wife abuse. This becomes legal grounds for divorce, and men could lose nearly everything they have over it. Legally it's known as "Loss of Consortium." One woman was awarded over $1.8 Million in a divorce case in New York in 2009.

RADICAL ISLAMIC SEXUALITY IS PURE EVIL

There is nothing about sexuality in Islam that is good or redeeming. It is top to bottom thoroughly evil. Women are considered sub-human animals, deficient in intelligence and damned to hell. Massive sexual disorder in little boys, as they are taught from the ages of three and four to hate women.[2]

"Women are your fields, go, then into your fields, whence you please." (Quran 2:223)

A woman's testimony often counts half of a man's testimony.[1,2]

"And let two men from among you bear witness to all such documents [contracts of loans without interest]. But if two men be not available, there should be one man and two women to bear witness so that if one of the women forgets (anything), the other may remind her." (Quran 2:282)

It seems that the foundational reason for having two women witnesses is that one of the women may "forget" something. Again, this goes to the nature of women. Philosophers teach us that one of the main differences between animals and humans lies in humankind's rationality. But this verse implies that a woman's mind is weak. How is this verse not misogynistic?[1,2]

CHAPTER TWENTY-FOUR: WHAT IS ISLAM?

Sura 2:282 removes any ambiguity about women; a lengthy discussion about the desirability of written contract: Mohammad said, "Isn't the witness of a woman equal to half of that of a man?" The women said, "Yes." He said, "This is because of the deficiency of a woman's mind." (Bukhari, emphasis added)

The reason for diminishing women's role in court is clear enough. Women have deficient minds, says Muhammad bluntly and tersely. Sura 2:282 says that a female witness may "forget," so the other female witness may need to remind the first. The Quran and the Hadith match up well in this matter. In the one area that sets humans apart—the mind—Muhammad says that womankind falls short by nature or Allah-endowed (in)abilities.

As for later legal opinions in Islam, Ibn Rushd again guides us. Sura 2:282 appears in a contractual business context, but legal scholars differ on whether woman may serve as witnesses in other contexts, like criminal cases.

For the "crime" of sexual immorality, which in Islam is punishable by death for adultery and whipping for fornication, four males must prove the crime. Females are excluded (Vol. 2, p. 559). So this means that if a wife suspects adultery from her husband, she cannot get four women to catch him in the act. She has to get four men. Would the "Old Boy's Club" prevent justice in Islamic patriarchal societies?

ANAL SEX CAUSES INFERTILITY

Infertility was reported to the U.S. military doctors in Afghanistan by Muslim men. Their women were thoroughly tested, and the doctors could not find anything wrong with them, when they asked the women what they did during sex, they reported to the doctors, that all the men were having anal sex with their wives. The men didn't know how to have sex with their women to produce children. This is due to the fact that the majority of Muslim men were all sodomized as children, so that's all they know. They didn't know how to have sex with their wives.

GENITAL MUTILATION

Muslim girls from the ages of seven to nine are put through this horrific ritual. Without any anesthetic, the men cut off their clitoris, so they will never experience any sexual pleasure, and then they cut off their labia and sew it up their vagina, leaving a hole the size of their anus. This makes sex excruciatingly painful. Genital mutilation is done on 90 percent of Muslim girls. Islamic hatred of women has led to rampant homosexuality. Islam teaches by *fatwa* (a fatwa is a religious declaration) that only a submissive homosexual "sins." The submissive partner is considered to be the sinner, not the dominant partner. Since there is no central Islamic authority as the Pope and the Catholic Church, every Imam is their own pope. They get to make their own rules for their village or community. The killing of Al-Zarqawi, "Thursday Night Club" which were male orgies. A fatwa stated that Allah was busy and couldn't see what you were doing on Thursday nights.[1,2]

MAN-BOY-PEDOPHILIA

A near universal Muslim phenomenon. Boys and men are taught that the ultimate sexual experience is to have sex with young boys, anally or orally. The American Psychological Association wants to legitimize pedophilia and call it, "minor attracted sexuality." Currently there are movements in Europe to legitimize incest and bestiality.

TOTAL GENDER SEGREGATION

Madrasas - schools Bucha Bazi (Afghanistan) little boys dress in drag, then are auctioned to the highest bidder, and men take them home to have their way with them sexually. Quranic Celebration of pedophilia — sex with both little boys and girls in Quran.

SEX WITH FEMALE CHILDREN

Quran 65:4 - Mohammed married Aisha at the age of six, he vaginally penetrated her at the age of nine. He writes about "thighing" her at the age of six. Frequently infants and toddlers are used for "thighing", which is dry humping, to the point of friction for masturbation. Psychologically healthy men should not be able to maintain an erection in the presence of a child. Dr. Salih bin Fawzin, a 2011 member of the highest Saudi Muslim Council, issued a fatwa declaring no minimum age for females to marry, and allows "husbands" to vaginally penetrate as soon as he "thinks" the child can "bear his weight."

PROSTITUTION AKA "TEMPORARY MARRIAGES"

Quran 4:24 "And all married women (are forbidden unto you) save those (captives) whom your right hands possess. It is a decree of Allah for you. Lawful unto you are all beyond those mentioned, so that ye seek them with your wealth in honest wedlock, not debauchery. And those of whom ye seek content (by marrying them), give unto them their portions as a duty. And there is no sin for you in what ye do by mutual agreement after the duty (hath been done). Lo! Allah is ever Knower, Wise

Incest: cousins, double cousins, uncle-niece, all causing massive genetic damage over 1,400 years. Muslims are susceptible to coercion and to lower I.Q.s because Muslims are overly inbred, they are developmentally disabled due to incest (i.e., generational curses). Incest makes them stupid, low I.Q., mentally, emotionally and spiritually retarded.

Bestiality: "A man can have sex with animals, such as sheep, cows, and camels and so on. However, he should kill the animal after he has his orgasm. He should not sell the meat to the people in his own village; however, selling the meat to the next door village should be fine." (Ayatollah Khomeini, "*Tahrirdvasyleh*" Volume 4, Darol Elm, Gom, Iran, 1990.)

"If a man commits the act of sodomy with a cow, an ewe, or a camel, their urine and their excrement become impure, and even their milk may no longer be consumed. The animal must then be killed and as quickly as possible and burned." (*The Little Green Book, Sayings of Ayatollah Khomeini*, Political, Philosophical, Social and Religious, p. 47, ISBN 0553-14032-9.)

Necrophilia: Fatwa: "Since a good Muslim couple will meet again in Heaven and since death does not alter the marital contract it is not hindrance to the husband's desire to have sexual intercourse with the corpse of his (freshly) deceased wife." ~ Imam Abdelbari Zemzami, May 2011, Morocco. Why won't mainstream culture (i.e., liberals) call out Muslim sexual perversions?[1,2]

LUCIFER AND THE MORNING STARS

Many do not know exactly who the stars of the morning are. Nor do they understand the Sons of God. But if we add them together, we come up with the "Angels of God." Genesis tells us that the "Sons of God" went after the daughters of men where we got giants from. Also we have in Isaiah the scene of Lucifer's fall, "O son of the morning." Then in Revelation we have Jesus Christ who is the "Morning Star." So when we understand this Scripture in Job 38, we see the Angels of God were singing, praising, and rejoicing before the Lord God. But He specifically describes the set of Angels who will fall from Grace as the "Sons of morning," and the faithful Angels led by Michael as the "Sons of God." And they were all together called the "Sons of the Morning Star," Jesus Christ, God Almighty. Now, how do Muslims miss this? They are not spiritually discerned.

This Scripture is difficult for Muslims to understand or explain –

"When the stars of the morning praised me together, and all the children of God (Bene Ha Elohim) rejoiced."

(Job 38:7)

Allah has NO power to forgive sins; his forgiveness is as empty as his power. All Muslims have to do is confess or agree that the Quran holds errors within it. Then we can officially call it a "Doctrine of Demons" and close the case against it.

Muslims claim, that a proof the Quran was from God, is that it contains scientifically accurate information about Embryology before man discovered it for himself. However, all the information in the Quran regarding Embryology is copied from three sources:

1. A Greek doctor named Galen, who lived of 150 AD.
2. A Jewish doctor named Samuel ha-Yehudi who lived 150 AD.
3. The Greek father of medicine Hippocrates who lived 400 BC.

It raises the question that in light of the fact that all the information contained in the Quran was already in print by these three doctors, how does this square with the argument on Embryology?[1] Supporting sources are lacking.

There are some verses from Quran that proves that Islam is from Paganism and Allah is Satan from Quran.

[1] This verse proves that Islam is from Paganism: Quran - Surat An-Najm Sura 53:15 Near it is the Garden of Abode. Behold, the Lote-tree was shrouded (in mystery unspeakable!) (His) sight never swerved, nor did it go wrong! Sura 53:17 The (Prophet's) vision (of Angel Gabriel) was never broken and it did not go wrong! Sura 53:18 Indeed he (the Prophet) saw from the Signs of his Lord, the Greatest! Have you thought upon Al-Lat and Al-'Uzza and Manat, the third, (goddess)? Are yours the male 'Allah' and His the females Al-Lat and Al-Uzza and Manat?[1,2]

"What! For you the male sex, and for Him, the female? Behold, such would be indeed a division most unfair!" (An-Najm 53:19-22)

For Information this Al-Lat, Al-Uzi and Al Manat are Three Pagan Daughters of Allah. Allah's Daughters: Al-Lat, Al-Uzza, and Manat.[1,2]

Al-Uzza, al-Lat and Manah, the three daughters of Allah, had their sanctuaries in the land which later became the cradle of Islam. In a weak moment, the monotheistic Muhammad was tempted to recognize these powerful deities of Makkah and al-Madinah and make a compromise in their favor, but afterwards, he retracted and the revelation is said to have received the form now found in Surah 53:19-20.

Muslims today do not worship Allah's daughters and view them as pagan deities. Having said that, it is important to note that Muhammad himself commanded his followers offer prayers to these "Allah's daughters." He later retracted it and blamed it on the Devil. It is this true event in Muhammad's life which was the topic of Salman Rushdie's book, *The Satanic Verses*.[1,2]

[2] This verse Proves that Allah is Satan: Quran 8:30 Allah is the best deceiver.

[3] Qur'an says that Allah desires to lead people astray (Quran Sura 6:39, 126). He does not help those who are led astray by him (Sura 30:29), and Allah desires to use them to populate hell (Sura 32:13).[2]

ISLAM: A RELIGION OF PEACE?

How can Islam be a religion of peace, when Muslims are constantly waging war with each other and non-Muslims? Truth be told, Islam is NOT a religion of peace, but a religion of war. Islam is a death cult. Islam is not even a religion, but a political agenda to achieve jihad, which means the struggle for dominance and control.

CHAPTER TWENTY-FOUR: WHAT IS ISLAM?

This makes Islam is a false religion. And those who do not identify with the extremists, are still blinded by their own beliefs and culture. The best course of action for Muslims, is to leave Islam. Thousands of Muslims are turning to Christ in Europe. Others have become atheists and secularists. They simply do not want to be associated with Jihadists. Jihad, is the core belief and root of Islam.

Question remains, how does a government on alert, sort out the cultural Muslims and those who hold the extreme radical jihadist beliefs? Just like there are many Jews and Christians, who never read their Bibles, and may know a little scripture, here and there, as the old saying goes, "a little knowledge is a dangerous thing," so it is with people born into the Muslim faith, who practice Muslim traditions as part of their culture and family life. Many do not even question it. Many are not aware of the extremism that lies within their own Quran and Hadith, which are the sayings and acts of the prophet Muhammad, both considered Bibles of Islam.

Sahih Muslim (1:33) The Messenger of Allah said: "I have been commanded to fight against people till they testify that there is no god but Allah, that Muhammad is the messenger of Allah, and they establish prayer and pay zakat." The first part of this condition is the Shahada, or profession of faith in Islam. Violence is sanctioned until the victims embrace Muhammad's religion.

Sahih Muslim (19:4294) - "When you meet your enemies who are polytheists (which includes Christians), invite them to three courses of action. If they respond to any one of these, you also accept it and withhold yourself from doing them any harm. Invite them to (accept) Islam; if they respond to you, accept it from them and desist from fighting against them ... If they refuse to accept Islam, demand from them the Jizya. If they agree to pay, accept it from them and hold off your hands. If they refuse to pay the tax, seek Allah's help and fight them." Osama bin Laden echoes this order from his prophet: "Does Islam, or does it not, force people by the power of the sword to submit to its authority corporeally if not spiritually? Yes. There are only three choices in Islam ... . Either submit, or live under the suzerainty of Islam, or die." (source: The al-Qaeda Reader p. 19-20)

Bukhari (8:387) - "Allah's Apostle said, 'I have been ordered to fight the people till they say: 'None has the right to be worshipped but Allah.' And if they say so, pray like our prayers, face our Qibla and slaughter as we slaughter, then their blood and property will be sacred to us and we will not interfere with them except legally and their reckoning will be with Allah.'"

Bukhari (53:392) - "While we were in the Mosque, the Prophet came out and said, "Let us go to the Jews" We went out till we reached Bait-ul-Midras. He said to them, "If you embrace Islam, you will be safe. You should know that the earth belongs to Allah and His Apostle, and I want to expel you from this land. So, if anyone amongst you owns some property, he is permitted to sell it, otherwise you should know that the Earth belongs to Allah and His Apostle."

Bukhari (2:24) - "Allah's Apostle said: "I have been ordered (by Allah) to fight against the people until they testify that none has the right to be worshipped but Allah and that Muhammad is Allah's Apostle, and offer the prayers perfectly and give the obligatory charity, so if they perform a that, then they save their lives and property from me except for Islamic laws and then their reckoning (accounts) will be done by Allah."

Bukhari (60:80) - "The Verse:--You (true Muslims) are the best of peoples ever raised up for mankind.' means, the best of peoples for the people, as you bring them with chains on their necks till they embrace Islam."

Bukhari (60:40) - "...:And fight them till there is no more affliction (i.e. no more worshiping of others along with Allah)."

Bukhari (59:643) - "Testify that none has the right to be worshipped except Allah, or else I will chop off your neck!"

Religion of peace? Let's take a look at Quran:

1. Kill any one who insults Islam or Mohammad. (Quran.33;57-61).
2. Kill all Muslims who leave Islam. (Quran.2;217/4;89/Bukhari.9;84-57).
3. Quran can not be doubted. (Quran.2;1).
4. Islam is the only acceptable religion. (Quran.3;85).
5. Muslims must fight (jihad) to non-Muslims, even if they don't want to. (Quran.2;216).
6. Non-Muslims are pigs and apes. (Quran. 2;62-65/Quran.5;59-60/Quran.7;166).
7. Non-Muslims cannot be friends with Muslims. (Quran.5;51).
8. Non-Muslims sworn enemies of Muslims and Islam. (Quran.4;101).
9. Non-Muslims can be raped as sex slave. (Quran.4;3 & 24/5;89/23;5/33;50/58;3/70;30).
10. Non-Muslims the vilest of creatures deserving no mercy. (Quran.98;6).
11. Muslim must terrorized us (non-Muslims). (Quran.8;12 &59-60/ Bukhari.4;52;220).
12. Muslims must strike terror into non-Muslims hearts. (Quran.8;60).
13. Muslims must lie to non-Muslims to strengthen and spread Islam. (Quran.3;28,16;106).
14. Muslims are allowed to behead non-Muslims (Quran.47;4).
15. Muslims are guaranteed to go to heaven if they kill non-Muslims. (Quran.9;111).
16. Marrying and divorcing pre-pubescent children is OK. (Quran.65;4).
17. Wife beating is OK. (Quran.4;34).
18. Raping wives is OK. (Quran.2;223).
19. Proving rape requires 4 (four) male Muslim witnesses. (Quran.24;13).
20. Muslims are allowed to crucify and amputate non-Muslims. Quran.8;12/47;4).

This is the playbook, the Islamic State, (ISIS/IS/ISIL/Jihadists) all take their cues out of. This is why the issue is not just the extremism, but the actual doctrine that was given

CHAPTER TWENTY-FOUR: WHAT IS ISLAM?

to Mohammed, by a fallen angel, the counterfeit Gabriel. When Mohammed alledged ascended into heaven, he most definitely ascened into the heavens, and was picked up by a spacecraft operated by the Annunaki.

One thing, that's important to discern, is, that not all Arabs are Muslims. The Arab race was created by the descendants of Ishmael. Many scholars believe it actually began with Esau. Arabs were not Muslims until after Mohammed left in around 750AD. Many Arabs are Christians, Atheists, Secularists. So to suggest that the world is 'racist' against Arabs, is simply not the case. The issue is with the belief system, that they call a religion, but it is essentially a political agenda which amounts to a death cult.

Many Muslims are leaving Islam because of the extremists. Just as many Christians left Christianity because of fundamentalists. The religious spirit is not respecter of persons, or religions, it seeks to divide and conquer and keep followers in bondage. Jesus came to set the captives free.

THE CALL TO JIHAD IN THREE STAGES

"When we turn to Islam's theological sources and historical writings (Quran, Hadith, Sira, and Tafsir), we find that there are three stages in the call to Jihad, depending on the status of Muslims in a society.[3]

"**STAGE ONE**—When Muslims are completely outnumbered and can't possibly win a physical confrontation with unbelievers, they are to live in peace with non-Muslims and preach a message of tolerance. We see an example of this stage when Muhammad and his followers were a persecuted minority in Mecca. Since the Muslims were entirely outnumbered, the revelations Muhammad received during this stage (e.g. "You shall have your religion and I shall have my religion") called for religious tolerance and proclaimed a future punishment (rather than a worldly punishment) for unbelievers.[3]

"**STAGE TWO**—When there are enough Muslims and resources to defend the Islamic community, Muslims are called to engage in defensive Jihad. Thus, when Muhammad had formed alliances with various groups outside Mecca and the Muslim community had become large enough to begin fighting, Muhammad received Quran 22:39-40:[3]

"Permission (to fight) is given to those upon whom war is made because they are oppressed, and most surely Allah is well able to assist them; Those who have been expelled from their homes without a just cause except that they say: our Lord is Allah." Although Muslims in the West often pretend that Islam only allows defensive fighting, later revelations show otherwise.[3]

"**STAGE THREE**—When Muslims establish a majority and achieve political power in an area, they are commanded to engage in offensive Jihad. Hence, once Mecca and Arabia were under Muhammad's control, he received the call to fight all unbelievers. In Surah 9:29, we read:

"Fight those who believe not in Allah nor the Last Day, nor hold that forbidden which hath been forbidden by Allah and His Messenger, nor acknowledge the Religion of Truth, from among the People of the Book, until they pay the Jizyah with willing submission, and feel themselves subdued.

"Notice that this verse doesn't order Muslims to fight oppressors, but to fight those who don't believe in Islam (including the "People of the Book"—Jews and Christians).

"Not surprisingly, we find similar commands in Islam's most trusted collections of a hadith (traditions containing Muhammad's teachings).[3]

"**Sahih al-Bukhari 6924**—Muhammad said: "I have been ordered to fight the people till they say: La ilaha illallah (none has the right to be worshipped but Allah), and whoever said La ilaha illahllah, Allah will save his property and his life from me."

"**Sahih Muslim 30**—Muhammad said: "I have been commanded to fight against people so long as they do not declare that there is no god but Allah."

"Here again, the criterion for fighting people is that the people believe something other than Islam.

"It's clear then that when Muslims rose to power, peaceful verses of the Quran were abrogated by verses commanding Muslims to fight people based on their beliefs. Islam's greatest scholars acknowledge this. For instance, Ibn Kathir (Islam's greatest commentator on the Quran) sums up Stage Three as follows: "Therefore all people of the world should be called to Islam. If anyone of them refuses to do so, or refuses to pay the Jizyah, they should be fought till they are killed."[3]

WHEN MUSLIMS REACH STAGE THREE

"Abrogation also accounts for shifting attitudes regarding Jews and Christians in the Quran. While Muslims are to be friendly to Jews and Christians when the former are outnumbered, the Islamic position changes when Muslims reach Stage Three, at which point Christians and Jews are to recognize their inferior status and pay the Jizyah (a payment made to Muslims in exchange for not being killed by them). Consider some of Muhammad's later teachings about Christians and Jews:[3]

"**Quran 5:51**—O you who believe! Do not take the Jews and the Christians for friends; they are friends of each other; and whoever amongst you takes them for a friend, then surely he is one of them; surely Allah does not guide the unjust people."

"**Quran 9:30**—And the Jews say: Uzair is the son of Allah; and the Christians say: The Messiah is the son of Allah; these are the words of their mouths; they imitate the saying of those who disbelieved before; may Allah destroy them; how they are turned away!"

"**Quran 98:6**—Those who reject (Truth), among the People of the Book and among the Polytheists, will be in Hell-Fire, to dwell therein. They are the worst of creatures."

"**Sahih Muslim 4366**—Muhammad said: "I will expel the Jews and Christians from the Arabian Peninsula and will not leave any but Muslim."

CHAPTER TWENTY-FOUR: WHAT IS ISLAM?

"**Al-Bukhari, Al-Adab al-Mufrad 1103**—Muhammad said: "Do not give the People of the Book the greeting first. Force them to the narrowest part of the road."

"Needless to say, these teachings can hardly be considered peaceful or tolerant."

It could be said then, that Islamic peace is situational.[3]

WHAT IS SHARIAH LAW?

Literally, *Shariah* means "path," or "path to water." It is also called "Allah's Law" - the body of commands that, if followed, will provide the path to salvation.[4]

According to Muslim scholars, the Prophet Muhammad laid down the laws. Some of the laws are said to be direct commands stated in the Quran. Other laws were based on rulings Muhammad is said to have given to cases that occurred during his lifetime. These secondary laws are based on what's called the Sunnah – the Prophet's words, example and way of life and *ijma* - the consensus of Islamic scholars; and *qiyas* - a kind of reasoning that uses analogies to apply precedents established by the holy texts to problems not covered by them, for example, a ban on narcotics based on the Quranic injunction against wine-drinking.[4]

One of the major concerns of people critical of Shariah law is that it is subject to interpretation and evolution. There is virtually no formal certification process to designate someone as being qualified to interpret Islamic law. Many of the Imans and so-called Islamic scholars, make it up as they go along. Imans are empowered to give *fatwas*, which essentially are rulings, commands and laws they tailor to each community. As it stands today, almost anyone can make rulings as long as they have the appearance of piety and a group of followers.

Shariah law is Islamic law dating back to the ninth century and is today the law of the land in Iran, Sudan, Saudi Arabia, parts of Nigeria and Indonesia. It is the ultimate authority among the Taliban, Al Qaeda, Hamas, and Hezbollah.

EXAMPLES OF SHARIAH LAW INCLUDE[4]:

1. The requirement of women to obtain permission from husbands for daily freedoms.
2. It forbids women from wearing jewelry and make-up and from making noise with their shoes when they walk.
3. If a woman does work outside the home, she is forbidden to sit beside the driver when traveling to and from work.
4. Stylish dress and decoration of women is forbidden.
5. The beating of disobedient woman and girls and insubordinate wives by men.
6. The execution of homosexuals and lesbians.
7. The engagement of polygamy and forced child marriages.

8. The testimony of four male witnesses to prove rape.
9. Honor killings of those, principally women, who have dishonored the family.
10. Death without trial to apostate Muslims who chose to leave Islam.
11. Inferior status of non-Muslims.
12. Capital punishment for those who "slander Islam."
13. Women are eligible for only half of the inheritance of men.
14. Virgins may be married against their will by a father or grandfather.
15. Arab women may not marry non-Arab men.
16. Muslim men may marry 4 women, including Christians and Jews.
17. Offensive war (military jihad) against non-Muslims is a religious obligation
18. Non-Muslims ruled by Islam must follow Sharia, including discriminatory *dhimmi* taxes and laws.
19. Non-Muslims may not receive Muslim charity ("zakat"), but may be bribed to convert to Islam.
20. Lying to infidels during jihad, or to promote Islam, is permissible.
21. Slavery is permitted and legitimate.
22. Muslim men have unlimited sexual rights over slave women, even married slaves.
23. Female sexual mutilation (cliterectomy) is obligatory.
24. Adultery is punished with death by stoning.
25. Women's testimony in court is worth half that of men (and is permitted only in property cases).
26. Non-Muslims may not testify in Sharia courts.

NOTES:

1. Ann Barnhardt, *Islamic Sexuality: A Survey of Evil*; -- 9/12/11 Colorado Springs lecture: http://tomohalloran.com/2013/06/10/watch-must-see-for-all-americans-ann-barnhardt-islamic-sexuality-a-survey-of-evil/
2. http://www.answering-islam.org/Authors/Arlandson/women_inferior.htm (http://ne3. "Allah" Wikipedia® The Free Encyclopedia, Wikipedia.com, 26Jan 2013, Web, August 18, 2013, Web.(http://en.wikipedia.org/wiki/Allah) 18 August 2013
3. http://www.answeringmuslims.com/p/jihad.html
4. Excerpts Text taken from: http://www.discerningthetimesonline.net/#!islam-shariah-law-/c15qj

CHAPTER TWENTY-FIVE

WHO IS THE BEAST?

"He also forced everyone, small and great, rich and poor, free and slave, to receive a mark on his right hand or on his forehead, so that no one could buy or sell unless he had the mark, which is the name of the beast or the number of his name.
This calls for wisdom.
If anyone has insight, let him calculate the number of the beast,
For it is man's number. His number is 666."

(Revelation 13:11-18)

It is written in the Book of Revelation that those who receive the mark of the beast will be subject to the wrath of God. Yet those who refuse to receive the mark of the beast will receive the wrath of the beast. This is why it's important to identify the beast of Revelation 13.

Many in the past recognized that the beast power was mentioned under various synonyms in Scripture. It was the little horn of Daniel 7, the man of sin, the son of perdition who introduces the mystery of iniquity in 2 Thessalonians 2, the antichrist of 1 John 2 and 4 and 2 John, Babylon of Revelation 14, 16, 17, 18, and the whore and scarlet beast of Revelation 17.

We are told that he is to arise from the fourth beast (the Roman Empire) of Daniel 7:7-8. That he displaced three of the ten kingdoms into which the Roman Empire disintegrated. (Daniel 7:8, 24). He possessed human qualities (Daniel 7:8). He spoke great words (Daniel 7:8). To be reptilian in a human body, a kind of Nephilim, i.e., reptilian-human hybrid.

His power will prevail because of a falling away from the truth, i.e., the apostasy (2 Thessalonians 2:3). He opposes God and true worship (2 Thessalonians 2:4). He exalts itself above God. (2 Thessalonians 2:4). He sits in the temple of God (i.e., the rebuilt Third Temple in Jerusalem) (2 Thessalonians 2:4). He accepts the mystery of iniquity. (2 Thessalonians 2:7). He will be destroyed at Christ's coming (2 Thessalonians 2:8). He will do the works of Satan (2 Thessalonians 2:9). He will use signs and lying wonders (2 Thessalonians 2:9). Will operate unjustly and will accept strong delusions (2 Thessalonians 2: 10-11).

The redeemed will have overcome the beast's mark (Revelation 15:2-3). Those with the mark of the beast receive the seven last plagues (Revelation 16:1-2). They will receive the wrath of God (Revelation 16:19).

THE GREAT COUNTERFEITER

This will be Lucifer/Satan's final curtain call as the great counterfeiter. He will manifest himself on earth as a man, not just as any man, but as a man with supernatural powers. He will claim he is the long-awaited Messiah, and he will claim that he is "god." He will display all kinds of signs and wonders which will deceive many into accepting him as the Prince of Peace, because initially, the Bible prophesy tells us, he will appear at a time of great chaos and trouble and bring peace between the nations of the Middle East, particularly to Israel.

> "For false messiahs and false prophets will appear and perform great signs and wonders to deceive, if possible, even the elect."
>
> (Matthew 24:24)

The present day UFO scenario is setting the stage for earth humans to accept him. The signs and wonders he is predicted to perform will come through alien technology and through UFOs which he will command. He will deceive the world into believing that he has come from outer space to save the world.

The stage has been set to prepare earth humans with the expectation that the gods return to earth after 2012 along with the belief in UFOs that is growing around the world. The implants inserted into the conversation on exopolitics is the belief and the expectation that we are not alone in the universe and that space aliens must be interested in earth and earth humans, otherwise why are there so many UFOs in our skies?

There is so much in the Bible about the being known as the Antichrist, who is literally the Devil-Incarnate. The scriptures gives him many titles, including "fierce king" (Daniel 8:23), "master of intrigue" (Daniel 8:23), "contemptible person" (Daniel 11:21), "the prince who is to come" (Daniel 9:26), "man of lawlessness" (2 Thessalonians 2:3), "son of destruction" (2 Thessalonians 2:3), "the Beast" (Revelation 13:1), "the Wicked One" (Psalm 10:2,4), and "the little horn" (Daniel 7:8) among others. He is the one the Bible says will arise within a ten kingdom confederacy at the end of days. Some scholars say it will be ten nations within the old Roman Empire. Other scholars say the world itself will be divided into ten regions of which he will rule over. It could be both or either.

> "He was given power to give breath to the image of the first beast, so that it could speak and cause all who refused to worship the image to be killed."
>
> (Revelation 13:15)

The image of the beast is a statute. How can a statute speak? It can speak if it's a robot or a hologram. This will be one of the signs of wonders he will demonstrate. He will use technology and try to pawn it off as supernatural miracles. But we also have to remember that earth humans are susceptible to idolatry, this is an historical pattern. Whether it may be golden calves or any other piece of artistry that dazzles the eye, earth

CHAPTER TWENTY-FIVE: Who Is The Beast?

humans like to stare at objects that represent the supernatural, extra-terrestrials, and what appears to be "godly." This is how Lucifer/Satan gets a foothold in pulling off his deception.

THE WORLD STAGE PREPARES FOR ANTICHRIST

Holograms are relatively new technology to earth humans. But not new to Lucifer/Satan, and his minions of fallen angels that have been using holographic technology on earth humans for centuries in the form of visions of heavenly beings, which coincidentally have always been accompanied by some kind of ensuing plague or disaster, along with reports of UFOs or mysterious lights in the sky.

There were six visions in Fatima, Portugal, which mysteriously occurred on the thirteenth day of the month for six consecutive months beginning May 13, 1917, to three young children. First there were reports of UFOs, then an angel appeared to them, then the Archangel Michael and the Angel of Peace, and finally a visit from the Virgin Mary, who swore the children to secrecy. If the first vision didn't identify itself as the Virgin Mary, then why keep changing the visions?

The messages given to the children was that "god" was angry with the world and was going to punish everyone. Then within months of the last vision came a deadly plague that killed billions, nearly 27 percent of the world's population at that time because of the Spanish flu of 1918. The fact that the vision changed itself to these children several times, and did not identify itself at first as the Virgin Mary, but ended with a "holographic image" (vision) because the children could relate to it, tells us that these visions of Fatima were technologically produced by the fallen angels, i.e., demons aliens, aka Grays.

The main question should be on every researcher's mind is, why would the "alleged" Virgin Mary swear three small children to secrecy? If she truly was the Virgin Mary, then why would she expect three small children to bear the burden of a secret about what "god" is allegedly planning for the world in the future. It's also important to note, that one of the children, who held the secret died at the age of ten. God's will? Or the manipulation of the "god of this world"?

In a recent Ancient Alien Series on the History Channel titled: *Aliens, Plagues and Epidemics,* the researchers documented and exposed that all the major plagues that have historically killed humankind were preceded by UFO sightings, "light events" in the sky that were recorded in the records as glowing golden bronze disks, that were seen in broad daylight, and then immediately thereafter there was an outbreak and multitudes died. They questioned, if the plagues were curses from the wrath of God or the wrath of ETs? Were these plagues sent to control and manipulate humanity? Or were they part of some kind of intergalactic warfare?

We need to remember that both Lucifer/Satan and his fallen angels lost their place in heaven, they know that the Almighty Creator Lord has ordained their ultimate downfall, but more importantly, they also know that it is within the Lord's plan of Divine Salvation for humans, that the redeemed humans will end up judging the angels in the end. Jealousy and hatred of earth humans is at the 'core' of these counterfeit messages to deceive earth humans, and bring an 'alien invasion' of viruses and bacteria from space upon them in the form of plagues and diseases. Is it the Creator who is angry at earth humans? Or is it Lucifer/Satan and his fallen ET angel hierarchy?

Today we have the equivalency of this type of alien holographic technology known as *Project Bluebeam*, which has the ability from HAARP stations situated around the planet to create holographic images high into the upper atmosphere. HAARP stands for *High Frequency Active Auroral Research Program*.

A holographic image sent from HAARP was projected to Oslo, Norway on the eve of when President Obama was being given his Nobel Peace Prize in December of 2009 for being elected President ironically just weeks after he committed 30,000 more troops to escalate the war efforts in Afghanistan. The strange spiral with a blue light beam (Project Blue Beam) was deliberately projected onto Oslo to send an alarming message to everyone around the world who witnessed and saw it, which many did as pictures and videos of it spread like wildfire around the Internet.

The HAARP antennae's are literally just a stone's throw away miles from Oslo. Some believe HAARP is considered to be the New World Order Mind Control and Weather Warfare Weapon. The Soviets were suspected for using the hypnotic spiral with the Blue Beam technology to send a message to Obama and the world. The 'Perfect Storm' is being planned. One really needs to ask the questions of how earth humans (Americans, Soviets, and Australians) obtained this level of technology?

Another train of thought amongst researchers, is that this blue light beam spiral, was done by aliens to open up a portal in space to enter through. What remarkable timing!

The reality is that UFOs have long been accepted by most people, but due to the government suppression of knowledge of UFOs, and their outright "official denials," which is oxymoronic in and of itself, has been frustrating for people to complete the missing pieces of the puzzle of what they know and suspect when having sightings, visitations, and experiences with UFOs and alien beings because the information is so fragmented. The military holds tight to its secrets until a new whistleblower emerges and leaks it to the rest of us, which sometimes may seem like big pieces, but pieces of the grand puzzle, nevertheless.

But what if the information is deliberately used to support a particular political agenda? The subject matter is confusing to the best of minds, to say the least, so how will humanity be prepared for the new wave of deceptions about to test earth humans? One really needs to hone in on one's powers of discernment here, which collectively is our biggest test of all time.

So many people are dying for disclosure, but disclosure of which truths? The truth that aliens are real and have been interacting and interfering with humans and earth governments for millennia? Or the Truth of who and what they really are and what their agendas are for earth humans?

Full disclosure may never happen, whereas partial disclosure seems more within reach. But as the old saying goes "a little knowledge is a dangerous thing," and that knowledge could easily be distorted which would deceive many. Deception always advances with a basic truth sandwiched between two lies.

Discernment is a very important tool and skill we all need to get us through these changing times. It can make or break someone as to whether or not to "drink" the Kool-Aid, and the many "illusions" that are thrust upon humans these days. How do you know when to slough something off or when to drink it in?

Truth is like oil, it will eventually always surface. So what if you've invested in lies and delusions, how would you know, until it is too late? Well, that's why we need to really hone our powers of discernment these days and pray for the "gift of discernment" from the Holy Spirit.

THE ANTICHRIST PROPHESY

> "And I saw a beast coming out of the sea. He had ten horns and seven heads, with ten crowns on his horns, and on each head a blasphemous name. The beast I saw resembled a leopard, but had feet like those of a bear and a mouth like that of a lion. The dragon gave the beast his power and his throne and great authority. One of the heads of the beast seemed to have had a fatal wound, but the fatal wound had been healed. The whole world was astonished and followed the beast. Men worshiped the dragon because he had given authority to the beast, and they also worshiped the beast and asked, "Who is like the beast? Who can make war against him?"
>
> (Revelation 13:1-4)

This is a loaded prophetic vision. As I've already gone over in my chapter "Ancient Technology and Biblical Astronauts" that the beast coming out of the sea, represents where Satan's army is located, inside the earth, and under the oceans. There are thousands around the planet who have witnessed flying saucers emerge out of the oceans, including myself, and take off into the sky and disappear into outer space.

The beast is a biblical term for the Nephilim, which are transgenic beings, and reptilian/draconian beings (serpents) that Lucifer/Satan and his fallen angels were cursed into. They live inside the earth. St. John is describing one of these Nephilim, Transgenics, which is some kind of mixture of a leopard, bear, and lion, who had had power and authority. The one who is wounded is healed, becomes the antichrist, and is convinced he is the supernatural messiah. This being will have the outward appearance of a human man, but the genetics of a Nephilim.

> "Then I saw another beast, coming out of the earth. He had two horns like a lamb, but he spoke like a dragon. He exercised all the authority of the first beast on his behalf, and made the earth and its inhabitants worship the first beast, whose fatal wound had been healed. And he performed great and miraculous signs, even causing fire to come down from heaven to earth in full view of men. Because of the signs he was given power to do on behalf of the first beast, he deceived the inhabitants of the earth.
>
> He ordered them to set up an image in honor of the beast who was wounded by the sword and yet lived. He was given power to give breath to the image of the first beast, so that it could speak and cause all who refused to worship the image to be killed.
>
> He also forced everyone, small and great, rich and poor, free and slave, to receive a mark on his right hand or on his forehead, so that no one could buy or sell unless he had the mark, which is the name of the beast or the number of his name. This calls for wisdom. If anyone has insight, let him calculate the number of the beast, for it is man's number. His number is 666."
>
> (Revelation 13:11-18)

Then the prophetic vision St. John is given tells of another beast that comes out of the earth. Another reptilian/draconian from the inner earth. This one makes sure that earth humans worship the first beast (the antichrist) and with alien technology causes fire to come down from heaven from UFOs in the first or second heaven, so that humans will witness it. He does this to gain power and, in doing so, deceives earth humans into the false belief that the aliens have arrived, and are here on earth to save us. Then he orders them to create an image of the antichrist, this could be some kind of holographic statute and then causes it to speak.

Besides the technological possibility of talking robots, holographic technology can produce a talking image as well, so much so that a person can think he is talking to a real person. The number 666 has been a conundrum. Many have interpreted it to mean a bar code, or have even used numerology to deduce a person's name to equal 666. This mystery will no doubt be revealed when the antichrist is revealed to the world. However, in my opinion, I believe this number represents technology, perhaps even the number of his fleet of UFOs.

Then the prophecy says that he has the power to force everyone to receive a mark. This could be a tattoo or an implant, or both, in order to do business on planet Earth. This tells us that this antichrist will come across to earth humans as some kind of financial genius who will set up through his "New World Order" an economic system at a time when all other systems have failed. Just like history tells us, when nations are economically depressed, they are willing to accept a dictator who promises them all provisions.

CHAPTER TWENTY-FIVE: Who Is The Beast?

The antichrist will set up global socialism, which will be the epitome of totalitarianism. It will fulfill George Orwell's visions of *1984*, where he saw everyone enslaved in a technologically advanced empire. This is the New World Order.

The Bible warns that the final "Empire" on Earth just before Messiah (Christ) returns will be a "re-united" Roman Empire of strong nations mixed with weak nations ("iron mixed with clay") over which the Antichrist will rise. Iron mixed with clay has been interpreted by most Bible scholars to mean the countries of Europe with the countries of the Middle East. Taking the meaning of iron, which relates to those countries who are technologically advanced, and clay, meaning those countries who are still somewhat primitive. Yet, we now have a Middle East that is becoming technologically advanced, which could be the meaning of this Bible prophecy, iron mixed with clay.

Another possible interpretation may be that "iron" representing technology may actually come from "alien technology" that is contracted to earth humans within these nations, which is what much of the official UFO whistleblowers have been touting for decades, that a number of nations around the world, including the United States, Russia, and China all have made contracts with aliens from inside the earth, for advanced technology.

In fact, World War II was fought over this technology, as was the ensuing Cold War between United States and the USSR, with the cover that it was about communism, when in reality it was about technological secrets with respect to alien technology to be used in a communistic regime. Is it any coincidence that our world has advanced exponentially in the past five decades, more than it has in the past two millennia?

> "Whereas you saw the feet and toes, partly of clay and partly of iron, the kingdom (Rome) shall be divided . . . (now re-uniting as modern Europe) And as the toes and feet were partly of iron and partly of clay, so the (re-united) kingdom shall be partly strong and partly fragile . . ." (Daniel 9:41-43) (This will be the "kingdom" of the Antichrist ... and Armageddon)

> "Then I stood on the sand of the sea. <u>And I saw a Beast (Satan's Antichrist) rising up out of the sea, having seven heads and ten horns, and on his horns ten crowns,</u> (other prophecies tell us these represent nations in Europe) and on his heads a blasphemous name . . . "<u>The dragon (Satan) gave him his power, his throne, and great authority</u>." (Revelation 13:1-2)

> "<u>The ten horns are ten kings who shall arise from (out of) this kingdom</u> (the Roman Empire). And another shall rise after them; he (the Antichrist) *shall be different* from the first ones, and shall subdue three kings . . ." (The end begins) (Daniel 7:24)

The Bible clearly says "in the last days" ten nations will rise out of the ancient Roman Empire. Many (not all) believe these ten nations could rise *out of* the European Union as we now see the "strong mixed with weak" nations of Europe reuniting into a powerful federation. Some also suggest the ten nations may represent worldwide trading blocs of nations, or the UN, or NATO, or nations out of the *Eastern* leg of the Roman Empire, which was based out of Constantinople in Turkey.

It is worth noting that the leaders of France, Italy, Germany, and England have called for the need to have a "powerful leader" lead and head the new and rising "European Union." In a moment of time, this man would immediately possess the power over all of Europe that eluded Adolph Hitler (Germany), Kaiser Wilhelm (Germany), Napoleon Bonaparte (France), and the royalties of England, Spain, and others to gain and restore the dominion and power of the ancient Roman Empire.

I found a book entitled *The Antichrist,* by Larry Harper. It's a different type of book as he brought together two separate works on the subject of the Antichrist and the Second Coming of Christ. It details what the Early Church Fathers believed some 1,800 years ago. I thought it was interesting in light of the present day interpretations of these prophesies. One work was that of the Church Father Irenaeus. The other was that of his disciple Hippolytus. Irenaeus' teacher was Polycarp. Polycarp was Bishop of Smyrna (today known as Izmir), a city on the west coast of Turkey.

Polycarp is said to have known the Apostle John, and was instructed by him in the Christian faith. Polycarp, in his turn, taught Irenaeus, who later became Bishop of Lyons in what is now France. Polycarp was then martyred by the Turkish government for his belief in Jesus Christ. Irenaeus then discipled Hippolytus.

The premise was that these two men preserved the apostolic teaching of the early Church. It is these two who clearly believed they were taught those things the original apostles received directly from Jesus Christ. As well, and not surprisingly, Irenaeus and Hippolytus agree on the basic points regarding the advent of Christ and Antichrist. These interpretations were handed down by the Apostle John himself through Polycarp! If this is true, then what follows cannot be ignored.

The beliefs that Irenaeus and Hippolytus held in common regarding the coming Antichrist can be summarized as follows:

1. Satan will appear as a man in the person of the Antichrist because he seeks to reign as king over mankind and desires to focus the worship of God on himself.
2. The Antichrist will be a Jew and will achieve his stated objectives by being accepted as the Christ, the messianic king of the Jews, taking his seat in the rebuilt third temple in Jerusalem, pretending to be God Himself, and thereby becoming the "abomination of desolation" spoken of by the prophet Daniel (Daniel 12:11), and mentioned also by Jesus (Matthew 24:15).
3. The Antichrist is the "little horn" of the fourth beast mentioned in Daniel 7. He will slay three of the other horns and reign as an eighth with the remaining seven horns.

CHAPTER TWENTY-FIVE: Who Is The Beast?

Hippolytus explains that those three horns are the rulers of Egypt, Libya, and Ethiopia (Interesting that there has been ongoing political upheaval in all of those countries recently). Israel has recently allied with Egypt, Jordan, and Saudi Arabia in a joint coalition against their fight to eradicate ISIS. There's that old Middle East saying coming into play: "The enemy of my enemy is my friend."

4. The Antichrist will achieve his objectives in the middle of the final seven-year period of this age. At that time, he will be proclaimed the messianic king of the Jews and will take his seat as God in the rebuilt temple in Jerusalem. He will reign for three and one-half years.
5. The Antichrist, during his reign, will deceive the majority of people living on the Earth at the time into believing he is God. However, he will persecute those who refuse to worship him because they are able to see through his delusion.
6. Irenaeus and Hippolytus believed that Jesus Christ will return to Earth at the end of the three and one-half year reign of the Antichrist, destroying Satan's kingdom and that the resurrection of the just will occur at that time.[1]

    The Bible tells us that Jesus Christ will return twice, once in stealth to rapture (lift up and gather) his Bride (his faithful believers) off the planet, who the Bible refers to as the "Restrainer." The reason for this is that these are the human vessels where His Spirit dwells. These are the humans who sanctify themselves to be the "temples of the Living God" on Earth, where God, through His Holy Spirit lives and dwells within them, to further the work of His Coming Kingdom on Earth. Together all of these humans make up what is called "the body of Christ" which the Lord refers to as His Bride. Their presence actually grounds the spiritual forces of the Christ on earth which "restrains" the antichrist from being revealed and reigning on earth.

    Once the Bride (the restrainer) is removed from the planet, then the antichrist begins his seven-year reign. Some scholars believe that this will happen at the three and half year mark, when the antichrist begins to persecute everyone who refuse to worship him.

    But keeping in line with the heart of God, who promises to save those who love him, the rapture will happen right before the Wrath of God is poured out on the planet which is during the great tribulation, but not necessarily at the beginning.

    I'd say, the sheer reality of nearly half the people on this planet disappearing suddenly, without warning, would most certainly be the jumpstart of the reign of Antichrist, by removing the restrainer off the planet, i.e., the body of Christ.[1].

    The False Messiah will in response, lie to the remaining world, that there was a mass abduction by aliens, and begin to gather those left behind to wage war on God for doing so, and take out his frustration on those who were left behind that realize what happened, because they were told it would happen, and are immediately convicted to repent to God, and become what is known as the Tribulation Saints, who resist the Antichrist and the New World Order. Most of whom become martyrs for Christ, but are rewarded with crowns in the Kingdom of Heaven.

The body of Christ is made up of many parts, through all cross sections of culture and religions. Remember there are nations on this planet that outlaw religion, outlaw Christianity, and outlaw Bibles, yet in spite of that, millions are turning to Jesus Christ as their personal Savior through the agency of the Holy Spirit. One really needs to ask, why? So many of these people go unaccounted for. Then there are the obvious believers who make up the world's churches.

Some people question whether the Bride of Christ is the body of Christ or the city of Jerusalem based on the words in Revelation 21:2: "And I John saw the holy city, New Jerusalem, coming down from God out of heaven, prepared as a bride adorned for her husband." Being that Jerusalem is the "eye of the storm," this could very well turn out to be true, when the grand mother ship, called the New Jerusalem, arrives out of the heavens, dripping with jewels, as Revelation goes on to describe, with twelve gates named after the twelve surviving "blessed" tribes of Israel. But the scripture says He is coming for His Bride, the parable of the ten virgins (Matthew 25) and their lamps are generally understood to mean the Bride of Christ, who are the true believers and followers of Jesus, who will soon meet and "marry" him at the long awaited wedding banquet, which could very well happen in the New Jerusalem, this grand mother ship that grounds to earth over the old destroyed Jerusalem, as the New City of Peace.

Remember the words of Christ about separating the sheep and the goats, not everyone who claims "Christian" status will be saved. Also the lukewarm will also be passed over, as Revelation clearly says, that the Lord will spew them out of his mouth (Revelation 3:16).

Then there will be millions left behind who have heard the good news but refused to repent and continue in unbelief. After the rapture, they will have another chance to repent and will receive salvation, but scripture tells us that they will be martyred through the harsh persecutions from the antichrist. These souls are the ones who will remember the scriptures that were witnessed to them about the antichrist, and they will be the ones who discern through his deceptions.

If after reading my books, *Who's Who In The Cosmic Zoo? Series,* and you still don't believe, hold on to them so that you can recognize the antichrist when he rises up. However, I pray for each reader to be given the grace to have the truth revealed before that time comes upon us. I hope each reader will take advantage of the window of grace offered to all now to receive Jesus Christ (Yahshua HaMashiach) as his or her personal savior. (For further elucidation on this, see my chapter, Ascension or Rapture? which is in Book Three: *Who Are The Angels?* of *Who's Who in the Cosmic Zoo*).

"And it shall be, that whosoever shall <u>call on the name of the Lord shall be saved</u>."
(Acts 2:21)

"Repent and be baptized, every one of you, in the name of Jesus Christ for the forgiveness of your sins. And you will receive the gift of the Holy Spirit."
(Acts 2:38)

CHAPTER TWENTY-FIVE: Who Is The Beast?

Then at the end of the seven year tribulation, the time known as "Jacob's Troubles" (Jacob was renamed Israel, which literally means, 'he who struggles with God, hence Jacob's), then the Lord Jesus Christ will return to win the final battle against the antichrist, Satan and his hosts, i.e., fallen angels, and claim his eternal victory over the earth and His Redeemed.

> "Together they will go to war against the Lamb, but the Lamb will defeat them because he is Lord of all lords and King of all kings. And his called and chosen and faithful ones will be with him."
>
> (Revelation 17:14)

He will appear to the world <u>with</u> his called and faithful one, that means that He will have already saved them, (Raptured them up) <u>before</u> He returns in what is known as the 'second coming' the prophecy tells us all will see him, and all those who pierced him will mourn.

> "They will look on me, the one they have pierced, and they will mourn for him as one mourns for an only child, and grieve bitterly for him as on grieves for a firstborn son."
>
> (Zechariah 14:5)

These are the souls (or soul group) who crucified Christ. How can that be, when the crucifixion happened over two thousand years ago? The only logical answer is that those souls will have reincarnated and will be on the earth at that appointed time.

Thomas R. Horn, writes in his book *Nephilim Stargates*, about the 'Father of Nephilim and the Son of Perdition': (emphasis mine)

> "Some believe that in the very near future a man of superior intelligence, wit, charm, and diplomacy will descend from the clouds or otherwise emerge on the world scene as a savior. He will seemingly possess a transcendent wisdom that enables him to solve problems and offer solutions to many of today's most perplexing issues. His popularity will be widespread, and his fans will include young and old, religious and non-religious, male and female. Talk show hosts will interview his colleagues, news anchors will cover his movement, scholars will applaud his uncanny ability at resolving what has escaped the rest of us, and the poor will bow down at this table. He will, in every human way, appeal to the best idea of society. But his profound comprehension and irresistible presence will be the result of an invisible network of thousands of years of collective knowledge. He will represent the embodiment of a very old and super intelligent spirit. As Jesus Christ was the "seed" of the woman, he will be the "seed" of the serpent (Gen. 3.15). Although his arrival in the form of a man was foretold by numerous

scriptures, <u>the broad masses of the world will not recognize him as the ultimate transgenic incarnation</u> - the "beast" of Revelation 13.1. [p. 198][2]

The way Horn brings the antichrist into modern-day terms, one could easily relate to how such a person could weave their way into the mainstream media, gain international popularity, particularly when our present mainstream media has already been compromised and taken over by the "spirit of the antichrist" as we have witnessed it's obvious bias with respect to favoring one politician over another, and protecting the irregularities and scandals of one president over another.

The very fact that the masses were sucked into believing in Barack Obama and voted him in for all the wrong reasons, only to have emerged with buyers' remorse years later and so many lies, indicates a precursor of the masses being charmed and thrilled with another man who displays superior intelligence, who is handsome and articulate, and tells people what they want to hear.

Many in the blogosphere thought Barack Obama was the antichrist; I do not. However, the one who is the final antichrist is supposed to be some kind of financial genius, who comes to solve the world's global problems, particularly the world's ailing global economy, and while Barack Obama may be many things, he is without a doubt, no financial genius!

"Concurrent with the political aspects of the NWO is the syncretistic and spiritual goals of New Agers and Dominionists. The blending of politics and spirituality, such as occurs in these movements, harmonizes perfectly with the ideas of an end-time marriage of government policy with the ideas of an end-time marriage of government policy and religious creed as was prophesied in the Bible. To that end, the tools necessary for paganism's ultimate incarnation — the god-king of the Great Tribulation (Satan in flesh) — are in place. The "gods" have been revived through modern mysticism. The pagan agenda of governing by "divine representation" is being constructed. The governments of the world are uniting beneath a one-world banner, and the earth's masses stand at the brink of a decisive moment in time."[2]

According to some Christians, this is the unfolding of an ancient scheme. At the core of the conspiracy, a leader of indescribable brutality is scheduled to appear. He will make the combined depravities of Antiochus Epiphanes, Hitler, Stalin and Genghis Khan, all of whom were types of the Antichrist, look like Pee Wee Herman's Playhouse. He will raise his fist, "speaking great things...in blasphemy against God, to blaspheme his name, and his tabernacle, and them that dwell in heaven." (Revelation 13.5-6)

As he champions worship of the gods who come through portals, he will cause "that as many as would not worship the image of the beast should be killed" (Revelation 13:15). "The King of Babylon," as he is called in Isaiah 14, will revive the Babylonian mystery religion — "the habitation of devils, and the hold of very

CHAPTER TWENTY-FIVE: Who Is The Beast?

foul spirit, and a cage of every unclean and hateful bird" where merchants of the earth trade in "souls of men" and where "the blood of prophets, and of saints" is found (Revelation 18:2, 13, 24).

THE GODS WHO COME THROUGH PORTALS

New Agers are being used in their seemingly "innocent" fascination for ancient gods to invoke these ancient gods through various types of rituals, invocations, and worldwide group meditations such as days with the numbers 11:11, 12:12 with the belief that they are tapping into and activating a stargate/portal, along with taking trips to various "portals" around the planet, i.e., ancient temples, megaliths, pyramids, sphinx, etc. These people who lead tours to these ancient sites believe they can reconnect with the gods of the past. In doing so, they are bringing these gods back through the portals, legally through invocation and unbeknownst to them, are inviting them back to strategically set themselves up for the final battle against Christ and two-thirds of heavens faithful extraterrestrial (angels).

> The book of Revelation details what follows the rise of Antichrist, culminating in a cataclysmic war called Armageddon, a time during which God Almighty judges the "gods" who come through portals, including, we would assume, so-called Zeus, Apollo, Demeter, Isis, and others.
>
> However futile, the *gods* will retaliate, and a war of indescribable intensity will occur. It will be fought on land and sea, in the heavens above, and in the earth below, in the physical and spiritual worlds. It will include "Michael and his angels [fighting] against the dragon; and the dragon [fighting] and his angels" (Revelation 12:7).
>
> Some humans will join the battle against God, calling on "idols of gold, and silver, and brass, and stone, and of wood" (Revelation 9:20) to convene their power against the Christian God, even uniting with "unclean spirits like frogs...the spirits of *devils* [the frog goddesses Heka?] Working miracles, which go forth unto the kings of the earth...to gather them to the battle of that great day... [to] a place called in the Hebrew tongue Armageddon ["Mount Megiddo"] (Revelation 16:13-14, 16).
>
> There, in the valley of Megiddo, the omnipotent Christ will utterly repel the forces of darkness and destroy the New World army. Blood will flow like rivers, and the fowl of the air will "eat the flesh of the mighty, and drink the blood of the princes of the earth" (Ezekiel 39.18). Besides Armageddon, battles will be fought in the Valley of Jehoshaphat and in the city of Jerusalem. Yet, the battle of Armageddon is the event that culminates the hostility between God Almighty and the lower gods that traverse portals." [Horn, 201, 202]

Over three thousand years ago, Satan and his "god" spirits, challenged Yahuah at Megiddo. They lost. On Mount Carmel, overlooking the Valley of Armageddon, the prophets of Baal dared the Hebrew God to answer by fire. He did, and according to Revelation 19:19-21; 20:11-12, 15; he will do it again.

CERN AND THE ANTICHRIST

The goal of CERN is time travel. The world's largest, most expensive, and extravagant science experiment is taking place in Switzerland, around Geneva. The scientists are using this giant hydron collider as their star gate, which is built some three-hundred feet into the earth. They claim to be searching for the "God Particle," but all the evidence points to the fact that they are working on opening dimensional doorways

The name CERN is derived from the acronym for the French Conseil Européen pour la Recherche Nucléaire, a provisional body founded in 1952 with the mandate of establishing a world-class fundamental physics research organization in Europe, which also happens to be located in Cern, Switzerland. CERN was started by twelve countries on September 29, 1954, on the Jewish New Year, Rosh Hashanah, which appears to be a symbol for counterfeit Israel. They are planning to reignite the collider in September of 2015 after several years of repairs and upgrades. September 28 is the fourth Blood Moon of a Tetrad of Blood Moons, which also begins the Feast of Tabernacles, also known as Sukkot.

The Bible tells us the antichrist number will be 666. The very logo/symbol of CERN are three 6's circling one another.

CERN is a forced hydron collider, forcing particles to collide. Beams of light are colliding to try to find the God particle. They want to replicate the Big Bang theory and collide these particles to see what comes off of them. They're trying to recreate the Big Bang. They claim they're trying to find what holds matter together, that they can't see. We know that is the spiritual dimensions, which is God.

They want to separate and isolate the natural from the supernatural. Here's the problem. When you separate the natural from the supernatural, which defines matter and anti-matter, you have matter that is positive spiritual energy from God, and negative energy which is ruled by the demonic realm.

The scientists take objects and rub them with spiritual energy, place them in the collider to see what happens. Infusing energy into a stone or piece of metal is an occult practice. They are experimenting by attaching negative and positive energies to specific objects. This is a common occult practice — putting curses on objects, through hexes, and spells which essentially attaches demonic spirits to objects.

In the same way they took rags and clothing from Peter and the Apostle Paul that was considered to be "anointed" with Christ's energy, and used them to do healings in the group, is the same concept that CERN is doing experiments with objects. They are using different energies and spirits and sending them deep into the earth through the collider.

CHAPTER TWENTY-FIVE: Who Is The Beast?

Then, they will sit back and see what happens when they connect the natural and the supernatural, which may not end up as they expected.

What CERN is doing is highly controversial, and many seers such as Jim Staley and Tom Horn connects the dots to them actually opening up a portal to the inner earth and literally opening up the bottomless pit, by fulfilling the prophecy in Revelation for the last days, when they eventually will release the fallen angel of the Abyss, which Revelation 9:2, 4, 7-11 says:

(Emphasis and commentary in brackets are mine)

"And the fifth angel sounded, and I saw a star fall from heaven to the earth (an extraterrestrial): and to him was given the key of the bottomless pit. And he opened the bottomless pit; and there arose a smoke out of the pit, as the smoke of a great furnace; and the sun and the air were darkened by reason of the smoke of the pit. And there came out of the smoke locusts on the earth: and to them was given power, as the scorpions of the earth have power. (Scorpions are metaphors for demons, however, scorpions are armored, these beings may be aliens, or it may also describe their spaceships, black, shiny and armored like a scorpion with power)

The locusts looked like horses prepared for battle. (Horses are metaphors for space chariots, locusts are insectoids, an alien race) On their heads they wore something like crowns of gold (space helmets), and their faces resembled human faces (Nephilim, fallen princes from the past). Their hair was like women's hair, and their teeth were like lions' teeth. They had breastplates like breastplates of iron, and the sound of their wings was like the thundering of many horses and chariots rushing into battle. (This line is clearly a description of a UFO) They had tails with stingers, like scorpions, and in their tails they had power to torment people for five months. (The tail had the power to torment people for five months, the tail of a spaceship that was actually a sophisticated weapon) They had as king over them the angel of the Abyss (the bottomless pit), whose name in Hebrew is Abaddon and in Greek is Apollyon (that is, Destroyer)."

Apollyon is one of Satan's Archdemonic Fallen Angels, he was fallen and bound into the pit since the last galactic battle with Lord and His Hosts (celestial armies).

Coincidentally or possibly intentionally planned, the ancient temple of Apollyon (Apollo) is situated in Cern, Switzerland. What's also extraordinary, is that the corporate offices of CERN has a giant statute of Shiva, who is a Hindu goddess as its mascot right outside its front door. This is odd, because most "scientific" corporations avoid connecting themselves with any kind of religion. However, when you compare this ancient statute of the Goddess of Destruction which depicts the goddess within a circle of fire, which the actual CERN stargate, it is almost identical. Proving that this ancient symbol, symbolized an extraterrestrial god moving through a stargate back and forth to earth. This Shiva statute is probably the most famous in the Hindu religion.

The Director for Research and Scientific Computing at CERN, Sergio Bertolucii had this to say about their experiment:

> "Something may come through the dimensional doors at LHC…and out of this door might come something, or we might send something through it."

St. Appolecum, the town was dedicated to Shiva or Horus. This city is the ancient god Apollyon, which today in Hindu is Shiva, the goddess of destruction, it is the only deity that intends to destroy the universe for the purpose of recreating it.

The purpose of CERN has been to open up a time space portal and theoretically creating a tear in the time-space continuum which could create a miniature black hole. The obvious danger is opening up a black hole could vacuum up not only earth but the entire universe into it, regardless of how big or small that black hole is. Yet they are moving forward with this, with the expectation that "something" will come through.

Perhaps these scientists are being taught by the fallen angels which were not bound in the pit, the ones who move through the dimensional doorways of earth, by teaching and guiding these scientists through giving them the technology and skills to actually succeed in their goals of opening up a stargate to a different dimension, meanwhile they are serving their fellow fallen angels, who are bound in the pit, by giving humans the keys and codes to releasing their friends?

It certainly appears that this is the case, particularly that this matches the prophecy in Revelation 9. These humans are not the only ones who have been used by the fallen angels to open up portals on earth. Aleister Crowley was used to open a portal in Egypt, and a being named "Lam" came through, who was a type of Gray in 1919.

The prophecies tell us that in the last days, the Nephilim, i.e., demonic alien beings, come back to the earth's surface from out of the bottomless pit for a final battle with the forces of light, who is Christ and His Celestial Army of Christed beings.

This being who gets released is somehow connected to the manifestation of the times of the final antichrist on Earth, which prophecy tells us will last for seven years.

The Shemitah cycles happen every seven years. There is a connection to the Shemitah cycles and the start of the seven year tribulation, which is the reign of the antichrist on earth.

This being may manifest himself within a human man, so that you do not "see" the true image of this being, which would freak everyone out, because he so damn ugly and scary looking, which the Bible refers to as "the beast," but instead, this being possesses a man, to use as his vessel, to situate himself in exactly the spot (or portal) he needs to be to have the seat of power to rule the world, and that will be the rebuilt third temple in Jerusalem, where he demands everyone worship him as a "god."

It is my opinion that this man will be of Jewish descent. He may even be Israeli. The prophecy tells us that only a quarter of the world follows the antichrist, and Israel leads the world because this man proves himself by initiating a peace treaty between Israel and

CHAPTER TWENTY-FIVE: Who Is The Beast?

her enemies, and actually is the first person to achieve peace for Israel, causing Israelis to respect him as the prince of peace, causing Arabs to worship him as well.

If the Jews are going to be deceived by this man, which the prophecies tell us is slated to happen for various reasons, the Lord allows Israel to be tested in this way, then it only makes sense that the antichrist will be a Jew; otherwise why would the Jews follow him? I realize there are several authors today following in Joel Richardson's theory that the antichrist is equivalent to the Islamic Mahdi, but there is no way Israeli Jews would follow a Muslim, let alone worship one. Certainly not in this universe! He gets Jews to worship him, because Jews follow science, and technology, and they become deceived by his alluring power and knowledge.

This is why I am asserting that the final antichrist will be a Jew, who will counterfeit the life of Yeshua, today known as Jesus Christ. He will do what the Jews felt Yeshua didn't do for them, which was to defeat Rome. He only stops the animal sacrifice halfway through because he demands human sacrifices, all those who defy him and refuse to take his mark to be in his "digital society."

Christians and some Jews whose eyes are open to be slaughtered in the worst way this world has seen. Animal sacrifices are retro, backwards, and do not affect anyone because a divine being came to Earth two thousand years ago and became the final blood sacrifice for both humans and animals, which can't be undone, nor outdone. This is the supernatural power, many believers rely on.

After all, God's Grace is sufficient for us. It is only by His Grace that we are given power to defeat demons, overcome the power of sin, and break curses. This is not something that can be done with clunky technology. This is the power of God, which is all anyone needs.

THE ANCIENT PORTAL OF MEGIDDO

The Bible writers speaks of this ancient battle site twelve different times. Further, Bible prophecy indicates that what took place at Megiddo has serious implications for our day. The long awaited "Battle of Armageddon" comes from the prophecy that the final battle between Satan and Christ will culminate over this ancient portal. The word "Megiddo" in Hebrew means "field of blood," the word "har" in Hebrew means "mount." Mount Megiddo is the location where the Lord will return, which stands in the midst of a valley plain known as Jezreel and Kishon.

Let us take a look at what both the Bible and archaeology say about this historic place. The books of Judges Chapters 4 and 5 tells of a battle at Megiddo, where victory was not won by the fruit of military prowess and equipment, but by supernatural intervention by Yahuah. Sisera's vastly superior troops were lured into the then-dry torrent valley of Kishon.

The Lord Yahuah gave Barak the signal to descend. 10,000 men marched down the mountain into the valley plain! But then, unexpectedly, Yahuah caused a thunderstorm.

Wind and rain now lashed into the face of the enemy. The Kishon River valley was turned into a raging torrent, immobilizing Sisera's war chariots in a sea of mud. Thrown into confusion, Sisera's troops fled in terror, only to be pursued and executed. "Not as much as one remained."

This stunning victory inspired the words: "Thus let all your enemies perish, O Yahuah, and let your lovers be as when the sun goes forth in its mightiness" (Judges 5:31). This victory brought forty years of peace in the land of Israel. Note: the word "thus" suggests that the battle was prophetic, pointing forward to a greater war in which all the enemies of the Lord would perish there.

However, history shows that Israel's enemies quickly forgot this disastrous encounter. This seems to be the pattern with history, which is why history repeats itself. Only forty-seven years later, a combination of nations under the lead of Midian "gathered together as one and proceeded to … camp in the low plain of Jezreel," the valley extending from Megiddo (Judges 6:33).

These encamped enemies were "as numerous as locusts." This time, however, the army of Israel was only a small but courageous band of three hundred men, standing "all around the camp" under the leadership of Gideon. At a signal, all three hundred of them blew horns, loudly smashed water jars, waved torches, and let out a terrifying war cry: "Yahuah's sword and Gideon's!" The Midianites panicked! "Lord Yahuah proceeded to set the sword of each one against the other," and Gideon's tiny band completed the rout! (Judges, Chapter 7). We today dare not make the mistake of the Midianites nor shrug off the significance of Megiddo.

Megiddo was known as the great crossroads of the ancient world. Megiddo, along with the cities of Hazor and Gezer, once dominated a major military and trade route connecting Asia and Africa. Megiddo laid between the other two cities and hence was the one most strategically located. From all directions, natural gateways, mountain passes, and roads converged into her valley plain. During the rains, this valley became a muddy plain, as Sisera and his armies experienced, however during the dry summer, this open plain was the place for chariots and charioteers to train for war (Song of Solomon 6:11, 12). Military troops often assembled there.

King Solomon took steps to fortify Megiddo: "Now this is the account of those conscripted for forced labor that King Solomon levied to build … the wall of Jerusalem and Hazor and Megiddo and Gezer" (1 Kings 9:15). A seventy-foot-high (twenty-one meters) mound, overlooking a wide, open valley, now marks the spot where Megiddo once stood. In ancient times, new buildings were often constructed on top of the ruins of old ones.

Each level of construction may, therefore, mark a particular time in history. Today, archaeologists, starting from the top, can dig their way down through layer after layer of history. At least, twenty of such layers have been discovered at Megiddo, indicating that the city was rebuilt many times.

CHAPTER TWENTY-FIVE: Who Is The Beast?

WHY SATAN IS OBSESSED WITH ISRAEL'S ANCIENT SPACE PORTALS

Israel is full of ancient space portals. The Temple Mount in Jerusalem is one of the most hotly contested portals in Israel. While ancient Israel was divided between northern Israel and southern Judea, both Jerusalem and Megiddo were in Judea. The end of our present timeline ends and culminates at the Temple Mount in Jerusalem and the ancient battlefield of Megiddo known as the seven-year tribulation, i.e., time of Jacob's troubles, and the "final" battle of Armageddon. It's important to distinguish the "final" battle from the "false" Armageddon, which is expected to take place before the final tribulation.

The promises and Bible prophesies cannot be ignored in light of our Israel current dilemmas. The Lord promises to return through these portals and establish His Throne in the coming Kingdom of God in the New Jerusalem which will overlay the old Jerusalem. This is why Satan is obsessed with taking over this portal — to try to prevent the Kingdom of God from coming to Earth. Jerusalem is the home of the Lord's heart. When King Solomon first built the glorious temple and dedicated it to the Lord, this is what the Lord said:

> "The LORD Yahuah said to him: "I have heard the prayer and plea you have made before me; I have consecrated this temple, which you have built, <u>by putting my Name there forever. My eyes and my heart will always be there.</u>"
>
> (1 Kings 9:3)

Jerusalem is the center of the Lord's attention, both on Earth and in heaven. For both men and for extraterrestrials (angels). The Heavenly Jerusalem is the meeting place of all of heaven's angels (extraterrestrial messengers and warriors) from all over the universe. When heaven comes to Earth, it will arrive through the downloading of the New Jerusalem, which is a city made of gold, precious jewels, and full of the glory of God (Shekinah presence) which comes down out of heaven, which is actually a huge mother ship city that descends and is laid over the old Jerusalem.

Jesus said at the end of this age, "I tell you the truth, not one stone here will be left on another; everyone will be thrown down" (Matthew 24:2). That means nothing here will last. We are told there will be a new heaven and a new earth in the end.

Israel is probably the most controversial piece of real estate on Earth and in the heavens. Every battle fought on Earth first starts in the heavens. We have to remember that this is an ancient spiritual battle.

> **"We war not against the flesh, but against principalities (despots), powers and rulers of the darkness and spiritual wickedness in the heavens."**
>
> (Ephesians 6:12)

These ancient space portals will end the world and begin the next world. Everyone who listens to God's word in the scriptures and follows Bible prophecy knows that every piece of news that happens on in the Middle East is happening because it is all part of the end of our present timeline unfolding and coming to an end.

After King Solomon's temple was destroyed in 586 BCE, the second temple was rebuilt and was again destroyed in 70AD. Bible prophecy tells us that a third temple will be rebuilt where the abomination of desolation will take place at the Temple Mount in Jerusalem, which will bring about the end of this world and precipitate the battle of Armageddon.

However, unlike the building of the first and second temples, which were all commanded and ordained by the Lord Yahuah, there is no command from Yahuah to rebuild the temple a third time. The rebuilding of the third temple is the work of man, not of God.

When Yahshua said, "Destroy this temple, and in three days I will raise it up" (John 2:19). He was referring to His body temple, which is exactly what happened after three days.

> "I am able to destroy the temple of God and build it in three days, after three days I will rise."
>
> (Matthew 26:61)

> "I will destroy this temple made with hands, and within three days, I will build another made without hands."
>
> (Mark 14:58)

Daniel was visited by the angel Gabriel (one of the Lord's extraterrestrial messengers) and was told that the temple was to be rebuilt during times of great trouble and then destroyed again.

But here's the rub, Gabriel mentions a prince, in the Hebrew text. It is a "Mashiach Nagi," which means Messiah Prince or King. This will cause the people of Israel to resume animal sacrifices in the newly rebuilt temple. All animal sacrifices were abolished after Yahshua. The Lamb of God became the final blood sacrifice for the atonement of humankind's sins. There has not been any animal sacrifices in Israel since then. Then Gabriel tells Daniel, that this prince will be cut off, who then establishes a covenant or treaty with the people of Israel.

This treaty essentially sets off all the events that precipitate the end. Everyone needs to discern, who is this end time prince? Almost every Bible scholar interprets this one to be the final antichrist, the one who will deceive all the nations of the world, including Israel. He entered the scene by bringing peace to World War III, which Bible prophecy calls the war of Gog and Magog, which starts over who rightfully owns Jerusalem. First he enters into a peace treaty with Israel, probably to settle the ongoing settlement issue of the Palestinians and Israel's neighboring enemies. But then he breaks the agreement three and half years into it, and literally all hell breaks loose on Israel, and the temple is destroyed by flood leading up to the final war.

It's important to add that, while most Christian scholars interpret these words to be talking about the future and final antichrist, these words have been misinterpreted particularly by Jews to relate to the coming Messiah, or Mashiach Nagid, (the Messiah King), which is why many Jews, particularly in Israel, will be deceived by this coming prince, and accept him as their Messiah, but in reality, this will be Satan's final curtain call to imitate Christ (Yahushua HaMashiach) and set himself up as God.

> "Seventy weeks are determined on your people and on your holy city, to finish the transgression, and to make an end of sins, and to make reconciliation for iniquity, and to bring in everlasting righteousness, and to seal up the vision and prophecy, and to anoint the most Holy. Know therefore and understand, that from the going forth of the commandment to restore and to build Jerusalem to the Messiah the Prince shall be seven weeks, and three score and two weeks: the street shall be built again, and the wall, even in troublous times. And after three score and two weeks shall Messiah be cut off, but not for himself: and the people of the prince that shall come shall destroy the city and the sanctuary; and the end thereof shall be with a flood, and to the end of the war desolations are determined. And he shall confirm the covenant with many for one week: and in the middle of the week (3-1/2 days) he shall cause the sacrifice and the oblation to cease, and for the overspreading of abominations he shall make it desolate, even until the consummation, and that determined shall be poured on the desolate."
>
> (Daniel 9:24-27)

David Flynn writes, in his article "Satan's Counterfeits: Judgment Day, UFOs, Angels & End Time Prophecy"[3]: "This king will make a seven-year treaty with the people, but after half that time, he will break his pledge and stop the Jews from all their sacrifices and their offerings. With the stroke of a pen the world will enter into a time of unparalleled upheaval lasting seven years until the return of Jesus Christ, Daniel's 70th week. There will be much more transpiring behind this treaty than two parties promising to resolve a land squabble. In fact, the importance of the last seven years of this present age is nearly unfathomable to the greater majority of mankind.

> "It shall be the time of judgment declared by God, not only of man, but of all the rebel angels of the universe. In the vast cosmos with all its billions of stars and untold myriads of worlds, earth will be the stage for the meting out of God's judgment. Why the earth? Because it is the very world God ransomed on a cross in Jerusalem c. 30 A.D."

> "The signing of the treaty reinstating sacrifice in Jerusalem will set into motion Satan's last effort to 'be like the most high.'

Satan's attempts to thwart the promises of God have long been directed at the children of Israel, and at the land of their promise. Satan knows how significant Jerusalem is to God."

"The Lord spoke to Ezekiel in a vision from the Temple:"...son of man, the place of My throne and the place of the soles of My feet, there where I will dwell among the sons of Israel forever...

(Ezekiel 43:6)

King David knew it was God's plan to live in Jerusalem (Mount Zion) forever:

"Great is the Lord Yahuah, and greatly to be praised in the city of our God, in the mountain of his holiness. Beautiful for situation, the joy of the whole earth, is mount Zion, <u>on the sides of the north, the city of the great King</u>."

(Psalm 48:1-2)

The north is the meeting place of the Lord Yahuah and the Elohim (the sons of God); Lucifer/Satan wanted to sit on mount Zion and exalt himself above the stars of God and be equal to the Almighty: David Flynn calls this "Satan's 'I will' speech," because it reveals his ambitions. It's interesting that, today, we have a whole self-improvement movement based on the use of the words: "I will."

"I will go up to the heavens,
I will raise my throne above the stars of God, and
I will sit in the mount of meeting, <u>in the sides of the north</u>.
I will rise over the heights of the clouds:
I will be compared to the Most High."

(Isaiah 14:13)

This not only reveals Lucifer/Satan's intentions, but reveals his abilities to go up the heavens, and his ambition to "rise over the heights of the clouds." As I've written in my chapter on the Mother Ships of the Lord, in my section on the *Cloudships*, that the use of the metaphor "the clouds" throughout the Bible describes the Lord's starships. So this passage reveals that it is Lucifer/Satan's intention to raise his ships (UFOs) above those of the Lord's ships, indicating that this final battle between the lord of darkness and the Most High God will culminate in a *Star Wars*-type cosmic battle of Biblical proportion.

The Lord's holy mountain is "Zion, in the sides of the north," will be the spotlight of attention for Satan and his fallen extraterrestrial angels, so that Lucifer/Satan's embodiment in the flesh as the final antichrist will exalt himself and claim to be God, "to be compared to the most high." His final agenda is the focal point of the Temple Mount in Jerusalem. Lucifer/Satan's ultimate rebellion will be concluded by his desolation of the Lord's rebuilt temple halfway through the Tribulation period, which is when the Israelis will realize that they chose the wrong the Messiah.

CHAPTER TWENTY-FIVE: Who Is The Beast?

"This is what the LORD YAHUAH Almighty says: "I am very zealous for Zion; I am burning with jealousy for Jerusalem."

(Zechariah 8:2)

Mount Zion has always been God's holy mountain, this is where the Lord promises to rule and take over the throne of David as King of the Kingdom of Heaven on Earth.

"The LORD says to my Lord: "Sit at my right hand until I make your enemies a footstool for your feet."

(Psalm 110:1)

That passage is so revealing, as well as prophetic, because the Lord Yahuah is speaking to the Lord Yahshua promising to bring all of his enemies under his feet. This will be fulfilled at the end of this timeline.

THE RIDER ON A WHITE HORSE

(Emphasis and commentary in brackets are mine)

"Behold, He is coming <u>with the clouds of heaven,</u> (*again, this verse says, 'with' the clouds, are the words that were used throughout the Bible to describe the Lord's spaceships*) and every eye will see Him..." (Revelation 1:7) (*Every eye will see Him, through actual eye witnessing the massive fleet of spaceships arriving in the Earth's skies, along with the vast amount of television coverage this will inevitably produce around the globe*).

"Then I saw heaven opened, and behold, a white horse! The one sitting on it is called Faithful and True, and in righteousness he judges and makes war. His eyes are like a flame of fire, and on his head are many diadems, and he has a name written that no one knows but himself. He is clothed in a robe dipped in blood, and the name by which he is called is The Word of God. [*This is the Lord and King Jesus Christ*]

And the armies of heaven, [*faithful extraterrestrials, aka the hosts' of heaven*] arrayed in fine linen, white and pure, were following him on white horses. [*Divine chariots, the Lord's spacecraft*] From his mouth comes a sharp sword [*the Word of God is the Sword of the Spirit*] with which to strike down the nations, and he will rule them with a rod of iron.

He will tread the winepress of the fury of the wrath of God the Almighty. On his robe and on his thigh he has a name written, King of kings and Lord of lords." [*None other than the Lord Jesus Christ, Yahshua HaMashiach, the Messiah and King of Israel, and King of the Universe.*]

(Revelation 19:11)

Horses have long been associated with "chariots." In St. John's vision, he saw horses because that was the means of transportation of his day. But he specifically saw them all as white, symbolizing "light" and "purity." However, what Jesus Christ and his celestial army will actually be riding through the heavens in, will not be physical flesh and blood white horses, but "divine chariots," otherwise known as spaceships.

Because the Lord's ships are always cloaked in clouds (see my chapter on the Mother Ships of the Lord and the section devoted to the *Cloudships*), this is probably what St. John saw in his vision, were white fluffy clouds and as many of us do, see shapes in the clouds, and his vision was given to him by God with a purpose, so he saw outlined the image of white horses being sent in battle, because that was what he could relate to. Cloudships with the power of thousands of white horses

What the Lord was revealing to him was that there will be a fleet of the Lord's spaceships coming with all of his faithful extraterrestrial warriors riding through space chariots with tremendous horse power, to assist Him in defeating the Dragon (Satan's hierarchy) and his dark fleet of UFOs.

> "Then I saw an angel standing in the sun, and with a loud voice he called to all the birds that fly directly overhead, "Come, gather for the great supper of God, to eat the flesh of kings, the flesh of captains, the flesh of mighty men, the flesh of horses and their riders, and the flesh of all men, both free and slave, both small and great." And I saw the beast and the kings of the earth with their armies gathered to make war against him who was sitting on the horse (Jesus Christ) and against his army. And the beast was captured, and with it the false prophet who in its presence had done the signs by which he deceived those who had received the mark of the beast and those who worshiped its image. These two were thrown alive into the lake of fire that burns with sulfur. And the rest were slain by the sword that came from the mouth of him who was sitting on the horse, and all the birds were gorged with their flesh."
>
> (Revelation 19:11-21)

The false prophet may in fact be an ancient deity that teams up with Lucifer, or one of the ancient fallen angels that were imprisoned and then let out at the end to deceive the world. They and all of their forces are defeated and thrown into the lake of fire. This is different and more permanent than the Abyss known as Hell. The birds are called in because of the millions of dead bodies that will happen when the Lord returns and defeats Satan's army and the false gods once and for all. Literally there will be rivers of blood on the ancient battlefield called the "field of blood" known as Har Megiddo at the time of Armageddon. This is the end of the battle and the end of the war between the cosmic forces of good and evil, light and darkness, God and Satan.

CHAPTER TWENTY-FIVE: Who Is The Beast?

"The LORD (YAHUAH) will be King over the whole earth.
On that day there will be one LORD,
And His name, the only name."

(Zechariah 14:6)

NOTES:

1. Larry Harper, *The Antichrist,* The Elijah Project; 2nd edition. 2003
2. Thomas R. Horn, *Nephilim Stargates*, *The Year 2012 And The Return Of The Watchers,* Anomolous Publishing, Crane, MO 2007
3. David Flynn, *Satan's Counterfeits: Judgment Day, UFOs, Angels & End Time Prophecy,* http://www.mt.net/~watcher/judgment.html

CHAPTER TWENTY-SIX

THE OFFICE OF CHRIST

"I AM who I AM."
(Exodus 3:14)

"I AM the Alpha and the Omega."
(Revelation 1:8, 11; 21:6; 22:13)

"I AM the First and the Last."
(Isaiah 44:6; Revelation 1:11, 17, 22:13)

The Office of Christ consists of all those in the cosmos who are faithful to the Divine Plan of Salvation, which was first written into the Stars. The Fifth Book in my series, of *Who's Who In The Cosmic Zoo?* Proves this through historical evidence, astronomy and scripture (See Book Five, *The Heavens*). Understanding the stars, is part of our ancient history.

That old saying, "It's written in the stars" couldn't be truer. The mythology is rich with stories that mark a particular star grouping. But just "who" wrote the mythology? Suffice it to say, it's a very long story, but for now, we know through scripture that when the fallen angels came to earth, (the 200 Bene HaElohim) they taught humans a corrupted version of astrology.

The word, 'Astrology' means *the language (logos) of the stars* created by the Creator of the Stars. However, the Bible scriptures tell us that all the stars were named by the Creator, and while He gave man the task of naming the animals on earth, it was the Creator's job to name the stars for a very specific reason, which reveals His Story, His Divine Plan of Salvation, and His coming Kingdom of Heaven.

Today's Astrology has been copied and corrupted as many times as there have been empires that have risen and fallen on the earth, leaving us with multiple versions of the star stories within stories, but when we peel those corrupted versions, what we see is the Gospel (the word for "Good News") written into the very constellations of the stars themselves by the hand of the Creator. "The Heavens Declare The Glory of God." (Psalm 19:1) Couldn't be truer. We see that that there was a suffering servant, a wounded hero for all the oppressed, who comes to save the faithful from the curse of evil in the cosmos, we also see that this super being becomes crowned King of the Heavens, and becomes known as the Cosmic Christ for all of Heaven's children.

Psalm 147:4 says, "He counts the number of the stars; He gives names to all of them." The Creator *named* all the stars, because they tell a story — His-Story. Over time, each civilization has rewritten His-Story, by copying their story over His-Story; some may call that counterfeiting. This is relevant to this chapter on the Cosmic Christ because you will see that what was put into place in the heavens was an "archetype," and many have come before us that have tried to fit into that archetype. Keep this in mind, as you read through these archetypes that have appeared, which all have many similarities, however, their differences can be distinguished through scripture and the revelation of the Living Holy Spirit, which is alive in the world, and testifies to the Word of God, both written into the Star Scroll, as well as the written word on earth.

Here is a brief understanding of how the meanings of the zodiac which is the path and circle of stars in the Milky Way, have become obscured through today's astrology, and as I prove in Book Five: *The Heavens,* how we lost the original meaning, and where those original meanings still exist both in scripture and today's Astronomical Star Charts.

PROPHETIC SIGNIFICANCE OF THE TWELVE SIGNS OF THE ZODIAC AND THE GOSPEL IN THE STARS[1]:

1.	Virgo	*The Seed of the Woman (Virgin)*-Christ the Incarnate Son	Isaiah 7:14
2.	Libra	*The Required Price Paid* - Christ the Redeemer	Isaiah 53:10
3.	Scorpio	*The Mortal Conflict* - Christ the Sufferer	Genesis 3:15; Ps. 91:13
4.	Sagittarius	*The Final Triumph* - Christ the Conqueror	Ps. 45:3-5; Ps 64; Isa 27:1
5.	Capricorn	*Life Out of Death* - Christ the Sacrifice	Isa 53:8; Lev 9:15; 16:22
6.	Aquarius	*Blessing Out of Victory* - Christ the Living Water	Isa 33:21; Joel 2:28-32
7.	Pisces	*Deliverance Out of Bondage* - Christ the Liberator	Jer 31; Isa 61:1; Zec 9:11
8.	Aries	*Glory Out of Humiliation* - Christ the Crowned Lamb	Is 62:3-5; 61:10; 54:5-8
9.	Taurus	*His Glorious Second Coming* - Christ the Judge	Is 34:2; 26:21; 60:1-3;
10.	Gemini	*His Rule On Earth* - Christ the King	Jer 33:14; 23:5; Is 59, 49
11.	Cancer	*His Possessions Held Secure* - Christ the Protector	Is 35; 51; 60; Jer 31; Ez 34
12.	Leo	*His Enemies Destroyed* - Christ the Victor	Rev.5:5; 20:2; Ps.75:8;11:6

However, the point is that, over time, the mythologies we have grown up with about the star constellations have obscured their original meaning. You can read about all these details, with full references in Book Five: *The Heavens.*

CHAPTER TWENTY-SIX: The Office Of Christ

All those created beings who have stayed faithful to the Almighty Creator, also known as extraterrestrial angels who did not rebel against the Creator, make up two-thirds of the heavens, are mentioned in the Gospel in the Stars, as well as in the written Word. The Lord of Hosts is the Lord of the Celestial Armies of the Heavens, which is made up of extraterrestrial angels from across the entire cosmos. Please refer back to my Cosmic Drama/Galactic Warfare Chart in Book One of *Who's Who in the Cosmic Zoo* of ETs and Aliens, (p.90-91) to discern who belongs to the Office of Christ and who belongs to the Office of Satan. Both have hierarchies and hosts (armies) that serve them in this cosmic warfare.[2]

It's important to read my chapters "The Divine Plan of Salvation as Written in the Stars," and "The Word of God in the Stars," (Book Five: *The Heavens*) to understand how many counterfeits have been sent to obscure the truth of God's original Divine Plan. Lucifer/Satan knew God's plan from the beginning, and after his rebellion to the Most High, who wanted to create his own plan of salvation many times, which has inevitably created an "archetype" of the Cosmic Christ, but fell short of the real One nonetheless.

Some ask, why would he do such a thing ahead of the appointed time? We need to keep in mind that the way we keep time on Earth and the way God keeps time in the heavens are not the same. Lucifer/Satan knew that the Most High was sending His Christ, so he purposely sent counterfeits ahead of him on Earth's timeline to confuse and confound followers all the way down the timeline, so others would eventually say with doubt in their hearts and minds, that when the real Christ arrived, that he copied the previous ones. Think of it as a form of time travel, a technology well within the powers of the Office of the Satans.

So let's look at the archetypes, there are many similarities, but more importantly, let's discern their differences, and let the real Christ please emerge.

THE ARCHETYPE OF THE COSMIC CHRIST

In the history of our earth after the floods, there are amazing similarities and parallels between the lives of Krishna, Mithras, and Jesus Christ. Some have postulated that these were three different incarnations of the same God/Divine Savior. Before Mithras, there was *Krishna* in India, *circa* 1200 BCE. Krishna is one of the most widely revered and most popular of all Indian divinities, worshipped as the eighth incarnation (avatar) of the Hindu god *Vishnu* and also as a supreme god in his own right. Let's compare their stories:

Krishna was born of the Virgin Mother *Devaki* after being visited by spirits to announce the impending birth of an immaculately conceived child who is the "son of God." Unlike the other archetypes of Christ, Krishna was no born nor associated with December 25. Based on the Vedic scriptures and astrological calculations, the date of Krishna's birth, who was also known as Janmashtami, was July 18, 3228 BCE. However, his birth was attended by wise men, as well as shepherds. Krishna was presented at birth with frankincense, myrrh, and gold. Krishna worked miracles, restored sight, casted out devils, and raised the dead.

Hundreds of years before both Mithras and Jesus, Krishna was baptised in the River Ganges, crucified between two thieves, died, buried, and resurrected in three days and worshipped as the "savior of men." He proclaimed himself the "Resurrection" and the "only way to the Father."

He was said to be without sin, of royal descent, and raised by a human father who was ... a carpenter. He preached of a great and final day of judgment and used parables to teach the people about charity and love. In death, he stood transfigured in front of his disciples. Krishna was called the "Shepherd God," "Lord of lords," "the Redeemer," and the "Universal Word." He was considered the "Alpha and Omega," as well as being omniscient, omnipresent, and omnipotent.

He was prophesised to return to battle evil forces in a second coming. His disciples bestowed on him the word *Jezeus* that means "pure essence."

Author Kersey Graves (1813-1883), compared the life of Jesus Christ (Yahshua) to Krishna's life. He found what he believed were 346 elements in common within Christian and Hindu writings. He reported on these amazing coincidences: Both Jesus and Krishna were called God and the Son of God; both were sent from heaven to Earth in the form of a man; both were called Savior, and both were the second person of the Trinity; both adoptive human fathers were carpenters; both had a spirit or invisible being as their actual father; both Jesus and Krishna were of royal descent; both were visited at birth by wise men and shepherds, both guided by a star (a spaceship); angels were sent in both cases to issue a warning that the local dictator, who planned to kill the baby and issued a decree for assassination; both parents fled — Mary and Joseph stayed in Mururea. Krishna's parents stayed in Mathura; both Yahshua and Krishna withdrew to the wilderness as adults, and fasted; both were identified as *"the seed of the woman bruising the serpent's head."*[3]

Jesus was called the *"the lion of the tribe of Judah;"* Krishna was called *"the lion of the tribe of Saki."* Both claimed: *"I am the Resurrection."* Both referred to themselves as having existed before their birth on Earth; both were "without sin." Both were god-men: being considered both human and divine. They were both considered omniscient, omnipotent, and omnipresent; both performed many miracles, including the healing of disease. One of the first miracles that both performed was to make a leper whole. Each cured *"all manner of diseases."* Both cast out demons and raised the dead. Both selected disciples to spread his teaching; both were meek and merciful. Both were criticized for associating with sinners. Both encountered a Gentile woman at a well. Both celebrated a last supper; both forgave their enemies; both descended into Hell, and both were resurrected. Many people witnessed their ascension into heaven.

Both Yahshua and Krishna were crucified between two thieves, at or between the ages of 30 to 36 by *"wicked hands."* The common orthodox depiction of Krishna's death relates that he was shot in the foot with an arrow while under a tree. However, the author

CHAPTER TWENTY-SIX: The Office Of Christ

Jacolliot stated in his book, *The Bible in India,* referring to the *Bagaveda-Gita and Brahminical Traditions,* that the body of Krishna was "suspended to the branches of a tree by his murderer, that it might become the prey of the vultures...later the mortal frame of the Redeemer had disappeared — no doubt it had regained the celestial abodes..."[4]

M. Guigniaut's *Religion de L' Antiquite* states: "The death of Krishna is very differently related. One remarkable and convincing tradition makes him perish on a tree, to which he was nailed by the stroke of an arrow." There are other references to Krishna being crucified, and being shown with holes in his feet, hands and side.[5]

The New Testament relates to Yahshua's crucifixion on a cross or stake as being "hung on a tree." "The God of our fathers raised up Jesus...hanging him on a tree" (Acts 5:30); "...hanging him on a tree" (Acts 10:39); "...they took him down from the tree..." (Acts 13:29); "Christ redeemed us from the curse of the law, having become a curse for us; for it is written 'Cursed is every one that hangeth on a tree" (Galatians 3:13); "...who his own self bare our sins in his body upon the tree..." (1Peter 2:24).

MITHRAS

After all, December 25 has long been the celebrated birthday of Mithras, which was known as Mithras, Mithra, or in *Sanskrit*, Mitra, in ancient Indo-Iranian mythology, he was the god of light, whose cult spread from India in the East to as far west as Spain, Great Britain, and Germany. The first written mention of the *Vedic* Mitra dates to 1400 BCE. His worship spread to Persia and, after the defeat of the Persians by Alexander the Great (356-323 BCE), throughout the Hellenic world.

In the third and fourth centuries CE, the cult of Mithras, carried and supported by the soldiers of the Roman Empire and was the chief rival to the newly developing religion of Christianity. The Roman emperors Commodus (161-192 CE) and Julian (331/332-363 CE) were initiates of Mithraism, and in 307 CE Diocletian (245-316 CE) consecrated a temple on the Danube River to Mithras, "Protector of the Empire." Worship of the sun (*Sol*) existed within the indigenous Roman pantheon, as a minor part, and always as a pairing with the moon.

However, in the East, there were many solar deities, including the Greek *Helios*, who was largely displaced by *Apollo*.

Christianity was spreading through Europe which marked the decline of Mithraism, as the Roman province Dacia was lost to the empire and invasions of the northern peoples resulted in the destruction of the temples of Mithras areas that were the main stronghold of the cult.

By 310AD - 411AD, during the rule of Constantine, Christianity began to eclipse Mithraism because Christianity admitted women while Mithraism did not, which limited its potential for growth.

The Vatican was built upon the grounds previously devoted to the worship of Mithras (600 BC). The Orthodox Catholic hierarchy is nearly identical to the Mithraic version. Virtually all of the elements of Orthodox Catholic rituals, from the miter, Eucharist, wafer, water baptism, altar, and doxology were adopted from the Mithraic and earlier pagan mystery religions. The religion of Mithras preceded Christianity by roughly six hundred years. Mithraic worship at one time covered a large portion of the ancient world. It flourished as late as the second century.

The similarities between Jesus Christ and Mithras are: both born of a virgin birth; both were considered to be a great travelling teacher and master; both had twelve companion followers or disciples; both were killed and resurrected; both performed miracles; both taught morality; both shared birthday celebration on December 25 (even though December 25 was clearly not the birth date of Jesus Christ) both were considered to be humankinds' savior; both known as the "Light of the World."

Mithras was born in a cave, similar to the manger setting for the nativity of Jesus. Both Jesus Christ and Mithras were referred to as the "Logos." Both were buried in a tomb and, after three days, rose again. Both resurrections are celebrated every year. Mithras had his principal festival at the time of the year which later became known as Easter (named after the goddess Ishtar/Ashtaroth) which was the time of the year both Mithras and Jesus Christ were resurrected.

Both Plato and Philo wrote, "Mithras is spiritual light contending with spiritual darkness, and through his labors, the kingdom of darkness shall be lit with heaven's own light; the Eternal will receive all things back into his favor, the world will be redeemed to God. The impure are to be purified, and the evil made good, through the mediation of Mithras, the reconciler of Ormuzd and Ahriman (the good and evil gods of Persia). Mithras is the Good, his name means Love. In relation to the Eternal he is the source of grace, in relation to man he is the life-giver and mediator."

Zoroaster lived 550 years before Jesus. He founded the doctrine of the struggle between light and darkness, a doctrine which is fully expounded in the Zeno-Avesta (Word of God), which is written in the Zend language, and according to tradition, was given to him by an angel from Paradise.

According to Zoroaster, Mithras (the sun) must be worshipped, from whom descended Ormuzd, the god of good, and Ahriman, the god of evil. They believe that the world will end when Ormuzd has triumphed over his rival, Ahriman, who will then return to his original source, Mithra.

Both Mithras and Christ performed miracles, both were called "the good shepherd," "the way, the truth, and the light; life, redeemer; savior; Messiah." Both Mithras and Christ were identified with both the lion and the lamb.

The International Encyclopedia states: "Mithras seems to have owed his prominence to the belief that he was the source of life, and could also redeem the souls of the dead into the better world ... The ceremonies included a sort of baptism to remove sins,

CHAPTER TWENTY-SIX: The Office Of Christ

anointing, and a sacred meal of bread and water, while a consecrated wine, believed to possess wonderful power, played a prominent part."

Both Christianity and Mithraism prided themselves in brotherhood and organized church congregations. Both religions purified themselves through baptism and each participated in the communion sacrament of bread and wine. Both religions considered Sunday their holy day, also known as the "Lord's Day," despite early Christian Jews observing the Jewish Sabbath for centuries. Both religions had a Eucharist or a "Lord's Supper."

Many have noted that the title of Pope was first found in Mithraic doctrine and was prohibited in Christian doctrine. However, the words, Peter (rock) and mass (sacrament) originated in Mithraism. Both religions considered abstinence, celibacy, and self-control to be among their highest virtues. Both held similar beliefs about heaven and hell, and the immortality of the soul. Both held almost identical concepts of the battles of good and evil. They both stated the existence of heaven was inhabited by beautiful beings and a hell populated by demons which was situated inside the bowels of the earth. Today the Pope still wears the mitre, the robes that came from Mithraism.

Both Mithraism and Christianity began their histories with the flood. Both believed in revelation as a key to their doctrine. Both believed in the judgment and resurrection of the dead after the final conflagration of the cosmos between the forces of light and darkness.

As far as symbolism goes, the followers of Mithras used to brand the sign of the cross on their foreheads, which is why many were attracted to Christ and the crucifix in the third and fourth centuries. In ancient art, the halo was the well-known depiction of Mithras, who was worshipped as the true sun god. Jesus Christ was depicted in exactly the same way.

In the catacombs at Rome therein lies a preserved relic of the old Mithraic worship. It is a picture of the infant Mithras seated in the lap of his virgin mother, while on their knees before him were Persian Magi adoring him and offering gifts. Some believe that this picture is that of the Baby Egyptian Sun God Horus being held by the virgin mother Isis-Meri.

"**I am** a star which goes with thee and shines out of the depths."

~ Mithras

"**I AM** the root and the offspring of David,
And the bright morning star."

~ Jesus (Revelation 22:16)

HORUS THE EGYPTIAN SUN GOD

Thousands of years before Krishna, Mithras, and Jesus was the Egyptian sun god Horus. Horus dates back to *circa* 3000 BC. Horus was born of the virgin *Isis-Meri* on December 25 in a cave/manger with his birth being announced by a star in the East and attended by three wise men.

Horus taught in the temple when he was a child. He was baptised when he was thirty years old by "*Anup* the Baptiser." Horus performed miracles and raised a man named *El-Azar-us*, from the dead. Not only did Horus walk on water, he was also crucified, buried in a tomb, and then resurrected.

Horus was known as "the Way," "the Fisher," "the Truth," "the Light," "God's Anointed Son," "the Son of Man," "the Good Shepherd," "the Lamb of God," and "the Word."

He was also called "the KRST," or "Anointed One." There was an Egyptian trinity with Horus the Son, *Atum* the Father, and *Ra* the Holy Spirit. In the later years of Horus, he had twelve disciples known as *Har-Khuttie*. Horus had an enemy (originally this was also the dark side of Horus, or his other face), this evil enemy was *Set* or *Sata* also known as *Seth*. Horus struggled with Sata for forty days in the wilderness. Some claim that this myth represents the triumph of light over dark. This triumph is most noted on December 25.

The Greek god *Attis*, born of the Virgin *Nana*, (or sometimes *Cybelem*) on December 25 and was reborn and rose from the dead on the third day. Attis was both the Father and the Divine Son. His crucifixion and subsequent resurrection were celebrated annually, with ritual communions of bread and wine. The wine represented the god's blood; the bread became the body of the savior.

WILL THE REAL SAVIOR PLEASE STEP UP?

We see there is an archetype that fits the Savior written in the Stars. Many have postulated that Horus, Krishna, Mithras and Jesus were actually all one and the same soul that appeared at different points on our timeline. But maybe not? Why would the same soul want to repeat their incarnation of suffering four different times? Maybe, these sons of God were sent to fulfill a role for their particular times, and for their particular race or group?

Some skeptics have noted the striking similarities between the four saviors, and have accused Jesus of plagiarism. This falls right into Lucifer/Satan's plot. This is exactly what he wanted when he time travelled and caused this to happen. Some believe that Horus, Krishna, Mithras, mimic the prophecies of Jesus Christ, which were prophesies intended for Jesus but were hijacked by Satan.

We have four saviors that seem to fit the archetype of that which is written in the stars — to suffer for the sins of the people, overcome death, and be resurrected. Horus,

CHAPTER TWENTY-SIX: The Office Of Christ

Krishna, and Mithras all lived in different ages, and were the saviors of their own ages. This Grand Experiment of the harvesting of earth humans and their path back to the Creator as written in the stars, of the Divine Plan of Salvation is a grand archetype to save souls from the curses of the darkness of this world, and from the bondage of the fallen angels, aka the satans and Lucifer.

What I am suggesting here is that these four sons of God, were not the same soul, but four different souls fulfilling their purposes for their time. However, they did not all fulfill the Divine Plan of Salvation/redemption as written first in the stars. Many of their groupings rewrote their stories over the original ones as written in the stars, as I prove in my chapters, "Divine Plan of Salvation as Written in the Stars" and "The Word of God in the Stars," in my final book of this series, Book Five of *Who's Who In the Cosmic Zoo?* titled *The Heavens*.

They all seem to fit the "archetype" that is written into the stars for the savior, and that even though their lives paralleled in so many ways, they all fell short in actually 'defeating' the god of this world, Lucifer/Satan, and redeeming back the keys of Death and Hades which Yahshua/Jesus Christ alone accomplished, as well as all the rest failed to pay the price for being the "final" blood sacrifice for the atonement for the sins of humanity. If they had succeeded, then Yahshua/Jesus Christ would not have had to come.

While there were similar characteristics in Mithras, Krishna and Horus, their inevitable religions that followed were manipulated by Lucifer/satan to divert attention away from Jesus Christ when he showed up on the timeline. The understanding of Time travel must be taken into account when viewing archetypes through history. For those who understand reincarnation, believe that these were all the same being, avatar, bodhisattva or god. They may have been the same being used to insert new religions into the grand experiment of humankind on earth. This is a thoughtform entertained by many researchers.

It's apparent, that Lucifer/Satan had a hand in spinning their offshoot religions to make sure that all those beings were inserted into the timeline in an attempt to fulfill the archetypal prophecy which is written into the stars, because it has been his plan all along to usurp and counterfeit the Office of Christ with his version of the counterfeit Christ or Antichrist.

Another viewpoint, which I am suggesting, is that these were all sons of heaven (Elohim) who may have all been great in their own rights, but all fell short to complete the 'final mission' that only Yahshua aka Jesus Christ successfully accomplished and is scheduled to complete at the end of this timeline, by ending the final battle with Satan with a simple breath and a Word (Revelation 19:11-16). All the armies that rise up against Him will be killed by the Words spoken out of His mouth. He was the Word became Flesh. In the beginning was the Word, and the Word was with God, and the Word was God (John 1:1).

Perhaps all of these sons of God belong to the council of Gods, known as the Elohim, or pantheon of gods, fulfilling the purposes of their Creator Father God Yahuah?

Perhaps they were sent along the timeline, but failed to complete the work that breaks the power of satan's kingdom? Yet when the end of this timeline is over, there will be One who has been given *all authority* over both the heavens and the earth, that all of these sons of God will submit to and serve.

They may all be related as sons of God, i.e., Elohim, but only Jesus "Yahshua" the Christ, fulfilled the Prophesy completely and was elevated above all the rest. Another difference is that Horus, Krishna, and Mithras were created beings, but Jesus "Yahshua" the Christ, was the Creator, the Word became flesh. There is a difference between a Creator and his creation. The difference between Lucifer and Yahshua, is that Lucifer was a created being/angel/cherub, Yahshua is not an angel; He is a Creator.

When the scripture says, that Jesus was the 'only begotten sons" The phrase "only begotten Son" occurs in John 3:16, which reads in the King James Version as, "For God so loved the world, that He gave His only begotten Son, that whosoever believeth in Him should not perish, but have everlasting life." The phrase "only begotten" comes from the Greek word *monogenes*. This word is translated into English bibles as "only," "one and only," and "only begotten." However the word means of one genetic, DNA. See the word 'gene' in *mono-gene;* i.e., 'one gene'.

The second definition is "pertaining to being the only one of its kind or class, unique in kind." This meaning is implied in John 1:14, 18; 3:18; 1 John 4:9. John was primarily concerned with demonstrating that Jesus is the Son of God (John 20:31), and he uses *monogenes* to highlight Jesus as uniquely God's Son—sharing the same divine nature as God—as opposed to believers who are God's sons and daughters by adoption (Ephesians 1:5). Jesus is God's "one and only" Son.

Jesus Christ (Yahshua) paid the price of the final sacrifice, through His blood. He was the Kinsman Redeemer, paying the price of sin, with His own life and blood, because the transgressions that were made, were made against God. We were bought with a price, (1 Corinthians 7:23) the price was His Divine Blood because He was God in the flesh. His final blood sacrifice ended the practice for the Jews to sacrifice the blood of lambs and goats for the propitiation of men's sins. His victory on the cross bought Him back the keys of Death and Hades from Satan, and Victory over the sins of humankind, the power of sin and the curses from sin.

> "Christ has redeemed us from the curse of the law, being made a curse for us: for it is written, Cursed is every one that hangs on a tree:
>
> (Galatians 3:13)

> "God made him who had no sin to be sin for us, so that in him we might become the righteousness of God."
>
> (2 Corinthians 5:21)

CHAPTER TWENTY-SIX: The Office Of Christ

The title, King of kings, Lord of lords and God of gods, indicates that this One will be the only One that completely fulfils the entire mission, and that is to defeat the powers of darkness once and for all, the One who has taken back the keys of death and Hades, which only Jesus Christ completely fulfilled.

This is what distinguishes Him from Krishna, Mithras, and Horus, while these sons, who were all noble and powerful in their own right, did fulfil *a* purpose for their time on the timeline, the final battle over the forces of darkness, not just on Earth, but in the entire universe, was accomplished by none other than Yahshua HaMashiach/Jesus Christ.

However, it is my opinion, that Krishna, Mithras, and Horus are all part of the "Office of Christ," and do have their places in the Kingdom of Heaven as kings and lords, in spite of having their stories used by Lucifer/Satan to confound the timeline and steal the glory from Christ. Be that as it may, there is only One who is crowned, King of all the kings and Lord of all the lords and God of gods, and that One is none other than "Yahshua" HaMashiach, aka Jesus Christ.

Many Christians believe that Jesus Christ is the Creator, a non-created being. Scripture says He was the Word who became flesh and lived among us (John 1:14). A Word is a thought, a word creates actions, a Word creates laws, a Word creates Life, A Word that is generated by Love, a Word that is Love, a Word that has the power to bless, and to curse.

> "I form the light, and create darkness: I make peace, and create evil:
> I the LORD do all these things."
>
> (Isaiah 45:7)

Scripture also tells us from the beginning in the story of Creation in Genesis that the Word spoke creation into existence. Many believe this to be Christ. There is a vast difference between "a son of God," and "The Only Begotten Son of God." Christians can claim the first, but only Jesus can claim the latter. The One who said "Let there be light," (Genesis 1:3) is Yahshua/Jesus Christ. He said, "I and the Father are One." (John 10:30)

"All of creation groans for the manifestation of the sons of god to be revealed." (Romans 8:19, 22)

He created humanity, and saved humanity. He has always existed, since before time, and is, in fact, the Creator of time-space, and all life that exists within it, spanning all existence, including the heavens. No other being can make this claim, or come anywhere near it. Angels are created beings, but the Creator is Almighty God. He created the angels. The angels serve Him. This sets Him apart from all others. No other being in all existence would be worthy to even accept the task that Yahshua/Jesus Christ took upon Himself, this is clearly stated in Revelation 5:12, where it is declared that only the Lamb was worthy, and Yahshua/Jesus Christ is the Lamb of God.

PROOF: CRUCIFIXION, RESURRECTION OF JESUS CHRIST

In Book One, of *Who's Who In The Cosmic Zoo?*, I reported on Project Pegasus, which was the code name for a secret time travel project orchestrated by the CIA and DARPA. See, pp. 308-324, with respect to the Mars Jump Room, which involved time travel to Mars. Andrew D. Basiago was one of the participants, and one of today's leading whistleblowers on the project. Something extraordinary occurred when one of the time travel participants was able to go back in time to the Crucifixion and Resurrection of Jesus Christ, through their chronovisor.

They were able to take a video of the hologram that they saw through the chronovisor, as if they were actually there. Andrew Basiago was given the privilege to view this when he was a young boy, as his father was also overseeing this secret project and gave him this opportunity as a reward for his participation in Project Pegasus. The chronovisor of Ernetti, Gemelli, and Fermi captured scenes of Jesus' Crucifixion and Resurrection, but the US government keeps such data "Top Secret" for obvious reasons, to protect the secret space technology program, and what they actually achieved.

While I have not seen the video, for obvious reasons, my friend Andrew Basiago has, and I do believe his reports. He has this story posted on his website sited below, and he was very kind to give me permission to reprint excerpts here. I have had discussions with Andrew D. Basiago about Project Pegasus, and if you read my Book One of *Who's Who In The Cosmic Zoo?*, you would have noticed that Andy actually edited my Mars chapter for accuracy in truth. I know Andrew Basiago to be a man of integrity. Andrew D. Basiago is a lawyer in private practice in Washington State, a writer, and a 21st century visionary. He holds five academic degrees, including a BA in History from UCLA and a Master of Philosophy from the University of Cambridge.

Andrew D. Basiago is a leading figure in the Truth Movement, who is presently heading a campaign to lobby the United States government to disclose such controversial truths as the fact that Mars harbors life and that the United States has achieved "quantum access" to past and future events.

I am including this story for continuity sake from Book One, as well as for those who need to have proof, that the story of Jesus Christ was in fact real, exactly as the Gospels report.

Andy Basiago runs several groups on Facebook to continue the ongoing discussion on time travel, life on Mars, as well as sharing his experiences with the type of time travel technologies that were experimented with in the 1970s and 80s. I am a member of those groups on Facebook, and one of the members asked him this pertinent question:

Question asked of Project Pegasus: I hope you don't mind, but this question has been bothering me since your Coast-to-Coast AM interview. I couldn't believe that George Noory passed on the opportunity to ask you about Christ's Crucifixion. He had the one man alive who claims to have seen the Crucifixion of Jesus and he

CHAPTER TWENTY-SIX: The Office Of Christ

failed to ask the obvious question. I was so disappointed, but I will ask you now. What did he look like? Have artists represented Christ accurately? I have included a picture from the new documentary *The Face of Jesus*. This likeness was taken from the *Shroud of Turin* and I think it accurately represents the face of Jesus. What is your opinion of the image?

Andrew D. Basiago, Project Pegasus: I had the privilege of viewing documentary footage of the Crucifixion of Jesus at a showing at the Sandia National Laboratory in Sandia, New Mexico in 1972. The documentary consisted of about 20 minutes of grainy, black and white footage on 16 mm film stock. The movie had been made by filming a hologram of the actual Crucifixion of Jesus produced by a chronovisor operated by a team of researchers working under the aegis of DARPA's Project Pegasus. Because it was a film of a hologram, the picture was not always clear but at times looked almost like a thunderstorm was pouring through the scene. At other times, the picture grew crystal clear and we could see very clearly both what was happening and what Jesus looked like.

Jesus was a Caucasian about 5'10" tall. He had dark brown hair and a full, dark brown beard. He had dark brown, sunken, very soulful eyes and an aquiline nose. During his agony on the Cross, Jesus' brow was pinched upward in an expression of intense suffering. This gave his eyes a droopy quality. His mouth was agape and we could see that he was in a great deal of distress. He had a thin body type, was very emaciated, and his rib cage protruded as he hung from the Cross. His appearance was Mediterranean and similar to some modern Italian and Spanish men. In my opinion, having seen the Crucifixion, the Face of Jesus shown in The History Channel program entitled *The Face of Jesus* is highly accurate, as are many historical renderings of Jesus that resemble it.

As I watched the film of Jesus on the Cross, I was struck by how much of the footage followed the Gospels. The film had been edited to show specific scenes. The totality showed much that confirmed the Biblical account. We could see that a jagged crown of thorns had been brutally thrust on Jesus' head. The wounds from the thorns had caused rivulets of blood to stream down the sides of his face. We could also see that Jesus was crucified on a hillside with two other men who were situated back and to the sides of his cross. At one point, a woman came to pray at the foot of Jesus' cross, and one of the centurions chased her away, violently pointing in the direction that she should go. At another point, the sky darkened, and I was terrified wondering what would happen next.

I was also struck by elements that could never have been discerned from the New Testament account of Jesus' Crucifixion and death. For one thing, the film revealed that Jesus was crucified on a thick pole, like a modern telephone pole, so that his feet were about 14 feet off the ground. He was so high off the ground that Longinus, the Roman centurion who pierced Jesus' side to hasten his death, had to hold the end of his spear handle and lunge up on one foot to reach Jesus' side. The Roman centurions' skirts were short, even effeminate, by contemporary standards. I noticed that the cross beam was only about the size of a 2"-by-4" and about six feet in length. The Cross was not cruciform but a large pole with a small board nailed to it. It was apparent that Jesus was nailed not through the palms, as has been shown in religious art down through the Ages, but through the wrists. It was overwhelming to watch, primarily because it showed a man being crucified, but especially because that man was Jesus of Nazareth, who from earliest childhood I had been educated to believe was the savior of all humankind. The film was so ghastly to watch that, midway through, I felt like evil had entered the room and was hovering in the middle of the room, buzzing like a demonic beehive.

In addition to me, my father had invited his longtime friend, Mary Constance Chavez [1928-1981], to view the film of the Crucifixion of Jesus. Connie was a devout Roman Catholic who went to Mass every day and throughout her life helped the nuns at the San Felipe de Neri Church in Old Town Albuquerque. During the viewing, Connie was having great difficulty watching the film, even hiding her face, at times, rather than look up at the screen. When the film concluded and the three of us walked out into the hallway, my father asked Connie why she was reacting the way she was. She exclaimed: "Because they were crucifying our Lord, Ray!"

My father then said something that astonished us: "I don't know why you're reacting that way, because we've also recovered footage of the Resurrection!" Connie was intrigued and asked my father to tell her what the film showed. He stated that the chronovisor revealed that as Jesus lay in his crypt, there was a flash of light, two angels appeared, Jesus stood up in his crypt, the angels helped him roll the rock away, and Jesus walked out of the crypt. My father said that seeing this was so moving to the men on his team that they spontaneously erupted in cries of "Praise be to God!" and "Jesus lives!"[6]

STARSHIPS WITH HORSEPOWER

In the final battle of Armageddon, when Jesus Christ returns to win the final battle with Lucifer/Satan through his anti-Christ and his armada of alien UFOs, Jesus Christ will return as Lord of Hosts, with His enormous fleet of spaceships and the hundreds of thousands of hosts of heaven (extraterrestrial armies) that will be gathered from one end of the cosmos to the other to complete Lucifer/Satan's defeat at the end of this timeline. It is my opinion, that the Lords Krishna, Mithras, and Horus will return with Him as part of His coalition federation forces to defeat the forces of darkness, with Jesus Christ as their Commander at the helm.

Revelation 19:11 talks about Christ returning on a white horse out of the heavens. The symbology is He will be riding out of the heavens on a Divine Chariot that will have "mega horsepower" which will be his starship(s). As I have already stated in my chapter,

CHAPTER TWENTY-SIX: The Office Of Christ

"Ancient Technology and Biblical Astronauts," that the language of the Bible when relating to beings travelling out of the heavens by using the lexicon of the ancient days, such as flying out of heaven on a white horse. We all know that flesh and blood horses don't fly, but we use the term "horsepower" which relates to the power a vehicle has to travel.

> "Then I looked, and there was <u>a white horse</u>! Its rider had a bow, and a victor's crown had been given to him. He went out as a conqueror to conquer."
> (Revelation 6:2)

> "Then I saw heaven opened, and behold, <u>a white horse</u>! The one sitting on it is called Faithful and True, and in righteousness he judges and makes war." "Their entire army was killed by the sharp sword that came from the mouth of the one riding <u>the white horse</u>. And the vultures all gorged themselves on the dead bodies."
> (Revelation 19:11, 21)

The one riding the white horse is Jesus Christ, He was given the Victor's crown, and He is the one called Faithful and True. The sword that came from his mouth is the Word of God. He ends the battle of Armageddon with a Word. The white horse is his spaceship. Whenever the Lord's spaceships were mentioned in the Bible, they were referred to as "clouds" (please refer back to my section on the *Cloudships*) or chariots of fire. Chariots are empowered by horses.

It is possible that when St. John were given these visions in Revelation, that he saw white horses, because that's what he could relate to, which represented starships, i.e., chariots of fire (star power), transportation vehicles that flew with great speed through the heavens. The fact that Ezekiel and many others all reported these spaceships as "clouds" and the glory of the Lord is that the color white may represent the cloud which was actually the tremendous light emanating from the starships. This could be why St. John described the transport vehicle he saw Christ returning on as a white horse. A vehicle of great white light, a chariot of white fire.

> **"All power and authority has been given to me."**
> ~ Jesus Christ (Yahshua HaMashiach)
> (Matthew 28:18)

> "And he made known to us the mystery of his will according to his good pleasure, which he purposed in Christ, to be put into effect when the times will have reached their fulfilment - to bring all things in heaven and on earth together <u>under one head, the authority of Christ</u>."
> (Ephesians 1:9-10)

"And being found in appearance as a man, He humbled Himself and became obedient to the point of death, even the death of the cross. Therefore God also has highly exalted Him and has given Him <u>the name which is above every name</u>, that <u>at the name of Jesus</u> every knee should bow, of <u>those in heaven</u>, and of <u>those on earth</u>, and of <u>those under the earth</u>, and that every tongue should confess that Jesus Christ is Lord, to the glory of God the Father."

(Philippians 2:8-11)

"Then I heard every creature in heaven and on earth and *under the earth* and on the sea, and all that is in them, singing: "To him who sits on the throne and to the Lamb be praise and honour and glory and power, forever and ever!"

(Revelation 5:13)

"And having disarmed the powers and authorities, he made a public spectacle of them, triumphing over them by the cross."

(Colossians 2:15)

"The message of the cross is foolish to those who are headed for destruction! But we who are being saved, know it is the very power of God."

(1 Corinthians 1:18)

"Who lays the beams of his chambers in the waters: who makes the clouds his chariot: who walks on the wings of the wind: He makes the winds His messengers, flaming fire His ministers."

(Psalm 104:3)

NOTES:

1. Kenneth C. Flemming, *God's Voice In The Stars: Zodiac Signs And Bible Truth,* Loizeauz Brothers, Neptune, New Jersey 1927. p.21
2. Ella LeBain, *Who's Who In The Cosmic Zoo? Book One, Third Edition,* pp.90-91
3. Author Kersey Graves, *The World's Sixteen Crucified Saviors:Christianity Before Christ,* 1875, *Adventures Unlimited Press;* 6 Revised edition (September 1, 2001)
4. Jacolliot, *The Bible in India,* Sun Pub Co (September 1992)
5. Joseph Daniel Guigniaut, George Friedrich Creuzer, *Religions de l' antiquite',* Published 1841, archives https://archive.org/details/europeanlibraries
6. Andrew D. Basiago, *The Face of Jesus*, Project Pegasus, http://www.projectpegasus.net/

CHAPTER TWENTY-SEVEN

THE CHRISTMAS GODS

*You cannot cut Christmas out of the calendar,
Nor out of the heart of the world.
Christmas is not a date. It is a state of mind.*

"Christ is all, and is in all."
(Colossians 3:11)

THE PISCEAN AGE IS THE AGE OF JESUS CHRIST

Since the birth of Jesus Christ, we've entered into a new era, and a new age, which according to the processional ages, is known as the Age of Pisces. Pisces is symbolized by the fish. The fish has long been the symbol for the Christ, particularly after Jesus left the earth, it was used as a sign for believers as it was etched into the ground to show that a meeting or assembly of believers was meeting at a certain place. Since then it has become the symbol for Christianity, which coincidentally corresponds to the Age of Pisces.

Jesus said, "And surely I am with you always, to the very end of the age." (Matthew 28:20) He also said, I AM coming back at the end of the age. He was referring to the end of the Age of Pisces, which accordingly to present calendars, is expected to end approximately between 2050 AD and 2100 AD. This astronomical timing is marked by when the sun rises on the Vernal Equinox in the stars of the constellation of Aquarius and not in Pisces.

Unlike our linear calendar, processional ages move backwards on the Milky Way. As of 2016, we are at 6 deg. 11 min of Pisces. We count backwards, 6, 5, 4, 3, 2, 1, "0". Zero point marks the end of the age and represents the beginning of the next Age of Aquarius. The controversy among today's astronomers and astrologers is, that the calendars we are using have been tampered with since the Common Era began after the disambiguation designated the change between the Julian and Gregorian calendars. Because of the margin of error along with calendar tampering, we could very well be further along the time line than we think.

The other controversy between astronomers has to do with measurement of the exact point in space the stars of the constellations of Pisces end, and the stars of the constellations of Aquarius begin. This boundary line is arbitrary to say the least. Suffice it to say, we are very close.

I believe that the older savior archetypes are no longer valid, as Jesus Christ has become the savior of our present age, and should anyone believe on Him, that He came in the flesh to be the final sacrifice for our sins and to break the curses of this world, he will be saved. (John 11:26) We are saved by grace and through faith, it is not something we can earn or boast about, it is a gift from God that only requires our faith. (Ephesians 2:8, 9)

This is why worship to the past Saviors is now considered idolatry in the eyes of the Lord, because their time has expired, and they are no longer the "ones" to return to save their people from the clutches of the god of this world, aka, Lucifer/Satan and his fallen angels, i.e., the dark forces, et. al. The timeline we are on, indicates that the Lord Jesus Christ (Yahshua HaMashiach) is returning, only this time to win the final battle with Satan over His people and over the rulership of the earth. Then everything will be transformed and the Kingdom of God will be established on Earth as it is in Heaven.

> "And many false prophets will arise and lead many astray" and "false messiahs and false prophets will appear and produce great signs and omens, and deceive many people, if possible, EVEN THE ELECT."
>
> (Matthew 24:11)

This is the purpose I felt led to write this book, that the increase in ETs, Alien contacts, and UFOs is precisely what will cause false prophets to rise up with signs and technological wonders that they will pawn off as "miracles" will deceive and lead many people astray, even the elect if they are not made aware. This is what leading UFO investigator Jacques Vallée was talking about when he said, "Human beings are under the control of a strange force that bends them in absurd ways, forcing them to play a role in a bizarre game of deception."

Spiritually speaking, what Jesus Christ did, was unprecedented and planned from the beginning of time to be the propitiation for man's sins. When Jesus said, "Forgive them for they know not what they do" (Luke 23:34), he knew that humans were under the control of alien forces. That they were oppressed and possessed by demons, fallen angels, and evil spirits. He knew that earth humans had been through several genetic manipulations, including the downgrading of the DNA to make earth humans slaves to the gods, causing great flaws in earth humans. This is why He said, "I have come to set the captives free." (Luke 4:18, Isaiah 61:1)

Jesus Christ is God's grace and mercy stretching out His arm to save, liberate, and deliver us from bondage. It is only through Him that Humans will be restored to their original "glory" bodies, before the fall of Adam, a time when humans walked with God and fellowshipped with Him. The restoration of the ten disabled strands of DNA, what today's geneticists call "junk DNA" is what is promised upon Christ's return.

> "In a flash, in the twinkling of an eye, at the last trumpet, when the trumpet sounds, the dead in Christ shall be raised incorruptible, and *we will all be changed.*"
>
> (1 Corinthians 15:52)

CHAPTER TWENTY-SEVEN: The Christmas Gods

"Do not be amazed at this, for a time is coming when all who are in their graves will hear His voice."

(John 5:28)

"For the Lord Himself will descend from heaven with a shout, with the voice of the archangel and with the trumpet of God, and the dead in Christ will rise first. Then we who remain alive on the earth, will be caught up together with them in the 'clouds' (starships/chariots of fire) to meet the Lord in the air (space), and so we shall always be with the Lord."

(2 Thessalonians 4:16-17)

Because He knew the dominion the fallen angels and Satan were given over other planets and star systems, it is therefore my conclusion that what Jesus Christ did for all of humanity on Calvary extended out to other planetary spheres of human experiments, making Him the "Cosmic Christ." This is why extraterrestrials are in alliance with Him and Yahuah and their massive fleet of starships all over the cosmos.

Jesus said, "In my father's house there are many mansions" (John 14:2). *Mansions* has long been a word used for stars, meaning we being the human experiment, would be dispersed among the stars to live after completing a series of earth lives meant to cultivate character in humans and to bring us into a closer intimate relationship with our Creator which was His will from the beginning.

However, the word *mansions* is also used to describe spaceships, as it was referenced in the Vedic scriptures multiple times which were called Vimanas and described as *mansions* in the sky. The Creator's Grace allows for many tries within the human experiment and has provided the way out through the Divine Plan of Salvation from the Dark forces (i.e., Satan, fallen angels, dark aliens & ETs) through faith in what Christ did. It's His way out, once that path is found.

THE RETURN OF THE SUN - DECEMBER 25

Following is a list of sixteen Pagan gods, some of whom I've already covered in my previous chapter that had "birthdays" or are associated with December 25th:

1. Adonis
2. Apollo
3. Attis
4. Bacchus
5. Dionysus the son of Zeus
6. Helios
7. Hermes
8. Hercules

9. Horus
10. Jupiter
11. Perseus
12. Prometheus
13. Mithras
14. Sol Invictus (The "Unconquered Sun")
15. Tammuz
16. Nimrod (who eventually came to be worshipped as Baal) – According to ancient Babylonian tradition, Semiramis (later known as the goddess Astarte/Asherah-/Ashtoreth/Isis/Ishtar/Easter in other pagan religions) claimed that after the untimely death of her son/husband Nimrod, a full grown evergreen tree sprang up overnight from a dead tree stump. Semiramis claimed that Nimrod would visit that evergreen tree and leave gifts each year on the anniversary of his birth, which just happened to be on December 25th. This was the true origin of the Christmas tree.

"By the time the Roman Empire legalized Christianity in the fourth century, most of the other religions in the empire were celebrating the birth of their gods on December 25th. Leading up to December 25th in ancient Rome, a festival known as Saturnalia was one of the biggest celebrations of the year. Saturnalia was a festival during which the Romans commemorated the dedication of the temple of their god Saturn. This holiday began on the 17th of December and it would last for an entire week until the 23rd of December. Saturnalia was typically characterized by gift-giving, feasting, singing and lots and lots of debauchery. The priests of Saturn would carry wreaths of evergreen boughs in procession throughout the pagan Roman temples. Later on, the Romans also started holding a festival on December 25th called Dies Natalis Solis Invicti, which means 'the birthday of the unconquered sun.' Basically it was a way for the empire to consolidate all of the December 25th 'sun god' birthdays throughout the empire into one holiday."[1]

In Jeremiah 10:1-4, God warns us against putting up these decorated trees like the pagans were doing, most Christians are totally unaware of this in their own Bibles:

"Hear what the LORD says to you, O house of Israel. This is what the LORD (Yahuah) says:
"Do not learn the ways of the nations or be terrified by signs in the sky, though the nations are terrified by them. For the customs of the peoples are worthless; they cut a tree out of the forest, and a craftsman shapes it with his chisel. They adorn it with silver and gold; they fasten it with hammer and nails so it will not totter."

CHAPTER TWENTY-SEVEN: The Christmas Gods

The early American Puritans understood this, who once banned Christmas trees in many areas of the United States during the seventeenth century, because they were considered to be pagan.

The date December 25 to celebrate the Cosmic Christ is nothing new. Astronomically speaking, December 25 is three full days and nights after the Winter Solstice, which is the day that the earth is furthest away from the Sun, creating the longest night of the year. The Earth orbits in an elliptical orbit around the sun, and when it reaches this pivotal point on the Winter Solstice, it is at the point of the curve of its ellipse and it takes three full days for it to turn that curve, which produces a standstill, which is known as Yule to the Pagans, a time where the earth stands still and the darkness reigns. A time to make merry, and focus on the light of the spirit from within.

December 25 is the day when the Earth moves forward along its orbit, at which point the light of the sun returns and is reborn for the coming year. This is the day when the days begin to lengthen by one minute a day earlier on the sunrise, and one minute a day later on the sunset, and is celebrated as the "return of the light." This day has been used as the celebration of these various gods throughout human history. It is purely astronomical.

The Greek god *Adonis* allegedly was born on December 25 as was the son of the virgin *Myrha*. Another Greek god *Hermes* was born on December 25 as was the son of the virgin *Maia*, as well as a member of a holy trinity *Hermes Trismegistus*. The god *Dionysus* was born on December 25 and turned water into wine. *Bacchus* was born on December 25 and was crucified in 200 BC. *Prometheus* was born on December 25 and descended from heaven as God incarnate as man, to save mankind, and was crucified, suffered, and rose from the dead.

Nimrod was represented in a dual role of God the Father and *Ninus*, the son of *Semiramis*. The olive branch of Semiramis was symbolic of this offspring produced through a "virgin birth." Ninus was also known as Tammuz, who was said to have been crucified with a lamb at his feet and placed in a cave. When a rock was rolled away from the cave's entrance three days later, his body had disappeared. Nimrod was symbolised by a fish and the origins of the Pope's mitre is shaped like a fish head. Nimrod was the son of *Cush*, who was the grandson of Noah. Nimrod was a Mason. The Tower of Babel was one of the most ancient traditions of Masonry, today known as Freemasonry.

The original Christmas festival originated in Babylon founded by Nimrod, the grandson of *Ham*, the son of *Noah*. Nimrod was a man of power on Earth; he created the Babylonian system of organised competition, man-ruled governments, and empires based upon the competitive and profit-making economic system. Nimrod who built the original tower of Babel, the first city of Babylon, Nineveh (the capital of Assyria) and many other commercial and pagan-religious centres.

Nimrod married his own mother, Semiramis. Legend has it, after his untimely death, she claimed that a full-grown evergreen tree sprang overnight from a dead tree stump, which symbolised the springing forth unto new life of the dead Nimrod. On each anniversary of his birth, she claimed Nimrod would visit the evergreen tree and leave gifts under it. December 25 was the birthday of Nimrod. It is from this incestual myth that we get the original Christmas tree.

King Solomon said, "There is nothing new under the sun" — the Son of God, the Sun Gods, or the Christmas gods, all represent the ancient veneration of the Sun.

Why are all these mythological ancient predecessors to Jesus Christ born on December 25? And why do all the other similarities transpire?

Firstly nobody knows the exact time of the birth of Jesus Christ, but the Bible does relate to the Hebrew month of *Tishri*, which is the seventh month that begins the Feast of Tabernacles, known as *Sukkot*, which usually happens around September/October, or the astrological month of Libra.

> Christmas gift suggestions:
> To your enemy, forgiveness.
> To an opponent, tolerance.
> To a friend, your heart.
> To a customer, service.
> To all, charity.
> To every child, a good example.
> To yourself, respect.

THE REAL BIRTHDAY OF JESUS CHRIST

"The Son of God became a man to enable men to become the sons of God."
~C.S. Lewis, *Mere Christianity*

Most biblical scholars and preachers readily admit and agree that Christ was **not**born on December 25. However, they claim that this day is as good as any other to celebrate the birth of Jesus, despite the fact that it was originally the pagan celebration, Saturnalia, which commemorated the birth of the sun god, Nimrod, Mithras, etc. But sun god or "son of God," it's all in the wording, and it seemed to fit. Someone definitely manipulated this for religious agendas, which began with the Church of Rome and was reinforced by the Catholic Church Fathers, who literally transformed the church of Mithras (Church of Rome), into the Roman Catholic Church, and took with it, all of its rituals, including the celebration of the birth of Mithras, which was December 25.

However, in spite of what they did, by manipulating the calendars and conveniently switching the birthday of Jesus Christ into their mold, they ignored what the Lord said in the Old Testament about appropriating pagan methods of worship and trying to honor Him with them:

CHAPTER TWENTY-SEVEN: The Christmas Gods

"Observe and obey all these words which I command you, that it may go well with you and your children after you forever, when you do what is good and right in the sight of the LORD your God. When the LORD your God cuts off from before you the nations which you go to dispossess, and you displace them and dwell in their land, <u>take heed</u> to yourself that you are not ensnared to follow them, after they are destroyed from before you, and <u>that you do not inquire after their gods, saying, 'How did these nations serve their gods? I also will do likewise.'</u> "<u>You shall not worship the LORD your God in that way</u>; for every abomination to the LORD which He hates they have done to their gods; for they burn even their sons and daughters in the fire to their gods. <u>Whatever I command you, be careful to observe it; you shall not add to it nor take away from it.</u>

(Deuteronomy 12:28-32)

Some people have actually figured out based on the scriptures when Jesus Christ was actually born. This is done by relating the conception and birth of Jesus (*Yahshua*) with the conception and birth of John the Baptist. Both are often confused with one another.

"There was in the days of Herod, the king of Judea, a certain priest named Zacharias, <u>of the division of Abijah</u>. His wife was of the daughters of Aaron, and her name was Elizabeth. And they were both righteous before God, walking in all the commandments and ordinances of the Lord blameless. But they had no child, because Elizabeth was barren, and they were both well advanced in years."

(Luke 1:5-7)

First, we need to understand "the division of Abijah." We find in 1 Chronicles 24:1-19 that the descendants of Aaron's twenty-four grandsons (the sons of Eleazer and Ithamar) were divided into twenty-four divisions or courses for the purpose of serving at the Temple. 1 Chronicles 24:10 tells us that the eighth division of service was assigned to Abijah's descendants.

Each of these divisions served at the Temple for an eight-day period (1 Chronicles 9:25). The service began and ended on the weekly Sabbath (2 Chronicles 23:8). In addition to their normal service, all twenty-four courses served at the Temple during the three holy seasons every year.

The Jewish *Mishnah* indicates that each course served a week during the first half of the year, the three annual festival weeks, and a week during the last half of the year, for a total of five weeks during a normal year.

A normal year on the Hebrew calendar consists of twelve lunar months of 29 or 30 days, for a total of 354 days. This is about eleven days less than a solar year (365.24 days). During a regular Jewish year (which occurs twelve times in a nineteen-year cycle), fifty-one weeks of coverage would be needed to ensure that the Temple was cared for every week throughout the year. Twenty-four (first half of the year) + 3 (festival weeks) + 24 (second half of the year) = 51 weeks

Between the first and the ninth week of the year, two of the three festival times when all twenty-four courses served occurred. Therefore, the course of Abijah, the eighth course, would serve its first regular week during the ninth or tenth week of the year (depending on how the Feast of Weeks fell on the calendar).

Now let's look at the conception of John the Baptist:

"So it was, that <u>while he [Zacharias] was serving as priest before God in the order of his division, according to the custom of the priesthood,</u> his lot fell to burn incense when he went into the Temple of the Lord. And the whole multitude of the people was praying outside at the hour of incense. Then an angel of the Lord appeared to him, standing on the right side of the altar of incense. And when Zacharias saw him, he was troubled, and fear fell upon him.

But the angel said to him, "Do not be afraid, Zacharias, for your prayer is heard; and your wife Elizabeth will bear you a son, and you shall call his name John. And you will have joy and gladness, and many will rejoice at his birth. For he will be great in the sight of the Lord, and shall drink neither wine nor strong drink. He will also be filled with the Holy Spirit, even from his mother's womb.

And he will turn many of the children of Israel to the Lord their God. <u>He will also go before him in the spirit and power of Elijah,</u> 'to turn the hearts of the fathers to the children,' and the disobedient to the wisdom of the just, to make ready a people prepared for the Lord."

And Zacharias said to the angel, "How shall I know this? For I am an old man, and my wife is well advanced in years." And the angel answered and said to him, "I am Gabriel, who stands in the presence of God, and was sent to speak to you and bring you these glad tidings. But behold, you will be mute and not able to speak until the day these things take place, because you did not believe my words which will be fulfilled in their own time."

And the people waited for Zacharias, and marveled that he lingered so long in the Temple. But when he came out, he could not speak to them; and they perceived that he had seen a vision in the Temple, for he beckoned to them and remained speechless. And so it was, <u>as soon as the days of his service were completed, that he departed to his own house.</u> Now <u>after those days his wife Elizabeth conceived</u>; and she hid herself <u>five months</u>, saying, "Thus the Lord has dealt with me, in the days when He looked on me, to take away my reproach among people."

(Luke 1:8-25)

Zacharias's wife Elizabeth would have conceived John the Baptist shortly following the week of his service at the Temple. This would have been sometime in late *Sivan* or early *Tamuz*.

CHAPTER TWENTY-SEVEN: The Christmas Gods

Let's switch our focus and take a look at Elizabeth's cousin Mary:

"Now <u>in the sixth month</u> [of Elizabeth's pregnancy] the angel Gabriel was sent by God to a city of Galilee named Nazareth, to a virgin betrothed to a man whose name was Joseph, of the house of David. The virgin's name was Mary. And having come in, the angel said to her, "Rejoice, highly favored one, the Lord is with you; blessed are you among women!" But when she saw him, she was troubled at his saying, and considered what manner of greeting this was.

Then the angel said to her, "Do not be afraid, Mary, for you have found favor with God. And behold, <u>you will conceive</u> in your womb and bring forth a son, and shall call his name JESUS. He will be great, and will be called the Son of the Highest; and the Lord God will give him the throne of his father David. And he will reign over the house of Jacob forever, and of his kingdom there will be no end." Then Mary said to the angel, "How can this be, since I do not know a man?"

And the angel answered and said to her, "The Holy Spirit will come upon you, and the power of the Highest will overshadow you; therefore, also, that Holy One who is to be born will be called the Son of God. Now indeed, <u>Elizabeth your relative has also conceived a son in her old age; and this is now the sixth month for her</u> who was called barren. For with God nothing will be impossible." Then Mary said, "Behold the maidservant of the Lord! Let it be to me according to your word." And the angel departed from her."

(Luke 1:26-38)

The Holy Spirit likely overshadowed Mary very soon after her encounter with the angel Gabriel. If John the Baptist was conceived in the two-week period after *Sivan* 19, Jesus would have been conceived about six months later, at the end of the Hebrew month *Kislev* or the beginning of the month *Tevet*. Mary would probably have conceived Jesus sometime from *Kislev* 24 to *Tevet* 7. *Kislev* 25 is the beginning of the Feast of *Chanukah*, also known as the Festival of Lights. This eight-day feast continues to *Tevet* 2.

Jesus observed the Feast of *Chanukah* (called the "Feast of Dedication" in John 10:22) while he was on Earth. John gives us an indication that Jesus was, in fact, conceived during this Festival of Lights (*Chanukah*) when he speaks of him at the beginning of his Gospel:

"In him was life, and the life was the light of men. And the light shines in the darkness, and the darkness did not comprehend it. There was a man sent from God, whose name was John. This man came for a witness, *to bear witness of the light* that all through him might believe. *He was not that light*, <u>but was sent to bear witness of that light</u>. That was the true light which gives light to every man coming into the world."

(John 1:4-9)

Quickly after Gabriel's visit, Mary went to see her relative Elizabeth:

> "Now <u>Mary arose in those days and went into the hill country with haste</u>, to a city of Judah, and entered the house of Zacharias and greeted Elizabeth. And it happened, when Elizabeth heard the greeting of Mary that the babe leaped in her womb; and Elizabeth was filled with the Holy Spirit. And <u>Mary remained with her about three months</u>, and returned to her house."
>
> (Luke 1:39-41, 56)

It appears that Mary stayed with Elizabeth right up to the time for her to give birth. The average time for the gestation of a human baby is nine months/40 weeks/280 days. Nine months from the time of John's conception in early *Tamuz* would bring us to Passover of the Jewish year 3756 in the 1st month called *Nisan*. This Hebrew date fell in the month of March in 5 BCE.

> "Now Elizabeth's <u>full time came for her to be delivered</u>, and she brought forth a son."
>
> (Luke 1:57)

It's highly symbolic that John the Baptist was born at the time of Passover. Even to this very day, there is still an expectation by religious Jews of the coming of Elijah the prophet during the time of Passover (Malachi 4:5-6). But many Jews did not recognize the reincarnation of Elijah in John the Baptist. In fact, a cup is set for Elijah at the annual Passover Seder, and children symbolically check for him at the door during the service. As Gabriel prophesied and Jesus confirmed (Matthew 11:14), John the Baptist was the prophet Elijah to prepare the way before the Messiah.

Signs in the heavens over Jerusalem on the fifteenth of *Nisan* in the Jewish year 3756 heralded the birth of John the Baptist. On that night, just after sunset, a spectacular full moon lunar eclipse was visible from Jerusalem in the astrological signs of the Full Moon in Libra/Sun in Aries.

Since Jesus was conceived during *Chanukah*, six months after John the Baptist was conceived, he would also have been born six months after John:

> "And it came to pass in those days that a decree went out from Caesar Augustus that all the world should be registered. This census first took place while Quirinius was governing Syria. So all went to be registered, everyone to his own city. Joseph also went up from Galilee, out of the city of Nazareth, into Judea, to the city of David, which is called Bethlehem, because he was of the house and lineage of David, to be registered with Mary, his betrothed wife, who was with child. So it was, that while they were there, <u>the days were completed for her to be delivered.</u> And she brought forth her firstborn son, and wrapped him in swaddling clothes, and laid him in a manger, because there was no room for them in the inn."
>
> (Luke 2:1-7)

CHAPTER TWENTY-SEVEN: The Christmas Gods

Since John was born on Passover, the fifteenth day of *Nisan* (the first Jewish month), Jesus would have been born six months later on the fifteenth day of *Tishri* (the seventh Jewish month). The fifteenth day of the seventh month begins the Feast of Tabernacles (Leviticus 23:34-35), also known as *Sukkot*. Jesus was born on the first day of the Feast of Tabernacles! In the year 5 BCE, this fell in the month of September.

This explains why there was no room at the inn for Joseph and Mary. A multitude of Jewish pilgrims from all over the Middle East had come to Jerusalem to observe the Feast of Tabernacles, as God required (Deuteronomy 16:16). Bethlehem, which was only a few miles outside of Jerusalem, was also overflowing with visitors at this time because of the Feast.

Just as it was six months earlier, signs in the heavens over Jerusalem on the first day of the Feast of Tabernacles (15 *Tishri*, 3757) proclaimed the birth of the prophesied Messiah. Another remarkable full moon lunar eclipse was visible in Israel on this night also, in the opposite astrological signs from John the Baptist with the Full Moon in Aries and the Sun in Libra. In addition to the hint of Jesus's conception during *Chanukah*, we also find an allusion to his birth during the Feast of Tabernacles in John's Gospel:

> "And the Word became flesh, and did TABERNACLE among us, and we beheld his glory, glory as of an only begotten of a father, full of grace and truth."
>
> (John 1:14)

The Greek word translated "tabernacle" above is *eskenosen*. This word is a form of *skenoo* (#4637 in *Strong's Greek Concordance*). While it is usually translated "dwelt," *Strong's* says this word literally means "to fix one's tabernacle, have one's tabernacle, abide (or live) in a tabernacle (or tent), tabernacle…"

Eight days after his birth, in accordance with the Law of Moses, Jesus was circumcised on the eighth day of Assembly (*Shemini Atzeret*), another holy day of God (Leviticus 23:36):

> "And <u>when eight days were completed for the circumcision of the child</u>, his name was called JESUS, the name given by the angel before he was conceived in the womb."
>
> (Luke 2:21)

It is also interesting to note that the time of the Feast of Tabernacles (*Sukkot)* always happens during the fall harvest and is always celebrated after the Jewish New Year *Rosh Hashanah* which is followed by *Yom Kippur*, the Day of Atonement. *Sukkot* is the feast to celebrate the harvest with a *Sukkah,* which is a shelter/tent (tabernacle) that is used to give shelter and protection, decorated by fruits.

The fact that Jesus was not born on December 25 distinguishes Him from all the other gods that have traditionally been celebrated on those days. This is just one more reason that sets Him apart from the rest. The fact that his birthday is celebrated on

December 25 shows that it was enforced by the Kingdom of Darkness to hold believers in ignorance, in Lucifer/Satan's attempt to counterfeit the true Christ, and keep believers in further darkness by getting them to celebrate their festivals out of sync with the Lord's calendar.

Messing with the calendar was originally done by Pope Gregory XIII, by a decree signed on February 24, 1582, hence the name "Gregorian Calendar." The Catholic Church replaced their celebration of the birthday of Mithras on December 25 with Jesus Christ, which was deliberately done by a thorough intervention of the 'satans' to confound the timeline, and keep earth humans, particularly believers, out of sync with the true sacred Feast days of the Lord, by obscuring his true birthday. This was done in a deliberate attempt to 'steal' blessings from the Lord in Heaven, which potentially is downloaded to all believers on appointed feast days. Remember Constantine outlawed all the feasts of the Lord, and decreed anyone who followed them, 'Judaizers' and anathema to Rome.

These days, it is no mystery to most people that Christmas has become a hodgepodge of holidays mixed into one. Between the Druid worship of trees to the celebration and traditions of an old man known as St. Nicholas, who brought gifts to children in old England, to the celebration of Yule and Saturnalia, which are all pagan holidays, to today's worship of Satan's capitalism, and the intense pressure people experience to spend money and buy expensive gifts in order to outdo and impress others, has become, without a doubt, the biggest commercial holiday of the year.

However, one thing that is important to mention, is, that true Christian believers, worship Jesus Christ on Christmas Eve and Christmas Day every year, most of whom, never even heard of these other sixteen pagan gods I listed here. So ask yourself this question, whose *spiritual* victory is now prominent on the timeline for the annual astronomical return of the Sun? (December 25).

It's important to know history, but for believers, it's also important to claim back ground stolen from the enemy for the Kingdom of Heaven. True Christians worship Christ every day, or twice a week in their respective churches. Choosing to worship Christ on Christmas is by no means, a sin, as many so called, *religious* folks would want you to believe. Those in the Hebrew Roots Movement (HRM), declare anyone who celebrates Christmas as an idolatrous sin, and therefore a false Christian. This is the *religious spirit* speaking, which is a counterfeit legalistic attitude (spirit), void of the true spirit of Christ (the Holy Spirit of Life, Resurrection and Victory over Darkness).

If most Christians never even heard of these other gods, nor even care what happened in the past, but choose nevertheless to worship the Lord Jesus Christ on Christmas, then who are these HRM grinches to say they shouldn't? The HRM folks might as well join the atheists, secularists and Muslims who wage war on Christmas every year.

Spiritually speaking, the *spiritual* victory lays with Yahshua Christ, who alone is worshipped every year on Christmas in churches all around the world. Nobody in

CHAPTER TWENTY-SEVEN: The Christmas Gods

Christianity even *remembers* nor memorializes the other gods on the timeline and that in and of itself is a victory for Christ, regardless of the fact that He wasn't even born on that day. Many people are comforted and healed by the presence of the Holy Spirit while worshipping Christ, whether it's on Christmas or any other day of the year. Christ is no respecter of persons, nor is He a legalist about days and times that He must be worshipped, which distinguishes Him from all the other legalistic religions and so called gods. Remember that, next time you judge someone who chooses to celebrate Christ on Christmas.

> "God made him who had no sin to be sin for us, so that in him we might become the righteousness of God."
>
> (2 Corinthians 5:21)

The purpose of the life, death, and resurrection of Yahshua was to be the final sacrifice for the sins of humankind. His scourging, the Bible tells us when he was whipped thirty-nine times, is the fulfilment of the Prophesy in Isaiah 53:5 which says, that it is by His stripes we are healed. While this is a mystery to many, we know today, according to the American Medical Association, that all medical diseases fall into thirty-nine different categories. Coincidence? I don't think so.

Many people are healed of all kinds of illnesses through the confession of this scripture alone. Matthew 8:17 says that Jesus carried every sickness and infirmity on Him on the cross, that it is through His blood that heals every infirmity known to humankind. It is not automatic, but needs to be appropriated through faith.

The crown of thorns placed on His head prior to His scourging which caused bleeding, was for the healing of mental illnesses. The piercings in his wrists were for all the sins of the hands, the piercings in his feet, were for all the sins that people commit as they walk in evil, and the sword into his side, which caused water to gush forth, was to pour out the rivers of living water upon humankind.

The fact that the Jewish priests ceased the practice of offering the blood of animal sacrifices on their altar for the atonement of sins after Jesus died on the cross, rose from the dead, and ascended back to heaven is historical evidence that His work on the cross became the final sacrifice for all humankind. Because it says, in Leviticus 17:11, only the blood can atone for sins.

Yes, lots of people died by crucifixion, but He was the only one who was resurrected, fully whole and healed, and continued to do miracles and walk the earth for another forty days thereafter, until He ascended, into God's throne in the heavens, via one of the Lord's starships. He didn't just disappear into thin space.

Always, the Bible is consistent, the Lord comes and goes in a Cloud (his heavenly chariot, which we would call today, starships). And the Ascension of Christ was no different as the Second Coming of Christ will be.

"But God chose the foolish things of the world to shame the wise; God chose the weak things of the world to shame the strong."

(1 Corinthians 1:27)

NOTES:

1. Michael T. Snyder, *The Mystery Of The Pagan Origin Of Christmas: Jesus Was Not Born On December 25th But A Whole Bunch Of Pagan Gods Were.*, 2009, http://unexplainedmysteriesoftheworld.com/archives/the-mystery-of-the-pagan-origin-of-christmas-jesus-was-not-born-on-december-25th-but-a-whole-bunch-of-pagan-gods-were

CHAPTER TWENTY-EIGHT

WHAT HAPPENS WHEN YOU DIE?

"The goal of all life is death."
~Sigmund Freud

"The LORD gives both death and life;
He brings some down to the grave but raises others up."
(1 Samuel 2:6)

"This is what the Sovereign Lord says: **My people, I am going to open your graves and bring you up from them; I will bring you back to the land of Israel**. Then you, my people, will know that I am the Lord, **when I open your graves and bring you up from them. I will put my Spirit in you and you will live, and I will settle you in your own land.** Then you will know that I the Lord have spoken, and I have done it, declares the Lord.'"

(Ezekiel 37:12-14)

What really happens to souls when they die? Is it just heaven or hell, as the Christian religion believes? Or is there an in between life? What about reincarnation? What about Purgatory? What do the scriptures REALLY say about rebirth? If the Lord says He gives both death and life, and He alone brings some people down to the grave, but raises others up, then doesn't God's Word settle the question once and for all that Rebirth and Reincarnation, aka being "born again" is really God's business? Let's discern.

REINCARNATION: GOD'S ORIGINAL PLAN

All souls return to the Creator God, i.e., the Lord of all Spirits. After death, angels escort souls through the afterlife. According to the scriptures, souls are directly sent to one of four places in the afterlife. 1) Paradise, also called "Abraham's Bosom" which is located inside the earth; 2) God's Holy Fire, which is called, "Purgatory," also located inside the earth; 3) some souls go to sleep in a resting place, also located inside the earth; 4) Hell, (Tartarus) also located inside the earth. How can all these places house so many different souls at the same time all be inside the earth? The scriptures tell us that these places are separated by chasms, otherwise known as dimensions, which I'll get more into later.

"Just as man is destined to die once, and after that to face judgment."

(Hebrews 9:27)

Many Christians misinterpret that scripture to mean there is no reincarnation, but what the verse is saying is that, after each death, there will be judgment. That judgment may be to end up in one of four places in the afterlife. Every soul is sent before the Lord to be judged, it's kind of like a trial, where the persecutor/accuser is Lucifer/Satan accuses the soul of ungodly behavior in their lifetime, which he keeps a record of. Because Earth is the battlefield for human souls, it is pretty much determined prior to death who belongs with whom and where, although there are many exceptions, depending on how a person dies. All deeds, both good and evil, and every word spoken are recorded by recording angels (extraterrestrial messengers).

> "But I tell you that men will have to give account on the Day of Judgment for every careless word they have spoken."
>
> (Matthew 12:36)

> "The tongue can bring death or life; those who love to talk will reap the consequences."
>
> (Proverbs 18:21)

PURGATORY, REINCARNATION IN THE HOLY BIBLE

Christians have a hard time with reincarnation, because a preexisting soul was condemned as heresy in the Second Council of Constantinople in 553AD and in the Roman Emperor's Constantine's Creed 365AD, which was against all things that were decreed by the God of Israel. His Creed stated that anyone who believed in such matters were considered to be a Judaizer and anathema to Rome. As a result, most Christians teach that reincarnation and purgatory are not in the Bible, but is this scripturally true? Let's discern. Truth be told, there are dozens of scriptures in the Bible that speak of "rebirth" and coming back from the dead.

Two of the most compelling scriptures in the Bible that literally prove not only the very definition of reincarnation but more importantly proves, that this process is God's plan and souls are judged according to His Mercy and Justice according to God's immutable laws.

According to the Merriam-Webster Dictionary, the definition of the word, 'reincarnation' means: the idea or belief that people are born again with a different body after death; someone who has been born again with a different body after death. The word is derived from Latin, as the word, 'carne' means flesh or meat. Reincarnation essentially is to return back into the life of the flesh.

"The LORD gives both death and life; he brings some down to the grave but raises others up." First Samuel 2:6 and Ezekiel 37:1-4, both promise and prophesy that the LORD (Yahuah) was going to breathe His spirit back into the Valley of the Dry Bones and give the dead Israelites new flesh. By every definition, that is reincarnation. I can be

CHAPTER TWENTY-EIGHT: What Happens When You Die?

a believer in the saving Grace of Jesus Christ and still accept reincarnation. Reincarnation is all about God's Grace. If God decides to send someone back to Earth in human form, then who am I to argue with that?

If Christians can believe in the resurrection, and Christians believe in resuscitation from death (raising of the dead into the same body), then what's the big deal with reincarnation? It's all done by the same God of Mercy, who is the God of second, third, fourth, etc. chances. Reincarnation is not a religion, it is not something man can do, but only the Lord can ordain and authorize a soul to return back to life.

SECOND CHANCES AND REBIRTH

In Ezekiel 37, the prophesy is to the dead Israelites in 585BC who the Lord promises He will breathe new life into them, attach flesh and tendons, and bring them all back to life. Many people, both Jews and Christians, believe wholeheartedly that this prophesy was fulfilled in 1948 when the Jews were given back the Land of Israel and were brought back to that land which was held in a 1,800-plus year drought, and was brought back to life, along with all of its descendants who were scattered for centuries in the Diaspora. All those who were called back to Israel were reincarnated from that Valley of Dry Bones, and were given another chance to cultivate the land under the laws of the Lord, as the Lord Yahuah promised in Ezekiel 37.

> "Then he said to me, "Prophesy to these bones and say to them, 'Dry bones, hear the word of the Lord! This is what the Sovereign Lord says to these bones: <u>I will make breath enter you, and you will come to life. I will attach tendons to you and make *flesh* come upon you and cover you with skin; I will put breath in you, and you will come to life</u>. Then you will know that I am the Lord.'"
>
> (Ezekiel 37:4-6)

> "But the rest of the dead lived not again until the thousand years were finished. This is the first resurrection."
>
> (Revelation 20:5)

This prophecy in Revelation clearly indicates that the dead will live again (reincarnate) after a thousand years. "Carne" means *flesh* in Latin, to reincarnate means for a soul to come back into the flesh. The Lord's promise in Ezekiel 37 couldn't be clearer, that He is the Lord of Reincarnation. And yes, reincarnation is in the Holy Scriptures, it is not some New Age or demonic belief, as many Christians believe.

Probably the best evidence of reincarnation in the Bible is found in Ezekiel Chapter 37:

THE VALLEY OF DRY BONES

"The hand of the Lord was on me, and he brought me out by the Spirit of the Lord and set me in the middle of a valley; it was full of bones. He led me back and forth among them, and I saw a great many bones on the floor of the valley, bones that were very dry. He asked me, "Son of man, can these bones live?"

I said, "Sovereign Lord, you alone know."

Then he said to me, "Prophesy to these bones and say to them, 'Dry bones, hear the word of the Lord! This is what the Sovereign Lord says to these bones:

I will make breath enter you, and you will come to life. I will attach tendons to you and make flesh come upon you and cover you with skin; I will put breath in you, and you will come to life. Then you will know that I am the LORD.'"

So I prophesied as I was commanded. And as I was prophesying, there was a noise, a rattling sound, and the bones came together, bone to bone. I looked, and tendons and flesh appeared on them and skin covered them, but there was no breath in them.

Then he said to me, "Prophesy to the breath; prophesy, son of man, and say to it, 'this is what the Sovereign Lord says: Come, breath, from the four winds and breathe into these slain, that they may live.' "So I prophesied as he commanded me, and **breath entered them; they came to life and stood up on their feet—a vast army**.

Then he said to me: "Son of man, these bones are the people of Israel. They say, 'Our bones are dried up and our hope is gone; we are cut off' therefore prophesy and say to them: 'this is what the Sovereign Lord says: **My people, I am going to open your graves and bring you up from them; I will bring you back to the land of Israel**. Then you, my people, will know that I am the Lord, **when I open your graves and bring you up from them. I will put my Spirit in you and you will live, and I will settle you in your own land.** Then you will know that I the Lord have spoken, and I have done it, declares the Lord.'"

(Ezekiel 37:1-14)

Both Constantine and the Seven Ecumenical Councils of Nicea wanted to suppress this truth that all Jews believed in for millennia because Rome had an agenda to control. You either followed the Church of Rome by toeing the church agenda or you went to hell. I would hope that today's Christian's would have the maturity to see through that political agenda and cease to continue perpetuating a false belief system that reincarnation is a lie. Truth be told, it's the other way around.

"Woe unto them that call evil good, and good evil; that put darkness for light, and light for darkness; that put bitter for sweet, and sweet for bitter!"

(Isaiah 5:20)

CHAPTER TWENTY-EIGHT: What Happens When You Die?

In addition to the fact that if a Christian is really following and listening to the Holy Spirit of Truth, the Holy Spirit will reveal this truth to them if they are willing to humble themselves and accept the fact that they have believed a lie all these years, that began in 365AD. Even Christians can get sent back to earth for a variety of reasons. Remember, God's ways are not our ways.

While many Christians want to put God in their boxes, The LORD cannot be limited. He alone is God and Judge over every soul. I believe the scripture in Hebrews 9:27, from Paul's writings, is grossly misinterpreted, that, "it is appointed unto man once to die and then judgment." There are several types of Judgments mentioned throughout the Bible. This makes an interesting research Bible study.

When I was learning Bible, one of the first things I was taught that in order to 'prove' scripture, there needed to be corroborating scriptures in both the Old and New Testaments to match or partner with, this confirmed the Word of God. Problem with Hebrews 9:27 is there is no corroborating scripture. This could be because the Church Fathers who edited the Bible canon may have edited some words out of this scripture, to change its meaning, or it could be a 'rogue' scripture, implanted into the canon to support their political agenda of Rome and that of Constantine's Creed, which became the law of the land.

I have challenged multiple Christians to prove this scripture with a corroborating Old Testament scripture, and no one is able to do so, because there is none. In fact, just the opposite is true, as there are dozens of both Old and New Testaments that prove reincarnation, which proves that the Church Fathers who edited the Bible Canon, didn't do a very good job of eliminating all scriptures relating to reincarnation.

There is the Judgment after each lifetime to access and review the life, and the Judgment of God also known as the terrible Day of the Lord, which happens during the Seven Bowls of God's Wrath being poured out upon the Earth. Then there is the Judgment that comes from Jesus when He returns when He judges His Church, separating His Sheep from the goats (Matthew 25:31-40), and finally the Great White Throne Judgment which takes place after all of God's plans are fulfilled when He closes up the world and creates a New Heaven and a New Earth, and we will remember the old one, no more (Revelation 20:11-15). The truth is there, and so is the Revelation of the Holy Spirit to those who have ears to hear.

Reincarnation has been an integral belief of Judaism, the early Christian movement, Hinduism, Buddhism, Sikhism, Jainism, Taoism, Theosophy, Kabbalah, Sufism, and the New Age movement. There is so much evidence in the scriptures as well as in the apocryphal texts that reincarnation was a common belief of both ancient Jews and early Christians, which was started by Jews, including Yeshua, aka Jesus Christ Himself, who taught this concept.

Again, while I may be stating the obvious, Jesus (Yahshua) was a Jewish Rabbi. I say this only because of the many watered down versions of Christianity today. These versions do not recognize Jesus as a Jew; instead, they project all kinds of misinterpretations and false beliefs on Him, which stems from what the Roman Catholic Church did to the scriptures, the Jews, and to the Jewish Messiah. There is an historical thread, as to when and why this belief and knowing in reincarnation, among our ancestors was deleted and considered heresy with the penalty of being excommunicated and even burned at the stake for these beliefs by the Catholic Church.

I ask you, my readers, isn't it time to end this lie and allow the Lord to free you from believing in the false implants which were implanted for the purpose of mind control by the Roman Empire? You can be free, right now, where you are, with a simple prayer of repentance to the Lord for believing in the lies inserted by Rome. Every prayer of repentance is answered and honored by God with the outpouring of His Grace through Christ. No exceptions!

"He sent forth his word and healed them; **he delivered them from the grave.**"
(Psalm 107:20)

If God doesn't allow reincarnation, then why is He delivering people from the grave? Why would King David, write such things? Today many Christians do not believe that reincarnation is possible, mainly because they have been taught that it was not true because of the false teaching that came down from the Catholic Church via Constantine from 325 AD through 375 AD, when reincarnation was removed from the Bible during Emperor Justinian's reign of the Constantine Empire, and later reinforced by the Nicean Council in 550AD. However, before that time, reincarnation was taught and believed by just about everyone in the ancient world for millennia.

Some argue, it was because Jesus Christ ended the cycle of rebirth. Really? Is this really what Jesus taught? I will prove to you through the words of Jesus Christ Himself, that just the opposite is true.

Believe it or not, reincarnation was actually taught in the Church of Rome until 325 AD when it was voted out (3-2) at the Council of Constantinople because it did not fit into the political agenda of the Roman Church at that time, which was to control religion and control its people. Reincarnation was widely believed by the Jews for millennia, both during and after Christ, until it was no longer in alignment with their agenda, which was to put the fear of God into people and let them think they only got one chance at life and they better fall in line with the church or else they would go to hell. This, however, was not and has never been God's will.

Reincarnation was taught throughout Judaism and Hinduism since the beginning of the fall of man. The Jewish Kabbalah is based on the wheels of the soul, which is all about reincarnation for the purpose of "tikune," which in Hebrew translates to "correction."

In Hinduism, the belief for reincarnation is based on karma, which is a Sanskrit word meaning "habit" based on the laws of cause and effect. Karma can be good or karma can be bad; in which case, it must be balanced. Justice is served in future lives. This explains

CHAPTER TWENTY-EIGHT: What Happens When You Die?

why people are born with different lots in life — some are born gifted, and others are born diseased, all in line with the laws of cause and effect. "Be not deceived; God is not mocked, as a man soweth, that shall he also reap." (Galatians 6:7) This is the meaning of Karma! The original scripture said "even though the reaping may come a thousand years hence" was later deleted out of the canon.

There are numerous reasons why the Lord sends the sinful back to Earth, instead of throwing them into Hell: because there's hell on Earth. To be born with a birth defect, or born into abject poverty, or being born in Somalia and starving to death as a child, being born in North Korea, or how about being born a female Muslim and be subjected to clitoral mutilation, repetitive anal rape and both sexual and physical abuse from male Muslims, is hell on earth. Or any other part of the planet which has severe oppression, human rights abuses; there are all sorts of bondages and afflictions a soul can experience, being born cursed, being orphaned, being born with an infirmity, being born to suffer all kinds of abuses, horrors, and traumas; these are all different levels and forms of hell on Earth.

The Lord allows all these varied states and conditions to be born into, for the higher purpose of soul correction, so that the soul would, through its suffering, have the opportunity to find salvation through the Lord by being humbled as a human, and learn some deep soul lesson while receiving its just punishment and correction for past mistakes by being purified through its suffering. And likewise, these birth conditions also serve as an opportunity for others born fortunate, to show compassion and kindness onto those who suffer, for this is the purpose of heaven on earth. This is the Grace of God, which is all about giving humans another chance to avoid being thrown into the Lake of Fire, which the scriptures say, was created for the devil and his angels, not for humans.

It's important to recognize the difference between hell and the lake of fire. Hell is a prison, which scripture proves is temporary, because souls do pass through it; however, the lake of fire is eternal death and damnation for the soul, which is created to destroy the soul, whereas hell is created to imprison the soul for correction, where the wicked end up. We know this because people have seen it and experienced it as part of a NDE (Near Death Experience) and it is mentioned as a real place over sixty-five times in the scriptures.

> "For we must all stand before Christ to be judged. We will each receive whatever we deserve for the good or evil we have done in this earthly body."
>
> (2 Corinthians 5:10)

Everyone faces Christ after each lifetime to be judged for what they've done. He decides where they go in the afterlife. For those who did not accept him or know him on earth, but were not necessarily wicked, receive his grace and mercy, because that's "who" He is, full of Grace, Mercy and Justice. They go through the holy fires of purgatory to "purge" themselves from all ungodly attitudes they acquired on earth. Then they await another chance at life, and are reborn.

Others may have lived such a godly life, they may get to enter into their eternal rest and sleep to await the final resurrection of the body for the coming Kingdom of God on earth. Others may enter paradise to be with him and live in his Heavenly Kingdom. While others who die in their iniquities may be sent to the torments and fires of the abyss. He is the judge of all.

> "The rest of the dead did not come to life until the thousand years were ended. This is the first resurrection. Blessed and holy are those who have part in the first resurrection. The second death has no power over them, but they will be priests of God and of Christ and will reign with him for a thousand years."
>
> (Revelation 20:5, 6)

> "For since death came through a man, the resurrection of the dead comes also through a man. For as in Adam all die, so in Christ all will be made alive."
>
> (1 Corinthians 15:21, 22)

> "But there is an order to this resurrection: Christ was raised as the first of the harvest; then all who belong to Christ will be raised when he comes back. After that the end will come, when he will turn the Kingdom over to God the Father, having destroyed every ruler and authority and power. For Christ must reign until he humbles all his enemies beneath his feet. And the last enemy to be destroyed is death."
>
> (1 Corinthians 15:23-25)

REINCARNATION: BEEN THERE, DONE THAT

Reincarnation was a fundamental belief of the early Christian church, because this was the way the Jews believed and the disciples were all Jews as was the early Church. The first five churches established after Jesus's death were located in Jerusalem, Antioch, Alexandria, Rome, and Constantinople. They did not all immediately call themselves Christians. "The disciples were called Christians first at Antioch" (Acts 11:26). The word *Christian* was first used as a derogatory term coined by the Romans against the Jews who believed in Yahshua, the Christ. The word stuck, and believers took it on and they became known as *Christians,* even though the early church were Jewish Christians.

Both the Gnostics and the Essenes were spiritual sects that pursued the belief of wisdom and the attainment of spiritual knowledge, which was the central focus of their beliefs, which included the belief and understanding of reincarnation. After the early church expanded into the world of the gentiles, there were a number of other significant writers and Saints of the early church that were fervent believers in reincarnation, such as

CHAPTER TWENTY-EIGHT: What Happens When You Die?

Saint Gregory of Nyssa, Saint Augustine, Saint Jerome and the profound and prolific Origen.

In his work *On First Principles*, Origen established his main tenets, including the pre-existence of souls, the Fall of Man, the rebirth of souls into temporal bodies, and the eventual return to enlightenment as our original state of consciousness. He was considered one of the greatest of all the early Christian theologians and most likely one of the primary people responsible for the onset of the ecumenical councils.[1]

Constantine was a Roman Emperor who allegedly became a Christian, but in the end, died worshipping Mithras, recognized that various religious sects were in conflict over scripture. As a result, he called the first ecumenical council directing them to resolve their conflicts and determine one doctrine for the Christian church. To today's eschatologists, this was a prelude to the New World Order's plan for a One World Religion. Spiritually speaking, the spirit behind Constantine's desire for everyone being under one religion was exactly the same spirit behind today's Pope who wants to unify the world under what he calls, *Chrislam,* the blending of Christianity and Islam, Roman Catholic-style.

An ecumenical council is an assembly of theologians and church dignitaries called together to discuss and establish the teachings of the church. The first ecumenical council, called the *Council of Nicea,* met in 325 AD, and was believed to have lasted over two months.[2]

The *Second Council of Constantinople*, which was actually the fifth ecumenical council, met in 553 AD under Pope Vigilius and Emperor Justinian I, this was nearly three hundred years after Origen's death. Emperor Justinian declared fifteen anathemas (condemnations) against Origen. At least, he wasn't hanged for it, because he was already dead.

ANATHEMA TO ROME

"The very first of the 'Anathemas against Origen' stated: 'If anyone asserts the fabulous pre-existence of souls, and shall assert the monstrous restoration which follows from it: let him be anathema' the fifteenth anathema stated in part: 'If anyone does not anathematize Arius, Eunomius, Macedonius, Apollinaris, Nestorius, Eutyches, and Origen as well as their impious writings...let them be anathema.' the condemnation of Origen's teachings was taken to imply rejection of pre-existence and reincarnation by the entire church."[3] Essentially speaking, if you didn't believe in their 'lie', you were excommunicated.

These "anathemas" created so much persecution amongst believers, and unfortunately, to this day, have followed church leaders into the formation of belief systems in forming churches that are denominations of Christianity, but are not connected to Catholicism. Anybody with a critical mind can glean from history, that both the Council of Nicea in 325 AD, followed by the Second Council of Constantinople in

553AD, had hijacked the truth from believers, by asserting their political agendas of their time into the church doctrine of their day.

Yet, even after the advent of the Renaissance (the period of rebirth), and the rise of enlightenment today, the Catholic and Christian churches never updated their records to match the truth. Christian denominations, all offshoots of Roman Catholicism continued in this false teaching and, for the most part, have never repented for it.

The truth of the matter is, when it comes to reincarnation, that all those before these councils believed in it, and it was spoken of and taught by Jesus Christ Himself, and that most traces (but not all) were deleted from their versions of the canonized Bible. Doesn't it occur to modern day believers, and those who study the Scriptures, why the books of the Gospels of Matthew, Mark, Luke, and John were almost identical? Did the disciples plagiarize each other? What are the odds of four different men who spent three years with Jesus writing practically the same four gospels verbatim? Does anyone with a critical mind really think that these were their "original" writings? Especially considering the fact that Matthew, Mark, Luke and John were all very different people, with different backgrounds and levels of education.

It is obvious that during the Councils of Constantinople that a great deal of editing by the Council took place. Then we have the apostle John say, "Jesus did many other wondrous things as well. If every one of them were written down, I suppose even the whole world would not have room for the books that would be written" (John 21:25). What if there were more wise words of Jesus that did not fit into the early church fathers' agenda that were deleted? What about more of his many miracles and testimonies that were written down, that were deemed too controversial for them at the time were also omitted?

The truth of the matter is that there are a number of religious scholars today that postulate that the early church fathers were elected to delete most of the original references of reincarnation in the Christian Bible. Furthermore, these scholars believe that the Bible over time has been periodically altered, implying new contextual meanings as well as having been edited to erase inconsistencies between the various writings.

"All scripture *is* given by inspiration of God,"

(2 Timothy 3:16)

Scripture is really the work of men, *inspired by God*, but still the work of men. Let's face it. The Council of Constantinople had a definite agenda, which was to put everyone on the same page, religiously speaking, and to eliminate all the debates and infighting between believers. Spiritually speaking, what entered into them at that time, was the *religious spirit*, which does not come from the Creator, but from the god of this world, who is Lucifer/Satan. These early church fathers were inspired by their political agenda to control the masses through doctrine.

Take the *Books of Enoch*, these scrolls were read by the early church. In fact the disciples themselves quoted Enoch on various occasions throughout the New Testament.

CHAPTER TWENTY-EIGHT: What Happens When You Die?

Enoch was the first to coin the phrase "the Son of Man," which was used by Jesus Christ Himself. Why weren't these books canonized into the "Holy Bible" by the Councils?

The answer is that Enoch's writing was counterintuitive to their political agendas. Enoch wrote of truths that were understood by the ancients, such as why God sent the floods to wipe out humankind, who were the Nephilim, who were the sons of God, who were the Watchers, and what were the purposes and meanings of the ten heavens. Enoch's writings were too controversial for Constantine to include. He wanted everyone on the same page, religiously speaking, so Enoch's writings were rejected, because they were too advanced for the average person to understand. Constantine wanted to appeal to the masses, not just the minority of scribes and scholars. Enoch's scrolls were read by the disciples and early Christians. Enoch was the first to prophesy about the coming of the "Son of Man", the coming of the Messiah, the Savior for humankind. He was also the first to coin the phrase, "Lord of all Spirits."

It's been said, that the Ethiopian bible is the oldest complete bible on earth. It has 81 books, not 66. The Coptic bible also includes Enoch's scriptures, as both the Ethiopians and Coptics resisted submitting to Roman auspices.

Eventually, after many spiritual battles, debates and conflicts over interpreting scripture, the Roman Church separated from the other Orthodox churches and formed the Roman Catholic Church in 1054 AD.[4]

According to various scholars, none of the original manuscripts of the entire Bible exist today. They are only copies of copies. However, the *Codex Vaticanus* is thought to be the oldest complete copy of the Bible still in existence, which dates as far back as the fourth century. It is housed in the Vatican Library, along with other controversial scriptures that contradict traditional Christian beliefs.[5] However, nobody can read it, or compare it to other bibles.

Knowledge is power, and many spiritual battles were fought over this power being transferred to earth humans between the god of this world, who is Lucifer/Satan and his fallen angels, and the angels that serve the Kingdom of Heaven on Earth. A compromise was agreed on, which is the manuscript we know today as the "Holy Bible."

From the Councils of Nicea in 325 AD to the Councils of Constantinople in 553 AD, followed by the Council of Trent in 1545 AD, the leaders of the Christian church over a period of time altered the original doctrine. What was considered accepted church doctrine immediately following the days that Jesus Christ walked the earth has been lost and stolen by the editors of the Holy Bible, and to many, has faded into the annals of time. The first ecumenical council took place over three hundred years after the death and resurrection of Jesus Christ. The fact that the ecumenical councils misinterpreted and were threatened by many of the teachings of Jesus is evident today.

Misunderstandings of His teachings happened while Jesus walked the earth, and continues to this day. The battles have always been spiritual against principalities, powers, rulers of the dark forces of this present world, and spiritual wickedness in the heavens (Ephesians 6:12), which have been ongoing for millennia over knowledge and over the empowerment of earth humans. The fact that there were so many conflicts over doctrine over time, that anyone who didn't accept all the edits that the ecumenical council dictated, were subject to condemnation, excommunication, all kinds of punishment, torture and many were burned to death. These actions were clearly not the Holy Spirit at work, nor was it the will of God, but the work of the counterfeit spirit also known as the "antichrist" spirit, which is still at work in the world today.

The last few scriptures at the end of the *Book of Revelation*, has been sorely misused by Christians, to prove that the rest of the Bible cannot be edited. Revelation 22:18, 19 is speaking specifically to the *scroll* of Revelation, later called the *Book of Revelation* when it became the sixty-sixth book added to the Bible canon.

> "I warn everyone who hears the words of the prophecy of *this scroll*: If anyone adds anything to them, God will add to that person the plagues described in *this scroll*. And if anyone takes words away from *this scroll of prophecy*, God will take away from that person any share in the tree of life and in the Holy City, which are described *in this scroll*."
>
> (Revelation 18, 19)

> "I am the Living One; I was dead, and now look, I am alive for ever and ever! And I hold the keys of death and Hades."
>
> (Revelation 1:17, 18)

JESUS TAUGHT REINCARNATION

The Gnostic text, *Pistis Sophia,* 200 AD, is one of the few ancient texts devoted wholly to the mysterious teachings of Jesus to his disciples. In it, Jesus Christ said: "Souls are poured from one into another of different kinds of bodies of the world." Jesus taught the concept of reincarnation to His disciples.[6]

Reincarnation is clearly no longer accepted today in most Christian churches, because of the edicts set down from the third and fifth centuries. However, reincarnation was willingly part of Jesus's original teachings. While the ecumenical councils deleted most of the scriptures relating to reincarnation, it is no surprise that it was not a perfect cover-up, as not all the scriptures were taken out of the Bible. Many of the scriptures were left in, which they probably didn't understand, so they missed deleting. The *Book of Revelation* is ripe with scriptures that prove rebirth, but the ecumenical councils were intimidated by its content, most likely thinking that most people wouldn't understand St. John's visions anyway. Oh and let's not forget about that curse attached to it at the very end.

The following are remnants that were left in the Holy Bible, which clearly describes that not only was this the accepted belief of the early church, but were the very teachings of Jesus Christ Himself.

CHAPTER TWENTY-EIGHT: What Happens When You Die?

Jesus said, "I AM the Gate, whoever enters through me will be saved. He will **come in and go out, and find pasture**." (John 10:9). Come in and go out, indicates rebirth.

He will come in and go out, this verse clearly indicates reincarnation. There are a myriad of reasons the Lord allows for rebirth. Think of how many people whose lives end abruptly, either through war, disaster, or disease. Many who never get to complete their missions, or share their gifts, or those who end up with unrequited love. Souls who never heard or understood the Divine Plan of Salvation, souls who were held in bondage by Satan all their lives, resulting in souls not fulfilling their God-given purposes along with thousands of other reasons. Souls need to feel complete; souls need to experience all that God has to offer, including all the learning experiences that earth life provides, along with character building, as well as the balancing of karmic debts.

What about those who have "karmic contracts," many of which gets carried over into their future lives? Jesus said, when you go "in" through Him (the Gate of both Heaven & Hell), you can come in, go out, and find pasture. Finding pasture is finding a new life which only He can authorize. Whether or not you believe Jesus Christ is the Lord of all the Spirits, as written in the ancient texts, **everyone** meets Him after they die, whether they believe in Him or not.

> "For we must all appear before the judgment seat of Christ; that every one may receive the things done in his body, according to that he hath done, whether it be good or bad" (2 Corinthians 5:10). This relates to Karma, the law of cause and effect, i.e., sowing and reaping.

> "But they which shall be accounted worthy to obtain that world, and the resurrection from the dead, neither marry, nor are given in marriage: **Neither can they die any more** [no more reincarnation]: for they are equal to the angels; and are the children of God, being the children of the resurrection" (Luke 20:35-36). Equal to the angels, means being immortal.

> "He who overcomes, I will make him a pillar in the temple of My God, **and he will not go out from it anymore**; and I will write on him the name of My God, and the name of the city of My God, the new Jerusalem, which comes down out of heaven from My God, and My new name."
>
> (Revelation 3:12)

'Not go out from it anymore,' clearly implies the cessation of the need to reincarnate. The fact that there will be humans who will be considered worthy, will end their cycles of reincarnation according to Luke 20:35, and will attain a heavenly status as "equal to the angels" to become known as the children of God, by being children of God's resurrection. There will be no more death and no more rebirth.

There are many people today who have had Near Death Experiences (NDEs), some of whose stories I will be including here and Book Three: *Who Are The Angels?* All were given another chance at coming back to life, being reborn, so to speak. Many were saved because they all met Jesus, who was the One who gave them their lives back, and literally sent them back into their bodies. It is this same Jesus, who grants souls new life, not necessarily to be resurrected back into the same body, but allows rebirth to occur in a new body, which is reincarnation.

> "And fear not them which kill the body, but are not able to kill the soul: but rather fear him which is able to destroy both soul and body in hell."
>
> (Mathew 10:28)

THE END OF REINCARNATION

However, reincarnation is not an eternal process, we are approaching a time on our timeline, which will end the cycle of reincarnation, which will happen at the end of this age, when Christ returns to set up His Kingdom on the Earth, after the Harvest of the Angels, Matthew 13:39, "The <u>harvest is at the end of the age, and the harvesters are angels.</u>" (God's faithful extraterrestrials). Those who are worthy will be translated into their non-corporeal bodies, and will be like the angels, immortal, to live forever in the Kingdom of God.

The words of the Lord YHUH (Yahuah) spoke through his prophet Hosea, and promised to redeem his people from the grave. This is one of the early promises of reincarnation in the Old Testament:

> "**<u>I will ransom them from the power of the grave; I will redeem them from death</u>**. Where, O death, are your plagues? Where, O grave, is your destruction?"
>
> (Hosea 13:14)

These words are later cross-referenced in the New Testament, "Where, O death, is your victory? Where, O death, is your sting?" (1 Corinthians 15:55)

So many Christians carry the *spiritual limitation device*, which is an implant originating from the Constantine and Nicean lies, that there is no reincarnation. Yet these same Christians who believe in the resurrection, and even believe in Christ and His Holy Spirit raises the dead on occasion (i.e., resuscitation, mistakenly think that God doesn't give rebirth/reincarnation to souls). Let me state the obvious that this implant obscures in their minds: He is the LORD, He is the God of gods, He has all the power of heaven and Earth, and He can do anything!

CHAPTER TWENTY-EIGHT: What Happens When You Die?

I have never understood why a Christian believer can believe in resurrection and resuscitation from the dead, but not reincarnation? Makes no sense at all. They put God in a box, limiting His power, to ... well, be God! They know that the only way to please God is with faith. So if you believe God can do anything, then don't doubt His mercy and grace to reincarnate souls. This is not something religion or religious people do. This is only authorized by the only One who has the authority to give life and rebirth to His created souls.

> "When the perishable has been clothed with the imperishable, and the mortal with immortality, then the saying that is written will come true: "Death has been swallowed up in victory." (v.54)

> "Now I say this, brethren, that <u>flesh and blood cannot inherit the kingdom of God</u>; nor does the perishable inherit the imperishable. Behold, I tell you a mystery; we will not all sleep, but we will all be changed, in a moment, in the twinkling of an eye, at the last trumpet; for the trumpet will sound, and the dead will be raised imperishable, and we will be changed...."
>
> (1 Corinthians 15:50-52)

The Lord said, "Before I formed thee in the belly I knew thee; and before thou camest forth out of the womb I sanctified thee, and I ordained thee a prophet unto the nations." (Jeremiah 1:5) This verse clearly illustrates, that before a person was conceived, the Lord knew them, which clearly shows that reincarnation was written into God's Divine Plan of Grace from the beginning of this human experiment we call earth life. There are many souls/spirits who are waiting on the Lord to allow them another chance at life. Again, only the Lord can authorize rebirth.

> "Lord you have been our dwelling throughout all generations...You turn man to destruction and then say, return, ye children of men; You carry them away as with a flood; **they are as asleep, yet in the morning they are like grass which grows back up**."
>
> (Psalm 90:1, 3, 5)

These scriptures clearly proves that rebirth is ordered by the Lord. The Lord is with us through <u>all generations</u>, yet man can only live one generation at a time if that. He can cause destruction to come on man, yet he will then return them back to life again to give them another chance. How many people die in floods or earthquakes, go to sleep, which is the Biblical metaphor for death, and yet are returned back to life to have another life on earth? This is the Grace of God that allows and governs the laws of rebirth. "Do not be deceived, God cannot be mocked, for whatsoever a man soweth, that shall he also reap." (Galatians 6:7)

"My little children, of whom I travail **in birth again until Christ be formed in you**." (Galatians 4:19) clearly illustrates reincarnation for the purpose of becoming perfect sons and daughters of God.

"And ye shall know the truth, and the truth shall make you free." (John 8:32) Free from rebirth on this planet of pain and suffering.

"**Your dead will live; their corpses (dead bodies) will rise**. You who lie in the dust, awake and shout for joy, for your dew is as the dew of the dawn, And **the earth will give birth to the departed spirits**." (Isaiah 26:19) This is the meaning of reincarnation, to be dead and then to live again. All departed spirits go inside the dimensions of the earth. When they are given rebirth, the earth releases them which is the meaning of this verse.

After each lifetime, each soul appears before the judgment seat of Christ, Lord of all Spirits for judgment. Depending on their lives and beliefs, some will get sent back (reincarnated); others will move on to the heavens, and others may be sent to hell. (See my chapter in Book Three: *Who Are The Angels?*, "Is Hell for Real?") Or they may pass through to Paradise where they spend eternity with God and complete their cycles of rebirth on Earth.

The Lord of Justice who balances His judgments with mercy and justice will determine through righteousness who ends up where, and with what lot in life, to either pay off karmic debts or learn soul lessons which are designed to bring us all back into "at-ONE-ment" with God, or those who come back to serve God with a mission. Yes, it's true. He does allow souls to be reborn, just to further His Kingdom on earth. Not because they are reaping what they've sown, or to atone — they're already saved — but because their desire to serve Him is so great that He appoints them to a life of ministry of some kind that draws souls back to Himself. How many true saints have you known whose only goal in life is to help, heal, and save others? These souls were sent from Heaven with a divine mission and divine assignment on Earth.

Think about this, if souls who are sent to the in-between holding place, which is known as purgatory, to purge from ungodly attitudes, how much more can earth life provide the same kind of "purging" through trials, tribulations, and adversities that we all face as human beings journeying through life on earth? The more we invest in purging, clearing, repenting, atoning for our errors, karma, (sins) on earth, the less our souls need to do in the afterlife, the freer we are as souls to enter into the Lord's rest.

Revelation 3 tells us in no uncertain terms, that there will be an end to the cycle of rebirth:

"Him who overcomes I will make a pillar in the temple of my God, and he will not go out from it anymore. (Never shall he leave it.) I will write on him the name of

CHAPTER TWENTY-EIGHT: What Happens When You Die?

my God and the name of the city of my God, the new Jerusalem, which is coming down out of heaven from my God; and I will also write on him my new name."

(Revelation 3:12)

I think the key words here are "he will not go out from it anymore" which again clearly indicates that reincarnation and the law of rebirth may come to an end to those who overcome this earth and become a Master of the planet. This is the real meaning of "Ascended Master."

There will be no more need for being "born again" in water (i.e., the water of the womb) or baptism. By overcoming the tests, trials, and tribulations in the kingdom of darkness (Lucifer/Satan's realm), Christ promises to make us "pillars" in His temple. A pillar is a support, a mainstay, a tower of strength that holds up its foundation. Another definition for a pillar is a leader or a rock. By being transformed out of the kingdom of darkness into the Kingdom of God, then there is no need to come back to Earth and live another life in the flesh. The corporeal then becomes the incorporeal; the translation has taken place and the new light body of eternal life has been given, instead of the body of flesh that dies.

"Giving thanks to the Father, which has made us meet to be partakers of the inheritance of the saints in light: <u>Who has delivered us from the power of darkness, and has translated us into the kingdom of the Son of His love,</u> in whom we have redemption.

(Colossians 1:12-14)

The end of this timeline will be the end of reincarnation. Wherever anyone is at, from their <u>cumulative lives</u> on Earth, they will be faced with a final judgment. There is what is called "the first death" and "the second death." The first death is the dying of the flesh, and the second death is having the soul thrown into eternal separation from God because the soul has repeatedly rejected God and therefore never found the path of redemption in its cumulative earth lives through the many cycles of reincarnation.

Reincarnation is all about God's Grace. It's about being given a second chance, and a third, and even up to 70 x 7 = 490 chances (lifetimes) along the timeline for the reincarnated soul to prove its faithfulness to God. Jesus revealed his standard of mercy to us in his *Parable of the Unforgiving Servant*:

"Then Peter came and said to Him, Lord, how often shall my brother sin against me and I forgive him? Up to seven times? Jesus said to him, I do not say to you, up to seven times, but up to *seventy times seven*. For this reason the kingdom of heaven may be compared to a king who wished to settle accounts with his slaves."

(Matthew 18:21-23)

Each life is designed to bring us closer to God on earth. After each life, the soul is returned to the Lord, who is the Creator of the soul and is known as the Lord of Spirits. He is the judge of whether or not that soul deserves His mercy and grace for another chance at earth life.

The Constantine and Nicean spiritual limitation implant deceives Christians into thinking reincarnation is not in the Bible, which is reinforced by the spirit of religion (Revelations 3) aka *religious spirit,* which is the cause of their spiritual blindness. As I've already proven, there are multiple scriptures in the Bible that relate specifically to rebirth (reincarnation). After the cycle of rebirth is complete, all the souls will face the final judgment. Yes, the Bible says, it is appointed to man once to die and then the judgment, (Hebrews 9:27), which is also true. As after each life, a soul goes back to the Lord for judgment, but that judgment can often result in being sent back to Earth to find the path of salvation through Him, instead of being sent to hell. That's Grace.

This is highly controversial to most Christians, mainly because they have been taught that there is no reincarnation. They've only been taught that there is just heaven and hell. They are obviously missing some important points. One is from history, which was the fact that all Jews, including those Jews who began the early church, i.e., the disciples, all believed in rebirth, as it is still to this day a Jewish tradition to name a baby with the first letter of the name of someone in the family who as passed on due to their traditional belief in rebirth. This belief is that new life will take on the *spirit* of the deceased family member, which is, in essence, what we today call, *reincarnation.*

The people of John the Baptist's day thought he had the *spirit* of Elijah, which is reincarnation. In addition, many thought Jesus was the reincarnation of Joshua, Jeremiah, or Elijah, as well. This "thought form" and belief was in place all the way through 325 AD, until the Church of Rome decreed it to be "deleted" from the canonized Bible. Both the Seven Ecumenical Councils and the Nicean Councils deliberately chose which books and which doctrines would be part of the Roman Church, and rejected the rest as heresy. This was all done under the auspices of Rome. Up until 325 AD, this is why reincarnation was taught in the church prior to 325AD.

"All great truths begin as heresy."

~George Bernard Shaw

Just because *they* decreed it heresy, didn't make the truth cease to exist. They decreed it heresy because they wanted everyone to be on the same page, and they used the extreme of heaven or hell as a tool to manipulate people into submitting to the church, and the religion they formed, instead of allowing them to know the truth. They thought, if people knew the truth, they would think they could live as they pleased because God would give them a second chance and allow rebirth. The earthly church fathers and the archons controlling them didn't want them to think this way.

CHAPTER TWENTY-EIGHT: What Happens When You Die?

The rejection of reincarnation was a form of mind control which exists to this day in the Christian churches, mainly because this is what they've been taught by the hierarchy, and this false teaching continues to permeate the leadership in today's churches, and let's face it, most church goers do not do their own homework, and readily accept what the pastors tell them as "gospel." Likewise, most Christian pastors are taught reincarnation is a lie; however, just the opposite is true, so they are being used as a portal for this ancient alien lie to perpetuate this lie to their flocks.

This "false belief" is actually an alien implant, aka "spiritual limitation control device" to oppress believers, keeping them in the "dark" about God's original plan. This spiritual limitation implant, is controlled by the *religious spirit,* as Revelation 3 calls it "the spirit of religion," which wars against the Holy Spirit. This is why those who were born into the Catholic Church, and all those recovering Catholics out there, must repent of Constantine's Creed, in order to be delivered and freed from these spiritual limitation implants and the demonic oppression caused by the evil *religious spirit.*

Think about this, why would a God who is full of Grace and Mercy, slow to anger, and is just, allow six million Jews who were exterminated in the Holocaust to go to Hell because they didn't believe in Jesus Christ? The truth is, He didn't. They had already been in Hell, and all the souls that suffered at the hands of the Nazis were reincarnated in the ensuing "baby boom" that followed immediately after WWII.

Many actually reincarnated with memories of torture and past life trauma to work through. Many also reincarnated with shame for being Jewish because of the humiliating persecution that they endured that was literally "seared" into their souls. Yet, God, in His infinite Grace and Mercy, gave them a new life, and with that a new opportunity to find Him, and find Healing and Respite for their souls. How do I know this? Because I am one of them. My entire story and testimony is being shared at the end of my five book series, in my sixth book, *CinderElla's Shadow.*

God is not as "black and white" as many Christians make Him out to be. Yes, there is a Hell, created for Satan and His Fallen angels, and all those who follow Satan and reject God. But there are also a lot of "gray" areas between heaven and hell. God understands that earth humans are tested and live in a kingdom of darkness that programs them to believe all kinds of lies about God, angels, ETs, aliens, heaven and hell. Yet, God knows the truth because God is Truth. God has more Love than we can imagine. There are all kinds of mitigating circumstances that cause a person to get sent back to Earth. There are all kinds of lives that never heard of the Salvation, Healing, and Deliverance offered through Christ.

The Lord Himself prophesied that His own people would suffer at the hands of their enemies because they rejected Him. The Holocaust was the ultimate punishment. But was it? The Bible tells us that when the abomination of desolation happens again (Daniel 9:27; 11:31; 12:11, Mark 13:14; Matthew 24:15) that Jews in Israel would suffer horrific persecution at the hands of the final antichrist, far worse than the Holocaust. Why does this happen? Because they rejected their own Messiah and still do not esteem the name of God. See, Zechariah 13.

> "In the whole land, declares the Lord (Yahuah), *"two-thirds will be struck down and perish; yet one-third will be left in it. This third I will put into the fire; I will refine them like silver and test them like gold.* They will call on my name and I will answer them; I will say, 'They are my people,' and they will say, 'The Lord is our God.'"
>
> (Zechariah 13:8-9 NIV)

During the Holocaust, two out of every three Jews were exterminated in Europe. During the time of the antichrist when he sets himself up in the resurrected third temple in Jerusalem and demands Israel to worship him, Jewish persecution will be at an all-time high. The prophets tell us, that the Lord will save only one-third of his people. This one-third will be His remnant. Why? Because one-third will "get it" and turn back to Him. Why does He allow these horrors to happen? Because He wanted Israel to acknowledge their sins toward Him, repent, and turn back to Him, who alone is their Lord and Savior. This entire cosmic drama is all about Him and His relationship with His people, which includes both Jews and Gentiles.

ON KARMA

Karma is a Sanskrit word which indicates the law of cause and effect. Simply put, your deeds, good or bad, will repay you in kind. This is defined in Scripture as: "Whatsoever a man soweth, that shall he also reap." (Galatians 6:7). This is Universal Law. God set this system up, and we are all subject to it. No matter what an individual's personal belief system is, the law of sowing and reaping is no respecter of persons or religion. Karma is created with every action, every thought, and every word.

"For every man shall bear his own burden." (Galatians 6:5). Clearly illustrates Karma, as each man must pay for what he has done, both good and bad, whether it be in the present or future life. Think about this, where is justice, when someone repeatedly abuses, steals, or murders in one life and no legal authority catches them or brings them to justice? All souls stand before God to be judged according to their deeds.

"His mischief shall return upon his own head, and his violent dealing shall come down upon his own plate" (Psalm 7:16); again another reference to Karma and Judgment. But what if his life ends before that can happen? He will return in his next body to reap what he has sown.

"Can a man take fire in his bosom and his clothes not be burned?" (Proverbs 6:27); clearly describes that nobody gets away with anything, even though it may *appear* that way in the physical life, every deed is judged in the afterlife at the Judgment seat of Christ.

CHAPTER TWENTY-EIGHT: What Happens When You Die?

"He who is pregnant with evil and conceives trouble gives birth to disillusionment. He who digs a hole and scoops it out falls into the pit he has made. The trouble he causes recoils on himself; his violence comes down on his own head." (Psalm 7: 14-16). Again, another reference to the fact that the laws of cause and effect (Karma) is at work in every life on Earth.

"God will render to every man according to his deeds" (Romans 2:6). Everybody is judged after each life, according to what he has done.

"But I tell you that men will have to give account on the Day of Judgment for every careless word they have spoken" (Matthew 12:36). This means that after each life, everyone will be held accountable to the Lord for what they say.

"For life and death is in the power of the tongue." (Proverbs 18:21) Every word spoken becomes a living thing, either to minister life or death. "You have been trapped by what you said, ensnared by the words of your mouth." (Proverbs 6:2). This is where the principle comes from that you possess what you confess. This law confirms that we can create our reality with the words of our mouth.

"He that leads into captivity shall go into captivity: he that kills with the sword must be killed with the sword." (Revelation 13:10) This scripture clearly indicates that what goes around comes around. For example, take a man who has taken unfair advantage of women all his life, who has raped and abused them. When he dies, he will be judged, and he will feel what it's like to be on the receiving end of his own abuse. He may be reincarnated as a woman who then is raped and abused. Some women come out of it with an awareness and make something of their lives; others will live their lives as victims without any awareness or consciousness that their souls may be reaping what they've sown in a past life. It seems like a vicious cycle, but the only end is awareness, confessing one's mistakes, and coming to God for healing and forgiveness to break the cycle of abuse in their lives, and in all their descendants.

> "And, behold, I come quickly; and my reward is with me, to give every man according as his work shall be."
>
> (Revelation 22:12)

"But I say unto you, that every idle word that men shall speak, they shall give account thereof in the Day of Judgment." (Matthew 12:36) "Ye judge after the flesh; I judge no man." (John 8:15) Without knowing what someone's karma is, how can one properly judge another? Only God can do that.

> "Give, and it shall be given unto you; good measure, pressed down, and shaken together, and running over, shall men give into your bosom. For with the same measure that ye mete withal it shall be measured to you again." (Luke 6:38) (Karma)

YE MUST BE BORN AGAIN

Jesus talks about being born again. Taken literally, John 3:7 couldn't be a clearer teaching about reincarnation. John, chapter 3 actually reveals an argument, which asks, how can a man be born again? While the Christian and born-again movement interpret this scripture to mean that we must be born again of spirit, by being baptized in the Holy Spirit and being baptized in water, the verse is so literal and so simple, that many miss its double meaning. As Jesus often spoke in parables:

> "There was a man of the Pharisees, named Nicodemus, a ruler of the Jews: The same came to Jesus by night, and said unto him, Rabbi, we know that thou art a teacher come from God: for no man can do these miracles that thou doest, except God be with him. Jesus answered and said unto him, Verily, verily, I say unto thee, except a man be born again, he cannot see the kingdom of God. Nicodemus said unto him, how can a man be born when he is old? Can he enter the second time into his mother's womb, and be born? Jesus answered, Verily, verily, I say unto thee, except a man be born of water and of the Spirit, he cannot enter into the kingdom of God. That which is born of the flesh is flesh; and that which is born of the Spirit is spirit. Marvel not that I said unto thee, <u>ye must be born again</u>".
>
> (John 3:1-7)

Ye must be born again. This part relates to rebirth, not just the rebirth of the spirit, but of water, which is what all babies live in inside the womb. There are so many people who may have a belief in God, but have so many other issues that only rebirth/reincarnation can resolve for the soul. Yes, this verse also means that we must be born again of Spirit while still living in the flesh, but how many people actually live it?

Reincarnation, which is allowed by the Grace of God and authorized by Jesus Christ, has a beginning and an end. Because we are approaching the end of this timeline, that will be the end of souls being allowed to reincarnate on Earth. This is why there are so many souls on Earth at this time, because time is getting short and the opportunity to reincarnate will end soon. Likewise, this is why there are so many souls on earth at this time, who have reincarnated with their "karma stacked," meaning they are living and purging up to three to four lifetimes on earth in one incarnation.

To those old souls reading this book, you will be able to relate to what I'm talking about because you have had such intense suffering with a number of different souls and soul mates. It might feel like your past was a past life, yet you are still in the same body.

Also reincarnation explains why there are so many children today who are born "old." They are born with all kinds of gifts, talents, and wisdom that is clearly beyond their years, that only having lived before can explain why they have already mastered certain talents that they were born with, which is second nature to them now at such a young age. In addition to the fact, that more and more children are being born with

CHAPTER TWENTY-EIGHT: What Happens When You Die?

accurate memories of their previous lifetimes, some of which have been proven and corroborated, which I go into in more detail in Book Three: *Who Are The Angels?*

However, on the flip side, there are many born into so much suffering, which is karma they are purging and atoning for from past lives. The scriptures talks about generational sins and the curses attached to those sins being sent down from the ancestry to the descendants, until someone in that family line says to themselves, "the buck stops here" and takes steps toward deliverance of family and generational curses that are attached to them and their ancestors. This is the deliverance work Jesus taught me, when He healed me of scoliosis, fibromyalgia, chronic pain, and depression, which — Praise the Lord! — is now a distant memory, and no longer my experience nor my identity.

Most Deliverance Ministers understand generational and family curses, but what most do not see is the connection to the individual's past lives. However, when doing Deliverance work, and applying the blood of Jesus to all sin, this too includes sins of the past, which are being reaped in the present life. Jesus didn't come to just cover our iniquities with His Divine Blood, but His Resurrection gives Him all the authority to break the *power of sin* over any one, or any bloodline. The more we invest in healing our spirits, the less work we have left to do in the afterlife.

Only Jesus Christ has the power to break curses. Christ redeemed us from the curse of the law by becoming a curse for us, for it is written: "Cursed is everyone who is hung on a tree." (Galatians 3:13) But what most Christians do not realize, is that this is not automatic, but the individual believer must *appropriate* the work of the cross to themselves, their ancestors, and the generational curses they inherited. Then the power of the cross may be fulfilled to them, and the power of the curses can be broken. (See, Book Three: *Who Are The Angels:* chapter on "Cosmic Karma & Ancient Curses" for further elucidation).

After the final battle of Armageddon, when the Lord returns to defeat Satan's Antichrist and his fallen angels for the last time, Satan will be bound for a thousand years. He will be allowed out of his prison one last time to test the nations and all those souls who have been born into the millennial age and have never been tested before. After that, he will be cast into the lake of fire for eternity, and then the promise is a new heaven and a new earth will manifest. That means the old earth will pass away; nothing will remain. The final judgment will determine which souls will end up in the Kingdom of Heaven for eternity and which souls who have consistently (through many lifetimes) aligned themselves with Satan and his counterfeit fallen angels and rebelled against God through all of their accumulated lifetimes. These souls will end up with them in the lake of fire.

"And just as each person is destined to die once and after that comes judgment, so Christ was sacrificed once to take away the sins of many people; and he will appear a second time, not to bear sin, but to bring salvation to those who are waiting for him."

(Hebrews 9:27)

"He said in a loud voice, "Fear God and give him glory, because the hour of his judgment has come. Worship him who made the heavens, the earth, the sea and the springs of water."

(Revelation 14:7)

"They are demonic spirits (aliens) who work miracles and go out to all the rulers of the world to gather them for battle against the Lord on that great judgment day of God the Almighty."

(Revelation 16:14)

"Behold, I will create new heavens and a new earth. The former things will not be remembered, nor will they come to mind."

(Isaiah 65:17)

"As the new heavens and the new earth that I make will endure before me," declares the Lord, "so will your name and descendants endure."

(Isaiah 66:22)

"Then I saw a new heaven and a new earth, for the first heaven and the first earth had passed away, and there was no longer any sea."

(Revelation 21:1)

Prophets of God Reincarnated

"Behold, I will send you Elijah the prophet before the coming of the great and dreadful day of the LORD." (Malachi 4:5) This scripture prophesies that Elijah will return to Earth.
"And if ye will receive it, this is Elias, which was for to come" (Matthew 11:14). This scripture reveals that Elias also known as Elijah was reincarnated as John the Baptist.
"And they said, some say that thou art John the Baptist: some, Elias; and others, Jeremiah, or one of the prophets."(Matthew 16:14) This scripture is relating to Reincarnation which was the common thought form and belief system of the Israelites and Jews of those days.
"And Jesus answered and said unto them, Elias truly shall first come, and restore all things. But I say unto you, that Elias is come already, and they knew him not, but have

done unto him whatsoever they listed. Likewise, shall also the Son of man suffer of them. Then the disciples understood that he spoke unto them of John the Baptist." (Matthew 17:11-13) In this scripture, Jesus Himself is saying that Elias (Elijah) has already reincarnated, but they did not recognize him and instead have persecuted and abused him, just as they have done to Jesus because the Jews did not recognize their own Messiah.

"<u>I tell you the truth</u>: among those born of women there has not risen anyone greater than John the Baptist; yet he who is least in the kingdom is greater than he. From the days of John the Baptist until now, the kingdom of heaven has been forcefully advancing, and forceful men lay hold of it. For all the Prophets and the Law prophesied until John. <u>And if you are willing to accept it, he is the Elijah who was to come</u>." (Matthew 11:11-14) Jesus said it Himself, that John the Baptist is the same soul as the prophet Elijah. Elijah had reincarnated into John the Baptist.

CAN A DECEASED SPIRIT RETURN TO EARTH?

Mediums channeling the dead are actually being duped by the demons (Watchers), who *watch* everything a person does in their life and have the power to imitate, in voice and even morph themselves into that person, which explains why people see ghosts. Not all ghosts are disembodied spirits; some of them are demons who are imitating those who have passed over to fool the living into thinking they are seeing ghosts. Many of whom are actually being purged in the light and the holy fire of purgatory while the demons are masquerading as them to the living. This ruse has been going on for millennia.

> "I will set my face against the person who turns to mediums and spiritists to prostitute himself by following them, and I will cut him off from his people."
>
> (Leviticus 20:6)

> "'Do not turn to mediums or seek out spiritists, for you will be defiled by them. I am the LORD your God."
>
> (Leviticus 17:10)

There is a reason these curses are in the Bible. The Lord knew how mediums and spiritists worked, and how the realm of the fallen angels set it up to dupe the living. These commandments and this advice was said for the people's own good because they would have opened themselves up for deception and demon spirits. This is the defilement the LORD warned against.

The New Living Translation writes Leviticus 20:6 like this, which takes on a slightly different meaning: "I will also turn against those who commit spiritual prostitution by putting their trust in mediums or in those who consult the spirits of the dead. I will cut them off from the community." Committing Spiritual Prostitution — that's a heavily loaded statement for someone who consults a medium or the spirits of the dead. Our culture is fascinated by those who can see ghosts, hear spirits, or talk to the dead.

There have been countless Hollywood movies made on the subject, along with a bunch of television shows where people are encouraged to participate in the audience while the medium talks to their dead loved ones. So many people are convinced that the medium is actually hearing from their dead loved one, especially when they tell them something personal that only they could know.

But the spiritual truth is, it is the evil spirits of the Nephilim, i.e., demons, aka the watchers, who literally watch and record every single thing a person does in his entire life, knows everything about a person's habits, personality, and character, as well as all the circumstances in their lives leading to their deaths. These spirits can deceive mediums and do so all the time, making them "think" they are hearing from the dead person's spirit, when in fact they are communing with demons. It's one of the oldest tricks in Satan's book. It truly is the original spiritual fraud and spiritual conspiracy.

Every sin and curse has demons attached to it. This is their spiritual legal ground giving them *legal rights* to perpetuate the torment of a curse; sin and its related curses, are Satan's realm. There is an age old parlor game, still going strong today, of "I'm hearing an initial, the letter 'M' Does anyone in the audience have someone who died that begins with the letter 'M'?" How broad is that? If the medium was truly in communication with someone's deceased loved one's spirit, then they would hear their full name. The fact that they don't indicates fraud and the fact that deceased spirits do not have a "soul tie" with the medium. Genuine soul ties allow lines of communications to be open via telepathic links that were already established in their relationship on Earth.

In addition to the facts, deceased spirits and souls have laws to follow in the afterlife about communicating with the living. They are not allowed to just go around haunting and talking to anyone. There are protocols which are all kept in place through ministering angels, under the authority of the Lord, depending on the different levels and holding places where the spirit/souls resides in the afterlife. These protocols are illustrated in the story of Lazarus, the beggar, and the rich man, who were separated by a chasm in the afterlife, in Luke chapter 16. The rich man ended up in hell, and Lazarus ended up in paradise, aka Abraham's Bosom. They were able to see each other, but not touch or connect. The rich man desperately wanted to get a message to his loved ones to warn them about hell, but it was too late, and he was not allowed out to the surface of the earth.

There has always been a fascination with the paranormal, to prove that ghosts are real. Yes, spirits are real, but they are *not* what people think they are. Demons, fallen angels, gray aliens are all real, and they orchestrate the things that go bump in the night, to lure and to entice the curiosity of humans.

The Book of Enoch was rejected by the Roman Catholic Church because it revealed the truth about fallen angels and the afterlife, and how the evil spirits will be stuck in the spirit realms around the earth, until the final Judgment. The following excerpts

CHAPTER TWENTY-EIGHT: What Happens When You Die?

specifically tells us, where they came from, which are also known as Nephilim spirits, in chapter 15: 8-12:

> "And now the giants, who have been begotten from body and flesh, will be called evil spirits on earth, and their dwelling-places will be upon the earth. Evil spirits proceed from their bodies; because they are created from above, their beginning and first basis being from the holy watchers, they will be evil spirits upon the earth, and will be called evil spirits. But the spirits of heaven have their dwelling-places in heaven, and the spirits of the earth, who were born on the earth, have their dwelling-places on earth."

This book is about discernment, and this is a huge area that requires discernment especially on the part of all those who put their trust in mediums for so-called consultations with their deceased loved ones. What a deeply personal and sensitive issue this is, especially for the one who has lost someone to be preyed upon by the spirit world by being duped and deceived. What if the soul is in hell? Do you really think they get to come out for a visit with their bereaved? By whose authority would someone be let out of prison? Certainly not a medium's.

Perhaps this is why the scripture calls it spiritual prostitution, because a prostitute is someone who stands in for the real thing, but is not, and also expects payment for the "pseudo-role" that they play.

So why would the fallen angels or demons go to all that trouble to trick people into thinking that they have been communicated with their deceased loved ones? Perhaps it's because they do not want humans to know the truth about what really happens after they die, that first the judgment and then a soul is sent to be cleansed and purged in purgatory awaiting reincarnation, or punished in hell, or sent to paradise in heaven. That all that feel good, love and light stuff is to keep one believing in a lie, which they are more comfortable with than the truth.

Can a person receive communication from a deceased loved one? Yes, but not through a medium. If there is a "soul tie" on Earth, a telepathic bond that has already been established, then that soul can send a message to their loved ones, in the form of a dream or a telepathy. There are souls whose assignment and work in purgatory is to work with their loved ones to complete unfinished business of all sorts. They are ordered to do so and work side by side with guardian angels who guide them to work within the laws.

Many souls, especially those in purgatory or awaiting their next incarnation, can have access to their loved ones on Earth through soul ties. The ones in hell, however, cannot and do not have access to their loved ones on Earth. However, this is the area where the demon watcher spirits masquerade as these deceased loved ones, getting the loved ones to believe that they are doing well on the other side, and "watching" over their loved ones on Earth. This is a lie, as no one who dies and is in the lower regions can watch anyone on Earth or in the other dimensions in afterlife. I explore this further in Book Three – *Who Are the Angels?*

The Word of God teaches that every human spirit RETURNS to God when the body dies, **"Then shall the dust return to the earth as it was: and the *spirit* shall return unto God who gave it"** (Ecclesiastes 12:7). In God's hands, that *spirit* will either be carried to Heaven by angels, or sent to Hell to suffer torment (Luke 16:22, 23).

Although hard to grasp, since God is often only viewed as a loving God, the Bible clearly teaches that God will take VENGEANCE upon those who die in their sins, having not obeyed the good news of salvation through Jesus Christ, "In flaming fire taking vengeance on them that know not God, and that obey not the gospel of our Lord Jesus Christ: Who shall be punished with everlasting destruction from the presence of the Lord..." (2 Thessalonians 1:8, 9). The punishment is to be cast out of God's presence.

It is clear from the Bible that the spirits of the dead cannot return to speak with us, nor send messages through psychic mediums. Mediums are empowered by Satan, who become willing channels of Satan's power. There's no doubt that some psychics are real, and do indeed possess Satanic power. Just because a supernatural phenomenon has been proved to be real, doesn't mean it comes from the source of all LIGHT.

The kingdom of darkness counterfeits all that the Kingdom of God created. It has been documented in multiple cases that some psychics have helped criminal investigators in missing person cases. This is because demonic intelligences are at work, and they masquerade as light. This is a counterfeit spirit of the gift of the Word of Knowledge from the Holy Spirit, who is perfectly capable of revealing truth and knowledge to those who trust in Him through Jesus.

Yes, it's true that people are gifted with ESP, intuition, psychic impressions, both visually and through telepathy. There is a clear light and dark to this realm, which is often clouded in confusion and misunderstanding.

However, when it comes to crimes and sin, the devil's job is not just to get someone to sin, but to torment them for doing so. Satan dispatches special demons to expose other demonic activity. There are tempters, seducers, and deceiver spirits and tormenting, guilt-ridden, accusing, and shaming spirits that depress and eventually destroy a soul. It's all in the name of spiritual legalism aka *Religious Spirit*.

Only repentance to Jesus can deliver from that entire minion of demons. Then, as scripture says, "there is no condemnation for those who are in Christ Jesus." (Romans 8:1)

I realize cognitive dissonance may set in for some here, what I learned and am sharing here, I learned from personal experiences. I go into more details of my experiences and personal testimony in my 6th book, *CinderElla's Shadow,* however, it's relevant here, as I grew up orphaned at age 6 by my mother through death and 15 by my father through estrangement, and eventual death. I consulted psychics and mediums. My motivation was to connect with my parents. I was an only child. I learned a lot about discernment, through psychics and mediums after being lied to so many times by them.

CHAPTER TWENTY-EIGHT: What Happens When You Die?

I had a near death experience in 2010 where I saw both my mother and father standing before me in a cloudy appearance, and then I saw Jesus, I was blacked out, asleep, and he took my hand and told me I was going to be OK and told me I was going to complete the editing of my books and share them for Him. Since then I repented of all involvement with mediums. I saw what I needed to see myself, where my parents were, just beyond a veil, and the Lord was close by. The afterlife is a real life, just as in the spirit realm. There are places of worship just as there are on earth. They worship the Creator, they continue their journey that that they started on earth, they grow in the light of the Lord. This may feel like heaven, but it's really not the 3rd heaven, but the heaven inside the earth, it's really just another one of multiple dimensions of earth. Paradise aka Abraham's Bosom.

Revelation 1:7 says, "Look, he is coming with the clouds, and every eye will see him, <u>even those who pierced him</u>; and all peoples on earth will mourn because of him. So shall it be! Amen."

How can that be possible? How those who pierced Him (crucified Jesus) over 2,000 years ago, could see Him when He returns? Didn't they die 2,000 years ago, too? Surely they can't still be alive? The only answer to explaining how those responsible for the crucifixion of Jesus Christ can be on Earth at the end of days to witness His Second Coming is that they have been reincarnated to witness His Power and His Glory as He fulfills His promise to return to Earth at the end of this age and save humankind.

Let's pray they don't doubt "who" He is this time, because it's their last and final chance to believe in Him and accept Him as their Lord and Savior.

NOTES:

1. G.W. Butterworth, *Origen: On First Principles*, Harper Torchbooks, The Cathedral Library, Harper and Row Publishers, New York, 1966.
2. Hans J. Hillerbrand, Martin Luther and the Bull "Exsurge Domine" Duke University, 2008
3. Stephen Lampe, *The Christian and Reincarnation,* Millennium, 1990
4. Patrick J. Pollack, *101 Heresies of Antipope Benedict XVI*, 2002
   http://www.patrickpollock.com/101heresiesofbenedictxvitract2.html
5. Bruce Fraser McDonald, PhD, *The Thomas Book,* Eloquent Books, CT. 2011
6. Gnostic text, *Pistis Sophia,* translated by G. S. R. Mead, 200 AD, http://gnosis.org/library/pistis-sophia/ps004.htm

CHAPTER TWENTY-NINE

WHO CREATED SEXISM?

"Thus saith the LORD:
My people perish because of lack of knowledge."

(Hosea 4:6)

"A lie can travel half way around the world,
Before the truth gets its boots on."

(Winston Churchill)

SHOULD WOMEN TEACH, PREACH, AND LEAD? WHAT DOES THE WORD OF GOD REALLY SAY?

I'm going to attempt to clear up this controversy that is used to divide the church and, most importantly, the sisterhood. The following two scriptures are constantly used to suppress and subjugate women from being used by God in the church, whether it's in the role of preaching, teaching, or pastoring.

> 1 Corinthians 14:34: "Let your women keep silence in the churches: for it is not permitted unto them to speak; but they are commanded to be submissive, as also says the law."

> 1 Timothy 2:12: "I do not permit a woman to teach or to exercise authority over a man; rather, she is to remain quiet."

Now, all of you who take these words literally, I want you to ask yourself, is this the will of the LORD, whom you serve? Because, if it is, then there needs to be corroborative scriptures in the Old Testament, to prove that the LORD is the same, yesterday, today, and forever (Malachi 3:6; Hebrews 13:8) and therefore confirms these scriptures in the New Testament to His Word in the Old Testament. Scripture must prove scripture. The Old Testament and the New Testament walk together like a right and left leg.

If these two scriptures cannot be proven and corroborated by the Word of the LORD Yahuah in the Old Testament, then it proves that the Roman Church Fathers who canonized the Bible we have today, inserted these rogue scriptures into the New Testament scriptures, particularly Paul's alleged writings, that served the agenda of the Roman Church of its time, which clearly contradicts and does not represent the will of the

LORD of Israel, whose name is YAHUAH, who sent His son YAHSHUA to save humankind.

Now, let's take a look at what the Tenakh, aka the Old Testament, also known as the Jewish Bible, has to say regarding women and the LORD's will for the feminine side of humanity:

> Jeremiah 31:22: "How long wilt thou go about, O thou backsliding daughter? For the LORD hath created a new thing in the earth, *a woman shall compass a man.*"(KJV)
>
> "How long will you go about, O you backsliding daughter? For the LORD has created a new thing in the earth, *a woman shall protect a man.*" (AKV)
>
> "How long will you go here and there, O faithless daughter? For the LORD has created a new thing in the earth-- *A woman will encompass a man.*" (NASV)

Two King James Versions, one uses the word "protect," the other "compass." Compass means to scope, to range, to extent, remit, breadth, to encompass an area. However, if we look at the original Hebrew, the word in Hebrew is *Tisovev,* which literally means to have an edge over.

So if this is the case, then that means women are supposed to protect, lead, and teach men, rendering the alien implants in Paul's alleged writing to be rogue and incompatible with the actual word of the LORD, and implanted by the Roman Catholic Church Editors to promote their patriarchal agenda of mind control.

Are Mothers not in charge of both boys and girls? Are Mothers not in charge of their son's education, nurturing, and protection? What about single Mothers, whose sole responsibility is to teach and guide boys into becoming men alone, without the help of a father figure? How does the scripture in 1 Timothy 2:12 apply to them? They clearly have authority over their young men. They certainly can't keep quiet, or otherwise, they would fail as their mothers and teachers.

Today you have Christian women defending these scriptures as if they are the Word of the LORD. How can they be the Word of the LORD, if it doesn't say, "Thus saith the LORD"? Paul was just a man, who was inspired by and used by the Lord because of his skills as a scribe. He was tasked with explaining the New Covenant Gospel of Jesus Christ to the Gentiles. However, these scriptures come out of letters he allegedly wrote to a group of Gentiles in Corinth, Greece, called the Corinthians, who were struggling with all kinds of sins and social problems.

Christians argue that the entire Bible is the Word of the Lord, that all scripture is to be used for reproof and correction (2 Timothy 3:16). Is it really? What if you were to learn that there are some rogue scriptures implanted into the New Testament, that completely contradict the original WILL and plan of the Creator LORD from the beginning, regarding the EQUALITY between men and women, that two very powerful

CHAPTER TWENTY-NINE: Who Created Sexism?

truths and mysteries were deliberately covered up by the Roman Catholic Church to disempower and control the masses. Is it any wonder why Karl Marx, who was a Jew, wrote, "Religion is the opiate of the masses?"

If everyone, both Jews and Gentiles, agrees that Jeremiah 31:22 truly is the Word of the LORD, then why would the LORD decree such a thing, and then relent or totally repent of it, approximately 1,800 years later, coincidentally when the Roman Catholic Church decided to canonize the Holy Scriptures into one book?

Furthermore, if Paul's writings are correct, then why do they completely contradict what the LORD did and said to and through His people in the Old Testament?

> Jeremiah 31:33 - "But this *shall be* the covenant that I will make with the house of Israel; After those days, saith the LORD, I will put my law in their inward parts, and write it in their hearts; and I will be their God, and they shall be my people." (includes men and women)

> Joel 2:28, 29 – "And it shall come to pass afterward, *that* I will pour out my spirit upon all flesh; and your sons and your daughters shall prophesy, your old men shall dream dreams, your young men shall see visions: Even on the male and female servants I will pour out My Spirit in those days...."

So the LORD says, it's His intention to pour out His spirit upon all flesh that includes men and women (sons and daughters) and even male and female servants. Then how on earth do Christian women justify believing in the lie implanted by the Roman Catholic Church in 1 Timothy 2, and 1 Corinthians 14? While, Joel 2:28, 29 is *foundational* core belief of the born again movements.

GOD'S ANOINTING ON WOMEN TO TEACH AND LEAD

If women are not supposed to lead, teach, or preach to men, then how does anyone explain how and why the LORD would raise up a woman named Devorah to lead Israel into forty years of peace for the land of Israel?

In Hebrew, the meaning of the name Devorah is Bee. Devorah was the Biblical prophetess who summoned Barak to battle against an army of invaders in ancient Israel. After the battle, she wrote a victory song which is part of the Book of Judges. The name Deborah is identical to the word *devorah*, meaning bee, both come from the magnificent root *Devar*, meaning to speak or pronounce. In this Bible story, this woman was true to her name, she spoke; the Israeli commander Barak listened, and she won victory for the ancient land.

Devorah was also a Judge of Israel, and being a woman, she made decisions to lead and teach both men and women of ancient Israel. The book of Judges tells us of the historical victory of Israel through the Judge and Prophetess Devorah:

Judges 4:4 "Now Deborah, a prophet, the wife of Lappidoth, was *leading* (judging) Israel at that time."

Judges 4:5-7 "She used to sit under the palm tree of Deborah between Ramah and Bethel in the hill country of Ephraim; and the sons of Israel came up to her for judgment. Now she sent and summoned Barak the son of Abinoam from Kedesh-naphtali, and said to him, "Behold, the LORD, the God of Israel, has commanded, 'Go and march to Mount Tabor, and take with you ten thousand men from the sons of Naphtali and from the sons of Zebulun. I will draw out to you Sisera, the commander of Jabin's army, with his chariots and his many troops to the river Kishon, and *I will give him into your hand*.'"

Judges 5:15 "And the princes of Issachar were with Deborah; even Issachar, and also Barak: he was sent on foot into the valley. For the divisions of Reuben there were great resolves of heart."

Deborah doesn't sound like a subjugated woman, a woman who's suppressed by power, or someone who is to "remain quiet." In fact, it's just the opposite; she was a leader of men, who all respected and followed her wise judgments and prophetic insights. This was a position she was anointed for and appointed to by the LORD, who gave her power and honor!

Today's Christian women, who choose to buy into the lie that was clearly implanted into the New Testament by the Roman Church, are suffering from mental confusion, because on one hand, they have a heart to follow and serve the LORD, but on the other hand, they are limiting and thwarting the LORD's power to use and raise them up, according to their gifts, to edify and serve the rest of the body of the Christ. So instead, what they do with their energy is tear down other women who are called to lead, the spirit of jealousy envelops them because they believe they are to remain quiet and powerless. This false belief, that women shouldn't speak, teach, preach, or lead men is a false identity programming that not only limits God's power in the Christian woman's life; it also condones Christian men to continue to practice this deceptive form of SEXISM on their wives.

Today, there is so much gender confusion, with men identifying as women and women identify as men, and all those in between in the transgender community, that Christian women are being attacked by the same type of confusion, which confuses their DIVINE ROLE in the body of Christ, which is not only to support men, but when called, to lead, protect, and encompass, which often means, having an edge on men over certain subjects.

And if ancient Israel's history isn't enough to convince you that the LORD (Yahuah) is still the same in His equality to use both men and women, in 1948, He called a Jewish woman from the state of Wisconsin, known today as Golda Meier, to lead the formation

CHAPTER TWENTY-NINE: Who Created Sexism?

of the rebirth of the State of Israel, who later became known as Israel's first Woman Prime Minister, whose role was to lead all of Israel, including men!

The scriptures are clear about the roles that the LORD wants for men and women in marriage, which is a *partnership*. Partners are designed to mutually support one another, not necessarily dominate one another, but partnership is about one partner offering one thing, and the other partner offering something completely different that the other one needs. Partners cooperate; they do not compete. The basis for the LORD's Divine Plan for marriage, is based on LOVE. First the LOVE of God residing in the man, who is COMMANDED to LOVE his wife.

Beating women into submission is NOT love. Muzzling women who have a voice and something to contribute to the betterment of the family and the community is NOT love. Subjugating women in the assembly of God is NOT love. The failure to LISTEN to women who have strong intuitions about situations and circumstances is NOT love.

Women are likewise commanded to submit to this LOVE, NOT submit to a man's blind authority over her, simply because she is a woman, but specifically, the scripture says, women are to submit to her husband's LOVE and respect him for it (Ephesians 5:33). If a husband is not walking in the LOVE of God, then a woman is not obligated to submit to him to follow him in his sins, whether that be sexual sins, anger, addictions, or various types of abuses — mental, emotional, sexual, and physical. These are, and have always been legal grounds for divorce. While divorce is not God's original plan, He does allow and justify it because God's will is NOT for women to be abused by their husbands. If Christian women think this is what the Word is saying, they are confusing the LORD's plan with Islam's manifesto to abuse and subjugate women, who are treated as second-class citizens or even lower than animals.

Genesis 5 tells us that the Elohim created the Evadamic race (aka humankind) who were a generation of humans that were created to repopulate the earth. This was not the first civilization to live on the earth, as Genesis 1:1 picks up after the first flood, also known as the floods of Lucifer, which was the sinking and flooding of the civilizations of Atlantis, which took place approximately 9600BC.

The book of Genesis is a synopsis of the story of creation. It actually tells the story of Adam and Eve in a nutshell. Today's Bible does not include the original Jewish books called, *The First and Second Books of Adam and Eve.,* also called, *The Conflict of Adam and Eve with Satan,* considered by the Roman Catholic Church to be pseudopigrapha; however, these books are found in the Jewish Talmud written like a Midrash and were later plagiarized into the Quran during the seventh century. Some Arab and Gentile scholars believe they were originally written in Arabic, but that is contrary to Jewish scholars. Yes, they are controversial, but they also reveal how real the battle is over human lives, human bodies, human minds, and human souls are, and more importantly, how deep Satan's hatred is for humanity, particularly women.

Both of these books go into much more detail about how much Satan hated them, which was much more than a temptation over a piece of fruit. These early scriptures tell the story of how Satan tried to kill them multiple times because he was so jealous that the Elohim placed them on the earth, to rule the earth, now a renewed earth, after the destruction of Satan's kingdom of Atlantis. The books tell about how, in each and every situation, Satan cornered them, so the LORD sent His angels to save them from death. Satan also uses the age-old lie that the curse was the woman's fault. This is the basis and foundation for all sexism, which is based on a lie.

Genesis 5 tells us that the Elohim created man both male and female, and both were <u>equally</u> blessed. It's important to note that EQUALITY does not mean sameness. Men and women are very different, but in God's eyes, they're equal. They may have different roles to play, but they were created equal. Here's an easy analogy to remember based on the Genesis myth of creation. Eve was made out of Adam's rib, not his head, not his feet, but his side, which relates to the fact that women were to be companions to men, equal partners, to walk side by side, not to dominate, not to be submissive doormats, but to be respected as equal partners. Sameness is like identical twins. Men and women are not the same, but they are equal nonetheless. Sameness implies competition, to remain the same, or to have one upmanship on others, as in the old game adage, "I'll match you and raise you one." Equality is not about competition, but about partnership.

Here are the instructions for God's plan for marriage in Paul's writings to Ephesus, in Ephesians 5: 27-33:

> "Husbands, **love** your wives, just as Christ loved the church and gave himself up for her to make her holy, cleansing her by the washing with water through the word, and to present her to himself as a radiant church, without stain or wrinkle or any other blemish, but holy and blameless. In this same way, husbands ought to love their wives as their own bodies. He who **loves** his wife loves himself. After all, no one ever hated their own body, but they feed and care for their body, just as Christ does the church— for we are members of his body. "For this reason a man will leave his father and mother and be united to his wife, and the two will become one flesh." (Genesis 2:24; Ephesians 5:31) This is a profound mystery—but I am talking about Christ and the church. However, each one of you also must **love** his wife as he loves himself, and the wife must respect her husband."

How many times does the scripture instruct men to LOVE their wives? It's all about LOVE, not power over another through blind submission. Women who are LOVED and cherished by their husbands, naturally submit to that LOVE in kind. When women are being treated with the LOVE they deserve, what's there to fight about? What could a woman possibly want more than to be LOVED, ADORED, and CHERISHED by her beloved husband? It's easy to respect a man when He is behaving with a loving spirit and treating you right. That's God's prescription for a healthy partnership. LOVE.

CHAPTER TWENTY-NINE: Who Created Sexism?

"When men learn the power of LOVE, instead of the love of power, then man will finally tamper with POWER." (Proteus)

What about the Queens and Matriarchs of Israel, Esther, Rachel, Rebecca, Sarah, Devorah? If God doesn't anoint women to lead and teach men, then how did He empower these women to lead and teach and become the female archetypes of ancient Israel? They have been looked upon by both Jewish and non-Jewish women for millennia as matriarchs and mothers of history.

Then came the lie from Rome to implant doubt and victim consciousness into women through Constantine's insertion into Paul's alleged writings that women shouldn't teach men, but remain quiet. Sounds more like Islam than the true Jewish Faith that Messiah was born into. Any woman who lives by these words needs deliverance! Deliverance from this religious implant, also called a "spiritual limitation device," held in place by demonic religious spirits, aka aliens and fallen angels, aka Grays.

Could there be a piece of church history that most people are missing here? That would be the controversy between Paul and Thekla, which is described in the *Book of Paul and Thekla*, a book that was rejected by Rome and never made it into the Bible canon. In this book, we learn of a remarkable story and testimony of God's power similar to the miracle God did for Daniel in the Lion's Den.[1]

Scholars agree that Thekla was a first-century feminist, and one of the early church's female leaders. The forgotten rejected book tells us that she traveled and ministered with Paul, leading hundreds to salvation through accepting the Gospel of Jesus Christ. Paul's teaching about celibacy is what attracted the young virgin as she felt she was married to the Lord Jesus and didn't need a man. She and Paul preached celibacy to the Roman women, which became increasingly popular, but the Roman men did not like this at all, as many of their wives refused to have sex with them. A major reason why the Roman Church banned this book from the canon was because they didn't want to shake up the status quo in the Roman Empire at the time. To put it bluntly, they didn't want women being celibate. Only the priests were obligated to be celibate; they wanted women for sex and procreation.

However, the story goes on to describe the controversy between Paul and Thekla over the issue of baptism. Thekla felt she didn't need a man to baptize her, as she knew the Lord and she could baptize herself in His name, which she ended up doing in front of thousands in the coliseum in a pool of seals!

This argument over the rights to Baptism, between Paul and Thekla is what inevitably caused her to be reported to the Roman authorities, who then threw her into the coliseum to be fed to a group of lions. Paul essentially turned his back on Thekla, a young virgin woman who he led to the Lord's salvation.

Thekla loved and looked up to Paul, yet the scriptures reveal he was indifferent to her. Now, that wasn't very "loving" and "Christ-like" of Paul to do that to Thekla! At this moment, God gave Thekla a miracle in front of the multitude of people watching. He caused the female lions to surround and protect her from the hungry male lions. After her life was spared from the lions, she jumped into the pool of seals and baptized herself in the name of the Lord. The Lord performed another miracle for Thekla, and that was to shut the mouths of the hungry seals, who never approached her as well.

Women cheered as Thekla was protected and her life was spared right before their very eyes. The fact that this story was omitted from the New Testament is a travesty and a shame, because not only does it glorify the Lord's faithfulness to His anointed women, it also proves that this argument about women not being able to teach men is a bogus lie from the whore of Babylon, aka the Roman Catholic Church, an organization that is steeped in the patriarchy since deep antiquity, which was Mithraism, the religion of Rome and Babylon.

You must know what was rejected in order to understand what was accepted into the Bible canon, and why. Because if you do not know Thekla, then you really can't have a full understanding of who Paul was either. There were political and social issues surrounding Paul which led him to pen his letters. Yes, there are some really insightful words of wisdom, but there are also some rogue scriptures, that stick out like a sore thumb and are incompatible with the rest of God's Word. Why did the Roman Church fathers only include the thirteen letters, which make up half the New Testament?

Yet, people tend to focus, for example, on the one text among Paul's attributed letters that most people seem to know even if they know nothing else about Paul. It is this sweeping accusation of what was clearly already in practice during Paul's time: "A woman must learn, listening in silence with all deference. I do not consent to them becoming teachers, or exercising authority over men; they ought not to speak" (1 Timothy 2:11-12).

There is a massive scholarly consensus based not externally on political correctness but internally on linguistic differences, that the three letters 1-2 Timothy and Titus, were written well over a half century after Paul's death. They were post-pseudo, and even anti-Paulian compositions created in his name but re-acting flatly to his radical views on equality for all those in the Christian community, whether they entered as Jews or Gentiles, females or males, or slaves or freeborn (Galatians 3:26-29). But what caused that reaction to females teaching and having authority?[2]

The obvious answer is patriarchal dominance; men did not want women to be equal to them, let alone have any authority over them. That certainly explains those negative commands in 1Timothy 2 that leaders cannot be female. It also explains those positive commands that Christian leaders must be male. But why does 1 Timothy 3:2, 4, 12, also insist that those male leaders - be they first-level or second-level ones - be "married" and have "children"?[2]

The deeper problem for 1 Timothy is not just female pedagogy but ascetic celibacy. That is why it warns, in thoroughly nasty language, about those who "forbid marriage and enjoin abstinence from certain kinds of foods" (4:3). What frightens 1Timothy's anonymous author(s) so profoundly is the challenge to Roman normalcy represented by

CHAPTER TWENTY-NINE: Who Created Sexism?

Christian celibacy, especially by female celibates thereby out of male control and, most especially, by female teenagers thereby out of parental control. Thekla is the specter that haunts 1Timothy.[2]

Women who choose to buy into this lie suffer from it in their personal lives, because they identify with a false identity programming, which is reinforced by the "spirit" of religion, causing a mental disorder of "fundamentalism," with the emphasis on the word *mental*. This alien implant inserted into the Bible to confuse and suppress women from expressing God's spirit through them, in whichever way God created them and equipped them to be, has created mental confusion and spiritual strongholds of spiritual limitation devices which networks with Jezebellian spirits to keep women bitching, moaning, and tearing down other women who actually take their orders from the spirit of Christ to empower others.

The symptoms of alien implants, the spiritual limitation device, which is held in place by the spirit of religion, aka *religious spirit,* are:

Mental depression, various types of mental disorders, some nagging condition in the body like irregularities of energy flowing through the body (i.e., emotional and physical constipation, hypo/hyper thyroid, high blood pressure, hypoglycemia, allergies, headaches, sinusitis, URIs, migraines, chronic pain, muscle spasms). All of these are symptoms of the "limitation" of the flow of God's spirit and life force flowing through you.

Wake up, ladies! Jesus came to set the captives free. These rogue scriptures are NOT God's will, nor does it reflect His personality, but the personality of the true enemy of humanity.

Satan hates humans, but he particularly has it in for the females because a woman gave the world the Messiah, who defeated him on the cross and spoiled principalities and powers.

> "And having spoiled principalities and powers, he made a public spectacle of them, triumphing over them through the cross."
>
> (Colossians 2:15)

In the book of Leviticus in the Old Testament in chapter nineteen, verse sixteen, it reads, "You shall not go about as a slanderer." But Jesus did say that there would be false accusations against his followers.

All women can be bitchy at times, often it's caused temporarily by raging female hormones, but also is accompanied by the curse of Eve, and a jealous and bitter spirit. However, Christian women should know better to avoid such negative spiritual states and thereby walking securely in the love of Christ. God hates backstabbing and gossip which is something some women can literally "chew the fat" over for hours on end.

> "Gossip is so tasty—how we love to swallow it!"
>
> (Proverbs 18:8)

Sure as sisters, we need to have an understanding ear. Sometimes girls just gotta talk, to vent, to process, to bounce off ideas with another, and sometimes when we have problems with another, we need to talk about it with a trusted female friend, a mother figure, or counsellor. This is healthy, and God is there to "walk us through" our issues. But the type of corporate campaigns against Christian women who happen to be natural leaders seem to come under the most attack from other so-called Christian women. This has got to stop!

Women can be mean, but Christian women do not represent Christ in this corporate gang-like campaign of criticism against what is clearly the work of the Lord to those outside and inside the faith, sometimes yet there's a group thought, which comes from the spiritual limitation device on them, that causes them to fail to discern which are the works of the Lord and which are the fingerprints of Satan.

Let's not overlook that it almost always seems to be a woman to volunteer to teach children Sunday school, which is why, we must in this controversy, go "outside" the scripture to get understanding, because if we didn't we would have NO Sunday school teachers. Bless their hearts. We generally don't make much of the women disciples who were with Jesus — nor of the deacon-ness Pheobe spoken of by Paul. In fact, the entire *Gospel of Mary of Magdal*, was completely rejected from the Roman Catholic canon, which reveals she was anything but a prostitute! Another lie implanted into the psyches of the church followers.

God has always used imperfect people perfectly. When people invite the Lord Jesus into their hearts, they allow themselves to be used by the Lord which fulfills God's purpose and Divine Plan, not only for them, but for Him. Then the fruits of those good works belong to the Gardner, who is the Lord. When the fruits of the Spirit are present, this is the fruit of Grace.

How can anyone on Earth, man or woman, to take issue with that? If you do, then you don't know God, and I encourage you to seek Him in spirit and in truth. Ask Him to reveal Himself to you. Test Him. The Lord has been known to show up in atheist's dreams, appear as a vision, speak to you audibly, and well, His usual way of revealing Himself, is to just show up in your life with His Presence! His Presence is all light, all love. When His Presence shows up, everything gets healed, adjusted, and filled up. It's perfectly ok if you do not take my word for it, so I encourage you to test the Lord, ask for Him to come into your life in a very personal way. Then relax, let it go, be patient, and see what happens.

Now, if you really want to speed up that process, and really want to get to know the Lord in a very intimate way, tell him you're a sinner in need of His love and salvation. Tell him you accept His son Jesus, and what He alone did for you on the cross. Tell Him you want to know the truth about Him. Invite Him into your life. This is an important discernment to always keep in mind, unlike Satan who seeks to possess and oppress people and use humans as his slaves, the Lord is a perfect gentleman, and will never

CHAPTER TWENTY-NINE: Who Created Sexism?

impose Himself upon you, unless you invite Him into your heart and life. Those are the rules of engagement.

I have written this piece, because not only I am tired of the lies, but I am tired of the controversy and strife this causes between women. Women who tear other "anointed" women down, because of this heresy, are servants of Satan, NOT the LORD. It is a great sin to tear down the LORD's anointed. Women who have certain strengths that other women do not have, should not be objects of jealousy and bitterness, but instead objects of admiration and respect, because those are their gifts from the LORD, who gives to each one accordingly. It's perfectly fine to dislike someone, for whatever reason (they rub you up the wrong way, or you don't like the way they talk or dress, all superficialities) but to declare a woman is a false teacher, simply because she is teaching the WORD to others is the epitome of the spirit of "bitchiness."

I hear Christian women, particularly on Facebook, declare other women who teach and preach are Jezebels. I always find it interesting when Christians are finger pointing, claiming others are false teachers or false prophets, that there are always three fingers pointing back on themselves. As Jesus said, "he or she who is without sin, let them cast the first stone." (John 8:7)

Let's discern just "who" was Jezebel? Jezebel was married to King Ahab of Israel. Jezebel was not of the Jewish faith. This was a fatal mistake for the King of Israel, as she caused him to lose his kingdom. This is a story and lesson in what happens to married couples who are unequally yoked, and what happens when you marry the wrong woman.

Jezebel worshipped Ashtaroth (Astarte), who was and continues to be the enemy of the LORD. Because she worshipped false gods, she was possessed by demons, influenced by fallen angels. Fallen angels are also known as Archdemons, and this Archdemon has been named "Jezebel," because of the misdeeds of the evil Queen Jezebel against the prophets of God and against Israel, but the demon came from who the evil Queen Jezebel worshipped, who was Astarte (Ishtar), which came from Semiramis, the mother of Nimrod. This traces back the serpent seed, Nimrod was a nightmare and rebelled against the Lord. He was totally influenced by the fallen angels, history proves it.

All demons are male by nature. They can pretend to be either gender. They may manifest themselves in either men or women; however the demon itself is still male by nature, because it's aggressive and is sent on assignment. Men can just as easily be possessed by the Jezebel demon as a woman can. However, both Jezebel and Ahab are archetypes in marriage relationships.

An Ahab personality is one who is easily manipulated, controlled, and dominated by a woman, also known as being "pussy-whipped," who doesn't consider the Lord or the consequences of aligning with someone who clearly worships the enemy of God. Ahab's are essentially spineless in character. They are appeasers and people pleasers, and have no integrity. Just because someone is a man, one shouldn't automatically assume they are Ahabs. They could easily be possessed by Jezebel, a spirit nearly every Pastor must contend with. This is a spirit that is sent to destroy men in positions of power and to oppose all of God's prophets. This spirit works to bring down marriages and kingdoms. This is an apostate spirit that rebels against the Holy Spirit.[3] See, my article on *Conquering the Jezebel Spirit,* at http://www.findingfreedom. name/conq-uering-the-jezebel-spirit.html

The Jezebel demon is associated with false prophets, as well as acting as a homewrecker demon between husbands and wives, the dominatrix spirit, and the spirit of gender confusion. Queen Jezebel had a daughter named Athaliah, who was just as evil as her mother, and had a blood lust for murdering children and babies. This is a reptilian thing to do. It is this spirit, which today is called the Athaliah's spirit/demon which influences women to kill the fruit of their womb. This demon is also related to the demon Lilith, which in Judaism is said to be responsible for the curse of infant death.

The Nephilim god Moloch, demanding sacrifices of infants and children to be burned on his altar. This should tell you that this being was not human. Those who are not human, want to destroy humans, and they start with preventing human life from ever occurring. This is the demon, behind abortions, which the book of Enoch 69:12 tells us, how to abort a fetus was taught by fallen angels.

Who was Athaliah? Athaliah in Hebrew means, "Afflicted of the Lord." Athaliah was the daughter of Ahab and Jezebel, who married Jehoram, the son of Jehoshaphat, king of Judah, and introduced into that kingdom of Judah the worship of Baal (B.C. 891.). After the great revolution by which Jehu seated himself on the throne of Samaria, she killed all the members of the royal family of Judah who had escaped his sword (2 Kings 11:1). From the slaughter of one infant, named Joash, the youngest son of Ahaziah, was rescued by his aunt Jehosheba, wife of Jehoiada the high priest (2 Chronicles 23:11). (2 Chronicles 24:6) The child was brought up under Jehoiada's care, and concealed in the temple for six years, during which period Athaliah reigned over Judah. At length Jehoiada thought it time to produce the lawful king to the people, trusting to their zeal for the worship of God and their loyalty to the house of David. His plan was successful, and Athaliah was put to death.[4]

The slaughter of infants has long been influenced by this demon who has a bloodlust for destroying humankind. Today's abortion industry is influenced by this same spirit. Athaliah worshipped Baal/Molech, who demands child sacrifices.

We can see today how spirits are named after evil people in history. This ties into archetypes. Women who bitch at other women's gifts or anointing, are repeating an even older more ancient archetype of female matriarchs, which are the archetypes of Leah and Rachel, the wives of Jacob, who later became Israel.

When women bitch and backstab other women, this is the spirit of Jezebel, who are jealous and bitter, and take pleasure in the tearing down of other woman, unlike themselves. This is not only the network of the Archdemon Jezebel at work, (a demon alive way before the evil Queen Jezebel appeared on the timeline), but rather represents the archetype demon in Leah, in her arranged marriage to Jacob. Jacob was obligated to marry Leah; however, Rachel was Jacob's beloved, whom He was truly in love with.

CHAPTER TWENTY-NINE: Who Created Sexism?

Leah was jealous of Rachel. Even though Leah had more children with Jacob than Rachel did, creating more tribes of Israel, she was always bitter toward her sister. Rachel, however, was chosen to give birth to Joseph and Benjamin. Joseph was destined to lead the Israelites.

In terms of archetypes, some women are Rachels, while others are Leahs. Which are you? Rachel listened to the Lord; she was anointed and blessed. She was given understanding of the mysteries of the Lord, and Rachel was the recipient and witness of the Lord's miracle power. Rachel understood and accepted Leah, in spite of Leah's jealousy of her. Leah, was never satisfied, always comparing herself with her sister and bitching and moaning, and greedy for attention, and she did not care if it was negative attention. These are emotional vampires and the proverbial drama queens that produce nothing but negativity within families and communities. Yet Rachel, who was barren at first, trusted in the Lord, who miraculously gave her two sons, Joseph and Benjamin.

There is a wonderful novel, called, *Rachel's Destiny As Written In The Stars* by Julie Bresciani Ph.D. which goes into the relationship between them and their relationships with both Jacob and the Lord, and reveals why the Lord chose Rachel's bloodline to lead the kingdom of Israel. Joseph was a forerunner for Jesus.[5]

Here is the final discernment: The difference between a religion and a relationship with the Living God, is that religion can be bought, manipulated, and is used to control the masses, whereas a relationship with the LORD God, has already been paid for in His Blood.

Jesus taught us to discern by being fruit inspectors: "You will know them by their fruits" Matthew 7:16. When women are successfully being used to grow God's kingdom, by preaching the gospel and leading people to salvation, healing and deliverance, which is available only through Jesus Christ, then those are the fruits that represent that it is the Lord's anointing on them to do His good work. Everyone is called to the great commission, which is to spread the good news of the Gospel of Jesus. The very word "gospel" means good news in Greek. No one is excluded from the great commission. Women are encouraged to share the good news, through preaching and teaching as well. For other women to say they have no right to do so, simply do not have the fruits of the Lord in them, which is understanding, compassion, and a passion for the Lord and His Truth. Knowledge empowers. (Hosea 4:6)

Just because the Roman Church fathers edited the Bible, doesn't mean anyone should throw the baby out with the bath water. Meaning, you need to learn to eat the meat, and throw out the bones. Those who become petty tyrants over the interpretation or misinterpretation of scripture are being misled by the *religious spirit,* and really need to take it to the Lord and ask to be delivered of these alien implants and false identity programming. The Word of the Lord is to empower, to deliver and to save <u>all flesh</u>, women are included. This is the truth to live by.

When Christians are confronted with contradictions, rogue scriptures and scriptures that do not comply to the character and Divine Plan of the Creator Lord, established in the Old Testament scriptures, they always invoke Revelation 22:18, as if to say, this can't be true, because it says in the scripture that no one can edit this book, and if they do they will come down with the plagues described in the book.

The only problem that most Christians mistakenly don't see is, that the Book of the Revelation of John, which appears as the sixty-sixth book of the Bible canon, was a separate *scroll* that was added to the canon. It is specifically a book of prophecy, describing the visions St. John was given by Jesus Christ. So, when this scripture is used to debate or negate the facts that 1 Timothy 1 was a bogus lie, implanted years after Paul died, they seem to think Revelation 22:18,19 is the answer. Read the exact words:

> "For I testify to every man that hears <u>the words of the prophecy of this book</u>, If any man shall add to these things, God shall add to him the plagues that are written in this book: And if any man shall take away **<u>from the words of the book of this prophecy</u>**, God shall take away his part out of the book of life, and out of the holy city, and from the things which are written in **<u>this book</u>**."

This book. This prophecy. This book. It is clear that the way this scroll of Revelation ended — to seal the prophecy with a curse, lest anyone alter its integrity. Approximately 400 years later, this scroll was added to the Bible canon, to become the last and final of the 66 books. Revelation 22:18,19 is speaking specifically to the prophecy in the Revelation, not the rest of the 65 books of the Bible canon, which didn't even exist in one book, during the time St. John wrote his vision on the scroll.

So Christians take this scripture out of context all the time as if to prove that every single word in the Bible must be God's word, no matter what. Not only has this been proven to be false, through the historicity of the timing of the writings of the books and scrolls added to the Bible, but a complete failure to take into account, the history behind the canonization and *editing* of the Bible, which was organized and controlled by the Roman Church.

In the end, does it really matter if Christians debate scripture over various doctrines? No, it means nothing but maybe wasted time, strained relationships, and giving way too much energy over to the spirit of strife. Ephesians 2:8 assures us, that it is "by grace are you saved through faith; and that not of yourselves: it is the gift of God: lest no man may boast."

Our salvation doesn't depend on the historical fact that the Roman Church edited the Bible, added books to it, or rejected a bunch of books that the ancients considered to be the "Word of God." Thank God our salvation doesn't depend on what they did and didn't do; it depends only on the Grace of our Lord through what Yeshua did for everyone on the cross. Yes, many Jews were crucified by the Romans. It was the cruelest of all punishments. But only Yeshua rose from the dead fully healed and restored. That's what sets Him apart from the rest. He came to establish the spiritual path back to God as being the blood sacrifice for the sins of humankind.

CHAPTER TWENTY-NINE: Who Created Sexism?

No animal sacrifice can ever match what He did, nor outdo it. Remember that, when Israel rebuilds its third temple and the Jewish Antichrist, most likely a Rabbi acting as High Priest, reestablishes animal sacrifices, demanding worship and declaring himself as God. If Christians can't discern rightly the Word of God from the inserts of men, then please, explain to me, how on Earth will they be able to discern the difference between the counterfeit Messiah and the true Lord and Savior?

Take a deep breath…Know that it's perfectly okay to accept the fact that there have been implants into the Bible canon to promote the agenda of a group of men, who were influenced by Satan's fallen angels. That shouldn't affect your *relationship* with the Lord. If you are truly walking with Christ, and His Holy Spirit resides in you, who is the revealer of all truths, all you need to do is humbly ask Him to reveal His truth to you. Give it time, breathe, give it to Him, go to sleep, and when you least expect it, He will put the thoughts and truth into your mind and heart, and you will know the truth that will set you free from the lies of the enemy, sent to thwart God's people from the empowerment through His Grace.

Remember all the thousands of people in this world who live in countries where it is illegal to even own a Bible. Yet missionaries report that there are literally tens of thousands coming to the Lord, through the workings of the Holy Spirit, through signs, wonders, and miracles, both men and women, equally being touched and delivered from all kinds of bondages, by the power of the Holy Ghost. These people do not know the Word of God. Maybe that's why God's Grace is being poured out on them, because they are poor in spirit, which attracts God's mercy. Maybe it's just as well they don't know the Bible, as they have no doctrine to argue over to divide them, but they do know the power of God in their lives nevertheless.

Think about that, if you can separate yourself from the manipulations of history, and just follow the Lord, and really just listen to His Spirit, I am sure, He will reveal to you His truth, and teach you how to read the word, and discern it rightly. The Grace of God is God's empowerment to overcome all that this world throws your way. That includes the power of sin, demons, curses, and the lies of alien implants.

The Bible, for the most part, is the written Word of God on Earth. God's Word has been fought over both in the heavens and on Earth. Human history is rife with all kinds of battles over the scrolls. Satan does not want humans to know "who" God is. He has blocked and destroyed so much of God's work on Earth. How about the burning of the Library of Alexandria? Our human memories of humanity's past and history were essentially wiped out. That's why we called it the Dark Ages, because it was very dark to navigate through a world, without our memory of "who" we are.

As a result, most people can't connect the dots to the past. There has been so much missing and stolen from earth humans that it's nothing but by the Grace of God that we are, where we are today. Nevertheless, the fundamental viewpoint needs to mature and see that they are not seeing the full picture, and that's why funda- "mentalists" have spiritual blindness.

Some things haven't changed, like the ancient gods of the past, who were ancient enemies of the LORD Yahuah. They are still fighting over the spirits, minds, and bodies of humans; they want your babies, your flesh, your mind, and your spirit to be their slaves. All three of these gods still operate today through a masquerade of aliens, space brothers, and ascended masters. As I indicated and proved in Book One, of *Who's Who In the Cosmic Zoo?*, today's "Ashtar Command" is a derivative name for the ancient goddess Archdemon Ashtoreth, who Jezebel worshipped. Ancient Baal is today's Allah.

Ancient Molech is today's Satan/Luciferian worship which demands live human sacrifices that continues to be done during annual ceremonies in Bohemian Grove. The abortion industry serves this ancient god Molech, aka Melech, Melqarth, Kronos, and Cronus. Moloch went by many names including, but not limited to, Apis Bull, Golden Calf, Chemosh, as well as many other names, and was widely worshipped in the Middle East.

The Molech idol was a large, hollow brass statue with the head of a bull and the bulging belly of a man. It was designed like an old fashioned pot-bellied stove, with the belly as the firebox. A child sacrifice laid on the hands, and would roll into the fire in the belly cavity and be burned alive. Scripture describes this practice as "passing through the fire to Molech" (Leviticus 18:21).

The good news is Jesus came to set all captives free. He truly is the Great Liberator. He alone holds the power for humankind to be free of the bondage of the sins of following false gods. That includes alien implants, which come from false gods, aka fallen angels.

The purpose of this essay is to edify, encourage, and promote deliverance and freedom through the Will, Word, and Grace of the Lord Jesus Christ.

NOTES:

1. The Acts of Paul and Thekla, from *The Apocryphal New Testament,* translated by J.K. Elliot, Oxford University Press, 1993.
2. John Dominic Crossan, *A New New Testament (Forward)* http://genius.com/John-dominic-crossan-a-new-new-testament-forward-annotated/, 2015 Genius Media Group Inc.
3. Ella LeBain, *Conquering The Jezebel Spirit*
   http://www.findingfreedom.name/conquering-the-jezebel-spirit.html
4. http://biblehub.com/topical/a/athaliah.htm
5. Julie Bresciani Ph.D., *Rachel's Destiny As Written In The Stars,* Astraea Ciara Pub. Co.; 1 edition (January 30, 1998)

CONCLUDING WORDS

*"The conclusion is always the same:
Love is the most powerful and still the most
Unknown energy of the world."*

~ Pierre Teilhard de Chardin

Religions were initially created to lead people into a faith-based relationship with God, but religions were sabotaged by *religious spirits* to actually turn people off of God and Christ which manifests throughout the bad behavior of religious people. Minds have been conditioned today to associate the name *Jesus Christ* with religion. This is a huge distortion of truth because Jesus didn't come to create a new religion but a new covenant with all people under the law of Grace. Grace invites all people of the Earth into an intimate and personal "relationship" with Him, which has little to do with religion. There is a huge difference between religions and a personal relationship with the Living God. This is the expression and outpouring of Christ's Spirit, aka the Holy Spirit. In this movement, people are touched through signs, wonders, and supernatural miracles, through the Grace of Christ, without knowledge of religion or the Bible.

We see this in countries where it is illegal to even own a Bible, let alone read one. Nations like China, Burma, and Afghanistan. In spite of not having access to a Bible, or even having a Bible translated into their own language, people are experiencing the Spirit of Christ through signs, wonders, and miracles, but certainly not without their fair share of persecution from their rigid and evil regimes. Today in China, Christian bookstores are allowed, but their titles are restricted and controlled by their government. This is unprecedented in China's history of atheism, yet the people of China are hungry for spiritual truths and are meeting secretly in home groups to pray and invite the Spirit of Christ to manifest in their lives.

The fastest growing religion today is the charismatic expression of Christianity, with nearly three billion believers around the globe. That's nearly half of the world's seven billion population. There is an end time prophecy scripture which reveals God's math when His plan for salvation of the world reaches his saturation point.

> "Two men will be in the field; one will be taken and the other left behind."
> "Two women shall be grinding at the mill; the one shall be taken, and the other left."
>
> (Matthew 24:40-41)

That is clearly a 2:1 ratio.

> "And this gospel of the kingdom will be preached in the whole world as a testimony to all nations, and then the end will come."
>
> (Matthew 24:14)

When the earth reaches its saturation point, which is getting close now, when believers in Jesus Christ become 3.5 billion, this prophecy of Matthew 24:14 will be fulfilled. There may never be an accurate count of the number of believers around the world, because many who practice their faith underground and in secret, and therefore a Census could never pick up on them, but God knows who they are.

The latest stats reveal that, in response to the rise of ISIS terrorism around the planet, the religion of Islam, once thought to be the fastest growing religion in the world, is now in crisis. Islam appears to be collapsing upon itself as more and more Muslims are leaving Islam in droves. Islam is facing a crisis due to the evil, over the top, wicked deeds of ISIS.

As a result, Muslims are leaving Islam because they don't identify with the radical Islam expressed through ISIS and fear being associated with them. Today's Muslims are so disgusted that many are becoming atheists, but even more Muslims are turning to Jesus Christ. Thousands have been worshipping Christ in secret for fear of being beheaded for their faith by ISIS. Many have already died for their faith.

The appalling deeds done in the name of Allah (who we know is really Satan), have horrified many Muslims causing them to question their faith. The dark night of Islam has arrived.[1]

More Muslims have converted to Christianity since 9/11 than throughout the entire history of Islam. Many keep their conversions a secret because they're afraid for their lives. Islam teaches that apostates and infidels must be killed. Because of ISIS, many have become Christian. There's a huge wave of atheism in the Muslim world, who are human beings that are emotionally and spiritually shattered that other Muslims would feel justified to carry out such horrific crimes against humanity in the name of their god Allah, and who wouldn't question that? The death cult of Islam is moving like a beast, seeking to devour everyone who does not join their death cult. Many Muslims are now saying, if ISIS is Islam, then I want no part of that. This rejection of Islam has led to a huge wave of conversions to Jesus Christ and baptisms in the Holy Spirit. They are learning that God is love.

However, in America and parts of Europe, political correctness has run amok, as so called, 'moderate' Muslims fear being marginalized and profiled because they are Muslim, who claim they do not believe in the more radical beliefs of the Jihadists. These are Muslims, who apparently do not read the Quran, or take the words of Mohammed literally, as the fundamentalists do. Just like thousands of Jews, who do not read their Bible, yet identify as Jewish, and likewise thousands of Catholics and Christians around the world, who are illiterate in what's in their Bible, yet identify as Christian. These types of Muslims, may consider themselves 'secular' or even 'moderate', and see Islam as more of a cultural identity than an actual 'religious' and 'political' path. But as I've proved in my chapters, *Who Is Allah* and *What Is Islam?,* that the radicals and Jihadists are playing right out of their own playbook, which is the Quran and Hadith.

Muslims are facing an identity crisis. Groups like the National Union of Students have refused to condemn ISIS on the grounds that this would justify Islamophobia. An ex-Muslim with a Bangladeshi background, who grew up in Saudi Arabia, says that, in many ways, he found the ex-pat compound in which he and his family lived in Saudi Arabia more progressive than Britain. "It was when my mother came here that she got really radicalized."[2]

Those who wrestle with political correctness in the Muslim world, need to realize that what creates radicalization is within the religion and ideologies of Islam itself. If the Quran didn't given credence to the killing of infidels (Jews, Christians and non Muslims), then perhaps Islam could be a religion of peace, but the facts are the Quran makes it clear, that Jihad is the ultimate expression of Islam. Muslims who do not identify with these viewpoints should be leading other Muslims away from it, but are failing in their efforts.

What's going on in Britain, France, and parts of America appears to be creating more radicals, because they are being trained in camps and radicalized on the internet. The Islamist movement in Britain has been to define the cultural identity primarily in terms of religion, whereas in Muslim countries in the Middle East, it really is more about political agendas.

Islamists believe the greatest power of Islam is the weakness of Christians. Islam is not God's instrument to judge the West. People are afraid of what they're seeing on the news as the signs of daily violence are signs of collapse. ISIS is at the core of the Quran. What many think is radical, or extreme, or an aberrant sect of Islam is actually at the very core and root of Islam, the teachings of the warrior-prophet Mohammed.

Many Muslims who do not identify with ISIS yearn for a God who loves them, a God who cares for their poor and their needy, a God who is mighty enough to save them from their bondages to Islam, a God who can give them peace which passes all human understanding in spite of and in the midst of dangers, and a God who will reach out and speak to them. Millions of Muslims are finding that God in Jesus Christ. As a result, many are taking refuge in Jesus, who is pouring out miracles to the Muslim people. Many face persecution and even death for their decision from other Muslims. Conversion is not tolerated in Islam.[3]

EXTRATERRESTRIAL SHEEP?

> "And I have other sheep that are not of this fold.
> I must bring them also, and they will listen to my voice. So there will be one flock, one shepherd."
>
> (John 10:16 - ESV)

It is my conclusion that Yeshua was referring to extraterrestrial humans that live on other planets and in other dimensions in space-time. In this verse, it refers to the sheep that are not of this fold, I believe this means that they are not of this Earth. The Divine Plan of Salvation was first written into the stars for all to see, and it is God's Divine Plan to bring Heaven to Earth. When the Lord returns to Earth, He will be setting up His Kingdom on Earth, through the downloading of the Holy City, the New Jerusalem, which comes out of the heavens and is overlaid over the old Jerusalem, which becomes trampled on by the Gentiles as Revelation 11:2 prophesies will happen.

Many have thought that John 10:16 always meant Yeshua was referring to the Gentiles, but clearly because the Gospel went out to the Gentile world, and because the time of the Gentiles is drawing to a close, John 10:16 is making reference to other sheep that are not here, not of this fold.

The New Jerusalem is most definitely a huge heavenly city that arrives on Earth because it is actually a Mother Ship that can travel in tact from the heavens to the Earth. As I've laid out, the fact that it has twelve gates that open up should tell anyone that this is a description of a Mother Ship. When this Holy City arrives on Earth, other sheep who believe in and trust in the King of Heaven will come with Him. The Millennial Reign of Christ on Earth will cause the Earth to become a kind of Grand Central Station of the Cosmos, where all the celestial races will converge together to listen to the voice of the King of Heaven. He clearly says, in John 10:16, that He must bring them also, which indicates that they are not here now, but are coming with Him. That's the Divine Plan.

So for all those who long to meet their extraterrestrial brothers and sisters, I encourage you to keep the faith, because if that desire is inside of you, it's because God put it in you, because He will fulfill it at His appointed time.

"I sought the LORD, and He heard me, and delivered me from all my fears."
(Psalm 34:4)

My Experiences With Religious Spirits

I once got into a debate about Yeshua with one of my oldest friends in the world, who happens to be Jewish. She just couldn't believe (there's that spirit of unbelief), that all sins could be forgiven if you believe in Yeshua. She, especially, had a problem with the fact that the sin of murder can be forgiven by those who believe in Jesus Christ. I knew that she had an abortion when she was engaged to be married, because they didn't want to embarrass their families, so they chose to abort the baby before the wedding. Then after they got married, she immediately got pregnant again and ended up with twin boys. It was as if God gave her that aborted baby back, plus one. Being liberal, she doesn't believe that abortion is murder, but after actually giving birth to two babies, her philosophy on that changed somewhat. So I asked her, don't you think Jesus can forgive abortion? She said yes. So why can't he forgive murder outside the womb? Still, she couldn't believe how murderers can be forgiven. This is because she was schooled in the Old Testament belief of an eye for an eye and a tooth for a tooth. It's the doctrine of

CONCLUDING WORDS

revenge. She considers herself a "religious Jew" and was clearly offended by my remarks about religious spirits being evil. This is cognitive dissonance.

This is why people get upset when you challenge what they hold most closely as their "core" beliefs, regardless of those core beliefs being rooted in lies. Cognitive Dissonance sets in, but eventually it must shift to adjusting one's attitudes and beliefs, especially when they learn the truth of their deception.

Another time, during my research and studies, I became friends with a female Baptist pastor, who took me under her wing to teach me Bible studies on deliverance. We would meet on the phone for ninety minutes a week, to pray, read Bible scriptures and discuss deliverance issues. This went on for about two months, until one day, knowing that I was writing books about ETs and aliens, she asked me why I thought so many Christians were being abducted by aliens? She had personally been asked to pray for several in her church who were still struggling with experiences with the Grays. One thing to mention is she had no problem believing that aliens existed. She followed the works of Stephen Quayle, and she was supportive of what I was writing about as well. She was always very kind, friendly and respectful of me, and we got along really well.

When I answered her about why I thought Christians were getting abducted by Gray aliens, she obviously could not accept my answer, and the relationship ended over it. Cognitive dissonance set in to her, and let me just say, her Roman Catholic implants were spluttering big time. She was raised Roman Catholic, but she left the church to become a Baptist minister. My answer was simple, that alien abductions are rooted in past lives. It's ok for deliverance ministers to believe in generational curses, but not past lives? So many of the generational curses in families are rooted in past lives, not only the past of the ancestors, but the past of the soul experiencing it now.

I told her all the scriptures where it was in the Bible (which I have already shared in this book). She went on about it being a 'core belief', and just couldn't get her head around ever reincarnating to this place. I didn't say she had to reincarnate here, that's between her and the Lord, what I was asked was what was the cause of the ongoing abductions? The fact that they are rooted in the past, doesn't necessarily equate them to the future. The Lord delivered me from the Grays, so why not them?

Women like this are known in the spiritual realm as "Charismatic Witches." They are controlled by the Jezebellic spirit, whose assignment is to attack God's people and true messengers. Jezebel networks with the religious spirit, because that was what her drama with Elijah was all about. Jezebel was eaten by dogs, Elijah won the battle, and Yahuah destroyed all of Jezebel's fake prophets through Elijah.

The religious spirit upon her, was keeping her in bondage to the lie that the Catholic Church implanted into the Bible that there is only one life to live, and if you don't get it right now, you're going to hell. Again, is it any wonder why Christians leave the church and turn to New Age circles? All New Agers accept and understand the concept of reincarnation, as do Jews, Hindus and Buddhists. Christians were lied to by the rogue scripture implant (Hebrews 9:27) and its subsequent edited version, has become part of the 'triple creeds' of Constantine, the Seven Ecumenical Councils, and the Nicean creeds, which all true believers in Yeshua/Jesus Christ must collectively repent from.

Then when I went crying to another church about how badly I was treated, the pastor's wife who was born Messianic, half-Jewish, half-Catholic, like myself, held both my hands, looked me straight in the eye and told me, she would never reject me for my knowledge or beliefs, and asked me what happened? When I told her, that's exactly what she did, because I told her that reincarnation was God's plan before Christ, and it's rooted in Judaism. Church politics is absolutely no different than corporate politics or national politics. All run by competitive, jealous and religious spirits. There is a Truth Embargo in some churches, they may preach repentance to their congregants, but they will never repent of believing in lies themselves.

Then I had another friend who was a believer. We had a very good rapport, and our daughters were good friends. They loved playing together. When she found out I wrote a book about aliens, she would have nothing to do with me after that. She insisted there weren't any aliens, that they were all just demons.

So to my readers, who wonder why I would compile such information, it's because so many people have been raised to believe in so many different lies, and if these core beliefs in 'lies' gets in the way of relationships and expressing the LOVE that Christ put in your hearts, which gets you to call yourself a "Christian", then please do act like a 'Christed' individual, who puts others first before yourself, and takes everything to God in prayer. Think always, what would Jesus do in this situation?

One thing good that came out of that experience was in all their gossip of me, due to my knowledge of reincarnation and aliens within the Bible, they all prayed fervently for me that the Lord would put upon me the spirit of discernment and download into me the gift of discerning of spirits, which evolved into the main message of this book series.

> "All things work together for good, to those who love God and are called according to His purpose."
>
> (Romans 8:28)

The Lord has brought me through much religious persecution, not only over this knowledge, but over "who" I am. My mother was an Italian Catholic; my father was an Orthodox Jew. They met during WWII. When they got married, my father's family ripped their clothes in mourning for him and considered him dead. They sat shiva for seven days, which is what Jews do to mourn for the dead. They actually mourned as if he had really died. My father was a sergeant in the infamous Battle of the Bulge, and survived the invasion of the beaches of Normandy. He was perfectly healthy. He'd only married a Gentile, yet he was dead to all of them.

Then when I was born in 1961, they would have nothing to do with me, because they considered me a "goy" because of my mother. In Judaism, they consider you to be Jewish only if your mother is Jewish. Even though, during the Jewish Holocaust, Jews were

CONCLUDING WORDS

singled out for even being one-eighth Jewish, regardless of what side of the family their Jewish genetics came from. But to this day, this remains how Jews are, in spite of Hitler's genocide. There has never been any question that my father was my father, because I have his nose (only a smaller version), and the older I get, the more I tend to look like him.

Then when I was six years old, all their cursing of my mother and my father actually manifested, and my mother came down with a rare form of cancer and died. My father was left alone with a six year old girl. I was an only child. About a year later, my father was sent on a blind date and was matched up to a Jewish divorcée with three daughters. Not long after, he married my step mother, and I acquired three stepsisters. They converted me to Judaism, when I was seven years old, before I could live with my stepmother, and they raised me Jewish and sent me to Hebrew school.

Then when I was fifteen, they sent me to Israel to complete my education. That's where I met Yeshua, in the Negev desert, not too far from a place called Nahal Zin, where many believe is where Yeshua/Jesus spent his forty days fasting and praying in the wilderness. Sde Boker was built right above the Wadi of Nahal Zin on the mesa.

Yeshua appeared to me in a vision and said, "I am the Messiah. Follow me." I had just finished reading *The Late Great Planet Earth* by Hal Lindsey, in July of 1979, and everything made sense to me. The Old and the New Testaments walked together like right and left legs. For the first time in my life, I felt whole. I felt like my life had meaning. I understood that my parents' merging of both Jew and Gentile was the fulfillment of the prayer of Yeshua/Jesus in John 17. I was one in Him. Jew and Gentile became one, and I am the fruit of that.

When I returned to New York and told them of my experience, they all rejected me for believing in Jesus. They mocked me and suggested I join a convent. I was never allowed back into my father's house again. One wonders how, after my father experienced this kind of rejection and persecution for marrying my mother, how he would be complicit in allowing my stepmother to do the same to me for accepting Yeshua/Jesus as my Messiah. The answer lies in the demonic religious spirits that my father never repented of, which I later learned were generational sins and generational curses.

Well, as the old saying goes, "the buck stops here." I have lived with the deleterious effects of religious spirits long enough. It was time to expose these demons for what they are, enemies of the God of Love, enemies of the Holy Spirit, and enemies of the Will of God. Religious spirits war against the Holy Spirit of Truth, Love, and Light. They do not want believers to be empowered with knowledge because knowledge empowers, and it's satan's motis operandi to keep believers spiritually handicapped with a little bit of truth sandwiched between lies.

The truth sets everyone free, if only they take the time to allow the Lord to make the necessary adjustment from the inside out. Repentance is key. If you're truly seeking truth and God, the promises of God are real, and the Lord says, those who seek me, will find me (Jeremiah 29:13; Matthew 7:7). Unloving spirits are not from God. All the hatred, all the racism, anti-Semitism and persecution does not come from the God of Love. Too often, God gets blamed for the works of the satans.

This book is being published for the purpose of those who got caught up in the crosshairs of religious spirits, and really just want a meaningful, intimate relationship with their Creator, no religious frills, just the real thing. The fruits of which are power, love, and a sound mind (1 Timothy 1:7) and supernatural peace, which is like a deep well within, in the face of all kinds of traumas, dramas, and stress. When the Spirit of Christ shows up, His very presence says, "Peace be still".

> "Be anxious for nothing, but in everything by prayer and supplication with thanksgiving let your requests be made known to God. And the peace of God, which surpasses all human comprehension, (its supernatural) will guard your hearts and your minds in Christ Jesus."
>
> (Philippians 4:6, 7-NIV)

"By their fruits, you will know them," are the very words of Yeshua/Jesus teaching his disciples how to discern between the wolves in sheep clothing from the real followers of Yeshua. All roots bear fruit. Unloving spirits are a manifestation of religious spirits, which is the "spirit" behind all false religious movements. They mix up truth with deceptions and distort and confuse the Hebrew language, like the Jehovah's Witnesses and Hebrew Roots Gentiles.

> ***Be careful when fighting a dragon that you don't become like one.***
> ~Ancient Chinese Proverb

Reincarnation was a core belief of ancient Israel and the Jews during the times of Christ. This is the reason why the disciples questioned Jesus about who He was. They recognized He was special, sent from God, so they assumed He must have been one of the prophets of old reincarnated. Why would the disciples think such a thing, unless reincarnation was the core belief among ancient Jews?

"Now when Jesus came into the district of Caesarea Philippi, he asked his disciples, "Who do people say that the Son of Man is?" And they said, "Some say John the Baptist, others say Elijah, and others Jeremiah or one of the prophets." He said to them, "But who do you say that I am?" Simon Peter replied, "You are the Christ, the Son of the living God." And Jesus answered him, "Blessed are you, Simon Bar-Jonah! For flesh and blood has not revealed this to you, but my Father who is in heaven. And I tell you, you are Peter, and on this rock I will build my church (people who assemble in my name), and the gates of hell shall not prevail against it. I will give you the keys of the Kingdom of Heaven, and whatever you bind on earth shall be bound in heaven, and whatever you loose on earth shall be loosed in heaven."

(Matthew 16:13-19)

The auspices and religious papacy of Rome knew that if they allowed such Jewish beliefs to pervade their empire, they would never be able to control the minds and spirits of the people. So they attempted to delete reincarnation out of the Bible canon. Of course, as the old sayings goes, the best laid plans of mice and men fail. Not only did they fail to accurately cover up this truth in God's Word, which I have proven already throughout this manuscript, but they did so with a big fat spiritual limitation implant, which is one of the three rogue scriptures implanted in the New Testament.

This is why Christians constantly quote Hebrews 9:27, till they turn blue in the face, literally when they argue that, in no uncertain terms, there is no reincarnation. Cognitive dissonance causes their spiritual limitation device to sputter because this is a lie and an implant straight from the pit of hell, inside the earth, from the Reptilian-Sauroid-Gray aliens that manipulated Rome and Rome's religious church leaders who agreed to implant the lie for them.

To those Christians who believe that Constantine was being inspired by the Holy Spirit, I invite you to please, check his fruits. Yes, it's true he had some supernatural experiences, he was shown a cross in the air, a hologram perpetrated by Draconian Grays. The symbol of the cross predated Yeshua/Jesus Christ, it began during the times of Nimrod in Babylon, which inspired him to take over the kingdoms. However, if he really met the real Lord, then why did he attempt to delete all evidence of the Jewish God, His feasts, Sabbath, beliefs in reincarnation, and dietary laws of purity from his Creed? Why did he change the scriptures to support his new religion, which history proves, wasn't really a new religion at all, but a refurbished religion of Mithraism and Nimrod? Was this really the work of the true Jesus? I don't think so.

All religions have lies implanted into them, in order to hold people in bondage to the religious spirits. Religious spirits use spiritual limitation devices and implantations of lies to thwart humans from having a personal relationship with Christ through the Holy Spirit. This is the Gospel. It's in relationship that the Good News lays. When people die, everyone stands before the Lord to be judged for their lives, souls are not judged based upon what church they belonged to, or what religion they tried to follow. Thank God for that! Souls are judged based on "who" they believe God is, and in their faith and relationship with God's Savior, the Messiah of humankind, Yeshua HaMashiach, aka the Lord Jesus Christ. It is God's Grace that restores our lives and makes us alive with Christ; it's truly a supernatural experience, so that no man can boast in themselves. Remember, pride was the original sin of Lucifer/Satan. God hates pride, especially spiritual and religious pride. Even atheists meet Jesus after they die.

In Book Three: *Who Are The Angels?* I give details of true stories of atheists who have had Near Death Experiences in hell, and were saved by Jesus Christ and brought back to life, to tell about it. This proves, that you do not need to 'believe' Jesus is Lord, in order for Him to actually be the Lord of the Spirits.

> "For by grace you have been saved through faith; and that not of yourselves, it is the gift of God; not as a result of works, so that no one may boast. For we are His workmanship, created in Christ Jesus for good works, which God prepared beforehand so that we would walk in them."
>
> (Ephesians 2:8-10)

God hates boasting. Refer back to Isaiah 14:12, when he called the fallen one, Heylel, (another name for satan), who boasts in a foolish rage. Boasting doesn't score you any points in heaven. Boasting about how religious you are, how big your church is, or how much authority you have on Earth, as is the case with the Vatican, is NOT the will of God. We are not saved by what we do to "earn" salvation. Salvation is FREE. But we will be judged by what we do with our lives after we accept God's free gift of Grace. We are created to be vessels to perform good works through Christ. Healing the sick, casting out demons (something I'm doing in this manuscript by exposing lies), and raising the dead.

Raising the dead can be both physical and spiritual. Everyone who has a personal encounter with Yeshua/Jesus is never the same. He puts life back into you, where you were hurt, confused, ashamed, guilt ridden, sick, lost, angry, rebellious, whatever the spiritual condition, "contact" with His Spirit forgives sin and restores the spirit of man. It's totally supernatural. He saves the soul from being used and stolen by satan's henchman (i.e., the alien army of Grays, Reptilians, Draconians, and Annunaki, etc). Humans are created to be vessels for either God or Satan, there is no neutral ground, or empty vessel, no matter what atheistic symptoms there may be. The spirit of unbelief blinds people to the supernatural. Denial is not a river in Egypt, but a state of mental illness. Just because a person denies the supernatural, doesn't mean it isn't real. Denying God, doesn't make God cease to exist, it does however, create spiritual blindness and hardens one's heart.

The Catholic Church implanted into the minds of Christendom that we need to accept a Savior in order to save us from the afterlife. But the truth is, humans need a Savior to save us NOW from the manipulations, witchcraft, and abuses from the alien races that have been preying on humankind for millennia. Again, just look at the history, and look what's behind the formation and controls of the world's religions. All those who carry the religious spirit and believe in their own "religiosity" including Catholics, Christians, Jews, Muslims, and New Agers are enemies of the Office of Christ and the Kingdom of Heaven. Only Yeshua/Jesus has the power to set the captives free.

Spiritual limitation implants are both etheric, as well as psychological, and some are even physical. I spend a lot of time discerning implants in Book Three: *Who Are The Angels?* And Book Four: *Covenants,* of this book series. Suffice it to say, implants are

CONCLUDING WORDS

used by Grays and Reptilians to control humans, by altering their spirit through oppression and possession, and controlling their minds and bodies. It's likened to having a demon, but this is a piece of technology, which is demonic. Remember, the word, demon is derived from Greek, which means, 'intelligences'.

This is the motis operandi behind many of the world's religions, which I am asserting were set up by aliens and ETs, who all have hidden agendas to control, manipulate and use humans as a resource for themselves. This is what is behind the truth embargo, the cover-ups of "who" these beings really were since deep antiquity.

Humanity is a species with severe amnesia, not only because of spiritual limitation devices and implantations, but because this ongoing spiritual battle over humans and planet earth has resulted in the cover up of the history of both alien and extraterrestrial interventions, some of which have been uncovered through archaeological finds.

Covering up the truth is an ancient practice done by the satanic forces, who can control humans better when they strip them of knowledge. The scriptures tell us that knowledge empowers (Hosea 4:6). Ignorance endangers. Therefore, knowledge is a threat to the dark forces, who prefer to operate in the dark, which creates confusion and despair, making humans vulnerable and ill-equipped to defend themselves against such an advanced group of beings.

"There is nothing new under the sun."

(King Solomon – Ecclesiastes 1:9)

This battle over knowledge and the truth is certainly nothing new to our planet. Consider the burning of the Library of Alexandria by the Roman Empire, which resulted in the loss of countless ancient scrolls and books. Its destruction has become a symbol for the loss of cultural knowledge and the beginning of amnesia for humanity, because future generations, that would be us, are scrambling around trying to connect the dots to our ancient past, and have our collective memories restored.

Even though sources differ on "who" is responsible for the burning of the Library of Alexandria, there is a mythology that the Library may have suffered several fires as well as other acts of destruction over several years. Records tells us that a fire was set by Julius Caesar in 48 BC, an attack was led by Aurelian in the AD 270s, and the decree of Coptic Pope Theophilus in 391AD either partially or completely destroyed the Library of Alexandria. Imagine if we still had all that knowledge which was lost. I bet you there would be less arguments over who we are, how we got here, who the ETs and angels are, and which god is the God of gods.

After the main library was fully destroyed, ancient scholars used a "daughter library" in a temple known as the Serapeum, located in another part of the city. According to Socrates of Constantinople, Coptic Pope Theophilus destroyed the Serapeum in AD 391.

These types of destructive acts of the past have been repeated recently with ISIS destroying the ancient site of the Bel Temple in Palmyra in Syria. Historians are weeping over these regressive and barbaric acts because there are so many pieces of our past that are both on the surface, underground and under water. Our planet tells us stories of our ancient past, which allows part of our collective memories to be restored.

The spirit and demon behind today's ISIS was the same demon behind the Roman Empire, as well as the Nazis, who also destroyed thousands of books containing knowledge from the past. I wrote about them in Book One, *Who's Who In The Cosmic Zoo?* One really needs to ask themselves, why are there always some group of people along our time line who are threatened by the knowledge of the past? Perhaps it's because it exposes "who" is behind their controlling influences? Or perhaps it is because they want to eradicate all traces of the truth of "who" God is? Or perhaps it has something to do with the alien and extraterrestrial presence on Earth from deep antiquity that the spirits and demons guiding these groups want all traces of removed, in order to give them a sense of "new" life, so humans can't connect the dots to "who" they were in the past, when these so called, 'gods' return?

Maybe their plan is so sinister, that when they return, which they will, as it's on the schedule of the prophetic calendars, that they want you to believe that they are your saviors, because they have more advanced technology than we do, and they can work some magic on our planet, which isn't really magic, but sophisticated technology, and they get you to believe that they are the one you've been waiting for.

Remember, for all those hypnotized by the 2008 U.S. Presidential Elections believed the lie that you were the ones we were waiting for. That hypnotic lie is nothing but a narcissist belief that you are god. The belief that "you are god" is a half-truth, which makes it a lie. When you get a hold of half truths, it's important to make sure you don't get a hold of the wrong half. So much of this deception is not necessarily what they are saying, but what they are not saying. What they are omitting. Just look at today's mainstream media. It's not necessarily what they report on, that gets people angry, but more importantly, what they choose to ignore, that is newsworthy.

When someone tells you that they are god or Christ, tell them to raise the dead, heal the sick and cast demons out of people, and if they can do that, that is a sure sign that they have Christ living in them, but only those who know that Christ is Lord of Lords could do that. That means, the human vessel is humbled by the presence of god within, and never claims "god" status. When that happens, that is the presence of a demon called "rebellion" against "who" God and Christ actually are.

The collective soul (i.e., the body of Christ) can only be god, when we have unity in spirit, knowledge, and faith. Most believers share unity in faith, but we most definitely are not unified in knowledge, and we are also collectively not unified in spirit. This is something that will get fixed, healed, and corrected when the Messiah returns. However, if we were truly unified in spirit, and when humans do achieve this community (common unity in spirit), we can be amazing! We know how to become a group mind, and together work as a team to really accomplish the changes we want. We can do that, have done

CONCLUDING WORDS

that, and we all need to continue to do that, in spite of all the problems we face as a planet. Humanity needs saving in more ways than one.

These ancient Annunaki gods are returning, as they do every 3600 years when the planet Nibiru orbits the Earth. It is clear they are returning at a divinely appointed time, at the time of the Second Coming of Christ, when the Bible tells us that every eye will see the battles in the air which are Armageddon, and then thousands upon thousands of white horses with Christ leading on a white horse come out of the heavens with the clouds of heaven (spaceships), and He ends the war with a breath and Word.

There will be a *Star Wars*-type event over the skies of Planet Earth soon, most definitely within this century, but maybe sooner, when all the prophecies on earth are fulfilled, mostly all regarding Israel. The eye of the storm.

Jerusalem is a space portal. There is a cosmic battle over it. Those who are alive on Earth will get to witness it. The scriptures tell us that, when the Lord returns, it will be terrible. Terrible for all those left on Earth. It's called the Terrible Day of the Lord in Isaiah 66. The Prophesies tell us that people will die from fear, that their hearts will fail them. It will be terrifying. Think of the types of scenes we have, in our generation, been conditioned to accept, which are considered science fiction films like *Star Wars*, *Star Trek*, etc. which give us so many of these space concepts, but what if the truth is stranger than fiction?

The Vatican is tracking Nibiru. The Vatican is also tracking aliens. They want to baptize them when they come. Ah, the best intentions often pave the path to hell. Point is, many people need to connect the dots here, in our history, that the spiritual implants that were inserted into our timelines in the past 1800 years, all point to the events leading up to the end of this Age, the Age of Processional Pisces, the Age of Religion, the Age of Grace, and the Age of the Gentiles. All of these are mentioned in the scriptures, all the scriptures, not just today's Catholic Bible Canon.

The Vatican has a lot to answer for. Here's a rule of thumb, if it's been debunked by Roman Catholics in the past, it's most likely the truth, as the Vatican is responsible for covering up truths from Jewish Scholars for millennia. They deliberately changed the names of God and Yeshua in their bibles and even changed the Lord's name for satan to be Lucifer, which means light bearer in Latin. As a result they've got the world's elite believing that Lucifer is Christ, but the name Lucifer became corrupted when Jerome inserted it to replace the name Heylel in Isaiah 14:12, creating a false god, mixing truth with a lie.

As I've already proved in this book, that the original Hebrew script called him Heylel, which means he who *boasts* in a foolish rage. Jerome deliberately changed that word to Lucifer when he penned the Latin Vulgate Bible. Lucifer is who the Vatican invokes in masses regularly. All true believers must repent from the Roman lies which were implanted to control the masses. Yeshua/Jesus came to set the captives free (Isaiah 61:1; Luke 4:18).

Spiritually speaking, here is the discernment: it's really quite simple, if your religion makes you a kinder person, one who is more loving, cooperative, community oriented, then that is a sign that the spirit of love is in you, but if your religion or cult is making you kill, hate, attack others because they think, believe, or behave differently than you, which is the most extreme expression of the religious spirit in today's Muslim Jihadists, then it's time you find another religion. Hate should not be part of any accepted religion on planet Earth. I remember going to a prophecy conference in the 1990s and hearing a prophecy that Islam was going to be dissolved and cease to exist in the future. As I've already mentioned, it appears that is what's happening, as Islam faces one of its worst crises in its history.

The Annunaki created Islam. Mohammed ascended into one of their spaceships. They used him to insert a competition religion because Christendom was spreading and taking over the ancient world. It is the ancient old war between Enlil and Enki, aka Satan and Yahuah. Nothing new under the sun.

If I was chosen to be the representative for planet Earth, because I embody within my DNA two of the world's major religions, I would say, both teach the importance of showing kindness, mercy, and goodness to others. Both teach relationship. Right relationship with God and right relationship with others. Somehow, spiritually speaking, both Judaism and Christianity really eventually merge into one, because the Lord Yahuah and Yahshua both rule them, and it's their Divine Will to make them One.

However, Islam, holds within it the tenets of a different alien god. Yes, Mohammed was abducted when he ascended. The angel Gabriel was not the same Gabriel in the Hebrew Bible; it was the counterfeit Gavriel, who is a fallen angel. I go into all those discernments in Book Three: *Who Are The Angels*?, proving that all the names of Heaven's Angels were counterfeited by the Fallen Angels and the Draconian Empire.

But suffice it to say, Mohammed's alleged manuscript, known as the Quran, contains hate and condones lies, which, spiritually speaking, is against the Words of Yahuah in the Bible. Point for point, they are opposite, diametrically opposed. Yahuah teaches his people to treat each other with respect. That means, not having sexual relations with your siblings, your parents, and, especially, no touching children sexually. The Judeo-Christian faith is unified on morals. We endeavour to protect the innocent, children are off limits for sexual pleasure, and we also teach godly forms of discipline on our children, not cruel and inhumane types of punishment. We do not dismember the body. Our God teaches mercy, therefore most people of the Judeo-Christian faith attempt to be good people, by being tolerant of others, forgiving and giving. When we are weak in these areas, we rely on the Lord's Spirit to strengthen us and carry us through.

Whereas Muslims are implanted to think it's ok to engage in every type of perversion that comes straight from the reptilian gods, who want to consume humans, in both flesh and blood and in soul essence, which is human spiritual energy. Fundamental Muslims carry in their spirit, a demon hell bent on killing, creating the death cult of today's Jihadists. Islam is in crisis; the religion is collapsing. The god who is Allah has

CONCLUDING WORDS

been exposed to be a demonic reptilian Draconian alien being, that wants to enslave, use, abuse, and vampirize humans. This is the presence of demons, of mean and evil reptilian demons, who have no mercy on humans. That's the spiritual battle.

So what we have is a clash between two kingdoms. Satan's kingdom of darkness and Christ's Kingdom of Heaven. This is a battle between two gods. Allah is Satan who was Baal, ancient Enlil, the enemy of Yahuah in the Old Testament. You know that a major showdown is coming between them over the Jerusalem Portal, which is located on the Temple Mount. This will be the final battle on Earth. It culminates into the end time battle of Armageddon.

This is why it's relevant for today's believers to give their prayers and attention to the people in this region, who are going through this battle on the ground. They are all suffering on both sides. However, the war between these two gods is resulting in the most wicked, sickest, perverted atrocities and persecutions on both Jews and Christians. They need to be supported in this war, not ignored. The Jihadists are not going to win.

The final chapter in prophesy is the rise and fall the New World Order. We know because the prophetic timeline has been right so far, so we can expect the ending to be just as accurate. The New World Order fails. Sorry to spoil the end of the story for you, but that's its destiny. Now, take a look at today's world, you wonder, how do you get all these people to share one belief? The Book of Revelation tells us that the last era on Earth, before the Second Coming of Christ arrives, will be a One World Government, sharing a global currency, and following the same religion. How on Earth could humanity share one religion? I don't know about you, but when I look at this world, that looks impossible.

But that is the Prophesy nevertheless. There are efforts under way within today's liberals and the ruling archons of this world, toward trying to merge Christianity with Islam, by calling it Chrislam. The Vatican is pushing for this mainly, with just a couple of the mainstream popular evangelists like Rick Warren and Joel Osteen, appearing to support this, almost blindly. Yet, based on the Word of God and prophecies, there is no merging of these two opposite doctrines.

The only way to connect Muslims with Jews and Christians is for Muslims to merge into Christianity, which is rooted in the true Hebraic faith, Judaism, which is fulfilled through Yeshua through God's Grace. That's the only possible circle it can take, in order for the world to become One faith. The world must unite within and through Christ, which is essentially the final outcome that gets completed in the coming New Age, the Millennial Reign of Christ. One thousand years of a Golden Age, Heaven is coming to Earth.

Today's Christians, mostly unaware, are still under the stronghold of Constantine's Creed, which resurrected Antiochus, the first antichrist, who was all about Jewish persecution and anti-Semitism. Today's Christians can't serve the true Jesus and hate Jews at the same time.

It is my assertion and discernment that the spirit and principality of satan that is behind all forms of anti-Semitism, which is hatred for Jews and anything Jewish, that includes hatred for the God of Israel, is rooted in JEALOUSY. They were jealous that the Lord Yahuah chose a group of people called the Israelites, aka Jews, over the pagan Gentiles to represent Him on Earth. These demons are still around today, they express themselves throughout the Muslim and Gentile worlds, and that includes some Christians who were taught the lies of replacement theology.

Rome was responsible for paganizing Christ, creating a new religion far removed from the God of Israel. Today's Christian denominations need to REPENT corporately of Constantine's Creed, and allow the LORD to set them free from alien implanted spiritual limitation devices which sits in the spirit bodies of all Christian believers who blindly follow the auspices of Rome. Rome has always been an enemy of God and His people, and Romans 11:11 says, Gentiles are grafted in, however, in doing so, they must REPENT of both the Nicean and Constantine's Creed because both are antichrist, anti-Semitic, anti-Yahuah, and lies.

What distinguishes what Yeshua did for us on the cross, from the Jewish priests sacrificing animals for the blood covering of sins is Yeshua's blood has the power to break the "power" of sin over our lives, not just to cover up the sin. This is not just some hypothesis. This is for real and has been proven over and over again in the lives of believers worldwide, especially in people who are illiterate of the Bible and religions.

This is what true deliverance is — no longer struggling with the flesh or mind, having freedom from the power of sin, that includes all related spiritual curses and assignments stemming from sin, both generationally and individually. This teaching unfortunately has been lost in many of today's churches, who are essentially asleep in the light.

The steps to take is repentance of not only one's individual sinful patterns, but also the family trances of their sinful patterns, that comes down through one's bloodlines and past lives, which are biblical foundations for freedom. Christian churches need to collectively repent of 'unconsciously' following after the Roman Empire's religion. Every prayer of repentance is heard and responded to with oceans of God's Grace, which is all anyone needs to be set free and restored to health. Only many of today's churches no longer teach this, which is why so many struggle with addictions and illness. Being saved means everything, including deliverance and freedom from the patterns of the past and old self.

> "Because the creation itself also shall be delivered from the bondage of corruption into the glorious liberty of the children of God. "For we know that the whole creation groans and travails in pain together until now."
>
> (Romans 8:21, 22 KJV2000)

CONCLUDING WORDS

CHILDREN OF GOD VS CHILDREN OF THE DEVIL

The Bible tells us that there is an actual genetic bloodline that belongs solely to Satan's seed. It begins in the story in Genesis, when the Lord curses the serpent (who was not yet a snake), into a snake and tells of his destiny to meet the seed of God through a woman, to crush his head (meaning authority in Hebrew), while he will only bruise His heel. In this prophetic scripture, the Lord acknowledges that Satan has a seed, because he curses his seed and tells him that he will always be at enmity with the Lord's seed. Genetics is speaking here.

> "The LORD God said to the serpent, "Because you have done this, Cursed are you more than all cattle, And more than every beast of the field; On your belly you will go, And dust you will eat All the days of your life; And I will put enmity Between you and the woman, And between **your seed and her seed;** He shall bruise you on the head, And you shall bruise him on the heel."
>
> (Genesis 3:14, 15)

The genetic bloodlines of satan's seed, are the serpent races, the alien hybrid races, stemming from several groups of renegade aliens on Earth, who all war against the bloodlines of Yahuah. This is the cause and foundation for all racism on Earth.

The Annunaki are circulating a lie that they created humankind. As I've detailed in Book One, *Who's Who In The Cosmic Zoo?,* this is a misnomer. The Annunaki did not create humans; they manipulated them genetically to turn humans into a slave race to serve them.

The human race was created perfectly in the image and likeness of the Elohim gods, with all twelve strands of DNA, as the original blueprint for the human race proves through genetics. Today's scientists are baffled by what they call "junk DNA," in the human genome. These are essentially the missing ten strands of DNA that have been switched off through genetic manipulation and genetic engineering. Humans are using only two of the twelve strands of DNA. The ten strands of DNA were disabled by these alien geneticists in order to control and enslave humans into their program.

The Cuneiform tablets that Zecharia Sitchin interpreted in his book series, *The Earth Chronicles,* tells us that the Annunaki ET gods, manipulated the DNA of humans, by mixing their DNA and human DNA together. It does not tell you "who" created the original humans that they were using to manipulate the DNA with, and the women that these gods found so attractive to mate with. The tablets do not tell you "who" put them on Earth.

However, the scriptures tell, between the book of Genesis and the rejected texts of Enoch, the story of "who" created the human race and put humans on Earth.

What we're dealing with is an "alien" presence on Earth, who wants to deceive humans into believing that they are not only humanity's creators, but also humanity's saviors. This is a huge ruse, with the agenda to enslave and control humans for their blood, and their soul essence.

> "Forasmuch then as the children are partakers of flesh and blood, he also himself likewise took part of the same; that through death he might destroy him that had the power of death, that is, the devil (the Reptilian Alien presence); and might free those who through fear of death were subject to slavery all their lives."
>
> (Hebrews 2:14, 15)

WHO IS THE SYNAGOGUE OF SATAN?

Are all Jews part of this? Or just a few elite Pharisaical types?

Message to the Church in Philadelphia:

> "I know your deeds. Behold, I have put before you an open door which no one can shut, because you have a little power, and have kept My word, and have not denied My name. Behold, I will cause those of the *synagogue of Satan, who say that they are Jews and are not*, but lie-- I will make them come and bow down at your feet, and make them know that I have loved you. Because you have kept the word of My perseverance, I also will keep you from the hour of testing, that hour which is about to come upon the whole world, to test those who dwell on the earth.
>
> (Revelation 3:8-10)

Here's the deal with Jews, there are many types of Jews. Not all the same. Jews are tribal. There are some Jews who belong to the Illuminati, the family of Rothschild, for one. They are hated by conspiracy theorists worldwide for being the puppet masters behind the funding of war on both sides, to keep that Militarized Industrial Complex going. So they would orchestrate a problem, to justify a solution, something called the Hegelian Principal, so people will accept another type of "social control."

However, not all Jews support each other, just look at Israel's Parliament. There are many types of viewpoints, but one thing Jews do unite on is Israel. However, there is a sect of religious Jews who do not. They are the Hasidim, and they believe the Jew is not supposed to return to Israel until the Messiah returns. They live outside of Israel. So these Jews confuse Gentiles, Jew haters, and those who are generally anti-Semitic in their views on Jews.

But the truth of the matter is nobody in Israel or the rest of the Jews in the world really care what the Hasidim think. The majority of Jews support Israel. Yes, then there is the BDS movement (Boycott, Divestment and Sanctions) that is led by American liberal Jews, who stump everyone in both Christian and Jewish communities. Why are they always voting against Israel? This is the nature of Jews. As the comedian Rodney Dangerfield once joked, "If you put two Jews in a room, you get ten opinions."

Just as perfect unity among Christians does not exist, so it goes among Jews as well. There are certain mindsets, in both religious and political circles, that are rooted in the past. On one level, they draw strength from it, but ironically they are handicapped and blinded by a kind of stubbornness as well, spiritually speaking.

If more Jews knew Yeshua personally, Israel would be in a whole different situation with respect to the rest of the world. But, this is what is destined to happen, at the end, so might as well prepare, heh?

I am convinced that when Gentiles behave in an anti-Semitic way toward their Jewish brethren, they block blessings from the Lord. The covenant of blessings and curses applies over and again, in Genesis 12:3. We see this manifest for every nation historically that has come against God's people. Empires fall, nations crumble, people end up reaping what they sow, when they sow hatred and genocide. It never works out well for the hater, never. So we should take note from history, and just stop it.

Because it is the Lord's will to bring the Jew and the Gentile together and join them as one, the only resistance, are unbelieving Jews, and anti-Semitic Christians. But hey, nothing's impossible with God!

The concept behind discernment is to recognize the fruits of what powers do. What is the end result of a belief system, or a policy, or new legislature? What are its fruits?

A Tree Recognized by its Fruit:

> "Either make the tree good and its fruit good, or make the tree bad and its fruit bad; for the tree is known by its fruit. You brood of vipers, how can you, being evil, speak what is good? For the mouth speaks out of that which fills the heart. The good man brings out of his good treasure what is good; and the evil man brings out of his evil treasure what is evil."...
>
> (Matthew 12:33-35)

When Christians love Jews, miracles seem to happen to them. They just do. I've witnessed firsthand, in Colorado, during annual Israel Awareness Days where Christians and Jews gather to unite for Israel and the Jewish People. Suffice it to say, "it's a God thing," meaning, that only the presence of God could make that happen.

It's pretty amazing stuff to get Orthodox Rabbis, Holocaust survivors and their families, along with Jewish community leaders to gather under one roof, that roof being a Christian non-denominational church of over three thousand Christians, to spend a day and night together honouring the history of the Jewish people and Israel.

Every year, the senior pastor, apologizes and repents to the Jewish people for centuries of persecution, misunderstanding, and anti-Semitism. It is something that is truly a godsend, and if you want to taste the presence of God, Yahuah, and Yeshua under one roof with over three thousand people, attend one of these Nights to Honor Israel, and you will see that, not only is this possible, the heart energy in the room is rich, moving, and joyful.

Nobody evangelizes Jews on that night. It is all about showing "Christ's love" to the Jewish people. Hundreds of thousands of dollars flow to Israeli charities that support Israeli orphans and special needs children in Israel, while a multi-talented group of musicians and dancers entertain, who regularly tour Israel as their "mission" to entertain and encourage the IDF, Israel's Defence Forces, to let them know they are not alone in this world. Many of whom feel that way, when fighting both physical and propaganda wars.

So it proves that it can happen because it is happening, and it's growing, growing exponentially every year, as Christians United for Israel. This is truly a piece of End Times Prophecy being fulfilled. All of Israel is supposed to get saved through Yeshua, and Gentile Christians are expected to love Jews, while being "grafted in" to Israel's covenants given to both Jews and Gentiles from Yahuah.

So, yeah, while the Pharisaical ones may be satan's strongholds on the Jews, the rest of the Jewish people, many of whom are secular, even atheists, liberal-minded, but Zionists nonetheless, unite through the homeland, Israel. These people should not be hated, many of them are poor, and there are many social problems in Israel. There are many Christian outreaches making a difference in the lives of Holocaust survivors, orphans, the IDF, and the poor of Israel, and should continue till the Messiah returns. This was what He wanted, when He said, "And the King shall answer and say unto them, Verily I say unto you, Since you have done it unto one of the least of these *my brethren*, you have done it unto me" (Matthew 25:40). His brethren, the Jewish people.

Every Christian should adopt a Jew to befriend. Show kindness, dissolve generations of hatred, anti-Semitism, repent, turn around from what conspiracy theorists says, stop believing in the lies perpetrated by anti-Semitic propaganda, that came straight out of Hitler's playbook, *Mein Kumpf*, which was, and still is, the anti-Semitic and anti-Zionist manifesto which every single Jew hater, anti-Israel, and anti-Zionist person quotes from; some of whom are completely unaware that they are in fact, regurgitating Hitler's words because it is spread around the world through various conspiracy circles and copied from person to person.

Those who do perpetuate this anti-Semitic propaganda, must track the source of their hatred of a race of people that has given them people who they honor, the likes of which are Jesus, Moses, Abraham, Albert Einstein, Sigmund Freud, Carl Sagan, Jonas Salk, Edward Teller, Fritz Haber, Roald Hoffman, Itzak Perlman, Julio Iglesias, Barbara Streisand, Bob Dylan, Paul Newman, Elizabeth Taylor, Stephen Spielberg, Harrison Ford, William Shatner, Leonard Nimoy, and the list goes on. Hundreds and thousands of Jews and those with Jewish DNA have made important contributions to this world, which most people could not live without. Israel is well-known for its long list of innovations in technology, medicine, and desert farming, which people in other desert countries have learned to adopt.

People need to stop hating and being jealous of Jews. You wouldn't have your salvation in Yeshua/Jesus without the Jewish race. That's the way God planned it.

When the Israelites were cast out of Israel after 70AD, they dispersed throughout the world, resulting in many mixed marriages, causing Jewish DNA to be spread throughout Europe, Asia, Japan, the Americas, Russia, etc. There are more people who have Jewish DNA than we realize, and this means that, if you're a hater, perhaps you should first check your family tree and see if any of your ancestors married a Jew.

Yes, the religious pharisaical Jews were chastised for being a "brood of vipers" by John the Baptist, who was truly the last of the Old Testament prophets. However, that doesn't make all Jews serpents. There were twelve tribes, many of whom were created from mixed marriages. Joseph married an Egyptian Princess, the tribes Manasseh and Ephraim were a result of the mixing of two types of DNA. Not all purely Jewish. I get into all the twelve tribes in detail, tracing "who" they are today in Book Four: *Covenants*.

So this should tell discerning Christians something; that it's the religious spirit that received all the Woes from Yeshua, not everyone was viewed equally in the ancient world, just as it is today, still on many levels. There were the poor and needy, who Yeshua's heart went out to, and then there were the ruling priests, who challenged Yeshua, but more importantly, it was Yeshua who challenged their hearts in the end, and cursed the spirits of hypocrisy.

Christians who are "grafted in" to Israel, must be mindful of this spiritual condition, which is the spiritual temptation to adopt the ancient attitudes of the Pharisees and Jewish Priests, who were cursed by both Yahuah in Malachi 2:2, and Yeshua in Matthew 23, which unfortunately happens to be prevalent in many of today's Christian churches because it's attached to Catholic Priests, Christian pastors and ministers, who are blinded by this evil spirit.

EIGHT WOES TO THE RELIGIOUS SPIRITS

Yeshua/Jesus, declared eight separate and distinct woes upon the Pharisees, all of whom carried the "religious spirit," or "spirit of religion," which was the very spiritual stronghold that conspired to kill and crucify him. A "woe" is a curse, a wretched miserable state of despair, much of which have come to pass on them after Yeshua left the earth. Just look at the history of Jews, the priesthood, and the millennia of persecution of Jews.

Nevertheless, a large part of Christ's ministry was teaching discernment and wisdom to Jews about the importance of following the "spirit" of the law versus the "letter" of the law. And as legalists, the priesthood was spiritually blinded to Yeshua's teaching.

Now, what we have today is a church that has morphed itself into expressing the very same spirit that crucified their Lord and Savior. How is that possible? Is it any wonder that Christians are now targets of the same kind of persecution that has for millennia affected Jews?

Just about every problem that comes out of religion, from the extremism of fundamentalism, through its expression of today's jihadists, to the extremism of atheism and the rebellion against any form of religion, and all the legalistic, cultic expressions in between, the spirit of religion is a spirit of control, which essentially is spiritual witchcraft. Ever wonder why so many people major on the minors and minor on the majors? How many people focus on looking good on the outside while being empty and dirty on the inside? This is the presence and evidence of a religious spirit in your life. Jesus spoke woes against religiosity, pompousness, pretentiousness, spiritual pride, snobbishness, and haughtiness.

A false prophet is one who falsely claims the gift of prophecy or divine inspiration, or who uses that gift for evil ends. Often, someone who is considered a "true prophet" by some people is simultaneously considered a "false prophet" by others, even within the same religion as the "prophet" in question. The term is, sometimes, applied outside religion to describe someone who fervently promotes a theory that the speaker thinks is false.

In today's Christianity, authors, pastors and speakers are labelled false prophets, even though none of them claim "prophet" status. Everybody calls everybody else "false," for all kinds of reasons. There is so much suspicion and fear that moves through Christians, coupled with ignorance, because they just get a "bee" in their bonnet about someone, that "bee" is a "spirit." Christians need to recognize that in themselves and work with Jesus to heal it.

Know this fact: It is this subtle, demonic, religious spirit that attacks God's anointed. You would expect this type of behavior from the unbeliever or the atheist. But more people who are actually "out there" serving God's Kingdom get attacked from fellow Christians. Those Christians who are constantly pointing fingers at other Christians, claiming they are false prophets, have this spirit on them.

Discernment is about love. The religious spirit, whose agenda is to keep people away from the power in the Holy Spirit, which is the Spirit of Love, Grace, Mercy, Forgiveness, Healing, and Power over the demonic realms, is "who" is getting assaulted when Christians finger point at other Christians. This spirit works for Satan's hierarchy to cast doubt on God's people, cast doubt on what the Spirit is doing within the "redeemed."

So let me get this out now, before you read further. I am of the redeemed. I am far from perfect, and just another sinner the Lord has rescued and has healed. I've been a writer all my life, and eventhough I'm a published author, I do not claim "prophet" status, nor do I claim to be the only voice out there. But I know what I know and, more importantly, "who" I know is where my discernment comes from.

One thing I will share briefly, of my testimony and personal past, at the end of my three and a half year education in Israel, after I had a vision of Jesus in the Negev Desert at Sde Boker, I travelled to South Africa. I was led to a group in Capetown, who were Messianic, and I was later baptized in both water and spirit in the Capetown Assemblies of God. I became one of their missionaries, and was sent on assignments in Hillbrow,

CONCLUDING WORDS

Johannesburg, Zululand, Kwa Sizabuntu, and Durban for two years. I was immersed into the outpouring of the Spirit in Apartheid South Africa, which was called a "revival" literally right before this stronghold was about to crumble.

I witnessed firsthand the source and foundation of South Africa's racism, which was rooted in the misunderstanding and misinterpretations of the Dutch Afrikaner's view of the book of Genesis, and the sons of Noah, which they used to justify their superiority over black people with.

The supernatural occurrings that were taking place two years before the end of Apartheid, became the "norm." I witnessed healings, demonic deliverances, and one twenty-three-year-old woman who died of kidney failure was raised from the dead, completely healed, with a compelling message from the Lord, one in which I never forgot.

She was shown, through her journey into the afterlife that she couldn't enter the gates of heaven, which was at the top of this mountain, where the Lord sat. As she was climbing the mountain to get to Him, she had strings around her ankles which weighed her down. The Lord showed her that those strings were her bitterness, her offenses, and her inability to forgive. He told her that He would heal her and send her back to her life, but He wanted her to tell everyone this: "That only forgiveness loosens the strings, and frees you to journey into heaven."

That was it. She was back in her body after being clinically dead for nearly an hour, completely healed full of joy from the Lord, and eager to start forgiving her family. Take note of this: Jesus didn't tell her to follow any religion, change what she was eating, and change the day she chose to worship and go to church in order to get through the gates of heaven. No, it was all about a change of the heart.

The religious spirit wants you to feel that you have to perform a particular way in order for God to love you, or to "earn" your ticket to heaven. This is a lie. God is Love. God doesn't just give Mercy. God is Mercy. He wants His children to learn to be more like Him, as challenging as it may be in this world full of disappointments, negativity, and wars. That's exactly why God needs humans to "invite" Him into their hearts, so His spirit can take over and teach us and work through us to be the light in the darkness, to a wounded, dying world.

This is what the "born-again" experience is about. It is about the embodiment of the Lord's strength. Where you are weak, you rely on the Lord's power; where you are powerless, you rely on the Lord's victory; where you are defeated, the Lord's healing where you are broken, sick and cursed, the Lord's blessings. This is a spiritual journey and a complete inside out spiritual experience. It is not a religion, but a wholehearted, daily, intimate "relationship" with the Living God.

Religion is truly the "enemy" of God, because it twists God's will, misinterprets God's Words, and puts God in a box with all kinds of limiting projections. This is NOT the presence of God's spirit because God is unlimited; otherwise, He wouldn't be the Almighty Creator, the Lord of lords, King of kings, and God of gods.

The spirit of unbelief and doubt literally causes mental illness in people. And eventually all mental illnesses creates physical dis-eases because the mind is not only out of alignment with God, but out of alignment with themselves and their bodies. This is the root cause of illness.

When we are put right with God, He heals us. He heals our spirits, our minds, and our bodies. Many people who are recipients of God's miracles are often undeserving of them. This is because it's not about what you do, but "who" you are to God that matters. He often takes the most unlikely people and uses them for His purposes because maybe they have something in them that He wants to work with. Maybe it's a passion, or a talent or a gift, and the world, the flesh, and the satanic curses distorted that. He can take a person and restore him or her back to what He divinely created that soul to be, to reveal not only "who" that person truly is, but in the end, the credit for this work goes to "who" God truly is. This is the transformative work that comes from abiding in Christ and inviting Him to abide in you.

Therefore, the religious spirit becomes like an attack dog, like any other demon out there that works for the Kingdom of Darkness, who seeks to put out the Light. Both psychologically and spiritually speaking, one really needs to look at a jealous spirit, rooted in pride that is at the bottom of Satan's Kingdom. He was ousted out of Heaven, so he's going to do everything in his limited power, to thwart you from getting there. John 10:10 tells us, "The thief cometh not, but for to steal, and to kill, and to destroy: I am come that they might have life, and that they might have it more abundantly."

An old wise teacher used to tell me when I was in my early twenties, when I was questioning this and that, that "sooner or later, we all come to realize, we're all hypocrites!" This is the dual nature of man. One part wants to reach a higher standard, but the other part is weak. This is why being "godly" can only come from God; it is not something people can do, nor can they do very well or achieve in their flesh.

Godliness comes from the indwelling Holy Spirit living in you. This is the only motivation toward change. Religion always ends up short.

So, here is the epitome of all hypocrisy. When Christians attack other Christians, they are essentially playing the role of the Pharisees, in how they treated Jesus.

Only Jewish believers know what it's like to be a Messianic Jew in this world. Not only do we experience complete rejection, as if we were "dead" coming from our Jewish family and friends for accepting salvation through Yeshua, but as believers in Yeshua, we enter into further persecution from Christians, some of whom are anti-Semitic and believe in "replacement theology," which is a distortion of Paul's writings that God gave the outpouring to the Gentiles to make the Jew jealous of all His supernatural miracles taking place through the spirit filled believers and that the church was eventually going to replace unbelieving Israel.

Come to think of it. It's not only the Jews that are provoked to jealousy, but other Gentiles and religious people as well, who claim they have religion, but do not have the presence of God in their lives and or their churches, because there is a disbelief that God doesn't even do miracles anymore.

The persecutory spirit comes from the spirit of religion. No spirit received as many **WOES** from Jesus as this one does. I see Christians on Facebook tearing down other Christians, actively engaged in smear campaigns against famous Christian leaders. There is very little unity within Christianity. Hebrew Roots Gentiles persecuting other believers for using the name Jesus. Each church denomination believes the other is false. I see Christians on Facebook unfriend and besmirch other Christians simply because they don't like what others post on their walls. How petty and shallow is that? Christians expect other Christians to be as funda<u>mental</u> as they are, and when they're not, or they're showing kindness, understanding, and compassion to outsiders, like gays, New Agers, Jews, etc., they think you're false. This is the spirit Jesus nailed in his 'Eight Woes to Religion', and this is the 'spirit' that was nailed to His Cross.

As soon as churches begin to grow, which is a movement by the Holy Spirit, then Christians go on the bandwagon to tear down its leader because they are preaching stuff that they don't like. Yes, Christians can and do have demons, and they are being called to clean house now in these End Times before it's too late.

Jesus Warns Against Hypocrisy:

"Then Jesus said to the crowds and to his disciples: "The teachers of the law and the Pharisees sit in Moses' seat. So you must be careful to do everything they tell you. But do not do what they do, for they do not practice what they preach. They tie up heavy, cumbersome loads and put them on other people's shoulders, but they themselves are not willing to lift a finger to move them.

"Everything they do is done for people to see: They make their phylacteries[a] wide and the tassels on their garments long; they love the place of honor at banquets and the most important seats in the synagogues; they love to be greeted with respect in the marketplaces and to be called 'Rabbi' by others.

"But you are not to be called 'Rabbi,' for you have one Teacher, and you are all brothers. And do not call anyone on earth 'father,' for you have one Father, and he is in heaven. Nor are you to be called instructors, for you have one Instructor, the Messiah. The greatest among you will be your servant. For those who exalt themselves will be humbled, and those who humble themselves will be exalted."

(Matthew 23:1-8-GWT)

The good news is, that the Eight Beatitudes of Matthew 5, and the Eight Woes of Matthew 23 are not only spiritual contrasts, but the very discernment of the spirit of love, which was Christ's main teachings as a Rabbi (the word *rabbi* in Hebrew literally translates to, "great one," or "great teacher"), versus the demonically implanted spirit of religion.

In the eight beatitudes, Yeshua/Jesus Christ taught that it will be the loving, the meek, the gentle, and the poor in spirit, who will inherit the Earth, these are the ones who will receive the Kingdom of God and be allowed into the Kingdom of Heaven and be called the Children of God.

I have found that the eight Beatitudes of Matthew 5:3-12 are best understood and discerned by contrasting them with the eight corresponding curses, or "Woes" of Matthew 23:13-33:

1. The first Woe is against the leaders who have shut the poor out of the Kingdom: "But woe to you, scribes and Pharisees, hypocrites, because you shut off the kingdom of heaven from people; for you do not enter in yourselves, nor do you allow those who are entering to go in."

(Matthew 23:13)

The first Beatitude: "Blessed are the poor in spirit, for theirs is the Kingdom of Heaven" this opens up the Kingdom to the poor.

(Matthew 5:3)

2. The second Woe is against the leaders who distressed the mourners rather than comforting them: "Woe to you, scribes and Pharisees, hypocrites, because you devour widows' houses, and for a pretense you make long prayers; therefore, you will receive greater condemnation."

(Matthew 23:14)

The second Beatitude: "Blessed are those who mourn for they will be comforted." This goes on today through the agency of the Holy Spirit.

(Matthew 5:4)

3. The third Woe is against the leaders who were not meek, but pompous fanatics who encompass the earth with their show: "Woe to you, scribes and Pharisees, hypocrites, because you travel around on sea and land to make one proselyte; and when he becomes one, you make him twice as much a son of hell as yourselves."

(Matthew 23:15)

The third Beatitude: "Blessed are the meek for they will inherit the earth."

(Matthew 5:5)

4. The fourth Woe is against the leaders who make up a false righteousness through trickery and deception: "Woe to you, blind guides, who say, 'Whoever swears by the temple, that is nothing; but whoever, swears by the gold of the temple is obligated.' "You fools and blind men! Which is more important, the gold or the temple that

sanctified the gold? And, 'Whoever swears by the altar, that is nothing, but whoever swears by the offering on it, he is obligated.' You blind men, which is more important, the offering, or the altar that sanctifies the offering? Therefore, whoever swears by the altar, swears both by the altar and by everything on it. And whoever swears by the temple, swears both by the temple and by Him who dwells within it. And whoever swears by heaven, swears both by the throne of God and by Him who sits upon it."

(Matthew 23:16-22)

> The fourth Beatitude: "Blessed are those who hunger and thirst for righteousness for they will be fulfilled to complete satisfaction."
>
> (Matthew 5:6)

5. The fifth Woe is against the leaders for omitting mercy altogether for things of lesser importance: "Woe to you, scribes and Pharisees, hypocrites! For you tithe mint and dill and cumin, and have neglected the weightier provisions of the law: justice and mercy and faithfulness; but these are the things you should have done without neglecting the others. You blind guides who strain out a gnat from your wine and swallow a camel!"

(Matthew 23:23-24)

> The fifth Beatitude: "Blessed are the merciful for they will receive mercy." (Matthew 5:7)

6. The sixth Woe is against the leaders who were spotless on the outside and without purity on the inside: "Woe to you, scribes and Pharisees, hypocrites! For you clean the outside of the cup and of the dish, but inside they are full of robbery and self-indulgence. You blind Pharisee, first clean the inside of the cup and of the dish, so that the outside of it may become clean also."

(Matthew 23:25-26)

> The sixth Beatitude: "Blessed are the pure in heart, for they will *see* God".
>
> (Matthew 5:8)

7. The seventh Woe is against the leaders who are full of hypocrisy and lawlessness: "Woe to you, scribes and Pharisees, hypocrites! For you are like whitewashed tombs which on the outside appear beautiful, but inside they are full of dead men's bones and all uncleanness. So you, too, outwardly appear righteous to men, but inwardly you are full of hypocrisy and lawlessness."

(Matthew 23:27-28)

> The seventh Beatitude: "Blessed are the peacemakers for they will be called the Children of God."
>
> (Matthew 5:9)

8. The eighth Woe is against the leaders because of their actions of being the persecutors against Kingdom people: "Woe to you, scribes and Pharisees, hypocrites! For you build the tombs of the prophets and adorn the monuments of the righteous, and say, 'If we had been living in the days of our fathers, we would not have been partners with them in shedding the blood of the prophets.' So you testify against yourselves, that you are sons of those who murdered the prophets. Fill up, then, the measure of the guilt of your fathers. You serpents, you brood of vipers, how will you escape the sentence of hell?"

(Matthew 23:29-33)

The eight Beatitude: "Blessed are those who are persecuted for the sake of righteousness, for theirs is the Kingdom of Heaven."

(Matthew 5:10)

Who Are the Children of God?

"Behold, what manner of love the Father has bestowed on us, that we should be called the sons of God: therefore the world knows us not, because it knew him not. Beloved, now are we the sons of God, and it does not yet appear what we shall be: but we know that, when he shall appear, we shall be like him; for we shall see him as he is. And every man that has this hope in him purifies himself, even as he is pure.

Whoever commits sin transgresses also the law: for sin is the transgression of the law. And you know that he was manifested to take away our sins; and in him is no sin. Whoever stays in him sins not: whoever sins has not seen him, neither known him. Little children, let no man deceive you: he that does righteousness is righteous, even as he is righteous. He that commits sin is of the devil; for the devil sins from the beginning. For this purpose the Son of God was manifested, that he might destroy the works of the devil.

Whoever is born of God does not commit sin; for his seed remains in him: and he cannot sin, because he is born of God. In this the children of God are manifest, and the children of the devil: whoever does not righteousness is not of God, neither he that loves not his brother."

(1 John 3:1-10-KJV)

The children of God are those whom God as has called back to be redeemed through His Son, which includes Jews and Gentiles. The children of God are the ones who trust the Creator God as their maker, Father, Mother, and Savior. I have detailed all the God of god's attributes, characteristics, and names within this book. The Children of God are the ones whose faith is in this one "*Who* has ascended up into heaven, or descended? *who* has gathered the wind in his fists? *who* has bound the waters in a garment? *who* has established all the ends of the earth? *what* is his name, and **what is his son's name**, if you can tell?" (Proverbs 30:4)

His name is Yahuah, and His son's name, Yahshua/Yeshua/Jesus, the kinsmen redeemer of those who have been enslaved by the alien presence.

> "Look your house is desolate. For I tell you, you will not see me again until you say, "Blessed is he who **comes in the name of the LORD.**"
>
> (Matthew 23:37-39)

WHO IS CHRISTIAN?

> "And when he had found him, he brought him to Antioch. And for an entire year they met with the church and taught considerable numbers; and the disciples were first called **Christians** in Antioch.
>
> (Acts 11:26 NAS)

The word *church* in the Greek is Ecclesia. The word *Christian* also began as a Greek word with formerly Pagan usage. The Mandaean deity of the sun god was titled "Christ Helios," the Alexandrian Osiris was titled "Christos," and the Romans via the Persians worshipped the sun under the title "Christos Mithras," where Christos took the Roman interpretation of good, or pure, sacred, or holy.

In Acts 11:26, the word, "Christian" refers to Messianic believers, true disciples of Yeshua, the called out ones, those who are sanctified and consecrated to Him. This word was never intended to refer to a building, like the 501c3 business entity called a church today, it was the ecclesia which assembled, and they first met in homes. The sign of the fish that is today's well-known symbol for Christianity, was etched into the dirt during ancient times to show believers where the group assembled. It was also meant to keep their meetings secret from the oppressive Romans.

The disciples were first called Christians by the Romans, which was originally meant as a derogatory term. However, we have NO record that Yeshua ever called His disciples "Christians" or that the disciples ever referred to themselves as "Christians," nor would they. To be a Christian meant one followed Rome. Christianity today still follows the Nicene and Constantine creeds.

Constantine instituted Christianity as the State religion of Rome in the third century. It was a deliberate, intentional separation and distancing from the true Hebraic faith, which was the faith of the prophets and apostles, and from anything "Jewish." Constantine essentially created Roman Catholicism by transforming Mithraism into Catholicism, which then spawned daughter churches i.e., Protestant, Methodist, Baptist Christian denominations. All of which still have roots in their pagan history.

Christianity keeps Sunday as the "Sabbath" in violation of the Fourth Commandment. Today's Christians celebrate Roman Catholic Church liturgical holidays like Christmas and Easter, which all have a Protestant papacy. They all commit ecclesiasticism, Nicolaitans, and instead of representing the indwelling Holy Spirit, they all carry the enemy of the Holy Spirit, which is the *Religious Spirit*. They all teach a different gospel and follow another "messiah" because they bought into the deception of Catholicism and all of its offshoot denominations and never completely repented from Roman Creeds and doctrines.

This is why today's so-called Christians, who are true believers, who know the Grace and Salvation of Yeshua, must repent from Constantine's Creed, because repentance will separate them from centuries of falsehoods perpetrated by Rome. And each time you repent to God for generational sins and curses, the Lord is mighty to heal and deliver. Try it, in case you need a new blessing.

I want my readers to know, that in this book, I have only attempted to scratch the surface. Between the mistranslations, mis-transliterations, and outright omissions of the rejected texts, which have caused so much confusion from all the lies, which began from Constantine's Creed, the Seven Ecumenical Councils, and the Nicean Creeds, all of whom inserted spiritual limitation implants to control the minds and spirits of humans. Their sins of omission have created amnesia in the souls of many, who have been living with amnesia their whole lives, as a generational curse, for eighteen centuries. It's time to stop. Wake up and repent from the lies.

The Hebrew Roots Movement may have uncovered many truths about how the Catholic Church manipulated Christianity, but most of them are no better than the Pharisees were during the times of Christ. The Pharisees were the ruling religious priests of ancient Israel who conspired to crucify Christ. They have, in essence, turned their knowledge of how Catholicism twisted and distorted scripture into another "legalistic" religion itself. This was and has never been the perfect and Divine Will of Christ, which was to come and set the captives free (See, Isaiah 16:1; Luke 4:18).

They preach to others that they must follow the "true Hebraic faith," by going back to keeping the laws of the Old Testament. They fail to see that the true Gospel was the pouring out of God's Spirit upon all flesh, which He promised to do in the End Times, by writing His law on our hearts, which was sufficient and intelligent, a plan that makes sense for everyone, levels the playing field and is not just for the educated, or "chosen few." One way sets people free; the other, creates mental, spiritual and physical bondage.

The legalists, and this includes all the Christian cults, Jehovah's Witnesses, Mormons, Seventh Day Adventist, the Hebrew Roots Movement, Catholicism, Judaism, and Islam, must all be tested on how much of the **"fruit of the Spirit of Love"** they have?

"The test of religion, the final test of religion, is not religiousness, but Love."

(Henry Drummond)

CONCLUDING WORDS

Legalists are often void of the Holy Spirit, which is the Spirit of Love. They fill the void with works, instead of being a vessel for the Spirit of Christ. They are quick to judge others, before showing compassion. They often miss the central message of the Gospel (Good News), which is freedom from Jesus Christ (Yeshua HaMaschiach) who taught, that the Greatest Commandment is this, and that upon these two things pivot the entire law of the prophets:

> "Hearing that Jesus had silenced the Sadducees, the Pharisees got together. One of them, an expert in the law, tested him with this question: "Teacher, which is the greatest commandment in the Law?"
>
> Jesus replied: "'Love the Lord your God with all your heart and with all your soul and with all your mind.' This is the first and greatest commandment. And the second is like it: 'Love your neighbor as yourself.' The entire Law and the Prophets hang on these two commandments."
>
> (Matthew 21:34-40)

Remember all roots eventually bear fruit. We are expected to be fruit inspectors, but how can a believer be a fruit inspector, if we can't discern between fruits? God wants spiritual fruits from us, not religious nuts.

As I've already proven, the name Jesus is just a transliteration, which has become another one of the Lord's "nicknames." We all have nicknames we answer to. Some of us even have pen names or stage names that we also answer to. Yes, it is true, when the Savior walked the Earth over two thousand years ago, He was not called Jesus, but He is by multitudes today. And for those who suggest this is false, reveals more about them, then it does about "who" Christ is.

Now, to be fair, if nothing ever happened in the name of Jesus, then I'd say to them, yeah, I think you have a point there. But the proof is in the pudding, as they say, as I and countless others have personally witnessed signs, wonders, miracles and demons flee in the name of Jesus! The Holy Spirit responds to ALL true translations of Messiah's names. True, He was named Yahushua, Yeshua for short. They also called him Emmanuel, just as we respond to nicknames, so does the Lord. Yah is the poetic version of the truncation of the Lord's name. That's where we get the word HalleluYah, which means "praise Yah."

It's perfectly all right for people to use the name Jesus. No rebellion, just has to do with language and culture, and God is in all of that. The Holy Spirit is the one "who" is responding. The Holy Spirit is All Wise, All Knowing, and All Powerful. Because the Holy Spirit comes from God, the Father (Yahuah) and God the Son (Yahushua), He is the very spirit that was inside and on Christ. The Holy Spirit was the "Dunamis" power of Christ, which was the power to resurrect Him from the dead. The word *dunamis* is Greek for resurrection.

First of all, all leaders are only human. No one is perfect, only the Lord. We can't let our search for perfection be the enemy of the good. Godliness comes from within. Once we see the show of it, through, let's say, all the silly hats, robes, pointy shoes, like the millennia old fashion of the Vatican, then it's all about what is projected on the outside, as a show to the world, while concealing what is going on inside. The Priesthood has been in crisis for decades now. Sexual scandals have plagued the Vatican, and instead of the priesthood growing around the world, it has been diminishing. This is because of the curse (Woes) upon the Priesthood, and that includes all religions, not limited to the Vatican.

I've witnessed Christians declare other Christian ministers false prophets, when they are actually the "true" leaders of God because their fruits prove it. The Kingdom is growing, people are getting healed, both mentally, spiritually and physically, accompanied with signs and wonders, and yes, with all that comes financial growth, because money is necessary in this world to provide for physical needs. The work I have witnessed churches doing behind the scenes through using their funds to sponsor missionaries to bring "light" into some of the darkest areas on this planet is nothing but courageous, and a passion to see God's Kingdom manifest on Earth.

Thy Kingdom Come....they Will be done....on earth, as it is in Heaven.

Christians need to cultivate a more "loving spirit." They are called through their faith to express Christ, in a dark world. Everyone has their individual assignment from God, in the end. It's between me and Him, not what you project onto me. I will follow His spirit, even when I feel the opposite. When I'm tired, weak, weary, angry, anxious, impatient, lost, confused and all alone, it doesn't matter, I will seek after His Spirit in me. That's when I experience peace, comfort, and a supernatural "inner" security restored in me, that I'd lost when my mother was taken away from me when I was six and then lost my father at fifteen. I have found peace in His Spirit.

So does that mean, we all need to do things the same way? No way, we need to be true to "who" God made us to be. I am a survivor of religious abuse. I am also the survivor of traumas and persecution. What matters is your individual relationship with the Lord, and that's it in the end. It's not about what church you belong to, although some are definitely better than others; it's about God's Grace in you.

I was wounded by religion through religious spirits. There was so much bigotry between both of my families that being a hybrid, allowed me to find the middle ground, and achieve balance. Jews and Italians are just as nutty as each other with their religious convictions (many of which do not hold water) because they are void of the Spirit of Grace.

Yes, God is our Judge, and yes, people need to be discerning, but when there is a distorted sense of judgment over others, to the point of snobbery, bigotry, and a refusal to be kind to another because of their "flaw," the Christian is not expressing Jesus in them, but the false spirit of religion. Christians really need to check themselves here daily. Why? Because Jesus is their Lord, and Jesus spoke more woes to the religious spirit, than any other. If I had the fear of the Lord in me, I'd take notice! It is to the shame of Christianity, that there is so much bickering, competition, jealousy, and confusion among Christians. We all share a common enemy, and that enemy blinds through jealousy, Jezebel, and a religious spirit. This is the "spiritual trinity of Lucifer/satan." Now is the time for repentance. Jesus said, "He who is without sin, let him cast the first stone." Churches, who enjoy "unity" in the Spirit, bear more fruit.

So what makes someone "false"? The spirit of error causes misperception and influences the mind to think everyone else is false when, in reality, they are true to the Spirit of Christ. It's flipped with the religious spirit. It can express itself from one extreme to another, and it's only a matter of swinging the pendulum. The spirit of error, which the religious name takes from archery, is "sin." Sin can be iniquity, transgressions of God's immutable laws of Love and Justice, or the perversion of His image. It's all in error.

To Err is Human, to forgive Divine.

~ William Shakespeare

Nobody is perfect, but when people surrender their lives to Christ, He does the perfecting, and everyone is judged according to His standards, not ours. What's more important to the Lord, is the state of our hearts, our spirits, how we relate to Him and to others. He's a relational God, through the indwelling Holy Spirit, the Ruach HaKodesh, this was the Spirit within Yeshua/Jesus who did miracles, and not only did he raise the dead, He overcame death, Hades, and the grave. That gives Him a lot of power and authority in the spiritual realms. All spirits have to obey him. Even the demons and aliens.

Why do the spirits fear the Lord? Because they know He is capable of destroying them, but He doesn't, He uses them for His purposes, to correct, to discipline and to punish. And sometimes, they do get bound up and held in prison. So, for my unbelieving readers, who are probably wondering, how do I know that all demons obey the Lord? Because all the demons I had to fight growing up abandoned, orphaned, and then rejected for believing in Yeshua, could only be cast out from me supernaturally, and that includes aliens. So, I want to say, in this book, I'm going to expose some big misunderstandings between both the Judeo and Christian faiths that just might ruffle the feathers of those who are deeply bound by religious spirits. But that's why I'm writing this, for you, so you can be free.

With humans, so often, we need to understand things before we can move on. We need a sense of closure in our minds, whether its wisdom or understanding. Otherwise the negative experience, then, becomes our greatest nemesis, and we can't be free or live free without resolution and healing.

Sometimes, it's all about just trusting in the Lord, who may keep Himself invisible to our realm most of the time, He nevertheless sees and hears our prayers. Most of us can't imagine the depth of His love because most of us never experienced that with our parents, or people in our lives, but His love is real, and no one can withstand the "presence" of God, which we call the "glory" cloud, and not be healed by it. It's the simple law of physics, if you turn on the light in a dark room, everything is revealed. But what is inside His Light is His Love, His Grace, His Mercy, His Loving-Kindness.

Religion seeks that, but religion falls short, because religion tries to do things on their own, and not through the Spirit. When you cooperate with the Holy Spirit's move in your life, all kinds of transformations happen. First, you get cleaned out. This can be a long process for some, but the first fruits are a transformed lifestyle and life. Second, the Spirit leads you into sanctification, where you renounce, rescind all agreements made mainly subconsciously through believing in lies, and you repent of all to God. Third, He adjusts you through healing your mind, your past, and revealing to you your true identity, which is in Him. Repenting of False Identity programming is a very important piece of the sanctification journey with God, otherwise, there is no real transformation if you're still identifying with your past.

> *"Sooner or later, we learn to throw the past away."* ~Sting

True deliverance comes out of repentance. Finally, you are ready to be used by God, as a new creation. But does that mean God can't use you until you've reached that stage? Not at all. God can use you every day to be kind to someone, to love your family, to serve your community; sometimes it's your very presence in a place that helps transforms it. God uses your process as a "catalyst" to change others. The Spirit of God is like electricity sparking one to another, like using a candle to light another candle.

I'm writing this book, because it's been my journey back to God, and just "who" He is, and "who" He is not. I hope that I can impart the understanding God gave me, to those who are seeking and to those who are confused by the behavior of people who claim to stand for Christ, yet do not.

If you don't know or you're not sure if you have the Holy Spirit, repent to God. The Holy Spirit is attracted to humans who have a contrite (humble) spirit. He longs to pour out His Grace on repentant humans.

> "The sacrifices of God are a broken spirit: a broken and a contrite heart, O God, you will not despise."
>
> (Psalm 51:17)

> "The LORD is near to them that are of a broken heart; and saves such as be of a contrite spirit."
>
> (Psalm 34:18)

CONCLUDING WORDS

The fact that the Holy Spirit responds to the names of Jesus in all languages on Earth today is manifested through answered prayers, miraculous healings, the raising of the dead, and the casting out of the demonic. This should tell anyone, who has a shred of "spiritual discernment" that the Lord Himself does not care if you do not call Him by His Hebrew name. No, Jesus is not Zeus. Just because satan conspired to change names doesn't mean satan wins in this area. The Holy Spirit is the Spirit of Solutions, He knows the history; He knows all the languages, and He also knows people's hearts.

Remember, this is far greater and bigger than us. It's not dependent on whether our knowledge is perfect or whether our lives are perfect because God knows; nobody's is. It's all dependent on what the Lord has done for us. All we need to do is have faith and believe. It's important to note, that the sins of unbelief block miracles. Unbelief is what stands in the way of seeing "who" God is, and knowing Him personally. Like I've already said throughout this book, that there is really no such thing as real atheists. Atheists claim, that there is no God, but what they are really saying is, "I don't know God." Many of them are 'mad at God', but 'who' they are really mad at, is the god of this world, the one who stole from them, who blinds them with unbelief and confuses them about 'who' the Creator God actually is.

Here's how it's all going to go down in the end. Everyone will be judged by God based on "who" you think He is because He created every soul and spirit with the knowledge of the Creator within its Creation. It's really quite simple, just as the entire tree blueprint is imprinted within its seed, so is the Creator God imprinted within all of His Creation, and that includes humans, animals, angels and extraterrestrials. This is why according to the mind of God, there is really no excuse for atheism, or unbelief, because the Lord God provides "evidence" of Himself in His Creation.

> "For the wrath of God is revealed from heaven against all ungodliness and unrighteousness of men, who hinder the truth in unrighteousness; because that which is known of God is manifest in them; for God manifested it unto them. **For the invisible things of him since the creation of the world are clearly seen, being perceived through the things that are made, even his everlasting power and divinity; that they may be without excuse**: because that, knowing God, they glorified him not as God, neither gave thanks; but became vain in their reasonings, and their senseless heart was darkened. Professing themselves to be wise, they became fools, and changed the glory of the incorruptible God for the likeness of an image of corruptible man, and of birds, and four-footed beasts, and creeping things."
>
> (Romans 1:18-23-ASV)

As I've proved throughout this book, that there is a difference between deliberate name changes, done in order to obscure and confuse, mis-translations, and mis-transliterations, which are rooted in linguistic misunderstandings and errors. Like the false made-up names, Yahusha and Jehovah. While Yahweh is merely a mispronunciation from the original Hebrew Yahuah (Yahuwah), I want my readers to keep in mind, that Yahweh is also the name of one of the first Nephilim, Yahweh Yaldabaoth, so this is important to remember, for those who worship the name Yahweh, or call your god Yahweh. You could be invoking the wrong god. I have witnessed this myself, firsthand, in the churches of those who worship the name Yahweh. This is one of the reasons why I was compelled to put this manuscript together. God knows your heart, but remember satan and his demonic henchmen are always on the prowl, looking for an angle to take advantage of ignorant believers.

This is what the Holy Spirit revealed to me about this controversy: There is much Grace over the name confusions. God is not judging people if they use His English name over His Hebrew one. Particularly with the name of the Messiah. Now, the Father's name has had some deliberate and intentional perversions to purposely confuse Gentiles, which was done by Masorete Jews from Babylon, and history tells us that they most definitely succeeded in confusing the Gentiles. This is why so many Christians are confused over this and have religious spirits on them because of this. Again, there is much Grace over this controversy. Knowledge empowers. The answer is really quite simple. Just repent. Every prayer of repentance is responded to with Grace and Forgiveness. Count on that!

> "But he said to me, 'My grace is sufficient for you, for my power is made perfect in weakness.' Therefore I will boast all the more gladly about my weaknesses, so that Christ's power may rest on me."
>
> (2 Corinthians 12:9)

The entire concept of Grace is foreign to those who have religious spirits. They think it's all about following a religion, a set of rules, laws, and ways of doing things. If you dot the "I" the wrong way, they freak out and reject you. That is a spiritual discernment of their fruits, which are not fruits of love and grace. They are legalists, and legalists are cold-hearted. They lack the spirit of understanding and loving-kindness, which are the true fruits and marks of the presence of the Holy Spirit within any believer, Jew or Gentile.

Religion says: God will love us if we change. However, the Gospel of Jesus Christ says: God's love changes us. If your theology doesn't lead you to love people, then perhaps it's time you should question your theology more.

The true religion is love. Taking care of the poor, feeding the hungry, clothing the naked, healing the sick, setting the captives free. That's how we will be judged. This was the original Word of God; these were the Words of Christ, and those who do these works do so through the Spirit of God, and are the blessed ones in the age to come.

CONCLUDING WORDS

"Religion that God our Father accepts as pure and faultless is this: to look after orphans and widows in their distress and to keep oneself from being polluted by the world."

(James 1:27)

The fruit of the Holy Spirit in one's life is supposed to make you "giving" and "forgiving." There is much discernment that is measured by and through the spirit of love. It not only tells people "who" you are, but more importantly, "who" lives inside of you. Love covers a multitude of sins, making religion, religiosity, and religious spirits irrelevant.

Nobody likes to learn that they've been betrayed for years, and taught to believe in lies, but being we are living in the Age of Knowledge, it's time we turn from of all the lies, and allow the truth to transform us, as is the perfect Will of God.

"Sometimes people hold a core belief that is very strong. When they are presented with evidence that works against that belief, the new evidence cannot be accepted. It would create a feeling that is extremely uncomfortable called cognitive dissonance and because it is so important to protect the core belief, they will rationalize, ignore and even deny anything that doesn't fit with the core belief."

~ Frantz Fanon

There is much Grace on the name confusions, and there is absolutely no issue with the Lord using His name in other languages. These are merely transliterations, but outright deceptions create counterfeit spirits and are spirits of error. Those who continue to perpetuate these will reap the fruit of deception.

Yeshua came from the tribe of Judah, the bloodline of King David. However, the counterfeit Messiah will come from the tribe of Joseph, a tribe that is not mentioned in the book of Revelation as the twelve surviving tribes of Israel, who each have gates named after them in the Grand Mother ship/Heavenly City/The New Jerusalem. Instead, Joseph's portion was doubled, and his sons Manasseh and Ephraim took his place. I go into more detail on these stories, why the original twelve tribes exchanged and deleted a few tribes in the Book of Revelation, due to generational curses and blessings in Book Four: *Covenants*.

Hebrew is also a poetic language. There is poetry in all the Psalms, and the Lord is given many names in the Old Testament. He answers to each and every one of them.

But if you are invoking one of the counterfeit names, which were deliberately born out of a schemed mass deception upon the Gentiles, then you are being fooled by a different spirit. This deceiving spirit is the spirit of religion, aka the religious spirit, which is one of satan's chief demons over the religions of the world.

This is why those who know God worship Him in Spirit and in Truth. There has been so many false gods, and their influence over the world has been great, but God's Spirit is greater, and it will prevail in the end, one way or the other.

> "You worship what you do not know; we worship what we know, for salvation is from the Jews. But an hour is coming, and now is, when the true worshipers will worship the Father in spirit and truth; for such people the Father seeks to be His worshipers. "God is spirit, and those who worship Him must worship in spirit and truth."
>
> (John 4:22-24)

The earth is going through a cleansing, a transformation, and a pole shift. When the pole shift is complete, that is when the Lord returns, literally at the 11th hour, to save the world. He's the Cosmic Messiah/Astronaut. He's not "alien," per se, because we're made in His image, and He was one of us, lived as a human. This is why He is the Son of Man, too. But He is most definitely out of this world. He identifies with our pain, our sorrow, our betrayals, our persecutions, and our heartbreak, because He experienced all that in His human body when He walked the earth a little over two thousand years ago.

He is the hope of glory. The heavens declare the glory of God (Psalm 19:1). He will return as the Lord of Hosts (Tzeveyot, in Hebrew means "celestial armies," which he commands), who will appear over earth's skies where every eye will see Him and His Heavenly Hosts, His army of celestial starships filled with the faithful extraterrestrial angels approaching the earth. It will be a glorious day. His glory is His starships, which shine brightly with His Presence, dripped in jewels and gold. So magnificent, so absolutely phantasmagorical, that our human imaginations just can't get our minds wrapped around such awesome power.

Believers, both Jews and Christians, need to keep the faith, and know that we're in store for something "right out of this world" to change this planet.

The Lord promises in both Old and New Testaments, to recreate the earth and the heavens. This is because He's going to clean up the toxic residue from the curse of Lucifer, and the dark stars, which will all be transformed into a new Heaven and a new Earth. Yes, I believe God's promises.

Earth will become a star, because the Kingdom of Heaven is coming to Earth. That's the promise of the Holy City, the New Jerusalem. What Atlantis was to Lucifer 26,000 years ago, the New Millennial reign of Christ will be on Earth, from His Throne which is located in the middle of the Mother Ship City, with twelve gates that open up, "It had a great, high wall with twelve gates, and with twelve angels at the gates. On the gates were written the names of the twelve tribes of Israel." (Revelation 21:12) This Mother Ship City will be overlaid over King David's Throne which is His Space Portal/Dimensional Doorway in Jerusalem.

CONCLUDING WORDS

THE LAST DAYS OF THE END TIMES

In the end times, what many are not prepared for is a battle between different groups of aliens and extraterrestrials. Right here on Earth. One minute you'll be seeing demons, the next angels. These are different sides. The so-called angels, are truly extraterrestrial messengers and warriors who stand for the Creator's truth, and they know all about our history of manipulation from the evil aliens, the controllers, the Archons of this world, the Annunaki slave masters.

Yeshua/Jesus said, "I have come to set the captives free," and that is what He's been doing through the work of the Holy Spirit now on Earth. One by one, He is revealing Himself and calling people back to the Creator of all Souls, to be restored, from the abuse of evil and being taken advantage of by the god of this world, who is Lucifer/Satan. The so-called Light Bearer Angel (son of heaven) turned rebel to steal the worship from the Lord who created Him.

The Father allowed Him to exist on different planes, which were much lower in density than the place of space where He was born. He was truly a fallen angel, and in his pity party, he managed to persuade one third of heaven's angels (extraterrestrials) to follow him in his rebellion against the Creator God of gods.

Being separated from the Father's love, he grew bitter and jealous, and he had to learn how to counterfeit what He knew about God's technology. But he has always been, along with all of his followers, unable to recreate a human soul. Souls are created by the Lord of Spirits, who creates all souls. The book of Enoch goes deep into this, and refers to the Lord as the Lord of Spirits multiple times. This is why, according to the Lord's plan of salvation, His intention and Divine Will is that all of His souls should be saved. This is why He sent His Son to be the bridge builder between man and God. It's the way back home. It's as simple as that.

If you can't find your way, ask for His Light. Call on His Holy name. Demons tremble to His name; they knew who knows him and who doesn't. Deliverance and Freedom can only happen in His mighty name.

Repentance has become a taboo word in America's churches. This taboo needs to be busted now, if people want to know God's power of Grace and Healing in your lives. Repentance isn't just about feeling sorry for your sins. Guilt is a spirit, that Christ has freed us from on the cross. You simply need to claim His healing for yourself, as it is available for everyone. Guilt comes from condemnation, but there is no condemnation for those who are in Christ, the old has passed away, the new inner man has been reborn (Romans 8:1). Christ living inside of us is our hope and glory. It's a spiritual relationship.

Human beings were created to be vessels of a higher intelligence, which is God. However souls get stolen by the fallen one, and this is where things get weird and crazy.

Remember, not every alien is an extraterrestrial, and not every extraterrestrial is an alien.

There are many human extraterrestrials, many human colonies. This is the true, deeper meaning in the John 10:16 scripture: "I have other sheep that are not of this sheep pen. I must bring them also. They too will listen to my voice, and there shall be one flock and one shepherd."

UFO WARS

Back in 1973, U.S. soldiers stationed in Vietnam were attacked by UFOs. The military lingo for UFOs are "enemy helicopters." These disk-shaped lighted metallic ships, hovered over them, causing the soldiers to fire at them. Then something very disturbing occurred, the UFOs took their weapons that the U.S. soldiers fired upon the UFOs, and reversed them back onto themselves. Then they moved upon them and beamed them with such an intense bright beam of light. The soldiers described said that it looked like an X-ray moving through their bodies, causing them to see their own skeletons, while creating excruciating pain. Once the light beam moved off of them, the saucer-shaped craft literally disappeared into the sky, the surviving soldiers became extremely sick, throwing up, disoriented, and drained of energy. Their fatigue lasted for weeks. They were psychologically and spiritually traumatized by the attack. This case was analyzed and documented by MUFON (Mutual UFO Network), and then aired on The MUFON Files – Hangar One.

This should give credence to the severity of the UFO phenomenon. What I've been saying throughout my books is that humans are sitting ducks and at the mercy of advanced technology. This event proved how powerless humans and most advanced human technology is. Contrary to popular New Age belief, humans cannot save themselves, Humanity needs a Savior, and there is only one power that is above all powers. Only one God, who is the God of gods. He is the Lord of Hosts, who is the Lord of the Celestial Extraterrestrial Armies of Light.

Everyone agrees that we are living in the End Times. The following prophetic scripture is happening today as your eyes read these very words.

> "Afterward, I will pour out my Spirit on **all people**. Your sons and daughters will prophesy, your old men will dream dreams, your young men will see visions."
>
> (Joel 2:28)

It doesn't say, only some people, or only Jews, or Christians, but it says, ALL PEOPLE. I really want to impress, how the outpouring of God's Spirit has absolutely nothing to do with following a specific religion or joining a cult or church or temple. This is what the God of gods is doing supernaturally to save humankind. If you're human through and through, then this applies to you.

CONCLUDING WORDS

CELESTIAL ARMIES OF FLYING WHITE HORSES

> "Then I saw heaven opened, and a white horse was standing there. Its rider was named Faithful and True, for he judges fairly and wages a righteous war. His eyes were like flames of fire, and on his head were many crowns. A name was written on him that no one understood except himself. He wore a robe dipped in blood, and his title was the Word of God. The armies of heaven, dressed in the finest of pure white linen, followed him on white horses. From his mouth came a sharp sword to strike down the nations. He will rule them with an iron rod. He will release the fierce wrath of God, the Almighty, like juice flowing from a winepress. On his robe at his thigh was written this title: King of all kings and Lord of all lords."
>
> (Revelation 19:11-16, NLT)

Horses that fly? Really? An army of white horses will be flying through the sky. This is a metaphor for a fleet of spacecraft. I've been an equestrian for nearly thirty years, and while I often wear my T-shirt that says: "You can touch the sky on a horse," I must report the truth here; horses don't fly. They can run really fast, and the rider may experience the feeling of flying, because the rider is about five-six feet off the ground, but the truth of the matter is flesh and blood furry horses, cannot and do not fly through the air, let alone fly out of some obscure place in the heavens and land on Earth.

What both Joel and St. John were perceiving in their vision, they related to horses, because in their vernacular, horses were used not only to pull chariots, but carried armies everywhere. Both were given visions of armies on horses. And in Joel 2:4, he specifically described his vision by writing, "they look like horses." Because in their day, that's all they had to relate it to.

But seriously folks, as much as I love riding horses, the last time I checked, horses don't fly. Now, if these scriptures said anything about horses with wings, then I could understand people thinking that an army of Pegasus horses (the mythical flying horse) were flying through the skies, making sounds and spitting fire, but that is simply not what the scripture is revealing by the description of their visions. The Chinese have a folklore of Flying Dragons spitting fire, which are metaphors for spaceships, just as these ancient scriptures are.

"Horsepower" is a term that many use for cars, trucks, boats and yes, even airplanes to measure their power of velocity. Likewise, both of these prophetic scriptures describe an army of spacecraft with the power of horses, but they are not literal flesh and blood furry horses; they are spacecraft with tremendous power and technology and weaponry that the Lord of Hosts of Celestial armies, who is the Lord Jesus Christ, also known as Yeshua HaMashiach, will be leading.

I want my readers to understand that the fleet of UFOs that are ruled by Satan's Fallen Angels, are counterfeit technology compared to what the Kingdom of Heaven has, which not only matches them in technology but exceeds them in their spacecraft.

Remember when the angels rebelled, only one-third followed Satan, two-thirds remained faithful to the Creator God, so Satan's ships are outnumbered 2:1. It's clear, that all the vernacular used within the prophetic verses with respect to fire coming down from heaven, can relate only to spaceships wielding nuclear power, and sophisticated weaponry that is more advanced than our present SDI systems.

What the celestial armies that John perceives as an army of white horses reveals that the Lord's enormous fleet of starships are all white, like clouds with tremendous speed, like that of horses. This is what will defeat the armies of the Antichrist in the end.

"He (the antichrist) performs great signs, so that he even makes fire come down out of heaven to the earth in the presence of men." (Revelation 13:13) He does this because he has control of the fleet of UFOs, because he is satan incarnate.

Remember, satan counterfeits God, God never counterfeits satan. If you think the Draconian Empire has some impressive spaceships, just wait till you see what the Lord of Hosts (Celestial Armies) have in store. And always remember the math, the fallen angels are outnumbered 2:1.

END TIME CONCLUSION

Worship is loving God for being God, for watching over us, protecting us, giving His Angels Charge over us (Psalm 91:11). Don't you wonder what "giving His Angels Charge" means? Due to the Renaissance, which produced so many stunning portraits depicting angels with white feathered bird wings, this image was implanted into our psyches to perceive that this is what angels look like.

But what if the artists were telling a story, that angels could fly like birds, but not exactly like birds on Earth? What if these beings had the ability to fly without wings, but the wings were symbolic to describe their skills? What if you learned that besides being able to interface in between dimensions and travel back and forth from Earth to heaven and heaven to Earth, that they weren't exactly flying like a bird, but knew how to move through dimensional doorways? One minute, they're here; then next, they're gone.

Another explanation is that these beings we call angels, the ones that God puts in charge of us, also have capabilities to fly in spaceships and protect our planet from being destroyed by gamma rays, asteroids, meteors, and well, alien spaceships!

I was watching footage from the space station for years that clearly reveals not only are there tons of UFOs around the earth, coming and going, moving around, but they appear to be fighting with each other. While many Christians may be reluctant to believe people who claim to see UFOs, it's important to note that they believe in the books of Ezekiel and Revelation, which are full of scriptures depicting spacecraft and aliens.

We see in NASA footage that appears to be a ship trying to enter into Earth's atmosphere, but is quickly shot at by other UFOs, only to do an about face and zip out into outer space, as if the ship that shot at it was acting like police protecting earth.

CONCLUDING WORDS

> "The powerful horses were eager to set out to patrol the earth. And the LORD said, "Go and patrol the earth!" So they left at once on their patrol."
>
> (Zechariah 6:7)

Let's face the reality. Horses don't fly. Real flesh and blood horses simply cannot lift themselves up into the air and fly through the sky. It's against the laws of physics, and God didn't make horses to fly. Now, I know what you're thinking, what about Pegasus? Pegasus was a type of Nephilim creature. The fallen angels experimented with mixing different types of DNA together, and I do believe there once was a horse like Pegasus.

But even if Pegasus wasn't a myth, or was real, whatever you believe, in today's world, horses can't fly. I must add. Isn't it interesting that, back in the 1980s, the CIA orchestrated Project Pegasus, which became their time travel experiments. I go into that in Book One of *Who's Who In The Cosmic Zoo?* (See, pp.308-324). Pegasus was their symbol for time travel. A flying horse.

So why do these types of scriptures keep showing up all over the Bible? The white horses of Revelation are all flying out of the sky coming to Earth. Here in Zechariah 6:7, the horses are commanded to go patrol the Earth. These are not physical horses on Earth, but the entire scripture tells us that these were powerful horses, and to put it into context, chapter six of Zechariah was a description of spaceships. The original Hebrew uses the same word that is used for both 'winds' and 'spirits'. Spaceships create winds and 'spirits' have been associated with extraterrestrials.

There are no real mountains on Earth made of bronze. There are, however, some manmade mountains made of iron and bronze. Back in Zechariah's day, they didn't have skyscrapers like we do today, nor do we have bronze mountains that house chariots? Sky chariots? A home for a few space chariots? Sounds like a parking garage for spaceships, spirits of heaven, i.e., angels, travelling in space chariots going in all four directions, patrolling the earth. These are the good ETs, because they were sent from heaven from the Lord of Hosts.

> "Then I looked up again and saw four chariots coming from between two bronze mountains. The first chariot was pulled by red horses, the second by black horses, the third by white horses, and the fourth by powerful dappled-gray horses. And what are these, my lord?" I asked the angel who was talking with me.
>
> The angel replied, "These are the four spirits of heaven who stand before the Lord of all the earth. They are going out to do his work. The chariot with black horses is going north, the chariot with white horses is going west, and the chariot with dappled-gray horses is going south."
>
> The powerful horses were eager to set out to patrol the earth. And the LORD said, "Go and patrol the earth!" So they left at once on their patrol."
>
> (Zechariah 6:1-7-NLT)

The white horses are coming. Thousands upon thousands of them. This is what is promised in Revelation 19. When I Google Revelation 19, I see hundreds of images of artistic renditions of this scene, with Jesus Christ on a White Horse with bright white light and hundreds of other men riding white horses coming out of the heavens approaching earth. Each artist depicts them as horses, but what if John saw something that he could only describe as what he could relate to, which were horses and chariots? But what he was really seeing were space vehicles with tremendous horsepower coming with the clouds of heaven, as depicted on my book cover.

> "And Jesus said, "I AM; and you shall see THE SON OF MAN SITTING AT THE RIGHT HAND OF POWER, and **COMING WITH THE CLOUDS OF HEAVEN.**"
>
> (Mark 14:62)

He didn't say "coming through the clouds of heaven." He said "coming with the clouds of heaven." Again the reference to the word "clouds" in biblical speak, means spaceships because the Lord's starships are cloaked in clouds. These are Merkabahs, which are living spaceships that operate on and through the very presence of God and the Elohim (who are all extraterrestrial gods), along with some very sophisticated types of technology, which are, out of this world.

The New International Version titles the following section which describes and headlines the scene of the Second Coming of Christ to Earth as "The Heavenly Warrior Defeats the Beast." Heavenly Warrior describes an Extraterrestrial with space powers. Warriors always carry weapons or are ones themselves. In this case, the scene St. John describes is one of celestial armies all riding on white horses coming to wage war against the Beast on Earth, and defeats all the Beasts, who are the Alien Draconian Reptilian armies which rule the Antichrist Revelation 19:11-21:

> "I saw heaven standing open and there before me was a white horse, whose rider is called Faithful and True. With justice he judges and wages war. His eyes are like blazing fire, and on his head are many crowns. He has a name written on him that no one knows but he himself. He is dressed in a robe dipped in blood, and his name is the Word of God. The armies of heaven were following him, riding on white horses and dressed in fine linen, white and clean. Coming out of his mouth is a sharp sword with which to strike down the nations. "He will rule them with an iron scepter." He treads the winepress of the fury of the wrath of God Almighty. On his robe and on his thigh he has this name written:

KING of kings and LORD of lords.

> And I saw an angel standing in the sun, who cried in a loud voice to all the birds flying in midair, "Come, gather together for the great supper of God, so that

you may eat the flesh of kings, generals, and the mighty, of horses and their riders, and the flesh of all people, free and slave, great and small.

Then I saw the beast and the kings of the earth and their armies gathered together to wage war against the rider on the horse and his army. But the beast was captured, and with it the false prophet who had performed the signs on its behalf. With these signs he had deluded those who had received the mark of the beast and worshiped its image. The two of them were thrown alive into the fiery lake of burning sulfur. The rest were killed with *the sword coming out of the mouth* of the rider on the horse, and all the birds gorged themselves on their flesh."

IT'S ALL ABOUT LOVE

"And in the end, the love you take, is equal to the love you make."

(Beatles)

Those who walk with Christ, walk in Light, Truth, and Love. Not because they are more special than the rest, but because they embody Christ, and are always seeking to get closer to Him through sanctification which requires repentance, a willingness to turn away from the old self, and an eagerness to embrace the transformation of the Christed Self, what New Agers call the Higher Self. This is the very world of the spirit of Christ within the believer.

If a believer doesn't have love in him or her, then that person is walking with another spirit. That's the biggest fruit, not knowledge, but love.

So many people don't know love. This world's darkness makes it difficult for some to see it, feel it, and be touched by it. But those who do know love know that it's only love if it's given away.

Sharing prayers is a transformation of spirit because, if you pray for the good of another, the protection of others, the health, healing, and well-being of another, that is the spirit of love. If you can serve another, in some way that helps them, that is love at work. Every human soul created by God is given a God spark. They can either embolden it, or smother it, based on the choices they make spiritually.

So what if you think that you have no one to love? Or that you feel that no one loves you? There is always something to love. God's creation would be a start. Rescuing an animal. Loving yourself. Nurturing a garden. Appreciating music. Talking to God. Doing random acts of kindness for strangers, like letting others in front of you in traffic. Holding doors open for others as you pass through. Helping strangers in need. This is what love does. This is where the angels are. Saving someone, filling a need somewhere, somehow, regardless of what you might perceive may be the smallest way. It is nevertheless a spark of light and love within a dark place and filling a need.

You do what you can. If you can share money with organizations that help and rescue others, like children, animals and relieve human suffering in some kind way that leaves them better off, as this is the kind of love that represents the Spirit of Christ and the Spirit of Love in action. This is the stuff that gets Angels who serve the Kingdom of Heaven excited. Small stuff, because when you add up all the God sparks doing the small stuff, it becomes big stuff, which is a God thing. Get it?

So if you're looking for fruits, look to those. The fruits of kindness matter most. Show mercy when you can, and when you can't, pray like crazy to ask Jesus to give it to you for them because let's be real, there are some things that are beyond forgiveness in this world. Things that can only be forgiven supernaturally.

The true spirit of forgiveness comes from God. Humans are not capable without their God spark to do so and even the most spirit filled believers, struggle to forgive in the face of severe persecution, mockery, abuse and maltreatment, but those truly filled with God's spirit, learn how to do that through Christ.

By abiding in Christ, Christ abides in us. It's really that simple. He has the solutions that we as flesh and blood, emotional beings, do not have. His Spirit gives life, raises the dead (both literally and figuratively), heals the sick, delivers from the demonic, and turns curses into blessings. This is something supernatural. It's something only God can do, and humans are complete and total failures at it. But that's why God loves humans because there are those who really seek Him, depend on Him, trust in Him, and He loves that. He responds through giving us supernatural comfort in the face of abandonment, supernatural provision in the face of loss, and supernatural peace in the midst of despair.

His Spirit cuts through the fog of confusion that so many humans are oppressed by. Confusing spirits. This is the realm of mental illnesses, because it is rooted in spiritual agreements with satan's spirits, which are lies. Lies create mental disorders; lies create confusion. Lies betray you. Believing in lies is kind of like self-sabotage; you give up your space to the darkness. Confusion is darkness, and it's like having a dark cloud around your mind. It creates double-mindedness, schizophrenia. Because confusing spirits have lost their way through unbelief in God and belief in lies. They give spiritual legal ground to the deaf, dumb, blind and mute spirit.

You want to know why so many people supernaturally hate Jews? Many really don't know why themselves, but they do nonetheless. It may be jealousy and resentment, which opens the door for satan's spirits to take over them. However, the underlying reason satan hates the Jews is because Jesus was Jewish and he has to answer to Him in the spirit world. Yeshua, being given all authority as the Lord of Spirits, has authority over satan and his spirits. It's that simple. That is the root of the spirit of anti-Semitism that oppresses so many Christians and Muslims.

Satan hates women because a woman gave birth to the Messiah. Satan hates that God has used women to give birth to all kinds of prophets. This is the spiritual root of sexism.

Those who cannot receive love, as well as those who can't give love, have a spirit on them. This is not the original blueprint for the soul. The Lord of Spirits is the creator of all souls. All souls have spirits. I call them God sparks, because they are literally light bodies. It's kind of an electrical and supernatural thing. You can't always see it, but you

CONCLUDING WORDS

know it's working in the background. Giving and receiving love is what the inner spirit of man is programmed to do. This is the true self because God is love. He created all the God sparks (i.e. soul-spirits). But people are born into all kinds of bondages, generational and family curses, which allows the soul to purge past life karma.

Spiritual strongholds like racism, anti-Semitism, and sexism are deeply rooted in the past, which are rooted in both alien and extraterrestrial bloodlines on earth. God's seed (DNA) verses satan's seed (alien DNA). When you understand the past, you can understand the present and change the future. If you can't understand the connection, then you will be doomed to repeat the past, and therefore be stuck in a pattern, a cursed pattern, that you have no power to change yourself.

That is why we all need a Savior; that is what Christ came to do — to be the bridge between us and God and restore us through His Grace and Forgiveness, Loving Kindness, and Faithfulness to our Higher Selves, by restoring our original "God sparks," back into right relationship with our Creator, the Lord of Spirits.

> "Man laughs at his greatness in taming the atom, but man has tamed nothing, and man is only a fool. When man can tame the power of LOVE, then man has tampered with power!"
>
> ~ Proteus

~Finis~

NOTES:

1. Dale Hurd, CBN News Reporter, Ex-Muslims Lighting the Way for Islam's Collapse? http://www.cbn.com/cbnnews/world/2015/June/Ex-Muslims-Lighting-the-Way-for-Islams-Collapse/, June 5, 2015
2. Andrew Anthony, Losing Their Religion, The Hidden Crisis of Faith Among Britain's Young Muslims, http://www.theguardian.com/global/2015/may/17/losing-their-religion-british-ex-muslims-non-believers-hidden-crisis-faith, May 17, 2015
3. Pat Robertson, CBN, 700 Club, June 15, 2015
4. https://en.wikipedia.org/wiki/Library_of_Alexandria

NOTES AND BIBLIOGRAPHY

All Bible quotes from www.biblehub.com

Chapter One – *Gods Or ETs?*
1. R.H. Charles, *The Books of Enoch*, 1912
2. Valerian, Val. *Matrix I and Matrix II*, Leading Edge Research 1994.
3. Dr. James Hurtak, *The Book Of Knowledge: The Keys of Enoch* ®, p.55, The Academy for Future Science.; Los Gatos, CA, 1977.

Chapter Two – *Ancient Technology & Biblical Astronauts*
1. Immanuel Velikovsky, Earth in Upheaval, 1955, Doubleday and Company, Inc., Garden City, New York.
2. Charles, R. H. (trans.). The Book of Enoch. 1917 < http://www.sacred-texts.com/bib/boe>.
3. Marian Apparitions - Angel of Light or Messenger of Deception? 2009- 2014 Rema Marketing http://www.fatimarevelations.com
4. Blumrich, Josef F., The Spaceships of Ezekiel (New York, NY: Bantam Press, 1974).
5. Ann Madden Jones, Yahweh Encounters, Bible Astronauts, Ark Radiations and Temple Electronics, Sandbird Publishing, North Carolina, 1995.
6. Robert Sephr, *Species With Amnesia: Our Forgotten History,* Atlantean Gardens, Encino, CA, 2015

Chapter Three – *Ancient Astronaut Theory*
1. Von Däniken, Erich, *Chariots of the Gods* (New York, NY: Bantam Books, 1969).
2. Sitchin, Zecharia, *The Earth Chronicles*: Sitchin, Zecharia, *Genesis Revisited* (Santa Fe, NM: Bear, 1991).
3. Gilbert, *Compassionate Mind,* pp. 170-171
4. Walter Burkert, *Homo Necans: The Anthropology of Greek Sacrificial Ritual,* trans. Peter Bing (Berkley, Los Angeles, and London, 1983), pp. 16-22
5. R. Cedric Leonard, PhD., *The Wheels of Ezekiel, A Possible Relationship To The UFO Phenomenon,* quotes used with permission. March, 2002. http://www.atlantisquest.com/Ezekiel.html
6. Joe Kovacs, *Shocked By the Bible,* Thomas Nelson, Nashville, Tennessee, 2008, p.67
7. UK Study, National Geographic Channel, *Chasing UFOs*, June 26, 2012

Chapter Four – *Mother Ships Of The Lord*
1. Swami Tapasyananda, *Sunkarakandam of Srimad Valmiki Ramayan, The Ramayana,* Published by The President, Sri Ramakrishna Math Printing Press, Mylapori, Chennai, India, 2006. pp.46-48

Chapter Five – *Cosmic Warfare On Earth*
1. *Mahabharata.* Sacred Texts. Ca. 400 BCE <http://www.sacred-texts.com/hin/maha/index.htm>.
2. Ella LeBain, Book One *Who's Who in the Cosmic Zoo of Aliens and ETs, Third Edition,* Tate Publishing, 2013
3. Charles, R. H. (trans.). *The Book of Enoch.* 1917 <http://www.sacred-texts.com/bib/boe>.

Chapter Six – *The Beasts Of The Sea And Earth*
1. Ella LeBain, *Book One, Who's Who In The Cosmic Zoo?,* Tate Publishing, 2013
2. Daniel H. Stern, *Jewish New Testament Commentary,* pp. 815-16
3. Tom Horn, *Apollyon Rising 2012, The Lost Symbol Found And The Final Mystery of the Great Seal Revealed,* Defender Books, Crane, MO. 2009

Chapter Seven – *Discernment of Gods, Angels & Demons*
1. Dr. Jacques Vallee citing the extensive research of Bertrand Meheust [*Science-Fiction et Soucoupes Volantes* (Paris, 1978); *Soucoupes Volantes et Folklore*(Paris, 1985)], in *Confrontations,* p. 146, 159-161
2. Whitley Strieber, *Communion: A True Story,* Beech Tree Books, New York; First Edition (1987)
3. G.H. Pember, *Earth's Earliest Ages and Their Connection with Modern Spiritualism, Theosophy and Buddhism*: Kregel Publications; 3rd edition (1982) (1605)
4. John A. Keel, *Why UFOs: Operation Trojan Horse,* Manor Books (1976)
5. Whitley Strieber, *Transformation: The Breakthrough,* Beech; First Edition (1988)
6. Ella LeBain, Book One *Who's Who in the Cosmic Zoo of Aliens and ETs, Third Edition,* pp.127-133. Tate Publishing, 2013
7. Dr. Jacques Vallée, *Confrontations: A Scientists Search For Alien Contact,* Anomalist Books (January 2, 2008)
8. Whitley Strieber, *Transformation: The Breakthrough,* Beech; First Edition (1988)

Chapter Eight - *Who Are The Gods?*
1. Von Däniken, Eric. *Chariots of the Gods?* 1968. Econ-Verlag (Germany), Putnam (USA), p. 26, p. 10
2. Thomas R. Horn, *Nephilim Stargates: The Year 2012 and the Return of the Watchers,* 2012. Defender Publishing, Crane, MO. p.25 (used with permission)

NOTES AND BIBLIOGRAPHY

3. Professor I.D.E. Thomas, *The Omega Conspiracy: Satan's Last Assault on God's Kingdom*

Chapter Nine – *The Return Of The Gods*
1. Thomas R. Horn, *Nephilim Stargates: The Year 2012 and the Return of the Watchers*, 2012. Defender Publishing, Crane, MO. pp., 26, 27, 146, 163,.201, 202 (used with permission)
2. Professor I.D.E. Thomas, *The Omega Conspiracy: Satan's Last Assault on God's Kingdom*
3. Nicholas Notovich, *The Unknown Life of Christ. The Lost Years of Jesus: The Life of Saint Issa*, 1894, India, http://reluctant-messenger.com/issa.htm
4. This article was first printed on http://www.jubilee.org.nz/articles/buddha-prophesied-jesus/ and is being used here with permission. Permission was granted to copy these Buddhist Scriptures from Wat Phra Sing in ChiangMai Province. The person who gave permission was Phra Sriwisutthiwong in Bangkok. It is guaranteed that there is no error in transmission, which is in the book of the district headman, the religious encyclopedia volume 23, book #29. This inquiry was made on October 13, 1954 AD, (Buddhist era 2497)) Phra Sriwisutthiwong is the Deputy Abbot and Director of Wat Pho Museum, Wat Pho Temple, Thailand.
5. Ella LeBain, Book One *Who's Who in the Cosmic Zoo of Aliens and ETs, Third Edition*, pp.326-329. Tate Publishing, 2013

Chapter Ten – *Gods Or ETs? What's Next?*
1. Steven Basset, http://www.paradigmresearchgroup.org/

Chapter Eleven – *Who Are The Biblical Gods?*
1. Rabbi Daniel Rendelman, *The YHWH Code*, Emet Ministries, http://www.emetministries.com

Chapter Twelve – *The Tetragrammaton*
1. Ann Spangler, *God's Word, The Names of God Bible,* Baker Publishing Group, 1995.
2. http://promotethetruth.com/id1.html

Chapter Thirteen – *The Name Above All Names*
1. http://faithlenders.weebly.com/uploads/5/5/3/7/5537776/constantines_creed.pdf
2. http://www.compellingtruth.org/Jesus-sabbath.html#ixzz3g5qEOpZg
3. http://www.touregypt.net/featurestories/serapis.htm

Chapter Fourteen – *Who Is The God of Gods?*
1. Selwyn Stevens, M.C.R., Ph.D., *God or Gods: How Many and Who?* http://jubileeresources.org/?page_id=608
2. *The Hebraic Roots Bible,* http://www.coyhwh.com/en/bibleDownloadPDF.php
3. Don Esposito, http://thekeytoredemption.blogspot.com/2009/05/who-is-don-esposito.html
4. *The Holy Scriptures: A Jewish Bible According To The Masoretic Text – Hebrew and English.* Sinai Publishing House, 72 Allenby Rd., Tel-Aviv, Israel. 1977.
5. Adam Clark, Bible Commentary, Published 1810-1826. http://www.preteristarchive.com/Books/1810_clarke_commentary.html
6. *The Ruling Class*, 1972 United Artists film, Directed by Peter Medak, screenplay by Peter Barnes.
7. *Gone To Texas*, 1986, Directed by Peter Levin, screenplay by John Binder, story by Frank Dobbs and John Binder, CBS Television Movies.

Chapter Fifteen – *Who Is Yahweh?*
1. Ella LeBain, *Who Is God?,* chapters *The God of This World* and *The Office of Satan, Who Is Yahweh?*
2. Chris Everard, *Feed Your Mind Magazine*, 2009. p.28
3. The *Hypostasis of the Archons,* Nag Hammadi Library; emphasis and commentary is mine.
4. James A. Michener, *The Source*, Random House, 1965, p. 205
5. *Apocryphon John* BG 38, 1-10

Chapter Sixteen – *Who Were The Archons?*
1. Apocryphon John III, 36:17, *The Apocryphon of John,* http://www.gnosis.org/naghamm/apocjn.html
2. Nag Hammadi Library, *The Apocryphon of John, On The Origin of the World* and *The Hypostasis of the Archons, The Complete Nag Hammadi Library* http://www.gnosis.org/naghamm/nhlalpha.html
3. Michio Kaku, *The Wall Street Journal*, September 23, 2011
4. Jan Erik Sigdell, *Is Yahweh An Annunaki?* http://www.christian-reincarnation.com/YahAn.htm
5. Ella LeBain, *Who's Who In The Cosmic Zoo? Book One – Third Edition,* Chapter – *Annunaki* pp. 110-119, Tate Publishing & Enterprises, LLC. 2013
6. Zecharia Sitchin, *The Earth Chronicles, Genesis Revisited,* Avon Books, NY, NY. 1990
7. Barbara Marciniak, Bringers Of The Dawn, Bear & Company (December 1, 1992)

NOTES AND BIBLIOGRAPHY

Chapter Seventeen – *Who Is Jehovah?*
1. Francis Brown, R. Driver, and Charles Briggs, *The Brown-Driver-Briggs Hebrew and English Lexicon,* Hendrickson Pub; Complete and Unabridged, fully searchable, with Strong Numbers and interactive Index edition (September 1, 1994)
2. Menahem Mansoor, *The Dead Sea Scrolls: A College Textbook and a Study Guide,* Eerdmans; First American Edition (1964)
3. Ella LeBain, *Who's Who In The Cosmic Zoo? Book One – Third Edition,* Chapter – Els – Elohim, pp.204-205, Tate Publishing & Enterprises, 2013.
4. Scott Thomas - Editor, *Funk & Wagnalls New Encyclopedia, 2000 Yearbook, 1999 Events,* Funk & Wagnalls, 2000
5. The Catholic Church, *The New World Dictionary-Concordance to the New American Bible*, p. 295. World Publishing (1970)
6. David Noel Freedman, Astrid B. Beck, Allen C. Myers, Editors *Eerdmans Dictionary of the Bible*, p. 682, William B. Eerdmans Publishing Company (October 23, 2000)
7. Louis F. Hartman, Bijbels Woordenboek (Translator), *Encyclopedic Dictionary of the Bible*, p. 1110, McGraw-Hill; 2nd Revised edition (1963)
8. *The Concise Columbia Electronic Encyclopedia*, Third Edition, Columbia University Press Houghton Mifflin; 3 Sub edition (October 12, 1994)
9. *Encarta Online Encyclopedia*, Microsoft, 2000
10. Philip W. Goetz, Robert McHenry, Dale Hoiberg, Editors, *Encyclopedia Britannica*, 15th Edition, 1999-2000
11. Cecil Roth, *The Concise Jewish Encyclopedia*, p. 277. Plume (April 1, 1980)
12. Isidore Singer, *The Jewish Encyclopedia*, vol. 9: p. 160, Ktav Publishing House; 1st edition (1901)
13. Ibid, vol. 7: p. 87
14. American Standard Version, Preface to the *Revised Standard Version* of the Bible (2nd Ed., 1971) p. 6-7, Thomas Nelson & Sons, NY.
15. Joseph Rotherham, Editor, *The Emphasized Bible*, p.24-25. Kregel Classics (June 30, 1959)
16. Paul Achtemeier, *Harper's Bible Dictionary*, p. 1,036. 1985 Harpercollins; First Edition edition (October 1985)
17. *World Book Encyclopedia* World Book Inc (November 2002)

Chapter Eighteen – *Like Father Like Son*
1. Jerry Siegel, Joe Schuster, creators, *Superman, The Movie*, Warner Brothers, 1978
2. Dr. Selwyn Stevens, *Gods or God: How Many & Who?*
3. Art Mathias, *Biblical Foundations of Freedom,* Wellspring Ministries of Alaska, 2000

Chapter Nineteen – *Who Is The Holy Spirit?*
1. Dr. Karl Payne, *Spiritual Warfare, Christians, Demonization and Deliverance,* WND Books, Washington, D.C., 2011

Chapter Twenty – *The God Of This World*
1. David Flynn, *Satan & Cherubim on Literal Planets - Stones of Fire* used with permission, http://www.mt.net/~watcher/)
2. John Milor, *Aliens and the Antichrist,* iUniverse, 2006
3. Fenis Dake, *God's Plan For Man,* Lawrenceville, Georgia: Dake Publishing Inc., 1977
4. Immanuel Velikovsky, *Worlds In Collision,* Dell; A Laurel Edition (1969)
5. David Flynn's research on *Cydonia Mars* http://www.mt.net/~watcher/
6. ibid, Flynn
7. Michael Tsarion, *Atlantis, Alien Visitation and Genetic Manipulation*: Angels at Work Publishing Santa Clara, California. 2002
8. Ella LeBain, *Who's Who In The Cosmic Zoo? Book One – Third Edition,* Chapter – Agartha/Agarthians p.98-p.105, Tate Publishing & Enterprises, 2013.
9. ibid, Flynn

Chapter Twenty – One – *The Office of Satan*
1. Eleanor D. Payson, MS.W., *The Wizard of Oz and other Narcissists* (Julian Day Publications, 2002).
2. Christopher Latch, *The Culture of Narcissim,* W. W. Norton & Company; Revised edition (May 17, 1991)

Chapter Twenty-Two – *Who Is Allah?*
1. Alberto Rivera, *The Prophet.* Chick Publications, 1979.
2. Hanna Jones, 2.2 Billion: World's Muslim Population Doubles, Time News Feed, Jan. 27, 2011, Web. 2011, Web. wsfeed.time.com/2011/01/27/2-2-billion-worlds-muslim-population-doubles/) 19 August, 2013.
3. Wellhausen, Juli Reste Arabischen Heidenthums, p. 221. Book. Berlin, Druck Und Verlag Von Geroge Reimer, 1897. Printed Book from the Collection of Harvard University. Digitilizing Sponsor: Google: Web. (http://archive.org/stream/restearabischen000wellgoog#page/n7/mode/2up.) 21 August 2013.
4. Arthur Jeffery, Islam: Muhammad, and His Religion, New York: The Liberal Arts Press, 1958, p.85
5. "Hadith" Wikipedia® The Free Encyclopedia, Wikipedia.com, 26 Jan 2013, Web, August 18, 2013, Web. (http://en.wikipedia.org/wiki/Hadith) 18 August, 2013

NOTES AND BIBLIOGRAPHY

6. "Judaism" Exposed, Abrahams Faith.Blogspot.com, Blogspot, March 30, 2011, Web, (http://abrahamsfaith.blogspot.com/2011/03/allah-god-of-ishmael-god-of-israel.html) 22 March, 2013
7. H.A.R. Gibb, Mohammedanism: An Historical Survey, New York: Mentor Books, 1955 Web, Google Books, (The Islamic Invasion – Ph. D. Dr Robert a Morey - Google Books – (http://goo.gl/HwKvGt)
8. "Arabic Lexicographical Miscellanies"; by J. Blau in the Journal of Semitic Studies, Vol. XVII, #2, 1972, pp. 173-190A
9. The Bible and Islam, or The Influence of the Old and New Testament on the Religion of Mohammed, New York, Charles Scribner's Sons, 1897, p 102
10. The Call of the Minaret, New York: Oxford University Press, 1956, p.31
11. William Montgomery Watt, Muhammad's Mecca, p.vii. Also see his article, "Belief in a High God in Pre-Islamic";, Journal of Semitic Studies, Vol. 16, 1971, pp. 35-40.
12. Islam: Beliefs and Observations, New York Barrons, 1987, p. 28
13. Encyclopedia of Religion, I:117, Washington DC, Corpus Pub, 1979
14. Encyclopedia Britannica, I:643
15. Encyclopedia of Islam, I:302, Leiden: E.J. Brill, 1913, Houtsma
16. Encyclopedia of Islam, I:406, ed. Gibb
17. Encyclopedia of World Mythology and Legend, I:41, Anthony Mercatante, New York, The Facts on File, 1983
18. G. J. O. Moshay, Who Is This Allah? 1994, pg. 138.
19. "Understanding Al-iLah – The god of Muhammad, Islam and Muslims (Part 1)", Welcome to Islam Watch, Islam Watch, 12 January, 2013, Web (http://www.islam-watch.org/authors/110-brokaan/1224-understanding-al-ilah-the-god-of-muhammad-islam-and-muslims-part-1.html)
20. Caesar E. Farrah, Ph.D., Islam: Its Beliefs and Observances [Barron's Educational Series, Inc., Sixth Edition, 2000; ISBN: 0764112058], p. 28
21. Encyclopedia of World Mythology and Legend, I:61.
22. Robert Morey, The Islamic Invasion, Eugene, Oregon, Harvest House Publishers, 1977, pp.50-51.

Chapter Twenty Three – *Babylonian History: Where It All Began*
1. Salemi, Peter. The Plain Truth About Islam, retrieved from - http://www.british-israel.ca/Islam.htm;
2. http://www.discerningthetimesonline.net/OriginOfCrescentandStar.html
3. DTTO - Showing You the World in Scripture
4. http://www.discerningthetimesonline.net/BabylonianHistoryWhereitallbegan.html
5. DTTO - Showing You the World in Scripture - The Harlot links with Turkey,
6. http://www.discerningthetimesonline.net/BabylonianHistoryWhereitallbegan.html
7. Tafrihul Askia Fil Ahwal Ul AMBIA, pages 134 - 139, Vol. 1.

8. http://www.discerningthetimesonline.net/BabylonianHistoryWhereitallbegan.html
9. Roberts, J.J.M., The Earliest Semitic Pantheon, Johns Hopkins University, Baltimore, 1972

Chapter Twenty Four – *What Is Islam?*
1. Ann Barnhardt, Islamic Sexuality: A Survey of Evil; -- 9/12/11 Colorado Springs lecture: http://tomohalloran.com/2013/06/10/watch-must-see-for-all-americans-ann-barnhardt-islamic-sexuality-a-survey-of-evil/
2. http://www.answering-islam.org/Authors/Arlandson/women_inferior.htm (http://ne3. "Allah" Wikipedia® The Free Encyclopedia, Wikipedia.com, 26Jan 2013, Web, August 18, 2013, Web.(http://en.wikipedia.org/wiki/Allah) 18 August 2013
3. http://www.answeringmuslims.com/p/jihad.html
4. Excerpts Text taken from: http://www.discerningthetimesonline.net/#!islam-shariah-law-/c15qj

Chapter Twenty Five – *Who Is The Beast?*
1. Larry Harper, *The Antichrist,* The Elijah Project; 2nd edition. 2003
2. Thomas R. Horn, *Nephilim Stargates*, *The Year 2012 And The Return Of The Watchers,* Anomolous Publishing, Crane, MO 2007
3. David Flynn, *Satan's Counterfeits: Judgment Day, UFOs, Angels & End Time Prophecy*, http://www.mt.net/~watcher/judgment.html

Chapter Twenty Six – *The Office Of Christ*
1. Kenneth C. Flemming, *God's Voice In The Stars: Zodiac Signs And Bible Truth,* Loizeaux Brothers, Neptune, New Jersey 1927. p.21
2. Ella LeBain, *Who's Who In The Cosmic Zoo? Book One, Third Edition,* pp.90-91
3. Author Kersey Graves, *The World's Sixteen Crucified Saviors: Christianity Before Christ,* 1875, *Adventures Unlimited Press;* 6 Revised edition (September 1, 2001)
4. Jacolliot, *The Bible in India,* Sun Pub Co (September 1992)
5. Joseph Daniel Guigniaut, George Friedrich Creuzer, *Religions de l' antiquite',* Published 1841, archives https://archive.org/details/europeanlibraries

Chapter Twenty Seven – *The Christmas Gods*
1. Michael T. Snyder, *The Mystery Of The Pagan Origin Of Christmas: Jesus Was Not Born On December 25th But A Whole Bunch Of Pagan Gods Were.*, 2009, http://unexplainedmysteriesoftheworld.com/archives/the-mystery-of-the-pagan-origin-of-christmas-jesus-was-not-born-on-december-25th-but-a-whole-bunch-of-pagan-gods-were

NOTES AND BIBLIOGRAPHY

Chapter Twenty Eight – *What Happens When You Die?*
1. G.W. Butterworth, *Origen: On First Principles*, Harper Torchbooks, The Cathedral Library, Harper and Row Publishers, New York, 1966.
2. Hans J. Hillerbrand, Martin Luther and the Bull "Exsurge Domine" Duke University, 2008
3. Stephen Lampe, *The Christian and Reincarnation,* Millennium, 1990
4. Patrick J. Pollack, *101 Heresies of Antipope Benedict XVI*, 2002 http://www.patrickpollock.com/101heresiesofbenedictxvitract2.html
5. Bruce Fraser McDonald, PhD, *The Thomas Book,* Eloquent Books, CT. 2011
6. Gnostic text, *Pistis Sophia,* translated by G. S. R. Mead, 200 AD, http://gnosis.org/library/pistis-sophia/ps004.htm

Chapter Twenty Nine – *Who Created Sexism?*
1. The Acts of Paul and Thekla, from *The Apocryphal New Testament,* translated by J.K. Elliot, Oxford University Press, 1993.
2. John Dominic Crossan, *A New New Testament (Forward)* http://genius.com/John-dominic-crossan-a-new-new-testament-forward-annotated/, 2015 Genius Media Group Inc.
3. Ella LeBain, *Conquering The Jezebel Spirit* http://www.findingfreedom.name/conquering-the-jezebel-spirit.html
4. http://biblehub.com/topical/a/athaliah.htm
5. Julie Bresciani Ph.D., *Rachel's Destiny As Written In The Stars,* Astraea Ciara Pub. Co.; 1 edition (January 30, 1998)

CONCLUDING WORDS
1. Dale Hurd, CBN News Reporter, *Ex-Muslims Lighting the Way for Islam's Collapse?* http://www.cbn.com/cbnnews/world/2015/June/Ex-Muslims-Lighting-the-Way-for-Islams-Collapse/, June 5, 2015
2. Andrew Anthony, *Losing Their Religion, The Hidden Crisis of Faith Among Britain's Young Muslims,* http://www.theguardian.com/global/2015/may/17/losing-their-religion-british-ex-muslims-non-believers-hidden-crisis-faith, May 17, 2015
3. Pat Robertson, CBN, *700 Club*, June 15, 2015
4. https://en.wikipedia.org/wiki/Library_of_Alexandria

ABOUT THE AUTHOR

Ella LeBain is the author of a book series entitled *Who's Who In The Cosmic Zoo? A Spiritual Guide to ETs, Aliens, Gods & Angels: An End Time Guide to the Mass Deception.*

Ella LeBain, who is originally from New York City, was educated in Israel. She received a Social Sciences Degree from the Biological Research Center of the Negev in 1979 where she was schooled in Biblical Hebrew. She then went on to receive an Astronomy Degree from the Hayden Planetarium in New York City in 1982. She spent two years working as a missionary in apartheid South Africa in the early 1980s, where she embarked on what has become a thirty-five year journey to get to the truth about UFOs, Aliens, ETs, gods, and angels and how they all fit into the end of our age scenario.

Ella has spent twenty-five years in the field of UFO research, investigating alien abductions, and she has had many supernatural experiences of her own along the way, many of which have shaped the writing of these books.

Ella has collected vast amounts of information from a variety of sources, in addition to her own experiences which have been incorporated into the Book set. Book One is a type of encyclopedia, covering *Who's Who in the Cosmic Zoo of ETs and Aliens* in an A-Z compendium.

Book Two - *Who Is God?* Focuses on the Cosmic Drama and identifies and discerns "who" are the so-called ET gods of ancient history based on both biblical and exobiblical scriptures.

Book Three – *Who Are The Angels?* Focuses on the hierarchy of angels (extraterrestrial messengers) both the fallen ET angels and those who have remained faithful to the Creator, how they have been interacting with humankind for millennia and the important roles they play at the end of this age.

Book Four – *Covenants* focuses on spiritual legal ground, and the spiritual contracts that are represented in the ancient Scriptures.

Book Five – *The Heavens* discerns the heavenly scroll and God's Word written first into the Stars before the downloading of the written scrolls on Earth, the afterlife, the millennial reign, and Heaven on Earth in the age to come.

Ella LeBain is also an International Deliverance Minister and a member of ISDM (International Society for Deliverance Ministers). While serving as a missionary in apartheid South Africa from 1979 – 1981, Ella witnessed front and center the spiritual revival that was taking place before the end of apartheid. Ella has witnessed the raising of the dead, demonic deliverances, supernatural healings, and miracles through the Living God.

Ella is a retired legal assistant of twenty-five years, where she made her living as a professional freelance paralegal, working on projects in New York City, Florida, and Colorado. Ella retired sixteen years ago to complete her books and become a stay-at-home Mom. Ella is the mother to a teenage daughter. She is happily married to her soul mate and shares a house with three cats. In her spare time, Ella likes to horse around with her equine partners every chance she gets. Horseback riding is her favorite past time and therapy, in Colorado.

Ella LeBain is available for interviews, lectures, and book signings.

Contact: ellalebain@skypathbooks.com

http://www.whoswhointhecosmiczoo.com

www.ingramcontent.com/pod-product-compliance
Lightning Source LLC
Chambersburg PA
CBHW080049190426
43201CB00035B/2139